SECOND EDITION

THE NATURE OF LEADERSHIP

Dedicated to these inspirational leaders who refuse to compromise their values:

Hoosen (Jerry) Coovadia
for his moral leadership against apartheid and AIDS.

Aung San Suu Kyi
for her principled leadership and defense of democracy in Burma.

SECOND EDITION

THE NATURE OF LEADERSHIP

EDITORS

DAVID V. DAY
University of Western Australia

JOHN ANTONAKIS
University of Lausanne

Los Angeles | London | New Delhi
Singapore | Washington DC

Los Angeles | London | New Delhi
Singapore | Washington DC

FOR INFORMATION:

SAGE Publications, Inc.
2455 Teller Road
Thousand Oaks, California 91320
E-mail: order@sagepub.com

SAGE Publications Ltd.
1 Oliver's Yard
55 City Road
London EC1Y 1SP
United Kingdom

SAGE Publications India Pvt. Ltd.
B 1/I 1 Mohan Cooperative Industrial Area
Mathura Road, New Delhi 110 044
India

SAGE Publications Asia-Pacific Pte. Ltd.
33 Pekin Street #02-01
Far East Square
Singapore 048763

Acquisitions Editor: Lisa Cuevas Shaw
Editorial Assistant: MaryAnn Vail
Production Editor: Kelle Schillaci
Copy Editor: Ellen Howard
Typesetter: C&M Digitals (P) Ltd.
Proofreader: Dennis W. Webb
Indexer: Sheila Bodell
Cover Designer: Gail Buschman
Marketing Manager: Helen Salmon
Permissions Editor: Karen Ehrmann

Copyright © 2012 by SAGE Publications, Inc.

Printed in the United States of America

Library of Congress Cataloging-in-Publication Data

The nature of leadership / editors, David V. Day, John Antonakis. — 2nd ed.

p. cm.
Includes bibliographical references and index.

ISBN 978-1-4129-8020-3 (pbk.)

1. Leadership. I. Day, David V., 1956–
II. Antonakis, John.

HD57.7.N377 2012 658.4′092—dc22 2010054158

This book is printed on acid-free paper.

11 12 13 14 15 10 9 8 7 6 5 4 3 2 1

Contents

Preface

Why The Nature of Leadership, 2nd Edition?

The answer to the question of why there should be a second edition of *The Nature of Leadership* was more fully considered than simply "why not?" Although the first edition of the book included timely knowledge and continued to be actively used in teaching and research, there have been many advances in leadership theory and research since the first edition was published in 2004. Through in-depth discussions between Lisa Shaw (Senior Executive Editor at Sage) and John Antonakis (lead editor on the first edition), they determined that the *Nature of Leadership* continued to provide a valuable resource to the field and that a revised and updated edition had the potential to become a high-impact handbook. To accomplish this goal, Lisa and John thought it best to alter the composition of the editorial team and also to include an accomplished leadership scholar whose primary area of research was leadership. This resulted in the addition of David Day as the coeditor of the second edition of the book.

As coeditors, we planned the second edition to better reflect the current streams that are driving leadership research. We expanded the volume from the original 14 chapters to 16 chapters, shuffled the chapter contents, and invited new contributions from several authors who are leaders in their respective fields. The final product is, in the spirit of the first edition, an edited book that provides a sufficiently broad yet focused and integrated cutting-edge review of leadership.

We have now revised the volume to appeal primarily to upper-level students of leadership (undergraduate and graduate level), as well as to leadership scholars. The original aims of our book are still reflected in the overarching goals:

1. To solidify and integrate the voluminous and seemingly disparate leadership literature

2. To separate the wheat from the chaff and science from myth

To accomplish this objective, we reviewed the literature to determine the most important areas of leadership research that should be incorporated in a complete yet concise handbook. In the new volume, we simplified the structure and focused on three themes, corresponding to the three sections of the book:

1. Leadership: Science, Nature, and Nurture

2. The Major Schools of Leadership

3. Leadership and Special Domains

We then worked with 23 subject-matter experts—ranging from the eminent to the up-and-coming—to provide readers with state-of-the-art reviews of these themes. In this way, we produced a book whose chapters, when taken together, are complementary and cohesive. As a concise volume, *The Nature of Leadership* is still unique in being unmatched, not only in breadth and depth but also in its thematic focus. We believe it fills an important gap in the leadership literature.

We distinguish our volume from comprehensive but very broad and bulky encyclopedic research volumes by including only the essential themes in a readable package. We also distinguish our volume from single-authored textbooks, which are limited by their author's perspective and knowledge. Finally, our edited book is not a simple collection of contributions. We worked closely with our contributors to provide them with a strategic overview of our volume and how their contribution helped to reify our vision. We reviewed every chapter to ensure that it complemented other chapters and that together the chapters fit seamlessly, enhancing the impression that the book was single or dual authored.

We trust that our volume will continue to create interest in leadership, which is arguably one of the most important functions of society. As John Gardner (1965), the eminent leadership scholar and politician, stated:

> Leaders have a significant role in creating the state of mind that is the society. They can serve as symbols of the moral unity of the society. They can express the values that hold the society together. Most important, they can conceive and articulate goals that lift people out of their petty preoccupations, carry them above the conflicts that tear a society apart, and unite them in the pursuit of objectives worthy of their best efforts. (p. 12; The antileadership vaccine. In *1965 Annual Report, Carnegie Corporation of New York* [pp. 3–12].)

Gardner's ideas are still valid, and possibly even more so, today. As Warren Bennis eloquently elaborates in this book's conclusion, in our time, we still witness scandals, bankruptcies, war, misery, and suffering, mostly because of corrupt and immoral leadership. Between here and Bennis's concluding chapter, readers will learn to bring to light the many facets of *The Nature of Leadership*.

—JA and DVD

Acknowledgments _____

We thank the chapter authors for their world-class contributions and their cooperation on this project. We are very grateful to the staff at Sage Publications for making this volume possible. In particular, we thank Lisa Shaw (Senior Executive Editor), MaryAnn Vail (Editorial Assistant), Kelle Schillaci (Production Editor), and Ellen Howard (Copy Editor). We also thank the reviewers who provided us with invaluable feedback on the second edition book proposal. Finally, we thank the countless leaders who have shared their time and experiences with leadership researchers over the decades. Without them, we would have no leadership science; their world is our lab.

David Day is grateful for the many years of mentoring and friendship from Bob Lord and for the patience and love of Patricia O'Connor.

John Antonakis owes an unpayable debt to Bruce Avolio and Robert House, who helped shape his ideas about leadership and who were instrumental in guiding his career. Most importantly, he expresses his deepest gratitude and love to Saskia, Athena, Artemis, and Baerli.

—DVD and JA

PART I

Introduction

1

Leadership: Past, Present, and Future

David V. Day

John Antonakis

In industrial, educational, and military settings, and in social movements, leadership plays a critical, if not the most critical, role, and is therefore an important subject for study and research.

(Bass, 2008, p. 25)

Leadership matters, according to prominent leadership scholars (see also Bennis, 2007). But what is leadership? That turns out to be a challenging question to answer. Leadership is a complex and diverse topic, and trying to make sense of leadership research can be an intimidating endeavor. One comprehensive handbook of leadership (Bass, 2008), covering more than a century of scientific study, comprises more than 1,200 pages of text and more than 200 additional pages of references! There is clearly a substantial scholarly body of leadership theory and research that continues to grow each year.

Given the sheer volume of leadership scholarship that is available, our purpose is not to try to review it all. That is why our focus is on the nature or essence of leadership as we and our chapter authors see it. But to fully understand and appreciate the nature of leadership, it is essential that readers have some background knowledge of the history of leadership research, the various theoretical streams that have evolved over the years, and emerging issues that are pushing the boundaries of the leadership frontier.

Further complicating our task is that more than one hundred years of leadership research have led to several paradigm shifts and a voluminous body of knowledge. On several occasions, scholars of leadership became quite frustrated by the large amount of false starts, incremental theoretical advances, and contradictory findings. As stated more than five decades ago by Warren Bennis (1959, pp. 259–260), "Of all the hazy and confounding areas in social psychology, leadership theory undoubtedly contends for top nomination. . . . Probably more has been written and less is known about leadership than about any other topic in the behavioral sciences." In a similar vein, Richard Hackman and Ruth Wageman (2007) more recently concluded that the leadership field is "curiously unformed" (p. 43).

For those who are not aware of the various crises leadership researchers have faced, imagine taking pieces of several sets of jigsaw puzzles, mixing them, and then asking someone to put the pieces together into one cohesive picture. Analogously, leadership researchers have struggled for most of the last century to put together an integrated, theoretically cohesive view of the nature of leadership, invariably leading to disappointment in those who attempted it. Also, the puzzle itself is changing. As noted recently, leadership is an evolving construct that reflects ongoing changes in the challenges that require leadership (Day, in press). For all these reasons, there has been much dissatisfaction and pessimism in the leadership field (e.g., Greene, 1977; Schriesheim & Kerr, 1977)—and even calls for a moratorium on leadership research (Miner, 1975).

Fortunately, a clearer picture is beginning to emerge. Leadership scholars have been re-energized by new directions in the field, and research efforts have revitalized areas previously abandoned for apparent lack of consistency in findings (e.g., leadership trait theory). Our accumulated knowledge now allows us to explain the nature (including the biological bases) of leadership, its antecedents, and consequences with some degree of confidence. This accumulated knowledge is reflected in our volume, which will provide readers with a thorough overview of leadership and its complexities, advanced methods used to study it, how it is assessed and developed, and evolutionary perspectives on the topic (see Part II). We include six major theoretical perspectives for studying leadership: individual differences, contingency, transformational and charismatic, relational, follower-centric, and shared (see Part III). We also focus on leadership and special domains such as culture, gender, identity, and ethics (see Part IV).

To provide the necessary background to understand the chapters that follow, we first acquaint readers with the concept of leadership and why leadership is necessary. Then we briefly trace the history of leadership research and examine its major schools, most of which are reviewed in our book. Our historical overview is also necessary as an organizing framework because chapter authors frequently refer to elements of the history of leadership research. We also discuss emerging issues in leadership research and how findings are being consolidated. Finally, we provide an overview of the book and a summary of each of the respective chapters.

What Is Leadership?

Leadership is one of social science's most examined phenomena. The scrutiny afforded to leadership is not surprising, given that it is a universal activity evident in humankind and in animal species (Bass, 2008). Reference to leadership is apparent throughout classical Western and Eastern writings with a widespread belief that leadership is vital for effective organizational and societal functioning. Nonetheless, leadership is often easy to identify in practice but it is difficult to define precisely. Given the complex nature of leadership, a specific and widely accepted definition of leadership does not exist and might never be found. Fred Fiedler (1971), for example, noted: "There are almost as many definitions of leadership as there are leadership theories—and there are almost as many theories of leadership as there are psychologists working in the field" (p. 1). Even in this absence of universal agreement, a broad definition of leadership is required before introducing the construct as a domain of scholarly inquiry.

Most leadership scholars would likely agree, at least in principle, that leadership can be defined in terms of (a) an influencing process—and its resultant outcomes—that occurs between a leader and followers and (b) how this influencing process is explained by the leader's dispositional characteristics and behaviors, follower perceptions and attributions of the leader, and the context in which the influencing process occurs. We recognize that this is a multifaceted definition that is heavily "leader centric" in describing mainly one-way effects associated with the personal characteristics of a leader; however, it also includes aspects of the interaction between leader and follower (in terms of perceptions and attributions) as well as a definition of leadership as an effect with regard to the resulting outcomes (e.g., goal achievement). We also acknowledge that leadership is rooted in a context, which may affect the type of leadership that emerges and whether it will be effective (Liden & Antonakis, 2009). Our broad definition of leadership thus incorporates the most commonly used definitional features: the leader as person (dispositional characteristics), leader behavior, the effects of a leader, the interaction process between a leader and follower(s), and the importance of context (Bass, 2008).

In setting forth any definition of leadership, it is also important that we differentiate it conceptually from power and management, respectively, because these concepts are often confused with leadership. Power refers to the means leaders have to potentially influence others. Examples include referent power (i.e., followers' identification with the leader), expertise, the ability to reward or punish performance, and the formal power that is accorded legitimately based on one's role (Etzioni, 1964; French & Raven, 1968). Thus, the ability to lead others requires that one has power.

Regarding its distinction from management, leadership as seen from the "New" perspective (Bryman, 1992) is purpose-driven action that brings about change or transformation based on values, ideals, vision, symbols, and emotional exchanges. Management is objectives driven, resulting in stability grounded in rationality, bureaucratic means, and the fulfillment of contractual obligations (i.e., transactions). Although some view leaders and managers as different sorts of individuals (Zaleznik, 1992), others argue that successful leadership also requires successful management, that leadership and management are complementary, but that leadership goes beyond management, and that leadership is necessary for outcomes that exceed expectations (Bass, 1985, 1998; Bass & Riggio, 2006).

At its essence, leadership is functional and necessary for a variety of reasons. On a supervisory level, leadership is required to complement organizational systems (Katz & Kahn, 1978), establish and recognize group goals and values, recognize and integrate various individual styles and personalities in a group, maximize the use of group members' abilities, and help resolve problems and conflicts in a group (Schutz, 1961, as cited in Bass, 2008). Thus, from a functional perspective, a leader is a "completer" who does or gets done whatever is not being adequately handled by a group (McGrath, 1962). At the strategic level, leadership is necessary to ensure the coordinated functioning of the organization as it interacts with a dynamic external environment (Katz & Kahn, 1978). That is, the organization must adapt to its context; for this to occur, its leaders must monitor the external and internal environments, formulate a strategy based on the strengths and weakness of the organizations and the opportunities presented by the environment, and monitor outcomes so that its strategic goals are met (Antonakis, House, Rowold, & Borgmann, 2010). Thus, leadership is required to direct and guide organizational and human resources toward the strategic objectives of the organization and ensure that organizational functions are aligned with the external environment (see Zaccaro, 2001).

The Study of Leadership

In this section, we discuss how the study of leadership has evolved. Our description is cursory because many of the details relating to the different theoretical perspectives of leadership are discussed in various chapters that follow. Our intention is to provide readers with a general understanding of how leadership theory evolved into the major paradigms presented in this book. We then discuss leadership in special domains and emerging issues relating leadership to culture, gender, ethics, and identity, among others. Finally, we discuss how leadership findings are being integrated into cohesive frameworks (i.e., hybrid approaches).

A Brief History of Leadership Research

We have divided leadership research into nine major schools (see Figure 1.1) and classified the schools on two dimensions: temporal (i.e., the time period in which the school emerged) and productivity (i.e., the indicative degree to which the school attracted research interest in a *specific* period of time). The derivation of the schools and the research productivity of the schools are based on our professional judgment; however, we have also been guided by a recent review of the literature that has appeared in the last decade in *The Leadership Quarterly* (Gardner, Lowe, Moss, Mahoney, & Cogliser, 2010). We have also relied on several historical reviews (e.g., Bass, 2008; Day, in

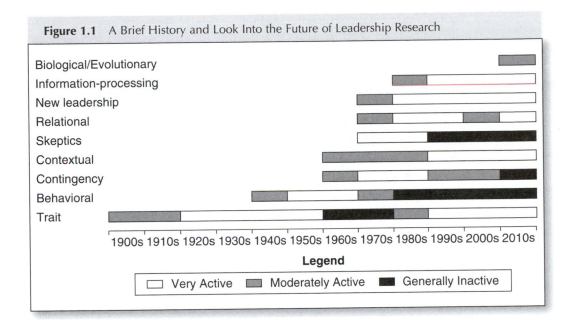

Figure 1.1   A Brief History and Look Into the Future of Leadership Research

press; House & Aditya, 1997; Lowe & Gardner, 2000; Van Seters & Field, 1990), to which readers can refer for more complete accounts of the history and development of leadership research.

Trait School of Leadership

The scientific study of leadership began at the turn of the 20th century with the "great man [sic]" or trait-based perspective, which saw the shaping of history through the lens of exceptional individuals. This school of thought suggested that certain dispositional characteristics (i.e., stable personality attributes or traits) differentiated leaders from nonleaders. Thus, leadership researchers focused on identifying robust individual differences in personality traits that were thought to be associated with effective leadership. In two influential reviews (Mann, 1959; Stogdill, 1948), traits such as intelligence and dominance were identified as being associated with leadership. However, trait research, for most intents and purposes, was shut down following the rather pessimistic interpretations of these findings by many leadership scholars (see Day & Zaccaro, 2007, for a more comprehensive discussion of the history of leadership trait theory).

This was the first major crisis reorientation of leadership research, and it took almost 30 years for this line of research to reemerge. The impetus for the re-emergence of leadership trait theory came from a reanalysis of Mann's data using a relatively new and innovative analytic procedure at the time—meta-analysis (Lord, De Vader, & Alliger, 1986). This analytic procedure proposed new ways of aggregating effects across studies to more accurately estimate effect sizes (Hunter & Schmidt, 1990). The meta-analytic results offered by Lord et al. suggested that the trait of intelligence was strongly correlated ($r = .50$) with *perceptions* of leadership (i.e., emergence rather than effectiveness) and that this effect was robust across studies included in Mann's data as well as studies published subsequent to Mann. More recent meta-analyses confirmed that objectively measured intelligence correlates ($r = .33$) with leadership effectiveness as well (Judge, Colbert, & Ilies, 2004). Studies by Kenny and Zaccaro (1983) and Zaccaro, Foti, and Kenny (1991) were also instrumental in demonstrating stable leader characteristics, such as traits related to leader emergence. David McClelland (1985), in the meantime, led another independent line of inquiry linking leader implicit motives (i.e., subconscious drives or wishes) to leader effectiveness (see also House, Spangler, & Woycke, 1991).

There have been a few high-profile reviews of the trait perspective on leadership and particularly the moderately strong relationship of the big-five personality factors with leader emergence and effectiveness (e.g., Judge, Bono, Ilies, & Gerhardt, 2002; Zaccaro, 2007); however, there has been a decline in the proportion of articles published in *The Leadership Quarterly* (*LQ*)—a prominent specialty journal devoted to leadership theory and research (Gardner et al., 2010). Research efforts in this area, however, shall probably continue as advances are made in psychometric testing and interest in other individual-differences areas (e.g., gender, diversity) increases.

Behavioral School of Leadership

Given the early pessimistic reviews of the trait literature, leadership researchers began, in the 1950s, focusing on the behavioral styles of leaders. Similar to the Lewin and Lippitt (1938) exposition of democratic versus autocratic leaders, this line of research focused on the behaviors that leaders enacted and how they treated followers. The influential Ohio State (Stogdill & Coons, 1957) and University of Michigan (Katz, Maccoby, Gurin, & Floor, 1951) studies identified two overarching leadership factors generally referred to as *consideration* (i.e., supportive, person-oriented leadership) and *initiating structure* (i.e., directive, task-oriented leadership). Others extended this research to organization-level effects (e.g., Blake & Mouton, 1964).

Nonetheless, leadership research found itself again in crisis because of contradictory findings relating behavioral "styles" of leadership to relevant outcomes. That is, there was no consistent evidence of a universally preferred leadership style across tasks or situations. From these inconsistent findings, it was proposed that success of the leader's behavioral style must be contingent on the situation. As a result, leadership theory in the 1960s began to focus on leadership contingencies. Interest in behavioral theories per se is currently very low (Gardner et al., 2010); however, many of the ideas of the behavioral movement have been incorporated into other perspectives of leadership (e.g., contingency theories, transformational leadership). In addition, recent meta-analytic results suggest that there is perhaps more consistent support for consideration and initiating structure in predicting leadership outcomes than has been generally acknowledged (Judge, Piccolo, & Ilies, 2004).

Contingency School of Leadership

The leadership contingency theory movement is credited in large part to Fiedler (1967, 1971), who stated that leader–member relations, task structure, and the position power of the leader determine the effectiveness of the type of leadership exercised. Another well-known contingency approach was that of House (1971), who focused on the leader's role in clarifying paths to follower goals. Kerr and Jermier (1978) extended this line of research into the "substitutes-for-leadership" theory by focusing on the conditions where leadership is unnecessary as a result of factors such as follower capabilities, clear organizational systems, and routinized procedures. Other lines of research, presenting theories of leader decision-making style and various contingencies, include the work of Vroom and associates (e.g., Vroom & Jago, 1988; Vroom & Yetton, 1973).

Whereas there is some ongoing interest in contingency theories (e.g., Fiedler, 1993; House, 1996), the overall influence of the approach appears to have tapered off dramatically. Only about 1% of the articles published in the last decade in *LQ* focused on contingency theories (Gardner et al., 2010). A contributing factor to this waning interest may be that parts of this literature have led to the development of broader contextual approaches to leadership, which are discussed under emerging issues below.

Relational School of Leadership

Soon after the contingency movement became popular, another line of research focusing on relationships between leaders and followers (i.e., the relational school) began generating substantial theoretical attention and became the focus of research. This movement was based on what originally was termed vertical dyad linkage theory (Dansereau, Graen, & Haga, 1975), which evolved into leader–member exchange (LMX) theory (Graen & Uhl-Bien, 1995). LMX theory describes the nature of the relations between leaders and their followers. High-quality relations between a leader and his or her followers (i.e., the "in group") are based on trust and mutual respect, whereas low-quality relations between a leader and his or her followers (i.e., the "out group") are based on the fulfillment of contractual obligations. LMX theory predicts that high-quality relations generate more positive leader outcomes than do lower quality relations, which has been supported empirically (Gerstner & Day, 1997; Ilies, Nahrgang, & Morgeson, 2007). This line of research continues to find new directions, and overall interest in relational approaches to leadership appears to be relatively strong, with approximately six percent ($N = 40$) of articles published in *LQ* between 2000 and 2009 addressing various relational perspectives, including growing interest in the role of followers (Gardner et al., 2010).

Skeptics-of-Leadership School

Leadership research faced yet other series of challenges in the 1970s and 1980s. The validity of questionnaire ratings of leadership was criticized as likely biased by the implicit leadership theories of those providing the ratings (e.g., Eden & Leviathan, 1975; Rush, Thomas, & Lord, 1977). This position suggests that what leaders do (i.e., leadership) is largely attributed based on performance outcomes and may reflect the implicit leadership theories that individuals carry "in their heads" (Eden & Leviathan, p. 740). That is, people attribute leadership as a way of explaining observed results, even if those results were due to factors outside of the leader's control.

In a related field of research, scholars argued that leader evaluations were based on the attributions followers make in their quest to understand and assign causes to organizational outcomes (Calder, 1977; Meindl & Ehrlich, 1987; Meindl, Ehrlich, & Dukerich, 1985). These researchers suggested that what leaders do might be largely irrelevant and that leader outcomes (i.e., the performance of the leader's group) affect how leaders are rated (see Lord, Binning, Rush, & Thomas, 1978). Another related line of research questioned whether leadership existed at all or was even needed, thus questioning whether it made any difference to organizational performance (Meindl & Ehrlich, 1987; Pfeffer, 1977).

Many of the above arguments have been addressed by leadership scholars who might be classified as realists rather than skeptics (e.g., Barrick, Day, Lord, & Alexander, 1991; Day & Lord, 1988; House et al., 1991; J. E. Smith, Carson, & Alexander, 1984). Interest in the skeptics' perspective appears to have waned, although there is increasing interest in followers' roles in leadership processes (Gardner et al., 2010). In addressing many of questions posed by the skeptics' school, the study of leadership has benefited from (a) using more rigorous methodologies, (b) differentiating top-level leadership from supervisory leadership and (c) focusing on followers and how they perceive reality. Furthermore, the study of followership and the resultant information-processing perspective of leadership have generated many theoretical advances that have strengthened the leadership field immensely.

Information-Processing School of Leadership

The major impetus for the information-processing perspective is based on the work of Lord and colleagues (e.g., Lord, Foti, & De Vader, 1984). The focus of the work has mostly been on understanding how and why a leader is legitimized (i.e., accorded influence) through the process of matching his or her personal characteristics (i.e., personality traits) with the prototypical expectations that followers have of a leader.

The information-processing perspective has also been extended to better understand how cognition is related to the enactment of various behaviors (e.g., Balkundi & Kilduff, 2005; Wofford, Goodwin, & Whittington, 1998). Also notable are the links that have been made to other areas of leadership, for example, prototypes and their relation to various contextual factors (see Lord, Brown, Harvey, & Hall, 2001; Lord & Emrich, 2000; Lord & Maher, 1991). Information-processing perspectives of leadership have generated much attention, and the interest in leader/follower cognitions among contributors to *LQ* continues to grow (Gardner et al., 2010). As a result, research in the areas of cognition, information processing— and emotions—should continue to provide us with novel understandings of leadership.

The New Leadership (Neo-Charismatic/Transformational/Visionary) School

At a time when leadership research was beginning to appear especially dull and lacking in any theoretical advances or insights, the work of Bass and his associates (Bass, 1985, 1998; Bass & Avolio, 1994; Hater & Bass, 1988) and others promoting visionary and charismatic leadership theories (e.g., Bennis & Nanus, 1985; Conger & Kanungo, 1987), reignited interest in leadership research in general (Bryman, 1992; Hunt, 1999) and in related schools of leadership (e.g., trait school).

Bass (1985) built on the work of Burns (1978), House (1977), and others to argue that previous paradigms of leadership were mainly transactional; that is, they were focused on the mutual satisfaction of transactional (i.e., social exchange) obligations. Bass believed that a different form of leadership was required to account for follower outcomes centered on a sense of purpose and an idealized mission. He referred to this type of leadership as *transformational leadership,* in which idealized and inspiring leader behaviors induced followers to transcend their interests for that of the greater good; the Bass model has federated much of the research in this area (Antonakis & House, 2002). Transformational and charismatic leadership, and other models categorized under the heading of "Neo-charismatic" approaches, make up the single most dominant leadership paradigm over the past decade; however, the overall proportion of published *LQ* articles stemming from this school has dropped from 34% between 1990 and 1999 to about 13% from 2000 to 2009 (Gardner et al., 2010). It holds the top spot in terms of published *LQ* articles. Gardner et al. attributed its proportional drop to the increase of various approaches classified as "New Directions" (e.g., contextual approaches, leadership development, authentic leadership) in the same time period—from 14% to more than 44%.

Biological and Evolutionary Perspectives _____

We are including a new research stream, which is related somewhat to the trait perspective of leadership in terms of measuring individual differences. This perspective, however, is more of a hard-science approach in terms of measuring directly observable individual differences (e.g., biological variables or processes) and also of considering why certain variables might provide an evolutionary advantage to an organism. This research stream is novel and is currently producing interesting research from looking at the behavioral genetics of leadership emergence (Ilies, Gerhardt, & Le, 2004) to leadership role occupancy, both in men and women (Arvey, Rotundo, Johnson, Zhang, & McGue, 2006; Arvey, Zhang, Avolio, & Krueger, 2007; Ilies et al., 2004). Other interesting avenues include studying the effect of hormones on correlates of leadership, for example dominance (Grant & France, 2001; Gray & Campbell, 2009; Sellers, Mehl, & Josephs, 2007; Zyphur, Narayanan, Koh, & Koh, 2009), neuroscientific perspectives of leadership (Antonakis, Ashkanasy, & Dasborough, 2009; Chiao, Mathur, Harada, & Lipke, 2009; Villarejo & Camacho, 2009), evolutionary points of view (Antonakis & Dalgas, 2009; Kramer, Arend, & Ward, 2010; K. B. Smith, Larimer, Littvay, & Hibbing, 2007; Van Vugt & Schaller, 2008), as well as integrative biological perspectives (Caldu & Dreher, 2007). This perspective might be poised to make major contributions in understanding the sociobiology of leadership. Interest in the area is spreading, as indicated by a forthcoming special issue of *The Leadership Quarterly* that is titled "Towards a Biology of Leadership."

Emerging Issues _____

We currently have a fundamental understanding of leadership, but there are still many areas that are in need of additional research. We briefly discuss some of these areas, which include context, ethics, and diversity issues related to leadership. We also discuss how future leadership research might be consolidated.

Related to the contingency movement is the Contextual School of leadership (e.g., (Hannah, Uhl-Bien, Avolio, & Cavaretta, 2009; Osborn, Hunt, & Jauch, 2002; Porter & McLaughlin, 2006; Shamir & Howell, 1999). From this perspective, contextual factors are seen to give rise to or inhibit certain leadership behaviors or their dispositional antecedents (Liden & Antonakis, 2009). These contextual factors can include leader hierarchical level, national culture, leader–follower gender, and organizational characteristics, among other factors (Antonakis, Avolio, & Sivasubramaniam, 2003). Understanding the contextual factors in which leadership is embedded is necessary for advancing a more general understanding of leadership. Simply put, leadership does not occur in a vacuum (House & Aditya, 1997), and context and leadership appear to be intertwined.

Ethics is another important emerging topic in leadership research (Brown & Treviño, 2006). It is surprising that ethics and ethical leadership has not been a mainstay of leadership researchers. Indeed, Bass (1985)—one of the most prominent figures in the field—did not make the distinction between authentic (i.e., ethical) and inauthentic (i.e., unethical) transformational leaders until more than a decade after he published his theory (see Bass, 1998; Bass & Steidlemeier, 1999). The ethics of leadership and a leader's level of moral development are increasingly becoming essential elements of leadership research and theory (Turner, Barling, Epitropaki, Butcher, & Milner, 2002). Future leadership models should consider the ethics of leader means and ends, as well as ways in which leader moral orientation can be developed and otherwise improved (Day, Harrison, & Halpin, 2009).

Issues regarding diversity and leadership have been highlighted as receiving relatively scarce attention in the literature (Eagly & Chin, 2010). In particular, the diversity of leaders and followers in terms of culture, gender, race and ethnicity, or sexual orientation has been infrequently addressed. Advances in theory and research are more notable in the areas of culture—thanks in large part to the Project GLOBE studies (House, Hanges, Javidan, Dorfman, & Gupta, 2004)—and gender through the work of Alice Eagly and colleagues (see Eagly & Carli, 2007, for a summary and overview of major findings). The literature with regard to leadership and race, ethnicity, and sexual orientation (in particular) is presently relatively unformed; however, there are some early attempts to identify and describe the challenges associated with leading across racial differences in organizations (e.g., Livers & Caver, 2003). Clearly, there is a need for additional theory building and empirical research directed at the numerous facets involved with diversity and leadership.

Given how much is currently known about the nature of leadership, we believe that researchers are in a position to integrate overlapping and complementary conceptualizations of leadership. Van Seters and Field (1990) argued that the new era of leadership research will be one of converging evidence and integration. In a similar vein—and almost 20 years later—Avolio (2007) urged the promotion of more integrative strategies for leadership theory building. It appears that our accumulated knowledge is such that we can begin to construct hybrid theories of leadership, or even hybrid-integrative perspectives (i.e., integrating diverse perspectives), including not only psychological and contextual variables but biological ones as well (Antonakis, 2011). An example of an integrative perspective includes the work of House and Shamir (1993), who integrated various "new" leadership theories. Zaccaro's (2001) hybrid framework of executive leadership links cognitive, behavioral, strategic, and visionary leadership theory perspectives. Zaccaro's work is also a good example of a hybrid-integrative perspective, given that he also integrated overlapping perspectives of leadership. Another recent example of a hybrid-integrative framework is the integrative approach to leader development proposed by Day et al. (2009) that seeks to connect the relatively disparate fields of expertise and expert performance, identity and self-regulation, and adult development.

There are many other ways in which hybrid approaches could be developed. For example, LMX theory—included under the "Relational School of Leadership"—has been criticized for not specifying behavioral antecedents of high- or low-quality relations (see House & Aditya, 1997). LMX could potentially be integrated with the transformational-transactional leadership theory, in that the style of leadership employed is thought to be related to the type of leader–follower relations and exchanges (see Deluga, 1990; Gerstner & Day, 1997; Howell & Hall-Merenda, 1999).

It is only through efforts to consolidate findings that leadership research will go to the next level where we may finally be able to construct and test more general theories of leadership. Previous research has laid the foundations for such theories. Now leadership researchers need to begin to conceptualize ways in which many of the diverse findings can be united and otherwise synthesized and integrated, examples of which are evident throughout the chapters of this book.

Organization and Summary of the Book _____

We have introduced readers to the major paradigms and current issues relating to leadership. In the remainder of this chapter, we provide a summary of the chapters that compose the second edition of the *Nature of Leadership*.

Part II: Leadership: Science, Nature, and Nurture

Chapter 2: Lord and Dinh (*Aggregation Processes and Levels of Analysis as Organizing Structures for Leadership Theory*) propose that theoretical integration in the leadership field requires a better system for addressing levels of analyses issues. They argue that it is necessary to distinguish among global, shared, and configural properties because each reflects a different form of aggregation from lower-level units. Lord and Dinh then apply this distinction to consider leadership at the level of events, individuals, groups, and organizations. Working with this system provides for new insights regarding the shared functions and antecedents of various leadership theories. It represents a major integrative advancement in leadership theory in exploring aggregation processes and levels of analysis as fundamental organizing structures for leadership theory.

Chapter 3: Zyphur, Barsky, and Zhang (*Advances in Leadership Research Methods*) describe five advanced quantitative techniques that they hope will prove useful to leadership researchers. The techniques are (a) latent polynomial regression, which introduces a new and improved congruence model; (b) multilevel member weighted modeling (MWM) that shows how observed variables may be used to weight the contributions of individual group members when estimating group averages in multilevel modeling; (c) intercept-as-mean latent growth modeling (IGM) that shows how researchers can set latent intercept factors to estimate each individual's average score across observations over time; (d) multilevel structural equation modeling that addresses noted limitations in regular structural equation modeling and multilevel models, respectively; and (e) latent class cluster analysis as a method for examining profiles among multiple observed variables such as leadership styles or personality traits. Zyphur and colleagues demonstrate how each model provides a novel mindset for asking new questions and studying traditional leadership questions in novel ways.

Chapter 4: Day (*The Nature of Leadership Development*) examines a number of fundamental questions with regard to the nature of leadership development and evaluates the available evidence regarding each question. The question of whether leaders are born or made has been addressed in a series of studies comparing identical and fraternal twins, suggesting that as much as 70% of leadership capability could be shaped by nurture (i.e., experience). Recent longitudinal evidence informing the question of whether leaders can and do develop over time is summarized, followed by an analysis of what is it that develops as a function of leadership development (i.e., what are the competencies or expertise facets that develop?). The chapter then reviews the available practices on how to best promote leadership development. It concludes with a look toward how to improve the science and practice of leadership development in terms of better supporting an evidence-based approach to the field.

Chapter 5: Van Vugt (*The Nature in Leadership: Evolutionary, Biological, and Social Neuroscience Perspectives*) proposes Evolutionary Leadership Theory (ELT) as a new approach to the study of leadership, connecting the diverse lines of research in the social, biological, economic, and cognitive sciences. It provides an overarching framework that is consistent with Darwin's evolutionary theory, which he refers to as "Darwin's Toolbox." Van Vugt argues that it is important to study the evolutionary origins and functions of leadership so as to better comprehend the veritable "nature" in leadership. In particular, ELT connects many older findings, helps generate novel hypotheses, and tests them with a diversity of methodologies from behavioral genetics to neuroscience and from experimentation to game theory.

Part III: The Major Schools of Leadership

Chapter 6: Judge and Long (*Individual Differences in Leadership*) urge students and scholars of the leadership field to keep three things in perspective. First, individual differences matter, and they provide a useful starting point for theory building. Second, leaders demonstrate different states and styles based on their dispositions as well as through the individual differences of followers. Third, leaders do not operate in a vacuum, and context can play a significant role in leadership outcomes. From these assumptions, Judge and Long propose and evaluate an evidence-based model of individual differences in leadership that links leader traits with leader states and styles as mediators predicting leader emergence and effectiveness. Moderators in the forms of leader and follower individual differences and contextual factors are also addressed. The authors also explore paradoxical effects associated with "dark side" facets of leader individual differences on emergence and effectiveness outcomes.

Chapter 7: Ayman and Adams (*Contingencies, Context, Situation, and Leadership*) review situational and contingency theories of leadership suggesting that relations between leader characteristics (e.g., traits, behaviors) and leader outcomes depend on the situation in which the influencing processes occur. They argue that the success of leadership is a function of contingencies, some contextual and some intrapersonal, which moderate the relations of leader characteristics to leader outcomes. Ayman and Adams also clarify a common misunderstanding that a leader's style is fixed. They differentiated style as either trait based, which is fairly consistent, or behavior based, which is malleable. They argue that leaders are capable of monitoring the environment and adjusting their responses to fit a particular context. A combination of leadership skills and competencies such as sensitivity, responsiveness, and flexibility may help leaders reach "mettle"—defined as the optimal match between leader characteristics and the situational context.

Chapter 8: Antonakis (*Transformational and Charismatic Leadership*) reviews the available evidence on "Neo-charismatic" theories of leadership, especially its transformational and charismatic forms. In his comprehensive historical analysis, he explains how these approaches came to fore and currently dominate the leadership landscape. He concludes that even though research in the field is mature, there is still much that needs to be done to improve these models. In particular, Antonakis points to outstanding needs for (a) more longitudinal and multilevel research, (b) the development of more inclusive and less biased questionnaire measures including objective measures, and (c) a fuller understanding of process models that also consider contextual effects and individual-difference antecedents. These are important issues to understand because as history attests, future leaders will continue to emerge who wield charismatic power.

Chapter 9: Uhl-Bien, Maslyn, and Ospina (*The Nature of Relational Leadership: A Multitheoretical Lens on Leadership Relationships and Processes*) adopt a multi-paradigmatic and multiple-theory lens to relational leadership. They draw from findings regarding relationships across a variety of literature and perspectives to provide a review of relational leadership from the standpoint of leader–follower relationships (e.g., dyadic relationship quality) and leadership "relationality" (e.g., relational processes and collective practices). Uhl-Bien and colleagues outline a broad, cross-disciplinary and multiple-method research program that focuses not just on LMX measures but on the wider examination of leadership relationships (dyadic and collective) and relational processes and practices. This agenda calls for including consideration of constructionist approaches that can help advance study of the nature of relationships, their development, and relational organizing (e.g., shared patterns of meaning making, conjoint agency, and coordinated behavior through which leadership is enacted). They conclude by challenging leadership scholars to take seriously the need to consider relationality in leadership research.

Chapter 10: Brown (*In the Minds of Followers: Follower-Centric Approaches to Leadership*) considers key assumptions about followers and the role that followers have played in much of the previous leadership literature. In furthering a follower-centric perspective on leadership, he argues that if we are to understand why followers behave as they do, a necessary first step is in understanding their thought processes, mainly in the form of information-processing activities. Two core questions are examined in the chapter. First, why is it that we understand the world through leaders? Second, what is the nature of our mental leader category and how does it influence followers' perceptions of leaders? Brown addresses these questions through a review of the foundational theory and research that informs our understanding of the information processing that is behind our leadership perceptions.

Chapter 11: Wassenaar and Pearce (*The Nature of Shared Leadership*) offer a foundational view of shared leadership defined as a dynamic, interactive influence process among individuals in groups where the objective is to lead one another to achieve group and organizational goals. The focus of shared leadership is not on *the* leader as with dominant leader-centric approaches but on how individuals in a team or organization can be *a* leader along with other members. The authors evaluate recent evidence on the antecedents and outcomes of shared leadership, review various approaches to the measurement of shared leadership, and explore future directions in theory and research on shared leadership.

Part IV: Leadership and Special Domains

Chapter 12: Den Hartog and Dickson (*Leadership and Culture*) take a contextual approach in reviewing research on the relation between leadership and national (i.e., societal) culture. They draw on literature from cultural anthropology and cross-cultural psychology to show that national culture equips individuals with common ways of perceiving and acting, which systemically affect what followers expect from leaders and how leaders enact their behaviors. They show that certain leader traits and behaviors may be context specific and that others may be universal, but differentially enacted according to national culture and context. Ultimately, Den Hartog and Dickson show that we should not take for granted that leadership models and theories developed in one culture will apply similarly in another. They describe culture at the societal and organizational level and show how culture can affect implicit leadership theories and behavior. Finally, they highlight the developing world in recognizing a new set of challenges to leadership scholars, given that most of our literature is steeped in cultural assumptions from the so-called developed countries of the world.

Chapter 13: Carli and Eagly (*Leadership and Gender*) focus on the contextual perspective of gender-based expectations of leaders and how they constrain the type of leadership that is enacted. They discuss the validity of arguments related to male–female difference from various perspectives, including societal, evolutionary, and prejudicial. Literature is reviewed demonstrating that women may not have the same opportunities to lead and that women are more constrained in the behaviors they can display than are men. They explore five explanations offered for women's scarce occupancy of high-level leadership positions and conclude that the evidence suggests the only plausible explanations reside in prejudice and discrimination against women leaders. Even though women leaders are disadvantaged by stereotypes and restricted role expectations, they are as effective as are men leaders, and women actually display certain prototypically effective leader styles more often than do men. Carli and Eagly ultimately conclude that economic necessity and fundamental issues of fairness require facilitating faster entry of women into the leadership ranks in the future.

Chapter 14: van Knippenberg (*Leadership and Identity*) provides an overview of the identity approach to leadership. Fundamental to this approach is the notion that identity shapes perceptions, attitudes, and behavior. In short, identity can be a powerful motivating force and a focus on leader and follower identity is instrumental in understanding leadership effectiveness. The research evidence is consistent that identity matters when it comes to understanding leadership processes and outcomes. van Knippenberg urges further development of the identity perspective on leadership as a possible means of fostering integration in the field and building more broad-ranging accounts of leadership.

Chapter 15: Ciulla (*Ethics and Effectiveness: The Nature of Good Leadership*) focuses on another emerging issue: ethics and leader effectiveness. She writes from the unique perspective of a philosopher, making clear the limitations of traditional leadership theorists' attempts to weave ethics into their theories by simply exhorting that ethical leadership is important. Although inroads have been made by some leadership scholars, Ciulla shows how philosophy can be used to highlight ethical dilemmas of leaders, how to judge the ethics of leader outcomes, and the implications for leader–follower relations. Ciulla sees leader ethics and leader outcomes as inextricably intertwined. In addition, she presents a persuasive argument that leaders cannot be considered effective unless they are ethical.

Part V: Conclusion

Chapter 16: Bennis (*The Crucibles of Authentic Leadership*) uses an engaging writing style in taking the reader along on an Odyssey of leadership. He provides practical examples, subtly integrating and applying many of the book's themes, and brings to light the nature of authentic leadership. He touches on numerous issues and how they relate to leader emergence and effectiveness, focusing on leader traits, experiential learning, coalition building, contexts and contingencies, national culture, and so forth. He concludes with how leadership research should be taken to the next level by studying it using multidisciplinary paradigms. He relates the issues discussed to historical events and to the interplay of factors that "make" leaders. These are the "crucibles" of leadership, conditions in which leaders face great tests and crises, from which they emerge, molded with a vision and values to inspire others to do what is morally correct.

We hope to introduce you to what we believe is a fascinating body of leadership literature. The complexity and mystique surrounding leadership evolve into understanding as you read the chapters that follow. In the last century, the often-misunderstood phenomenon of leadership has been tossed and battered while social scientists tried to make sense of a force they knew was important, but which seemed beyond the reach of scientific inquiry. Remarking about the difficulties leadership researchers have faced, Bennis (1959, p. 260) noted: "Always, it seems, the concept of leadership eludes us or turns up in another form to taunt us again with its slipperiness and complexity."

The concept is still complex—perhaps more so than at any other point in history—but it is better understood and less elusive. We still have much to learn about leadership, but we are guided by a spirit of optimism emanating from the findings of those researchers before us who went through their own "crucibles." Bloodied in a sense but unbowed, they continued to study leadership and to inspire succeeding generations of scientists to continue their exploration. All the while, leaders influenced followers and will continue to do so, regardless of the fads, follies, and folderol that have distracted leadership researchers in the past.

References

Antonakis, J. (2011). Predictors of leadership: The usual suspects and the suspect traits. In A. Bryman, D. Collinson, K. Grint, B. Jackson & M. Uhl-Bien (Eds.), *Sage handbook of leadership*. Thousand Oaks, CA: Sage, 269–285.

Antonakis, J., Ashkanasy, N. M., & Dasborough, M. T. (2009). Does leadership need emotional intelligence? *The Leadership Quarterly, 20*, 247–261.

Antonakis, J., Avolio, B. J., & Sivasubramaniam, N. (2003). Context and leadership: An examination of the nine-factor full-range leadership theory using the Multifactor Leadership Questionnaire. *The Leadership Quarterly, 14*, 261–295.

Antonakis, J., & Dalgas, O. (2009). Predicting elections: Child's play! *Science, 323*(5918), 1183.

Antonakis, J., & House, R. J. (2002). An analysis of the full-range leadership theory: The way forward. In B. J. Avolio & F. J. Yammarino (Eds.), *Transformational and charismatic leadership: The road ahead* (pp. 3–34). Amsterdam, Netherlands: JAI.

Antonakis, J., House, R. J., Rowold, J., & Borgmann, L. (2010). *A fuller full-range leadership theory: Instrumental, transformational, and transactional leadership*. Unpublished manuscript.

Arvey, R. D., Rotundo, M., Johnson, W., Zhang, Z., & McGue, M. (2006). The determinants of leadership role occupancy: Genetic and personality factors. *The Leadership Quarterly, 17*, 1–20.

Arvey, R. D., Zhang, Z., Avolio, B. J., & Krueger, R. F. (2007). Developmental and genetic determinants of leadership role occupancy among women. *Journal of Applied Psychology, 92*, 693–706.

Avolio, B. J. (2007). Promoting more integrative strategies for leadership theory-building. *American Psychologist, 62*, 25–33.

Balkundi, P., & Kilduff, M. (2005). The ties that lead: A social network approach to leadership. *The Leadership Quarterly, 16*, 941–961.

Barrick, M. R., Day, D. V., Lord, R. G., & Alexander, R. A. (1991). Assessing the utility of executive leadership. *The Leadership Quarterly, 2*, 9–22.

Bass, B. M. (1985). *Leadership and performance beyond expectations*. New York: Free Press.

Bass, B. M. (1998). *Transformational leadership: Industrial, military, and educational impact*. Mahwah, NJ: Lawrence Erlbaum.

Bass, B. M. (2008). *The Bass handbook of leadership: Theory, research, and managerial applications* (4th ed.). New York: Free Press.

Bass, B. M., & Avolio, B. J. (1994). *Transformational leadership: Improving organizational effectiveness*. Thousand Oaks, CA: Sage.

Bass, B. M., & Riggio, R. E. (2006). *Transformational leadership* (2nd ed.). Mahwah, NJ: Lawrence Erlbaum.

Bass, B. M., & Steidlemeier, P. (1999). Ethics, character, and authentic transformational leadership behavior. *The Leadership Quarterly, 10*, 181–217.

Bennis, W. (1959). Leadership theory and administrative behavior. *Administrative Science Quarterly, 4,* 259–301.

Bennis, W. (2007). The challenges of leadership in the modern world. *American Psychologist, 62,* 2–5.

Bennis, W., & Nanus, B. (1985). *Leaders: The strategies for taking charge.* New York: HarperCollins.

Blake, R. R., & Mouton, J. S. (1964). *The managerial grid.* Houston, TX: Gulf.

Brown, M. E., & Treviño, L. K. (2006). Ethical leadership: A review and future directions. *The Leadership Quarterly, 17,* 595–616.

Bryman, A. (1992). *Charisma and leadership in organizations.* Newbury Park, CA: Sage.

Burns, J. M. (1978). *Leadership.* New York: Harper & Row.

Calder, B. J. (1977). An attribution theory of leadership. In B. M. Staw & G. R. Salancik (Eds.), *New directions in organizational behavior* (pp. 179–204). Chicago: St. Clair.

Caldu, X., & Dreher, J. C. (2007). Hormonal and genetic influences on processing reward and social information. In C. Senior & M. J. R. Butler (Eds.), *Social cognitive neuroscience of organizations* (Vol. 1118, pp. 43–73). Oxford, UK: Basil Blackwell.

Chiao, J. Y., Mathur, V. A., Harada, T., & Lipke, T. (2009). Neural basis of preference for human social hierarchy versus egalitarianism. In S. Atran, A. Navarro, K. Ochsner, A. Tobena & O. Vilarroya (Eds.), *Values, empathy, and fairness across social barriers* (Vol. 1167, pp. 174–181). Oxford, UK: Basil Blackwell.

Conger, J. A., & Kanungo, R. N. (1987). Toward a behavioral theory of charismatic leadership in organizations. *Academy of Management Review, 12,* 637–647.

Dansereau, F., Jr., Graen, G., & Haga, W. J. (1975). A vertical dyad linkage approach to leadership within formal organizations: A longitudinal investigation of the role making process. *Organizational Behavior and Human Performance, 13,* 46–78.

Day, D. V. (in press). Leadership. In S. W. J. Kozlowski (Ed.), *The Oxford handbook of organizational psychology.* New York: Oxford University Press.

Day, D. V., Harrison, M. M., & Halpin, S. M. (2009). An integrative approach to leader development: Connecting adult development, identity, and expertise. New York: Routledge.

Day, D. V., & Lord, R. G. (1988). Executive leadership and organizational performance: Suggestions for a new theory and methodology. *Journal of Management, 14,* 453–464.

Day, D. V., & Zaccaro, S. J. (2007). Leadership: A critical historical analysis of the influence of leader traits. In L. L. Koppes (Ed.), *Historical perspectives in industrial and organizational psychology* (pp. 383–405). Mahwah, NJ: Lawrence Erlbaum.

Deluga, R. J. (1990). The relationship of leader-member exchanges with laissez-faire, transactional, and transformational leadership in naval environments. In K. E. Clark, M. B. Clark, & D. P. Campbell (Eds.), *Impact of leadership* (pp. 237–247). Greensboro, NC: Center for Creative Leadership.

Eagly, A. H., & Carli, L. L. (2007). *Through the labyrinth: The truth about how women become leaders.* Boston, MA: Harvard Business School Press.

Eagly, A. H., & Chin, J. L. (2010). Diversity and leadership in a changing world. *American Psychologist, 65,* 216–224.

Eden, D., & Leviathan, U. (1975). Implicit leadership theory as a determinant of the factor structure underlying supervisory behavior scales. *Journal of Applied Psychology, 60,* 736–741.

Etzioni, A. (1964). *Modern organizations.* Englewood Cliffs, NJ: Prentice Hall.

Fiedler, F. E. (1967). *A theory of leadership effectiveness.* New York: McGraw-Hill.

Fiedler, F. E. (1971). *Leadership.* Morristown, NJ: General Learning.

Fiedler, F. E. (1993). The leadership situation and the black box in contingency theories. In M. M. Chemers & R. Ayman (Eds.), *Leadership theory and research: Perspectives and directions* (pp. 1–28). San Diego, CA: Academic Press.

French, J. R. P., & Raven, B. H. (1968). The bases of social power. In D. Cartwright & A. Zander (Eds.), *Group dynamics: Research and theory* (3rd ed., pp. 259–269). New York: Harper & Row.

Gardner, W. L., Lowe, K. B., Moss, T. W., Mahoney, K. T., & Cogliser, C. C. (2010). Scholarly leadership of the study of leadership: A review of *The Leadership Quarterly's* second decade, 2000–2009. *The Leadership Quarterly, 21,* 922–958.

Gerstner, C. R., & Day, D. V. (1997). Meta-analytic review of leader–member exchange theory: Correlates and construct issues. *Journal of Applied Psychology, 82,* 827–844.

Graen, G. B., & Uhl-Bien, M. (1995). Relationship-based approach to leadership: Development of leader-member exchange (LMX) theory of leadership over 25 years: Applying a multi-level multi-domain perspective. *The Leadership Quarterly, 6,* 219–247.

Grant, V. J., & France, J. T. (2001). Dominance and testosterone in women. *Biological Psychology, 58,* 41–47.

Gray, P. B., & Campbell, B., C. (2009). Human male testosterone, pair-bonding, and fatherhood. In P. T. Ellison & P. B. Gray (Eds.), *Endocrinology of social relationships* (pp. 270–293). Cambridge, MA: Harvard University Press.

Greene, C. N. (1977). Disenchantment with leadership research: Some causes, recommendations, and alternative directions. In J. G. Hunt & L. L. Larson (Eds.), *Leadership: The cutting edge* (pp. 57–67). Carbondale, IL: Southern Illinois University Press.

Hackman, J. R., & Wageman, R. (2007). Asking the right questions about leadership. *American Psychologist, 62,* 43–47.

Hannah, S. T., Uhl-Bien, M., Avolio, B. J., & Cavaretta, F. L. (2009). A framework for examining leadership in extreme contexts. *The Leadership Quarterly, 20,* 897–919.

Hater, J. J., & Bass, B. M. (1988). Superiors' evaluations and subordinates' perceptions of transformational and transactional leadership. *Journal of Applied Psychology, 73,* 695–702.

House, R. J. (1971). A path-goal theory of leader effectiveness. *Administrative Science Quarterly, 16,* 321–338.

House, R. J. (1977). A 1976 theory of charismatic leadership. In J. G. Hunt & L. L. Larson (Eds.), *Leadership: The cutting edge* (pp. 189–207). Carbondale, IL: Southern Illinois University Press.

House, R. J. (1996). Path-goal theory of leadership: Lessons, legacy, and a reformulated theory. *The Leadership Quarterly, 7,* 323–352.

House, R. J., & Aditya, R. N. (1997). The social scientific study of leadership: Quo vadis? *Journal of Management, 23,* 409–473.

House, R. J., Hanges, P. J., Javidan, M., Dorfman, P. W., & Gupta, V. (Eds.). (2004). *Culture, leadership, and organizations: The GLOBE Study of 62 societies.* Thousand Oaks, CA: Sage.

House, R. J., & Shamir, B. (1993). Towards an integration of transformational, charismatic, and visionary theories of leadership. In M. M. Chemers & R. Ayman (Eds.), *Leadership: Perspectives and research directions* (pp. 81–107). New York: Academic Press.

House, R. J., Spangler, W. D., & Woycke, J. (1991). Personality and charisma in the U.S. presidency: A psychological theory of leader effectiveness. *Administrative Science Quarterly, 36,* 364–396.

Howell, J. M., & Hall-Merenda, K. E. (1999). The ties that bind: The impact of leader-member exchange, transformational and transactional leadership, and distance on predicting follower performance. *Journal of Applied Psychology, 84,* 680–694.

Hunt, J. G. (1999). Transformational/charismatic leadership's transformation of the field: An historical essay. *The Leadership Quarterly, 10,* 129–144.

Hunter, J. E., & Schmidt, F. L. (1990). *Methods of meta-analysis: Correcting error and bias in research findings.* Newbury Park, CA: Sage.

Ilies, R., Gerhardt, M. W., & Le, H. (2004). Individual differences in leadership emergence: Integrating meta-analytic findings and behavioral genetics estimates. *International Journal of Selection and Assessment, 12,* 207–219.

Ilies, R., Nahrgang, J. D., & Morgeson, F. P. (2007). Leader-member exchange and citizenship behaviors: A meta-analysis. *Journal of Applied Psychology, 92,* 269–277.

Judge, T. A., Bono, J. E., Ilies, R., & Gerhardt, M. W. (2002). Personality and leadership: A qualitative and quantitative review. *Journal of Applied Psychology, 87,* 765–780.

Judge, T. A., Colbert, A. E., & Ilies, R. (2004). Intelligence and leadership: A quantitative review and test of theoretical propositions. *Journal of Applied Psychology, 89,* 542–552.

Judge, T. A., Piccolo, R. F., & Ilies, R. (2004). The forgotten ones? The validity of consideration and initiating structure in leadership research. *Journal of Applied Psychology, 89,* 36–51.

Katz, D., & Kahn, R. L. (1978). *The social psychology of organizations* (2nd ed.). New York: John Wiley.

Katz, D., Maccoby, N., Gurin, G., & Floor, L. G. (1951). *Productivity, supervision and morale among railroad workers.* Ann Arbor, MI: Institute for Social Research, University of Michigan.

Kenny, D. A., & Zaccaro, S. J. (1983). An estimate of variance due to traits in leadership. *Journal of Applied Psychology, 68,* 678–685.

Kerr, S., & Jermier, J. (1978). Substitutes for leadership: Their meaning and measurement. *Organizational Behavior and Human Performance, 22,* 375–403.

Kramer, R. S. S., Arend, I., & Ward, R. (2010). Perceived health from biological motion predicts voting behaviour. *Quarterly Journal of Experimental Psychology, 63,* 625–632.

Lewin, K., & Lippitt, R. (1938). An experimental approach to the study of autocracy and democracy: A preliminary note. *Sociometry, 1,* 292–300.

Liden, R. C., & Antonakis, J. (2009). Considering context in psychological leadership research. *Human Relations, 62,* 1587–1605.

Livers, A. B., & Caver, K. A. (2003). *Leading in black and white: Working across the racial divide in corporate America.* San Francisco: Jossey-Bass.

Lord, R. G., Binning, J. F., Rush, M. C., & Thomas, J. C. (1978). The effect of performance cues and leader behavior on questionnaire ratings of leadership behavior. *Organizational Behavior and Human Performance, 21,* 27–39.

Lord, R. G., Brown, D. J., Harvey, J. L., & Hall, R. J. (2001). Contextual constraints on protoype generation and their multi-level consequences for leadership perceptions. *The Leadership Quarterly, 12,* 311–338.

Lord, R. G., De Vader, C. L., & Alliger, G. M. (1986). A meta-analysis of the relation between personality traits and leadership perceptions: An application of validity generalization procedures. *Journal of Applied Psychology, 71,* 402–409.

Lord, R. G., & Emrich, C. G. (2000). Thinking outside the box by looking inside the box: Extending the cognitive revolution in leadership research. *The Leadership Quarterly, 11,* 551–579.

Lord, R. G., Foti, R. J., & De Vader, C. L. (1984). A test of leadership categorization theory: Internal structure, information processing, and leadership perceptions. *Organizational Behavior and Human Performance, 34,* 343–378.

Lord, R. G., & Maher, K. J. (1991). *Leadership and information processing: Linking perceptions and performance.* Boston, MA: Unwin Hyman.

Lowe, K. B., & Gardner, W. L. (2000). Ten years of *The Leadership Quarterly:* Contributions and challenges for the future. *The Leadership Quarterly, 11,* 459–514.

Mann, R. D. (1959). A review of the relationships between personality and performance in small groups. *Psychological Bulletin, 56,* 241–270.

McClelland, D. C. (1985). How motives, skills, and values determine what people do. *American Psychologist, 40,* 812–825.

McGrath, J. E. (1962). *Leadership behavior: Some requirements for leadership training.* Washington, DC: U.S. Civil Service Commission, Office of Career Development.

Meindl, J. R., & Ehrlich, S. B. (1987). The romance of leadership and the evaluation of organizational performance. *Academy of Management Journal, 30,* 90–109.

Meindl, J. R., Ehrlich, S. B., & Dukerich, J. M. (1985). The romance of leadership. *Administrative Science Quarterly, 30,* 78–102.

Miner, J. B. (1975). The uncertain future of the leadership concept: An overview. In J. G. Hunt & L. L. Larson (Eds.), *Leadership frontiers* (pp. 197–208). Kent, OH: Kent State University Press.

Osborn, R. N., Hunt, J. G., & Jauch, L. R. (2002). Toward a contextual theory of leadership. *The Leadership Quarterly, 13,* 797–837.

Pfeffer, J. (1977). The ambiguity of leadership. *Academy of Management Review, 2,* 104–112.

Porter, L. W., & McLaughlin, G. B. (2006). Leadership and organizational context: Like the weather? *The Leadership Quarterly, 17,* 559–576.

Rush, M. C., Thomas, J. C., & Lord, R. G. (1977). Implicit leadership theory: A potential threat to the internal validity of leader behavior questionnaires. *Organizational Behavior and Human Performance, 20,* 756–765.

Schriesheim, C. A., & Kerr, S. (1977). Theories and measures of leadership: A critical appraisal. In J. G. Hunt & L. L. Larson (Eds.), *Leadership: The cutting edge* (pp. 9–45). Carbondale, IL: Southern Illinois University Press.

Sellers, J. G., Mehl, M. R., & Josephs, R. A. (2007). Hormones and personality: Testosterone as a marker of individual differences. *Journal of Research in Personality, 41,* 126–138.

Shamir, B., & Howell, J. M. (1999). Organizational and contextual influences on the emergence and effectiveness of charismatic leadership. *The Leadership Quarterly, 10,* 257–283.

Smith, J. E., Carson, K. P., & Alexander, R. A. (1984). Leadership: It can make a difference. *Academy of Management Journal, 27,* 765–776.

Smith, K. B., Larimer, C. W., Littvay, L., & Hibbing, J. R. (2007). Evolutionary theory and political leadership: Why certain people do not trust decision makers. *Journal of Politics, 69,* 285–299.

Stogdill, R. M. (1948). Personal factors associated with leadership: A survey of the literature. *Journal of Psychology, 25,* 35–71.

Stogdill, R. M., & Coons, A. E. (Eds.). (1957). *Leader behavior: Its description and measurement.* Columbus, OH: Ohio State University, Bureau of Business Research.

Turner, N., Barling, J., Epitropaki, O., Butcher, V., & Milner, C. (2002). Transformational leadership and moral reasoning, *Journal of Applied Psychology, 87,* 304–311.

Van Seters, D. A., & Field, R. H. G. (1990). The evolution of leadership theory. *Journal of Organizational Change Management, 3,* 29–45.

Van Vugt, M., & Schaller, M. (2008). Evolutionary approaches to group dynamics: An introduction. *Group Dynamics: Theory, Research, and Practice, 12,* 1–6.

Villarejo, A., & Camacho, A. (2009). Neuropoliticis: Neuroscience visits politics. *Neurologia, 5*(Suppl. 1), 8–11.

Vroom, V. H., & Jago, A. G. (1988). *The new leadership: Managing participation in organizations.* Englewood Cliffs, NJ: Prentice Hall.

Vroom, V. H., & Yetton, P. W. (1973). *Leadership and decision making.* Pittsburgh, PA: University of Pittsburgh Press.

Wofford, J. C., Goodwin, V. L., & Whittington, J. L. (1998). A field study of a cognitive approach to understanding transformational and transactional leadership. *The Leadership Quarterly, 9,* 55–84.

Zaccaro, S. J. (2001). *The nature of executive leadership: A conceptual and empirical analysis of success.* Washington, DC: American Psychological Association.

Zaccaro, S. J. (2007). Trait-based perspectives of leadership. *American Psychologist, 62,* 6–16.

Zaccaro, S. J., Foti, R. J., & Kenny, D. A. (1991). Self-monitoring and trait-based variance in leadership: An investigation of leader flexibility across multiple group situations. *Journal of Applied Psychology, 76,* 308–315.

Zaleznik, A. (1992, March/April). Managers and leaders: Are they different? *Harvard Business Review,* 126–133.

Zyphur, M. J., Narayanan, J., Koh, G., & Koh, D. (2009). Testosterone-status mismatch lowers collective efficacy in groups: Evidence from a slope-as-predictor multilevel structural equation model. *Organizational Behavior and Human Decision Processes, 110,* 70–77.

PART II

Leadership

Science, Nature, and Nurture

2

Aggregation Processes and Levels of Analysis as Organizing Structures for Leadership Theory

Robert G. Lord

Jessica E. Dinh

University of Akron

Theories accomplish two goals of science: first to predict, and second to understand diverse phenomena (Dubin, 1969). Leadership research has made considerable progress toward attaining these goals, and during the past 100 years, the field has witnessed the development of a number of theories that attempt to explain the antecedents, consequences of, and more generally, the nature of leadership. Yet, despite the thousands of studies and years of research, our understanding of leadership remains incomplete. What makes leadership research complex is that the field lacks a single unifying conception or theory that defines leadership (Hunt, 2004). What we have instead is an impressive number of leadership theories that represent a diverse range of theoretical perspectives (e.g., trait, information-processing, systems, complexity), span different levels of analysis (e.g., micro, meso, macro), and incorporate ideas from a variety of neighboring disciplines (e.g., sociology, psychology, economics, political science). Importantly, each has contributed to the field by offering its own unique assumptions and perspectives on leadership. Although these theories have done well in advancing

AUTHORS' NOTE: Please address correspondence concerning this chapter to Robert G. Lord and Jessica E. Dinh, Department of Psychology, University of Akron, Akron, OH 44325–4301, USA. Phone: 330–972–7018; e-mail: rlord@uakron.edu, jd62@zips.uakron.edu.

research and providing a broader understanding of leadership, there is little cohesion among the theories that would allow us to understand how they all tie together.

Part of the problem is that leadership is a complex phenomenon. Although leaders may directly affect outcomes at multiple levels (individuals, groups, organizations), often their effects are indirect, operating through others and taking place over substantial periods of time (Day & Lord, 1988; Lord & Brown, 2004). Thus, different researchers may focus on different aspects of a relatively long causal chain. For example, consider that one leader may have a productive work group, while another does not. Where should we look to explain this difference? Typically theorists would look to a leader's personality or behavior for an explanation. But it might be more appropriate to focus on how the two leaders' actions prime individual versus collective identities in followers (Lord & Brown, 2004); how those different identity levels affect individual self-regulatory processes producing competition versus cooperation in their groups (De Cremer & Van Knippenberg, 2002); and how these different member-to-member interactions encourage social loafing versus social engagement. The complexity of leadership can also be appreciated by acknowledging the impact that context (e.g., national and organizational culture) may have on leaders, which may in turn, constrain their effect on outcomes (Jones & Olken, 2005; Liden & Antonakis, 2009). As these examples illustrate, we often overestimate the direct effects of leaders (Meindl & Ehrlich, 1987) and fail to appreciate how their actions alter the nature of active identities, social exchanges, and motivational processes in followers.

Although most leadership theory emphasizes the top-down effects of hierarchical leaders, bottom-up or more inclusive views of leadership have gained increased attention in the last decade. Accompanying this shift in focus, leadership has been viewed as a shared process (Carson, Tesluk, & Marrone, 2007; Day, 2000; Pearce & Conger, 2003); follower contributions to leadership processes have gained more attention (Liden & Antonakis, 2009; Shamir, Pallai, Bligh, & Uhl-Bien, 2007); theory relating leadership and social network processes has been developed (Balkundi & Kilduff, 2005; Zohar & Tenne-Gazit, 2008); and complexity science has been applied to leadership (Marion & Uhl-Bien, 2001; Uhl-Bien, Marion, & McKelvey, 2007). However, much of the literature in this area is primarily conceptual, and different views on bottom-up and top-down processes have not been integrated. Our position in this chapter is that this problem aligns with the application of level of analysis issues and that a careful consideration of levels of analysis can help to provide a basis for more comprehensive theorizing that allows for both top-down and bottom-up processes in leadership research. In this chapter, we begin by articulating the linkages with the levels of analysis literature, and then we move on to show how a more comprehensive approach can be developed at alternative levels of analysis: levels pertaining to events, individuals, groups, and organizations.

Levels of Analysis and Leadership Theory

Current State of the Field

Along with many others, we believe that the majority of leadership research has not paid sufficient attention to level of analysis issues, even though persuasive arguments for specifying the level for a theory are an important part of our literature (Dansereau, Alutto, & Yammarino, 1984; Klein, Dansereau, & Hall, 1994; Rousseau, 1985). For example, in a recent review of 348 published articles in the leadership field, Yammarino, Dionne, Chun, and Dansereau (2005) reported that less than 30% of the research explicitly considered levels in discussing theory and about one in six empirical articles used multilevel techniques to analyze data. Failure to specify the level of analysis in which researchers are most interested can result in confusion, affecting the conclusions and inferences that can ultimately be drawn from the data (Klein et al., 1994). This concern has been emphasized by several recent articles (Bamberger, 2008; Hall & Lord, 1995; Klein et al., 1994; Kozlowski & Klein, 2000; Whetten, Felin, & King, 2009; Yammarino et al. 2005). In particular, Klein et al. (1994) argue that "greater attention to levels issues will increase the clarity, testability, comprehensiveness, and creativity of organizational theories" (p. 224). Such advances enable appropriate theory generalization across various contexts and the development of multilevel theories.

Klein et al. (1994) also emphasize that level of analysis issues are foremost theory issues, but as with the broader organization science literature (Bamberger, 2008), concern with levels of analysis is often driven by available technology. The widespread availability of random coefficients modeling procedures in the past decade has made it easier to see how processes at one hierarchical level constrain processes at lower levels. Similarly, we have statistical tools that address measurement issues, helping researchers decide whether it is appropriate to aggregate data from individual to group levels (Bliese, 2000). Although these are important technological advances, they have not spawned integrative theory, and to some extent, they put the cart before the horse in that they can raise technical issues that obfuscate theoretical issues central to understanding the appropriate level of analysis.

Leadership and the Combination of Individual Outputs

We propose that greater clarity in understanding leadership can be developed from addressing one fundamental issue: *How do subunit inputs and processes combine to produce unit-level outcomes and how does leadership affect this process?* For example, transformational leaders are often thought to have their greatest effect by changing how work groups (rather than individuals) function (DeGroot, Kiker, & Cross, 2000). Although the substantive processes involved in combining lower level inputs to produce higher level outcomes will vary with level and the nature of work tasks, much can be gained by considering this issue at an abstract level. Kozlowski and Klein (2000), make the useful distinction between *compositional* models of combination, in which lower level inputs are combined to produce a higher level output that has essentially the same form (is isomorphic) as the lower level units, and *compilational* models, in which aggregation produces a fundamental change in the nature of a phenomena when aggregated to a higher level. They also note that some properties (global unit properties) exist only at the level of a specific unit. They maintain that compositional models have been emphasized in the literature, often positing that inputs are simply added together to produce an output at a higher level, although D. Chan (1998) illustrates that there are several interesting alternatives to simple addition that can explain compositional processes. An example of a compositional model of, say, self-efficacy for shared leadership would be that group-level beliefs could be adequately represented as the sum of group members' beliefs about their own shared leadership capability. In contrast, a compilational model would emphasize an understanding of how group-level processes emerge over time through the interactions of group members and an understanding of how one group member's unique capacities can complement those of another. Here, social interaction changes one's understanding of collective efficacy and creates a different construct—an assessment of unique group processes, rather than a simple aggregation of individual-level attributes.

This example can also be used to illustrate an important issue that goes to the heart of understanding leadership processes. Consider the case in which groups within an organization show high within-group agreement in shared leadership efficacy, but there are substantial mean differences among groups on this variable. Such a pattern could result from some leaders empowering group members and encouraging them to develop shared leadership capabilities, while other leaders hold on to power, limiting the leadership skills that their group members develop. In other words, this pattern of within-group homogeneity but between-group differences reflects a cross-level effect of formal group leaders. Alternatively, leaders may be relatively uniform in terms of their willingness to empower others, but some groups may have diverse preferences while other groups have similar preferences on achieving certain outcomes. Page (2007) notes that diverse preferences produce conflict in groups, and shared leadership processes are not likely to work as well with high-conflict groups (Carson et al., 2007). Consequently, groups with highly diverse preferences could be expected to develop low shared leadership efficacy over time because of the frequent conflict they experience. However, groups with low diversity in preferences would function differently, experiencing lower conflict and being more able to develop shared leadership capability. Again, the resulting pattern is one of between-group differences in shared leadership efficacy and homogeneity within groups regarding this belief. However, in this second situation, the key causal factor is differences in bottom-up emergent processes engendered by different degrees of agreement in group member preferences, not the top-down effects of group leaders.

The point of these two contrasting examples is to illustrate the importance of focusing on how inputs are combined and a leader's role in this process, not just descriptive aspects of the resulting outcomes that have implications for whether one can aggregate measures. Note that in both examples, homogeneity in within-group beliefs about shared leadership capacity would suggest that we have a group-level phenomenon. Yet in the first case, we have strong effects of formal leaders on emergent group processes, whereas in the second case, effects of a formal leader may be absent.

Leadership, Dynamics, and Processes

Our focus on how leadership affects dynamic processes runs counter to the predominant trend in leadership research that is to underemphasize process-based understanding of how leaders actually affect group-level outputs (Kaiser, Hogan, & Craig, 2008). Processes are often underemphasized in the leadership area because people can rely on their implicit understanding of leadership as a guide to theory development (Calder, 1977; Shondrick, Dinh, & Lord, 2010), and implicit beliefs often emphasize the role of individual-level leadership effects such as traits or behavioral tendencies. Indeed, Yammarino et al. (2005) note that most leadership research focuses on individuals as the appropriate level of analysis, reflecting the predominant concerns with individual leader-style phenomena. For the most part, research focused on individual leaders does not consider cross-level effects or the compositional or compilational processes that produce outcomes at higher levels of analysis.

In addition, a focus on individual leaders fails to recognize that leaders encounter many different types of events. Thus, the critical causal dynamics associated with individual differences (Mischel & Shoda, 1998), or a leader's effect on group outcomes, may need to be examined at the level of events from a person-parts perspective (Klein et al., 1994). Ironically, although it is generally recognized that leadership skill develops from experience (Day, Harrison, & Halpin, 2009; Lord & Hall, 2005), how event-related learning and experience are aggregated to the level of personal qualities or skills is not addressed with the same concern for level of analysis issues that we find in aggregating individual to group-level effects. Yet many alternative compositional or compilation processes may characterize the development of skills or behavioral tendencies from event-level experiences. We propose that any framework for understanding leadership from a level of analysis perspective should be extended downward to include events within individuals. As Yammarino et al. (2005) note, theoretical revolutions in science often occur when scientists consider levels above *and below* their typical focus, so this tendency to ignore the event level may limit discovery in our field. For example, Avolio (2005) has argued that it is unusual and extreme events, often called trigger events, that are crucial in developing transformational leaders. In addition, the leader sensemaking literature (Weick, 1995) recognizes the important role of leaders in shaping others' interpretation of events.

Leadership theories have not fully considered level of analysis issues, in part, because leadership theory often relies on cross-sectional survey research, which is the primary methodology used in the field (Hunter, Bedell-Avers, & Mumford, 2007). Because of this static emphasis, causal dynamics are often grounded in commonsense theories, which emphasize the effects of individual leaders (Meindl & Ehrlich, 1987), rather than a more scientific analysis of causality, which includes specification of appropriate levels of analysis. Also, by relying extensively on an organizational member's casual memory for leadership processes rather than real-time observation of specific leadership events, this approach often misses the moment-to-moment dynamics in leadership events. Instead of detailed assessments of the consequence of one event for another, researchers often rely on raters' implicit aggregation of leadership events in forming overall perceptions of leadership (Shondrick et al., 2010), which may fundamentally distort the nature of leadership processes, yielding simpler interpretations that overemphasize the effects of individual leaders.

In short, understanding how leaders influence the way that individual-level inputs are combined to produce collective outputs may need to include the level of events within individuals, considering emergent compilational as well as compositional processes. Alternative methodologies that allow precise measurement of such events are also needed.

Developing an Integrated Typology

We suggest that leadership theories can be classified according to event, individual, group, and organizational levels of analysis (Drazin, Glynn, & Kazanjian, 1999; Hall & Lord, 1995; Klein et al., 1994; Morgeson & DeRue, 2006). Attention to how inputs are combined at one level to create outputs at another level also needs to be integrated with these levels of analysis concerns. We have laid out a preliminary system for such classification in Table 2.1, which was created by crossing these four levels of analysis with three types of unit-level properties previously described. To help our readers navigate through these levels of analysis and unit properties, we will discuss each cell in this table moving from global to configural properties for each level. This creates both a structure for examining the effects of leadership on aggregations and a structure for organizing various leadership theories in terms of functional similarity. As we will address throughout this chapter, these concerns have important consequences for theory building and theory generalization (Whetten et al., 2009).

Table 2.1 Basis for Formation of Unit-Level Properties by Level of Analysis

Levels	Global ULP: Descriptive characteristic of unit does not apply to lower levels	Shared ULP: Property emerges from composition of lower level unit properties	Configural ULP: Property emerges from compilation of lower level unit properties
Individual property from aggregated events	1. Time pressure	1. Knowledge structures expanded by accumulation of facts 2. Perfecting skills and abilities by learning from previous errors	1. Conscious understanding emerges from interaction of different events 2. Self-complexity increases by self-reflective processing of emotional events
Individual (whole) from individual (parts)	1. Traits	1. Global self-efficacy	1. Increased self-complexity via CAPS and hot/cool networks 2. Self regulation from hierarchically organized motivational elements 3. Effects of default and affective networks on use of cognitive resources
Group from individual	1. Group demographic/ skill diversity and network structure	1. Team mental models and team performance through addition of individual skills, actions, and thoughts 2. Group affective tone, task knowledge, and motivation	1. Team transactive memory and specialized group-member functions that require frequent member-to-member interaction 2. Strong collective identities result in emergent group processes via cooperation (e.g., team efficiency)
Organization from group	1. Organizational characteristics (e.g., structure, strategy, workforce composition)	1. Organizational demographic composition and network density 2. Collective values, goals, and human resources	1. Development of organizational ethical culture 2. Organizational identity and complexity
Common thread among theories	Stable attributes are important antecedents to processes at each level	Individuals function independently; individuals fulfill similar function	Outcomes emerge from interactions of different units; individuals and groups perform different functions

NOTE: ULP = unit-level property; CAPS = cognitive and affective processing system.

Taxonomy for Leadership Theory

As shown in Table 2.1, theories can be organized into four levels of analysis that include *events, individuals, groups,* and *organizations.* Following Kozlowski and Klein (2000), we also distinguish among three types of properties at each level: global, shared, and configural unit properties. *Global unit-level properties* reflect single-level phenomena—such as an organization's age. Shared and configural properties reflect aspects of units that originate at lower levels but are manifest at higher levels. That is, they reflect aggregation processes. *Shared unit-level properties* are similar across levels and reflect compositional forms of emergence; whereas *configural unit-level properties,* which differ across levels in fundamental ways, reflect compilational forms of emergence. As we discuss this framework, we will describe several popular theories that correspond to each cell in Table 2.1, which are identified in Table 2.2.

Micro-Micro Level: Importance of Events and Leadership

Type of Unit

Event-level processes as a level of analysis have only recently received attention from the research field (Morgeson & De Rue, 2006). Events, which we define as "occurrences that interrupt the routines of organizational life and prompt controlled processing" (Morgeson & De Rue, 2006, p. 272), are an important part of our developing framework. Some events may require a direct intervention from a leader to be resolved. To provide a good example of an event and how events may directly involve leaders, one can consider the BP oil spill catastrophe in the Gulf of Mexico, which that was one of the worst environmental disasters in recent history. From the scale and severity of the event, leaders across multiple levels, from local to federal government agencies, have responded in various ways to help resolve the situation. Though the BP oil incident is itself unique, it is important to note that across the board, leaders may respond to multiple smaller events that vary in criticality, duration, and urgency—all within a relatively short period of time.

Prior to detailing the ways in which leaders can change how events are assimilated to form higher level constructs, we first must clarify the types of leadership processes that will be considered. Part of the difficulty with the leadership literature is that the field itself is expansive—extending from how leaders develop internal qualities such as skills, attitudes, and values; to how leaders influence the processing of events in others by guiding sensemaking processes; to how others perceive leaders. In the sections to come, we will focus only on the first two of these processes. Our focus on events addresses how experiencing different events cumulates to produce behavioral tendencies or leadership skills and how leaders can influence the way in which events combine to produce performance outcomes in others. Aggregation

Table 2.2 Classification of Leadership Theories by Their Unit-Level Property (ULP) and Level of Analysis

Levels	Global ULP: Descriptive characteristic of unit does not apply to lower levels	Shared ULP: Property emerges from composition of lower level-unit properties	Configural ULP: Property emerges from compilation of lower level-unit properties
Individual property from aggregated events	1. Affective events theory 2. Adaptive response to events 3. Event-related motivational processing	1. Skill development 2. Trust and attachment to leaders 3. Affective priming and sensemaking processes	1. Ethical or moral development via self-reflection 2. Developing scripts, schemas, general leadership roles, and metacognitive structures increase self-complexity
Individual (whole) from individual (parts)	1. Trait theory 2. Chronic self-regulatory processes and leadership behavioral styles 3. Genetic determinants of leadership	1. Developing leader human and social capital 2. Priming self-identity and influencing motivational processing	1. Self-complexity and willingness to lead 2. Leader's effects on self-regulatory hierarchies of others 3. Supportive or threatening leadership 4. Broadening effects of leader's positive affect
Group from individual	1. Group demographic diversity as resources for leadership complexity	1. Establishment of a safety climate/goal-orientation climate 2. LMX and relative LMX theories, dyadic-level leadership processes 3. Transformational leadership directed at individual-level perceptions	1. Group-focused collective and complexity leadership theories 2. Safety- and goal-oriented climates 3. Group processes (e.g., affective tone, sensemaking, sense-giving, shared leadership) 4. Social identity theory
Organization from group	1. Punctuated equilibrium (e.g., mergers, spinoffs, strategic choices made by leaders) 2. Theory of organizational structure and culture	1. Attraction-selection-attrition models of organizational climate 2. Emotional capacity theory of organizational learning	1. Organizational ethical culture 2. Complexity leadership theory
Common thread among theories	Stable attributes are important antecedents to leadership	Leadership is focused on the individual; individuals fulfill similar function	Leadership outcomes emerge from interactions of different units; individuals and groups perform different functions

NOTE: ULP = unit-level property; LMX = leader–member exchange.

across events to form leadership perceptions will be addressed briefly in a later section of the paper.

Global Unit-Level Properties of Events

As indicated in Table 2.1, the most basic representation of an event is something that is shared by the unit as a whole such as *time pressure*. Applied to theory however, events (as a global property) can in their own right have important effects on leaders and leadership processes. For instance, Weiss and Cropanzano's (1996) *Affective Events Theory* describes how affective reactions to events can directly affect behavior, a process that may be better understood by focusing on event-related affective processes than on how these processes cumulate to create more aggregate structures in individuals. Other theories at an event global level include *adaptive leadership* responses, in which specific events produce general appraisals that influence leadership behavior (Hannah, Uhl-Bien, Avolio, & Cavarretta, 2009). Specific events can trigger alternative motivational structures (*motivational processing*), which influence how a leader behaves, leading to various leadership outcomes (Lord & Brown, 2004, chap. 6). Although such globally oriented theories (see Table 2.2, first row, leftmost cell) are useful in providing a general description of the unit's structure or function within a singular event, they also leave out the complexity that is characteristic of many emergent leadership processes. To have a more thorough understanding of leadership processes, leadership theories must account for emergence via both composition and compilation. Beginning with composition, in the following sections, we will focus on how events are aggregated within leaders and how leaders influence the aggregation of events in others to create shared unit properties.

Composition by Memory and Leadership

A problem with cross-sectional studies is that they create theories that are isolated in scope, explaining phenomena as a whole rather than considering how different elements or parts sum to produce higher level entities or phenomena. In general, events may be described as being compositional if each event fulfills the same function (Whetten et al., 2009) such as strengthening cognitive or emotional tendencies. For instance, by reflecting on past experiences and events, leaders may reaccess similar memories that are added together, such as in the accumulation of task-related knowledge over a lifetime (Table 2.1, first row, middle cell, entry 1). In this sense, learning processes can create compositional aggregation by influencing the pattern of neural network consolidation—by incrementally strengthening specific pathways in these networks (Hanges, Lord, & Dickson, 2000). Applied to leadership, several theories also posit that the composition of different events has important influences on leadership outcomes (Table 2.2, first row, middle cell, entries 1 and 2). *Skill development* (Lord & Hall, 2005), for instance, may result from a leader's repeated efforts to perfect a particular skill. Just like a pianist may practice hours on end to memorize a piece, a leader may work diligently to develop speaking or management skills. Similarly, Dirks and Ferrin's (2002) concepts of *trust development* and *attachment to leaders* (i.e., attachment theory; Keller, 2003; Popper & Amit, 2009) are also compositional in that trust and one's sense of attachment build progressively over time through repeated leader–follower interactions.

Composition and the Effects of Leaders on Others

Our description of how events affect a leader's skills can apply to others (or followers) as well. Because leaders are important role models and can structure aspects of the situation, they can directly influence how experiences with different events cumulate in others (Zohar & Tenne-Gazit, 2008). One important effect of leaders is that they can influence follower development through learning by error processes. For instance, rather than pressuring followers to avoid errors, leaders can encourage active learning processes by allowing followers to make errors and to use errors as a learning device (Keith & Frese, 2005). This orientation also facilitates the refinement of metacognitive processes and increases cognitive complexity that leads to nonlinear shifts in performance (Keith & Frese, 2005). For the most part, however, we would expect compositional processes to describe the enhancement of skills as individuals build many specific productions (if → then rules) through experience (Anderson, 1987), as shown in the corresponding cell in Table 2.1 (first row, middle cell, entry 2).

As we suggested, events can cumulate in an additive fashion through automatic learning. For example, the tendency of an individual to respond to a specific type of social situation with a positive response may be strengthened by experiencing many good event outcomes, and reduced with bad outcomes. Thus, a person's affective tendency may reflect an accumulation of similar responses to many events. However, leaders could also influence this process through *affective priming* or *sensemaking* (see Table 2.2, first row, middle column, entry 3), which shifts the emphasis placed on positive or negative events (Pescosolido, 2002). Consequently, leader sensemaking activities can also affect how events are interpreted and how they are cumulated to form higher person-level constructs. To illustrate, leaders can provide feedback that facilitates learning in a way that emphasizes comparisons among individuals, thereby making performance goal orientations more relevant; or they can focus feedback on task skills, making learning goal orientations more salient (Dragoni, 2005). If leaders shift an individual's goal orientation from his or her chronic tendency through such processes, we might expect a discontinuous change in person-level learning or performance that reflects different types of bottom-up combinations of events.

An important aspect of sensemaking is for leaders to help others see the relevance of an event to their personal identities, increasing the potential affective impact of an event and accessing relevant cognitive structures (O'Malley, Ritchie, Lord, Gregory, & Young, 2009). Indeed, transformational leaders may excel at this process, repeatedly shaping an individual's general sense of efficacy in ways that can be both good and bad (Kark, Shamir, & Chen, 2003). Such processes would likely be compositional, and they may operate through conscious or unconscious social communication. Likewise, Pygmalion effects, in which the expectations of leaders for followers influence follower behavior and self-efficacy, provide another example of a leader's effect on how events are cumulated in others (Eden, 1992).

In general, leadership theories that have compositional effects involve processes that operate on individuals and their personal reactions to events. They involve processes such as skill learning, use of feedback, sensemaking, affective reactions, or self-efficacy. These reactions then cumulate over time through repeated interactions with a leader around specific events, but such accumulation is compositional because no qualitative transformation of the follower's cognition or affect occurs.

Compilation, Affective Processes, and Leadership

Although events are individually bounded and confined within a span of time, different events also may interact with each other through human memory and other cognitive systems, resulting in compilational aggregation that creates a integrative cognition or emotion that is fundamentally different than reactions to the specific constituent events (see Table 2.1, first row, rightmost cell, entry 1). Such configural unit properties can occur when conscious processes integrate diverse information, such as how a leader could encourage a subordinate after one event but be critical after another. This outcome is particularly likely with salient and emotionally tinged events because they are automatically encoded into episodic memory and are easily recalled (Allen, Kaut, & Lord, 2008).

To understand how such processes operate to produce configural unit properties, it is necessary to look at conscious processes in a bit more detail because consciousness is itself an aggregation processes that integrates diverse information from various parts of the brain. As detailed in Baars's Global Workspace Theory of Consciousness (Baars, 1983, 2002; Dehaene & Naccache, 2001; Newman, Baars, & Cho, 1997), consciousness is an emergent state in a richly connected network ("Global Workspace," in Baars's terms) extending from many parts of the brain. It involves a portion of this network that momentarily attains high activation and, thereby, can be connected to, and integrated with, other units in the brain that are also momentarily active. Once information becomes conscious, it is then broadcast to other units to cue relevant information, and it is integrated with other consciously held information. Thus, conscious experience is hypothesized to have a synergistic effect that can integrate constructs like current perceptions, past experiences or memories, goals, self-structures, and experienced affect to produce a coherent whole. One function of this system may be to compilationally integrate events into an aggregated emergent structure or understanding that is fundamentally different from its constituent parts, reflecting a configural unit property. For example, one might notice that a coworker has responded to several events during a morning with variability in emotions or outcomes and conclude that he is having a bad day, is stressed, or fatigued—a conscious inference that goes beyond the perceived information.

The relevance of this theory to leadership is that it shows how self-reflection can integrate past behaviors with current understandings to facilitate the emergence of skills like leadership. For example, Avolio, Rotundo, and Walumbwa (2009) found that individuals who engaged in modest rule breaking during youth were more likely to emerge as leaders later on as working adults. As Avolio and colleagues suggest, modest rule breaking forces individuals to confront and overcome the challenges and consequences that accompany their actions, which can create an opportunity for one to learn from his or her mistakes through self-reflective processes. We suggest that *self-reflection* (see Table 2.1, first row, rightmost cell, entry 2) can reactivate earlier memories and, through compilation, may lead to greater self-complexity, moral reasoning, and the ability to entertain different perspectives. Such capacities are predictive of leadership (Avolio et al., 2009). Furthermore, the ability to challenge one's current mental models, beliefs, and assumptions is also an important leadership skill that can be learned through this process (Avolio et al., 2009). In fact, similar findings have also been shown by Bray, Campbell, and Grant (1974), where managers who experienced challenging events early in their careers became the most successful managers 10 years later, arguably through similar compilational processes.

As these examples illustrate, different events can challenge an individual's self-concept, which influences growth and future behavioral tendencies (Joseph & Linley, 2005) of leaders and followers alike, especially if acts are interpreted as being courageous rather than just rule breaking (Worline, Wrzesniewski, & Rafaeli, 2002). As shown in the corresponding section of Table 2.2 (first row, rightmost cell, entries 1 and 2), several leadership theories describe how events compile and interact over time. For instance, a leader's *moral values and beliefs* may interact and cumulate across different events as a leader moves through different stages of moral development (Day et al., 2009). The critical idea in such theories is one of qualitative change as various events are assimilated. The same interactional processes may underlie how different *leadership scripts, schemas* (Lord, Brown, Harvey, & Hall, 2001; Wofford & Goodwin, 1994), and *generalized roles* (Sluss & Ashforth, 2007) develop through unique experiences as individuals interact with and learn from others. The development of *metacognitive structures,* which are higher level self-regulatory structures, may also emerge from integrative assimilation of events. These nonlinear and often dramatic within-person changes can also increase the complexity of a leader's self-structure (Hannah, Woolfolk, & Lord, 2009).

In short, the point that we emphasize is that events can fundamentally change individuals in additive or nonlinear and unpredictable ways by directly changing one's self-concept, affective orientation, or the kinds of skills and knowledge that can be learned by using conscious memory processes to aggregate events. These processes affect the development of skills in both leaders and others, and leaders may be important influences on this process.

Micro Level: Individual, Traits, Personality, Skills, and Leadership

Traits as Global Unit-Level Characteristics of Leaders

Personality and *individual traits* are often treated as being global properties of individuals, in which the individual is seen to be stable, invariant, and unchanged across time and context (McCrae et al., 2000; McCrae & Terracciano, 2005). In level of analysis terms, this represents a wholes perspective (Klein et al., 1994). Moreover, when applied to leadership, one important implication of this perspective is that leaders would not be able to influence the "construction" of personality in others, nor would they be able to modify their own personality. Personality, instead, is seen as a fundamental cause of both leader behaviors (Day, in press; Judge, Bono, Ilies, & Gerhardt, 2002) and the behavior of others.

David Day (in press) has recently reviewed the long history of research that views leadership as a result of traits. Indeed, numerous meta-analytic results have consistently identified several traits (e.g., intelligence, charisma, kindness, strength, honesty) that are highly associated with perceived leadership (Lord, Foti, & De Vader, 1984; Offermann, Kennedy, & Wirtz, 1994). However, as Day (in press) notes, one needs to carefully distinguish between *perceptions* of leaders (i.e., emergence) and a leader's *effects* on organizational outcomes (i.e., effectiveness), as these are two completely different ways of operationalizing leadership that are often muddled in research. In addition to *traits,* other global individual-level theories (see Table 2.2, second row, leftmost cell, entries 1–3) include Kark and Van Dijk's (2007) theoretical framework that addresses how a leader's *chronic self-regulatory focus* influences follower outcomes, or how specific *behavioral styles* are predictive of leadership effectiveness (Kerr, Schriesheim, Murphy, & Stogdill, 1974). More recently, research has investigated the *genetic underpinnings of leadership* emergence (Arvey, Zhang, Avolio, & Krueger, 2007), which provides a different example of a global (but endogenous) individual-level property. What is common among all these leadership theories is the tendency to see leadership as emerging from an enduring, global quality of an individual that typically is conceptualized as a trait, as shown in the leftmost cells in the second row of Tables 2.1 and 2.2.

Problems with a global trait perspective. Despite the importance of this line of research, there are several problems with trait theory and similar approaches to leadership. One is that they are descriptive and do not offer an explanation of leadership processes (Calder, 1977). It has also become clear that any explanation of the relationship between leadership behavior and task or organizational outcome needs to view leaders and followers within the context of the entire environmental and social system (Liden & Antonakis, 2009; Zaccaro, Kemp, & Bader, 2004). Another problem with this perspective is that important event-level processes are ignored, yet processes at this level are important in understanding the observed variability (rather than stability) of behavior at different points in time (Fleeson, 2001; Tett & Burnett, 2003). For instance, using experience sampling methodologies, Fleeson (2001) found that individuals expressed a wide range of trait-relevant behaviors as they exhibited most levels on all of the Big Five trait dimensions throughout the course of a normal day. The importance of this finding is that it suggests the need to reconceptualize personality from being a static and stable structure to one that depends on micro-level processing that varies across different environmental contexts.

Explanations for and examples of variability. In contrast to the rigidity of trait theory, personality has been reconceptualized to include both stable dispositions and intra-individual differences that are influenced by external and internal situational demands (Fleeson, 2001; Mischel & Shoda, 1998; Tett & Burnett, 2003). In fact, the application of cognitive and social-cognitive sciences to personality constructs offers a means to reconcile the differences between dispositional and process views of personality by envisioning personality as a stable, but dynamic, system of interconnected networks of self-relevant constructs (Hannah et al., 2009; Shoda, Tiernan, & Mischel, 2002). From this perspective, thoughts, beliefs, and actions are actively generated in response to specific situations and across different contexts, yet they remain based on enduring individual characteristics that are collectively termed the "self-structure" that reflects the stable interconnections of units within the network (Mischel & Shoda, 1998; Shoda et al., 2002). Thus, rather than describing how an individual typically behaves as a function of his or her specific value on each of the Big Five trait dimensions, it is more accurate to understand one's actions as tendencies that can change flexibly in response to different contextual and situational cues (Fleeson, 2001; Tett & Burnett, 2003). Such cues provide variable input into stable processing structures, and this variable input (i.e., sensory information) allows the same structures to produce variable outputs (i.e., behavior) in different situations. Neural network models of information processing provide one model that can explain this flexibility because they are systems for aggregating inputs using either compositional or compilational processes, which will be detailed in a subsequent section. Because of this capacity to model different types of processes, neural networks have been applied to a wide range of domains: personality (Mischel & Shoda, 1998), the integration of affective and cognitive systems (Metcalfe & Mischel, 1999), and hierarchical regulatory systems (Lord, Hannah, & Jennings, 2011).

It is important to recognize that such research represents a different level of analysis than typical trait views of personality, reflecting what Klein et al. (1994) referred to as a person-parts perspective rather than a person-wholes perspective associated with traits. Whereas *parts* are elements that are internal to a person, *events* are externally based; however, both can be aggregated to create more encompassing entities that can be classified as wholes. It is also important to note that this distinction applies to static or dynamic aggregation processes occurring over a period of time, which can be either compilational or configural. We cover these types of aggregation processes in the following sections.

Emergence of Individual Capacities Through Composition and Leadership

Compositional forms of emergence may occur in the following ways. As we have mentioned previously, self-efficacy can be classified as a shared unit-level property, and when applied to the level of an individual, it suggests that experiencing self-efficacy in various life domains can accumulate to create constructs such as global self-efficacy (see Table 2.1, second row, middle cell). Compositional views also apply to understanding general leadership capacities. For example, we can think of the automaticity of various leadership skills as being produced by the strengthening (i.e., summing) of different capacities within individuals when we think in terms of *human capital* of a leader. Alternatively, if we think of a leader's *social capital* (i.e., personal resources that are embedded within the network of social relationships), we might aggregate across social relations (Day et al., 2009; see Table 2.2, second row, middle cell, entry 1). Leaders could also affect *motivation* by clarifying various paths to goals (House, 1971) or by priming follower *identities* and *self-concepts* through cognitive and active actions (Lord & Brown, 2004). Because affecting motivation and activating follower identities require repeated and consistent primes, we propose that these theories are compositional in form as these effects cumulate in followers (see Table 2.2, second row, middle cell, entry 2). More interesting theory regarding individual differences, however, has developed from compilational views of aggregation, which we now discuss.

Emergence of Individual Capacities Through Compilation and Leadership

How network models can explain individual variability. Several theories explain how individual elements are aggregated to produce personality and individual variability. Mischel and Shoda's (1998) cognitive and affective processing system (CAPS) for instance, views personality as a network of interconnected mental constructs (including our beliefs, goals, expectations, memories, and knowledge) that combine to produce more aggregate constructs such as behavior or personality. Because these networks are built up from one's personal experiences, they can also be thought of as stable, internal structures that differ from person to person. What makes the network of cognitive and affective processing systems unique, however, is that it is capable of producing different behavioral outcomes (seen as one's personality) because as different situational demands arc assimilated, very different network patterns become active (Hannah et al., 2009).

Although CAPS systems (see Table 2.1, second row, rightmost cell, entry 1) may seem to be a simple feed-forward network that merely transfers situationally related input patterns into consistent outputs of behavioral responses, the complexity of the model can increase due to the number of mediating layers (hidden units) and the degree of interaction of units at each layer. Thus, compilational aggregation can be produced by multilevel neural networks because the intermediate or "hidden" levels can represent interactions or nonlinear combinations of activation from prior input layers in the neural network (Churchland & Sejnowski, 1992). These networks can also construct sophisticated patterns that reflect interactions among variables and become "tuned" to specific situations. Consequently, even though the underlying network of associations that characterizes an individual's personality structure remains relatively invariant across diverse situations, people can adjust behavior to situations in sophisticated ways according to the precise pattern of activation within the network (Shoda et al., 2002).

A second theory that explains individual variability is Metcalfe and Mischel's (1999) conceptualization of how cognition and affect are integrated. They view the *hot emotional system* and the *cool cognitive system* as interacting through richly interconnected networks in which activation flows from hot to cool systems (or vice versa) and back again. This process can create momentary structures, which are patterns of activation that reflect the integration of both hot and cool inputs. Self-regulatory theories also use networks to hierarchically organize constructs such as goals and self-structures to explain behavior (Hannah et al., 2009; Lord, Diefendorff, Schmidt, & Hall, 2010) in a manner that explains not only variability in behavior but how it can produce adaptation to situational changes (see Table 2.1, row 2, rightmost column, entries 1 and 2).

These types of theories provide an important basis for understanding both leadership as an outcome and a leader's effects on others. In the former case, leader qualities (e.g., personality, integrations of cognitions and affect, or self-regulation) are the output of processes involving various types of internal inputs; and in the latter case, leaders can affect how others process different inputs (CAPs units, affect/cognition, or goals/identities) or they can have important influences on such inputs directly (e.g., by emphasizing cognitions over affect). These leadership effects are detailed in the following two sections.

Aggregation of self-attributes of leaders. A large part of leadership research has emphasized the effects leaders have on followers as a top-down process. What has not received nearly as much attention, however, are the bottom-up processes that stem from the effects followers have on leaders. As we have shown in the previous section, people are complex systems in which different processes (e.g., self-regulation, goals, affect) emerge as leaders experience a variety of different emotions or interact with others in their social environments (Lord et al., 2011). Social interactions may be especially important to compilational processes because the influence of others can prime different individual self-identities (i.e., *working self-concepts;* Lord & Brown, 2004; Shah, 2003) and mental structures (e.g., affective and cognitive systems) that may interact and aggregate in ways that produce very different behavioral outputs.

This process is illustrated by *self-complexity* research in leadership. Here, the self is seen as a confederation of "self-attributes," such as one's acquired skills, memories, and behavioral competencies that are typically thought of as traits (e.g., being friendly, authoritative, dependable, supportive) and are unique to the individual (Hannah et al., 2009). Generally, self-complexity increases with the number of self-attributes a leader has and as the number of interconnections among these attributes increases. Thus, leadership may involve an integration of such characteristics within a particular role (e.g., teacher). Leadership can also reflect an integration of capacities across roles in creating a general quality such as willingness to lead (K. Y. Chan & Drasgow, 2001). Both types of integration increase the complexity of a leader (Table 2.2, second row, rightmost cell, entry 1).

Greater complexity, in turn, allows a leader to effectively respond to a wider range of situational demands and challenges (Hannah et al., 2009). Thus, complex individuals can tailor responses to specific situation by appropriately engaging this rich network (a compilational process) rather than by merely drawing on a generic response such as how to be a directive leader learned in a previous context (a compositional process). Consequently, this perspective has the capacity to explain how behavior or performance changes in response to different contexts or events (Tett & Burnett, 2003). Similar arguments have been used to explain *creative responses of leaders* to ill-defined or novel situations (Mumford & Peterson, 1999; Mumford, Zaccaro, Harding, Jacobs, & Fleishman, 2000). In retrospect, the leadership field has come a long way from emphasizing a strict one-way correspondence between traits and behaviors (i.e., traits → behaviors), to one that reconceptualizes human self-regulatory structures as a complex system that responds and adapts to its social surroundings. In the following section, we extend this perspective to address how leaders facilitate aggregation in others.

Leadership and aggregation in others. There are many possible routes for leaders to influence how others integrate information and develop. We have mentioned several in the section on aggregation of events, so we will merely note here that leaders can influence processes related to *sensemaking*

(O'Malley et al., 2009; Weick, 1995) and *feedback interpretation* (Levy, Cober, & Miller, 2002) because newer information may interact with past information and experiences to create new internal structures. *Goal orientation* (Dragoni, 2005), *regulatory focus* (Kark & Van Dijk, 2007), or *self-identity* (Lord & Brown, 2004; van Knippenberg, van Knippenberg, De Cremer, & Hogg, 2004) are also compilationally integrated by individuals as they self-regulate using hierarchies of loosely connected networks (Lord et al., 2010) and create momentary structures that guide information processing and behavior (see Table 2.2, second row, rightmost cell, entry 2). Leadership theories have been developed that focus on each of these elements in isolation (goal orientation, regulatory focus, and self-identity), but they have not yet addressed how leaders should guide the combination of these elements.

Two processes related to default and affective networks (Table 2.1, second row, rightmost cell, entry 3) have so much potential to influence how thoughts and feelings are integrated to produce behavior that they deserve additional attention in relation to leadership. One involves whether an individual is self-focused or task-focused when generating behavior. As described by Gusnard (2005), neurocognitive research shows that people have large, specialized networks called *default networks* for assessing the personal relevance of tasks and creating autobiographical memory. However, because these self-relevant networks consume so many metabolic resources, they must be inhibited to allocate attentional and memory resources to other tasks. The exception is when tasks are seen as being potentially harmful, which causes these networks to remain active when specific tasks are performed. This theory is relevant to leadership because by creating *supporting* as opposed to *threatening situations,* leaders can influence whether individuals fear potential harm while doing a task (Table 2.2, second row, rightmost cell, entry 3). Consequently, leaders who are able to create positive and supportive environments may increase a subordinate's capacity to manage complex tasks or to learn from their mistakes because such a climate allows individuals to effectively suppress default networks. Research on creativity also supports these arguments. George and Zhou (2007) for instance, found that although experiencing positive and negative emotions are important inputs to creative processing, leadership support is the key that enables individuals to maximize their creative potential. By creating nonthreatening environments, leaders can profoundly influence individuals' capacity to mobilize their attentional and working memory resources, which in turn, affect their resulting task performance. This type of indirect influence of leaders may be particularly important when tasks are complex or novel and the need for processing resources is at its peak.

Leaders can also affect how others combine information through their communication of affect. Emotions are contagious (Hatfield, Cacioppo, & Rapson, 1993) and through leader–follower interactions, a leader's expressions of positive emotion may affect individuals (Cherulnik, Donley, Wiewel, & Miller, 2001), groups (Barsade, 2002), and eventually an entire organization. Charismatic and transformational leaders are thought to be particularly good at creating positive emotional reactions in followers (Bono &

Ilies, 2006; Naidoo & Lord, 2008). Positive emotions (e.g., joy), in turn, can lead to broadened thought-action repertoires such as increasing followers' preference for variety (Kahn & Isen, 1993), creativity (Isen, Daubman, & Nowicki, 1987), integration (Isen, Rosenzweig, & Young, 1991), exploration, and the capacity to consider alternative world views or perspectives (Leslie, 1987). Such processes (see Table 2.2, second row, rightmost cell, entry 4) can be part of the short-run effects of emotions, or they may lead to spirals that, over time, can increase individual qualities such as cognitive complexity or self-complexity. Work by Staw and Barsade (1993) offers a concrete illustration of the influences of upward spirals. Focusing on MBA students, these authors found that experiencing positive emotions increased cognitive functioning (e.g., in decision-making tasks) and interpersonal skills. At a broader level, positive emotions also can enhance momentary desires to become a "doer of good deeds" (Haidt, 2000, p. 4), which can eventually lead to organizational change and transformation (Fredrickson, 2003).

As we have shown, several theories can be specified that rely on compilational processes that relate to leadership and are included in the rightmost cell in the second row of Table 2.2, entries 1–4. Higher level constructs can also emerge over time. Using experience sampling procedures for instance, Bledow, Schmidt, and Frese (2010) found that high levels of work motivation among software developers resulted from the interaction of varying emotions (i.e., positive, negative affect) experienced throughout the course of a day. This implies that not only are configural patterns important in compilational forms of emergence, but how these patterns emerge and interact across time should also be considered.

In sum, although personality dispositions and traits are thought to be stable across contexts, more process-oriented views of personality have merit and allow for greater influence of leaders on individuals. By influencing how individuals combine various internal cognitive and affective structures, as well as by priming alternative self-regulatory processes, leaders can produce important effects on others. Because such effects are indirect and may take place over time, they can be easily overlooked as a potential area for developing leadership theory.

Meso Level: Group Processes, Attributes, and Leadership

Global Group Properties and Leadership

Several global properties of groups may reflect leadership decisions. For example, *demographic diversity* and *diversity in skills* or *backgrounds* are often affected by the staffing decisions of leaders that favor or reduce diversity. How individuals are configured into networks can also have important affects on leadership processes (Balkundi & Kilduff, 2005). For example, leaders could support outreach activities that connect diverse individuals or they could encourage more traditional interaction patterns that are based on functional similarity. Network properties of groups likely reflect the input of formal leaders as well as the emergence of structure from individual interactions. Although such global properties are important (see the third rows of Tables 2.1 and 2.2, leftmost column), the framework we have developed emphasizes how individual-level inputs combine to produce group-level qualities.

Compositional Processes, Group Attributes, and Leadership

Compositional aspects of groups might reflect the addition of thoughts, emotions, or actions to create group-level processes like *team mental models* (DeChurch & Mesmer-Magnus, 2010; Kozlowski & Ilgen, 2006) or *team performance* (Kozlowski & Klein, 2000; see Table 2.1, third row, middle cell, entry 1). The critical distinguishing factor for compositional aggregation is that the individual-level capacities and the group-level capacities are isomorphic. For example, team mental models reflect the information that is shared among team members, whereas team *transactive memory* pertains to information that is distributed among group members and may require the interaction of members to be used (DeChurch & Mesmer-Magnus, 2010; Kozlowski & Ilgen, 2006; see Table 2.1, third row, third column, entry 1). Thus, team mental models are compositional, and team transactive memory is compilational. A key factor in understanding the difference between compositional and compilational aggregation of member contributions may lie in the function performed by individuals, as Whetten et al. (2009) suggest. When everyone is performing the same function, additive combinations are likely; but when individuals perform different functions, more compilational combinations seem likely. The problem for leadership theory is that how individual inputs combine to produce group outputs reflects the net effects of many types of group processes.

In general, when leadership processes affect individuals independently of other group members, we might expect leadership to produce compositional effects on group characteristics or processes. This process illustrates a classic top-down effect of hierarchical leadership, which may be effective if leader complexity (an individual's ability and resources to perceive and react to a situation adequately) matches the complexity required by the situation (Lord et al., 2011). Individual coaching, for instance, would be an example of such leadership process. Individually focused concerns for specific aspects of climate such as safety climate (Zohar & Tenne-Gazit, 2008) would also create a group *safety climate* through compositional aggregation as group members repeatedly observe and mimic their leaders. *Dyadic-level leadership processes* (i.e., leader–member exchanges) would also fit within this category, as we will explain next, although they may be influenced by group and organizational attributes (Henderson, Liden, Glibkowski, & Chaudhry, 2009; see Table 2.2, third row, middle cell, entries 1 & 2).

Flynn (2005) proposes that different types of exchanges are associated with different identity levels and, together, exchanges and identities can affect the way that group contributions are aggregated. Because individual-level identities emphasize differences among group members and convey worth through favorable social comparison, they are likely to lead to a climate of within-group competition and the isolation of individuals. Under such circumstances, compositional processes seem more likely and aspects such as a *groups affective tone* (George, 2002), *goal orientation climate* (Dragoni, 2005), or *task knowledge* and *motivation,* are likely to reflect additive composition (see Table 2.1, third row, middle cell, entry 2). In addition, because individuals tend to negotiate rewards for their contributions on an event-by-event level when individual identities are salient (Flynn, 2005), group processes may change substantially as different events are encountered.

Alternatively, if leaders create a relational orientation by priming relational identities, a sense of trust in one's partner develops, and one's sense of worth is based on enduring roles rather than on differentiation from others. Such situations lead to more stable exchanges than event-by-event negotiation, and differentiated within-group structures develop over time (Flynn, 2005). This is precisely the type of structure and role relations that dyadic level leadership theory (Gerstner & Day, 1997; Graen & Scandura, 1987) addresses in focusing on the development of role relations. Because leader–member exchange (LMX) theory emphasizes hierarchical linkages, we believe compositional aggregation processes are likely; but if member-to-member interactions are critical, compilational processes may be more likely as team-level structures (e.g., cognition) emerge from the increased group synergy (DeChurch & Mesmer-Magnus, 2010). Interestingly, D. Chan (1998) notes that in some compositional models, the comparison of an individual to group means is also important. This "frog pond" effect has been labeled Relative LMX by Henderson, Wayne, Shore, Bommer, and Tetrick (2008), where group member perceptions of psychological contract fulfillment affected in-role performance and organizational citizenship behaviors. Thus, in addition to individual LMX effects, there were individual within-group effects; but as D. Chan notes, both can be viewed as types of compositional aggregation (see Table 2.2, third row, middle column, entry 2).

To summarize, individual inputs can aggregate isomorphically in ways that create group-level outcomes such as safety and goal-orientation climates. They also develop automatic team processes, as well as team skill and motivational structures. These processes are also greatly influenced by leaders and the kinds of member-to-member interactions that are emphasized. Although team processes may be compositional during periods when members are independent of other members, sometimes teams must dynamically interact to better adapt to particularly complex situations (DeChurch & Mesmer-Magnus, 2010). In these instances, compilational processes are likely, which are considered next.

Compilational Effects, Group Identity, and Leadership

When group inputs are interactively combined, as in integrative problem solving or in creative endeavors, these inputs may create an entirely new outcome that goes beyond any contribution that can be made by any one member alone. Leaders can support such combination by processes that emphasize *collective* rather than *individual outcomes* (see Table 2.1, third row, rightmost cell, entry 2). For example, when leaders foster collective identities, group members define themselves in terms of group membership and their sense of worth stems from contributions to and membership in groups. Also, social exchanges are more general, focusing mainly on the collective value of the group (Flynn, 2005), which blunts status and role differences among individuals. In such situations, the behavior of both group members and leaders is often prescribed by group norms, and individuals may prefer to be treated similarly by leaders (Hogg et al., 2005)—but that does not mean that individual inputs are identical or combine through additive processes. It is also possible that strong collective identities lead to cooperative interactions in which new properties emerge over time that are qualitatively different from individual-level phenomena—for example, team leadership or team efficacy processes may be fundamentally different than individual-level processes, reflecting compilational combination. Applications of *complexity leadership theory* to group levels (Hogue & Lord, 2007) are characterized by such emergent processes (see Table 2.2, third row, rightmost cell, entry 1). Importantly, DeGroot et al. (2000) found that transformational leadership directed at the group level had an effect size that was double the effect of focusing at the individual level, illustrating the potential effects of focusing leadership on group-level processes associated with collective identities.

Recent work regarding the effects of *transformational leaders* on *organizational safety climate* strength shows two mechanisms for a leader's influence that are consistent with our framework (Zohar & Tenne-Gazit, 2008). Specifically, one mechanism that enables leaders to influence group climate perceptions involves the direct effect of transformational leaders on individual-level climate perceptions of group members, which we have argued engenders compositional aggregation (see Table 2.2, third row, middle column, entry 3). The other mechanism is through the effects of transformational leaders on group-level climate perceptions, which may be more compilational (see Table 2.2, third row, rightmost column, entry 2). There are also a number of other leadership theories that emphasize interactive processes among differentiated group members. For example, interactions among individuals may change *affective tone* through empathetic and supportive interactions so that the resulting group-level affect differs from specific individual emotions. *Sense-giving processes* and *sensemaking* of group members also reflect the interaction of group members (Foldy, Goldman, & Ospina, 2008; O'Malley et al., 2009; Weick, 1995). Finally, leadership and *social identity theory* (van Knippenberg et al., 2004), self-managed work teams (Carson et al., 2007), and the notion of shared leadership (Pearce & Conger, 2003) also stress the creation of collective attributes from the interaction of group members (see Table 2.2, third row, right cell, entries 3 and 4).

One potential value of the typology we have developed is that grouping leadership theories by the cells shown in Table 2.2 may reveal similarities in what might otherwise be considered unrelated theoretical approaches. For example, social identity theory (van Knippenberg et al., 2004), theories of safety climate (Zohar & Tenne-Gazit, 2008), goal orientation theory (Dragoni, 2005), and shared leadership (Pearce & Conger, 2003) address very different content, but they are highly similar in that they all emphasize leadership processes that create conditions under which individual input coalesces into a group climate or identity through processes that could be either compositional or compilational. Consequently, leaders who stress individual goals and values, individual identities, individual safety, and individual leadership may produce very different forms of group processes than leaders who stress common goals, shared values, collective identities, and shared leadership. Moreover, leaders who adopt consistent stances in all these domains are likely to have the greatest effect.

Perhaps one of the most important processes leaders can influence is how their actions influence group members' sense of identity. This is because identity serves as an important constraint for self-regulation (Lord et al., 2010), provides a cognitive structure for sensemaking, is a conduit for social justice effects (Johnson & Lord, 2010), and is associated with the nature of social exchanges in groups (Flynn, 2005). Consequently, by priming individual, relational, or collective identities through their language or actions, leaders can change the way that individual behaviors or qualities are combined to create a group output (Lord & Brown, 2004).

Macro Level: Theories of Leadership From an Organization Perspective

As we move down the rows shown in Table 2.1, the potential for top-down influence associated with leadership increases. Moreover, the effects of leaders on aggregate structures like organizational or group climate may be an important way that they influence behavior. Thus, leadership at macro levels can cascade down to groups and individuals. Research on ethical climate (Brown & Trevino, 2006) provides an example of such effects. However, the potential for bottom-up emergence of many macro-level qualities and a leader's potential to catalyze such emergence have only recently gained attention in the leadership literature (Marion & Uhl-Bien, 2001; Uhl-Bien et al., 2007). Although complexity theory is most consistent with compilational aggregation as emergence occurs, other forms of aggregation are also important. We take a brief look at these possibilities in this section.

Global Unit Qualities of Organizations

Many important organizational characteristics reflect aggregate properties of the organization such as *structure, strategy,* or *workforce heterogeneity,* and so forth (see Table 2.1, bottom row, first column). Leaders can affect these qualities through decisions regarding processes such as *mergers, spin-offs, plant closings, workforce reductions,* and *strategic choices* as indicated in the bottom row of Table 2.2, first column, entry 1. Further, structural properties of organizations may reflect the orientations and personalities of top management, particularly founders of organizations. For example, Miller and colleagues found that the personality (e.g., locus of control) of chief executives affected the strategy and structure of organizations (Miller, Kets de Vries, & Toulouse, 1982; Miller & Toulouse, 1986; see Table 2.2, bottom row, first column, entry 2). In most instances, however, organizational qualities result from more collective activities, but leaders can still influence the way individual and group inputs are combined.

Compositional Qualities of Organizations and Leadership

Many demographic aspects of organizations reflect the aggregation of group-level qualities. For example, the *number of employees* or *heterogeneity* in terms of gender, age, race, and ethnicity all reflect aspects that exist at group levels and can be aggregated to create organizational-level properties of the same form (see Table 2.1, bottom row, middle cell, entries 1 and 2). Leaders can affect these variables through the formulation and implementation of personnel policies, and also by creating a climate that *attracts, selects,* and *retains* certain types of individuals (Schneider, 1987). Individual differences in skills, ability (e.g., emotional capacity), or personality can also cumulate isomorphically from group to organizational levels, and as already discussed, leaders can affect these variables in many ways see (Table 2.2, bottom row, middle cell, entries 1 and 2).

Compilational Qualities of Organizations and Leadership

Many important leadership theories deal with the compilational aggregation of individual or group properties to create an organizational-level construct. According to Schein (1985), for example, cultures develop over time through individual and group interactions and, therefore, may be best thought of as compilational processes. Importantly, such interactions can be shaped by the cumulative behavior of many leaders, but because these actions are distributed over time and organizational units, there is no definable locus for culture. The *ethical culture* of an organization provides a good example of such processes (see the lower, rightmost cell of Tables 2.1 and 2.2, entry 1). Ashforth, Gioia, Robinson, and Trevino (2008) note that corrupt ethical cultures can reflect macro qualities such as top-management behavior that then becomes modeled at lower levels and develops into a code of conduct ("bad barrel," in their terms). Alternatively, they may reflect the micro-level behaviors of specific individuals ("bad apples," in their terms) that are modeled by others and cumulate into cultures that vary in terms of their ethical orientation. Thus, bad leadership can have pervasive effects as it spreads to create a collective culture.

Because of these multilevel, multidirectional aspects of culture, it is hard to change through organizational-level actions, but leadership actions directed at the group level may dramatically alter the emergence of group culture (Schein, 1985). Charismatic or transformational leaders are often expected to be able to change organizational qualities such as culture or other organizational features (Shamir & Howell, 1999). However, though they may directly affect individual-level qualities such as values or beliefs, these individual qualities may not merely aggregate through isomorphic compositional processes to create organizational characteristics. Instead, individual values and beliefs may be transformed as they cumulate to group-level entities, and these group-level qualities may also change dramatically as they emerge to create organizational characteristics. Consequently, changes in ethical cultures may require prolonged interventions involving multiple leaders operating at multiple levels (Ashforth et al., 2008). Moreover, such multilevel compilational aggregation may alter the intended effects of charismatic leaders. For this reason, many argue that the consequences of leadership actions often cannot be foreseen in complex organizations (Cilliers, 1998; Marion & Uhl-Bien, 2001).

Other emergent qualities of organizations, such as *organizational identity* and *complexity,* may also result from compilational processes as shown in the lower right corner of Table 2.1, entry 2. Although these constructs may exist at individual or group levels, they cumulate to create organizational-level phenomena that may be very different constructs and may fulfill different functions. Thus, it may be hard to develop an appropriate theory for understanding how leaders can affect this emergent process because dissimilarity in functions across levels may limit the generalizability of theory (Morgeson & Hofmann, 1999; Whetten et al., 2009).

These issues are particularly germane to *complexity leadership theory* (Marion & Uhl-Bien, 2001; Uhl-Bien et al., 2007). This theory (see Table 2.2, bottom row, rightmost cell, entry 2) emphasizes compilational, emergent processes at multiple levels; but because it is a relatively new theory, the specifics of underlying processes are unknown. For example, it is frequently asserted that leaders need to catalyze emergent processes to facilitate the development of complexity, which in turn will allow organizations to better adapt to changing environments. However, where leaders should focus to achieve such results is unknown. The framework we developed suggests that there are many possible ways different entities may emerge through different types of aggregation. Thus, this framework could help clarify how catalytic processes operate.

In short, because organizational-level qualities can constrain the operation of lower level processes, as well as emerge from these levels, it is difficult to develop appropriate theory. Most leadership theory has emphasized top-down effects, using homogeneity in lower level units as evidence for top-down effects, which often are attributed to higher level leadership practices. We maintain, however, that bottom-up, emergent processes may be equally important; and how leaders influence these emergent processes is a challenging issue for leadership scholars. Thinking in terms of the aggregation processes we have described may be helpful in addressing this challenge.

Limitations and Extensions

Consideration of Context, Time, and Dynamics

The focus of this chapter has primarily considered how leaders might influence individuals, groups, and organizations, and how key forms of emergence are important in these processes. Although context and its effects on leadership processes have not been thoroughly addressed, understanding one without the other may offer a rather myopic view of leadership. This is because leadership is embedded within a larger social context and, as such, can be influenced by micro- and macro-level forces (e.g., legal, economics, culture, national politics), which moderate a leader's efficiency and ability to effect change. Different country-level governance structures (e.g., democratic vs. autocratic regimes), for instance, have been shown to affect leadership processes to the extent that they limit a leader's power and autonomy (Jones & Olken, 2005). Similarly, other macro-level forces (e.g., the strength of governance structure within firms) may supersede and directly affect important organizational outcomes beyond leaders themselves (Core, Holthausen, & Larcker, 1999). Thus, both micro- and macro-level factors are important sources that can lead to different forms of aggregation and should be considered more fully.

Whether the focus is on top-down or bottom-up processes, it is also important to realize that different processes take different durations of time to occur. For example, changes in motivation or value salience that occur through leader priming (Lord & Brown, 2004) may be rapid, requiring only a few seconds to occur. In contrast, increasing self-efficacy in others may require weeks or months (e.g., Eden & Aviram, 1993), and learning complex leadership skills may take several years (Day et al., 2009; Lord & Hall, 2005). Although we have not explicitly addressed the time dimension, understanding how leadership affects aggregation processes needs to be considered with the appropriate time frame in mind.

One also needs to consider the form of change over time. Many compilational emergent processes could be expected to be discontinuous, perhaps exhibiting periods with little change and then finally dramatic change. For example, several models of individual development focus on stages, which would likely show this discontinuous pattern (Day et al., 2009, chap. 6). The way that knowledge is organized and used as adults develop may also show such qualitative differences (Ericsson & Charness, 1994; Lord & Hall, 2005). Groups also alternate between different phases (Marks, Mathieu, & Zaccaro, 2001). Such qualitative changes may create different types of aggregation and create different leadership demands as development occurs. For example, Nahrgang, Morgeson, and Ilies (2009) used latent growth curve modeling to show that personality factors such as subordinate extroversion and leader agreeableness were important determinants of LMX early in an exchange, but both subordinate and supervisor performance determined LMX after the initial interaction period.

Leadership Perceptions

Due to length considerations, we chose not to focus on leadership perceptions as a substantive issue. However, aggregation processes across events and individuals are just as relevant to this topic. Individuals cumulate perceptions of themselves and others across events, and social interactions may influence the accumulation of individual perceptions to a group level. Empirical evidence has shown, in fact, that leadership is not a stable characteristic. Rather, it is one that varies as individual perceivers adjust their own perceptions to be more in line with other perceivers in a group (Kenny & Zaccaro, 1983) or in an even larger social context such as an organization. Thus, a seemingly simple process of perceiving another as a leader (or follower), in truth, may be only the surface of a more dynamic and iterative underlying social process (DeRue & Ashford, 2010).

These issues could be addressed by future theory that focuses on the nature of these aggregation processes. Such issues have both practical and research-related implications. Practically, leadership is fundamentally an influence process, and influence is tied to the perception of leadership (Lord & Maher, 1991). Thus, being perceived as a leader not only helps one manage his or her career (Kaiser et al., 2008) but also allows one a greater latitude of acceptable influence in organizations. In terms of research, it is worth stressing that most of our measures of leadership ask individuals to aggregate perceptions across events as they produce frequency ratings on Likert-type scales. However, these ratings will be accurate only if aggregation is compositional. When aggregation processes are compilational (e.g., a single violation undercuts trust in a leader), such ratings will not accurately describe typical leadership processes. Indeed, to understand how leadership processes are perceived, it may be necessary to move down to an event level and emphasize episodic rather than semantic memory (Shondrick et al., 2010).

Conclusions

We have argued that theoretical integration in the leadership field requires a better system for addressing level of analysis issues. Following Kozlowski and Klein (2000), we argued that it is necessary to distinguish among global, shared, and configural unit properties, as each reflects a different form of aggregation from lower level units. As shown in Tables 2.1 and 2.2, we have applied this distinction to consider leadership at the level of events, individuals, groups, and organizations. In working with this system, we found that it helped us to develop new insights regarding the shared functions and antecedents of several different leadership theories. However, like many developmental processes, the full value of this approach will only be revealed by its effects over time on the emergence of future leadership theory.

One advantage of our framework is the potential to organize the leadership field in terms of a more encompassing structure, as we have done in Table 2.2. Considering this table as a whole suggests theoretical questions not addressed by prior leadership research and highlights important cross-theory similarities and differences. For example, considering the three columns in Table 2.2, global theories all focus on stable attributes that specify the antecedents for leadership or the context in which leadership occurs. In contrast, the shared properties column highlights leadership theory that is focused on individuals or separate units, whereas the configural properties column focuses on groups of individuals or units. We need to know whether this distinction is an important boundary variable for leadership theory. For example, a common linkage in the shared properties column is that leadership is focused on individuals. Consequently, relevant leadership capacities may relate to empathy, understanding, and dyadic social relations. This is a very different orientation than a focus on how systems of events, individuals, or groups interact, which is the common thread in the configural properties column. Thus, general principles regarding leadership may hold within theories located in the same column of Table 2.2, but they may not generalize across columns. For example, an understanding of skill development may have more similarity to understanding how trust or attachment develops than to understanding moral development.

Similar issues apply to the rows of Table 2.2. Can leadership theory that pertains to how external events cumulate also be used to guide leadership theory focusing on how individuals integrate internal properties such as cognitive and affective reactions, or do the first and second rows reflect important boundaries for leadership theory? Likewise, the individual-to-groups distinction has received extensive attention in the leadership field, but is there a similar boundary from groups to organizations that has not received enough attention? We propose that careful consideration of such issues can be a first step in developing a more integrated field of leadership theory.

Discussion Questions

1. How might events affect compositional and compilational processes at higher levels of analysis (e.g., person, group, organizational)?

2. Think of dynamic team–leader relationships. Could different events trigger compositional and compilational processes at different points in time?

3. Which is more important in determining the efficiency and success of a collaborative group of individuals (i.e., a work team): compositional or compilational processes? Why so?

4. How might contextual and situational factors influence different forms of emergence at an event, person, group, and organizational level of analysis?

5. Select a leadership phenomenon or theory that interests you. How might examining this leadership process at different levels of analysis, while considering different forms of emergence, aid in understanding this phenomenon or theory?

6. Case Study Topic: Using the framework proposed in this chapter, explain how leaders at Pixar foster creativity. (See Supplementary Reading/Case Study in the next paragraph.) That is, how might leaders influence creative processes at the level of events, individuals, groups, and organizations? Be sure to address how notions of emergence (e.g., compositional, compilational processes) may be involved in this process.

Supplementary Reading/Case Study

Catmull, E. (2008, September). How Pixar fosters collective creativity. *Harvard Business Review, 86*(9), 64–72.

References

Allen, P., Kaut, K., & Lord, R. (2008). Emotion and episodic memory. In E. Dere, A. Easton, L. Nadel, & J. P Huston (Eds.), *Handbook of behavioral neuroscience: Vol. 18. Handbook of episodic memory* (pp. 115–132). Amsterdam, Netherlands: Elsevier Science.

Anderson, J. R. (1987). Skill acquisition: Compilation of weak-method problem solutions. *Psychological Review, 94*, 192–210.

Arvey, R. D., Zhang, Z., Avolio, B. J., & Krueger, R. F. (2007). Developmental and genetic determinants of leadership role occupancy among women. *Journal of Applied Psychology, 92*, 693–706.

Ashforth, B. E., Gioia, D. A., Robinson, S. L., & Trevino, L. K. (2008). Re-viewing organizational corruption. *The Academy of Management Review, 33*, 670–684,

Avolio, B. J. (2005). *Leadership development in balance: Made/Born.* Mahwah, NJ: Lawrence Erlbaum.

Avolio, B. J., Rotundo, M., & Walumbwa, F. O. (2009). Early life experiences as determinants of leadership role occupancy: The importance of parental influence and rule breaking behavior. *The Leadership Quarterly, 20*, 329–342.

Baars, B. J. (1983). Conscious contents provide the nervous system with coherent, global information. In R. J. Davidson, G. E. Schwartz, & D. Shapiro (Eds.),

Advances in Research and Theory, Vol. 3. Consciousness and self-regulation (pp. 45–76). New York: Plenum Press.

Baars, B. J. (2002). The conscious access hypothesis: Origins and recent evidence. *Trends in Cognitive Sciences, 6,* 47–52.

Balkundi, P., & Kilduff, M. (2005). The ties that lead: A social network approach to leadership. *The Leadership Quarterly, 16,* 941–962.

Bamberger, P. (2008). Beyond contextualization—Using context theories to narrow the micro-macro gap in management research. *Academy of Management Journal, 51,* 839–846.

Barsade, S. G. (2002). The ripple effect: Emotional contagion and its influence on group behavior. *Administrative Science Quarterly, 47,* 644–675.

Bledow, R., Schmidt, A., & Frese, M. (2010). The affective underpinnings of work engagement: The dynamic interplay of positive and negative affect. Manuscript submitted for publication.

Bliese, P. D. (2000).Within-group agreement, non-independence, and reliability: Implications for data aggregation and analysis. In K. J. Klein & S.W.J. Kozlowski (Eds.), *Multilevel theory, research, and methods in organizations* (pp. 349–381). San Francisco: Jossey-Bass.

Bono, J. E., & Ilies, R. (2006). Charisma, positive emotions and mood contagion. *The Leadership Quarterly, 17,* 317–334.

Bray, D., Campbell, R. J., & Grant, D. L. (1974). *Formative years in business: A long-term AT&T study of managerial lives.* New York: John Wiley.

Brown, M. E., & Trevino, L. K. (2006). Ethical leadership: A review and future directions. *The Leadership Quarterly, 17,* 595–616.

Calder, R. J. (1977). An attribution theory of leadership. In B. M. Staw and G. R. Salancik (Eds.), *New directions in organizational behavior* (pp. 179–204). Chicago: St. Clair Press.

Carson, J. B., Tesluk, P. E., & Marrone, J. A. (2007). Shared leadership in teams: An investigation of antecedent conditions and performance. *Academy of Management Journal, 50,* 1217–1234.

Chan, D. (1998). Functional relations among constructs in the same content domain at different levels of analysis: A typology of compositional models. *Journal of Applied Psychology, 83,* 234–246.

Chan, K. Y., & Drasgow, F. (2001). Toward a theory of individual differences and leadership: Understanding the motivation to lead. *Journal of Applied Psychology, 86,* 481–498.

Cherulnik, P. D., Donley, K. A., Wiewel, T. S. R., & Miller, S. R. (2001). Charisma is contagious: The effect of leaders' charisma on observer's affect. *Journal of Applied Social Psychology, 31,* 2149–2159.

Churchland, P. S., & Sejnowski, T. J. (1992). *The computational brain.* Cambridge, MA: MIT Press.

Cilliers, P. (1998). *Complexity and postmodernism: Understanding complex systems.* London: Routledge.

Core, J. E., Holthausen, R. W., & Larcker, D. F. (1999). Corporate governance, chief executive officer compensation, and firm performance. *Journal of Financial Economics, 51,* 371–406.

Dansereau, F., Alutto, J., & Yammarino, F. J. (1984). *Theory testing in organizational behavior: The variant approach.* Englewood Cliffs, NJ: Prentice Hall.

Day, D. V. (2000). Leadership development: A review in context. *The Leadership Quarterly, 11,* 581–613.

Day, D. V. (in press). Leadership. In S. W. J. Kozlowski (Ed.). *The Oxford hand-book of industrial and organizational psychology.* Oxford, UK: Oxford University Press.

Day, D. V., Harrison, M. M., & Halpin, S. M. (2009). *An integrative approach to leader development.* New York: Routledge.

Day, D. V., & Lord, R. G. (1988). Executive leadership and organizational perfor-mance: Suggestions for a new theory and methodology. *Journal of Management, 14,* 453–464.

DeChurch, L. A., & Mesmer-Magnus, J. R. (2010). The cognitive underpinnings of effective teamwork: A meta-analysis. *Journal of Applied Psychology, 95,* 32–53.

De Cremer, D., & van Knippenberg, D. (2002). How do readers promote coopera-tion? The effects of charisma and procedural fairness. *Journal of Applied Psychology, 87,* 858–866.

DeGroot, T., Kiker, D. S., & Cross, T. C. (2000). A meta-analysis to review organi-zational outcomes related to charismatic leadership. *Canadian Journal of Administrative Sciences, 17,* 356–371.

Dehaene, S., & Naccache, L. (2001). Towards a cognitive neuroscience of conscien-tiousness: Basic evidence and a workspace framework. *Cognition, 79,* 1–37.

DeRue, D. S., & Ashford, S. J. (2010). Who will lead and who will follow? A social process of leadership identity construction in organizations. *Academy of Management Review, 35,* 627–647.

Dirks, K. T., & Ferrin, D. L. (2002). Trust in leadership: Meta-analytic findings and implications for research and practice. *Journal of Applied Psychology, 87,* 611–628.

Dragoni, L. (2005). Understanding the emergence of state goal orientation in orga-nizational work groups: The role of leadership and multilevel climate percep-tions. *Journal of Applied Psychology, 90,* 1084–1095.

Drazin, R., Glynn, M. A., & Kazanjian, R. K. (1999). Multilevel theorizing about creativity in organizations: A sensemaking perspective. *Academy of Management Review, 24,* 286–307.

Dubin, R. (1969). *Theory building.* New York: Free Press.

Eden, D. (1992). Leadership and expectations: Pygmalion effects and other self-ful-filling prophecies in organizations. *The Leadership Quarterly, 3,* 271–305.

Eden, D., & Aviram, A. (1993). Self-efficacy training to speed reemployment: Helping people to help themselves. *Journal of Applied Psychology, 78,* 352–360.

Ericsson, K. A., & Charness, N. (1994). Expert performance: Its structure and acqui-sition. *American Psychologist, 49,* 725–747.

Fleeson, W. (2001). Toward a structure- and process-integrated view of personality: Traits as density distributions of states. *Journal of Personality and Social Psychology, 80,* 1011–1027.

Flynn, F. J. (2005). Identity orientations and forms of social exchange in organiza-tions. *Academy of Management Review, 30,* 737–750.

Foldy, E., Goldman, L., & Ospina, S. (2008). Sensegiving and the role of cognitive shifts in the work of leadership. *The Leadership Quarterly, 19,* 514–529.

Fredrickson, B. L. (2003). Positive emotions and upward spirals in organizations. In K. S. Cameron, J. E. Dutton, & R. E. Quinn (Eds.), *Positive organizational scholarship: Foundations of a new discipline* (pp. 163–175). San Francisco: Berrett-Koehler.

George, J. M. (2002). Affect regulation in groups and teams. In R. G. Lord, R. J. Klimoski, & R. Kanfer (Eds.), *Emotions in the workplace: Understanding the structure and role of emotions in organizational behavior* (pp. 183–218). San Francisco: Jossey-Bass.

George, J. M., & Zhou, J. (2007). Dual tuning in a supportive context: Joint contributions of positive mood, negative mood, and supervisory behaviors to employee creativity. *Academy of Management Journal, 50,* 605–622.

Gerstner, C. R., & Day, D. V. (1997). Meta-analytic review of leader–member exchange theory: Correlates and construct issues. *Journal of Applied Psychology, 82,* 827–844.

Graen, G. B., & Scandura, T. A. (1987). Toward a psychology of dyadic organizing. *Research in Organizational Behavior, 9,* 175–208.

Gusnard, D. A. (2005). Being a self: Considerations from functional imaging. *Consciousness and Cognition, 14,* 679–697.

Haidt, J. (2000). The positive emotion of elevation. *Prevention and Treatment, 3,* 1–5.

Hall, R. J., & Lord, R. G. (1995). Multi-level information-processing explanations of followers' leadership perceptions. *The Leadership Quarterly, 6,* 265–288.

Hanges, P. J., Lord, R. G., & Dickson, M. W. (2000). An information-processing perspective on leadership and culture: A case for connectionist architecture. *Applied Psychology: An International Review, 49,* 133–161.

Hannah, S. T., Uhl-Bien, M., Avolio, B. J., & Cavarretta, F. L. (2009). A framework for examining leadership in extreme contexts. *The Leadership Quarterly, 12,* 129–131.

Hannah, S. T., Woolfolk, R. L., & Lord, R. G. (2009). Leader self-structure: A framework for positive leadership. *Journal of Organizational Behavior, 30,* 269–290.

Hatfield, E., Cacioppo, J. T., & Rapson, R. L. (1993). Emotional contagion. *Current Directions in Psychological Science, 2,* 96–99.

Henderson, D. J., Liden, R. C., Glibkowski, B. C., & Chaudhry, A. (2009). LMX differentiation: A multilevel review and examination of its antecedents and outcomes. *The Leadership Quarterly, 20,* 517–534.

Henderson, D. J., Wayne, S. J., Shore, L. M., Bommer, W. H., & Tetrick, L. E. (2008). Leader–member exchange, differentiation, and psychological contract fulfillment: A multilevel examination. *Journal of Applied Psychology, 93,* 1208–1219.

Hogg, M. A., Martin, R., Epitropaki, O., Mankad, A., Svensson, A., & Weeden, K. (2005). Effective leadership in salient groups: Revisiting leader–member exchange theory from the perspective of the social identity theory of leadership. *Personality and Social Psychology Bulletin, 31,* 991–1004.

Hogue, M., & Lord, R. G. (2007). A multilevel, complexity theory approach to understanding gender bias in leadership. *The Leadership Quarterly, 18,* 370–390.

House, R. J. (1971). A path goal theory of leader effectiveness. *Administrative Science Quarterly, 16,* 321–338.

Hunt, J. G. (2004). What is leadership? In J. Antonakis, A. T. Cianciolo, & R. J. Sternberg (Eds.), *The nature of leadership* (pp. 19–46). Thousand Oaks, CA: Sage.

Hunter, S. T., Bedell-Avers, K. E., & Mumford, M. D. (2007). The typical leadership study: Assumptions, implications, and potential remedies. *The Leadership Quarterly, 18,* 435–446.

Isen, A. M., Daubman, K. A., & Nowicki, G. P. (1987). Positive affect facilitates creative problem solving. *Journal of Personality and Social Psychology, 52,* 1122–1131.

Isen, A. M., Rosenzweig, A. S., & Young, M. J. (1991). The influence of positive affect on clinical problem solving. *Medical Decision Making, 11,* 221–227.

Johnson, R. E., & Lord, R. G. (2010). Implicit effects of social justice on self-identity. *Journal of Applied Psychology, 95,* 681-695.

Jones, B. F., & Olken, B. A. (2005). Do leaders matter? National leadership and growth since World War II. *The Quarterly Journal of Economics, 120,* 835–864.

Joseph, S., & Linley, P. A. (2005). Positive adjustment to threatening events: An organismic valuing theory of growth through adversity. *Review of General Psychology, 9,* 262–280.

Judge, T. A., Bono, J. E., Ilies, R., & Gerhardt, M. W. (2002). Personality and leadership: A qualitative and quantitative review. *Journal of Applied Psychology, 48,* 765–780.

Kahn, B. E., & Isen, A. M. (1993). The influence of positive affect on variety seeking among safe, enjoyable products. *Journal of Consumer Research, 20,* 257–270.

Kaiser, R. B., Hogan, R., & Craig, S. B. (2008). Leadership and the fate of organizations. *American Psychologist, 63,* 96–110.

Kark, R., Shamir, B., & Chen, G. (2003). The two faces of transformational leadership: Empowerment and dependency. *Journal of Applied Psychology, 88,* 246–255.

Kark, R., & Van Dijk, D. (2007). Motivation to lead, motivation to follow: The role of the self-regulatory focus in leadership processes. *Academy of Management Review, 32,* 500–528.

Keith, N., & Frese, M. (2005). Self-regulation in error management training: Emotion control and metacognition as mediators of performance effects. *Journal of Applied Psychology, 90,* 677–691.

Keller, T. (2003). Parental images as a guide to leadership sensemaking: An attachment perspective on implicit leadership theories. *The Leadership Quarterly, 14,* 141–160.

Kenny, D., & Zaccaro, S. J. (1983). An estimate of variance due to traits in leadership. *Journal of Applied Psychology, 68,* 678–685.

Kerr, S., Schriesheim, C. A., Murphy, C. J., & Stogdill, R. M. (1974). Toward a contingency theory of leadership based upon the consideration and initiating structure literature. *Organizational Behavior and Human Performance, 12,* 62–82.

Klein, K. J., Dansereau, F., & Hall, R. J. (1994). Level issues in theory development, data collection, and analysis. *Academy of Management Review, 19,* 195–229.

Kozlowski, S. W. J., & Ilgen, D. R. (2006). Enhancing the effectiveness of work groups and teams. *Psychological Science in the Public Interest, 7,* 77–124.

Kozlowski, S. W. J., & Klein, K. J. (2000). A multilevel approach to theory and research in organizations: Contextual, temporal, and emergent processes. In S. W. J. Kozlowski & K. J. Klein (Eds.), *Multilevel theory, research and methods in organizations: Foundations, extensions, and new directions* (pp. 3–90). San Francisco: Jossey-Bass.

Leslie, A. M. (1987). Pretense and representation: The origins of "theory of mind." *Psychological Review, 94,* 412–426.

Levy, P. E., Cober, R. T., & Miller, T. (2002). The effect of transformational and transactional leadership perceptions on feedback-seeking intentions. *Journal of Applied Social Psychology, 32,* 1703–1720.

Liden, R. C., & Antonakis, J. (2009). Considering context in psychological leadership research. *Human Relations, 62,* 1587–1605.

Lord, R. G., & Brown, D. J. (2004). *Leadership processes and follower self-identity.* Mahwah, NJ: LEA.

Lord, R. G., Brown, D. J., Harvey, J. L., & Hall, R. J. (2001). Contextual constraints on prototype generation and their multilevel consequences for leadership perception. *The Leadership Quarterly, 12,* 311–338.

Lord, R. G., Diefendorff, J. M., Schmidt, A. M., & Hall, R. J. (2010). Self-regulation at work. *Annual Review of Psychology, 61,* 543–568.

Lord, R. G., Foti, R. J., & De Vader, C. L. (1984). A test of leadership categorization theory: Internal structure, information processing, and leadership perceptions. *Organizational Behavior and Human Performance, 34,* 343–378.

Lord, R. G., & Hall, R. J. (2005). Identity, deep structure and the development of leadership skill. *The Leadership Quarterly, 16,* 591–615.

Lord, R. G., Hannah, S. T., & Jennings, P. L. (2011). A framework for understanding leadership and individual requisite complexity. *Organizational Psychology Review 1,* 1-29.

Lord, R. G., & Maher, K. J. (1991). Leadership and information processing: Linking perceptions and organizational performance. Boston: Unwin Hyman.

Marion, R., & Uhl-Bien, M. (2001). Leadership in complex organizations. *The Leadership Quarterly, 12,* 389–418.

Marks, M. A., Mathieu, J. E., & Zaccaro, S. J. (2001). A temporally based framework and taxonomy of team processes. *The Academy of Management Review, 26,* 356–376.

McCrae, R. R., Costa, P. T., Jr., Ostendorf, F., Angleitner, A., Hrebickova, M. Avia, M. D., et al. (2000). Nature over nurture: Temperament, personality, and life span development. *Journal of Personality and Social Psychology, 78,* 173–186.

McCrae, R. R., & Terracciano, A. (2005). Universal features of personality traits from the observer's perspective: Data from 50 cultures. *Journal of Personality and Social Psychology, 88,* 547–561.

Meindl, J. R., & Ehrlich, S. B. (1987). The romance of leadership and the evaluation of organizational performance. *Academy of Management Journal, 30,* 91–109.

Metcalfe, J., & Mischel, W. (1999). A hot/cool-system analysis of delay of gratification: Dynamics of willpower. *Psychological Review, 106,* 3–19.

Miller, D., Kets de Vries, M. F. R., & Toulouse, J. M. (1982). Top executive locus of control and its relationship to strategy-making, structure, and environment. *Academy of Management Journal, 25,* 237–253.

Miller, D., & Toulouse, J. A. (1986). Chief executive personality and corporate strategy and structure of small firms. *Management Science, 32,* 1389–1409.

Mischel, W., & Shoda, Y. (1998). Reconciling processing dynamics and personality dispositions. *Annual Review of Psychology, 49,* 229–258.

Morgeson, F. P., & DeRue, D. S. (2006). Event criticality, urgency, and duration: Understanding how events disrupt teams and influence team leader intervention. *The Leadership Quarterly, 17,* 271–287.

Morgeson, F. P., & Hofmann, D. A. (1999). The structure and function of collective constructs: Implications for multilevel research and theory development. *Academy of Management Review, 24,* 249–265.

Mumford, M. D., & Peterson, N. G. (1999). The O*NET content model: Structural considerations in describing jobs. In N. G. Peterson, M. D. Mumford, W. C. Borman, P. R. Jeanneret, & E. A. Fleishman (Eds.), *An occupational* *information system for the 21st century: The development of O*NET* (pp. 21–30). Washington, DC: American Psychological Association.

Mumford, M. D., Zaccaro, S. J., Harding, F. D., Jacobs, T. O., & Fleishman, E. A. (2000). Leadership skills for a changing world: Solving complex social problems. *The Leadership Quarterly, 11,* 11–35.

Nahrgang, J. D., Morgeson, F. P., & Ilies, R. (2009). The development of leader–member exchanges: Exploring how personality and performance influence leader and member relationships over time. *Organizational Behavior and Human Decision Processes, 108,* 256–266.

Naidoo, L. J., & Lord, R. G. (2008). Speech imagery and perceptions of charisma: The mediating role of positive affect. *The Leadership Quarterly, 19,* 283–296.

Newman, J., Baars, B. J., & Cho, S. B. (1997). A neural global workspace model for conscious attention. *Neural Networks, 10,* 1195–1206.

Offermann, L. R., Kennedy, J. K., & Wirtz, P. W. (1994). Implicit leadership theories: Content, structure, and generalizability. *The Leadership Quarterly, 5,* 43–58.

O'Malley, A. L., Ritchie, S. A., Lord, R. G., Gregory, J. B., & Young, C. M. (2009). Incorporating embodied cognitions into sensemaking theory: A theoretical examination of embodied processes in a leadership context. *Current Topics in Management, 14,* 151–182.

Page, S. E. (2007). *The difference: How the power of diversity creates better groups, firms, schools, and societies.* Princeton, NJ: Princeton University Press.

Pearce, C. L., & Conger, J. A. (2003). *Shared leadership: Reframing the hows and whys of leadership.* Thousand Oaks, CA: Sage.

Pescosolido, A. T. (2002). Emergent leaders as managers of group emotion. *The Leadership Quarterly, 13,* 583–599.

Popper, M., & Amit, K. (2009). Attachment and leader's development via experiences. *The Leadership Quarterly, 20,* 749–763.

Rousseau, D. (1985). Issues of level in organizational research: Multilevel and cross-level perspectives. In L. L. Cummings & B. M. Staw (Eds.), *Research in organizational behavior* (Vol. 7, pp. 1–37). Greenwich, CT: JAI Press.

Schein, E. (1985). *Organizational culture and leadership.* San Francisco: Jossey-Bass.

Schneider, B. (1987). The people make the place. *Personnel Psychology, 4,* 437–453.

Shah, J. (2003). The motivational looking glass: How significant others implicitly affect goal appraisals. *Journal of Personality and Social Psychology, 85,* 424–439.

Shamir, B., & Howell, J. M. (1999). Organizational and contextual influences on the emergence and effectiveness of charismatic leadership. *The Leadership Quarterly, 10,* 257–283.

Shamir, B., Pallai, R., Bligh, M. C., & Uhl-Bien, M. (2007). *Follower-centered perspectives on leadership: A tribute to the memory of James R. Meindl.* Greenwich, CT: Information Age.

Shoda, Y., Tiernan, S. L., & Mischel, W. (2002). Personality as a dynamical system: Emergence of stability and distinctiveness from intra- and interpersonal interactions. *Personality and Social Psychology Review, 4,* 316–325.

Shondrick, S. J., Dinh, J. E., & Lord, R. G. (2010). Developments in implicit leadership theory and cognitive science: Applications to improving measurement and understanding alternatives to hierarchical leadership. *The Leadership Quarterly, 21,* 959-978.

Sluss, D. M., & Ashforth, B. E. (2007). Relational identity and identification: Defining ourselves through work relationships. *Academy of Management Review, 34,* 533–551.

Staw, B. M., & Barsade, S. G. (1993). Affect and managerial performance: A test of the sadder-but-wiser vs. happier-and-smarter hypothesis. *Administrative Science Quarterly, 38,* 304–331.

Tett, R. P., & Burnett, D. D. (2003). A personality trait-based interactionist model of job performance. *Journal of Applied Psychology, 88,* 500–517.

Uhl-Bien, M., Marion, R., & McKelvey, B. (2007). Complexity leadership theory: Shifting leadership from the industrial age to the knowledge era. *The Leadership Quarterly, 18,* 298–318.

van Knippenberg, D., van Knippenberg, B., De Cremer, D., & Hogg, M. A. (2004). Leadership, self, and identity: A review and research agenda. *The Leadership Quarterly, 15,* 825–856.

Weick, K. (1995). *Sensemaking in organizations.* Thousand Oaks, CA: Sage.

Weiss, H. M., & Cropanzano, R. (1996). Affective events theory: A theoretical discussion of the structure, causes and consequences of affective experiences at work. In B. M. Staw & L. L. Cummings (Eds.), *Research in organization behavior* (Vol. 19, pp. 1–74). Greenwich, CT: JAI Press.

Whetten, D. A., Felin, T., & King, B. G. (2009). The practice of theory borrowing in organizational studies: Current issues and future directions. *Journal of Management, 35,* 537–563.

Wofford, J. C., & Goodwin, V. L. (1994). A cognitive interpretation of transactional and transformational leadership theories. *The Leadership Quarterly, 5,* 161–186.

Worline, M., Wrzesniewski, A., & Rafaeli, A. (2002). Courage and work: Breaking routines to improve performance. In R. G. Lord, R. Klimoski, and R. Kanfer (Eds.), *Emotions in the workplace: Understanding the structure and role of emotions in organizational behavior* (pp. 295-330). San Francisco: Jossey-Bass.

Yammarino, F. J., Dionne, S. D., Chun, J. U., & Dansereau, F. (2005). Leadership and levels of analysis: A state-of-the-science review. *The Leadership Quarterly, 16,* 879–919.

Zaccaro, S. J., Kemp, C., & Bader, P. (2004). Leader traits and attributes. In J. Antonakis, A. T. Cianciolo, & R. J. Sternberg (Eds.), *The nature of leadership* (pp. 101–123). Thousand Oaks, CA: Sage.

Zohar, D., & Tenne-Gazit, O. (2008). Transformational leadership and group interaction as climate antecedents: A social network analysis. *Journal of Applied Psychology, 93,* 744–757.

3

Advances in Leadership Research Methods

Michael J. Zyphur

University of Melbourne

Adam P. Barsky

University of Melbourne

Zhen Zhang

Arizona State University

The study of leadership has seen many advances with regard to the methods used to describe, predict, and measure good and poor leadership in their multifarious forms (see Antonakis et al., 2004). Many of these advances have occurred as a function of the conceptualization and/or reconceptualization of leadership associated with the zeitgeist of leadership research. The current chapter is meant to advance leadership research by discussing quantitative methods that will allow scholars to examine leadership questions in new ways. Specifically, our aim is to allow researchers to rethink old techniques and learn about new techniques so they may switch (a) "analytical mindsets" (Zyphur, 2009) or (b) the way theory and research are framed in relation to particular quantitative techniques. This should allow the creation of new theoretical models that previously would have been culled or not

AUTHORS' NOTE: Please address correspondence concerning this article to Michael J. Zyphur, Department of Management and Marketing, Level 10, 198 Berkeley Street, University of Melbourne, Victoria 3010, Australia. Phone: +61-3-90355826. e-mail: mzyphur@unimelb.edu.au.

conceived because of statistical limitations, as well as allow new theoretical postulations in an inductive fashion by beginning with a new statistical model and then trying to understand how it may be used to address leadership questions (Edwards, 2008).

Although there are many techniques leadership researchers use, including agent-based simulations for testing complexity theories of leadership (e.g., Dionne & Dionne, 2008), social network-based approaches to study shared leadership (e.g., Carson, Tesluk, & Marrone, 2007; Ensley, Hmieleski, & Pearce, 2006), the life narrative method for examining leadership development (e.g., Ligon, Hunter, & Mumford, 2008), and various biological approaches (e.g., Zhang, Ilies, & Arvey, 2009), these are outside the scope of our current discussion.

Topics to Discuss

We begin by discussing structural equation modeling (SEM). We then describe a recent advance in SEM capabilities in the form of latent variable interactions, which allows analyzing moderated relationships among different latent variables as well as the nonlinear effects of latent variables that we term latent polynomial regression (LPR). We show how LPR allows for a more complete method for addressing congruence in leadership research.

Next we describe multilevel modeling (MLM) and how this has been used by leadership researchers to predict outcomes across multiple levels of analysis. We then describe a little known and underutilized modeling technique that allows differential relationships between group members and the random coefficients that represent the group at higher levels of analysis.

We then describe latent growth modeling (LGM) as a method for modeling change over time. Leadership researchers have seldom put LGM to use in their studies. We note that LGM allows hypothesis testing at multiple levels of analysis. As a part of this exposition, we use our previous formulations for SEM and MLM as a basis for showing how these models allow for equivalent solutions to similar problems. We then present a new LGM where the mean of all observations over time may be explicitly modeled for each person as an "intercept factor." We call this the intercept-as-mean growth model (IGM), which is relevant because the mean of multiple scores is the most reliable and is their maximum likelihood estimate.

Then we discuss the intersection of SEM and MLM in the form of multilevel structural equation modeling (MSEM), a technique that incorporates the advantages of both the SEM and MLM paradigms. We note how full MSEM provides capabilities beyond both SEM and MLM for answering questions in leadership research. Particularly, we note that it's possible to model higher-level outcome variables in MSEM (i.e., bottom-up in addition to the typical top-down relationships; K. J. Klein & Kozlowski, 2000)—something that is not possible in traditional MLM—and something that allows for complex mediation analyses across levels of analysis.

Finally we explore latent class cluster analysis (LCCA), a relative of latent profile analysis (LPA). We note where logic similar to that of LCCA is used by leadership researchers to profile personality as a method for understanding leadership style and effectiveness (Michael, 2003). We show how LCCA can be used with widely accepted taxonomies of personality such as the Big 5 to profile personalities based on the patterns that exist in the data rather than, for example, dichotomizing scores along the dimensions that make up individual difference constructs (e.g., "high" versus "low" along extraversion). One key argument throughout this discussion is that LCCA allows for more of a person-centered analysis rather than a variable-centered analysis.

Throughout this chapter, we assume that predictors are exogenous, meaning that they are not influenced by causal factors that influence the relationship between predictors and criteria. In other words, the predictors do not correlate with the error terms of criterion variables when only the causal effect of predictors on criteria is accounted for. As discussed by Antonakis, Bendahan, Jacquart, and Lalive (2010), when predictors are endogenous, there is a variety of explanations for the observed relationship between predictors and criteria, such as omitted variables (e.g., the "third variable" or "common cause" problem), sample selection, simultaneity, and common methods variance, among others. When endogeneity is an issue, model estimates are not consistent, meaning these estimates will not converge to the appropriate population parameter as sample size increases. As such, these estimates should not be interpreted as supporting or failing to support hypotheses. In fact, in some if not most cases, these estimates cannot be meaningfully interpreted at all. Antonakis et al. (2010) explicitly discussed the pervasive problem of endogeneity in leadership research and offered various remedies to overcome this problem (e.g., two-stage least squares estimation, regression discontinuity models, difference-in-difference models, selection models), which fortuitously can allow for making causal inferences with correlational data in certain cases. For simplicity purposes, in this chapter we assume the predictors in our examples are exogenous, although we emphasize the serious problem endogeneity represents and the benefits of accounting for endogeneity, which can be done in multiple ways (see Hamilton & Nickerson, 2003; Wooldridge, 2002).

Additionally, for all models shown in the figures, we provide code for their estimation in the statistical modeling program Mplus (L. K. Muthén & Muthén, 1998–2008)—our program of choice, given its ability to model variables with many underlying distributions with a variety of estimators (e.g., asymptotic distribution free, Bayes) in multifarious model specifications, such as mixture models, multilevel structural equation models, and models with latent interaction, just to name a few.

Introduction and the Form of the Model

Until structural equation models were developed, researchers struggled with the limitations of existing statistical techniques such as OLS regression, ANOVA, and exploratory factor analysis (EFA). Namely, specifying complex relationships among latent variables (i.e., unobserved variables) in a confirmatory fashion was not possible (Bollen, 1989). This is of issue because OLS regression and ANOVA do not account for measurement error in outcomes and do not allow complex structural paths among variables, and although EFA accounts for measurement error, it is not a confirmatory technique and does not allows complex structural paths among factors. SEM was developed by scholars such as Jöreskog and Sörbom (1979) to solve these problems by (a) allowing latent variables that are measured by multiple observed indicators and (b) specifying structurally complex relationships among these latent variables (see Kline, 2005).

As in factor analysis, an interpretation of latent variables is that they represent constructs that cause scores along observed variables, such as personality items (for discussion see Bollen, 2002). In these models, latent variables account for/explain covariance among observed variables. Unlike in factor analysis, however, regression among latent and observed variables is possible. This has the benefit of reducing measurement error in the measure of a given construct—via latent variables—and allowing complex structural paths among them.

Put simply, SEMs allow researchers to specify relationships among observed variables and latent variables (through factors loadings), as well as relationships among latent variables (through regression or covariation). During parameter estimation, the likelihood associated with each estimated parameter is maximized in relation to observed data—a likelihood is the conditional probability of observing the data (D), given that the model-estimated parameters (M) are true (Bollen, 1989), which we can write as $P(D \mid M)$. The parameters allowing the greatest degree of fit to the data are estimated in an iterative fashion, until the likelihood is sufficiently maximized (i.e., changes in the likelihood are minimized around an assumed global maximum).

One form of an SEM may be shown as follows:

$$\mathbf{y}_i = \mathbf{\Lambda}\mathbf{\eta}_i + \mathbf{K}\mathbf{x}_i + \mathbf{\varepsilon}_i, \text{ and} \tag{3.1}$$

$$\mathbf{\eta}_i = \mathbf{\alpha} + \mathbf{B}\mathbf{\eta}_i + \mathbf{\Gamma}\mathbf{w}_i + \mathbf{\zeta}_i, \tag{3.2}$$

where $\mathbf{y}_i$ is a vector of observed variables for a person i; $\mathbf{\Lambda}$ is a matrix of factor loadings for the latent variables; $\mathbf{\eta}_i$ is a vector of latent variables for a person i; $\mathbf{K}$ is a matrix of regression coefficients of $\mathbf{y}_i$ on a vector of observed exogenous predictors $\mathbf{x}_i$; $\boldsymbol{\varepsilon}_i$ is a vector of error terms for person i; $\boldsymbol{\alpha}$ is a vector of latent variable means; $\mathbf{B}$ is a matrix of regressions among latent variables; $\boldsymbol{\Gamma}$ is a matrix of regressions among observed predictors of the latent variables; $\mathbf{w}_i$ is a vector of observed exogenous predictors; and $\boldsymbol{\zeta}_i$ is a vector of latent variable disturbances for person i. The variances and covariances of errors are specified in a matrix $\boldsymbol{\Theta}$, and the variances and covariances of latent variables are specific in a matrix $\boldsymbol{\Psi}$. Here, Equation 3.1 contains the measurement model, whereas Equation 3.2 contains the structural model.

Because SEM is a system of regression paths among observed and latent variables, it subsumes many other statistical techniques, such as OLS regression, ANOVA and MANOVA, path analysis, factor analysis, and a variety of models for handling longitudinal data, with each of these being a special case of the model presented in Equations 3.1 and 3.2 (Bollen, 1989). Considering OLS regression, ANOVA, and ANCOVA, continuous predictors and dummy-coded variables indicating group membership can be contained in $\mathbf{x}_i$ and coefficients of effect in $\mathbf{K}$, with vectors and matrices in Equation 3.2 left empty. For factor analysis, factor loadings would be contained in $\boldsymbol{\Lambda}$ and, as in exploratory factor analysis, different numbers of factors specified to explain covariance among variables in $\mathbf{y}_i$ would be contained in $\boldsymbol{\eta}_i$, with non-orthogonality specifications possible by allowing covariance among the factors in $\boldsymbol{\Psi}$. As an example of an SEM using all terms in Equations 3.1 and 3.2, see Figure 3.1a (see Appendix A1 for Mplus code—an exclamation mark "!" refers to a comment not included in the program code).

The assumptions underlying SEM estimation with maximum likelihood include large sample sizes and multivariate normality—including the independent variables (Bollen, 1989). In cases where these assumptions do not hold, normalizing the variables, bootstrapping, maximum likelihood estimators robust to non-normality, and asymptotically distribution free estimators such as weighted least squares may be used (for an introduction, see Kline, 2005). Additionally, categorical variables—count, ordered categorical, dichotomous, and nominal—may be introduced by specifying mixed multivariate distribution functions and using weighted least squares or maximum likelihood estimation using numerical integration.

Issues surrounding model identification and the assessment of fit are many. In brief, "global" identification requires more information than estimated parameters (i.e., positive degrees of freedom), whereas "local" identification requires enough information to estimate parameters in a given part of a model (see Bollen, 1989). In terms of model fit, likelihood ratio tests with a chi-square distribution are used to test the discrepancy between model-implied covariances and observed covariances—also used when assessing differences between model-implied covariance matrices when comparing nested models such as in multigroup invariance testing. Significant differences indicate that the estimated model does not fit the observed data.

Figure 3.1a   A basic structural equation model specification following Equations 3.1 and 3.2, with items in $\mathbf{y}_i$ reflecting latent variables in $\boldsymbol{\eta}_i$ via factor loadings in $\boldsymbol{\Lambda}$, influenced by a predictor in $\mathbf{x}_i$ with a regression weight in $\mathbf{K}$, errors in $\boldsymbol{\varepsilon}_i$, latent variable intercepts in $\boldsymbol{\alpha}$, regression among the latent variables in $\mathbf{B}$, latent variables influenced by a predictor in $\mathbf{w}_i$ with a regression weight in $\boldsymbol{\Gamma}$, and latent variable disturbances in $\boldsymbol{\zeta}_i$. Similar notation will be used for all figures presented in this chapter.

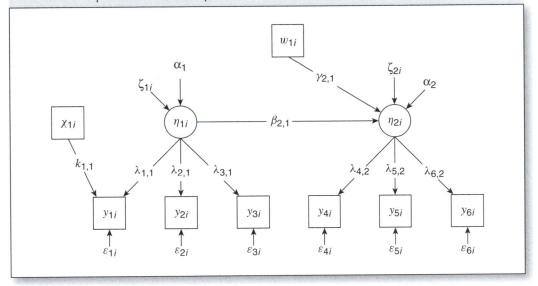

A common point of contention surrounding such tests is that they become too sensitive as sample size increases—although as with other tests, the power associated with larger sample sizes is useful. Additional fit indices such as approximate/standardized and unstandardized indices are often employed for this reason, but all are based on the log likelihood. A discussion of these indices, the information each provides, and reporting standards is beyond the scope of this chapter (readers may see Chen, Curran, Bollen, Kirby, & Paxton, 2008; McDonald & Ho, 2002; "Structural," 2007; Yuan, 2005).

Importantly, the model-estimated mean for each variable y can be determined by fixing a column in $\boldsymbol{\Lambda}$ to unity, where the corresponding element in $\boldsymbol{\eta}_i$ would be the mean for each individual i, the corresponding element in $\boldsymbol{\alpha}$ would be the grand mean across all individuals, and the corresponding element in $\boldsymbol{\zeta}_i$ would be the deviation away from this grand mean for each individual. *This fact is relevant because it will inform below how multilevel modeling and SEM allow for equivalent specifications in latent growth models.*

SEM is used for many purposes in the pursuit of understanding the properties of various measures and the relationships among latent variables (Williams, Edwards, & Vandenberg, 2003). For example, Antonakis, Avolio, and Sivasubramaniam (2003) show invariance in the measurement properties of the multifactor leadership questionnaire (MLQ-5X) across genders and contexts. Barling, Loughlin, and Kelloway (2002) show that safety-specific transformational leadership predicts occupational injuries through safety climate and other variables.

Latent Interaction Terms

Although such analyses are commonplace, one shortcoming of the way scholars think about the SEM framework is that testing interactions (i.e., moderation) among latent variables is difficult if not impossible (Edwards, 2008). Variables that interact with important leadership processes have long been of interest—more or less defining the entire area of contingency approaches to leadership (Howell, Dorfman, & Kerr, 1986)—and testing for interactions among variables that could be modeled as latent is common for leadership researchers (e.g., Ng, Ang, & Chan, 2008). Also, analyses that require the multiplication of variables that could be considered latent, yet lie outside the domain of tests of interaction, such as curvilinear relationships in congruence modeling, are also popular (e.g., Colbert, Kristof-Brown, Bradley, & Barrick, 2008).

The ability to examine latent interactions and quadratic effects are critical for a number of reasons. First, the reliability of observed product terms is a function of their reliability as well as their correlation, and quadratic terms are similarly affected (Dimitruk, Schermelleh-Engel, Kelava, Moosbrugger, 2007). In all cases, the reliability of these resulting variables is lower than the original variables, reducing the power to detect effects when they exist. Second, because researchers do not often consider SEM a solution for modeling interactions and quadratic effects, they are limited to less structurally complex regression models (Edwards & Lambert, 2007).

To overcome these issues, the Latent Moderated Structural Equations (LMS; A. Klein & Moosbrugger, 2000) and the Quasi-Maximum Likelihood approaches (QML; A. Klein & Muthén, 2007) allow specifying latent variables that represent the multiplication of other latent variables. Importantly, such interactions not only can take the form simply of interactions among different latent variables, and between a latent variable and an observed variable, but also can allow for latent quadratic terms. Although other methods for estimating such latent variables exist (e.g., Bollen, 1996; Jöreskog & Yang 1996, 1997), they are unwieldy and suffer from a variety of shortcomings mitigated by LMS and QML—such as underestimated standard errors, low efficiency and power, and issues surrounding multicollinearity (Kelava, Moosbrugger, Dimitrik, & Schermelleh-Engel; 2008; Moosbrugger, Schermelleh-Engel, & Klein, 1997; Schermelleh-Engel, Klein, & Moosbrugger, 1998)—this is because of the non-normality that is created in product terms, quadratic terms, and, thus, endogenous variables. Given the application of LMS in Mplus (see B. Muthén & Asparouhov, 2003), we reference LMS in this section.

Because the complexity of LMS is great, the approach is presented here by simply adding any interaction or quadratic latent variables to the $\boldsymbol{\eta}_i$ vector and the $\boldsymbol{\Lambda}$, $\boldsymbol{B}$, and $\boldsymbol{\Psi}$ matrix—they are treated like latent variables. Just as with other methods of estimating interactions (e.g., Cohen, Cohen, West, & Aiken, 2003), the effects of latent variables and their interaction are estimated and may be used to plot interaction effects and estimate changes in R^2. Again, one of the variables may be observed, and for a discussion of interactions without latent variables, see Edwards and Lambert (2007). To grasp the versatility of the LMS approach, researchers could simply substitute latent variables for all variables found in Edwards and Lambert (2007).

Implications for Leadership Researchers

Aside from testing latent interactions, LMS allows addressing another question asked by leadership researchers: the degree of congruence (i.e., fit, similarity, etc.) among leaders and followers. A common method for addressing this question is polynomial regression (see Edwards, 1993, 1995, 2002, 2007; Edwards & Parry, 1993). However, Cheung (2009) notes this method suffers from (a) measurement error, (b) an inability to examine measurement equivalence across leaders and followers, and (c) a lack of allowing complex relationships among variables.

To alleviate these problems, Cheung (2009) proposes a latent congruence model (LCM) to capture the average level along a construct for leaders and followers as well as model the deviation away from this average. However, Cheung notes that without the ability to model latent interaction and quadratic terms, the LCM is limited in its applicability, given the many possibilities for more general latent polynomial regression models (LPR; e.g., latent response surface modeling) as well as latent interactions among his latent congruence variables.

By using the LMS approach, the following issues that have confronted researchers for congruence modeling with latent variables may be overcome: (a) all shortcomings of polynomial regression identified by Cheung (2009), (b) limitations of the LCM in not being able to model latent interaction and quadratic terms, and (c) problems involving the non-normality of endogenous latent and observed interaction terms (as well as exponentiated latent variables).

The classic polynomial regression model for congruence modeling shown in Edwards and Parry (1993) takes the following form:

$$y_i = b_0 + b_1 x_i + b_2 z_i + b_3 x_i z_i + b_4 x_i^2 + b_5 z_i^2, \qquad (3.3)$$

where constraints on the coefficients may be imposed to examine squared differences between leader and follower. An equivalent LPR model may be estimated using the LMS procedure (Dimitruk et al., 2007), where the structural part of the model in Equation 3.2 for an endogenous variable η_1 (see Figure 3.1b; see Appendix A2 for Mplus LPR code) can be shown as

$$\eta_{1i} = \alpha_1 + \beta_{1,2}\eta_{2i} + \beta_{1,3}\eta_{3i} + \beta_{1,4}\eta_{2i}\eta_{3i} + \beta_{1,5}\eta_{2i}^2 + \beta_{1,6}\eta_{3i}^2 + \zeta_{1i}, \quad (3.4)$$

where constraints may be placed on model parameters of interest, likelihood ratio tests may be conducted with nested models, and researchers may save time in computing the parameters required for response surface models by including such parameters as outcomes of appropriate equations estimated in SEM programs (e.g., in the "model constraint" portion in Appendix A2). Additionally, several followers may be nested within a single leader. To accommodate this nonindependence of observations, standard errors can be

Figure 3.1b A latent polynomial regression model (LPR) following Equation 3.4, where all terms are as in Figure 3.1a. Here, three latent variables are specified to capture the interaction between the two latent variables acting as predictors, as well as their squares. Such a model allows testing fit/congruence in a latent variable framework.

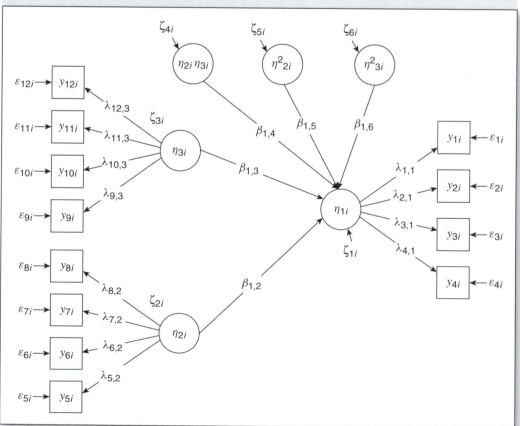

computed using a robust estimator (i.e., Huber-White or sandwiched estimator). This is made possible in Mplus by specifying Type = Complex in the Analysis command and identifying the grouping variable in the Variable command (see Appendix A2). In addition, because the multivariate normality assumption typically does not hold for models with latent interactions, researchers could use bootstrapped confidence intervals instead of parametric approaches to null-hypothesis significance testing.

In summary, the modeling possibilities allowed by the LMS framework are vast for leadership researchers. It solves problems of low reliability and the integration of interaction and quadratic terms in complex structural equations. Also, LMS allows examining congruence in a way that goes beyond both polynomial regression and LCM by integrating their logic into a single latent variable framework with complex structural relations.

Multilevel Modeling

Just as with SEMs, the logic of MLMs was developed in order to solve statistical issues confronted by researchers (for discussion, see Searle, Casella, & McCulloch, 1992). Specifically, many researchers collect and analyze data that are nested in one way or another. For example, two pioneers in the domain of MLM, Raudenbush and Bryk (1986, 2002), often analyze data from students nested within classrooms, which are themselves nested within schools and school districts. These observations are said to be nonindependent to the extent that scores from individuals in similar units are correlated (i.e., when there exists a significant amount of between-unit variance). When this occurs, there are both threats and opportunities for researchers.

One threat is that standard errors are downwardly biased because the number of independent observations are overestimated, leading to higher Type-I error rates. Another threat is that higher-level representations of lower-level observations are latent, and therefore, using unit averages does not account for sampling error (Raudenbush & Bryk, 2002).

An opportunity for researchers is that observed variables may be partitioned into components at different levels of analysis, and effects may be estimated among lower-level outcome variables and predictors at the same or higher level. Another opportunity is that lower-level relationships among variables within units may be predicted by higher-level variables (i.e., a random slope or a slopes-as-outcomes model).

One way to represent an MLM is as follows:

$$\mathbf{y}_j = \mathbf{x}_j \boldsymbol{\eta}_j + \boldsymbol{\varepsilon}_j, \text{ and} \tag{3.5}$$

$$\boldsymbol{\eta}_j = \boldsymbol{\alpha} + \mathbf{B}\boldsymbol{\eta}_j + \boldsymbol{\Gamma}\mathbf{W}_j + \boldsymbol{\zeta}_j, \tag{3.6}$$

where $\mathbf{y}_j$ is a vector of observed data for all n_j people in a group j; $\mathbf{x}_j$ is a matrix of predictors, where all values in the column linked to the random intercept are set to unity; $\mathbf{\eta}_j$ is a matrix of random regression coefficients that vary by group, where an element in the matrix is the "random inter-cept" for the jth group and all other random coefficients could be "random slopes" (it is notable that these are all latent variables, just as in SEM); $\mathbf{\varepsilon}_j$ is a vector of errors; $\mathbf{\alpha}$ is a vector of random coefficient means; $\mathbf{B}$ is a matrix of regression coefficients among the variables in $\mathbf{\eta}_j$, which is not typically modeled in MLM but is included here to show the link between MLM and SEM; $\mathbf{\Gamma}$ is a matrix of regressions among observed predictors of the random coefficients, both random intercepts and slopes; $\mathbf{W}_j$ is a vector of observed predictors; and $\mathbf{\zeta}_j$ is the disturbance for a group j. Equation 3.5 may be thought of as a Level-1 equation whereas Equation 3.6 may be thought of as existing at Level 2. As we later discuss, MLM equations are structurally equivalent to SEM equations (Curran, 2003; Mehta & Neale, 2005), and thus the SEM and MLM can be conceptualized as alternate ways of viewing the same latent variable problem.

Leadership researchers have used this powerful modeling technique, avoid-ing the threats and availing themselves of the opportunities noted above. For example Hofmann, Morgeson, and Gerras (2003) showed that the relationship between LMX and safety-specific citizenship behaviors (individual-level vari-ables) was moderated by safety climate (a group-level variable).

In light of the endogeneity issue discussed above, Antonakis et al. (2010) note that an often overlooked, yet critical, issue in multilevel and longitudinal analyses with panel data is the possibility that error/disturbance terms are cor-related with the lower-level predictors (elements in $\mathbf{x}_j$). This is possible because many level-1 variables can have both within-group and between-group vari-ance, and when between- and within-group effects of x_{ij} on y_{ij} diverge (i.e., contextual or composition effects), then estimating a single regression weight will lead to a correlation among predictors and errors/disturbances (see similar thought in Zhang, Zyphur, & Preacher, 2009). As in other forms of regression, this correlation is a violation of a critical assumption in MLM, rendering the estimates for the level-1 predictors inconsistent. Researchers can use the Hausman (1978) test on single or multiple parameters to ascertain whether the lower-level estimates are consistent. When inconsistent, fixed-effects mod-els in various forms may be estimated: variables dummy coded to represent each group, group-mean centering the lower level predictor (and possibly including the group means at a higher level of analysis), and including the group means at a higher level without group-mean centering (see Raudenbush & Bryk, 2002). (It is notable that in MSEM—discussed below—the within-level variables are specified to contain no between-group variance, and thus the within-level estimates are always consistent.)

Another important issue is that one important possibility for MLM specifications has gone overlooked by multilevel researchers. The traditional representation of an MLM (e.g., Raudenbush & Bryk, 2002) leaves out an important element in Equation 3.5: The link between group members and their higher-level representations do not have to be uniform across individuals. It is possible to weight lower level scores by placing weights in $\mathbf{x}_j$ to alter the contribution of score in $\mathbf{y}_j$ to a random intercept. In other words, it is possible to change the contribution of each individual's score to the model-estimated group average in the same way that factor loadings change the contributions of observed variables to latent variables in SEM. In an MLM, the criterion $\mathbf{y}_j$ is a function of $\mathbf{x}_j{}^*\boldsymbol{\eta}_j$—meaning that when $\mathbf{x}_j$ is smaller, values in $\boldsymbol{\eta}_j$ must be larger to predict $\mathbf{y}_j$. Therefore, the weighting variable should be reverse coded, or a nonlinear transformation could be used such as the reciprocal $\mathbf{x}_j$ (i.e., $1/\mathbf{x}_j$).

This idea can be represented diagramatically using traditional notation (see McDonald & Ho, 2002). With four people in each group, Figure 3.2a shows how, in the traditional MLM, each group member's score is equally important when estimating the group average (i.e., each member's score is regressed onto the random intercept at unity). However, given Equation 3.5, Figure 3.2b shows how this is not necessary (see Appendix B for Mplus code). By suppressing the random intercept, researchers may impose their own weights relating group members' scores to the model-estimated group average (i.e., a model-estimated weighted average). In Figure 3.2b, the latent variable is a random slope representing the model-estimated weighted average, the weights would be contained in $\mathbf{x}_j$ ($1/\mathbf{x}_j$), and $\mathbf{y}_j$ is regressed on $\mathbf{x}_j$.

The traditional MLM (Figure 3.2a) operationalizes a state of affairs where each group member has an equal influence in terms of the group's standing

Figure 3.2a   A multilevel model following Equations 3.5 and 3.6, except an individual i is nested within a group j, rather than items being nested within individuals. The latent variable in this case is a random intercept from a traditional multilevel model.

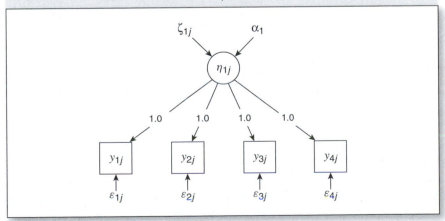

Figure 3.2b   A member-weighted multilevel model (MWM) following
Equations 3.5 and 3.6, where individuals' scores are weighted
by a variable in $\mathbf{x}_j$ and the random intercept is suppressed.

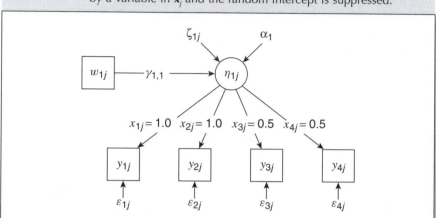

along the variable of interest. The alternative specification (Figure 3.2b) operationalizes a state of affairs where this influence varies across group members as a function of values in $\mathbf{x}_j$. Here, we call this the multilevel member-weighted model, or MWM, which we frame below.

The possibility that group members may have different relationships with a group as a whole is relevant for leadership research. For instance, in contrast to the dominant leadership model of the time—the average leadership style (ALS) model (Kerr, Schriesheim, Murphy, & Stogdill, 1974)—the vertical dyad linkage (VDL) approach (Dansereau, Graen, & Haga, 1975) suggests that superiors divide their group of subordinates into in-groups and out-groups, and that they become leaders for in-group but not out-group members.

The theoretical progenies of VDL, LMX (Graen & Uhl-Bien, 1995) and individualized leadership (Dansereau et al., 1995), accept the basic premise that leaders have different relationships with different subordinates, yet research in these areas tends to focus on individuals or dyadic relationships as the core level of analysis. Problematically, this does not account for the fact that leaders have different relationships with subgroups of subordinates within a workgroup. With a differential in the extent to which leaders interact with and appreciate followers, understanding how such differentials can be operationalized in an MLM becomes crucial, and the MWM may be a method of modeling such relationships.

Consider also that there is often an unequal distribution of power, status, and influence across group members, and members are often implicitly or explicitly aware of such intragroup distributions (Fiske, 1993). For example, work on corporate board composition notes the differences in power and status that exist across group members, differences that are recognized

(R. C. Anderson, Mansi, & Reeb, 2004). Even in groups without an explicit holder of power and status, such an individual emerges over time to steer the functioning of the group (Yukl & Van Fleet, 1992).

Differences in power and status have important corollaries, such as voice and dominance behaviors (C. Anderson & Berdahl, 2002; Kipnis, 1976, 1984) and control over resources (Keltner, Gruenfeld, & Anderson, 2003), which lead to disproportionate influences on the group across group members (see Salancik & Pfeffer, 1977). This has the consequence that not every group member may be an equal contributor to group processes and outcomes (Tiedens, Ellsworth, & Mesquita, 2000). Similar arguments can be made for constructs such as group identification, network centrality, and the like, where these variables could be used to weight group members' scores in $\mathbf{x}_j$ along any variable of interest $\mathbf{y}_j$ when estimating their mean η_{1j}.

To give an applied example (see Figure 3.2b), consider that individuals are measured along their individual performance in $\mathbf{y}_j$, and a researcher wishes to predict this individual-level performance with the leadership style of each group's manager in $\mathbf{w}_j$. However, problematically, some group members may work full-time whereas other group members work part-time. In this case it is reasonable to assume that to represent the individuals' performance as a whole with η_{0j}, the full-timers should have more weight than part-timers. This is shown in Figure 3.2b, where full-timers are the first two group members and have twice the weight of the part-timers.

Importantly, the values in $\mathbf{x}_j$ may be set to any value. For example, as noted above, $\mathbf{x}_j$ could be data collected along LMX, group identification, and within-group status or power. The model-estimated weighted average η_{0j} would then take into account the differential relationship between each group member and the representation of the group along $\mathbf{y}_j$.

Finally, it is notable that a similar weighting is possible by multiplying or dividing $\mathbf{x}_j$ by $\mathbf{y}_j$ and using the result as the outcome variable in MLM. This would effectively weight $\mathbf{y}_j$ by $\mathbf{x}_j$. However, in doing this, the resulting variable will be a function of the reliability of both variables as well as their correlation, which is not ideal (Cohen et al., 2003). Further, by keeping $\mathbf{x}_j$ and $\mathbf{y}_j$ separate in the model and adding to Equations 3.5 and 3.6 so that $\mathbf{x}_j$ may act as an outcome variable, both $\mathbf{x}_j$ and $\mathbf{y}_j$ may be used dynamically to predict and be predicted by other latent and observed variables. Therefore, the MWM has the unique advantage of weighting individuals' score when estimating the group means without having to alter $\mathbf{y}_j$ directly.

Latent Growth Modeling

Modeling and predicting change over time has long been a challenge for researchers. This largely has to do with modeling change statistically, given that such data are multilevel (Singer & Willett, 2003). With modern statistical techniques, researchers have the opportunity to model change over time with versatile structural equations (Bollen & Curran, 2006).

The state of the art in modeling change is latent growth modeling (LGM), also called latent change modeling (Hertzog, Dixon, Hultsch, & MacDonald, 2003), growth trajectory modeling (Stoolmiller, Kim, & Capaldi, 2005), and latent curve modeling (McArdle & Epstein, 1987). With observations over time, LGM allows estimating (a) a latent intercept that estimates scores along the variable at a particular point in time and (b) latent linear, quadratic, and higher-order slope factors that capture changes over time away from the intercept. The change as linear or nonlinear depends on model specification. Also, predictors and outcomes of the observed variable as well as these latent intercept and slope factors may be added in a structural model.

Many model extensions exist, such as the autoregressive latent trajectory (ALT) model (Bollen & Curran, 2004; Curran & Bollen, 2001; Zyphur, Chaturvedi, & Arvey, 2008), second-order factor models where latent variables are used as indicators for LGM, piecewise growth models (e.g., Bollen & Curran, 2006), and survival models (e.g., Singer & Willett, 2003). Here, we introduce LGM generally and then present a new type of LGM that will be useful to leadership researchers, which we call the intercept-as-mean growth model (IGM).

The Form of the Model

Note that SEM and MLM provide equivalent solutions (Curran, 2003; Mehta & Neale, 2005). By examining Equations 3.1, 3.2, 3.5, and 3.6, Equations 3.1 and 3.5 are shown to be measurement models or equivalently Level-1 models, whereas Equations 3.2 and 3.6 are structural models or equivalently Level-2 models. Here, items (SEM) are to people (MLM) as individuals (SEM) are to groups (MLM). Factor loadings in Λ from Equation 3.1 are equivalent to the values in x from Equation 3.5—the only difference is that the values in x are allowed to vary across individuals, whereas the values in x are fixed across individuals. Further, latent variables are found in η from Equations 3.1, 3.2, 3.5, and 3.6. Thus, the LGM (and other SEM and MLM models) may be specified either as SEMs or MLMs.

In MLMs, observations over time are treated as nested within individuals, whereas in SEM observations over time are treated as items. In both cases, the latent variables capture individual-level parameters. Proceeding with MLM notation and assuming five measurement occasions (see Figure 3.3), observed data in y is a vector of data over time along one variable. The initial time of observation, perhaps the first observation of performance after an employee is hired, is the first data point. To estimate an intercept factor, a vector in x is fixed to unity (as Λ is in SEM). Then x is used to specify latent slope factors that capture different types of change. By specifying values starting at zero and increasing in increments of 1.0 over time

Figure 3.3   A latent growth model following Equation 3.7, and indicating the specification required to estimate an intercept-as-mean growth model (IGM) as in Equation 3.9. This model follows Equations 3.1 and 3.2 when observations over time are treated as items in a structural equation model, or it can follow Equations 3.5 and 3.6 when observations over time are treated as nested within individuals.

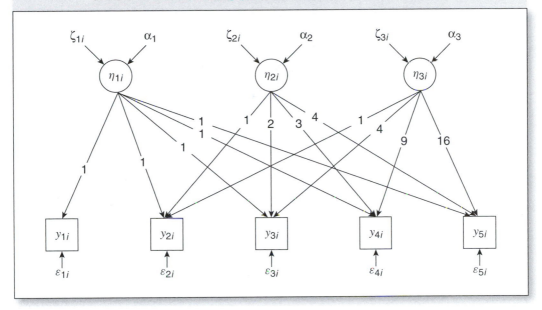

for each observed variable (e.g., 0, 1, 2, 3, . . . T), linear change over time is modeled, where the difference between each observation is modeled as being equivalent because increases in the time coding are the same across all times of observation, that is, +1.0 at each incremental observation. Quadratic and cubic forms of change can be specified by adding additional vectors in $\mathbf{x}$. For example, to model quadratic growth, values in $\mathbf{x}$ associated with the linear slope factor would be squared (e.g., 0, 1, 4, 9, . . . T^2), whereas for cubic change, the values are cubed (e.g., 0, 1, 8, 27, . . . T^3). The latent variables that now make up $\boldsymbol{\eta}$ would describe linear, quadratic, and cubic trends in the data (see Figure 3.3).

It is helpful momentarily to consider how this model functions. The point of this demonstration is to consider how the model to the right of the "=" sign attempts to recreate the observed data to the left of the "=" sign—the SEM and MLM are maximizing the likelihood of the values in $\boldsymbol{\eta}$ and $\boldsymbol{\varepsilon}$. Using the following data:

$$
\begin{bmatrix} 4 \\ 5 \\ 6 \\ 7 \\ 8 \end{bmatrix} = \begin{bmatrix} 1 & 0 & 0 \\ 1 & 1 & 1 \\ 1 & 2 & 4 \\ 1 & 3 & 9 \\ 1 & 4 & 6 \end{bmatrix} \begin{bmatrix} 4 \\ 1 \\ 0 \end{bmatrix} + \begin{bmatrix} 0 \\ 0 \\ 0 \\ 0 \\ 0 \end{bmatrix},
\tag{3.7}
$$

where the first column **y** is observed performance each month; time codings are in the **x** matrix (where each row is associated with a performance observation and each column is associated with a latent variable); in the second column vector **η** are values along the latent variables for the individual; and the final vector are errors in **ε**. Values in **η** and **ε** are estimated. The first row of time codings in **x** makes the first latent variable in **η** estimate the first performance observation—with all zeros except for the first latent variable in **x**, the most likely value for the first observation is 4 (i.e., what value for the first entry in **η**, when separately multiplied by 1, 0, and 0 in **x**, will equal the 4 in **y** when all the products are summed?).

Multiplying **x** and **η** shows that beginning with the observation 4, the linear time coding found in the second column of **x** accounts for all of the values in **y** over time. The value of 1 in **η** in the second row, which is associated with the second column in **x**, indicates the average amount of change in performance over time, which is an increase of 1 unit at each time point. The remaining value in **η** indicates the quadratic variable accounts for nothing in **y**. Also, the zeros in **ε** indicate that all data in **y** is accounted for by scores along the latent variables.

What this example also indicates is that the time codings may be adjusted to set a different time point to be the latent intercept variable, yet maintaining equivalent levels of model fit (Hancock & Choi, 2006). For example,

$$\begin{bmatrix} 4 \\ 5 \\ 6 \\ 7 \\ 8 \end{bmatrix} = \begin{bmatrix} 1 & -2 & 4 \\ 1 & -1 & 1 \\ 1 & 0 & 0 \\ 1 & 1 & 1 \\ 1 & 2 & 4 \end{bmatrix} \begin{bmatrix} 6 \\ 1 \\ 0 \end{bmatrix} + \begin{bmatrix} 0 \\ 0 \\ 0 \\ 0 \\ 0 \end{bmatrix}, \tag{3.8}$$

where the results are unchanged except that the latent intercept factor now captures performance in **y** at the third observation. By keeping the distance between the time codings in **x** unchanged (i.e., a distance of 1.0 for each time point), the value along the slope factor is unchanged.

The latent variables in **η** may now be used as outcomes or predictors in the structural part of the model. Almost exclusively, researchers use these variables as outcomes in analyses, for example, predicting changes in performance over time with personality variables (e.g., Zyphur, Bradley, Landis, & Thoresen, 2008). However, they may also be used as predictors of such dependent variables as turnover or promotion.

Variables at Level 1 (i.e., variables that vary over time,) may be added in **x** to predict **y**—these may be called time-varying covariates. The associated latent variables are traditional random slopes from an MLM. For example, consider the time spent in training as a predictor of performance, where the amount of training varies each month. The mean of the latent variable associated with this predictor is the overall effect of training on performance, and variance in the latent variable is differences across people in this relationship. The effect of training on performance may be predicted by individual-level or Level-2 variables—these may be called time-invariant covariates. For example, training is likely to have a greater effect on performance for individuals with high levels of intelligence. This individual-level variable would predict the relationship between performance and training over time.

Model Specification

To know if latent growth factors are justified (i.e., explain incremental variance in y), likelihood ratio difference testing with nested models is recommended. For example the fit of models with and without quadratic growth factors may be compared. With such tests, the observed p value should be halved because the variance in the constrained model is at the boundary of its space (i.e., the variance is zero and variances cannot be less than zero; see Self & Liang, 1987). Also, different types of covariance structures may be modeled and tested against one another (Singer & Willett, 2003).

Next, the time metrics used may be altered. In the above example, the incremental increase of 1.0 in the time codings in x for the linear growth factor makes the value along the latent variable in η the amount of increase from one observation to the next. In the example, there was one month between observations, so the value of 1.0 in η indicates there is a +1.0 unit of change each month. However, if the time codings were in increments of .50 (i.e., −1.0, −.50, 0, .50, 1.0), then the resulting value in η would be the average amount of increase in performance every half month (i.e., half the distance between the observations). These are baseline scaling coefficients, whereas the position of the intercept they determine with the location of 0.0 is called the baseline shift coefficient (Hancock & Choi, 2006).

Next, the model can incorporate individually varying times of observation. For example, consider two people, one measured every month, and another measured twice a month. The time codings for the first person could be in increments of 1.0 whereas the second person could have time codings of .50. These codings would make the standings of these individuals comparable along the latent growth variable (because half a month is to a month as .50 is to 1.0).

Next, in the SEM framework, freely estimated time codings may be estimated in Λ (the same matrix as x in the current discussion). The resulting "factor loadings" would be the best estimates of the nature of change over time (B. Muthén & Curran, 1997). Finally, second-order factor models of LGMs are possible, where the variable for each measurement is a latent variable measured by multiple observed indicators—for example, leadership ratings along a multi-item scale over time, where the scale items indicate a latent factor for each occasion of observation. In all cases, traditional indices of model fit may be used for model evaluation.

Making Means Meaningful in LGM

The question of how to make intercept factors meaningful for researchers by setting them to estimate the average for each person has not received attention. The estimate of an observed variable that has the greatest likelihood of predicting the variable is its mean. Consider also that the mean is the most reliable estimate for an individual measured on multiple occasions.

Although change over time as modeled in LGM indicates uncertainty in an individual's position along a construct, the average for each person may still be useful in a structural model. For example, it could be used to control for average differences in change over time by regressing slope factors onto the intercept factor. It may be predicted or act as a predictor as well. Here, we show how to specify a model where the intercept factor estimates the mean value over time along an observed variable, in the form of our intercept-as-mean growth model (IGM).

Using Equation 3.9, the way to specify an IGM is as follows:

1. Determine the average value along y for an individual i, which we will call μ and is

$$10 = (2 + 7 + 12 + 12 + 17)/5.$$

2. Find the place in y where μ exists between two periods of observation:

   a. The lower we will call y_L and in Equation 3.9 is y_2, the second observation: 7.

   b. The upper we will call y_U and in Equation 3.9 is y_3, the third observation: 12.

3. Subtract y_L from y_U, which we will call Δ_{U-L}, which is $5 = 12-7$.

4. Subtract μ from y_L, which we will call $\Delta_{L-\mu}$, which is $-3 = 7-10$.

5. Divide $\Delta_{L-\mu}$ by Δ_{U-L}, which we will call x_L, which is $-.6 = -3/7$, and is the time coding for y_L.

6. Add 1.0 to this value, which we will call x_U, and is the time coding for y_U.

7. The time codings for each additional x variable below x_L merely require subtracting 1.0 from each, whereas all coding above x_U merely require adding 1.0.

Now each individual in the sample will have an intercept that estimates his or her mean and everyone will have a unit difference between the time codes in x (assuming each time coding has already been computed for each person at each time point; see Appendix C1 for Mplus code for an IGM as MLM; see Appendix C2 for Mplus code for an IGM as SEM). Researchers may use this design to obtain the model-estimated mean for each individual, as captured by the intercept factor, for use in complex structural models. Also, with two points that could be the mean for an individual, for example with data along y of 3, 9, 3, it is irrelevant if a researcher chooses to set the zero point in x between y_1 and y_2, or between y_2 and y_3; the results will be equivalent.

$$\begin{bmatrix} 2 \\ 7 \\ 12 \\ 12 \\ 17 \end{bmatrix} = \begin{bmatrix} 1 & -1.6 \\ 1 & -.6 \\ 1 & .4 \\ 1 & .4 \\ 1 & 2.4 \end{bmatrix} \begin{bmatrix} Intercept \\ Linear\ Slope \end{bmatrix} + [Residual]. \tag{3.9}$$

MSEM

As described above, the MLM and SEM paradigms were developed to address different statistical modeling issues faced by researchers. The MLM framework correctly models the dependence among nested and other hierarchically arranged observations and allows testing "cross-level" hypotheses (Raudenbush & Bryk, 2002). Problematically, this approach permits the estimation of neither complex structural parameters nor a measurement model. Alternatively, SEM overcomes these shortcomings but does not directly allow separating variance into between- and within-group components as in MLM. This has the consequence of forcing researchers to choose between correctly modeling the multilevel influences in their data with MLM or examining relationships without the biasing effects of measurement error and with the possibility of complex structural relations with SEM.

Moving beyond these two model types, MSEM has been developed (e.g., B. Muthén, 1994; Skrondal & Rabe-Hesketh, 2004) and implemented in various software packages (e.g., Mplus, L. K. Muthén & Muthén 1998–2008). The MSEM has SEMs and MLMs as special cases, allowing for measurement and structural models at multiple levels (e.g., Zyphur, Narayanan, Koh, & Koh, 2009), as well as random slopes and a mixture of underlying variable distributions (Rabe-Hesketh, Skrondal, & Pickles, 2004). A simplified expression for the MSEM is

$$\mathbf{y}_{ij} = \mathbf{y}_{Bj} + \mathbf{\Lambda_W}\mathbf{\eta}_{Wij} + \mathbf{\varepsilon}_{Wj}, \tag{3.10}$$

$$\mathbf{y}_{Bj} = \mathbf{\alpha_B} + \mathbf{\Lambda_B}\mathbf{\eta}_{Bj} + \mathbf{\varepsilon}_{Bj}, \tag{3.11}$$

$$\mathbf{\eta}_{Wij} = \mathbf{B_W}\mathbf{\eta}_{Wij} + \mathbf{\Gamma_W}\mathbf{W}_{Wij} + \mathbf{\zeta}_{Wij}, \text{ and} \tag{3.12}$$

$$\mathbf{\eta}_{Bj} = \mathbf{\alpha} + \mathbf{B_B}\mathbf{\eta}_{Bj} + \mathbf{\Gamma_B}\mathbf{W}_{Bj} + \mathbf{\zeta}_{Bj}. \tag{3.13}$$

All terms are as in Equations 3.1 and 3.2, except the subscripts W and B indicate within- and between-group terms, respectively, where within-group terms predict deviations away from the model-estimated group mean, and between-group terms predict the model-estimated means.

Before continuing, a few comments on this structure are warranted. First, eliminating the measurement part of the model creates a multilevel path model. Also, the variables in the between part of the model that are linked to a y_{ij} are latent (i.e., "random intercepts" in y_{Bj}) just as in a MLM. Also, it is possible to treat the coefficients in $\mathbf{B}_w$ as randomly varying across groups, i.e., random slopes that are entered in the between part of the model (for elaboration on such models, see Preacher, Zyphur, & Zhang, 2010). Further, by expanding Equation 3.13, observed outcome variables are allowed at the between-group level of analysis (an option not possible in MLM), which allows 1-1-2 and 1-2-2 mediation models (Preacher et al., 2010).

As in SEM, variance in y has been decomposed into "true" and "error" variance in the latent variables and error variances (Lord & Novick, 1968), except it is now separated into between- and within-group parts. Because of this, with equality constraints placed on $\mathbf{\Lambda}$ and $\mathbf{\varepsilon}$ for the same item p across B and W parts, this allows a "multilevel variance components model" (Rabe-Hesketh et al., 2004), where variance in a latent factor is disaggregated into between- and within-group parts (see Figure 3.4a, where filled circles indicate a random coefficient, i.e., latent variable; see Appendix D1 for Mplus code). This model allows comparisons across the within- and between-group latent variables, which is useful for estimating multilevel reliability and error-free intra-class correlations (ICC).

Reliability is the proportion of true score to total variance (Lord & Novick, 1968). However, with multilevel data, without disaggregation into within- and between-group parts the within- and between-group variance is confounded in reliability computations. To avoid such a problem, it is possible to compute a reliability coefficient for both the within- and between-group variables (B. Muthén, 1991), where the reliability of a latent variable η_1 would be

$$\text{Reliability}_w = VAR(\eta_{W1})/(VAR(\eta_{W1}) + VAR(\varepsilon_{W1\ldots P})), \text{ and} \quad (3.14)$$

$$\text{Reliability}_B = VAR(\eta_{B1})/(VAR(\eta_{B1}) + VAR(\varepsilon_{B1\ldots P})). \quad (3.15)$$

For a guide on conducting such computations, see Raykov and Shrout (2002). Determining reliability in this fashion is important because a majority of error variance exists at the within-group level of analysis (B. Muthén, 1991). It is notable that the reliability estimated in Equation 3.15 already accounts for sampling error (i.e., unreliability in the group means, which could be measured with ICC(2)), because at the group level each item is a latent variable, a precision-weighted estimate of the group mean.

Figure 3.4a   A multilevel confirmatory factor analysis model following Equations 3.10–3.13, where variance in variables observed at the individual level of analysis is decomposed into within- and between-group components via random intercepts.

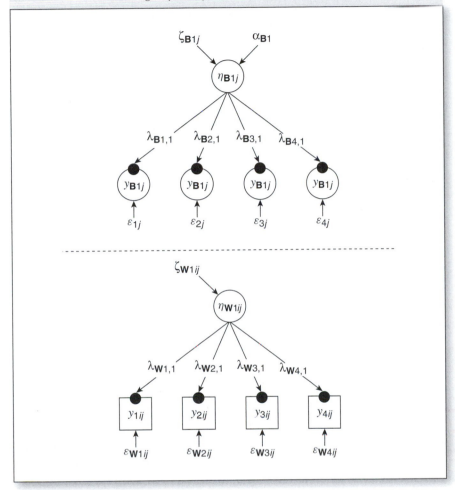

In terms of ICCs, researchers often desire to know the proportion of variance that lies at a between-cluster level, which can be thought of as a measure of the reliability of an individual's score as an assessment of the group mean (Bliese, 1998). This ICC(1) is

$$\rho = \sigma_B^2 / (\sigma_B^2 + \sigma_W^2) \, , \tag{3.16}$$

where σ_2 is the amount of variance in a variable. However, variance terms in practice contain true and error variance. ICC estimates are biased by measurement error when scale aggregates are used rather than the variance of latent variables. This is problematic because, again, a majority of error variance in a variable is at the within-group level, which will downwardly bias ICC estimates. Computing a true score ICC can be done as follows (B. Muthén, 1991; see Appendix D1 for details):

$$\rho_{1T} = VAR(\eta_{\mathbf{B1}})/(VAR(\eta_{\mathbf{B1}}) + VAR(\eta_{\mathbf{W1}})). \qquad (3.17)$$

Implications for Leadership Researchers

As noted by Liden and Antonakis (2009), MSEM is uniquely positioned to address questions about context (see also Marsh, Lüdtke, Robitzsch, et al., 2009). This is important because, as mentioned previously, contextualizing leadership styles and their effectiveness has been a major endeavor in leadership research. With the possibility of entering contextual variables into the between-group portion of an MSEM, leadership scholars gain an opportunity to examine the moderating effects of higher-level variables on lower-level relationships as well as complex interactions at multiple levels. Given the violation of multivariate normal distribution assumption due to latent interactions, bootstrapped confidence intervals could be used instead of normal distribution-based hypothesis testing—although this is currently not an option in available statistical modeling programs.

For example, consider a model where a contextual variable is used as a moderator of the relationship between leadership style and individual-level performance, which could be noted as a 2*2-1 model. Also, context acts as a predictor of the leadership style adopted by leaders, which in turn predicts individual performance, which could be noted as a 2-2*2-1 model—as shown in Figure 3.4b (see Appendix D2 for Mplus code). It is notable that mediation models such as 2-1-1 and 2-2-1 always exist at the between-group level of analysis (Preacher et al., 2010). Finally, in this model, the contextual variable predicts the relationship between a lower-level predictor and individual performance, effectively moderating the lower-level relationship. One example of this within-group relationship is the association between relative LMX and individual performance. Relative LMX refers to the relative standing of a member in the group with regard to his or her LMX quality (Henderson, Liden, Glibkowski, & Chaudhry, 2009). Given this definition, this variable's antecedents and outcomes are naturally examined at the within-group level of analysis.

This model is shown in Figure 3.4b, where the contextual variable ($w_{\mathbf{B1}}$) is observed, leadership style ($\eta_{\mathbf{B2}}$) is latent and measured by multiple variables at the between level (e.g., a peer's rating of a leader), and individual performance indicators are latent at the between-group level and used to indicate a group-level latent factor ($\eta_{\mathbf{B1}}$). At the within-group level, the predictor of individual performance, relative LMX, is latent ($\eta_{\mathbf{W2}}$), as is the performance variable ($\eta_{\mathbf{W1}}$). Their relationship is the random slope of interest, which is

Figure 3.4b   A multilevel structural equation model following Equations 3.10–3.13, where variance in variables observed at the individual level of analysis is decomposed into within- and between-group parts via random intercepts, random slopes are specified, an interaction among latent variables is specified, and a group-level predictor is included.

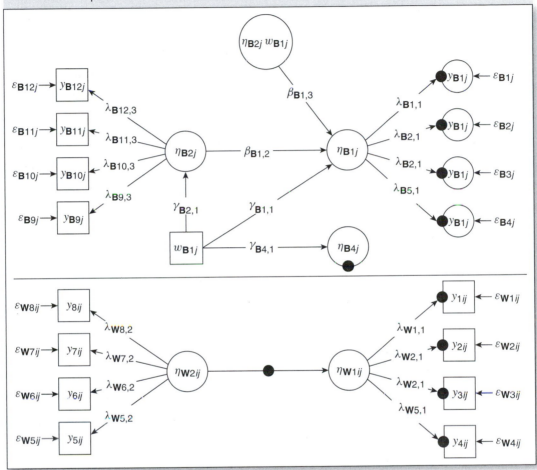

latent (η_{B4}) at the between-group level. At the between level, all means and variance are omitted for the sake of clarity.

Before concluding, a few practical aspects of MSEM that can make it problematic in practical application are worth noting. For example, model estimation is difficult when there is little between-group variation in variables, when random slopes have very little variance, when models are very complex, when error/disturbance variances tend toward zero (common at the between-groups level), and when between-groups sample sizes are small. These issues are beyond the scope of the current chapter, but with adequate sample sizes and adequate levels of variance at the between level of analysis, MSEM is a useful tool for researchers.

Latent Class Cluster Analysis (or Latent Profile Analysis)

Approaches to the study of social phenomena may be divided into two forms: those that are variable centered and those that are person centered (B. Muthén & Muthén, 2000). The variable-centered approach focuses on looking at relationships among variables, such as the effects of personality on leadership outcomes, whereas the person-centered approach looks at relationships among people, such as which individuals have similar profiles of personality and what types of leadership outcomes they collectively tend to experience (e.g., Foti & Hauenstein, 2007). This latter approach is virtually never adopted, likely because of (a) unfamiliarity with modern clustering techniques and how they may be embedded into larger structural models that exemplify the variable-centered approach and (b) trepidation over the fact that clustering is largely exploratory and inductive. With an obsession for deductive methodology, fears over Type-I error rates drive researchers toward other more confirmatory techniques.

Here, we propose latent class cluster analysis (LCCA) as a solution to both issues. The first issue is solved by incorporating continuous and observed variables into LCCA and allowing for complex structural models. We address the second issue by noting the possibility of introducing parameter constraints and testing nested models for the justification of such constraints as well as additional latent classes (which are all deductively oriented, confirmatory practices), and we note that LCCA generally outperforms other clustering techniques.

The technique known as LCCA—a more general version of latent class analysis (see Gibson, 1959; Lazarsfeld & Henry, 1968)—has its roots in work by researchers such as Lazarsfeld (1950) and Goodman (1974) and is used to explain heterogeneity across subpopulations in sociological, medical, and psychological data (for discussion of the history and many names of LCCA, including latent profile analysis, see Vermunt & Magidson, 2002). LCCA is a probabilistic, model-based, and more general version of traditional cluster analytic methods (DiStefano & Kamphaus, 2006). LCCA specifies a categorical latent variable that serves to group individuals together who have a similar latent profiles across multiple observed variables—The profile is latent because it is not directly observed (see Figure 3.5, where the first latent variable in the model is the latent class variable with a mean for each k latent class).

As discussed by Vermunt and Magidson (2002), with normally distributed variables, the model may be expressed as

$$f(\mathbf{y}_i|\theta) = \sum_{k=1}^{K} \pi_k f_k(\mathbf{y}_i|\theta_k), \tag{3.18}$$

where, as above, $\mathbf{y}_i$ is individual's standing along multiple y variables; K is the total number of clusters specified; π_k is the probability of belonging to the *k*th cluster (which, given the sample size, is the estimated number of individuals within a cluster *k*); and model parameters are in θ.

Here, the means, variances, and covariances among the *y* variables are estimated, with the latter contained in a matrix Σ_k for each class. This matrix itself may take many forms. Most notably the covariances among all variables may be restricted to zero. This common model is called the local independence model, as all variables are specified as independent, conditional on the latent class variable. One way to interpret this model is that all covariance among observed variables is captured or explained by the latent class variable—similar to confirmatory factor analysis where covariance among items is explained by a factor and the justification of the covariance restrictions may be tested across nested models.

Before continuing, a number of points can be made that distinguish this model from other more common forms of clustering. First, LCCA is model-based. A model is specified with a number of classes *K*, and variances and covariances are also specified. The likelihood of the model-estimated parameters is then maximized to achieve the greatest fit to the observed data. This allows the comparison of, for example, nested models with different specifications of Σ_k across all *K* classes or different specifications within a given class, or equality constrained placed on means across classes—with comparisons using traditional likelihood ratio difference testing.

For example, the variances in Σ may be allowed to vary across classes to reflect the possibility of different degrees of homogeneity across the classes—although model parsimony is important in this respect, as well as an eye toward maintaining adequate degrees of freedom. Further, traditional factor analytic or SEM models could be estimated within each class.

Additionally, because LCCA is model based, it allows the comparison of models with different numbers of classes to determine the class structure with the greatest degree of fit. It is notable that this process of class enumeration is often subjective and may rely on comparisons using unstandardized fit indices (e.g., the Bayesian information criterion), bootstrapped likelihood ratio difference tests, entropy statistics, as well as a great number of more substantive checks (see B. Muthén, 2003; Nyland, Asparouhov, & Muthén, 2007).

Second, LCCA is a probabilistic clustering approach, meaning that results from LCCA reflect the fact that cluster membership is not fully determined. Given model-estimated parameters and individuals' raw data, the probability that each individual belongs to a given class may be estimated. Using these posterior probabilities, it is common to assign individuals to the class with which they have the highest probability of membership, termed model allocation (Vermunt & Magidson, 2002). When individuals have very high probabilities of membership in a single class and very low probabilities of membership in other classes, then the quality of classification for a given model may be considered high—measured by an entropy statistic, where values above .80 are considered acceptable (B. Muthén & Muthén, 2000).

Third, results are insensitive to the scaling of variables. Obviously, estimates of means and variances of the variables will be influenced by their scaling, but linear transformations of any given y will not influence π_k, nor will it influence the probability of any given individual belonging to a class k. This is not the case with other methods of clustering, such as k-means cluster analysis where variables' variances have a very marked impact on results (DiStefano & Kamphaus, 2006), which presents substantial problems with noncontinuous variables.

Fourth, the model may be extended to allow a mixture of underlying distributions for any given y. This is made possible by specifying mixed multivariate distribution functions, with the model taking the form of

$$f(\mathbf{y}_i|\theta) = \sum_{k=1}^{K} \pi_k \prod_{p=1}^{P} f_k\left(y_{ip}|\theta_{pk}\right), \qquad (3.19)$$

where, as above, P is the total number of indicator variables and p is any given indicator, and y_{ip} is an element in $\mathbf{y}_i$ (Vermunt & Magidson, 2002). This allows variables with virtually any underlying distribution to be incorporated into the model without making subjective judgments about scaling in order to equate them with other variables, as required for most cluster analysis.

Next, and interestingly, the LCCA model may be extended to include observed and latent covariates, as well as traditional SEM forms within each class, with complex measurement and structural paths that may have a variety of implications. For example, cluster membership may be conditioned on covariates, which can be shown with an extension to Equation 3.19 as

$$f(\mathbf{y}_i|\mathbf{x}_i, \theta) = \sum_{k=1}^{K} \pi_{k|\mathbf{x}_i} \prod_{p=1}^{P} f_k\left(y_{ip}|\theta_{pk}\right), \qquad (3.20)$$

where values for any given variable x are linked to the latent class variable with a multinomial logit function. In this case, class membership may be thought of as being predicted by an individual's standing on a variable x, such that clustering is now "informed" by x. This model may be extended with more complex specifications in the place of $\mathbf{x}_i$, such as measurement and structural components typical in SEM for the purposes of, for example, predicting class membership with latent factors or, perhaps, latent interaction terms from LPR.

Within each class, it is also possible to specify such structures by taking the SEM elements in Equations 3.1 and 3.2, and then making them class dependent by adding them to LCCA. These types of models are called mixture models, factor mixture models, or structural equation mixture models, and they allow for models such as latent growth mixture models, where the variance in growth trajectories from LGM may be clustered together to group individuals who have similar levels of change over time (B. Muthén, 2004; Wang, 2007).

Finally, this model may be extended to the multilevel case where individuals are nested in groups. Combined with a SEM, such a model can be termed a multilevel structural equation mixture model, where individuals' probabilities of class membership as well as parameters from a SEM could be allowed to vary across levels of analysis (Lubke & Muthén, 2005).

Implications for Leadership Researchers

Although it can take many complex forms, LCCA is useful even in its simplest forms. Consider classifying individuals into personality types by assigning individuals to "high" versus "low" categories—as is still done with the MBTI in applied contexts (Michael, 2003), a less than desirable practice (Garden, 1991; McCrae & Costa, 1989; Pittenger, 1993; Sipps & DiCaudo, 1988). One allure of such a procedure is that instead of providing continuous values along the various dimensions to describe personality, individuals are placed into a single profile or type of personality, which has intuitive appeal. For example, in conjunction with one another, how does one interpret scores of 3.85 along agreeableness, 2.86 along conscientiousness, and the like?

By using LCCA, people can be clustered with discrete profiles along valid measures of personality, such as the Big 5, while retaining the appeal of discrete personality profiles and removing the need for an arbitrary distinction such as "high" versus "low," with the properties associated with each profile driven by the data (Marsh, Lüdtke, Trautwein, & Morin, 2009). Additionally, however, variables such as those in the Big 5 may be used to predict latent class membership. For example, consider a researcher who desires to profile individuals along the multifactor leadership questionnaire (MLQ), capturing trends shared by subpopulations of individuals along the MLQ variables. Consider also that from a theoretical perspective, dispositional variables such as the Big 5 may be thought of as partially underlying individuals' standings along the constructs measured by the MLQ. With such an idea, an LCCA may be specified that creates profiles along the MLQ and informs the creation of these profiles with individuals' standings along the Big 5. Importantly, this is done with latent variables. (See Figure 3.5, where the first latent variable is a latent class variable (η_1), whereas the predictors of this variable could be personality variables; see Appendix E for Mplus code.)

In closing, although the above exploration of LCCA indicates vast possibilities for its application, it is important to note that key decisions about model configuration (e.g., the identification of the number of classes) should be based on both relevant theory as well as the observed data, meaning a

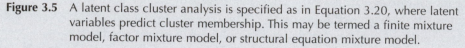

Figure 3.5 A latent class cluster analysis is specified as in Equation 3.20, where latent variables predict cluster membership. This may be termed a finite mixture model, factor mixture model, or structural equation mixture model.

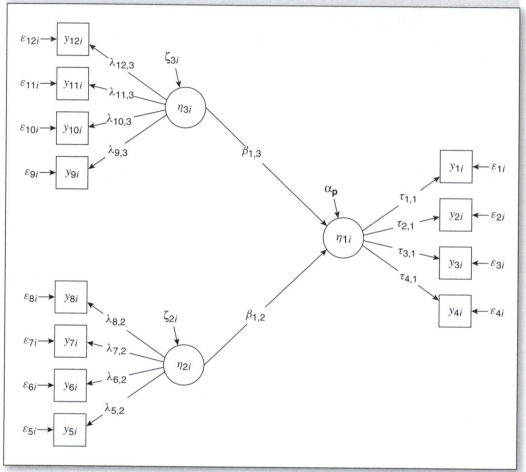

check based on substantive and statistical concerns (B. Muthén, 2003). This is particularly important for researchers who wish to test formal hypotheses rather than to simply explore alternative ways to represent and model data in a purely exploratory manner.

Summary

The methods described above are meant to provide insights into how researchers may utilize existing techniques in new ways and to show how underutilized techniques may be useful. The importance of understanding statistical methods and their underlying assumptions cannot be overstated (Antonakis et al., 2010). By understanding how to operationalize theory and hypotheses with quantitative techniques, researchers not only gain the chance to test existing theory in more precise ways but also have the ability to (a) conjure new and complex theories without the threat of not being able to test them with statistical analyses and (b) use the possibilities embedded within a statistical model as a basis for inductive theory construction (Zyphur, 2009). The statistical techniques discussed above will allow researchers to do this.

Discussion Questions

1. Using quantitative methods to answer questions in leadership research is a very common practice. What aspects of leadership do you think are not, and never will be, addressable with quantitative methods?

2. That team members contribute unequally to a team as a whole is obvious in most applied settings. Some team members are louder than others, and some get paid more attention to by leaders. However, most of this unequal influence occurs not because of different amounts of direct upward contribution, but instead by more lateral and informal influences among team members. What types of lateral, social, and political influences among team members allow some team members to contribute more or less to team outcomes? Consider also how this allows more or less recognition for high performance across team members.

3. Performance, cohesion, and many other factors that define teams tend to fluctuate over time. Although we can describe a team's average performance or cohesion, what are the implications of change over time for measuring and describing phenomena in teams? With high levels of change over time, what might be the best ways to describe a team's characteristics?

4. People tend to describe each other along a collection of attributes simultaneously, such as, "she's a hardworking, goal-driven manager who is appreciated for her charisma and dedication to helping those who need it most in her team." This means we describe people with profiles that consist of multiple attributes. Interestingly, the attributes that we use to describe people can differ depending on who they are. For example, men (women) tend to be described along more male (female) characteristics. Given the fact that masculine traits are generally considered more desirable for management positions, what are the implications of describing men and women using different profiles of traits?

5. Both scientists and practitioners are interested in fully explaining differences across people or situations. For example, the more we know

about what explains fluctuations in team or organization performance, the better we will be able to manage them. One problem with trying to explain the things in which we are interested is that it can lead us to consider a large number of variables, so many variables that the models we use for explanation become unwieldy and too large to be practical. At what point should we decide that we have enough variables in the model we're using to explain something? How might this differ across situations and the type of phenomenon we're interested in explaining?

Appendix A1

(Throughout appendices, text following an exclamation mark "!" refers to a comment.)

TITLE: A Structural Equation Model;

DATA: FILE IS ...; ! insert data file here

VARIABLE: NAMES ARE y1-y6 x1 w1; ! all observed variables

USEVARIABLES ARE y1-y6 x1 w1; ! indicates variables to use in the model

MODEL: ! portion where model is specified

y1 ON x1;

n_1 BY y1-y3; ! indicates first latent variable Eta_1 is measured by y1-y3

n_2 BY y4-y6; ! indicates second latent variable Eta_2 is measured by y4-y6

Appendix A2

TITLE: A Latent Polynomial Regression (LPR) Model;

DATA: FILE IS ...; ! insert data file here

VARIABLE: NAMES ARE y1-y12 cluster; ! all observed variables

USEVARIABLES ARE y1-y12; ! indicates variables to use in the model

CLUSTER = cluster; ! defines variable indicating group membership

ANALYSIS: TYPE = RANDOM; ! indicates random variables will be modeled

TYPE = COMPLEX; ! indicates that standard errors are computed with a sandwich estimator

! to accommodate the nonindependence of followers of the same leader

ALGORITHM = INTEGRATION; ! indicates numerical integration will be used

MODEL: ! portion where model is specified

n_1 BY y1-y4; ! indicates first latent variable Eta_1 is measured by y1-y4

n_2 BY y5-y8; ! indicates second latent variable Eta_2 is measured by y5-y8

n_3 BY y9-y12; ! indicates third latent variable Eta_3 is measured by y9-y12

n_2Xn_3 | n_2 XWITH n_3; ! defines the interaction between Eta_2 and Eta_3

n_2Xn_2 | n_2 XWITH n_2; ! squares Eta_2

n_3Xn_3 | n_3 XWITH n_3; ! squares Eta_3

n_1 ON ! regresses n_1 on all latent variables and labels the coefficients as beta2–beta6

n_2 (beta2)

n_3 (beta3)

n_2Xn_3 (beta4)

n_2Xn_2 (beta5)

n_3Xn_3 (beta6);

MODEL CONSTRAINT: ! portion of the model where labeled parameters may be used

NEW (slope_c slope_i curv_c curv_i); ! name the newly generated parameters, "c" refers to

! the congruence line and "i" refers to incongruence line

slope_c = beta2 + beta3; ! slope along the congruence line when n_2 = n_3 = 0

slope_i = beta2—beta3;

curv_c = beta4 + beta5 + beta6; ! curvature along the congruence line when n_2 = n_3 = 0

curv_i = – beta4 + beta5 + beta6;

Appendix B

TITLE: A Multilevel Member Weighted Model (MWM);

DATA: FILE IS ...; ! insert data file here

VARIABLE: NAMES ARE y x w cluster; ! all variables

USEVARIABLES ARE y x w; ! indicates variables to use in the model

CLUSTER = cluster ! defines variable indicating group membership

WITHIN = x y; ! indicates both variables will only be used on the lower level of analysis

ANALYSIS: TYPE = TWOLEVEL RANDOM; ! indicates multilevel model with random slope

MODEL: ! portion where model is specified

%WITHIN% ! lower level of the model

S | y on x; ! defines regression of y on x as random slope (i.e., weighted average)

%BETWEEN% ! higher level of the model

S on w; ! regresses observed variable on the random slope (i.e., weighted average)

! note that the random intercept (i.e., model-estimated mean) of y is suppressed by not

! mentioning it in the Between portion of the model

Appendix C1

TITLE: An Intercept as Mean Growth (IGM) Model setup as a multilevel model

DATA: FILE IS ...; ! insert data file here

VARIABLE: NAMES ARE y x cluster; ! variable names, where x is the time codings

USEVARIABLES ARE y x; ! indicates variables to use in the model

CLUSTER = cluster ! defines variable indicating group membership

WITHIN = x ; ! indicates time codes only used at the lower level of analysis

ANALYSIS: TYPE = TWOLEVEL RANDOM; ! indicates multilevel model with random slope

MODEL: ! portion where model is specified

%WITHIN% ! lower level of the model

S | y on x; ! defines regression of y on x as a random slope, which is the linear slope factor

%BETWEEN% ! higher level of the model

y S; ! specifies the intercept in "y" and the linear slope factor in "S" as existing at the higher level

Appendix C2

TITLE: An Intercept as Mean Growth (IGM) Model setup as a structural equation model

DATA: FILE IS ...; ! insert data file here

VARIABLE: NAMES ARE y1-y5 a1-a5; ! variable names

USEVARIABLES ARE y1-y5 a1-a5; ! indicates variables to use in the model

TSCORES = a1-a5; ! indicates which variables have the time codings for each individual

MODEL: i s | y1-y5 AT a1-a5; ! defines an intercept and slope factor, using the time codings

Appendix D1

TITLE: Multilevel Model with a Latent Factor

DATA: FILE IS ...; ! insert data file here

VARIABLE: NAMES ARE y1-y4 cluster; ! variable names, where x is the time codings

USEVARIABLES ARE y1-y4; ! indicates variables to use in the model

CLUSTER = cluster; ! defines variable indicating group membership

ANALYSIS: TYPE = TWOLEVEL; ! indicates multilevel model

MODEL: ! portion where model is specified

%WITHIN% ! lower level of the model

n_w1 BY y1-y4; ! defines Eta_W1

n_w1 (W); ! labels the within group variance of the latent variable as "W"

%BETWEEN% ! higher level of the model

n_b1 BY y1-y4; ! defines Eta_B1

n_b1 (B); ! labels the between-group variance of the latent variable as "B"

MODEL CONSTRAINT: ! portion of the model where labeled parameters may be used

NEW (ICC) ! defines a new variable that will not explicitly be a part of the estimated model

ICC = B/(B+W); ! Computes the ICC(1) of the latent variable

Appendix D2

TITLE: Multilevel Structural Equation Model with a random slope and latent interaction

DATA: FILE IS …; ! insert data file here

VARIABLE: NAMES ARE y1-y12 w cluster; ! variable names

USEVARIABLES ARE y1-y12 w; ! indicates variables to use in the model

BETWEEN = y9-y12 w; ! indicates variables measured at the between level, no within variance

CLUSTER = cluster; ! defines variable indicating group membership

ANALYSIS: TYPE = TWOLEVEL RANDOM; ! indicates multilevel model with random slope

MODEL: ! portion where model is specified

%WITHIN% ! lower level of the model

n_w1 BY y1-y4; ! defines Eta_W1

n_w2 BY y5-y8; ! defines Eta_W2

S | n_w1 ON n_w2; ! defines the regression of Eta_W1 on Eta_W2 as a random slope

%BETWEEN% ! higher level of the model

n_b1 BY y1-y4; ! defines Eta_B1

n_b2 BY y9-y12; ! defines Eta_B2

n_b1Xn_b2 | n_b1 XWITH n_b2; ! defines interaction between Eta_B1 and Eta_B2

n_b1 ON n_b2 n_b1Xn_b2 w; regresses n_b1 on other variables

S ON w; ! regresses the random slope on w

Appendix E

TITLE: LCCA with 2 classes, membership informed by latent variables

DATA: FILE IS ...; ! insert data file here

VARIABLE: NAMES ARE y1-y12; ! variables names

USEVARIABLES ARE y1-y12; ! indicates variables to use in the model

CLASSES = c (2); ! number of classes to be estimated

ANALYSIS: TYPE = MIXTURE; ! mixture model specified

ALGORITHM = INTEGRATION; ! numerical integration used

MODEL:

%OVERALL% ! indicates overall model, no variance within classes is specified here

n_2 BY y5-y8; ! defines Eta_2

n_3 BY y9-y12; ! defines Eta_3

c ON n_2 n_3; ! regresses the latent variable Eta_1 on Eta_2 and Eta_3

! note that the latent class variable as indicated by y1-y4 need not be specified directly

! by not using y1-y4 in the model they are used as indicators for the latent class variable

References

Anderson, C., & Berdahl, J. L. (2002). The experience of power: Examining the effects of power on approach and inhibition tendencies. *Journal of Personality and Social Psychology, 83,* 1362–1377.

Anderson, R. C., Mansi, S. A., & Reeb, D. M. (2004). Board characteristics, accounting report integrity, and the cost of debt. *Journal of Accounting & Economics, 37,* 315–342.

Antonakis, J., Avolio, B. J., & Sivasubramaniam, N. (2003). Context and leadership: An examination of the nine-factor full-range leadership theory using the Multifactor Leadership Questionnaire. *The Leadership Quarterly, 14,* 261–295.

Antonakis, J., Bendahan, S., Jacquart, P., & Lalive, R. (2010). On making causal claims: A review and recommendations. *The Leadership Quarterly, 21,* 1086–1120.

Antonakis, J., Schriesheim, C. A., Donovan, J. A., Gopalakrishna-Pillai, K., Pellegrini, E. K., & Rossomme, J. L. (2004). Methods for studying leadership. In J. Antonakis, A. T. Cianciolo, & R. J. Sternberg (Eds.), *The nature of leadership* (pp. 48–70). Thousand Oaks, CA: Sage.

Barling, J., Loughlin, C., & Kelloway, E. K. (2002). Development and test of a model linking safety-specific transformational leadership and occupational safety. *Journal of Applied Psychology, 87,* 488–496.

Bliese, P. D. (1998). Group size, ICC values, and group-level correlations: A simulation. *Organizational Research Methods, 1,* 355–373.

Bollen, K. A. 1989. *Structural equations with latent variables.* New York: John Wiley.

Bollen, K. A. (1996). An alternative two-stage least squares (2SLS) estimator for latent variable equations. *Psychometrika, 61,* 109–121.

Bollen, K. A. (2002). Latent variables in psychology and the social sciences. *Annual Review of Psychology, 53,* 605–634.

Bollen, K. A., & Curran, P. J. (2004). Autoregressive latent trajectory (ALT) models: A synthesis of two traditions. *Sociological Methods & Research, 32,* 336–383.

Bollen, K. A., & Curran, P. J. (2006). *Latent curve models: A structural equation perspective.* Hoboken, NJ: John Wiley.

Carson, J. B., Tesluk, P. E., & Marrone, J. A. (2007). Shared leadership in teams: An investigation of antecedent conditions and performance. *Academy of Management Journal, 50,* 1217–1234.

Chen, F., Curran, P. J., Bollen, K. A., Kirby, J., & Paxton, P. (2008). An empirical evaluation of the use of fixed cutoff points in RMSEA test statistic in structural equation models. *Sociological Methods and Research, 36,* 462–494.

Cheung, G. W. (2009). Introducing the latent congruence model for improving the assessment of similarity, agreement, and fit in organizational research. *Organizational Research Methods, 12,* 6–33.

Cohen, J., Cohen, P., West, S. G., & Aiken, L. S. (2003). Applied multiple regression/correlation analysis for the behavioral sciences (3rd ed.). Hillsdale, NJ: Lawrence Erlbaum.

Colbert, A. E., Kristof-Brown, A. L., Bradley, B. H., & Barrick, M. R. (2008). CEO transformational leadership: The role of goal importance congruence in top management teams. *Academy of Management Journal, 51,* 81–96.

Curran, P. J. (2003). Have multilevel models been structural equation models all along? *Multivariate Behavioral Research, 38,* 529–569.

Curran, P. J., & Bollen, K. A. (2001). The best of both worlds: Combining autoregressive and latent curve models. In L. M. Collins & A. G. Sayer (Eds.), *New methods for the analysis of change* (pp. 107–135). Washington, DC: American Psychological Association.

Dansereau, F., Alutto, J. A., Nachman, S. A., Alkelabi, S. A., Yammarino, F. J., Newman, J., et al. (1995). Individualized leadership—A new multiple-level approach. *The Leadership Quarterly, 6,* 413–450.

Dansereau, F., Graen, G., & Haga, W. J. (1975). Vertical dyad linkage approach to leadership within formal organizations: A longitudinal investigation of role making process. *Organizational Behavior and Human Performance, 13,* 46–78.

Dimitruk, P., Schermelleh-Engel, K., Kelava, A., & Moosbrugger, H. (2007). Challenges in nonlinear structural equation modeling. *Methodology, 3,* 100–114.

Dionne, S. D., & Dionne, P. J. (2008). Levels-based leadership and hierarchical group decision optimization: A simulation. *The Leadership Quarterly, 19,* 212–234.

DiStefano, C., & Kamphaus, R. W. (2006). Investigating subtypes of child development: A comparison of cluster analysis and latent cluster analysis in typology creation. *Educational and Psychological Measurement, 66,* 788–794.

Edwards, J. R. (1993). Problems with the use of profile similarity indices in the study of congruence in organizational research. *Personnel Psychology, 46,* 641–665.

Edwards, J. R. (1995). Alternatives to difference scores as dependent variables in the study of congruence in organizational research. *Organizational Behavior and Human Decision Processes, 64,* 307–324.

Edwards, J. R. (2002). Alternatives to difference scores: Polynomial regression analysis and response surface methodology. In F. Drasgow & N. Schmitt (Eds.), *Measuring and analyzing behavior in organizations: Advances in measurement and data analysis* (pp. 350–400). San Francisco: Jossey-Bass.

Edwards, J. R. (2007). Polynomial regression and response surface methodology. In C. Ostroff and T. A. Judge (Eds.), *Perspectives on organizational fit* (pp. 361–371). Mahwah, NJ: Lawrence Erlbaum.

Edwards, J. R. (2008). To prosper, organizational psychology should . . . overcome methodological barriers to progress. *Journal of Organizational Behavior, 29,* 469–491.

Edwards, J. R., & Lambert L. S. (2007). Methods for integrating moderation and mediation: A general analytical framework using moderated path analysis. *Psychological Methods, 12,* 1–22.

Edwards, J. R., & Parry, M. E. (1993). On the use of polynomial regression equations as an alternative to difference scores in organizational research. *Academy of Management Journal, 36,* 1577–1613.

Ensley, M. D., Hmieleski, K. M., & Pearce, C. L. (2006). The importance of vertical and shared leadership within new venture top management teams: Implications for the performance of startups. *The Leadership Quarterly, 17,* 217–231.

Fiske, S. T. (1993). Social cognition and social perception. *Annual Review of Psychology, 44,* 155–194.

Foti, R. J., & Hauenstein, N. M. A. (2007). Pattern and variable approaches in leadership emergence and effectiveness. *Journal of Applied Psychology, 92,* 347–355.

Garden, A. (1991). Unresolved issues with the Meyers-Briggs Type Indicator. *Journal of Psychological Type, 22,* 3–14.

Gibson, W. A. (1959). Three multivariate models: Factor analysis, latent structure analysis, and latent profile analysis. *Psychometrika, 24,* 229–252.

Goodman, L. A. (1974). Exploratory latent structure analysis using both identifiable and unidentifiable models. *Biometrika, 61,* 215–231.

Graen, G. B., & Uhl-Bien, M. (1995). Relationship-based approach to leadership: Development of leader-member exchange (LMX) theory over 25 years: Applying a multi-level multi-domain perspective. *The Leadership Quarterly, 6,* 219–247.

Hamilton, B. H., & Nickerson, J. A. (2003). Correcting for endogeneity in strategic management research. *Strategic Organization, 1,* 51–78.

Hancock, G. R., & Choi, J. (2006). A vernacular for linear latent growth models. *Structural Equation Modeling, 13,* 352–377.

Hausman, J. A. (1978). Specification tests in econometrics. *Econometrica, 46,* 1251–1271.

Henderson, D. J., Liden, R. C., Glibkowski, B. C., & Chaudhry, A. (2009). LMX differentiation: A multilevel review and examination of its antecedents and outcomes. *The Leadership Quarterly, 20,* 517–534.

Hertzog, C., Dixon, R. A., Hultsch, D. F., & MacDonald, S. W. S. (2003). Latent change models of adult cognition: Are changes in processing speed and working memory associated with changes in episodic memory? *Psychology and Aging, 18,* 755–769.

Hofmann, D. A., Morgeson, F. P., & Gerras, S. J. (2003). Climate as a moderator of the relationship between leader-member exchange and content specific citizenship: Safety climate as an exemplar. *Journal of Applied Psychology, 88,* 170–178.

Howell, J. P., Dorfman, P. W., & Kerr, S. (1986). Moderator variables in leadership research. *Academy of Management Review, 11,* 88–102.

Jöreskog, K. G., & Sörbom, D. (1979). *Advances in factor analysis and structural equation models.* Cambridge, MA: Abt Books.

Jöreskog, K. G., & Yang, F. (1996). Nonlinear structural equation models: The Kenny-Judd model with interaction effects. In G. A. Marcoulides & R. E. Schumacker (Eds.), *Advanced structural equation modeling* (pp. 57–88). Hillsdale, NJ: Lawrence Erlbaum.

Jöreskog, K. G., & Yang, F. (1997). Estimation of interaction models using the augmented moment matrix: Comparison of asymptotic standard errors. In W. Bandilla and F. Faulbaum (Eds.), *SoftStat '97: Advances in Statistical Software* (6th ed., pp. 467–478). Stuttgart, Germany: Lucius.

Kelava, A., Moosbrugger, H., Dimitrik, P., & Schermelleh-Engel, K. (2008). Multicollinearity and missing constraints: A comparison of three approaches for the analysis of latent nonlinear effects. *Methodology, 4,* 51–66.

Keltner, D., Gruenfeld, D. H, & Anderson, C. (2003). Power, approach, and inhibition. *Psychological Review, 110,* 265–284.

Kerr, S., Schriesheim, C. A., Murphy, C. J., & Stogdill, R. M. (1974). Toward a contingency theory of leadership based upon the consideration and initiating structure literature. *Organizational Behavior and Human Performance, 12,* 62–82.

Kipnis, D. (1976). *The powerholders.* Chicago: University of Chicago Press.

Kipnis, D. (1984). The use of power in organizations and in interpersonal settings. In S. Oskamp (Ed.), *Applied social psychology annual* (Vol. 5, pp. 172–210). Beverly Hills, CA: Sage.

Klein, A., & Moosbrugger, H. (2000). Maximum likelihood estimation of latent interaction effects with the LMS method. *Psychometrika, 65,* 457–474.

Klein, A., & Muthén, B. O. (2007). Quasi maximum likelihood estimation of structural equation models with multiple interaction and quadratic effects. *Multivariate Behavioral Research, 42,* 647–673.

Klein, K. J., & Kozlowski, S. W. J. (2000). From micro to meso: Critical steps in conceptualizing and conducting multilevel research. *Organizational Research Methods, 3,* 211–236.

Kline, R. B. 2005. *Principles and practice of structural equation modeling.* New York: Guilford Press.

Lazarsfeld, P. F. (1950). The logical and mathematical foundation of latent structure analysis & The interpretation and mathematical foundation of latent structure analysis. In S. A. Stouffer et al. (Eds.), *Measurement and prediction* (pp. 362–472). Princeton, NJ: Princeton University Press.

Lazarsfeld, P. F., & Henry, N. W. (1968). *Latent structure analysis.* Boston: Houghton Mifflin.

Liden, R. C., & Antonakis, J. (2009). Considering context in psychological leadership research. *Human Relations, 62,* 1587–1605.

Ligon, G. S., Hunter, S. T., & Mumford, M. D. (2008). Development of outstanding leadership: A life narrative approach. *The Leadership Quarterly, 19,* 312–334.

Lord, F. M., & Novick, M. R. (1968). *Statistical theories of mental test scores.* Reading, MA: Addison-Wesley.

Lubke, G. H., & Muthén, B. (2005). Investigating population heterogeneity with factor mixture models. *Psychological Methods, 10,* 21–39.

Marsh, H. W., Lüdtke, O., Robitzsch, A., Trautwein, U., Asparouhov, T., Muthén, B., & Nagengast, B. (2009). Doubly-latent models of school contextual effects: Integrating multilevel and structural equation approaches to control measurement and sampling error. *Multivariate Behavioral Research, 44,* 764–802.

Marsh, H. W., Lüdtke, O., Trautwein, U., & Morin, A. J. S. (2009). Classical latent profile analysis of academic self-concept dimensions: Synergy of person- and variable-centered approaches to theoretical models of self-concept. *Structural Equation Modeling, 16,* 191–225.

McArdle, J. J., & Epstein, D. (1987). Latent growth curves within developmental structural equation models. *Child Development, 58,* 110–133.

McCrae, R. R., & Costa, P. T. (1989). Reinterpreting the Meyers-Briggs Type Indicator from the perspective of the five-factor model of personality. *Journal of Personality, 57,* 17–40.

McDonald, R. P., & Ho, M. H. R. (2002). Principles and practice in reporting structural equation analyses. *Psychological Methods, 7,* 64–82.

Mehta, P. D., & Neale, M. C. (2005). People are variables too: Multilevel structural equation modeling. *Psychological Methods, 10,* 259–284.

Michael, J. (2003). Using the Myers-Briggs Type Indicator as a tool for leadership development? Apply with caution. *Journal of Leadership & Organizational Studies, 10*(1), 68–81.

Moosbrugger, H., Schermelleh-Engel, K., & Klein, A. (1997). Methodological problems of estimating latent interaction effects. *Methods of Psychological Research, 2,* 95–111.

Muthén, B. O. (1991). Multilevel factor analysis of class and student achievement components. *Journal of Educational Measurement, 28,* 338–354.

Muthén, B. O. (1994). Multilevel covariance structure analysis. *Sociological Methods and Research, 22,* 376–398.

Muthén, B. O. (2003). Statistical and substantive checking in growth mixture modeling. *Psychological Methods, 8,* 369–377.

Muthén, B. (2004). Latent variable analysis: Growth mixture modeling and related techniques for longitudinal data. In D. Kaplan (Ed.), *Handbook of quantitative methodology for the social sciences* (pp. 345–368). Newbury Park, CA: Sage.

Muthén, B.O., & Asparouhov, T. (2003). Modeling interactions between latent and observed continuous variables using maximum-likelihood estimation in Mplus. Mplus Web Notes No. 6.

Muthén, B. O., & Curran, P. J. (1997). General longitudinal modeling of individual differences in experimental designs: A latent variable framework for analysis and power estimation. *Psychological Methods, 2,* 371–402.

Muthén, B., & Muthén, L. K. (2000). Integrating person-centered and variable-centered analyses: Growth mixture modeling with latent trajectory classes. *Alcoholism: Clinical and Experimental Research, 24,* 882–891.

Muthén, L. K., & Muthén, B. O. (1998–2008). *Mplus user's guide: Statistical analysis with latent variables* (5th Ed.). Los Angeles, CA: Muthén & Muthén.

Ng, K. Y., Ang, S., & Chan, K. Y. (2008). Personality and leader effectiveness: A moderated mediation model of leadership self-efficacy, job demands, and job autonomy. *Journal of Applied Psychology, 93,* 733–743.

Nyland, K., Asparouhov, T., & Muthén, B. O. (2007). Deciding on the number of classes in latent class analysis and growth mixture modeling: A Monte Carlo simulation. *Structural Equation Modeling, 14,* 535–569.

Pittenger, D. J. (1993). The utility of the Myers-Briggs Type Indicator. *Review of Educational Research, 63,* 467–488.

Preacher, K. J., Zyphur, M. J., & Zhang, Z. (2010). Testing multilevel mediation in the social sciences: A complete theoretical and empirical framework. *Psychological Methods, 15,* 209–233.

Rabe-Hesketh, S., Skrondal, A., & Pickles, A. (2004). Generalized multilevel structural equation modeling. *Psychometrika, 69,* 167–190.

Raudenbush, S. W., & Bryk, A. S. (1986) A hierarchical model for studying school effects. *Sociology of Education, 59,* 1–17.

Raudenbush, S. W., & Bryk, A. S. (2002) Hierarchical linear models: Applications and data analysis methods (2nd ed.). Thousand Oaks, CA: Sage.

Raykov, T., & Shrout, P. E. (2002) Reliability of scales with general structure: Point and interval estimation using a structural equation modeling approach. *Structural Equation Modeling, 9,* 195–212.

Salancik, G., & Pfeffer, J. (1977). Who gets power—and how they hold on to it: A strategic contingency model of power. *Organizational Dynamics, 5,* 2–21.

Schermelleh-Engel, K., Klein, A., & Moosbrugger, H. (1998). Estimating nonlinear effects using a latent moderated structural equations approach. In R. E. Schumacker & G. A. Marcoulides (Eds.), *Interaction and nonlinear effects in structural equation modeling* (pp. 203–238). Mahwah, NJ: Lawrence Erlbaum.

Searle, S. R., Casella, G., & McCulloch, C. E. (1992). *Variance components.* New York: John Wiley.

Self, S. G., & Liang, K.-Y. (1987). Asymptotic properties of maximum likelihood estimators and likelihood ratio tests under nonstandard conditions. *Journal of the American Statistical Association, 82,* 605–610.

Singer, J. D., & Willett, J. B. (2003). *Applied longitudinal data analysis: Modeling change and event occurrence.* New York: Oxford University Press.

Sipps, G. J., & DiCaudo, J. (1988). Convergent and discriminant validity of the Meyers-Briggs Type Indicator as a measure of sociability and impulsivity. *Educational and Psychological Measurement, 48,* 445–451.

Skrondal, A., & Rabe-Hesketh, S. (2004). *Generalized latent variable modeling: Multilevel, longitudinal and structural equation models.* Boca Raton, FL: Chapman & Hall/CRC.

Stoolmiller, M., Kim, H. K., & Capaldi, D. M. (2005). The course of depressive symptoms in men from early adolescence to young adulthood: Identifying latent trajectories and early predictors. *Journal of Abnormal Psychology, 114,* 331–345.

Structural equation modeling [Special issue]. (2007). *Personality and Individual Differences, 42*(5).

Tiedens, L. Z., Ellsworth, P. C., & Mesquita, B. (2000). Stereotypes about sentiments and status: Emotional expectations for high- and low-status group members. *Personality and Social Psychology Bulletin, 26,* 560–574.

Vermunt, J. K., & Magidson, J. (2002). Latent class cluster analysis. In J. A. Hagenaars & A. L. McCutcheon (Eds.), *Applied latent class analysis* (pp. 89–106). Cambridge, UK: Cambridge University Press.

Wang, M. (2007). Profiling retirees in the retirement transition and adjustment process: Examining the longitudinal change patterns of retirees' psychological well-being. *Journal of Applied Psychology, 92,* 455–474.

Williams, L. J., Edwards, J. R., & Vandenberg, R. J. (2003). Recent advances in causal modeling methods for organizational and management research. *Journal of Management, 29,* 903–936.

Wooldridge, J. M. (2002). *Econometric analysis of cross section and panel data.* Cambridge, MA: MIT Press.

Yuan, K. H. (2005). Fit indices versus test statistics. *Multivariate Behavioral Research, 40,* 115–148.

Yukl, G. & Van Fleet, D. D. 1992. Theory and research on leadership in organizations. In M. D. Dunnette and L.M. Hough (Eds.), *Handbook of industrial and organizational psychology* (Vol. 3, pp. 147–197). Palo Alto, CA: Consulting Psychologists Press.

Zhang, Z., Ilies, R., & Arvey, R. D. (2009). Beyond genetic explanations for leadership: The moderating roles of the social environment. *Organizational Behavior and Human Decision Processes, 110,* 118–128.

Zhang, Z., Zyphur, M. J., & Preacher, K. (2009). Testing multilevel mediation using hierarchical linear models: Problems and solutions. *Organizational Research Methods, 12,* 695–719.

Zyphur, M. J. (2009). When mindsets collide: Switching analytical mindsets to advance organization science. *Academy of Management Review, 34,* 677–688.

Zyphur, M. J., Bradley, J. C., Landis, R. S., & Thoresen, C. J. (2008). The effects of cognitive ability and conscientiousness on performance over time: A censored latent growth model. *Human Performance, 21,* 1–27.

Zyphur, M. J., Chaturvedi, S., & Arvey, R. D. (2008). Job performance over time is a function of previous performance and latent performance trajectories. *Journal of Applied Psychology, 93,* 217–224.

Zyphur, M. J., Narayanan, J., Koh, G., & Koh, D. (2009). Testosterone-status mismatch lowers collective efficacy in groups: Evidence from a slope-as-predictor multilevel structural equation model. *Organizational Behavior and Human Decision Processes, 110,* 70–79.

4

The Nature of Leadership Development

David V. Day

University of Western Australia

Discerning the nature of leadership development is not altogether easy or straightforward. Leadership alone is a complex construct, which some commentators have claimed is "curiously unformed" as a scholarly discipline (Hackman & Wageman, 2007, p. 43). Development is an equally complex construct of study, especially given that it inherently involves change and the consideration of the role of time in underlying theory and research. Although much progress has been made in terms of the statistical modeling of change (e.g., McArdle, 2009; Nagin, 1999; Raudenbush, 2001), aspects of development pertaining to time and the timing of when things occur continue to be theoretically underdeveloped and often imprecisely specified in theory and research (Mitchell & James, 2001).

Given the vast number of publications on the topic of leadership development, it is easy to assume that a great deal is known about it from a scientific perspective. Unfortunately, this does not appear to be the case. As noted by others in the field, volume does not necessarily correlate with quality when it comes to the leadership development literature (Avolio, Sosik, Jung, & Berson, 2003). More generally and historically, there is wide gap between leadership theory and practice (Zaccaro & Horn, 2003). Partly as a result of this gap, the field of leadership development is mainly a collection of disparate best practices (e.g., 360-degree feedback, coaching, on-the-job experience, mentoring) rather than a coherent, theoretically

AUTHOR'S NOTE: Please address correspondence concerning this chapter to David V. Day, University of Western Australia Business School, 35 Stirling Highway (M261), Crawley, WA 6009, Australia. Phone: +61–8–6488–3516; e-mail: david.day@uwa.edu.au.

guided, and evidence-based process (Day, 2000). Because of these and other reasons, it has been suggested that the field of leadership development "is going nowhere fast" (Howard & Wellins, 2008, p. 4).

Despite such pessimistic characterizations of the leadership development field, I am considerably more sanguine about the possibility of building an evidence-based science of leadership development than I was just a few years ago. Although the field is still dominated by practitioners and those of dubious motives who are prescribing *the* answer [sic] on how to best develop leaders and leadership in organizations or are using assessment instruments of suspect validity to diagnose leadership needs, others have begun to explore some of the underlying process issues theoretically and empirically. One example is a recent meta-analysis of 200 lab and field studies evaluating the impact of leadership interventions (Avolio, Reichard, Hannah, Walumbwa, & Chan, 2009). Results indicated overall positive effects for leadership training and development interventions, but with noted variability in respective effect sizes associated with the underlying theoretical approach. One purpose of this chapter is to review the emerging literature and integrate it with several key questions and underlying assumptions about the nature of leadership development. A relevant place to begin is with defining what is meant by leadership development.

It is surprising and perhaps a bit unsettling how often an operational definition of leadership development is assumed rather than clearly stated. The thinking appears to be that it must seem pretty straightforward that leadership development involves developing leadership; however, there are reasons to question this simplicity. Although leadership has proven difficult to define precisely, a widely acknowledged ontology—although not a definition—is that it is composed of a leader, followers, and a shared goal (Bennis, 2007). Another way of viewing this is that leadership must involve a social interaction among two or more individuals in pursuit of a mutual goal. For this reason, it has been proposed that most of what passes for leadership development is more properly termed leader development (Day, 2000). Whereas leaders can work to develop their leadership-related knowledge, skills, and competencies, because of its interpersonal and relational nature, leadership cannot be developed directly unless intact dyads, work groups, or the organization as a whole are the focus of development.

Based on this distinction between leader and leadership development, some scholars have defined the focal constructs in these ways: *Leader development* is the expansion of an individual's capacity the be effective in leadership roles and processes, whereas *leadership development* is the expansion of an organization's capacity to enact basic leadership tasks needed to accomplish shared, collective work (Van Velsor & McCauley, 2004). Instead of focusing mainly on organization position, hierarchy, or status to denote leadership, the notion of roles and processes refers to behaviors or other actions enacted by anyone—regardless of whether or not considered as a formal leader—that facilitate setting direction, creating alignment, and building commitment. These fundamental "leadership tasks" have been proposed as an adaptable leadership ontology that is more fitting for the ever-increasing kinds of challenges that require collaborative forms of leadership (Drath et al., 2008). With acknowledgement of the distinction between leader and leadership development, the latter term will be generally used in this chapter as the more overarching or inclusive construct.

This presents us with the first general question or underlying assumption about leadership development: What is the available evidence that people can become better leaders? Perhaps it is the case that great leaders are born with their talent and little can be done for those without this natural ability. This ultimately boils down to the age-old debate regarding nature (born) versus nurture (made). It is typically concluded that it is likely some combination of both nature and nurture, but nonetheless it is an interesting and relevant issue to put to the literature. Specifically, how much of leadership is because of heritable factors (i.e., genetics), and how much is because of the environment? Realistically, what percentage of the total leadership equation might be developed through structured interventions and experience?

Are Leaders Born or Made?

It has been estimated that organizations invest between USD$20B and USD$40B annually in leadership development programs and other supporting management education activities in the United States alone (Lamoureux, 2007; O'Leonard, 2008). Given these considerable estimates, it would appear that organizations firmly believe that leadership can be developed. Otherwise, why spend so much for something that could be entirely determined by genetics and other inherited characteristics? Nonetheless, there is a difference between inferring that leadership is something that potentially can be developed based on financial investments and demonstrating it with hard data.

No one has isolated the leadership gene yet; however, research designs comparing monozygotic (identical) and dizygotic (fraternal) twins have yielded some interesting and encouraging results. Based on methodological and analytical procedures advanced in the field of behavioral genetics, Arvey and colleagues (Arvey, Rotundo, Johnson, Zhang, & McGue, 2006) estimated the heritability (i.e., h^2) of *leadership role occupancy* among a sample of male twins. From this research perspective, leadership was defined and measured in terms of the various self-reported formal and informal role attainments of twins in work and other professional settings. This was measured using bio-history methods in which individuals reported past or present participation in leadership roles. Note that this could be considered mainly a measure of leadership emergence, in that no data were collected regarding the actual effectiveness of these individuals in their respective leadership roles. Another challenge is that it equates leadership mainly with position. Nonetheless, results indicated that about 30% of individual differences in leadership role occupancy could be attributed to latent genetic factors (i.e., $h^2 = .30$). This estimate was subsequently replicated in a separate sample of female twins (Arvey, Zhang, Avolio, & Krueger, 2007). Additional analyses suggested that work experiences explained approximately 11.5% of the variance in leadership role occupancy, with other environmental influences (and error) explaining the remainder.

Subsequent research using this general twins study approach (Zhang, Ilies, & Arvey, 2009) sought to examine potential environmental moderators of the noted relationship between genetic influences and leadership role occupancy. The general approach is grounded in theory and research on gene–environment interactions, in which aspects of the social environment modify the influence of an individual's genetic makeup, either strengthening or weakening the effects of genes on phenotypes (Plomin, DeFries, & Loehlin, 1977). Results suggested that the genetic influences on leadership role occupancy were weaker for individuals reared in enriched social environments, as defined by higher family socioeconomic status, higher perceived parental support, and lower perceived conflict with parents. Conversely, genetic effects were stronger for twins reporting generally poorer social environments.

These findings appear to offer relatively good news to both scientists and practitioners interested in the topic of leadership development. Although some nontrivial proportion of inherited capabilities is associated with ascendency into leadership roles (approximately 30%), a far larger proportion of the variance was associated with nonshared environmental influences. Put somewhat differently, by virtue of "good genes," some individuals appear to have a genetic advantage when it comes to emerging or ascending into leadership roles; however, the results also suggest that anyone could become a better leader and increase his or her odds of occupying formal or informal leadership roles through practice and other interventions. Individuals lacking a genetic advantage might need to work a little harder to achieve the same results relative to those individuals gifted with better genetic makeup for leadership, but the evidence suggests that development as a leader is possible regardless of inherited characteristics.

The results of the Zhang et al. (2009) study also pose some intriguing practical implications when it comes to leadership development. On the positive side, interventions aimed at improving the family environment through increased parental support and decreased conflict with parents might offer ways to enhance the future success of developing leaders, regardless of genetic background. It also suggests that environmental influences on subsequent leadership outcomes might be framed relatively early in life and that life span approaches might help to better understand the early family influences on leadership and leadership development (e.g., Avolio & Gibbons, 1988; Avolio, Rotundo, & Walumbwa, 2009; Cox & Cooper, 1989). What awaits future empirical scrutiny is whether growing up in an enriched social environment is a factor that enhances individual readiness when it comes to leadership development or whether work-related developmental programs implemented later in life are more successful for those who experienced enriched environments in adolescence. These are important questions that fortunately do not require samples of fraternal and identical twins to answer.

Having answered the question affirmatively that leadership development is more than a matter of genetics, the next question to consider is what is the available evidence that leaders actually can develop over time.

Do Leaders Develop?

Although the research base is not large, there is emerging evidence gathered from longitudinal designs on the question of whether leaders develop over time, and if so, what factors predict this development. The studies reviewed in this section all take a longitudinal perspective and focus on the development of various indicators of leadership emergence and/or effectiveness as a leader. Because of some challenges associated with generalizing from case studies, a decision was made to exclude them and other forms of anecdotal evidence (e.g., biographies of leaders) in this review of the evidence of longitudinal leader development (see Notes and Case Studies for example cases for readers interested in this approach).

AT&T Management Progress Study

The earliest published study of psychological factors related to leadership advancement (a form of emergence) was the AT&T Management Progress Study (Bray, Campbell, & Grant, 1974) that pioneered the use of the assessment center for selection as well as development. The study began in 1956 and was still active several decades later. The focus of the longitudinal research was to address three core questions (Bray, 1982):

- What significant changes take place as lives develop in a large business enterprise?
- What expected changes do not occur?
- What lies behind these changes and stabilities?

The study director (Douglas W. Bray) wrote that he thought "the most significant single finding . . . is that success as a manager is highly predictable" (1982, p. 183). Note that Bray frames the study in terms of predicting success as a manager rather than as a leader; however, contemporary researchers frame similar career advancement issues in terms of leadership role occupancy (e.g., Arvey et al., 2006; 2007). Nonetheless, one of the most important personality factors in the study was *leadership motivation*, which was significantly related to all seven assessment factors of Administrative Skills, Leadership Skills, Advancement Orientation, General Mental Ability, Stability of Performance, Work Motivation, and Independence of Others. Other personality factors related to at least five of these assessment factors were *ambition* and *optimism*. It is interesting to note the parallel between these results and more recent efforts directed at developing and testing a motivation-to-lead construct (Chan & Drasgow, 2001) as well as the role of optimism as a positive psychological capacity that is thought to be developed as part of authentic leadership development (Luthans & Avolio, 2003).

United States Military Academy Studies

Switching the focus from business to the military, understanding what factors are associated with leader development is of utmost importance in military organizations. All uniformed leaders are developed from within the system—none are hired externally—and development is a lifelong commitment. Military officers and noncommissioned officers can be members of their respective organizations for much of their adult lives. As noted by General (Ret.) Eric Shinseki, the former U.S. Army Chief of Staff: Every day the Army trains soldiers and grows leaders.

A study that investigated factors associated with leader emergence and leader effectiveness in the military tracked the development of 236 male cadets at the United States Military Academy (USMA) across four years (Atwater, Dionne, Avolio, Camobreco, & Lau, 1999). Cognitive ability, physical fitness, prior leadership (i.e., influence) experiences, and self-esteem measured in the first year of the study predicted those who emerged as leaders and assumed formal leadership positions in the fourth year. Physical fitness and prior experiences measured in the first year also predicted ratings of leader effectiveness in the fourth year. Whereas moral reasoning as measured by the Defining Issues Test (Rest, 1986) increased over time across cadets, it was unrelated to either leader emergence or leader effectiveness. Of the null findings, hardiness did not distinguish between more and less effective leaders or who advanced into leadership roles, nor did it increase over time as expected. As with the AT&T study (Bray, 1982; Bray et al., 1974), the present research demonstrated that leader emergence and effectiveness could be predicted using individual difference measures, although the overall amount of variance explained in the developmental outcomes was relatively small.

Another longitudinal study of leader development at USMA is the Baseline Officer Leader Development Study (BOLDS). In this project, a single cohort of cadets ($N = 1,143$) was tracked from their arrival at West Point in 1994 until their graduation four years later (with attrition). An extensive set of potential predictor measures was collected on members of the cohort in their first year (e.g., biodata, cognitive and problem-solving abilities, personality, psychosocial level). Four years later, the leader effectiveness ratings were gathered in the form of an overall Military Development grade reflecting overall performance as a leader and a Cadet Performance Report containing ratings from multiple sources (e.g., supervisors, peers, instructors, subordinates) on several leadership qualities (e.g., influencing others, supervising, delegating, developing others).

In an effort to more clearly establish the cognitive and personality (i.e., Big Five) predictors of leader effectiveness, researchers split the overall BOLDS sample into separate test and validation samples and controlled for leader sex in examining potential relationships with leader performance (military development grades) averaged over junior and senior years (Bartone, Snook, & Tremble, 2002). Overall, the results were inconsistent across the test and hold-out validation samples and were generally weak (R^2 change in the .01–.03 range). Assessing the total combined sample results suggested that sex (females performing better), college entrance exam (cognitive ability), social judgment (ability to exercise sound judgment in regard to self, social, and organizational relations), and the Big Five personality factor of conscientiousness were all significant predictors of leader performance. Again, the R^2 change estimates were relatively small (.01–.02) but statistically significant with the overall multiple R^2 of .05. Although the various effect sizes are modest, it should be noted that there was a gap of two to three years between when the predictor and criterion data were collected.

A second published BOLDS study focused on assessing cadets' psychosocial level of development and linking it with leader effectiveness (Bartone, Snook, Forsythe, Lewis, & Bullis, 2007). The study was grounded in Kegan's theory of human development (Kegan, 1982, 1994), which is one type of constructive-developmental theory used to understand leadership and leader development (McCauley, Drath, Palus, O'Connor, & Baker, 2006). Developmental assessments of cadets were conducted using the intensive subject-object interview technique in which interviewees describe and elaborate on a series of prompts provided by an interviewer, who also asks follow-up probing questions to elicit the underlying meaning structure behind the content of the narrative (Lahey, Souvaine, Kegan, Goodman, & Felix, 1988). Because of the extensive amount of time needed to conduct each face-to-face interview (approximately one to two hours) and to subsequently score the interview transcript, Bartone et al. (2007) randomly selected participants at Year 1 of the study ($N = 38$) from the larger BOLDS cohort and reinterviewed those remaining in the sample in Years 2 and 4. Although limited by the relatively small sample sizes across measurement periods, the authors concluded that there was "an overall picture of substantial psychosocial development" in approximately half of the sample (Bartone et al., p. 498). Growth in development level was found to be positively and significantly related to overall leadership effectiveness ratings (Cadet Performance Report) provided by peers and subordinates, but was unrelated to supervisor ratings of cadet leadership.

Across both of the published BOLDS studies (Bartone et al., 2002; 2007), there is some (albeit modest) evidence that leader effectiveness can be predicted using individual difference measures of cognitive and personality factors and that psychosocial development may also play a role in the growth of effective leaders, at least in relatively early career stages. Along with the Atwater et al. (1999) study, it points to the military in general and USMA in particular as drivers of the post-AT&T studies of longitudinal leader development research. This makes sense, given the importance of leader development and leader effectiveness to military organizations. Longitudinal studies using nonmilitary samples are further enhancing our understanding of the leader development process.

Fullerton Longitudinal Study

The Fullerton Longitudinal Study (FLS) is an ongoing long-term project designed to study child development through adolescence and into adulthood. The project began in 1979 with 130 participants receiving yearly assessments through age 17, then again at age 24 and age 29. Leadership assessments were gathered at the last assessment period to date (participant age 29). This study provides—among other things—a unique opportunity to trace the developmental pathways from individual differences in early childhood to self-rated adult leadership potential as well as leadership role occupancy (self-reported frequency of engagement in work-related leadership duties). Results from one set of analyses indicated that children who were more approaching of new people, places, and experiences at ages from 2 to 16 tended to become more extraverted adolescents (age 17), with greater social skills as adults (age 29) and more frequent work-related leadership responsibilities and higher transformational leadership potential (Guerin et al., in press).

A second study from this larger FLS project (Gottfried et al., in press) sought to investigate potential relationships between intelligence, childhood intrinsic motivation, adolescent intrinsic motivation, and motivation to lead (Chan & Drasgow, 2001) in adulthood. There were no significant relationships between intelligence and any of the motivation outcomes (intrinsic or leadership motivation); however, childhood intrinsic motivation was related to adolescent intrinsic motivation, which in turn, predicted the affective-identity ("I like to lead") and noncalculative ("I will lead even if there are no personal benefits to me") components of motivation to lead. There was no relationship between adolescent motivation and social-normative ("I have a duty to lead") motivation to lead.

Taken together, these studies from the ongoing FLS provide insights into the early influences on leader development. Childhood intrinsic motivation and approach temperaments appear to be related to adolescent motivation and personality (extraversion) that predict aspects of motivation to lead and self-appraised leadership potential in adulthood. One potential implication of these findings is that more introverted children and adolescents might benefit from youth leadership initiatives designed to help draw out and prepare them for future leadership roles. In this regard (and consistent with the literature on personality and leadership; Judge & Bono, 2000; Judge, Bono, Ilies, & Gerhardt, 2002), more extraverted individuals might have an advantage in emerging as a leader, although there may be less of an influence on their subsequent effectiveness. Going forward with the impressive project, FLS researchers are urged to collect independent leadership ratings as these study participants move further into adulthood and have the opportunity to take on additional leadership responsibilities.

Developmental Trajectory Studies

A general term used to describe the evolution of an outcome over time is *developmental trajectory* (Nagin, 2005). Trajectories are relevant to the study of leader development in that the respective leadership skills, competence, and effectiveness evolve over time and may traverse much of the adult life span (Day, Harrison, & Halpin, 2009). Charting and predicting leader development trajectories has the potential to provide further insight into different forms or shapes of trajectories, given that individuals are unlikely to develop in the same way or at the same time, and to identify individual factors that predict within-trajectory as well as between-trajectory differences. The statistical procedures for estimating and comparing developmental trajectories are relatively new and have not been widely applied to the leader development field. Nonetheless, there are at least two studies that have adopted this approach in longitudinal studies of leader development.

Using data from the National Longitudinal Survey of Youth 1979 (U.S. Department of Labor), researchers examined aspects of leader emergence (i.e., leadership role occupancy and leader advancement) across 10 years with a sample ($N = 1,747$) of full-time working adults (Li, Arvey, & Song, in press). The researchers examined the influence of general mental ability, self-esteem, and family socioeconomic status on these two forms of leader emergence, and they also examined the moderating role of gender. Leadership data were collected on five separate occasions and modeled using two-part random effect modeling for semicontinuous longitudinal data (Muthén, 2004). Results suggested that a linear growth model fit the data better than alternatives (e.g., no growth; quadratic model) and that there was no evidence for additional latent subclasses of trajectory forms. Self-esteem had a significant and positive effect on leadership role occupancy for both men and women and on leadership advancement in terms of supervisory scope (number of employees supervised) over time for women. Family socioeconomic status was found to have a negative effect on the leadership advancement of women, and general mental ability was found to have no significant effect on leader emergence over time for either sex.

Perhaps the most intriguing results from this study are that women leaders raised in higher socioeconomic environments were more likely to stall in their careers as leaders compared to women raised in lower economic status families. Although these results are interesting, Li et al. (in press) do not have a clean post hoc explanation for this finding. It is not that more affluent women are leaving work, because everyone in the sample was employed full-time across the 10-year period. Instead, the authors point to work in the fields of child development (Luthar, 2003; Luthar & Becker, 2002) and counseling psychology (Lapour & Heppner, 2009) to suggest that there is a price for privilege and that it may affect women to a greater extent than men when it comes to career development. Why this would be the case is unclear.

General mental ability was not found to predict developmental trajectories of either leader role occupancy or leader advancement. Null findings can be difficult to interpret, given that alternative explanations cannot be easily ruled out; however, the relatively large sample size in the study suggests that it was unlikely an issue of statistical power. Furthermore, the null effects for general mental ability are consistent with those of Gottfried et al. (in press) that indicated no relationship between intelligence and either intrinsic motivation or motivation to lead in their sample from the Fullerton Longitudinal Study. Taken together, these null results are intriguing in suggesting that the motivation to lead and long-term leader emergence may not be just a simple function of intelligence. It also further underscores the need for conducting longitudinal studies of leader development using effectiveness as the criterion rather than emergence. Such studies may show that leader intelligence is a robust predictor of leaders' effectiveness, even if it does not predict emergence in the form of leader role occupancy or advancement.

Another study using the general approach of estimating and predicting developmental trajectories examined university students ($N = 1,315$) engaged in community service action learning projects in conjunction with a course on leadership and team building (Day & Sin, in press). The participants worked in project teams across 13 weeks to conceptualize, design, implement, and evaluate a service project that would benefit the local community in some way. Each team consisted of approximately six members plus a peer learning adviser (i.e., coach). There were no formal leaders appointed in each team. Among other things the peer adviser did was provide ratings of each team member four times on his or her effectiveness as a leader in the team. The research was designed as a partial test of a recently proposed integrative model of leader development (Day et al., 2009). Central to the model are the proposed underlying processes of leader identity construction and self-regulation, which are further supported at the deepest level by the adult development processes associated with selective adaptation and compensation proposed by Baltes and colleagues (Baltes, 1997; Baltes & Baltes, 1990).

A surprising finding from the Day and Sin (in press) study was that the prevailing trajectory of leader effectiveness was primarily negative with a slight positive upturn at the final rating period (quadratic model). This reinforces an important point that development is not universally or inherently a positive, linear function. In the present case, putting young adults into a team environment in which they need to both perform and learn under stressful conditions involving a tight timeline can challenge their effectiveness as leaders. Nonetheless, there were conditions that moderated this overall trajectory. Identifying more strongly as a leader and adopting a stronger learning goal orientation (Dweck, 1986; Dweck & Leggett, 1988; Elliott & Dweck, 1988) were shown to be related to more effective (less negative) trajectories. Using growth mixture modeling procedures (Wang & Bodner, 2007), a second class of trajectories was identified for about 10% of the sample consisting of positive and linear development trajectories of rated leadership effectiveness. Additional evidence suggested that certain aspects of adult development processes differentiated reliably between the two subclasses of developmental trajectories.

This provides clear evidence that individuals do not benefit from or experience leader development in the same ways. Furthermore, various theoretically driven individual differences in the form of leader identity construction, goal orientation, and adult development processes were demonstrated to be associated with more effective trajectories of leader development. These individual difference factors, as well as those identified in other longitudinal studies reviewed in this section (e.g., personality, psychosocial developmental level, motivation to lead, self-esteem) might eventually prove to be important in enhancing and otherwise facilitating the development of effective leaders.

This section reviewed longitudinal investigations demonstrating that leaders can and do develop over time and that individual difference variables can be used to predict development and its forms (i.e., trajectories). The next section examines what it is, more specifically than leader emergence or effectiveness, that develops through leadership development initiatives. Put differently, if leaders can emerge or become more effective through taking part in developmental initiatives, then what is developed that is associated with this enhanced emergence and effectiveness?

What Develops in Leadership Development?

The issue of determining what develops through leadership development initiatives is critically important in terms of research as well as practice. On the research side of things, the answer to this question determines the outcome variable(s) of interest that are measured in evaluating the degree of change that has occurred. It also anchors the espoused theory of change that undergirds any developmental initiative and is essential in *pathway mapping*, defined as the process of specifying a program's desired outcomes and linking those outcomes to program activities and strategies (Gutiérrez & Tasse, 2007). From a practice perspective, it is important to first identify the criterion or desired outcome(s) before choosing or designing an appropriate developmental intervention. You should always know what you are aiming for when you implement something as complex—and expensive—as leadership development.

Despite its importance scientifically and practically, it should be noted that there is a wide range of potential criteria to consider. What have become extremely popular—and controversial—are leadership competency models. Although the term *competency* apparently "has no meaning apart from the particular definition with whom one is speaking [sic]" (Schippmann et al., 2000, p. 706), one way to consider competencies is as bundles of leadership-related knowledge, skills, and abilities. Critics have argued that competency models are a so-called best practice "that defies logic, experience, and data" (Hollenbeck, McCall, & Silzer, 2006, p. 399), but those on the pro side of the argument (see Silzer's arguments in the Hollenbeck et al. article) have countered that competency models provide an overarching framework that helps focus individuals and organizations in developing leadership skills. Specifically, competency models help individuals by (among other things) outlining a leadership framework that can be used (a) to help select, develop, and understand leadership effectiveness and (b) as a basis for leadership training and development initiatives within an organization. Such models also potentially help organizations by communicating which general forms of leader behaviors are important and by purportedly offering a leadership framework that is relevant across positions and situations (Hollenbeck et al., pp. 402–403).

Developing the Expert Leader

Regardless of one's perspective on the merits of leadership competency models, what they have in common is providing a taxonomy of various leadership-related skills, sub-skills, and skills bundles (i.e., competencies). One example of a generic model of leadership skill requirements across organizational levels is the so-called leadership skills "strataplex" (T. V. Mumford, Campion, & Morgeson, 2007). At its core, the model proposes that leadership skills requirements can be understood in terms of four general categories: (a) cognitive, (b) interpersonal, (c) business, and (d) strategic skills. Various sub-skills for each general category have also been proposed and tested (see Table 4.1).

A different model has been offered by researchers with regard to individual capabilities thought to enable leadership that also can be developed (Van Velsor & McCauley, 2004). The three general categories of "developable" capabilities or competencies include (a) self-management capabilities, (b) social capabilities, and (c) work facilitation capabilities. Supporting capabilities for each of the general competencies are also provided in Table 4.1. What is interesting is that there is relatively little overlap between these two frameworks.

A relevant question to ask is which of these models is the correct one? The answer is that they both could be right or that one or both could be wrong. The illustrative point is that trying to distill leadership into a set of skills or competencies will likely become unwieldy and still omit important things. It is reminiscent of what happened with leadership trait theory before the Big Five personality framework was introduced. There were too many traits and no way

Table 4.1   Two Views on Essential Leadership Skills Requirements

Leadership Strataplex	T. V. Mumford, Campion, & Morgeson (2007)	Developable Leadership Capabilities	Van Velsor & McCauley (2004)
GENERAL SKILLS	**SUBSKILLS**	**GENERAL CAPABILITIES**	**SUBSKILLS**
Cognitive	Speaking Active listening Writing Reading comprehension Active learning	Self-management	Self-awareness Ability to balance conflicting demands Ability to learn Leadership values
Interpersonal	Social perceptiveness Coordination Persuasion	Social	Ability to build and maintain relationships Ability to build effective work groups Communication skills Ability to develop others
Business	Management of material resources Operations analyses Management of personnel resources Management of financial resources	Work facilitation	Management skills Ability to think and act strategically Ability to think creatively Ability to initiate and implement change
Strategic	Visioning Systems perception Identification of consequences Identification of key causes Problem identification Solution appraisal		

to winnow down the list to those traits that were most important universally for leadership. It also reinforces the point that there are various perspectives on what can and should be addressed in leadership development initiatives.

Nonetheless, understanding leadership as a set of skills or competencies has some advantages. For one thing, a skills-based approach is consistent with the assumption that individual leadership capabilities can be developed (Lord & Hall, 2005). In addition, skills provide a bridge between trait theories and behavioral theories of leadership and may help to identify the missing components that allow effective leaders to generate the right behaviors at the right time (M. D. Mumford, Zaccaro, Connelly, & Marks, 2000). It is also a desirable quality that skills can be more readily assessed relative to other constructs (e.g., traits).

A question that needs to be addressed regarding a skills-based perspective on leadership is what is the expected time frame for such complex skills and competencies to develop? There are recent approaches that have conceptualized leadership skills development in terms of an expert performance model (Day et al., 2009; Lord & Hall, 2005). That is, developing leadership skills and competencies is comparable to developing expertise in other domains such as science, music, chess, and sports (Bloom, 1985; Chi, Glaser, & Farr, 1988; Ericsson, Charness, Feltovich, & Hoffman, 2006). A robust finding from the expert performance literature is that it takes a minimum of 10 years or 10,000 hours of dedicated practice to achieve minimal expert status in a given domain (Ericsson et al., 2006; Ericsson, Krampe, & Tesch-Römer, 1993). If this is indeed the case in the leadership domain, what would help to motivate the kinds of *deliberate* practice during such an extended time period to become an expert leader? This was the basis for the integrative approach to leader development proposed by Day et al. (2009).

Within the area of skill acquisition and development, there are two distinct traditions in adult development, including leader development. One tradition is based in behaviorist origins focusing on the acquisition of micro-level skills and abilities. The emphasis here is on demonstrating skill acquisition through observable task performance. The other tradition has its historical origins in Gestalt psychology, focusing mainly on changes in abstract reasoning and psychosocial ego development. This tradition is concerned almost entirely with mental processes and structures, without much attention to observable behaviors. An example of this tradition is constructive-developmental theory, which as noted previously in this chapter is a general class of adult development theories focusing on the growth and elaboration of a person's way of understanding the self and broader world (McCauley et al., 2006). A comprehensive approach to leadership development needs to incorporate both of these traditions. Thus, an expert leader has not only sophisticated reasoning skills and complex knowledge structures but also a repertoire of observable skills and competencies that is both broad and deep.

Underlying Processes of Identity, Self-Regulation, and Adult Development

In attempting to integrate theoretically across the two traditions of skills development, Day et al. (2009) proposed that the observable level of leadership skills and competence (i.e., expertise) was supported by deeper level processes associated with the more Gestalt-like mental structures and frameworks. In particular, the development of a leader identity is seen as important in forming positive spirals of identity and leader development. Identity formation is a key process in motivating one to seek out developmental experiences and opportunities for deliberate practice of desired leadership skills and competencies. If one does not think of oneself as a leader or aspire to lead, then there is little motivation to develop or serve as a leader (Chan & Drasgow, 2001). In addition, self-regulation processes (e.g., self-regulatory strength, goal orientation, leadership self-efficacy) support the proposed leader-development spirals in terms of contributing the motivational resources for persistence in and across development experiences. Positive spirals of leader development continue to the extent that perseverance is applied toward ongoing development to more expert or elite levels of leader performance. In this way, individual differences in self-regulatory strength is thought to be a key resource in forming and maintaining identity-development spirals and the determination to achieve higher levels of development as a leader.

An important context in which leader development occurs is that of adult development (Day et al., 2009). Whereas child development is driven mainly by biologically based maturational processes that contribute to positive growth and development, there are unique aspects of development in adults relative to children and adolescents. Experience is a much more potent force for development in adults, yet there also are physiological changes in adulthood that have important implications for leader development across the life span. Noted deficits in certain kinds of processing because of aging (e.g., basic information processing, fluid intelligence) could present barriers to leader development in adulthood. Thus, understanding how to compensate for such deficits and optimize available resources would be extremely important in enhancing leader development. But as we will see (and as some of us already know from personal experience), it is a constant battle to try and maximize developmental gains and minimize losses associated with the aging process.

The eminent developmental psychologist, Paul Baltes, has noted that "*any* process of [adult] development entails an inherent dynamic between gains and losses [and] no process of development consists only of growth or progression" (Baltes, 1987, p. 611). This statement is a cornerstone of life span developmental psychology. It is also an important consideration because any growth or progression associated with leadership development occurs in the broader context of an aging and declining organism. How is development even possible under such adverse conditions?

In attempting to address this question, Baltes and colleagues have described adult development as a process of selective adaptation and transformation. Specifically, individual differences in the "orchestrating processes" of development—selection, optimization, and compensation—are thought to play pivotal roles in the inherent dynamic between gains and losses mentioned above. The selection-optimization-compensation (SOC) metamodel rests on the fundamental assumption that across all stages of human development, individuals who manage their lives successfully do so through these processes. Collectively, SOC processes provide the backbone of developmental regulation in adulthood (Baltes, 1997; Baltes & Baltes, 1990; Freund & Baltes, 1998, 2002).

In terms of the orchestrating processes of development, *selection* refers to setting goals as well as reconstructing one's goal system in the face of loss; *optimization* involves acquiring and investing goal-relevant means in terms of resource allocation of time and effort, deliberate practice, and acquiring new skills/resources; and *compensation* refers to using alternative means to maintain a given level of functioning when specific goal-relevant means are no longer available (Freund & Baltes, 2002). Keys to positive development include efforts to select appropriate goals, manage resources optimally, and compensate and adapt when thwarted in one's goal striving.

Overall, there has been a missed opportunity for advancing the notion of leader development as embedded in ongoing adult development processes (also see M. D. Mumford & Manley, 2003). This is a major oversight because it results in the overly simplistic assumption that what changes in leadership development solely involves the building of specific and observable skills and competences. It ignores the role of knowledge structures and mental models (e.g., leader identity), as well as supporting processes associated with self-regulation and the deeper regulatory processes associated with healthy aging and successful adult development (e.g., SOC processes). Considering these and other potential sources of deep-level support offers new avenues for advancing leader development theory and research in ways that could potentially accelerate or otherwise enhance developmental processes in growing the expert leader.

In building on the previous questions of whether leadership development can occur, evaluating the longitudinal evidence that it does develop, and understanding what develops in the process, the next section will examine ways in which leadership development is cultivated in individuals and organizations. Specifically, what are some methods for developing leadership skills and competencies and corresponding knowledge structures in individuals?

_____How to Best Promote Leadership Development?

Most of the attention in the leadership development literature has been devoted to proposing ways in which to promote it. This has led to a focus on programs, practices, and other experiences mainly from a practitioner standpoint. An alternative perspective is that more needs to be done to enhance a science of leader and leadership development (Day & Zaccaro, 2004) with a greater focus on underlying process issues (Day & O'Connor, 2003; Van Velsor, Moxley, & Bunker, 2004). Nonetheless, aspects of how to develop leaders and leadership are important but need to be better integrated with theoretical and empirical concerns. This section will first review two types of developmental practices: (a) structured programs, and (b) experiences, followed by some suggestions on how to integrate the practice concerns with those associated with better understanding the leader development process.

Structured Programs to Develop Leadership Talent

When discussing structured programs, the referent is formal initiatives that can last anywhere from a few hours to many months. Programs also vary in terms of the focus of their content. Conger (2010) has suggested that leadership development initiatives can be classified into four general categories: (a) individual skill development, (b) socialization of organizational vision and values, (c) strategic leadership initiatives to foster large-scale change, and (d) action learning initiatives targeted to address organizational challenges and opportunities.

Individual skill development is an extremely popular approach to leader development, with many organizations and consulting firms offering open enrollment as well as customized programs that are delivered off-site or in-house. Other terms for these kinds of initiatives include assessment for development and feedback-intensive programs (Guthrie & King, 2004). They are so termed because participants complete a number of individual difference measures (e.g., personality, values, leadership skills assessments) and also receive the results of a 360-degree assessment completed by self, subordinates, peers, and superiors (and possibly others). The goals of these kinds of initiatives are to build self-awareness regarding individual strengths and developmental needs and to enhance an understanding of how one is perceived by others. Especially when linked with coaching and an action-oriented development plan (Day, 2000), these initiatives offer a blueprint of sorts for building needed leadership skills while acknowledging and leveraging identified strengths.

Nonetheless, there are a few caveats with regard to the success of skills development programs. In a comprehensive meta-analytic review of the feedback intervention literature, it was found that nearly 40% of the interventions had a negative effect on performance and almost 15% were found to have no effect (Kluger & DeNisi, 1996). These results suggest that merely providing feedback is no guarantee of positive developmental outcomes. Although research has indicated that working with a coach can help improve 360-degree feedback ratings over time (Smither, London, Flautt, Vargas, & Kuchine, 2003), and that meeting with direct reports to discuss their upward feedback is positively related to subsequent improvement (Walker & Smither, 1999), positive change is not a given. For example, if direct reports are held accountable for their upward feedback in the form of nonanonymous ratings, it is likely to result in inflated ratings of the supervisor's performance (Antonioni, 1994). Improvement is most likely when the following conditions apply: (a) feedback indicates that change is necessary, (b) individuals have a positive feedback orientation (i.e., feedback is viewed positively), (c) change is feasible, (d) appropriate goals are set to regulate behavior, and (e) actions are taken that can lead to skills improvement (Smither, London, & Reilly, 2005).

Related to this last point (e), other research suggests that it is not just actions taken that lead to skills development, but the amount of deliberate practice that is undertaken (Ericsson & Charness, 1994; Ericsson et al., 1993; Ericsson, Prietula, & Cokely, 2007). As noted previously in this chapter, deliberate practice is thought to be critically important for developing leadership skills and expertise (Day et al., 2009). Thus, it is not solely or even primarily what happens during the program that matters as much as the motivation and perseverance to engage in practicing desired skills during an extensive period of time.

Leadership development programs are also used to *socialize* either new or newly promoted individuals with the *vision and values of the organization.* Along with setting direction and building commitment, researchers have argued that creating alignment is a key leadership process (Drath et al., 2008). An important form of alignment is in developing a shared understanding of what the organization is about and how it should operate (Conger, 2010). As compared with leadership skills development programs, these kinds of initiatives tend to be in-house (i.e., internally developed and delivered), using company leaders as the teachers. Whereas such programs are becoming increasingly popular, their use is still relatively rare as compared with other categories of leadership development programs. Regardless of its popularity, this approach illustrates how a process designed to socialize leaders on the basic values and operating philosophy of the company has evolved into leadership development.

The *active strategic change management* of an organization has also become a driving reason behind leadership development in terms of addressing shifts in the requisite leadership capabilities needed to implement widespread change. These kinds of initiatives are typically highly customized to an organization's strategy, with emphases on communication of strategic objectives (especially if they are changing), creating alignment among organizational leaders in terms of the strategy—what Conger (2010) refers to as building "strategic unity" (p. 301)—and also to develop change agents across organizational levels that can help facilitate change and enhance progress toward strategic priorities. Such programs have potential to be effective for building individual and organizational change-related skills and competencies; however, a key component for success of the approach is that the senior leadership team has a clear change agenda and knows what leadership requirements are needed. It (almost) goes without saying that this is not always a given.

The final category of structured leadership programs involves *action learning initiatives.* As the name implies, such programs involve working together in teams to address problems of strategic importance (action) while simultaneously building self-awareness and learning about leadership through individual and group reflection (learning). The focus of such initiatives is on holistic leader development as compared with action training (Frese, Beimel, & Schoenborn, 2003) that focuses on learning by doing through more structured practices such as role play with feedback to develop specific skills and competencies. The origins of action learning can be traced to the pioneering work of Revans (1980), and it is essentially a semistructured form of learning by doing. The process of action learning has evolved since its early roots in Great Britain, but there are certain core components that are suggested as requisite components for maximizing its developmental effects (Marquardt, Leonard, Freedman, & Hill, 2009):

- important or intractable problem of strategic importance;
- group(s) of four to eight members, ideally from diverse functional backgrounds;
- emphasis on questioning (rather than asserting) and reflective communications;
- development of action strategies, presented to senior management, and possibly implemented;
- individual and group commitment to learning; and
- learning facilitated by an independent team coach.

Another helpful component in the action learning process is to have a project sponsor. This is typically a senior leader who has a vested interest in the particular problem or project that is being addressed by a team.

Action learning can be a powerful tool for leader and leadership development; however, there are potential downsides. It is a very intense program that requires a major investment in terms of time and other resources for it to be effective, yet most participants take on action learning on top of their day-to-day job responsibilities. The value in terms of leadership development can be lost or seriously diluted if the focus becomes mainly on getting the project completed (action) with little commensurate attention to development (learning). This is why an independent team coach is recommended in action learning. Despite the potential downside to action learning, the evidence suggests that such initiatives are widely used (76% of survey respondents reported "extensive use") for leadership development purposes (Conger & Xin, 2000).

In summary, structured programs are a popular method for addressing leadership development needs in organizations. Although the variety of programs might be combined into four general categories, there is great diversity within categories in terms of program length, intensity, focus, and so forth. There also is the overarching risk of thinking about leadership development in programmatic terms, which contributes to the tendency to result in episodic thinking. That is, if development is thought of as occurring only during a designated formal program, then the critical development that must continue when an individual returns to the job is overlooked or downplayed. Individual change and development requires an extended period of dedicated practice, as the research from the expert performance domain has demonstrated (e.g., Ericsson et al., 1993). Put differently, if you only try to develop during a formal program, then it is unlikely that you will ever acquire the sophisticated levels of leadership skills and expertise needed to be effective in senior leadership roles.

Developing Leadership Through Experiences

Although leadership development programs are popular with organizations, when you ask successful senior executives about how they developed as leaders, researchers found that they claim it was through experience. Specifically, it was the lessons of experience that were reported to be the most potent forces for development (McCall, Lombardo, & Morrison, 1988). These findings parallel those from the job performance literature in noting that job experience can have a substantial indirect effect on work performance through its effect on job knowledge (Schmidt, Hunter, & Outerbridge, 1986).

The notion of development through experience has reached almost the status of "received doctrine" in terms of becoming an unanalyzed article of faith for a group of scholars (Means, 1965). What tends to be overlooked in espousing experience-based approaches to development is that experience is an extremely complex construct incorporating both qualitative and quantitative dimensions (Tesluk & Jacobs, 1998). Further complicating matters, two individuals placed in the identical experience often learn very different things from it, if anything is learned at all (Day, 2010). A related problem is that a lot of on-the-job learning is informal and ad hoc because of its unstructured nature.

In an attempt to provide some structure to identifying and measuring the developmental components of managerial jobs, McCauley and colleagues developed the Developmental Challenge Profile (McCauley, Ruderman, Ohlott, & Morrow, 1994). Factor analyses of the responses of nearly 700 managers suggested three general underlying categories of developmental job challenges: (a) *job transitions* (e.g., unfamiliar responsibilities, proving yourself), (b) *task-related characteristics* (e.g., creating change, handling external pressure, influencing without authority), and (c) *obstacles* (e.g., lack of top management support, difficult boss). As noted, each of these general categories was multidimensional in nature. Subsequent research on the measure revealed significant gender differences in reported job challenges, with men reporting greater task-related challenges, whereas women managers reported experiencing greater developmental obstacles in their jobs (Ohlott, Ruderman, & McCauley, 1994).

More recent research on developing leaders through experience examined the potential boundary conditions associated with highly challenging experiences. Using the Developmental Challenge Profile (McCauley et al., 1994), researchers linked leadership skills development with the amount of challenge in the experience (DeRue & Wellman, 2009). As hypothesized, the relationship between developmental challenge and leadership skill development showed a pattern of diminishing returns. That is, after a certain point, adding more challenge to a developmental experience became less predictive of further skills development. But the researchers also found that aspects of the context in terms of access to feedback offset the diminishing returns associated with high levels of developmental challenge.

These empirical findings are consistent with a proposed leader development model in which any experience can be made more developmentally powerful to the extent that it includes aspects of assessment, challenge, and support (Van Velsor & McCauley, 2004). It could be argued that having good feedback availability is an important support resource (e.g., reinforcement, knowledge of results), such that even when the developmental challenge is very intense, resources in the form of feedback can help to facilitate further leadership skill development. Without the access to feedback, the challenge may become overwhelming, which serves as an obstacle to additional development from the experience.

McCall (2010) recently has proposed recasting leadership development to make better use of experience, while also recognizing that "using experience effectively to develop leadership talent is a lot more complicated and difficult than it appears to be" (p. 3). Part of the issue contributing to this complexity is that experience can be so wide ranging, including job rotations, strategic job assignments, action learning projects, as well as experientially based development programs. In other words, what isn't experience? In order to address this challenge, some have proposed that organizations need to develop frameworks or taxonomies that identify and link experiences, competencies, relationships, and learning capabilities that individuals will need to develop as they move through job assignments in the organization (Yost & Mannion Plunket, 2010).

Developing this sort of comprehensive taxonomy is a major undertaking. The advantage of having such a framework is that it can be used in identifying the experiences most important for development, redesigning certain jobs to make them more developmental, and evaluating the overall level of leadership capacity in the organization in terms of the breadth and depth of leadership talent. Although potentially very useful, this taxonomy approach appears to ignore the human element in the learning process. Specifically, learning from experience is not always a given.

Brehmer (1980) contrasted experientially based learning with more formal approaches such as teaching-based approaches. Results of his study suggested that learning from experience was more difficult because (a) there is not always an awareness that there is something to learn, (b) even if such an awareness exists, it is not always clear what is to be learned, and (c) there is a good deal of ambiguity and uncertainty in determining if or when learning has occurred (also see Feldman, 1986). Other research has demonstrated that experience does not improve expert performance if the access to timely feedback is missing (Summers, Williamson, & Read, 2004). Such issues are magnified when the experience in question is a challenging stretch assignment where there are major career implications at stake and the primary focus is on performing well rather than learning well.

In summary, experience is often thought of as the most promising and potentially powerful developer of leaders (McCall, 2010). This makes sense at a general level; however, when the nature of experience is unpacked, it proves more complicated than it sounds. First, everything related to leader development could be cast in terms of experience, from the shortest classroom workshop to intense stretch assignments or ongoing work experiences. If anything could be seen as experience, then they could be made more developmental by incorporating and enhancing aspects of assessment, challenge, and support (Van Velsor & McCauley, 2004). Second, experience is complex and multifaceted, making it difficult to quantify and categorize (Tesluk & Jacobs, 1998). Nonetheless, researchers have demonstrated that it is possible to obtain an estimate of the degree of developmental challenge in work experiences and to link it with relevant outcomes (DeRue & Wellman, 2009; McCauley et al., 1994). Third, learning from experience is not always easy or straightforward (Brehmer, 1980; Day 2010; Feldman, 1986; Summers et al., 2004), so more attention needs to be given to helping individual learners gain the desired lessons of experience as part of the developmental process.

Looking ahead to the final chapter section, future directions in the science and practice of leadership development are considered. Specifically, what remains to be done to further improve and advance the field? Where are the major gaps between what we know and what we need to know?

How to Improve Leadership Development Science and Practice?

Theory

There is a recognized need for promoting more integrative theory-building strategies in the general field of leadership (Avolio, 2007), and this certainly also applies to leadership development. In moving to the next level of integration, theory could more fully consider the dynamic interplay between leaders and followers, in addition to taking into greater account the context in which these interactions occur (Avolio & Gardner, 2005; Gardner, Avolio, Luthans, May, & Walumbwa, 2005). Another way of thinking about this proposed integrative strategy is in terms of inclusiveness. Historically, leadership theory mainly has been about the leader. More integrative theories recognize that the leadership landscape includes leaders, followers, and the situational context as essential ingredients in this dynamic interaction.

New ontology of leadership can also help inform leadership development. A good example is the theoretical work of Drath et al. (2008), who have recast the basic parameters of leadership around the fundamental tasks of direction, alignment, and commitment. As a possible replacement for the traditional leadership "tripod" of leaders, followers, and a shared goal (Bennis, 2007), an alternative ontology for leadership was organized in terms of the leadership outcomes associated with (a) widespread agreement in a collective on the overall goals, aims, and mission (*direction*); (b) the organization and coordination of knowledge and work in a collective (*alignment*); and (c) the willingness of individuals to subsume their own interests and benefit within the collective interest and benefit (*commitment*).

Drath et al. (2008) argue that the traditional tripod ontology is too narrow to support emerging leadership theories associated with shared or distributed leadership, applications of complexity science, and relational approaches to leadership. That aside, the new ontological framework offers fresh ways to conceptualize leadership development as well. Anything that can help develop ways to enhance direction, alignment, or commitment at the individual, group, or organizational level would be viable leadership development.

Another area of future theoretical interest is in moving toward more integrative and inclusive leadership development of a different kind. Leadership is a dynamic, evolving process. As such, it incorporates behaviors, perceptions, decision-making, and a whole host of other constructs. Thus, leadership by nature is an eclectic phenomenon, and attempting to conceptualize and study its development from any one theoretical perspective (e.g., motivational, emotional, behavioral) will yield only limited results. More inclusive and integrative perspectives are needed that cut across a number of theoretical domains. One example is the integrative theoretical approach to leader development that links the otherwise disparate domains of adult development, identity and self-regulation, and expertise acquisition (Day et al., 2009). Using this as just one example, leadership development theory will continue to advance by integrating across multiple domains and disciplines in a more diverse and eclectic manner.

Research

The leadership development field incorporates several challenging features that need to be considered in moving forward with a research agenda. One such consideration is that of *levels*. Avolio (2004), for example, has commented that leadership development is inherently a multilevel process. Relevant levels to consider include within-person and between-person; higher dyadic levels involving relationships with followers, peers, and subordinates; as well as team and organizational levels. Going forward, researchers will need to be very clear as to the appropriate level(s) in which they are working and to choose the type of research design, measures, and analyses that are most suitable for the respective focus. In particular, it appears that cross-level approaches (e.g., effects of organizations and teams on individuals) hold great promise for furthering our understanding of developmental processes.

Leadership development also is a dynamic and longitudinal process, which inherently involves the consideration of *time*. As noted at the beginning of this chapter, we need better theory and more research that explicitly address time and the specification of when things occur (Mitchell & James, 2001). There is no area of research where this is truer than leadership development. As noted, the development of leaders can be conceptualized as a process occurring across the entire adult life span (Day et al., 2009). Clearly there are limits in terms of what any one research study can tackle in terms of time frame; however, it is encouraging to see studies such as the Fullerton Longitudinal Study (Gottfried et al., in press; Guerin et al., in press) that are adopting more of a life span development perspective in addressing issues related to leader development. Going forward, acknowledging the longitudinal feature of leader development will ideally challenge researchers to give careful attention to when they measure things, how often they measure, and how many times they measure, and linking these measurement concerns with a theoretical framework that lays out when (and how) developmental changes are thought to unfold. This is indeed a high standard for researchers, but is one that is likely to reap huge dividends in terms of better understanding leader development and ultimately devising ways to accelerate the underlying processes.

Another research recommendation is to more fully consider the *individualized* nature of development. Leaders do not develop in the same way, following identical growth patterns (e.g., Day & Sin, in press). People often learn different things from the same experience, and some learn the key lessons of experience more readily than others. Methodological and analytical approaches that take a more individualized approach to leader development will likely yield more insight than those that only attempt to model average trends across a given sample (see chapter 3 of this volume for additional details on methods in leadership research).

Raudenbush (2001) has proposed a personal trajectory approach to developmental research. Although it may be infeasible to conceptualize and model a unique trajectory for each and every developing leader, there are other individualized approaches such as group-based modeling of development (Nagin, 2005) and growth mixture modeling (Wang & Bodner, 2007) that can identify and potentially predict different latent trajectory classes. These are powerful techniques that can help researchers better understand the individualized nature of leader development, especially when used in conjunction with informed decisions about time and the timing of key processes, and rigorous theorizing about the appropriate levels on which development is thought to occur.

Related to the individualized nature of development is how motivated or ready (or not) someone is for maximizing developmental opportunities. The general term for this state is *developmental readiness* and, unfortunately, there is not much empirically based research on the topic in the leader development literature. If the focus is on enhancing the likelihood of learning from a developmental experience, then having a relatively strong learning goal orientation (Dweck, 1986) would likely be an important consideration. What is unclear is to what extent a learning goal orientation is a trait (stable across time) or a state (variable to situational demands) phenomenon (DeShon & Gillespie, 2005). Ideally, the factors associated with developmental readiness are things that can be intervened on prior to an individual engaging in a developmental project, which makes general cognitive ability or personality unlikely candidates in practice. But what is needed first is theory-driven research that links various malleable individual differences variables with initial levels (intercepts) and trajectories (slopes) of development over time.

Practice

There is a longstanding perspective that leaders are ill-prepared to handle future challenges. Drucker (1995) noted some time ago that no more than one third of executive selection decisions turn out right, about one third are minimally effective, and fully one third are outright failures. The distressing aspect of these estimates is that even though leadership development is a strategic human capital concern of many organizations, current and past data suggest that it is not being done very effectively.

One issue that has undermined the effectiveness of leadership development initiatives is the focus on relatively short-term, episodic-based thinking in terms of how development occurs. Too often the thinking about leadership development has viewed it as a series of unconnected, discrete programs, with little assistance in integrating across these developmental episodes (Vicere & Fulmer, 1998). Contemporary thinking about leadership development views it as a continuous and ongoing process throughout the adult life span (Day et al., 2009). In short, just about any experience has the potential to contribute to learning and development and will likely do so to the extent that it incorporates aspects of assessment, challenge, and support (Van Velsor & McCauley, 2004).

The primary focus in the field is on developing individual leader skills; however, there is no guarantee that better leadership will result. After all, leadership involves a dynamic social interaction within a given situational context. Thus, effective followers are needed along with effective leaders (Hollander, 2009). In addition, leadership development will likely require intervention at more collective group, team, or organizational levels. Despite the distinction drawn here and in other places between leader development and leadership development (e.g., Day, 2000), it is not an either-or proposition. Instead, state-of-the-art initiatives seek to find ways to link individual leader development with more collective leadership development to enhance overall leadership capacity in teams and organizations.

Conclusions

There are good reasons to be hopeful about the future of leadership development, especially on the scientific side of the scientist-practitioner equation. During the past decade there has been increasing attention paid to theorizing about leadership development processes, especially in terms of moving beyond any single, bounded theoretical approach to conceptualizing leadership. It is an inherently dynamic, multilevel, and multidisciplinary process, and as such it makes sense to build theoretical frameworks that reflect these features.

Although the absolute number of empirically based publications on the general topic of leadership development is still relatively small, it is a growing area that is beginning to contribute to a stronger evidence-based understanding of important aspects of the leadership development process. It is also encouraging to note the increasing attention to using longitudinal designs in the study of leadership development. But it is a daunting task going forward because of the lengthy time frame involved in the development of leaders and because of all the interrelated issues associated with development. But rather than posing a threat, these issues present a wealth of opportunities for researchers. There are countless possible issues to investigate; however, one thing is certain, and that is that single-shot, survey-based research designs are unlikely to add much value to this nascent science of leadership development. Research designs that incorporate multiple measurement perspectives, mixed methods, as well as a longitudinal component are more likely to provide scientific insight to the leadership development process.

Given the recent evidence that the practice of leadership development is slipping in terms of perceived quality and added value in organizations (Howard & Wellins, 2008), it may be time to take a step back and rethink what is needed to better support an evidence-based approach to leadership development. Specifically, what may be most needed is not only strong, continuing interest in the field theoretically and empirically, but also systematic efforts devoted to translating ideas into action and science into sound practice.

Discussion Questions

1. Are there certain kinds of leaders who are "high potential?" If so, what makes them so and what are the kinds of knowledge, skills, abilities and other factors that they would have relative to others?

2. Were there any particular experiences that you learned a great deal from in terms of leadership? If so, what were they and what made them so impactful in terms of learning? When have you found it most difficult to learn from experience?

3. What are some of the unanswered questions in the field of leadership development? In other words, what are some things we need to know about leadership development that we do not know at present?

4. In your estimation, what are reasonable estimates on the return on investment (ROI) for leadership development in financial and non-financial terms? What are your reasons for these estimates?

Notes and Case Studies

Datar, S. M., Garvin, D. A., & Knoop, C.-I. (2009, May). *The Center for Creative Leadership*. Harvard Business School note (#9–308–013).

Snook, S. A. (2008, June). *Leader(ship) development*. Harvard Business School note (#9–408–064).

Leadership Development in the Military:
http://www.slideshare.net/hcsugarman/a-case-study-in-leadership-development-u-s-navy

Leadership Development in the Private Sector:
http://www.thiagi.com/leadership-development-case-study.html

Leadership Development in the Public Sector:
http://www.idea.gov.uk/idk/core/page.do?pageId=7116876

Supplementary Readings

Conger, J. A., & Fulmer, R. M. (2003). Developing your leadership pipeline. *Harvard Business Review, 81*(12), 56–64.

Hannah, S. T., & Avolio, B. J. (2010). Ready or not: How do we accelerate the developmental readiness of leaders? *Journal of Organizational Behavior*. Retrieved from www.interscience.wiley.com; DOI: 10.1002/job.675

Ready, D. A., & Conger, J. A. (2003). Why leadership development efforts fail. *MIT Sloan Management Review, 44*(3), 83–88.

Thomas, R. J. (2008). Crucibles of leadership development. *MIT Sloan Management Review, 49*(3), 15–18.

References

Antonioni, D. (1994). The effects of feedback accountability on upward appraisal ratings. *Personnel Psychology, 47*, 349–356.

Arvey, R. D., Rotundo, M., Johnson, W., Zhang, Z., & McGue, M. (2006). The determinants of leadership role occupancy: Genetic and personality factors. *The Leadership Quarterly, 17*, 1–20.

Arvey, R. D., Zhang, Z., Avolio, B. J., & Krueger, R. F. (2007). Developmental and genetic determinants of leadership role occupancy among women. *Journal of Applied Psychology, 92,* 693–706.

Atwater, L. E., Dionne, S. D., Avolio, B., Camobreco, J. F., & Lau, A. W. (1999). A longitudinal study of the leadership development process: Individual differences predicting leader effectiveness. *Human Relations, 52,* 1543–1562.

Avolio, B. J. (2004). Examining the Full Range Model of leadership: Looking back to transform forward. In D. V. Day, S. J. Zaccaro, & S. M. Halpin (Eds.), *Leader development for transforming organizations: Growing leaders for tomorrow* (pp. 71–98). Mahwah, NJ: Lawrence Erlbaum.

Avolio, B. J. (2007). Promoting more integrative strategies for leadership theory-building. *American Psychologist, 62,* 25–33.

Avolio, B. J., & Gardner, W. L. (2005). Authentic leadership development: Getting to the roots of positive forms of leadership. *The Leadership Quarterly, 16,* 315–338.

Avolio, B. J., & Gibbons, T. C. (1988). Developing transformational leaders: A life span approach. In J. A. Conger, R. N. Kanungo, & Associates (Eds.), *Charismatic leadership: The elusive factor in organizational effectiveness* (pp. 276–308). San Francisco: Jossey-Bass.

Avolio, B. J., Reichard, R. J., Hannah, S. T., Walumbwa, F. O., & Chan, A. (2009). A meta-analytic review of leadership impact research: Experimental and quasi-experimental studies. *The Leadership Quarterly, 20,* 764–784.

Avolio, B. J., Rotundo, M., & Walumbwa, F. O. (2009). Early life experiences as determinants of leadership role occupancy: The importance of parental influence and rule breaking behavior. *The Leadership Quarterly, 20,* 329–342.

Avolio, B. J., Sosik, J. J., Jung, D. I., & Berson, Y. (2003). Leadership models, methods, and applications. In W. C. Borman, D. R. Ilgen, & R. J. Klimoski (Eds.), *Handbook of psychology: Industrial and organizational psychology* (Vol. 12, pp. 277–307). Hoboken, NJ: John Wiley.

Baltes, P. B. (1987). Theoretical propositions of life-span developmental psychology: On the dynamics between growth and decline. *Developmental Psychology, 23,* 611–626.

Baltes, P. B. (1997). On the incomplete architecture of human ontogeny: Selection, optimization, and compensation as foundation of developmental theory. *American Psychologist, 52,* 366–380.

Baltes, P. B., & Baltes, M. M. (1990). Psychological perspectives on successful aging: The model of selective optimization with compensation. In P. B. Baltes & M. M. Baltes (Eds.), *Successful aging: Perspectives from the behavioral sciences* (pp. 1–34). New York: Cambridge University Press.

Bartone, P. T., Snook, S., Forsythe, G. B., Lewis, P., & Bullis, R. C. (2007). Psychosocial development and leader performance of military officer cadets. *The Leadership Quarterly, 18,* 490–504.

Bartone, P. T., Snook, S. A., & Tremble, J. T. R. (2002). Cognitive and personality predictors of leader performance in West Point cadets. *Military Psychology, 14,* 321–338.

Bennis, W. (2007). The challenges of leadership in the modern world. *American Psychologist, 62,* 2–5.

Bloom, B. S. (Ed.). (1985). *Developing talent in young people.* New York: Ballantine.

Bray, D. W. (1982). The assessment center and the study of lives. *American Psychologist, 37,* 180–189.

Bray, D. W., Campbell, R. J., & Grant, D. L. (1974). *Formative years in business: A long-term AT&T study of managerial lives.* New York: John Wiley.

Brehmer, B. (1980). In one word: Not from experience. *Acta Psychologica, 45,* 223–241.

Chan, K.-Y., & Drasgow, F. (2001). Toward a theory of individual differences and leadership: Understanding motivation to lead. *Journal of Applied Psychology, 86,* 481–498.

Chi, M. T. H., Glaser, R., & Farr, M. J. (Eds.). (1988). *The nature of expertise.* Hillsdale, NJ: Lawrence Erlbaum.

Conger, J. A. (2010). Developing leadership talent: Delivering on the promise of structured programs. In R. Silzer & B. E. Dowell (Eds.), *Strategy-driven talent management: A leadership imperative* (pp. 281–311). San Francisco: Jossey-Bass.

Conger, J. A., & Xin, K. (2000). Executive education in the 21st century. *Journal of Management Education, 24,* 73–101.

Cox, C. J., & Cooper, C. L. (1989). The making of the British CEO: Childhood, work, experience, personality, and management style. *Academy of Management Executive, 3,* 241–245.

Day, D. V. (2000). Leadership development: A review in context. *The Leadership Quarterly, 11,* 581–613.

Day, D. V. (2010). The difficulties of learning from experience and the need for deliberate practice. *Industrial and Organizational Psychology: Perspectives on Science and Practice, 3,* 41–44.

Day, D. V., Harrison, M. M., & Halpin, S. M. (2009). *An integrative approach to leader development: Connecting adult development, identity, and expertise.* New York: Routledge.

Day, D. V., & O'Connor, P. M. G. (2003). Leadership development: Understanding the process. In S. Murphy & R. Riggio (Eds.), *The future of leadership development* (pp. 11–28). Mahwah, NJ: Lawrence Erlbaum.

Day, D. V., & Sin, H.-P. (in press). Longitudinal tests of an integrative model of leader development: Charting and understanding developmental trajectories. *The Leadership Quarterly.*

Day, D. V., & Zaccaro, S. J. (2004). Toward a science of leader development. In D. V. Day, S. J. Zaccaro, & S. M. Halpin (Eds.), *Leader development for transforming organizations: Growing leaders for tomorrow* (pp. 383–399). Mahwah, NJ: Lawrence Erlbaum.

DeRue, D. S., & Wellman, N. (2009). Developing leaders via experience: The role of developmental challenges, learning orientation, and feedback availability. *Journal of Applied Psychology, 94,* 859–875.

DeShon, R. P., & Gillespie, J. Z. (2005). A motivated action theory account of goal orientation. *Journal of Applied Psychology, 90,* 1096–1127.

Drath, W. H., McCauley, C. D., Palus, C. J., Van Velsor, E., O'Connor, P. M. G., & McGuire, J. B. (2008). Direction, alignment, commitment: Toward a more integrative ontology of leadership. *The Leadership Quarterly, 19,* 635–653.

Drucker, P. F. (1995). *Managing in a time of great change.* New York: Truman Talley Books/Dutton.

Dweck, C. S. (1986). Motivational processes affecting learning. *American Psychologist, 41,* 1040–1048.

Dweck, C. S., & Leggett, E. L. (1988). A social cognitive approach to motivation and learning. *Psychological Review, 95,* 256–273.

Elliott, E. S., & Dweck, C. S. (1988). Goals: An approach to motivation and achievement. *Journal of Personality and Social Psychology, 54,* 5–12.

Ericsson, K. A., & Charness, N. (1994). Expert performance: Its structure and acquisition. *American Psychologist, 49,* 725–747.

Ericsson, K. A., Charness, N., Feltovich, P. J., & Hoffman, R. R. (Eds.). (2006). *The Cambridge handbook of expertise and expert performance.* New York: Cambridge University Press.

Ericsson, K. A., Krampe, R. T., & Tesch-Römer, C. (1993). The role of deliberate practice in the acquisition of expert performance. *Psychological Review, 100,* 363–406.

Ericsson, K. A., Prietula, M. J., & Cokely, E. T. (2007, July-August). The making of an expert. *Harvard Business Review, 85,* 114–121.

Feldman, J. (1986). On the difficulty of learning from experience. In H. P. Sims, Jr. & D. A. Gioia (Eds.), *The thinking organization: Dynamics of organizational social cognition* (pp. 263–292). San Francisco: Jossey-Bass.

Frese, M., Beimel, S., & Schoenborn, S. (2003). Action training for charismatic leadership: Two evaluations of studies of a commercial training module on inspirational communication of a vision. *Personnel Psychology, 56,* 671–697.

Freund, A. M., & Baltes, P. B. (1998). Selection, optimization, and compensation as strategies of life management: Correlations with subjective indicators of successful aging. *Psychology and Aging, 13,* 531–543.

Freund, A. M., & Baltes, P. B. (2002). Life-management strategies of selection, optimization, and compensation: Measurement by self-report and construct validity. *Journal of Personality and Social Psychology, 82,* 642–662.

Gardner, W. L., Avolio, B. J., Luthans, F., May, D. R., & Walumbwa, F. (2005). "Can you see the real me?" A self-based model of authentic leader and follower development. *The Leadership Quarterly, 16,* 343–372.

Gottfried, A. E., Gottfried, A. W., Reichard, R. J., Guerin, D. W., Oliver, P. H., & Riggio, R. E. (in press). Motivational roots of leadership: A longitudinal study from childhood through adulthood. *The Leadership Quarterly.*

Guerin, D. W., Oliver, P. H., Gottfried, A. W., Gottfried, A. E., Reichard, R. J., & Riggio, R. E. (in press). Childhood and adolescent antecedents of social skills and leadership potential in adulthood: Temperamental approach/withdrawal and extraversion. *The Leadership Quarterly.*

Guthrie, V. A., & King, S. N. (2004). Feedback-intensive programs. In C. D. McCauley & E. Van Velsor (Eds.), *The Center for Creative Leadership handbook of leadership development* (2nd ed., pp. 25–57). San Francisco: Jossey-Bass.

Gutiérrez, M., & Tasse, T. (2007). Leading with theory: Using a theory of change approach for leadership development evaluations. In K. M. Hannum & J. W. Martineau (Eds.), *The handbook of leadership development evaluation* (pp. 48–70). San Francisco: Jossey-Bass.

Hackman, J. R., & Wageman, R. (2007). Asking the right questions about leadership. *American Psychologist, 62,* 43–47.

Hollander, E. P. (2009). *Inclusive leadership: The essential leader-follower relationship.* New York: Routledge.

Hollenbeck, G. P., McCall, M. W., Jr., & Silzer, R. F. (2006). Leadership competency models. *The Leadership Quarterly, 17,* 398–413.

Howard, A., & Wellins, R. S. (2008). *Global leadership forecast 2008|2009: Overcoming the shortfalls in developing leaders.* Pittsburgh, PA: Development Dimensions International.

Judge, T. A., & Bono, J. E. (2000). Five-factor model of personality and transformational leadership. *Journal of Applied Psychology, 85,* 751–765.

Judge, T. A., Bono, J. E., Ilies, R., & Gerhardt, M. W. (2002). Personality and leadership: A qualitative and quantitative review. *Journal of Applied Psychology, 87,* 765–780.

Kegan, R. (1982). *The evolving self: Problem and process in human development.* Cambridge, MA: Harvard University Press.

Kegan, R. (1994). *In over our heads: The mental demands of modern life.* Cambridge, MA: Harvard University Press.

Kluger, A. N., & DeNisi, A. (1996). The effects of feedback on performance: A historical review, a meta-analysis, and a preliminary feedback intervention. *Psychological Bulletin, 119,* 254–284.

Lahey, L., Souvaine, E., Kegan, R., Goodman, R., & Felix, S. (1988). *A guide to the subject-object interview: Its administration and interpretation.* Cambridge, MA: Harvard University Graduate School of Education.

Lamoureux, K. (2007, July). *High-impact leadership development: Best practices, vendor profiles and industry solutions.* Oakland, CA: Bersin & Associates.

Lapour, A. S., & Heppner, M. J. (2009). Social class privilege and adolescent women's perceived career options. *Journal of Counseling Psychology, 56,* 477–494.

Li, W.-D., Arvey, R. D., & Song, Z. (in press). The influence of general mental ability, self-esteem and family socioeconomic status on leadership role occupancy and leader advancement: The moderating role of gender. *The Leadership Quarterly.*

Lord, R. G., & Hall, R. J. (2005). Identity, deep structure, and the development of leadership skill. *The Leadership Quarterly, 16,* 591–615.

Luthans, F., & Avolio, B. (2003). Authentic leadership development. In K. S. Cameron, J. E. Dutton, & R. E. Quinn (Eds.), *Positive organizational scholarship: Foundations of a new discipline* (pp. 241–258). San Francisco: Berrett-Koehler.

Luthar, S. S. (2003). The culture of affluence: Psychological costs of material wealth. *Child Development, 74,* 1581–1593.

Luthar, S. S., & Becker, B. E. (2002). Privileged but pressured? A study of affluent youth. *Child Development, 73,* 1593–1610.

Marquardt, M. J., Leonard, H. S., Freedman, A. M., & Hill, C. C. (2009). *Action learning for developing leaders and organizations: Principles, strategies, and cases.* Washington, DC: American Psychological Association.

McArdle, J. J. (2009). Latent variable modeling of differences and changes with longitudinal data. *Annual Review of Psychology, 60,* 577–605.

McCall, M. W., Jr. (2010). Recasting leadership development. *Industrial and Organizational Psychology: Perspectives on Science and Practice, 3,* 3–19.

McCall, M. W., Jr., Lombardo, M. M., & Morrison, A. M. (1988). *The lessons of experience: How successful executives develop on the job.* Lexington, MA: Lexington Books.

McCauley, C. D., Drath, W. H., Palus, C. J., O'Connor, P. M. G., & Baker, B. A. (2006). The use of constructive-developmental theory to advance the understanding of leadership. *The Leadership Quarterly, 17,* 634–653.

McCauley, C. D., Ruderman, M. N., Ohlott, P. J., & Morrow, J. E. (1994). Assessing the developmental components of managerial jobs. *Journal of Applied Psychology, 79,* 544–560.

Means, R. L. (1965). Weber's thesis of the Protestant ethic: The ambiguities of received doctrine. *Journal of Religion, 45,* 1–11.

Mitchell, T. R., & James, L. R. (2001). Building better theory: Time and the specification of when things happen. *Academy of Management Review, 26,* 530–547.

Mumford, M. D., & Manley, G. R. (2003). Putting the development in leadership development: Implications for theory and practice. In S. E. Murphy & R. E. Riggio (Eds.), *The future of leadership development* (pp. 237–261). Mahwah, NJ: Lawrence Erlbaum.

Mumford, M. D., Zaccaro, S. J., Connelly, M. S., & Marks, M. A. (2000). Leadership skills: Conclusions and future directions. *The Leadership Quarterly, 11,* 155–170.

Mumford, T. V., Campion, M. A., & Morgeson, F. P. (2007). The leadership skills strataplex: Leadership skill requirements across organizational levels. *The Leadership Quarterly, 18,* 154–166.

Muthén, B. (2004). Latent variable analysis: Growth mixture modeling and related techniques for longitudinal data. In D. Kaplan (Ed.), *Handbook of quantitative methodology for the social sciences* (pp. 345–368). Thousand Oaks, CA: Sage.

Nagin, D. S. (1999). Analyzing developmental trajectories: A semiparametric, group-based approach. *Psychological Methods, 4,* 139–157.

Nagin, D. S. (2005). *Group-based modeling of development.* Cambridge, MA: Harvard University Press.

Ohlott, P. J., Ruderman, M. N., & McCauley, C. D. (1994). Gender differences in managers' developmental job experiences. *Academy of Management Journal, 37,* 46–67.

O'Leonard, K. (2008). *The corporate learning factbook 2008: Statistics, benchmarks, and analysis of the U.S. corporate training market.* Oakland, CA: Bersin & Associates.

Plomin, R., DeFries, J. C., & Loehlin, J. C. (1977). Genotype-environment interaction and correlation in the analysis of human behavior. *Psychological Bulletin, 84,* 309–322.

Raudenbush, S. W. (2001). Comparing personal trajectories and drawing causal inferences from longitudinal data. *Annual Review of Psychology, 52,* 501–525.

Rest, J. R. (1986). *Moral development: Advances in research and theory.* New York: Praeger.

Revans, R. W. (1980). *Action learning.* London: Blond & Briggs.

Schippmann, J. S., Ash, R. A., Battista, M., Carr, L., Eyde, L. D., Hesketh, B., et al. (2000). The practice of competency modeling. *Personnel Psychology, 53,* 703–740.

Schmidt, F. L., Hunter, J. E., & Outerbridge, A. N. (1986). Impact of job experience and ability on job knowledge, work sample performance, and supervisory ratings of job performance. *Journal of Applied Psychology, 71,* 432–439.

Smither, J. W., London, M., Flautt, R., Vargas, Y., & Kuchine, I. (2003). Can working with an executive coach improve multisource feedback ratings over time? A quasi-experimental field study. *Personnel Psychology, 56,* 23–44.

Smither, J. W., London, M., & Reilly, R. R. (2005). Does performance improve following multisource feedback? A theoretical model, meta-analysis, and review of empirical findings. *Personnel Psychology, 58,* 33–66.

Summers, B., Williamson, T., & Read, D. (2004). Does method of acquisition affect the quality of expert judgment? A comparison of education with on-the-job learning. *Journal of Occupational & Organizational Psychology, 77*, 237–258.

Tesluk, P. E., & Jacobs, R. R. (1998). Toward an integrated model of work experience. *Personnel Psychology, 51*, 321–355.

Van Velsor, E., & McCauley, C. D. (2004). Our view of leadership development. In C. D. McCauley & E. Van Velsor (Eds.), *The Center for Creative Leadership handbook of leadership development* (2nd ed., pp. 1–22). San Francisco: Jossey-Bass.

Van Velsor, E., Moxley, R. S., & Bunker, K. A. (2004). The leader development process. In C. D. McCauley & E. Van Velsor (Eds.), *The Center for Creative Leadership handbook of leadership development* (2nd ed., pp. 204–233). San Francisco: Jossey-Bass.

Vicere, A. A., & Fulmer, R. M. (1998). *Leadership by design.* Boston: Harvard Business School.

Walker, A. G., & Smither, J. W. (1999). A five-year study of upward feedback: What managers do with their results matters. *Personnel Psychology, 52*, 393–423.

Wang, M., & Bodner, T. E. (2007). Growth mixture modeling: Identifying and predicting unobserved subpopulations with longitudinal data. *Organizational Research Methods, 10*, 635–656.

Yost, P. R., & Mannion Plunket, M. (2010). Developing leadership talent through experiences. In R. Silzer & B. E. Dowell (Eds.), *Strategy-driven talent management: A leadership imperative* (pp. 313–348). San Francisco: Jossey-Bass.

Zaccaro, S. J., & Horn, Z. N. J. (2003). Leadership theory and practice: Fostering an effective symbiosis. *The Leadership Quarterly, 14*, 769–806.

Zhang, Z., Ilies, R., & Arvey, R. D. (2009). Beyond genetic explanations for leadership: The moderating role of the social environment. *Organizational Behavior and Human Decision Processes, 110*, 118–128.

5

The Nature in Leadership

Evolutionary, Biological, and Social Neuroscience Perspectives

Mark Van Vugt

VU University Amsterdam

University of Oxford

When a honey bee returns to its hive after foraging for nectar, it performs a dance for the other bees. The bee skips around making a figure-eight movement, waggling its abdomen as it does so. In 2005, scientists found out that the dancer is indicating through its moves the location and quality of a foraging site (Riley, Greggers, Smith, Reynolds, & Menzel, 2005). The direction the bee is facing points to the direction of the food source relative to the sun; the duration of the waggle dance represents how far the source lies and its quality. Scientists proved it by setting up artificial food sources and monitoring the behavior of the bees that scrutinized a waggle dance. When the hive was moved 250 meters, the follower bees flew to a site that was 250 meters away from the artificial source, proving that the follower bees were following navigational instructions encoded in the waggle dance. It proved a theory first put forward by the Nobel Prize–winning biologist, Karl von Frisch, in the 1960s. The dancer bee is in fact acting as a leader by scouting out food resources for the hive. The best dancers recruit the most followers, and this interaction produces a very efficient group performance.

AUTHOR'S NOTE: Please address correspondence concerning this chapter to Mark Van Vugt, VU University Amsterdam/University of Oxford, van der Boechorsstraat 1, 1081 BT Amsterdam, the Netherlands. e-mail: m.van.vugt@psy.vu.nl.

The waggle dance of the honey bee is one of many leadership and follow-ership displays that take place in the animal kingdom, from the migration patterns of relatively brainless species, such as fish, to food sharing among our brainier primate cousins, the chimpanzees.

Humans are animals too. Although our leadership patterns are, in many ways, more sophisticated than that of our animal relatives, maybe there are lessons to be learned from taking a closer look at the evolutionary history of leadership. In this chapter, I will explain why leadership might have emerged in various social species, such as ours, and what forms it takes. Questions about the origins and evolved functions of leadership are seldom asked by social scientists studying leadership. They tend to be primarily interested in the mechanics of leadership—How does it work?—rather than questions about the nature of leadership.

Yet there is an increasing awareness among leadership theorists of the importance in building a comprehensive theory by integrating knowledge from the natural, biological, and social sciences that all have something inter-esting to say about leadership (Antonakis, 2011; Bennis, 2007; Hogan & Kaiser, 2005). For instance, anthropologists, biologists, cognitive neuroscien-tists, economists, political scientists, primatologists, psychologists, and zoolo-gists have been studying various aspect of leadership emergence; yet so far, there has been very little cross-fertilization between these areas in developing models and theories of leadership that are consistent with each other (King, Johnson, & Van Vugt, 2009). In addition, social scientists studying leadership have provided many good middle-level theories—such as personality, cogni-tive, situational, and contingency theories of leadership (for excellent recent reviews, see Avolio, Walumbwa, & Weber, 2009; Graen & Uhl-Bien, 1995; Hackman & Wageman, 2007; Yukl, 2006)—yet they are often not very well connected to higher order theories (cf. Bennis, 2007; Van Vugt, Hogan, & Kaiser, 2008).

Evolutionary theory (as I will explain shortly) may provide such an over-arching framework that can connect these separate lines of inquiry. Darwin's theory of evolution through natural selection (1871) makes clear that human psychology is ultimately a product of biological evolution—in the same way that our bodies are evolutionary products—consisting of many different traits that evolved because they enabled our ancestors to cope better with the demands of the environments in which they were living.

In this chapter, I will put forward a new theoretical perspective on leadership—evolutionary leadership theory, or ELT—which is guided by the principles of Darwin's evolutionary theory, and explains how our leadership and followership psychology may have been shaped through natural selection pressures. I will define leadership broadly here in terms of a process of influ-ence to achieve coordination between individuals for the pursuit of mutual goals. In this chapter, I will first provide a very brief introduction into evolu-tionary theory and focus in particular on the growing field of evolutionary psychology. This field applies Darwinian thinking to human psychology and behavior. Second, I will argue why evolutionary psychology may be particularly relevant for understanding leadership and will address the likely evolved functions of leadership. Third, I will present evidence from across the behavioral sciences—from biology to psychology, and from cognitive neuroscience to game theory—suggesting that leadership and followership may be psychological adaptations—evolved mechanisms—for solving coordination problems between individuals. Much of this research is done by my collaborators and me, who work together in multidisciplinary teams around the world on various aspects of evolutionary leadership theory. Fourth, I will put forward a short, speculative natural history of leadership, addressing how leadership may have evolved in small steps from a rather crude device for synchronizing the activities of simple organisms to complex structures able to coordinate the activities of millions of individuals dispersed across space and time. Fifth and finally, I will address some implications of evolutionary leadership theory for developing research on leadership and good leadership practice.

The Evolutionary Psychology of Leadership

Evolutionary leadership theory starts with the recognition that the physiological, neurological, and psychological processes involved in producing human behavior are products of biological evolution. It follows, therefore, that conceptual insights of evolutionary theory, when applied with rigor and care, can produce novel discoveries about human behavior, too (Buss, 2005; Nicholson, 2000; Van Vugt & Schaller, 2008). Charles Darwin is the father of modern evolutionary theory. In his 19th-century voyage on the *Beagle* to the Galapagos Islands, Darwin noted that different species were beautifully adapted to their environments. After much study, he concluded that different species were not created by a divine hand, but they arose as a consequence of their environment. Members of a species displaying certain features—say, a giraffe boasting a long neck—flourished in their environment better than less well-equipped members—short-necked giraffes. A long-necked giraffe would have access to more food (leaves high in the tree tops), and this advantage would give long-necked members a survival advantage. This would result in differential reproduction: Long necks would out-reproduce short necks and, given enough time, long necks would become a universal feature of giraffes. This feature is then referred to as an adaptation. This, Darwin reasoned, explained why creatures seemed so perfectly suited to their environments.

Darwin postulated that natural selection operates via three very simple rules: (1) There is variation in traits between individuals within the same species; (2) some of this variation is heritable (which is why offspring resemble parents); and (3) some of these trait variations give individuals an edge in the competition for resources. These three rules form the backbone of evolutionary theory.

Darwin's insights have been proved right so many times that evolutionary theory is no longer treated as a hypothetical possibility but, rather, as a law of nature. To understand evolutionary theory, one does not necessarily need to know anything about biology, heritability, or genes. Yet it is good to realize, first, that adaptations (such as the giraffe's neck) are underpinned by genes. Any gene first emerges as a random mutation and usually only spreads through a population if it gives the organism an edge in the competition for resources. Thus, at some point in history, a baby giraffe was born with a spontaneous gene mutation giving him or her a longer neck than the other giraffes. Because this gene produced a giraffe that was better adapted to the environment, this particular gene survived, and over many generations, it has spread through the population such that every giraffe nowadays carries the "long neck" gene—in evolutionary terms, this trait has gone to fixation. It is also important to realize that when evolutionary biologists talk about a "gene for trait X," this is overly simplistic because most traits are underpinned by multiple genes operating in combination. Finally, when evolutionary biologists talk about "traits," they refer to any feature of an organism that is expressed when an organism's genes interact with their environment, including their morphology (such as height and eye color), neurophysiology (such as brain areas, neurotransmitters, and hormones), and behaviors (such as risk taking, sociability, and leadership). Natural selection can operate on any aspect of an organism's design, if it is under the control of genes. For further details on evolutionary theory and biology and evidence for evolution, I refer readers to popular science books written by distinguished evolutionary theorists such as Richard Dawkins (2009) and David Sloan Wilson (2007).

Evolutionary leadership theory is inspired by *evolutionary psychology*, which is a relatively new discipline that applies the principles of evolutionary theoretical biology to human psychology (Barkow, Cosmides, & Tooby, 1992; Buss, 2005; Schaller, Simpson, & Kenrick, 2006). Evolutionary psychology has the potential to integrate theory and research from different branches of psychology and connect it with knowledge from the biological and behavioral sciences to generate a unifying theoretical framework based on the premise of evolutionary theory. Its core tenet is that the human mind is a product of evolution through natural selection: Evolution has shaped the human brain (and its products in terms of hormones and behaviors) in the same way as it has shaped the human body and the bodies and minds of other animals. In effect, this means that humans are viewed as part of the animal kingdom and are subject to the same laws of biology and evolution.

Evolutionary psychology proposes that our brains contain many specialized cognitive mechanisms—or adaptations—that enable humans to solve many different problems affecting their reproductive success (Buss, 2005; Kenrick, Li, & Butner, 2003). For instance, humans likely possess specialized mechanisms for heat regulation, finding food, avoiding predators, searching for mates, face recognition, gossip, reputation, and dealing with strangers. These psychological mechanisms are likely to be functional and domain-specific, in the sense that they are good at solving particular problems and not others (Barrett & Kurzban, 2006). For instance, language is a highly efficient device for gossiping, but it is probably not so good for arousing positive emotions—laughter probably works much better for this purpose.

It is instructive to think of these mechanisms as evolved if–then decision rules that were selected to produce adaptive behaviors in fitness-relevant situations. An example of an evolved social decision rule would be something like: "Follow an individual whom you trust." (It is easy to see that this is a superior decision rule to that of "follow any individual," and it is therefore more likely to have evolved.) These psychological mechanisms were shaped through natural selection pressures operating in ancestral environments, which means that they may not necessarily produce adaptive behavior in modern environments. For instance, in ancestral times it could have been advantageous to follow a physically strong leader, but in today's society where physical strength matters less, this may not be adaptive anymore—or it may even be maladaptive. This constitutes what we refer to as an "evolutionary mismatch" (Van Vugt, Johnson, Kaiser, & O'Gorman, 2008).

Evolutionary psychology often uses the four questions approach, first coined by Aristotle and then further developed by the Nobel Prize–winning Dutch ethologist Niko Tinbergen (1963) to search for evidence of biological and psychological adaptations. For instance, to the question of why animals have vision, one answer would be that it helps them find food and avoid danger. This is the question about the evolutionary function of vision. An additional question concerns through what particular series of evolutionary steps vision evolved (phylogeny). Other questions concern the mechanics of the eye (form), and even the process of an individual's eyesight across his or her life span (ontogeny). The first two questions address the evolutionary explanations for a particular phenomenon (ultimate causes), and the second two address the proximate explanations. Although the answers to these questions are likely very different, they complement each other.

In the same way, we could ask about the function, phylogeny, form, and ontogeny of leadership to get a complete account of the phenomenon (Van Vugt, Hogan, et al., 2008). For instance, the first question is whether leadership and followership may have been instrumental in fostering the survival and reproduction rates of humans in ancestral environments, such that they became part of our evolved psychology. This question most interests evolutionary-minded biologists and psychologists. The second question is through what series of steps did leadership emerge in humans and other animals, and where were these traits present in a common ancestor (Brosnan, Newton-Fisher, & Van Vugt, 2009). This question most interests biologists, primatologists, and zoologists studying leadership. The third question concerns the mechanics of leadership—How does it work?—and this is what most interests social and industrial/organizational psychologists studying leadership. For instance, what kinds of people make good leaders or followers, and under what conditions is a particular leader style most effective? In terms of proximate mechanisms, we can also examine the neuroscience of leadership, examining what brain regions and hormonal factors are involved in producing leadership and followership behavior. For instance, individual differences in testosterone underlie the effectiveness of acting as a leader (Josephs, Sellers, Newman, & Metha, 2006), and a leader's punishment of group defectors produces higher activation in the brain reward regions (Fehr & Camerer, 2007).

The final question concerns the developmental aspects of leadership and asks questions such as whether some people are born leaders—given the complexity of this trait, there is unlikely to be a single gene for leadership!—or whether leadership is learned, and whether leadership styles vary as a function of age, experience, and so forth. This most interests developmental and personality psychologists studying leadership (Hogan, 2006; Simonton, 1994).

Each of Tinbergen's four questions analyzes leadership from a different angle, and together they offer a more complete account. Yet these questions should not be confused. Various well-established psychological theories assume, for instance, that leadership involves identifying obstacles between groups and their goals and then finding ways to remove these obstacles (Hackman & Walton, 1986; House, 1971). Such theories offer a proximate explanation for leadership because they identify which particular leaders emerge and are effective in particular situations. For example, a directive leader is more effective when tasks are stressful or ambiguous. These theories can be complemented with questions about the evolved functions of leadership—for instance, How and why did the capacity for directive leadership evolve? Again, it is very important not to confuse these levels of explanations. For instance, if we find that people are attracted to charismatic leadership, we still need to explain why charismatic leadership emerged in the first place and how it evolved. Did it perhaps coevolve with the capacity for language some 100,000 to 200,000 years ago (Van Vugt, 2006)?

The Coevolution of Leadership and the Social Brain

Humans are ultrasocial animals (Baumeister & Leary, 1995; E. O. Wilson, 1975). For most of our history—the genus Homo is approximately between two and two and a half million years old—our ancestors lived on the African savannah in small, highly interdependent, interconnected hunter-gatherer societies that were relatively egalitarian (Richerson & Boyd, 2006). Group living is an adaptation. For many species, group life is a buffer against the perturbations of the natural environment, so this creates selection pressures for mechanisms fostering social interaction and group coordination. Living in groups poses significant challenges, and to deal with these requires relatively big brains.

The social brain hypothesis (Dunbar, 2004; Van Vugt & Kameda, in press) argues that early humans evolved large brains in order to survive and thrive in large, complex social groups. In support of the social brain hypothesis, comparative studies have found a positive correlation between the size of the neocortex (the thinking part of the brain) and group size when comparing humans with other primates and comparing primates with other mammals (Dunbar, 2004). Humans come out on top, having both a relatively large neocortex and large social network size. From the brain data, the extrapolated maximum social network size for humans is approximately 150 individuals, also known as Dunbar's number. This corresponds roughly to the size of a small community like a neighborhood or religious society, which can be held together through informal social control. Incidentally, 150 is the number of seats in the parliament of the Netherlands—a highly egalitarian country. It is also the median number of recipients on people's Christmas card lists, according to a U.K. study (Hill & Dunbar, 2003).

Early humans may have reaped the benefits of large social networks in terms of getting and sharing food, protection, information sharing, and perhaps communal parenting (Kenrick et al., 2003). Yet, with these benefits also came substantial costs of managing and maintaining large social networks. To reap the benefits and avoid the costs of increasingly large and complex social networks, a host of psychological adaptations likely evolved. Some of these are uniquely human, such as the capacity for language and religion. Other traits were co-opted and served new purposes, such as the capacity for intelligence, laughter, culture, and perhaps leadership.

Why did early humans need leadership? Phylogenetically speaking, perhaps the most ancient leadership problem is group movement (as a nomadic species, early human groups were always on the move). House's (1971) path-goal theory acknowledges this primary function of leadership: Effective leaders clarify the path to help their followers get from where they are to where they want to be, and they make the journey along the path easier by removing roadblocks. Our ancestors needed to move in search of resources, and the risk of predator attacks made it functional to move together as a group (King et al., 2009). But how does a group decide when to go where? This coordination problem can be solved easily by some individuals seizing the initiative and others following in their footsteps. Leadership in group movement has been documented throughout the animal kingdom, from the social insects to fish, birds, and mammals (for a review see King et al., 2009), suggesting that it does not require a lot of brain power. A simple decision rule, such as "If one individual moves, I move along," can produce something akin to followership and, by default, leadership. If we assume stable individual differences in adhering to this decision rule—some individuals will always make a first move—it will automatically produce "leaders" and "followers."

Once these rudimentary mechanisms are there, they can easily be co-opted in brainier species to solve a wider range of problems. Evolutionary leadership theory suggests at least six crucial fitness problems in ancestral environments selecting for leadership: (1) finding resources, (2) conflict management, (3) warfare, (4) building alliances, (5) resource distribution, and (6) teaching (Van Vugt & Ahuja, 2010). The first problem concerns exploring resource opportunities, and the honey bee example shows that worker bees take on leadership roles as scouts in pointing the group to explore new foraging sites.

Something akin to scout leaders can be found in hunter-gatherer societies—regarded as models of early human group life (Foley, 1997)—where individuals move around in hunting parties in search of food.

The second problem concerns conflict management and selects for peace leaders. Living in relatively large groups intensifies conflict between individuals. The social lives of our hunter-gatherer ancestors involved constant conflict, and homicide must have been a leading cause of death (Alexander, 1979; Chagnon, 1997; Van Vugt, De Cremer, & Janssen, 2007). Our closest phylogenetic relatives—the great apes: chimpanzees, bonobos, and gorillas—practice peacekeeping. Therefore, we think it was almost surely a feature of early human groups as well (Boehm, 1999; De Waal, 1996). De Waal (1996) describes an instance of peacemaking leadership: "A quarrel between Mama and Spin got out of hand and ended in fighting and biting. Numerous apes rushed up to the two warring females and joined in the fray. A huge knot of fighting, screaming apes rolled around in the sand, until Luit [the alpha male] leapt in and literally beat them apart. He did not choose sides in the conflict, like others; instead anyone who continued to act received a blow from him" (p. 129).

A next set of adaptive problems that our ancestors faced would have been dealing with out-groups, which may have introduced a niche for war and alliance-building leaders (diplomats). In human evolution, increasingly large groups would have competed with one another for scarce resources such as water holes, food, and mates, and this may have induced severe intergroup conflict (Van Vugt et al., 2007). Archaeologists and anthropologists suggest that warfare created a strong selection pressure for the evolution of a range of important group behaviors such as coalitional aggression, altruism, loyalty, and intergroup behavior (Van Vugt & Hart, 2004). Leadership may play a role in coordinating group activities to defeat other groups. In war and in other external threats, it makes sense for groups to defer to a leader (Vroom & Jago, 1978). In traditional societies such as Native American tribes, different chiefs emerge in war or peacetime, depending on the relationship with other tribes (Johnson & Earle, 2000).

The fifth leadership niche concerns the allocation of scarce group resources, such as food and water. For instance, if a large animal is killed, how should the meat be distributed to ensure that everyone gets a share? This problem would have opened up opportunities for an individual to step in as resource allocator. In traditional societies, Big Men leaders emerge to take on these roles (Van Vugt, Hogan, et al., 2008).

The final adaptive problem is how to train and socialize individuals to become good group members who contribute to group survival and effectiveness. This requires leaders who can teach newcomers relevant knowledge about the physical and social environment and introduce them to the culture and social norms of a group.

In sum, evolutionary leadership theory (Van Vugt & Ahuja, 2010) assumes that leadership evolved as solutions to distinct coordination problems involving group movement for foraging (scouts), policing in groups (peace-keepers), organizing attacks against out-groups (war leaders), establishing peaceful alliances with other groups (diplomats), managing the group resources (managers), and socializing newcomers to become productive and loyal group members (teachers).

Successful execution of these leadership and followership roles in each of these domains would have enhanced the reproductive success of individuals and their groups. As a thought experiment, imagine two groups of humans living in the same region and competing for the same resources such as water holes, food, and safe sleeping sites. One group is characterized by internal discord and in-group violence, poor decision making, and poor socialization practices. The second is characterized by relative intragroup harmony, aggression toward out-groups, and good socialization practices. There is no doubt that over time, the second group will prevail and thus the genetic material underlying these adaptive behaviors will spread through the population—maybe via a combination of individual and group selection (D. S. Wilson, Van Vugt, & O'Gorman, 2008)—leading to the fixation of these traits.

Testing Evolutionary Hypotheses About Leadership: Darwin's Toolbox

Evolutionary psychology represents an enormously diverse set of theories, methods, and analytical perspectives (Buss, 2005; Van Vugt & Schaller, 2008). This conceptual and methodological diversity results, in part, from the fact that evolutionary psychology attracts contributions from scientists with an unusually diverse range of scholarly backgrounds—not just scholars with different kinds of training within psychology, but scholars from biology, primatology, zoology, anthropology, economics, political science, and many other academic disciplines. This diversity is a functional response to the high evidentiary standards that attend theories and hypotheses in evolutionary psychology. A truly convincing support for an evolutionary-informed theory or hypothesis about leadership needs to show not only that it is activated in evolutionarily-relevant situations but also that it functions in ways that would have promoted individuals' reproductive interests in ancestral times. The first part is relatively easy. The second part is hard.

Barring the unlikely invention of a time machine, it is impossible to collect behavioral data in ancestral environments or to empirically track the actual evolution of an alleged adaptation. Instead, evolutionary psychologists must rely on a multitude of other, often indirect sources of evidence to build an evolutionary theory of leadership (Schmitt & Pilcher, 2004).

Evolutionary scientists frequently begin with a general theory—often from the core principles of evolutionary biology—that heuristically guides their attention toward potential psychological adaptations. Common theories used by evolutionary psychologists include parental investment theory, inclusive fitness theory, life-history theory, costly signaling theory, and evolutionary game theory (Gangestad & Simpson, 2007). If a hypothesized adaptation such as leadership flows directly from a theory under the general paradigm of evolution, then evolutionary psychologists can express more confidence in the existence of an adaptation. For instance, a higher parental investment from females leads to the hypothesis that women are interested in sexual partners who can provide resources and that males signal their mate value through achieving high-status positions—because status is linked to resources. This yields testable predictions about leadership, such that (1) women should find male leaders (sexually) more attractive and (2) men should enact leadership behaviors in the presence of (attractive) women. We are currently testing these predictions in our evolutionary social and organizational psychology laboratory (ESOP) at the VU University.

Second, evolutionary theorists can apply computer simulations to study the evolution of various group dynamic processes such as leadership and followership. Simulation studies suggest that leadership evolves quicker when the interests of individual agents are aligned, versus conflicting (Van Vugt & Kurzban, 2007). Computer simulations also help in identifying conditions under which democratic leaders produce better results than dictatorial leaders—for instance, when followers have exit options (Van Vugt, Jepson, Hart, & De Cremer, 2004).

Third, experimental methods of behavioral economics and social psychology are also useful in testing evolutionary hypotheses about leadership. The experimental (economics) games method studies interactions between players in games such as the prisoner's dilemma game, the ultimatum game, the dictator game, and the public goods game in which players allocate money. This can produce insights into many questions, for instance, regarding which personality types are more likely to take the lead in games with or without a conflict of interest between players.

Fourth, evidence for any hypothesized leadership and followership adaptation may emerge from recent advances in neuroscience. The nascent field of neuroeconomics applies neuroscience tools to economic games (Fehr & Camerer, 2007). Brain imaging studies, for instance, have the potential to provide data attesting to specific physiological structures associated with specific kinds of social behaviors (Adolphs, 1999). For instance, fMRI research can be used to detect where there is brain activity when leaders successfully coordinate group activities, make fair allocation offers, or punish individuals harming group goals (Fehr & Camerer, 2007). A very recent technique called TMS, or transcranial magnetic simulation, has emerged that disrupts activity in brain areas thought to be responsible for social and economic decisions. This technique has found, for example, that disruption of the left frontal precortex hinders people's ability to build a favorable reputation, with important implications for leadership emergence (Knoch, Schneider, Schunk, Hohmann, & Fehr, 2009).

Hormonal studies can help identify the hormonal correlates of particular leadership or followership experiences. Individual differences in baseline hormone levels, such as testosterone, predict how well individuals perform in high-status positions. Josephs et al., (2006) showed in an experimental study that high-testosterone individuals do better on a complex cognitive task in a high-status position, whereas low-testosterone individuals performed better on this task in a low-status position. In addition, research suggests that when individuals climb up in the hierarchy of their group, their testosterone levels increase to make them look more leader like (Van Vugt, 2006). We expect that the more competitive the organization is in terms of the rewards and stresses on leadership, the higher the rise in testosterone is likely to be. This is currently being tested in our ESOP lab.

Fifth, behavior genetics studies may help to provide an indication of whether leadership emergence has a substantial genetic component. A high heritability index suggests that there may be important individual differences in these traits. Although we are unlikely to find a single gene responsible for leadership, there are some promising results of studies showing that personality differences that systematically relate to leadership emergence (such as extraversion and intelligence) have a substantial heritable component (Ilies, Arvey, & Bouchard, 2006).

Sixth, methods of experimental cognitive psychology are also often used by evolutionary psychologists to find evidence for adaptations. For instance, cognitive experiments have shown that men perform better, on average, on spatial rotation tasks, whereas women perform better, on average, on spatial memory tasks (Buss, 2005). One evolutionary interpretation of this result is that ancestral men—the primary hunters—have evolved these capacities in order to navigate through an unfamiliar terrain and track prey on the move. Ancestral women—the primary gatherers—have evolved greater competencies in remembering locations where fruits and nuts can be collected.

Regarding leadership, cognitive experiments can be used to find out if people have evolved cognitive leadership prototypes about who should lead in particular situations. In our research, we examine if people have automatic associations with leadership when they rate people's faces. We have shown that people prefer a more masculine looking leader during war and a more feminine looking leader during peace (Van Vugt & Spisak, 2008). If these prototypes are cross-cultural and they can be found in children and young adults, then we have strong indication that these prototypes are evolved decision rules rather than learned rules, unlike what is suggested by implicit leadership theory (Lord, De Vader, & Alliger, 1986). Indeed, a recent study found that children as young as 5 years old can pick the winners of political election outcomes based on the faces of the candidates (Antonakis & Dalgas, 2009). Furthermore, there is cross-cultural agreement on what the face of a leader looks like (Berggren, Jordahl, & Poutvarra, 2010), suggesting that these are evolved prototypes.

Seventh, psychological surveys can provide support for evolutionary hypotheses about leadership by examining self-reported data about people's experiences with leadership and followership in the real world. For instance, survey evidence from around the globe reveals that there are some traits that are universally perceived to be associated with good leadership, such as vision, integrity, and trustworthiness (Den Hartog, House, Hanges, Ruiz-Quintanilla, & Dorfman, 1999). In addition, there are traits that are more important considerations in some cultures but not in others, such as a leader's generosity and dominance (Den Hartog et al., 1999). This suggests that some decision rules are relatively biologically fixed, such as "I will only follow a leader I can trust." Yet other rules are more flexible and influenced by culture (such as the rule "follow a generous leader").

In addition, anthropological and ethnographic databases can provide additional evidence for evolutionary hypotheses about leadership, testing the extent to which leadership phenomena are universal across human cultures. This kind of evidence is necessary to differentiate between phenomena that are evolutionary adaptations, and those that are more superficial, culture-specific manifestations. For instance, research on Western and Eastern cultures suggests that whereas the need for leadership is universal, between these cultures, people differ in what they expect from their leaders (Dorfman, Hanges, & Brodbeck, 2004; Hofstede, 1980).

Ninth, cross-species evidence is instrumental in testing speculations about the evolutionary history of any alleged adaptation such as leadership. In both humans and elephants, for instance, older individuals take on leadership positions when there is a knowledge problem—the matriarch elephant takes the lead to a long-forgotten water hole (King et al., 2009). This finding implies that the underlying evolved psychological mechanism or decision rule—follow an older individual when the group does not know where to go—predates the divergence of primates and elephants from their immediate common mammalian ancestor.

When considered in conjunction, the findings from these diverse lines of inquiry can produce new insights into leadership and its evolutionary functions. The utility of an evolutionary approach becomes apparent to just about anyone who seriously employs such an approach. For illustrative purposes, I have made a list of 10 recent empirical findings that have been discovered by biologically inspired research programs on leadership with a diverse methodology, ranging from mathematical models to behavioral and neuroscience studies. Although not one of these findings tells a definitive story about the evolutionary significance of leadership, together they point to the existence of a specialized cognitive machinery for dealing with leadership problems. A growing body of empirical evidence, in other words, shows the generativity of adopting an evolutionary approach to leadership.

1. Mathematical models suggest that in groups in which information is distributed among many individuals, democratic leadership works better than despotic leadership (Conradt & Roper, 2003; Van Vugt, 2009).

2. A laboratory experiment shows that individuals with high testosterone levels perform better on cognitive tasks when assigned to a leadership position, whereas low-testosterone individuals perform better in a followership position (Josephs et al., 2006).

3. A brain imaging study shows that when a follower receives an unfair offer from the leader in an ultimatum game, it elicits brain activity in areas related to emotion (anterior insula), suggesting that emotions play a role in deciding whether to follow a leader or not (Sanfey, 2007).

4. Archival data from traditional societies suggest that despotic leaders, such as emperors and tyrants, have greater reproductive success than democratic leaders (Betzig, 1986).

5. Swarming experiments with humans show that with just a few informed individuals, large groups of individuals can coordinate their activities (Couzin, Krause, Franks, & Levin, 2005).

6. Experiments with capuchin monkeys show that they respond negatively to unfair outcome allocations from (human) experimenters, suggesting an early evolutionary origin of injustice aversion in interacting with leaders (Brosnan, Newton-Fisher, & Van Vugt, 2009).

7. Data from traditional hunter-gatherer societies suggest that they have a host of different devices to keep overbearing leaders in check, such as through gossip, ridicule, exclusion, and assassination (Van Vugt, Hogan, et al., 2008).

8. Survey data show that men in top management positions in Western societies have more sexual liaisons than men in lower ranked functions in the organization (Perusse, 1993).

9. Laboratory experiments show that groups with leaders—who can punish free riders—do much better than groups without leaders; furthermore, groups with a leader achieve the same level of cooperation as groups where everyone can punish (O'Gorman, Henrich, & Van Vugt, 2009; Van Vugt & De Cremer, 1999).

10. When men and women watch someone being punished who has behaved unfairly, there is brain activation in the reward regions of the brain for men only, and this is accompanied by feelings of revenge (Singer et al., 2006).

A Game Theory Analysis of Leadership

Evolutionary scientists sometimes use the tool of game theory to speculate on the evolutionary origins of particular social phenomena. I have done this for leadership and followership, and this has produced a number of interesting insights into the origins and emergence of leadership (Van Vugt, 2006; Van

Vugt, Hogan, et al., 2008). Game theory emerged from the analysis of strategic interactions between combatants in World War II, but it has since become a basic model for studying human choice across the behavioral sciences (Gintis, 2007). Game theory is a helpful tool in identifying under which conditions certain social traits (or strategies) evolve, especially when they are competing with alternative traits (strategies).

For instance, the well-known prisoner's dilemma game has been used to model the evolution of cooperation. This model shows that the dominant strategy—which is the trait that is most likely to evolve—is to defect, resulting in a noncooperative equilibrium. Only by making additional assumptions, such as repeated play (Axelrod, 1984) or reputation-building (Hardy & Van Vugt, 2006), does a cooperative strategy survive.

Leadership and followership can be modeled as (evolved) game strategies, too. Framing leader–follower relations in terms of game theory can test the idea that leadership and followership evolved as two complementary strategies for achieving social coordination (Van Vugt, 2009). Key to leadership is, indeed, the need for coordination. A simple coordination game, depicted in Figure 5.1a, can make clear how leadership evolves. Figure 5.1a depicts a pure coordination game where the players have symmetrical interests. It is best illustrated with an example. (Although we present the simplest dyadic version, this analysis can be easily extended to larger, more complex groups.) Suppose Jamie and Pat are on the African savannah, our ancestral environment. They must choose between two water holes, A or B. For protection against predators, they must move together. Leadership offers a solution. Where do they go? If one of them takes the lead and moves on to his or her preferred choice, the other has no option but follow. It does not matter where they end up, at hole A or hole B, as long as they go together. This coordinating leadership is observed in many group-living animals who are regularly on the move, such as buffaloes, baboons, and humans. It does not require any brain power, just one individual who moves and the other follows. Essentially a dictator can solve this game (Van Vugt, 2009). Figure 5.1a indicates that

Figure 5.1a   A Pure Coordination Game

| | | Pat | |
		Hole A	Hole B
Jamie	Hole A	1, 1*	0, 0
	Hole B	0, 0	1, 1*

NOTE: A simple coordination game in which the payoffs are indicated for Jamie and Pat, respectively, within each square. So, if Jamie and Pat choose the same hole, they each get a +1 payoff. The game equilibria are indicated with asterisks. They each get a +1 payoff in reproductive units.

both leaders and followers benefit from coordinated action, and this is why these strategies evolved in tandem (Van Vugt, 2006).

Evolutionary game theory (Maynard-Smith, 1982), a special branch of game theory, assumes that game strategies are underpinned by gene alleles that compete with each other in a Darwinian contest. Winning strategies (genes) spread through the population at the cost of inferior ones via the process of natural selection. This simple model suggests that leadership is likely found in any situation (or species) where the benefits of coordination outweigh the costs, which theory is supported by reviews of animal leadership (King et al., 2009).

In nature, there is usually no convergence of interests between players. Indeed, in complex social groups such as where humans live, conflicts are often the rule rather than the exception. How does leadership come about then? The picture is more complicated. I have given an example in Figure 5.1b, a game I have labeled the Leader Game (also known as Battle-of-the-Sexes or Ultimatum Game). Rather than assuming equality of payoffs, Jamie might prefer to move to water hole A, which would give him an outcome of 3, whereas Pat might want to move to water hole B, which would give him a payoff of 3, too. The payoffs of the game suggest that both are still better off moving to the same hole (outcomes of either 1 or 3), yet there is a conflict of interests as to what hole to move to. What are the implications of this for how leadership is negotiated?

First, we should expect leadership will emerge more slowly in situations in which there is a conflict of interest because both individuals have an incentive to take the lead as they profit more from getting to their preferred water hole (van Vugt & Kurzban, 2007). Historically it is true that leaders have enjoyed better health, greater wealth, and more reproductive success than followers (Betzig, 1986; Chagnon, 1997; Perusse, 1993). The imbalance in payoffs between leaders and followers is the cause of constant tension and greater payoff differences create more reluctant followership. It is perhaps not surprising that in human leadership, generosity and fairness are crucial factors in leader endorsement (De Cremer & Van Vugt, 2002; Dorfman et al., 2004; Epitropaki & Martin, 2004).

Figure 5.1b   The Leader Game (or Battle-of-the-Sexes)

| | | Pat | |
		Hole A	Hole B
Jamie	Hole A	3, 1*	0, 0
	Hole B	0, 0	1, 3*

NOTE: The Leader Game in which payoffs (in reproductive success) are for Jamie and Pat respectively, within in each square. So if Jamie and Pat go to Hole A, Jamie gets a better payoff (+3) than Pat (+1). Game equilibria are indicated with asterisks.

Second, the game analysis of leadership suggests that leadership across both games should correlate with measures of initiative taking, because the one who moves first is more likely to emerge as leader. In support of this analysis, leadership correlates with various indices of initiative taking, such as boldness, ambition, self-esteem, excitement seeking, and extraversion—all linked to leadership emergence (Judge, Bono, Ilies, & Gerhardt, 2002). Furthermore, more intelligent individuals are better at "reading" the payoff preferences of others and in using fair and collectively sustainable first- and second-move strategies (Burks, Carpenter, Goette, & Rustichini, 2009). Not surprising, studies show consistent links between leadership and general measures of intelligence (with an average correlation of .33 between objectively measured intelligence and leader effectiveness; Judge, Colbert, & Illies, 2004). Links have also been established between leadership and social perceptiveness, indicating that leaders might be superior at responding flexibly to social situations (Kellett, Humphrey, & Sleeth, 2002; Zaccaro, Gilbert, Thor, & Mumford, 1991). Yet it remains to be seen whether leaders are more empathic than nonleaders (Antonakis, Ashkanasy, Dasborough, 2009). A final implication, in comparing the two games, is that when there is greater conflict of interest, personality factors associated with aggression, dominance, and authoritarianism should become relatively more important because there are incentives to force other individuals to do what you want.

This game analysis also explains the evolution of a diversity of leadership styles and strategies because one strategy may be suited to one situation and another to another situation. A game approach suggests that different leader strategies represent situations with (slightly) different payoff structures, which affect the relationship dynamics between leaders and followers (Van Vugt, 2009). Task leadership is likely to develop as a solution to Figure 5.1a when payoffs for leaders and followers are identical and the leader's task is primarily to coordinate group activity. Relational leadership is most effective when there are noticeable payoff differences and there are opportunities for leaders to exploit and for followers to defect. In this case, the primary task of leaders is to preserve group cohesion (Fiedler, 1967; Van Vugt, 2009).

Payoff differences (Figure 5.1b) account for the distinction between transactional and transformational/charismatic leadership. Transactional leaders appeal to followers' self-interest, by providing them with favorable outcomes in return for support (Bass, 1985; Hollander & Offermann, 1990). Transactional relationships follow the payoff matrix of the Leader Game, where followers are rewarded by leaders, and the higher their rewards the more dedicated followers are. Transformational leaders use charisma and vision to inspire followers beyond their immediate self-interest (Bass, 1985; Burns, 1978). Language seems a prerequisite for this kind of leadership, which suggests that it is uniquely human (charismatic leaders are known to use a lot of metaphors in their speeches; Mio, Riggio, Levin, & Reese, 2005).

Transformational leaders effectively change the game payoffs so that followers do better than their leaders—self-sacrifice is an important aspect of transformational leadership (De Cremer & Van Knippenberg, 2002). It is also possible, of course, that through clever use of language, charismatic leadership makes followers believe that they are better off—whereas in fact, the leader has the upper hand. Leaders with Dark Triad personalities (a lethal combination of high scores on Machiavellianism, Narcissism, and Psychopathy) have charismatic qualities and may use their appeal to manipulate group members into believing that they have their interests at heart, whereas in reality they pursue only their selfish interests.

The distinction between transactional and transformation leadership is akin to the difference between selfish and servant leadership (Gillet, Cartwright, & Van Vugt, 2010; Greenleaf, 2002). In some situations, an individual may take the lead by moving to the water hole that the other player prefers—Jamie might suggest to Pat to go to Pat's preferred hole. This is essentially servant leadership because doing so contains a sacrifice. This is not unlike what is found in other animals, such as when hyenas share a carcass and one hyena takes the lead in deterring other predators from access to the meat. It is not easy to see how servant leadership could ever evolve, because of the costs of this strategy. Perhaps this has evolved through kin selection, where the self-sacrificial leadership act helps their relatives, or though reciprocal altruism, where the hyenas take turns in taking on this leadership role. In human societies, an alternative payoff is the heroic status that the individual receives in compensation for his or her bravery, which may ultimately produce a payoff.

As an empirical test of this idea, we studied in the lab how groups of four players were able to solve coordination games with varying levels of conflict (much like the example in Figure 5.1b). In this game—where players were anonymous and there was no reputation building—we found evidence for servant leadership. Those who took the lead in the coordination game received a lower payoff than those who moved afterwards. Moreover, leadership in the game was positively associated with a prosocial personality and negatively associated with a selfish personality (Gillet et al., 2010)

Finally, game theory analyses can illuminate the origins of despotic versus democratic leadership. When there is no conflict of interest between players (as in Figure 5.1a), any individual can take the lead, and it does not matter what he or she chooses. Thus, pure coordination problems can be solved by despotic leaders. Yet, in the Leader Game, the payoff differences in the game inevitably cause resentment among players. Once individuals obtain the position of leader, they may be reluctant to give it up (Kipnis, 1972). If followers threaten to defect or revolt, then leaders will have to make concessions to stay in power. They can promise their followers a greater share of outcomes, but followers may (and often do) fear that leaders will not keep their promises. Followers might demand some control over the group's decision making, in order to protect their long-term interests.

In sum, a game theory analysis is helpful in illuminating the evolutionary origins of leadership and different leadership styles. The simplest coordination game selects for leadership, and this explains why it is common throughout the animal kingdom (King et al., 2009). Any individual who moves first can emerge as the leader, and he or she is effectively a dictator. Leadership is more complicated in situations (or species) in which there is frequent conflict of interest between group members, such as in humans. This selects for a richer variety of leadership styles in which, depending on the conditions, a relational, charismatic, transformational, or servant-style leader emerges to keep large groups of individuals together. We do not know enough yet about the evolution of these different leadership styles and in which situations they emerge, but it seems that language is an important evolved mechanism to support them.

A Brief Natural History of Leadership

Moving away from the evolutionary functions of leadership, what can we say about its phylogeny? How did leadership evolve across evolutionary time, and what can we say about the evolution of leadership in humans and nonhumans? A review of the human and nonhuman leadership literature suggests at least four major transitions in the evolution of leadership (King et al., 2009; Van Vugt, Hogan, et al., 2008): (1) Leadership emerged in prehuman species as a mechanism to solve simple group coordination problems, where any individual initiated an action and others followed; (2) leadership was co-opted to foster collective action in situations involving significant conflicts of interest, such as internal peacekeeping, in which dominant or socially important individuals emerged as leaders; (3) dominance was attenuated in early human egalitarian societies, which paved the way for democratic and prestige-based leadership; and (4) the increase in social complexity of societies that took place after the agricultural revolution produced the need for more powerful and formal leaders to manage complex intra- and intergroup relations—the chiefs, kings, presidents, and CEOs—who at best provide important public services and at worst abuse their power to dominate and exploit followers (see Table 5.1). Here, I discuss these different stages briefly (see Van Vugt, Hogan, et al., 2008, for more details on the natural history of leadership).

Stage 1: Animal Leadership

The phylogenetic evidence suggests that cognitive preadaptations for leadership long precede human and nonhuman primates. Simple leader–follower structures for coordinating group movement are observed in various social species, such as the foraging patterns of many insects, the swimming patterns of schools of fish, and the flying patterns of migrating birds. The important issue is that species lacking large brains and complex sociocognitive capacities

Table 5.1   A Natural History of Leadership

Stage	Time Period	Society	Group Size	Leadership Structure	Leader	Leader–Follower Relations
1	> 2.5 million years ago	Pre-human	Variable	Situational	Any individual, often the dominant group member	Situational or hierarchical (nonhuman primates)
2	2.5 million–13,000 years ago	Band, clan, tribe	Dozens to hundreds	Informal, expertise-based	Big man, head man	Egalitarian
3	13,000–250 years ago	Chiefdoms, kingdoms, warlord societies	Thousands	Centralized, hereditary	Chiefs, kings, warlords	Hierarchical
4	250 years ago–present	Nations, states, large businesses	Thousands to millions	Centralized, democratic	Heads of state, CEOs	Hierarchical, but participatory

From M. Van Vugt, R. Hogan, and R. Kaiser. (2008). Leadership, followership, and evolution: Some lessons from the past. *American Psychologist, 63,* 182–196.

can display followership, using a decision rule as simple as "follow the one who moves first." The individual moving first then automatically emerges as the leader.

Stage 2: Band and Tribal Leadership

Leadership was further shaped by the unique evolutionary history of humans. The emergence of hominids about 2 to 2.5 million years ago until the end of the last ice age, about 13,000 years ago, and the accompanying growth in brain and social network size had substantial implications for leadership development. During this stage, the Pleistocene era, humans lived in seminomadic hunter-gatherer bands and clans consisting of from 100 to 150 closely related individuals (Dunbar, 2004). Modern hunter-gatherers such as the !Kung San of the Kalahari desert and the Aborigines in Northern Australia may provide our best model for human social organization in this stage. The living conditions in this stage are likely to have been fairly egalitarian, as there were no resource surpluses. There were no formally recognized leaders. (There are various anecdotes of White missionaries visiting exotic places and, on encountering the natives, they would ask to be brought to their leader, which bewildered the natives as they did not know the concept of leadership). This period ended with the advent of agriculture some 13,000 years ago.

Stage 3: Chiefs, Kings, and Warlords

It is unlikely that our evolved leadership psychology has changed much since the agricultural period. Yet our social structures have somewhat changed since the agricultural revolution. Agriculture and dependable food supplies enabled groups to settle and populations to grow exponentially. For the first time in our history, communities accumulated surplus resources, and leaders played a key role in their redistribution (Diamond, 1997; Johnson & Earle, 2000). As communities grew, so did the potential for within- and between-group conflict. Leaders acquired extra power to deal with such threats, resulting in more formalized authority structures that paved the way for the first chiefdoms and kingdoms (Betzig, 1986; Johnson & Earle, 2000). In their expanded role, leaders could siphon off resources and use them to create groups of dedicated followers—sometimes by establishing hereditary leadership.

Stage 4: Modern State and Business Leadership

The fourth leadership period corresponds to the beginning of the Industrial Revolution in the 18th century. Communities merged into states and nations, and large businesses developed, all of which had implications for leadership practices. Citizens of states and employees in organizations are relatively free from the predations of their leaders and may defect to other states or organizations. This freedom shifts the balance of power away from leaders and produces conditions more akin, but not equivalent, to the reverse dominance hierarchy of the ancestral period. Although modern bureaucratic arrangements make business sense, they may be constrained by our evolved leadership psychology.

Implications of Evolutionary Leadership Theory for Research and Practice

In this final section, I will note some implications of my evolutionary leadership theory (ELT) for leadership research and practice. Granted some of these implications could be derived from other proximate psychological theories of leadership, for example, path-goal theory, leader–member exchange theory (LMX), and transformational or leadership categorization theories (Avolio et al., 2009; Graen & Uhl-Bien, 1995). Yet, each of these theories must ultimately turn to evolution to explain its own assumptions (e.g., Why do human groups have charismatic leadership? Where do cognitive leadership prototypes come from?). Furthermore, ELT also sheds light on core leadership questions that have not yet been sufficiently addressed in the literature, such as why people follow leaders in the first place; why leadership is consistently linked to intelligence, when leaders prioritize their own needs over the needs of the group; why there is a consistent preference for tall and healthy looking leaders; and why women CEOs attract so much hostility. Finally, an evolutionary framework also seems to generate a broader variety of practical implications than other theoretical perspectives about the way we should design our organizations in light of the constraints of our evolved leadership psychology.

Why Follow?

First, ELT highlights the importance of studying the origins of followership. The natural psychology of followership is more complicated and interesting than that of leadership, yet it is hardly studied (see Chapter 10 of this volume for a follower-centric approach to leadership). ELT suggests that followership evolved in response to specific ancestral coordination problems such as group movement, group defense, internal peacekeeping, and teaching. This implies that followership should emerge more quickly and be more effective in these evolutionarily relevant situations and that there are differences in follower styles.

Although this hypothesis has not been tested explicitly, it is consistent with prior findings. People are more likely to follow a leader under conditions of external threat, such as a natural disaster or bystander emergency situation (Baumeister, Chesner, Senders, & Tice, 1989; Hamblin, 1958). Intergroup conflicts also pave the way for followership and leadership. In the famous Robber Cave experiment, individuals who did not know each other were brought together, and they promptly chose team leaders to represent them (Sherif, 1966). Finally, conformity research suggests that when people are uncertain about what to do, they are more likely to follow the advice of another individual who then effectively becomes the leader. The famous Milgram and Asch experiments demonstrate that followership emerges spontaneously in such situations, even if it is the (morally) wrong option. This implies that our brains are effectively tuned to followership—a heritage of our ancestral past—which is consistent with ELT.

A different implication of ELT is that individuals may not want to follow anyone when they face a relatively evolutionarily new problem (such as global warming) or a simple coordination problem. The latter is consistent with the research on leadership substitutes (Kerr & Jermier, 1978). Exercising leadership outside these adaptive problem domains could even undermine team performance. For instance, highly cohesive groups do less well in performing a routine task with a formally appointed leader (Haslam et al., 1998). An important lesson that emerges from this is that except in certain important and well-defined situations, having a formal leader is both unnecessary and detrimental.

The leadership literature could benefit from adopting an evolutionary approach by studying followership motives in different situations and the personality correlates of good and bad followership (Altemeyer, 1981; Wayne

& Ferris, 1990). Followership styles may be at least as variable and differentiated as leadership styles (Kellerman, 2008). For instance, people may follow a leader with different levels of commitment, from being an indifferent follower to a diehard follower (Kellerman, 2008). In addition, followers' motives may differ in that some people follow because they want to become leaders themselves (apprentices), whereas others follow because they are uncertain (disciples) or simply because they do what they are told by individuals higher up the group hierarchy (subordinates). An evolutionary approach places followership at the forefront of the study of leadership and is a good starting point for developing new followership theory and research (Van Vugt & Ahuja, 2010).

Who Leads? The Savannah Hypothesis of Leadership

A second implication of ELT is that who we get and want as our leaders nowadays is likely to be affected by our ancestral past. Reviewing the literature on both humans and nonhumans, we have found that individual differences in temperament, motivation, dominance, and knowledge—all linked to personality—are consistently associated with leadership emergence across species (King et al., 2009). This makes a lot of sense in light of the evolutionary game analysis of leadership. ELT predicts that first movers in a coordination game will be leaders. A recent meta-analysis indicates that of the Big Five personality dimensions, extraversion (a sign of both temperament and motivation) is most strongly related to leadership emergence ratings (Judge et al., 2002). Other studies report correlations between leadership and such traits as assertiveness, boldness, initiative, need for achievement, proactivity, and risk taking (e.g., Ames & Flynn, 2007; Bass, 1990; House & Aditya, 1997)—all these traits increase the likelihood of being the first to act. In the cognitive domain, knowledgeable people—those who quickly recognize situations requiring coordination—are more likely to become leaders. This explains the reliable relationship between general intelligence and leadership (i.e., average correlation of .33; Burks et al., 2009). Perhaps, across evolutionary time as groups got larger and socially more complex, coordination tasks also became more complicated, and this selected for a higher intelligence, especially in leaders. Thus, we may find that as tasks become more complex—being president of a larger country—intelligence becomes a better predictor of leadership.

Another implication of ELT is that good leaders (those who attract followers) should be perceived as both competent and benevolent because followers want leaders who can acquire resources and then be willing to share them. The first claim is supported by research showing that task expertise correlates with leadership (Bass, 1990) and that low expertise disqualifies individuals from leadership positions (Hollander & Offermann, 1990). Leaders' willingness to share is reflected in such traits as trustworthiness, fairness, generosity, and self-sacrifice—universally desirable leader attributes (Dorfman et al., 2004; Epitropaki & Martin, 2004; Hardy & Van Vugt, 2006; Lord et al., 1986).

Finally, ELT explains why leadership (still) correlates with such factors as age, height, weight, and health—something not explained by existing leadership theories. Given the risks associated with following the wrong leader, people should prefer leaders who look like they have qualities that, at least in ancestral times, would produce benefits. I have labeled this the Savannah Hypothesis of Leadership (Van Vugt & Ahuja, 2010). For instance, in ancestral savannah environments, having specialized knowledge—the location of water holes during a drought, for instance—may have been vital (Boehm, 1999). In baboons and elephants, group movement is also decided by the older, not the most dominant, troop member (King et al., 2009). Older individuals are more likely to have specialized knowledge. This explains why age is correlated with leadership, at least in knowledge domains (such as university professors).

In contrast, when group activities require strength and stamina (group defense in ancestral times, grueling travel schedules in modern business), physical indices such as energy level and health are better predictors of leadership emergence (Nicholson, 2000; Van Vugt, 2006). Modern voters prefer physically fit political candidates (Simonton, 1994). Interestingly, seemingly irrelevant physical factors like height predict leadership status even today (Judge & Cable, 2004). In ancestral times, taller leaders may have been better peacekeepers within groups and more intimidating foes to rival groups.

Consistent with this Savannah hypothesis, ELT suggests that our implicit leadership theories have been shaped through natural selection and that different cognitive prototypes are salient in different evolutionary-relevant situations. As an example, U.S. voters tend to choose hawkish presidents when threatened by war (McCann, 1992) and show an increased preference for charismatic leaders—and a decreased preference for participative leaders— when reminded of their mortality (Cohen, Solomon, Maxfield, Pyszczynski, & Greenberg, 2004). Similarly, CEO charisma is positively related to organizational effectiveness, but only under conditions when subordinates experience uncertainty (Waldman, Ramirez, House, & Puranam, 2001). Finally, groups prefer a masculine-looking leader when they are in conflict with another group, but they switch to a more feminine-looking leader when they want to establish a peaceful relationship with another group (Spisak & Van Vugt, 2010; Van Vugt & Spisak, 2008).

Contingency Approaches of Leadership

Another strength of ELT is that it provides a solid foundation for contingency approaches to leadership by showing that different adaptive ancestral problems elicit different styles of leadership. Extrapolating from hunter-gatherer evidence, leadership was flexible and, depending on conditions, different leaders emerged—for instance, the best hunter leads the hunting party, the wisest elder resolves internal conflicts, the fiercest warrior leads the fight (Van Vugt, Johnson, et al., 2008). An implication is that despite stable individual (and heritable) differences in the likelihood of leadership and followership emergence across situations, these roles can also be adopted more flexibly. Twin research suggests, indeed, that only about 25% of variance in leadership emergence is due to heritable differences in personality (Ilies, Gerhardt, & Le, 2004). In addition, ELT assumes that different leadership styles reflect adaptations to different situations with (slightly) different payoff structures, such as the distinction between task and relational leadership, transformational and transactional leadership, and despotic and democratic leadership.

ELT also accounts for the fact that some leadership attributes are universally valued in leaders (such as integrity and fairness)—they are evolved cognitive prototypes—whereas the importance of other attributes is culturally more variable, as it depends on the specific challenges posed by an organization's physical and social environment (Dorfman et al., 2004; Hofstede, 1980; Richerson & Boyd, 2006). For instance, participative styles prevail in the Netherlands and Australia, where harsh natural conditions forced authorities to share power with citizens, creating a strong egalitarian ethos (cf. Den Hartog et al., 1999). In contrast, more authoritarian leadership styles are found in places in which infectious diseases are prevalent (such as sub-Sahara Africa) and strong social norms, conformity, and punitive measures are necessary to reduce infection risks (Fincher, Thornhill, Murray, & Schaller, 2008).

The Ambivalence Model of Leadership

Another implication of ELT is that it explains when and why leaders prioritize their personal goals above the group goals and what groups can do to prevent this. An evolutionary approach suggests that there are, in fact, two forms of group hierarchies in the animal world. The first is the dominance hierarchy that results from competition for scarce resources, where the strongest and most determined individual prevails and controls group resources and activities (E. O. Wilson, 1975). The second form of hierarchy emerges by consensus when hierarchical structures are perceived to benefit the group. These two forms offer very different accounts of leadership. The dominance model characterizes species in which alpha males control group activities and others are intimidated or forced to acquiesce. The picture is quite different for humans, because our hierarchies are much flatter and are often based on prestige rather than dominance (Henrich & Gil-White, 2001). The evolutionary transition from dominance to prestige-based leadership was pivotal, making it possible for humans to function in highly coordinated, cohesive, and democratic units.

Dominance, however, is part of our primate heritage, and there is always a risk that leaders will try to force followers into submission (Betzig, 1986;

Boehm, 1999; Padilla, Hogan, & Kaiser, 2007). Furthermore, dominance is often taken as a cue for competence (Anderson & Kilduff, 2009). This makes leader–follower relations inherently problematic, and I suggest that these two hierarchies have produced a different set of adaptations. On one hand, there will always be the temptation to dominate for individuals in leadership positions because that is the easiest way to get others to do what you want. Thus, humans should have evolved a leadership psychology with a set of decision rules that should elicit dominance behaviors in appropriate situations (such as when they hold power). On the other hand, we should also have evolved a followership psychology which includes a set of mechanisms, or decision rules, to avoid being dominated and exploited when we follow a leader.

This tension emerging from the conflict of interest between leaders and followers probably created an "arms race" in human evolution between adaptations aimed at enhancing personal power versus reducing the power of others. The anthropological, ethnographic, and psychological literatures reveal several mechanisms that individuals possess to increase their power base. Leaders are known to redistribute resources fairly and generously, and this enhances their influence—these are universally desirable leadership attributes (Brown, 1991; Dorfman et al., 2004). Leaders also sometimes induce external group threats to consolidate their power (Cohen et al., 2004). Leaders sometimes "buy" support through nepotistic and corruptive practices (Altemeyer, 1981), and cronyism is a common strategy for retaining power in both humans and chimpanzees, our closest primate cousin (De Waal, 1982; Gandossy & Sonnenfeld, 2004). Finally, with the advent of language, another powerful tool emerged to enhance power—the invention of ideologies. Throughout history, leaders have used or even created religions to maintain power—for example, the Sun Language religion of Kemal Ataturk—and turned their rule into a hereditary position to benefit their kin, a clear indication of nepotism (Betzig, 1986; Diamond, 1997).

Various antiexploitation devices have evolved in human evolution to ensure that humans were able to benefit from following without being exploited. The first is to accept and endorse authority only in areas where leaders have proven expertise. A second mechanism is language, which allows individuals to gossip about and ridicule those in powerful positions and hold them under public scrutiny. For instance, in hunter-gatherer bands, if a chief misbehaves, he is publicly criticized, and if he tries to give commands, he is often rebuffed (Boehm, 1999).

Shunning exploitative leaders is also a powerful tool to level relationships. Ostracism presumably had severe health and safety consequences for the ostracized in the past, and this is why people still respond negatively to ostracism in the present (Williams & Sommer, 1997) although the consequences nowadays are less severe—people do not die anymore if they are thrown out of their peer group. Another decision rule is to abandon overbearing individuals. Van Vugt et al. (2004) showed that the attrition rates in autocratically led groups are four times greater than in democratically led groups. A final mechanism to avoid exploitation is homicide. In hunter-gatherer societies, a dominating individual runs the risk of being killed. In the United States, disgruntled citizens have attempted to assassinate 15 of 43 presidents, making it one of the most dangerous jobs in the world.

These leveling mechanisms are critical for the welfare of groups; historical evidence suggests that tyrants and dictators emerge whenever followers are unable to protect themselves against exploitative leaders (Betzig, 1986; Padilla et al., 2007).

The Mismatch Hypothesis

Finally, ELT provides an answer to why modern leadership often fails, by suggesting that there is likely a mismatch between our evolved leadership psychology and the challenges of modern environments. Our leadership psychology evolved over several million years, during which time our ancestors lived among kin in small egalitarian bands in which leadership was informal, consensual, and situational. ELT assumes that this psychology may still affect the way we respond to our leaders, and this sometimes creates a mismatch between our evolved psychology and the requirements of modern leadership. Here are several examples of potential mismatches (Van Vugt, Hogan, et al., 2008; Van Vugt, Johnson, et al., 2008).

First, leadership in the ancestral environment was distributed, democratic, and situational. The individual most qualified for the task at hand had the greatest influence on collective actions. Rarely would one individual make decisions affecting each group member. Yet with bureaucracy, came formal leadership roles in which one individual is responsible for managing all these functions within an organization. We are not adapted to take on so many different formal leadership roles. Few leaders have the right skills to perform a wide array of duties—this is often referred to as leader versatility (i.e., the ability to perform multiple, even competing, roles; Kaiser, Lindberg, & Craig, 2007). This may account for the high failure rate of senior managers, estimated to be about 50% to 60% in modern businesses (Hogan & Kaiser, 2005). It may also explain growing interest in the notion of distributed leadership—the idea that leadership is a process that can be shared because that is closest to our evolutionary leadership prototype.

The current selection process of leaders may create another mismatch. In ancestral times, leaders emerged from the group bottom-up through their skill, personality, or ambition. In modern industrial and bureaucratic organizations, leaders are appointed by managers senior to them in the organizational hierarchy. Pleasing superiors is more important to career success than pleasing subordinates, and this is at odds with our evolved leadership psychology. It is noteworthy that executives are more likely to succeed if subordinates are included in the selection process (Sessa, Kaiser, Taylor, & Campbell, 1998) as predicted by ELT.

The payoff differences between leaders and followers in modern times may also be at odds with our evolved leadership psychology. In ancestral times, there were minimal status and wealth differences, although successful leaders in war or trade may have had greater reproductive success (Chagnon, 1988). In modern business environments, the average salaries for CEOs are almost 200 times the average pay for workers. Research shows that this difference increases the potential for abuse (Kipnis, 1972) and decreases the ability to empathize with subordinates (Galinsky, Magee, Inesi, & Gruenfeld, 2006). The highly asymmetric payoffs for modern business leaders may be at odds with human nature and encourage a kind of management that employees naturally resist.

What about transformational and charismatic leadership? As societies grew in human evolution, there was a niche for leadership in enforcing social norms and fostering social cohesion. The need for such leadership activities is probably even greater today when genetic strangers must work together in large groups and the size of businesses and other kinds of organizations makes group identification difficult. Interestingly, research indicates that transformational leadership works, in part, by influencing followers to identify with the group and by emotionally bonding them (Van Vugt & De Cremer, 1999). Transformational leaders change the way followers see themselves—from self-interested individuals to members of a group—through emphasizing the similarity and shared fate among group members, almost as if they are kin. Transformational leadership may have been necessary to make the leap from small to large interconnected groups in human evolution. Although these individuals are rare in the modern world (Bass, 1985; Burns, 1978), their success suggests that people are naturally attracted to such leaders. We are currently studying whether transformational/charismatic leadership enhances the emotional bonding of individuals to groups and whether their influence works via the release of endorphins and oxytocin among followers.

Another mismatch concerns the scale of modern organizations compared to small hunter-gatherer societies. Interestingly, organizations like Toyota, GoreTex, and Virgin are designed and structured in a way that resembles hunter-gatherer bands. For instance, these companies delegate decision making to managers far down the chain of command, so that the size of functional units approximates that of a hunter-gatherer band (anywhere up to 150 individuals, as predicted by Dunbar's number). Additionally, decentralized decision making is associated with greater employee morale, involvement, and commitment, which in turn are associated with greater productivity, financial results, and customer satisfaction.

Male and Female Leadership Biases

A final potential mismatch is the preference for tall, older, and masculine leaders, which may be another legacy of our evolutionary past (as discussed under the Savannah hypothesis). The preference for these savannah traits may provide clues about one current social issue, the prejudice against female leadership. Male leadership may have been the norm in ancestral environments—although there must have been a niche for female leaders as peacekeepers (Van Vugt & Spisak, 2008). It remains to be seen—and here is the potential for a mismatch—how beneficial the bias toward male leadership is in organizations that increasingly emphasize interpersonal skills and network building (Eagly & Carli, 2003). Despite many similarities, men and women are biologically somewhat different, and as a result of facing different adaptive problems in ancestral times (e.g., mate choice, parental care, hunting), they have likely evolved different psychologies as well (Geary, 1998). Thus, unlike what social role theorists claim, some sex differences in social behavior are hardwired rather than learned or socialized (Pinker, 2002). Women, on average, have better verbal memory, empathy, and communication skills—presumably as a result of evolutionary selection pressures on females to maintain close social networks for protection and child rearing (Van Vugt, 2006). Women leaders are also more democratic, which is consistent with this peacekeeping hypothesis (Eagly & Carli, 2003), whereas male leaders are more authoritarian and warmongering—human males have evolved a specific warrior psychology to deal with the ancient challenges of intergroup conflict (Van Vugt et al., 2007; Van Vugt & Spisak, 2008).

Men, on average, are also more status and power driven, and therefore they apply earlier to leadership posts. The male bias may be difficult to overcome, especially when the perks and privileges associated with leadership roles are substantial. Because of differences in parental investment, women chose men who were good resource providers and, as a result, men have evolved a stronger status drive. Thus, when leadership comes with status, then men should be more interested in getting such positions. Indeed there is evidence suggesting that when women and men work together on group tasks, the men are quicker to claim leadership roles, even if the women are better qualified (Mezulis, Abramson, Hyde, & Hankin, 2004). In addition, regardless of their talent, men are also more likely to assume leadership roles when being observed by women, perhaps because women prefer status in potential mates. The glass ceiling effect may be a manifestation of this male leadership bias that is rooted in our ancestral past.

Conclusions

Evolutionary leadership theory (ELT) is a new approach to the study of leadership, which connects the diverse lines of research in the social, biological, economic, and cognitive sciences and provides an overarching framework that is consistent, ultimately, with Darwin's evolutionary theory. I have argued why it is important to study the evolutionary origins and functions of leadership. I have shown what evolutionary psychology can contribute to the science of leadership, connecting many old findings and generating many novel hypotheses and testing them with a diversity of different methodologies, from behavioral genetics to neuroscience and from experimentation to game theory. I hope this new field of enquiry will generate interest from leadership researchers and practitioners who are interested, as I am, in the Nature of Leadership.

Discussion Questions

1. Do nonhuman animals have leadership? If so, how is it different from human leadership?

2. How can neuroscience research contribute to understanding leadership?

3. Does power corrupt? Discuss evidence for or against this claim using insights from evolutionary psychology.

4. Why would there have been a preference for taller leaders in ancestral environments? How would you investigate this?

Supplementary Readings

Antonakis, J., & Dalgas, O. (2009). Predicting elections: Child's play. *Science, 323,* 1183.

Fehr, E., & Camerer, C. (2007). Social neuroeconomics: The neural circuitry of social preferences. *Trends in Cognitive Sciences, 11,* 419–427.

King, A. J., Johnson, D. D. P., & Van Vugt, M. (2009). The origins and evolution of leadership. *Current Biology, 19,* R911–R916.

Van Vugt, M., & Ahuja, A. (2010). *Naturally selected: Why some people lead, why others follow, and why it matters.* London: Profile

Van Vugt, M., & De Cremer, D. (1999). Leadership in social dilemmas: The effects of group identification on collective actions to provide public goods. *Journal of Personality and Social Psychology, 76,* 587–599.

Van Vugt, M., Hogan, R., & Kaiser, R. (2008). Leadership, followership, and evolution: Some lessons from the past. *American Psychologist, 63,* 182–196.

References

Adolphs, R. (1999). Social cognition and the human brain. *Trends in Cognitive Sciences, 3,* 469–479.

Alexander, R. D. (1979). *Darwinism and human affairs.* Seattle: University of Washington Press.

Altemeyer, B. (1981). *Right-wing authoritarianism.* Winnipeg, Canada: University of Manitoba Press.

Ames, D. R., & Flynn, F. J. (2007). What breaks a leader? The curvilinear relation between assertiveness and leadership. *Journal of Personality and Social Psychology, 92,* 307–324.

Anderson, C., & Kilduff, G. J. 2009. Why do dominant personalities attain influence in face-to-face groups? The competence-signaling effects of trait dominance. *Journal of Personality and Social Psychology, 96,* 491–503.

Antonakis, J. 2011. Predictors of leadership: The usual suspects and the suspect traits. In A. Bryman, D. Collinson, K. Grint, B. Jackson, & M. Uhl-Bien, *Sage Handbook of Leadership* (pp. 269–285). Thousand Oaks, CA: Sage.

Antonakis, J., Ashkanasy, N. M., & Dasborough, M. (2009). Does leadership need emotional intelligence? *The Leadership Quarterly, 20,* 247–261.

Antonakis, J., & Dalgas, O. (2009). Predicting elections: Child's play. *Science, 323,* 1183.

Avolio, B., Walumbwa, F. O., & Weber, T. J. (2009). Leadership: Current theories, research, and future directions. *Annual Review of Psychology, 60,* 421–449.

Axelrod, R. (1984). *The evolution of cooperation.* New York: Basic Books.

Barkow, J., Cosmides, L., & Tooby, J. (1992). *The adapted mind: Evolutionary psychology and the generation of culture.* New York: Oxford University Press.

Barrett, H. C., & Kurzban, R. (2006). Modularity in cognition: Framing the debate. *Psychological Review, 113,* 628–647.

Bass, B. M. (1985). *Leadership and performance beyond expectations.* New York: Free Press.

Bass, B. M. (1990). *Bass and Stogdill's handbook of leadership: Theory, research, and managerial applications* (3rd ed.). New York: Free Press.

Baumeister, R. F., Chesner, S. P., Senders, P. S., & Tice, D. M. (1989). Who's in charge here? Group leaders do lend help in emergencies. *Personality and Social Psychology Bulletin, 14,* 17–22.

Baumeister, R. F., & Leary, M. (1995). The need to belong: Desire for interpersonal attachments as a fundamental human motivation. *Psychological Bulletin, 117,* 497–529.

Bennis, W. (2007). The challenges of leadership in the modern world. *American Psychologist, 62,* 2–5.

Berggren, N., Jordahl, H., & Poutvaara, P. (2010). The looks of a winner: Beauty and electoral success. *Journal of Public Economics, 94,* 8–15.

Betzig, L. (1986). *Despotism and differential reproduction: A Darwinian view of history.* New York: Aldine.

Boehm, C. (1999). *Hierarchy in the forest.* London: Harvard University Press.

Brosnan, S. F., Newton-Fisher, N. E., & Van Vugt, M. (2009). A melding of minds: When primatology meets personality and social psychology. *Personality and Social Psychology Review, 13,* 129–147.

Brown, D. (1991). *Human universals.* Boston: McGraw-Hill.

Burks, S. V., Carpenter, J. P., Goette, L., & Rustichini, A. (2009). Cognitive skills affect economic preferences, strategic behavior, and job attachment. *Proceedings of the National Academy of Sciences, 106,* 7745–7750.

Burns, J. M. (1978). *Leadership.* New York: Harper & Row.

Buss, D. M. (2005). *Handbook of evolutionary psychology.* Hoboken, NJ: John Wiley.

Chagnon, N. A. (1988). Life histories, blood revenge, and warfare in a tribal population. *Science, 239,* 985–992.

Chagnon, N. A. (1997). *Yanomamo.* London: Wadsworth.

Cohen, F., Solomon, S., Maxfield, M., Pyszcynski, T., & Greenberg, J. (2004). Fatal attraction: The effects of mortality salience on evaluations of charismatic, task-oriented, and relationship-oriented leaders. *Psychological Science, 15,* 846–851.

Conradt, L., & Roper, T. (2003). Group decision-making in animals. *Nature, 421,* 155–158.

Couzin, I. D., Krause, J., Franks, N. R., & Levin, S. A. (2005). Effective leadership and decision-making in animal groups on the move. *Nature, 433,* 513–516.

Darwin, C. (1871). *The descent of man.* London: Appleton & Co.

Dawkins, R. (2009). *The greatest show on earth: The evidence for evolution.* New York: Free Press.

De Cremer, D., & van Knippenberg, D. (2002). How do leaders promote cooperation? The effects of charisma and procedural fairness. *Journal of Applied Psychology, 87,* 858–866.

De Cremer, D., & Van Vugt, M. (2002). Intra- and intergroup dynamics of leadership in social dilemmas: A relational model of cooperation. *Journal of Experimental Social Psychology, 38,* 126–136.

Den Hartog, D. N., House, R. J., Hanges, P. J., Ruiz-Quintanilla, S.A., & Dorfman, P. W. (1999). Culture-specific and cross-culturally generalizable implicit leadership theories: A longitudinal investigation. *The Leadership Quarterly, 10,* 219–256.

De Waal, F. B. M. (1982). *Chimpanzee politics: Power and sex among apes.* New York: Harper & Row.

De Waal., F. B. M. (1996). *Good natured: The origins of right and wrong in humans and other animals.* Cambridge, MA: Harvard University Press.

Diamond, J. (1997). *Guns, germs, and steel.* London: Vintage.

Dorfman, P. W., Hanges, P. J., & Brodbeck, F. C. (2004). Leadership and cultural variation: The identification of culturally endorsed leadership profiles. In R. J. House, P. J. Hanges, M. Javidan, P. W. Dorfman, & V. Gupta (Eds.), *Culture, leadership, and organizations: The GLOBE study of 62 societies* (pp. 669–719). Thousand Oaks, CA: Sage.

Dunbar, R. I. M. (2004). *Grooming, gossip, and the evolution of language.* London: Faber & Faber.

Eagly, A. H., & Carli, L. L. (2003). The female leadership advantage: An evaluation of the evidence. *The Leadership Quarterly, 14,* 807–834.

Epitropaki, O., & Martin, R. (2004). Implicit leadership theories in applied settings: Factor structure, generalizability, and stability over time. *Journal of Applied Psychology, 89,* 293–310.

Fehr, E., & Camerer, C. (2007). Social neuroeconomics: The neural circuitry of social preferences. *Trends in Cognitive Sciences, 11,* 419–427.

Fiedler, F. E. (1967). *A theory of leadership effectiveness.* New York: McGraw-Hill.

Fincher, C., Thornhill, R., Murray, D., & Schaller, M. (2008). Pathogen prevalence predicts human cross-cultural variability in individualism/collectivism. *Proceedings of the Royal Society B, 275,* 1279–1285.

Foley, R. A. (1997). The adaptive legacy of human evolution: A search for the environment of evolutionary adaptedness. *Evolutionary Anthropology, 4,* 194–203.

Galinsky, A. D., Magee, J. C., Inesi, M. E., & Gruenfeld, D. H. (2006). Power and perspectives not taken. *Psychological Science, 17,* 1068–1077.

Gandossey, R., & Sonnenfeld, J. A. (2004). *Leadership and governance from the inside out.* London: Wiley.

Gangestad, S., & Simpson, J. A. (2007). *The evolution of the mind.* New York: Guilford.

Geary, D. (1998). *Male/female: The evolution of human sex differences.* Washington, DC: APA Press.

Gillet, J., Cartwright, E., & Van Vugt, M. (2010). Selfish or servant leadership? Leadership personalities in coordination games. *Personality and Individual Differences.* doi:10.1016/j.paid.2010.06.003

Gintis, H. (2007). A framework for unifying the behavioral sciences. *Behavioral and Brain Sciences, 30,* 1–16.

Graen, G. B., & Uhl-Bien, M. (1995). Development of leader-member exchange (LMX) theory of leadership over 25 years: Applying a multi-level domain perspective. *The Leadership Quarterly, 6,* 219–247.

Greenleaf, R. (2002). *Servant leadership.* Google Books.

Hackman, J. R., & Wageman, R. (2007). Asking the right questions about leadership. *American Psychologist, 62,* 43–47.

Hackman, J. R., & Walton, R. E. (1986). Leading groups in organizations. In P. S. Goodman (Ed.), *Designing effective work groups* (pp. 72–119). San Francisco: Jossey-Bass.

Hamblin, R. L. (1958). Leadership and crises. *Sociometry, 21,* 322–335.

Hardy, C., & Van Vugt, M. (2006). Nice guys finish first: The competitive altruism hypothesis. *Personality and Social Psychology Bulletin, 32,* 1402–1413.

Haslam, A., McGarty, C., Brown, P., Eggins, R., Morrison, B., & Reynolds, K. (1998). Inspecting the emperor's clothes: Evidence that random selection of leaders can enhance group performance. *Group Dynamics, 2,* 168–184.

Henrich, J., & Gil-White, F. (2001). The evolution of prestige: Freely conferred deference as a mechanism for enhancing the benefits of cultural transmission. *Evolution and Human Behavior, 22,* 165–196.

Hill, R. A., & Dunbar, R. (2003). Social network size in humans. *Human Nature, 14,* 53–72.

Hofstede, G. (1980). *Culture's consequences: International differences in work-related values.* Beverly Hills, CA: Sage.

Hogan, R. (2006). *Personality and the fate of organizations.* Hillsdale, NJ: Lawrence Erlbaum.

Hogan, R., & Kaiser, R. (2005). What we know about leadership. *Review of General Psychology, 9,* 169–180.

Hollander, E. P., & Offermann, L. (1990). Power and leadership in organizations: Relationships in transition. *American Psychologist, 45,* 179–189.

House, R. J. (1971). A path-goal theory of leader effectiveness. *Administrative Science Quarterly, 16,* 321–339.

House, R. J., & Aditya, R. N. (1997). The social scientific study of leadership: Quo vadis? *Journal of Management, 23,* 409–473.

Ilies, R., Arvey, R., & Bouchard, T. (2006). Darwinism, behavioral genetics, and organizational behavior: A review and agenda for future research. *Journal of Organizational Behavior, 27,* 121–141.

Ilies, R., Gerhardt, M., & Le, H. (2004). Individual differences in leadership emergence: Integrating meta-analytic findings and behavior genetics estimates. *International Journal of Selection and Assessment, 12,* 207–219.

Josephs, R. A., Sellers, J. G., Newman, M. L., & Metha, P. (2006). The mismatch effect: When testosterone and status are at odds. *Journal of Personality and Social Psychology, 90,* 999–1013.

Johnson, A. W., & Earle, T. (2000). *The evolution of human societies.* Stanford, CA: Stanford University Press.

Judge, T. A., Bono, J., Ilies, R., & Gerhardt, M. (2002). Personality and leadership: A qualitative and quantitative review. *Journal of Applied Psychology, 87*, 765–780.

Judge, T. A., & Cable, D. M. (2004). The effect of physical height on workplace success and income: A preliminary test of a theoretical model. *Journal of Applied Psychology, 89*, 428–441.

Judge, T. A., Colbert, A. E., & Ilies, R. (2004). Intelligence and leadership: A quantitative review and test of theoretical propositions. *Journal of Applied Psychology, 89*, 542–552.

Kaiser, R., Lindberg, J., & Craig, S. (2007). Assessing the flexibility of managers: A comparison of methods. *International Journal of Selection and Assessment, 16*, 40–55.

Kellerman, B. (2008). *Followership*. Boston: Harvard Business School Press.

Kellett, J. B., Humphrey, R. H., & Sleeth, R. G. (2002). Empathy and complex task performance: Two routes to leadership. *The Leadership Quarterly, 13*, 523–544.

Kenrick, D., Li, N. P., & Butner, J. (2003). Dynamical evolutionary psychology: Individual decision rules and emergent social norms. *Psychological Review, 110*, 3–28.

Kerr, S., & Jermier, J. (1978). Substitutes for leadership: Their meaning and measurement. *Organizational Behavior and Human Performance, 22*, 374–403.

King, A. J., Johnson, D. D. P., & Van Vugt, M. (2009). The origins and evolution of leadership. *Current Biology, 19*, R911–R916.

Kipnis, D. (1972). Does power corrupt? *Journal of Personality and Social Psychology, 24*, 33–41.

Knoch, D., Schneider, F., Schunk, D., Hohmann, M., & Fehr, E. (2009). Disrupting the prefrontal cortex diminishes the human ability to build a good reputation. *Proceedings of the National Academy of Sciences of the United States of America, 106*, 20895–20899.

Lord, R. G., De Vader, C. L, & Alliger, G. M. (1986). A meta-analysis of the relation between personality traits and leadership perceptions: An application of validity generalization procedures. *Journal of Applied Psychology, 71*, 402–410.

Maynard-Smith, J. (1982). *Evolution and the theory of games*. Cambridge, UK: Cambridge University Press.

Mezulis, A., Abramson, L., Hyde, J. S., & Hankin, B. L. (2004). Is there a universal positivity bias in attributions? A meta-analytic review of individual, developmental, and cultural differences in the self-serving attributional bias. *Psychological Bulletin, 130*, 711–746.

McCann, S. J. H. (1992). Alternative formulas to predict the greatness of U. S. presidents: Personological, situational, and zeitgeist factors. *Journal of Personality and Social Psychology, 62*, 469–479.

Mio, J. S., Riggio, R. E., Levin, S., & Reese, R. (2005). Presidential leadership and charisma: The effects of metaphor. *The Leadership Quarterly, 16*, 287–294.

Nicholson, N. (2000). *Managing the human animal*. New York: Thomson.

O'Gorman, R. O., Henrich, J., & Van Vugt, M. (2009). Constraining free-riding in public goods games: Designated solitary punishers can sustain human cooperation. *Proceedings of Royal Society B, 276*, 323–329.

Padilla, A., Hogan, R., & Kaiser, R. B. (2007). The toxic triangle: Destructive leaders, vulnerable followers, and conducive environments. *The Leadership Quarterly, 18*, 176–194.

Perusse, D. (1993). Cultural and reproductive success in industrial societies: Testing the relationship at the proximate and ultimate levels. *Behavioral and Brain Sciences, 16,* 267–322.

Pinker, S. (2002). *The blank slate.* London: Penguin Classics.

Richerson, P. J., & Boyd, R. (2006). *Not by genes alone: How culture transformed human evolution.* Chicago: Chicago University Press.

Riley, J. R., Greggers, U., Smith, A., Reynolds, D., & Menzel, R. (2005). The flight paths of honey bees recruited by the waggle dance. *Nature, 435,* 205–207.

Sanfey, A. (2007). Social decision making: Insights from game theory and neuroscience. *Science, 318,* 598–602.

Schaller, M., Simpson, J., & Kenrick, D. (2006). *Evolution and social psychology.* London: Psychology Press.

Schmitt, D. P., & Pilcher, J. J. (2004). Evaluating evidence of psychological adaptation: How do we know one when we see one? *Psychological Science, 15,* 643–649.

Sessa, V. I., Kaiser, R., Taylor, J. K., & Campbell, R. J. (1998). *Executive selection.* Greensboro, NC: Center for Creative Leadership.

Sherif, M. (1966). *In common predicament.* Boston: Houghton Mifflin.

Simonton, D. K. (1994). *Who makes history and why?* New York: Guilford.

Singer, T., Seymour, B., O'Doherty, J. P., Stephan, K. E., Dolan, R. J., & Frith, C. D. (2006). Empathic neural responses are modulated by the perceived fairness of others. *Nature, 439,* 466–469.

Spisak, B., & van Vugt, M. (2010). *Face masculinity and femininity as predictors of electoral success.* Unpublished manuscript.

Tinbergen, N. (1963). On the aims and methods in ethology. *Zeitschrift for Tierpsychology, 20,* 410–433.

Van Vugt, M. (2006). The evolutionary origins of leadership and followership. *Personality and Social Psychology Review, 10,* 354–372.

Van Vugt, M. (2009). Despotism, democracy, and the evolutionary dynamics of leadership and followership. *American Psychologist, 64,* 54–56.

Van Vugt, M., & Ahuja, A. (2010) *Naturally selected: Why some people lead, why others follow, and why it matters.* London: Profile.

Van Vugt, M., & De Cremer, D. (1999). Leadership in social dilemmas: The effects of group identification on collective actions to provide public goods. *Journal of Personality and Social Psychology, 76,* 587–599.

Van Vugt, M., De Cremer, D., & Janssen, D. (2007). Gender differences in cooperation and competition: The male warrior hypothesis. *Psychological Science, 18,* 19–23.

Van Vugt, M., & Hart, C. M. (2004). Social identity as social glue: The origins of group loyalty. *Journal of Personality and Social Psychology, 86,* 585–598.

Van Vugt, M., Hogan, R., & Kaiser, R. (2008). Leadership, followership, and evolution: Some lessons from the past. *American Psychologist, 63,* 182–196.

Van Vugt, M., Jepson, S. F., Hart, C. M., & De Cremer, D. (2004). Autocratic leadership in social dilemmas: A threat to group stability. *Journal of Experimental Social Psychology, 40,* 1–13.

Van Vugt, M., Johnson, D., Kaiser, R., & O'Gorman, R. (2008). Evolution and the social psychology of leadership: The mismatch hypothesis. In J. B. Ciulla (Set Ed.) and C. R. Hoyt, G. R. Goethals, & D. R. Forsyth (Vol. Eds.), *Leadership at the crossroads: Vol. 1. Leadership and psychology* (pp. 267–282). London: Praeger.

Van Vugt, M., & Kameda, T. (in press). Evolutionary approaches to group dynamics. In J. Levine (Ed.), *Handbook of group processes*. London: Sage.

Van Vugt, M., & Kurzban, R. K. (2007). Cognitive and social adaptations for leadership and followership: Evolutionary game theory and group dynamics. In J. Forgas, W. von Hippel, & M. Haselton (Eds.), *Sydney Symposium of Social Psychology: Vol. 9. The evolution of the social mind: Evolutionary psychology and social cognition* (pp. 229–244). London: Psychology Press.

Van Vugt, M., & Schaller, M. (2008). Evolutionary perspectives on group dynamics: An introduction. *Group Dynamics, 12,* 1–6.

Van Vugt, M., & Spisak, B. R. (2008). Sex differences in leadership emergence during competitions within and between groups. *Psychological Science, 19,* 854–858.

Vroom, V. H., & Jago, A. G. (1978). On the validity of the Vroom-Yetton model. *Journal of Applied Psychology, 63,* 151–162.

Waldman, D. A., Ramirez, G. G., House, R. J., & Puranam, P. (2001). Does leadership matter? CEO leadership attributes and profitability under conditions of perceived environmental uncertainty. *Academy of Management Journal, 44,* 134–143.

Wayne, S. J., & Ferris, G. R. (1990). Influence tactics, affect and exchange quality in supervisor-subordinate interactions: A laboratory experiment and field study. *Journal of Applied Psychology, 75,* 487–499.

Williams, K. D., & Sommer, K. L. (1997). Social ostracism by co-workers: Does rejection lead to loafing or compensation? *Personality and Social Psychology Bulletin, 61,* 570–581.

Wilson, D. S. (2007). *Evolution for everyone*. New York: Delta.

Wilson, D. S., Van Vugt, M., & O'Gorman, R. (2008). Multilevel selection theory and major evolutionary transitions: Implications for psychological science. *Current Directions in Psychological Science, 17,* 6–9.

Wilson, E. O. (1975). *Sociobiology: The new synthesis*. Cambridge, MA: Harvard University Press.

Yukl, G. A. (2006). *Leadership in organizations* (6th ed.). Englewood Cliffs, NJ: Prentice Hall.

Zaccaro, S. J., Gilbert, J. A., Thor, K. K., & Mumford, M. D. (1991). Leadership and social intelligence: Linking social perceptiveness and behavioral flexibility to leader effectiveness. *The Leadership Quarterly, 2,* 317–342.

PART III

The Major
Schools of Leadership

6 Individual Differences in Leadership

Timothy A. Judge

University of Notre Dame

David M. Long

University of Florida

To varying but generally high degrees, all mammalian species are social animals (i.e., individual mammals are organized into clans and collectives). How are these collectives organized? What dictates their behavior beyond the instincts and motives of the individuals comprising the group? What explains the varying rates of success both within and between collectives or groups? *Leadership*—which we define as actions by individuals which serve to direct, control, or influence the group's behavior toward collective goals—may not be the only answer to these questions, but it is probably the most important. It is fair to surmise that whenever there is social activity, a social structure develops, and one (perhaps the) defining characteristic of that structure is the emergence of a leader or leaders. Leaders may then be argued to be a human universal: Where there are humans, there is a collective social structure, and where there is a social structure, there is a leader at the head and center of it.

Yet, as with many complex social phenomena, answering one question only stimulates others. As noted by R. Hogan and Kaiser (2005), two of those questions are: "Who *shall* rule?" and "Who *should* rule?" (p. 169).

AUTHORS' NOTE: Please address correspondence concerning this chapter to Timothy A. Judge, Mendoza College of Business, University of Notre Dame, Notre Dame, IN 46556, USA. e-mail: tjudge@nd.edu.

More generally, in studying a group, one quickly wonders: What has caused this leadership structure to emerge? Why has one animal (the alpha) emerged to lead the collective? And how does this leadership cause this collective to flourish—or flounder?

Given these questions, it is of no surprise that the earliest conceptions of leadership focused on individual differences. The most famous of these is Thomas Carlyle's "great man" theory, in which he argued, "For, as I take it, Universal History, the history of what man has accomplished in this world, is at bottom the History of the Great Men who have worked here" (Carlyle, 1840/2008, p. 1). Despite its intuitive appeal, this "great man" (or, more accurately in contemporary society, "great person") approach, and the trait perspective in general, fell out of favor. Reviewers of the literature commented that the approach was "too simplistic" (Conger & Kanungo, 1998, p. 38), "futile" (House & Aditya, 1997, p. 410), and even "dangerous" and a product of "self-delusion" (see Andersen, 2006, p. 1083).[1]

What caused this apparent failure? To some degree, it was a product of the times. The intellectual movements in mid-20th century psychology (between, say, 1930 and 1980)—humanistic psychology, behaviorism, the cognitive revolution, finally and most importantly, social psychology—not only did not emphasize individual differences, but they were, in some cases, openly hostile to them. Behavioral genetics provided a devastating and durable rebuttal to the dismissal of individual differences, as did many of the conceptual advances offered in response to Mischel's (1968) critique. Still, intellectual traditions die hard, and there remain not small pockets of resistance to trait research (R. Hogan, 2005). It is an insoluble limit to scientific inquiry that belief does not always yield to evidence, especially when the evidence falls short of lawful relations (always the case in social scientific inquiry).

Another reason for the resistance to traits was unintentionally self-inflicted. Personality theory was and is fragmented by issues both pragmatic (how to measure personality) and philosophical (whether to focus on individual differences [nomothetics] or individual development [idiographics]). There is not—and probably never will be—consensus on how to define personality, how to distinguish related terms (traits, temperament), what comprises personality psychology, and how to measure personality. Though this may indicate a "weak paradigm" (Kuhn, 1970), all social sciences are "weak" or uncertain in that variation in human behavior is so complex in its nature and origins as to defy lawful explanation. In our opinion, the solution to such "weak" disciplines is not to attempt to forge a false consensus or to proffer mathematically rigorous but unrealistic methods or models (the problem with the dominant approach—Samuelsonianism—in economics [McCloskey, 2002]). Rather, a discipline is healthiest that embraces debate and engages itself toward addressing intellectual disagreements. The best of personality psychology does this. Yet, this process yields slow and uneven gains in understanding.

Still another reason for the limited impact of trait theory on leadership research was at once a very practical and a very deep one: What traits are "cardinal"—as opposed to "central" or "secondary" (Allport, 1937)? Some of the most important midcentury personality research was inventory based (e.g., Gough's California Psychological Inventory; Cattell's 16 PF; Guilford-Zimmerman Temperament Survey). Although there was some overlap in these inventories, mostly, it was a rather confusing exercise to distill common cardinal and central traits from these inventories. No matter what its critics maintain, a path out of this wilderness was provided by working on the five-factor model, or the "Big Five" (Costa & McCrae, 1992; Digman, 1990; Goldberg, 1990; Norman, 1963; Tupes & Christal, 1961). Though not a formal or comprehensive theory of personality (does one exist?), the five-factor typology provided both an organizing structure and a reasonable measurement approach. The structure has been related to virtually all applied criteria.

Concomitant with the acceptance of the five-factor model was growth and application of a methodology: meta-analysis. Meta-analyses of a diverse set of topics caused re-examination of many previously held assumptions—In general, these meta-analyses showed that subjective eyeballing of data across studies generally leads reviewers to overestimate the variability in the data and underestimate central tendencies. The intersection of these trends—meta-analyses using the five-factor model as an organizing framework—has produced powerful insights into many, if not most, organizational behaviors (see R. Hogan, 2005; Ones, Dilchert, Viswesvaran, & Judge, 2007).

Capitalizing on these two trends, Judge, Bono, Ilies, and Gerhardt (2002) conducted a meta-analysis of the leader trait approach, organizing the traits according to the five-factor model. Judge et al. (2002) meta-analyzed 222 correlations from 73 samples. They found that four of the Big Five traits had nontrivial correlations with leadership emergence and effectiveness: extraversion, conscientiousness, emotional stability, and openness to experience. When the criterion was regressed on the five traits, the five-factor model had a multiple correlation of $R = .53$ with leader emergence and $R = .39$ with leadership effectiveness. Despite the apparent success of this effort and other attempts to link the five-factor model to organizational criteria, critics of the trait approach remain, and many of these criticisms are relevant to the leader trait perspective, even if they were not specifically directed at it.

First, some remain unimpressed by the size of the validity coefficients. These criticisms pertain mostly to the relations of the Big Five traits to job performance, but since the leader trait correlations are not dramatically different, the same criticisms may apply. In comparing the personality literature to an oft-cited, earlier review (Guion & Gottier, 1965), Murphy and Dzieweczynski (2005, p. 345) concluded with respect to job performance, "One major concern was that the validity of personality inventories as predictors of job performance and other organizationally relevant criteria seemed generally low. An examination of the current literature suggests that this concern is still a legitimate one." Andersen (2006), in commenting on the leader trait approach specifically, concluded (p. 1088): "The main point is that the relationship (measured as correlation) is low. Consequently, personality has low explanatory and predictive power."

A second criticism pertains to the ways in which leadership is measured. Some argue that whereas personality measures may reveal whether an individual is perceived as leader-like, such measures are less successful in identifying whether those leaders are successful in an objective sense. Kaiser, Hogan, and Craig (2008) criticized the Judge et al. (2002) study for this (failed) distinction, noting that the study focuses on "how leaders are regarded and tells us little about leading effective teams" or how such traits "help organizations prosper" (p. 102). Morgeson, Campion, Dipboye, Hollenbeck, Murphy, & Schmitt (2007) also criticize the Judge et al. (2002) meta-analysis on these grounds, arguing, "Perceived influence is not equivalent to effectiveness, and showing that there is a correlation of a personality dimension with perceived influence does not provide a strong basis for use of this measure to select managers who will be effective" (p. 1044). Though Judge et al. (2002) did distinguish between leader emergence—who is recognized as a leader of a group—and leadership effectiveness—how well that leader performs in that role—it is fair to conclude that most of the studies they cumulated for leadership effectiveness still relied on subjective evaluations. Objective measures of leadership, of course, have their own problems, including contamination (financial success of a leader's unit may depend on many factors unrelated to the effectiveness of his or her leadership) and faux objectivity (are historian ratings of U.S. presidential greatness really objective?).

Third and finally, the five-factor model is not the sole statement on the structure of personality. There are critics of the epistemological origins of the model, and of its ontological status (Block, 1995, 2001; McAdams, 1992). Another line of research, although not necessarily standing in opposition to the five-factor model, argues in favor of either fewer (e.g., Digman, 1997) or more (e.g., Benet-Martinez & Waller, 1997) core factors. Goldberg, for example, despite being a strong advocate of the notion that the most salient individual differences become encoded in natural language (i.e., lexical hypothesis), favors a circumplex model of trait interactions (Abridged Big Five Dimensional Circumplex [AB5C]; Hofstee, de Raad, & Goldberg, 1992), whereby blends of the five traits are treated as more valid indicators of personality than the otherwise distinct five factors. Moreover, despite widespread use of the five-factor model, including facets of subdimensions of these factors (see DeYoung, Quilty, & Peterson, 2007), there still is not widespread agreement on the lower order facets.

The purpose of this chapter is to review the leader trait approach in such a way as to organize thinking, present a perspective, and provide an agenda for future research. In so doing, beyond addressing the above criticisms, we borrow from two recent perspectives in personality research. First, we focus not only on the Big Five traits, but consider the leadership implications of more narrow, but also possibly more powerful, personality traits. Second, we draw from recent thinking on the paradoxical implications of traits for fitness (Nettle, 2006). We do consider the advantages of positively valenced ("bright") traits and the disadvantages conferred by negatively valenced ("dark") traits. However, we also consider the possible advantages of "dark side" traits, and the possible disadvantage of "bright side" traits (Judge & LePine, 2007).

Before our specific discussion of traits, we first review a critical theoretical perspective that underlies our analysis to follow. Specifically, we briefly review research on evolutionary theory and evolutionary psychology and focus in particular on the issue of trait paradox. That perspective then guides the trait discussion that follows, which focuses on the bright and dark sides of the specific traits.

Evolutionary Psychology and Trait Paradox

Evolutionary theory does many things relevant to the leader trait perspective, including: (a) providing a theory for the existence of certain traits, and of leadership, in humans (or other species [Gosling, 2008; Van Vugt, Hogan, & Kaiser, 2008]); (b) providing an explanation, if only in part, for the efficacy of certain traits and of leadership (Van Vugt et al., 2008); and (c) also providing a prediction, at least in a general form, for trait paradoxes. Given that evolutionary approaches are considered elsewhere in the book (see Van Vugt's chapter), here we focus on what is particularly germane to our approach to follow: trait paradox.

Paradox of Traits

The interaction of species with their environment is often paradoxical. What leads to fitness at one time or in one context might be reversed at another time or in a different situation. Moreover, the two evolutionary selection processes—survival fitness and sexual fitness—may contradict one another: Males sometimes die or are damaged in mating rituals, and females' impregnation endangers their survival both pre- and post-partum (M. Kirkpatrick & Ryan, 1991). Here we focus on three evolutionary paradoxes relevant to the leader trait perspective: (a) the benefits of a trait at one time or in one context may be reversed when times or situations change; (b) traits rarely have unalloyed advantages (or disadvantages) even in a single context at a single point in time; and (c) there are nonlinearities in the effect of a trait on fitness or leadership outcomes.

First, a trait that promotes fitness at one time (or in one situation) may become irrelevant or, worse, counterproductive, when situations change. An individual with a slow metabolism or greedy appetite might do well when food is scarce. But that same individual might become morbidly obese in a munificent environment. As applied to the leader trait perspective, this paradox suggests a possible mismatch between the traits of leaders and contemporary demands. Evolution is, as judged against the length of life span, an extraordinarily long process. The high mutation rate of humans notwithstanding (Penke, Denissen, & Miller, 2007), many if not most characteristics we have today evolved over tens of thousands and hundreds of thousands of years. Yet civilization today is radically different from that of 10,000 years ago—what is a very short period in human evolution is a very long period in human civilization. Just as some characteristics, both physical (e.g., good vision) and psychological (e.g., alertness) might have waned in importance to survival, so might other characteristics become more important (e.g., refinement, demureness) only relatively recently. In short, the traits that caused us to rise to the top of the food chain, and our leaders to rise highest, may not be as well suited to contemporary society (Van Vugt et al., 2008).

Second, even when confined to a singular environment at one point in time, trait paradox occurs. This form of paradox might be labeled "antagonistic pleiotropy" (Penke et al., 2007), where polymorphisms (i.e., a specific genetic variant or mutation that is discernable) have a positive effect on one fitness-related trait and a negative effect on another. Given the complex set of behaviors that underlie solving adaptive problems, one might expect most traits, even those very helpful to fitness, to contain antagonistic pleiotropy. What causes one to be attractive to mates often involves taking risk and, in so doing, trading one type of fitness (reproductive) for another (survival). At this juncture, one might ask: "It is all fine and good to talk about reproductive fitness when one's subject is mating rituals, but that subject is not germane to organizational leadership." We think this argument misunderstands the nature of genes. We value height in our leaders (Judge & Cable, 2004), not because it is rational to do so but because at one time height helped solve adaptive problems or suggested reproductive fitness. Natural selection led to humans having those instincts, and those same instincts will take a very long time to dissipate, even when they cease to be important to fitness (and, of course, some traits remain important to survival or reproductive fitness). People do not discard their genes when they enter the door to their workplace.

Adapting this to the topic at hand, these observations suggest that just as certain characteristics may have countervailing effects on fitness, so too might they have similar effects on leader effectiveness. A trusting, gentle, compassionate leader might earn the affection of her followers, but she also might be vulnerable to being manipulated or duped by others. A shrewd, scheming, cunning leader might be despised and distrusted by those who know him well, but he might gain many advantages at the expense of the uninitiated.

Third, traits may not have linear effects—on fitness or on leadership outcomes. Comparing two leaders being one standard deviation apart on openness may mean one thing if both leaders are below the overall openness mean and may mean something quite different if both leaders are above the mean. The higher scoring leader might be seen as more innovative, entrepreneurial, and autonomous in the former case but as sensation seeking, radical, or unmanageable in the latter case. Similarly, bold and assertive actions position one to "claim" valuable resources for oneself and one's clan (Ames & Flynn, 2007), and first mover advantages are often important to group survival (Van Vugt et al., 2008). However, overly bold actions can become foolhardy and expose oneself or one's collective to unwanted attention, counterattacks, and resource depletion. Thus, for some traits, curvilinear relations should exist.

Similarly, the fitness implications of traits may be complex, and may be affected by the presence or absence of other traits. The evolutionary biologist Ernst Mayr noted, "The genotype . . . is always in the context with other genes, and the interaction with those other genes make a particular gene either more favorable or less favorable" (Diamond, 2001, p. 39; see also Mayr, 2001). A genotypic predisposition toward conscientiousness may reveal a phenotypic manifestation in many different ways, perhaps depending on the presence of other traits. Whether the conscientious leader is effective may depend on how that conscientiousness is expressed.

A Note on Behavioral Genetics

Genetic sources of personality traits are now so well established that one might reasonably call it a law (Turkheimer, 2000). *Leaders are born* in the sense that identical twins reared apart share striking similarities in terms of their leadership emergence. Numerous studies now show that various measures of leadership—from indicators of leader emergence (leadership offices held) to leadership effectiveness measures (measures of transformational leadership behavior)—show significant heritabilities, often in the 30%–60% range (Arvey, Rotundo, Johnson, Zhang, & McGue, 2006; A. M. Johnson, Vernon, Harris, & Jang, 2004; A. M. Johnson et al., 1998). A significant part of the heritability of leadership is no doubt because of the heritability of individual differences associated with leadership (Ilies, Gerhardt, & Le, 2004).

It is reasonable to ask how evolutionary theory and behavioral genetics can be reconciled. After all, if a phenotype is helpful to reproductive success or survival, then variation in that trait should become attenuated over time as those who are low on the characteristic are disproportionately selected out. Put another way, if mutation adds variation, then evolution removes it (by selecting out those with counteradaptive variation).

Evolutionary selection, however, has its own process, and there are various reasons why genetic individual differences persist (Penke et al., 2007). First, there is *selective neutrality*, where selection is blind to an individual difference (i.e., the characteristic is unrelated to fitness). One might, for example, observe characteristics in some leaders (say, sensitivity to criticism) that say little about their effectiveness or their evolutionary fitness. Second, there is *mutation-selection balance*, where selection does not perfectly eliminate the individual difference, often because the nature of the context has changed (i.e., some of the characteristics that led to fitness in the early stages of humanity may not apply to fitness in contemporary life). Third, there is *balancing selection,* where selection itself maintains genetic variation (i.e., a characteristic may be positively related to fitness in some environments or contexts, and negatively related to fitness in others). There are also more complex mechanisms that allow genetic mutation and evolutionary adaptation to maintain individual differences. One possibility was mentioned earlier: frequency-dependent selection, where the fitness implications of a particular trait depend on its prevalence in other members of the species (see Ilies et al., 2004). The benefits of psychological collectivism, for example, may accelerate as collectivism in a species or sub-population increases (i.e., the payoff to collectivism increases as others in one's population are similarly collectivistic [positive frequency-dependent selection]).

What are the implications of behavioral genetics for the leader trait perspective? As noted above, it provides an explanation for why, at least in part, leaders are born. To a significant degree, leadership is rooted in individual genes, namely, their genetic predispositions to have psychological (personality, intelligence) and physical (height, attractiveness) characteristics that predispose them to seek leadership positions, to be selected by others to such positions, and to thrive in such positions once selected.

Model of Individual Differences in Leadership _____

Based on the foregoing review, and based substantially on an earlier work (Judge, Piccolo, & Kosalka, 2009), Figure 6.1 presents a conceptual model. Following prior leader trait research (Judge et al., 2002), the model distinguishes between leader emergence and leadership effectiveness. Based on criticisms of the leader trait paradigm (Kaiser et al., 2008), it also draws a distinction between subjective leadership effectiveness—follower ratings of leaders, follower affective reactions to leaders—and objective effectiveness—as reflected in group performance, group survival. The model posits trait effects on both emergence and effectiveness. Because one must first emerge as a leader to be effective as one, it also shows a link from leader emergence to leadership effectiveness. Moreover, because both the process of emerging as leader and becoming an effective leader after emerging as one depend on behaviors, leader states and styles mediate the trait effects. Finally, the model also suggests various moderating influences through the model.

Having presented the model in a general sense, we turn our attention to the core of our model. Specifically, we discuss in detail: (a) the *paradox of leader individual differences*—the ways in which leader individual differences (personality, ability) exert paradoxical effects on leader emergence, leadership states and styles, and leadership effectiveness; (b) *mediators of individual differences*—leadership states and styles as explanations for the relationship of leader traits to leader emergence and to leadership effectiveness; and (c) *moderators of individual differences*—the degree to which follower and leader individual differences, as well as context, moderate the linkages within the model. In the following sections, we discuss each of these processes in turn.

Figure 6.1 Model of individual differences in leadership

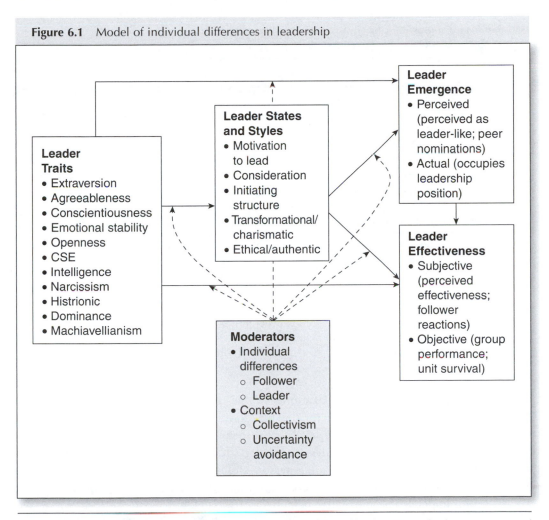

NOTE: CSE = core self-evaluations. Bold lines represent direct effects of leader traits on leader emergence and on leader effectiveness. Dashed lines represent moderating influences.

_____ **Paradox of Leader Individual Differences**

As shown by prior quantitative reviews (Judge et al., 2002), many socially desirable personality traits—so called "bright" traits—are likely to be valuable for leader emergence and leadership effectiveness across situations. Yet these same traits could be counterproductive in particular contexts. Thus, bright traits, albeit favorable for leadership in general, also carry with them paradoxical utility. We would also observe a similar phenomenon for socially undesirable (i.e., "dark") traits, such that these traits might compromise leader effectiveness in general but actually might enhance group survival and fitness in some.

Thus, the framework for trait paradox, as shown in Table 6.1, considers four possible implications for leader emergence and leadership effectiveness of traits: (a) socially desirable traits that in most cases, have positive

Table 6.1   Paradoxical Effects of Leader Individual Differences on Leader Emergence or Leadership Effectiveness

Trait Social Desirability	Actual Effects in Specific Context or Situation	
	Bright effect	*Dark effect*
Bright trait	Socially desirable trait has positive implications for leaders and stakeholders	Socially desirable trait has negative implications for leaders and stakeholders
	Example: Conscientious leader displays high ethical standards in pursuing agenda in long-term interest of organization.	*Example*: Conscientious leader has difficulty adapting strategy when confronted with environmental turbulence.
Dark trait	Socially undesirable trait has positive implications for leaders and stakeholders	Socially undesirable trait has negative implications for leaders and stakeholders
	Example: Narcissistic leader's self-confidence causes him/her to emerge from chaotic context when no one else is willing to assume responsibility.	*Example*: Narcissistic leader manipulates reward structure (e.g., stock price based on granted options) to personal advantage at long-term expense to organization.

implications; (b) socially undesirable traits that in most situations, have negative implication; (c) socially desirable traits that in particular situations and at extreme levels, have negative implications; and (d) socially undesirable traits that in particular situations, have positive implications. In so doing, we draw on a person–situation interactionist model of behavior and performance (Tett & Burnett, 2003) to describe the conditions under which particular personality traits relate to leader effectiveness. We consider seven "bright side" individual differences: The Big Five traits, core self-evaluations, and intelligence. Based on Judge et al. (2009), we consider four "dark side" traits that are among the most widely investigated socially undesirable traits: narcissism, dominance, histrionic personality, and Machiavellianism. Of course, other bright and dark side traits could be considered. (Table 6.2 and Table 6.3 highlight these traits and their potential implications.)

Table 6.2   Possible Leader Trait Paradoxes Involving "Bright" Five-Factor Model Traits

		Leadership Benefits and Costs	
		Leader Benefits	*Leader Costs*
	Extraversion	More likely to emerge as leader; More charismatic and inspiring; Greater ambition	More impulsive and risky decisions; Less likely to listen to followers; May lack persistence and commitment to long-term vision

		Leadership Benefits and Costs	
		Leader Benefits	Leader Costs
"Bright" (Big Five) Traits	Agreeableness	More considerate; More positive interpersonal interactions and helping behavior; Lower conflict; Lower deviance and turnover	Lower ambition to lead or excel; Less initiating structure; Easily "rolled" off course by influential followers
	Conscientiousness	Greater desire to lead; More effective at setting and maintaining goals; More ethical	Reduced adaptability; More controlling; More likely to lose visionary focus (in favor micro-management)
	Emotional stability	Greater desire to lead; More positive vision; More ethical	Less able to detect risks; Less concerned with danger (more susceptible to illusions); More likely to choose "easy" wins that verify self-concept
	Openness	More innovative; More visionary; More adaptable	Nonconformists; More likely to lead group in dangerous or independent direction; Less likely to accept leadership from above

Table 6.3 Possible Leader Trait Paradoxes Involving "Dark" Traits

		Leadership Benefits and Costs	
		Leader Benefits	Leader Costs
"Dark" Traits	Narcissism	More likely to emerge as leader; More willing to defend territory against threats; More charismatic	Inflated self-views in terms of leadership; Exploitive and manipulative leadership; Derogation of perceived competitors
	Histrionic	More likely to emerge as leader; More likely to be viewed as charismatic and innovative; Good social skills, especially in new environments	Vanity (overly concerned with looks, overly sensitive to disapproval; attention-seeking); Overly dramatic and unstable; Low tolerance for frustration
	Dominance	More motivated to lead; More likely to emerge as leader; More effective at taking charge	Perceived as controlling or domineering; May be conflict-seeking; Difficult interactions with dominant followers
	Machiavellianism	Greater motivation to lead; More politically astute; May win greater gains for group	Less considerate; More manipulative; Overly political and "distributive" (win-lose) leadership

Bright Side of Bright Traits

Each of the Big Five traits—being "bright" or socially desirable traits—may have positive effects for leaders.

Conscientiousness. Because conscientious individuals are detail-oriented and deliberate in their decision making (Costa & McCrae, 1992; R. Hogan & Hogan, 2001), conscientiousness may facilitate leader effectiveness through initiating structure activities. Moreover, conscientious leaders tend to be disciplined in pursuit of goal attainment, suggesting that conscientious leaders will clearly and consistently define role expectations and fairly deliver on informal contracts (Bass, 1985). Conscientious leaders will exhibit integrity (J. Hogan & Ones, 1997) and more tenacity and persistence in pursuit of organizational objectives (Goldberg, 1990), explaining perhaps, why conscientious leaders foster work climates regarded as fair and just (Mayer, Nishii, Schneider, & Goldstein, 2007).

Extraversion. Because extraverts are assertive, of all the Big Five traits, extraversion should be the strongest predictor of leader emergence, and that is the case (Judge et al., 2002). Because extraverts are energetic, upbeat, talkative, and enthusiastic (Costa & McCrae, 1992), they should be more charismatic as well. It is therefore no surprise that Bono and Judge (2004) recognized extraversion as "the strongest and most consistent correlate of transformational leadership" (p. 901).

Agreeableness. Agreeableness is manifested in modesty and altruistic behavior (Costa & McCrae, 1992), which means that agreeable leaders should be more considerate. Agreeable leaders are likely to promote cooperation and helping behavior among team members (Hurtz & Donovan, 2000), be empathetic when delivering critical feedback, and encourage a pleasant, friendly, and fair work environment (Mayer et al., 2007).

Emotional stability. Emotionally stable leaders are calm, relaxed, consistent in their emotional expressions, and not likely to experience negative emotions such as stress, anxiety, or jealousy (Judge & LePine, 2007). Leaders who exhibit emotional stability are likely to remain calm in moments of crisis, be patient with employee development, and recover quickly from group and organizational failures.

Openness to experience. Openness to experience is linked to creativity, imagination, and insight (John & Srivastava, 1999), suggesting that visionary leadership is more likely for open individuals. In their meta-analytic review, Bono and Judge (2004) found that open individuals receive high scores on the intellectual stimulation and inspirational motivation components of transformational leadership, as these leaders have a vivid imagination, are able to challenge conventional wisdom on critical issues, and visualize a compelling future for the organization.

Core self-evaluation. The Big Five, of course, do not exhaust the "bright side" individual differences that are characteristics of relevant leadership. One such individual difference is core self-evaluations (CSE). According to Judge (2009), "Core self-evaluations are fundamental, bottom-line evaluations that people make of themselves" (p. 58). Hiller and Hambrick (2005) offer a comprehensive review of the literature linking the core traits and executive leadership, noting that in many situations a positive self-concept underlies many required behaviors of executive leadership, including innovation and risk-taking. Moreover, Hiller and Hambrick (2005) also suggest that high levels of core self-evaluations in CEOs will be associated with simpler and faster strategic decision processes, a greater number of large stake initiatives, and more enduring organizational persistence in pursuit of those initiatives. Supporting this line of reasoning, a recent study found that CSE was linked to the success of chief executives of major league baseball organizations (Resick, Whitman, Weingarden, & Hiller, 2009).

Intelligence. The final bright side individual difference we consider here is not a personality trait, but rather an ability, namely general mental ability or intelligence. Few individual differences are more valued in modern Western society than cognitive ability (i.e., intelligence; Judge, Colbert, & Ilies, 2004). Judge and his colleagues found that the relationship between intelligence and leadership is indeed significant, albeit not as strong as the relationship between intelligence and job performance. Intelligence, of course, helps leaders solve the problems that confront their unit and, perhaps, decide on a vision and mission that is effective and appealing to stakeholders.

Dark Side of Dark Traits

Narcissism. Narcissism is a personality trait that is characterized by arrogance, self-absorption, entitlement, and hostility (Rosenthal & Pittinsky, 2006). As a self-regulatory defense mechanism against a grandiose, yet shallow, self-concept (Morf & Rhodewait, 2001), narcissists tend to view others as inferior to themselves and tend to derogate those whom they see as competitors. Narcissist leaders are more likely to interpret information with a self-serving bias and make decisions based on how those decisions will reflect on their reputations. Van Dijk and De Cremer (2006) found that narcissistic managers were more self-serving than their more humble counterparts, with an inclination to allocate scarce organizational resources to themselves. Whereas narcissistic leaders may be prone to enhance self-ratings of leadership, attractiveness, and influence, these same leaders are generally viewed negatively by others, which reveals itself in lower job performance and fewer examples of organizational citizenship among subordinates (Judge, LePine, & Rich, 2006).

Histrionic personality. Those who have a histrionic personality tend to be dramatic, colorful, seductive, social, manipulative, exhibitionistic, and emotional. The reader might wonder whether these characteristics might well describe charismatic leaders. Indeed, recent evidence suggests that individuals who score high on histrionic personality measures tend to score high on measures of transformational leadership (Khoo & Burch, 2008). R. Hogan and Kaiser (2005) describe the benefits of a histrionic personality to leadership, which include being entertaining and engaging. Another study suggested that innovative managers were more likely to score high on aspects of histrionic personality—manipulative, dramatic, and eccentric (Zibarras, Port, & Woods, 2008). This suggests that histrionic individuals may be particularly likely to be viewed as leader-like, and thus more likely to emerge as leaders.

Dominance. Whereas dominance is often regarded as a lower level facet of extraversion (Judge et al., 2002), it often is not, and need not be, subsumed under extraversion (Judge et al., 2009). Dominant individuals prefer to take charge, to control conversations, and to direct others. As noted by Judge et al. (2009), dominant leaders may lead through brute force and may be unlikely to lead their followers to feel their views are supported or even considered. In a study of personality and authority in families, for example, Altemeyer (2004) found that highly dominating individuals were regarded as power hungry and manipulative. Nicol (2009) found that socially dominant leaders were less likely to be described as considerate by their followers. Van Vugt (2006) challenges the conventional wisdom in evolutionary psychology that leadership emerges from dominance and submission, arguing, "The literature suggests that people do not support dominant leaders, quite possibly because of fears of being exploited by them" (p. 359).

Machiavellianism. Machiavellianism is a term used to define a personality trait characterized by both awareness—political astuteness and cunning—and an ability to use that awareness to achieve one's ends. Embedded in Machiavellianism is the encouragement to deceive, manipulate, and forcefully persuade others towards the leader's goals. Machiavellian leaders are more likely to employ "hard" political influence behaviors (Reimers & Barbuto, 2002) and tend to avoid motives of organizational concern and prosocial values (Becker & O'Hair, 2007). Machiavellians are less likely to share knowledge with others (Liu, 2008). Though Machiavellian leaders may have greater influence over people (Goldberg, 1999), that influence is generally used for personal power rather than the collective good.

Dark Side of Bright Traits

Conscientiousness. Highly conscientious individuals tend to be cautious and analytical and, therefore, often less willing to innovate or take risks. Cautious leaders avoid innovation, resist change, and delay critical decision-making processes, hampered by their need to gather compelling information and evidence in support their preferences (R. Hogan & Hogan, 2001). Leaders who are highly conscientious may be threatened by turbulent circumstances and organizational change, and they experience stress when impending deadlines and daunting workloads compromise their strong desires to follow strict and organized procedures. Indeed, conscientious individuals tend to be less adaptable to change (LePine, Colquitt, & Erez, 2000), which suggests that conscientious leaders may be poorly equipped to handle the very changes they are charged with envisioning, anticipating, and/or responding to. Moreover, highly conscientious leaders may be seen as difficult to please, prone to micromanagement, and bureaucratic about procedures and policies (R. Hogan & Hogan, 2001).

Extraversion. Extraverts tend to be bold and aggressive. As a result, extraverts are more likely to have conflictual relations with others (Bono, Boles, Judge, & Lauver, 2002), suggesting that extraverted leaders may produce more conflicts with followers and colleagues. Because of their sociability and broader social networks (Forret & Dougherty, 2001), extraverted leaders may also engage in short, shallow communications with many people in an organization, thus failing to provide a clear strategic focus for followers. Third, extraverted groups may be more prone to risky shift (Rim, 1982), suggesting that groups working for extraverted leaders may be similarly predisposed toward risky decisions. Finally, as sensation seekers who maintain short-lived enthusiasm for projects, people, and ideas (Beauducel, Brocke & Leue, 2006), extraverted leaders may make hasty or overly aggressive decisions or may not have the persistence to see elongated projects to their conclusion.

Agreeableness. Because agreeable individuals are cooperative, accommodating, gentle, and conflict-avoidant (Graziano & Eisenberg, 1997), agreeable leaders may avoid making tough decisions and may seek to minimize conflict to suboptimal levels. Further, because agreeable managers are prone to giving lenient performance ratings (Bernardin, Cooke, & Villanova, 2000), followers of agreeable leaders may be deprived of honest appraisals of their work and, thus, may fail to benefit from criticism. If leaders communicate their preferences through the feedback they provide (Kaiser et al., 2008), then the gentle and lenient feedback provided by agreeable leaders suggests a preference for social harmony over all else (competition, achievement, making hard choices necessary for survival). Agreeable leaders who use a nonconfrontational style may be ideally suited for positions that demand complacent adherence to the status quo. Thus, it may be unlikely to find highly agreeable leaders proposing radical process innovations or challenging the status quo. The problem, of course, is that leaders often must be willing to assert themselves to challenge the status quo. R. Hogan, Curphy, and Hogan (1994) describe the results of a study which found that the most common reason for managerial incompetence was "managers' unwillingness to exercise authority (e.g., 'is reluctant to confront problems and conflict')" (p. 494).

Emotional stability. Leadership is an inherently emotional process (Dasborough & Ashkanasy, 2002). Leaders with high levels of emotional stability are less likely to use inspirational appeal as an influence tactic (Cable & Judge, 2003), relying instead on objective and rational arguments. Yet of all the influence tactics that managers use, inspirational appeal is the most effective in gaining commitment from followers (Yukl & Tracey, 1992). Another potential downside of emotionally stable leaders is that they may not perceive threats from the environment. D. D. P. Johnson (2004) documents how many leader decisions to go to war—often with catastrophic consequences to the leader's followers—were born from positive illusions.

Openness to experience. McCrae (1996) characterized individuals scoring high on measures of openness to experience as nonconformists, those who pride themselves on antiauthoritarian and antiestablishment attitudes, whereas Judge and LePine (2007) considered high openness as a potential hazard in hierarchical, conventional, or traditional work settings. Because open leaders are willing to try most anything in the pursuit of organizational success, these leaders might get easily distracted with vogue ideas, therefore pursuing short-term strategies that defy deeply held corporate values and traditions, potentially compromising an organization's long-term stability. Indeed, openness to experience is negatively correlated with continuance commitment (Erdheim, Wang & Zickar, 2006). Open leaders might lack focus on organizational objectives and, instead, focus on skeptical or alternative viewpoints. Thus, open leaders might compromise a group's ability to fit within a broader collective (Judge et al., 2009).

Core self-evaluations. Extremely positive self-views—what Hiller and Hambrick (2005) describe as hyper-CSE—can be very dysfunctional in a leader. Hyper-CSE might cause leaders to underappreciate risk or to have "rosy view" about the future. Thus, overly confident leaders might make overly risky decisions because they deny the risk that is there (Simon & Houghton, 2003). Or, high CSE leaders might overpay in acquiring another company because they believe the future brighter than it is (Hayward & Hambrick, 1997). Although positive self-regard is positive for interpersonal and leadership functioning in general, hyper-CSE will most likely hamper the objectivity of strategic judgments, whereby leaders with hyper-CSE might craft organizational strategies that serve their own best interests, rather than those of the organization's stakeholders. Finally, because individuals with high self-esteem react defensively to critical feedback (Baumeister, Campbell, Krueger & Vohs, 2003), leaders high in CSE might react to negative feedback by questioning the competence of the evaluator and the validity of evaluation technique (Kernis & Sun, 1994).

Intelligence. Although intelligence is positively associated with both leader emergence and leader effectiveness (Foti & Hauenstein, 2007), as noted by

Judge et al. (2009), "It is not uncommon for individuals with exceptionally high IQs to be perceived as atypical and treated as outsiders to a work group" (p. 869). Bass (1990) and Stogdill (1948) hypothesized that it could be detrimental to a group if the leader's intelligence substantially exceeds that of group members. This speculation inspired Judge et al. (2004) to suggest that group intelligence, a group's collective intellectual capacity, would moderate the relationship between leader intelligence and leader effectiveness, such that groups with a high IQ would be more receptive to a highly intelligent leader than groups with low IQs. Thus, intellect in and of itself may not be perfectly effective, especially if there exists a mismatch of IQs between group members and the group's leader. Finally, highly intellectual individuals have a high need for cognition (Cacioppo, Petty, Feinstein, & Jarvis, 1996), suggesting that very intelligent leaders may be indecisive because they are pensive and may make problems more complex than they really are.

Bright Side of Dark Traits

Narcissism. Narcissistic individuals maintain exaggerated views of their own self-worth, but the multidimensional trait appears to have some positive associations in the leadership process. The authoritative component of narcissism (Emmons, 1984) predicted ratings of leader emergence in four-person leaderless discussion groups (Brunell et al., 2008). Deluga (1997), in an archival analysis of U.S. presidential personalities, suggested that narcissistic entitlement and self-sufficiency were positively associated with charismatic leadership and ratings of executive performance. Because narcissistic leaders favor bold and aggressive actions that are likely to draw attention to their vision and leadership, there are times when such actions are beneficial to the leader's organization. Chatterjee and Hambrick (2007), for example, used an unobtrusive measure of narcissism among 111 CEOs and evaluated strategic innovation and performance over a 12-year period. Narcissism was positively related to the number and size of corporate acquisitions, a benchmark the authors regard as a proxy for strategic dynamism. Although these narcissistic CEOs ultimately achieved organizational performance that fluctuated over time, their firms' performance was essentially no different from those with less self-aggrandizing leaders.

Histrionic personality. As Conger (1993) notes, charismatic leadership is based on a self-construed "hero" mentality, where the leader must convince others of his or her "extraordinariness" (p. 285). This self-construal of one's heroic qualities fits with the histrionic personality, where individuals put themselves on a pedestal and need to be the center of others' attention. Moreover, histrionic individuals are often thought to have attractive social skills, though their skills are directed at focusing attention on themselves and manipulating others for their personal goals. Finally, R. Hogan and Kaiser (2005) note that histrionic leaders are likely to be impulsive, attention seeking, and may lead by crisis. As Willner (1984) noted, if a crisis is not present, a charismatic leader will often create one.

Dominance. Dominance was among the first traits associated with leadership and leader emergence (Mann, 1959). Dominant individuals command the attention of others, and consistently attain high levels of influence (Anderson & Kilduff, 2009). As such, individuals who get high scores on ratings of dominance are more likely to emerge as leaders and more likely to be promoted to positions of authority (Foti & Hauenstein, 2007; Hing, Bobocel, Zanna, & McBride, 2007; Judge et al., 2009). In addition, socially dominant leaders display a strong desire for achievement and control (Cozzolino & Snyder, 2008), making them attractive to willing followers. Anderson and Kilduff (2009), for example, argued that trait dominance is associated with the appearance of competence, which may explain why Hare, Koenigs, and Hare (1997), in a field study of 260 managers, reported that both managers and coworkers believed that "model" managers should be more dominant than they are usually rated to be.

Machiavellianism. Although most descriptions of Machiavellianism are understandably derogatory, the original discussions of power contained in Machiavelli's *The Prince* [*Il Principe*] are far less derisive. Moreover, evidence suggests some benefits to being a Machiavellian leader. Machiavellians have a high motivation to lead (Mael, Waldman & McQueen, 2001). Moreover, Machiavellian leaders show considerable flexibility in handling structured and unstructured tasks (Drory & Gluskinos, 1980). In addition, Machiavellians engage in a variety of influence tactics—such as strategic self-disclosure—conducive to building political connections (Dingler-Duhon & Brown, 1987). Perhaps for these reasons, Simonton (1986) demonstrated that Machiavellians tend to serve the most years in national elective offices, and Machiavellianism among U.S. presidents was positively associated with legislative success in Congress.

Mediators of Individual Differences

Important to research on leader individual differences is investigation of the mechanisms that connect leader traits to leader outcomes. Our model suggests that leader traits link not only directly to leader outcomes but also indirectly. These indirect links help to explain how the personality of leaders influences their actions and, ultimately, their outcomes. If broad personality traits form the backbone of how and why individuals behave in a certain way, then specific traits are possibly the marrow. In fact, scholars have argued that specific leader traits do matter when predicting leader actions and outcomes (S. A. Kirkpatrick & Locke, 1991). The actions of a leader include the behaviors, states, and styles displayed when making decisions, executing strategies, and interpersonally connecting with others. In the following sections, we discuss how these actions and behaviors potentially mediate the linkages in our model.

Initiating Structure and Consideration

In the 1940s and 1950s, leadership scholars undertook a collaborative effort at Ohio State University to address a growing list of leader behaviors. Researchers of the Ohio State Studies took this comprehensive list of more than 1,000 behavioral dimensions and combined them into two separate but not necessarily unrelated categories. The first category, initiating structure, is defined as the extent to which a leader defines his or her role and the roles of followers, is goal oriented, and establishes well-defined communication standards (Bass, 1990). Leaders high on this dimension often emphasize task strategy, work and role organization, deadlines, work relationships, and goals. The second category, consideration, is defined as the degree to which a leader shows care and respect for followers, looks out for their welfare, and expresses appreciation and support (Bass, 1990). Considerate leaders often place focus on interpersonal strategy and tend to show regard, compassion, and gratitude for followers. These two categories, which form the core of leadership behavioral theory, have been meta-analytically connected to important leadership outcomes (Judge, Piccolo, & Ilies, 2004).

Although we are not aware of published research linking a leader's standing on the Big Five dimensions to his or her initiating structure, personality scholars have, as previously noted, linked the Big Five to behaviors that seem to possess a structuring component. For example, studies have linked conscientiousness to voice behavior in teams (LePine & Van Dyne, 2001), autonomous goal setting (Barrick, Mount, & Strauss, 1993), and goal-setting motivation (Judge & Ilies, 2002). These three outcomes have initiating, organizing, and production commonalities, suggesting that leader conscientiousness could stand as a significant predictor of initiating structure. Another mediating possibility, albeit for a different Big Five dimension, could occur if insecure leaders (a facet of neuroticism) displayed tendencies to either control their employees or resist ideas. These actions are often typical of leaders high in initiating structure behaviors. Similar arguments could also be made for dark side traits. As an example, individuals high in dominance have a strong desire for control (Cozzolino & Snyder, 2008). Perhaps dominant leaders also value control. Control behaviors would be more typical of a leader high in structure.

We are also unaware of any published research linking a leader's Big Five dimensions to his or her consideration. However, researchers have shown that Big Five dimensions do relate to behaviors that are similar to consideration. For example, studies have revealed a positive relationship of agreeableness to interpersonal facilitation (Hurtz & Donovan, 2000) and to benevolence (Roccas, Sagiv, Schwartz, & Knafo, 2002), and a negative relationship to vengefulness (McCullough, Bellah, Kilpatrick, & Johnson, 2001). These results suggest that agreeableness is potentially related to leader consideration, because these outcomes align closely with the actions of a more sympathetic and warm leader, who focuses on membership, integration, and representation. As another possibility, egocentric leaders (e.g., narcissistic, histrionic, hyper-CSE, or hubristic) show tendencies to focus on grandiosity and impression management and to place value on praise and recognition (Chatterjee & Hambrick, 2007; Hayward & Hambrick, 1997; Judge et al., 2009). It is conceivable that these leaders will demonstrate consideration behaviors as a tactic of self-enhancement to their followers. A somewhat related argument could be made as well for sociable and bold leaders (facets of extraversion). In fact, research has shown that extraversion predicts successful performance in jobs that require social interaction (Mount & Barrick, 1998).[2]

Transformational and Charismatic Leadership

Leaders are often faced with challenges that are unexpected or which seem insurmountable at an initial glance. Hence, leaders must motivate followers to perform beyond expectations. Transformational leaders inspire followers to commit to a shared vision that provides meaning to their work, while also serving as role models who help followers develop their own potential and view problems from new perspectives (Bass, 1985; J. M. Burns, 1978). Four behavioral dimensions of transformational leadership, listed in increasing degree of involvement and effectiveness (Avolio, 1999), are individualized consideration (leader mentors follower), intellectual stimulation (leader challenges follower creativity), inspirational motivation (leader inspires a vision), and idealized influence (leader acts as an admirable role model). This final behavior, idealized influence, is considered by many to be charisma (Judge & Piccolo, 2004). House (1977), building on previous work by sociologist Max Weber, argued that charismatic leaders act in a way that is extraordinary or heroic. The functional equivalency of charismatic and transformational leadership measures to various criteria has opened a debate as to whether or not the two are the same or if charismatic leadership is simply a facet of a broader transformational construct (Bass, 1985; Conger & Kanungo, 1998). That debate is beyond the scope of this chapter, and our discussion of linkages with traits and the Big Five treats them as interchangeable (see Yukl, 1999).

There are empirical reasons to expect that transformational and charismatic leader behaviors mediate the links between leader traits and outcomes. First, and as noted earlier, Big Five dimensions have been shown to be associated with leader outcomes. Second, Big Five dimensions have been shown to be associated with both transformational and charismatic leadership (Bono & Judge, 2004). Although some results have been mixed as to which dimensions have the strongest and weakest correlations, all five are related to both types of leadership (Bono & Judge, 2004; Judge & Bono, 2000). Finally, both transformational and charismatic leadership are significantly related to leader outcomes. In a meta-analysis of more than 600 correlations, Judge and Piccolo (2004) found an overall moderate relationship ($r = .44$), which generalized over temporal and multisource conditions.

There are conceptual reasons for transformational and charismatic behavior mediation as well. For example, extraversion has facets that include key similarities to charisma, including assertiveness, verboseness, and vigor (Saucier, 1994). These facets, particularly in a time of crisis or unpredictability, allow charismatic leaders to emerge as followers look to them to help reduce uncertainty. In fact, extraversion was the Big Five trait most highly correlated with idealized influence (charisma) when meta-analyzed (Bono & Judge, 2004). There are also reasons to expect transformational leadership to mediate the effects of emotional stability on leader effectiveness. Emotionally stable (low neuroticism) leaders often demonstrate a calmness and sense of security that are seen as admirable and appealing by followers, particularly during times of high uncertainty. As opposed to extraversion, which helps leaders emerge, emotional stability helps leaders leverage their charismatic qualities to be both emergent and effective (Judge et al., 2002). Also, transformational leadership potentially mediates the relationship that open leaders have with key follower and leader outcomes. Open leaders are creative, curious, and often sophisticated. These leaders are typically more willing to take risks and remain open to follower ideas and suggestions. These qualities are closely tied to highly effective aspects of transformational leadership.

Ethical and Authentic Leadership

The actions of nefarious leaders such as Enron's Jeffrey Skilling, WorldCom's Bernard Ebbers, and Bernard Madoff (all of whom are in prison) have undeniably given traction to a more recent focus on leader morality. Ethical leadership has been defined as the "demonstration of normatively appropriate conduct through personal actions and interpersonal relationships, and the promotion of such conduct to followers through two-way communication, reinforcement, and decision-making" (Brown, Treviño, & Harrison, 2005, p. 120). Authentic leadership, although related to ethical leadership via moral underpinnings, is unique in that rather than emphasizing transactional components of the moral management of others, it emphasizes that both self-awareness and self-expression should be in accordance with inner thoughts and feelings. As defined in the literature, authentic leaders are those who are acutely aware of how they think and behave and are perceived by others as being aware of their own and others' moral and value perspectives, knowledge, and strengths (Avolio & Gardner, 2005). These two leadership types are connected by the premise that they result in followers who at some level mimic their leader's actions—an effect that might not occur were they led by less moral leaders. Because of their commonality, our arguments for mediation assume that both ethical and authentic leadership have similar influences on leader outcomes.

Scholars have suggested that moral leaders are trustworthy, fair, apathetic, and altruistic (Treviño, Hartman, & Brown, 2006). Furthermore, qualitative and quantitative research has shown that these leaders attempt to influence the morality of their followers through role modeling, rewards, and discipline (Sosik, 2005; Treviño, Brown, & Hartman, 2003). In a theoretical framework, Brown and Treviño (2006) proposed that ethical leadership should be associated with an increase in follower satisfaction, motivation, and commitment. Furthermore, they argue that ethical leadership will result in a decrease in follower deviance. Scholars have proposed that authentic leadership is related to follower authenticity, self-regulation of behaviors, and self-realization of emotion and values (Gardner, Avolio, Luthans, May, & Walumbwa, 2005). Authentic leadership has also been linked to follower commitment and citizenship behaviors (Walumbwa, Avolio, Gardner, Wernsing, & Peterson, 2008).

There are reasons to expect relationships between leader individual differences and moral behaviors. Conscientious leaders should possess a strong sense of self-direction and discipline (Costa & McCrae, 1992; John & Srivastava, 1999). Such tendencies often convey the type of self-awareness that underlies authentic and ethical leadership. Another trait, emotional stability, allows leaders to maintain consistency with respect to emotions and to be more secure in how those emotions are expressed (John & Srivastava, 1999)—both closely aligned with authenticity and self-knowing. Previous findings also show that agreeable individuals are often kind and sympathetic (Costa & McCrae, 1992; Saucier, 1994) and, if placed into a status role, have ties with ethical dimensions of leadership (Judge & Bono, 2000). Such leaders are seen as trustworthy and altruistic, and they frequently inspire followers to emulate these behaviors. This emulation often results in followers who make ethical decisions, increase prosocial behaviors, and decrease counterproductive behaviors (Brown & Treviño, 2006). And finally, leaders high in core self-evaluation likely carry a sense of assurance and efficacy about their tasks and duties. These leaders, because of positive self-appraisal and overall confidence, may be less likely to use unethical tactics as a getting-ahead maneuver.

Leader Motives

Socioanalytic theory (R. Hogan, 1983, 1986) maintains that individual differences relate to success and attainment via interpersonal actions. As this theory articulates, the interpersonal actions of individuals manifest as personal motivation either to get along (communion) or to get ahead (agency), as societies and work groups become structured with status and hierarchies (see Judge, Piccolo, & Kosalka, 2009, for a review). This dual motive theory has been expanded to a third motive—finding meaning—which is driven by a personal desire to find order and sensibility during times of chaos and randomness (R. Hogan & Shelton, 1998). As a theory of status and achievement striving, we argue that socioanalytic theory is one mechanism that links leader traits to leader emergence, primarily through the motives that certain traits elicit. In essence, socioanalytic theory helps explain "why" behaviors and outcomes of leaders are a result of their personalities.

The first two motives of socioanalytic theory, getting along and getting ahead, have clear associations with traits. Research has suggested that agreeable individuals are motivated to get along with others (communion), and both conscientious and extraverted individuals are motivated to get ahead (agency; Barrick, Stewart, & Piotrowski, 2002). Although these motivations often positively influence outcomes, there is a potential countereffect as well. One can certainly envision how being overly cooperative and ambitious can be detrimental if, as a result, ethics are compromised (Uhl-Bien & Carsten, 2007). The final motive, finding meaning, also has straightforward connections to leader individual differences. Researchers have noted that people try to avoid chaos, randomness, and uncertainty, striving for order, sensibility, and predictability (R. Hogan & Shelton, 1998). These desires are typical of someone high in conscientiousness and are likely to result in behaviors that satisfy these inclinations.

Moderators of Individual Differences

In addition to mediating mechanisms that link leader traits to leader outcomes, moderators potentially exist that can influence the links of our model. For the purposes of this chapter, we have separated our list of moderators into three categories. The first category, leader individual differences, includes variables that moderate the link between leader traits and leader styles or behaviors. The second category, follower individual differences, includes variables that affect how leader behaviors relate to leader outcomes. The final category, contextual differences, discusses conditions that potentially influence the paths from traits to behaviors, and from behaviors to traits.

Leader Individual Differences

We argue that either intelligence or creativity will interact with a leader's personality, such as extraversion, to moderate a leader's actual and perceived transformational leadership behaviors. We offer three separate arguments to support our assertion. First, Schmidt & Hunter (1998) found that intelligence is a significant predictor of job performance ($r = .51$), with even higher correlations for more complex jobs. Intelligence could give extraverted leaders the efficacy needed to feel comfortable articulating a vision, thus increasing their transformational behavior. Second, individuals seem to share the common understanding that prototypical leaders are intelligent (Rubin, Bartels, & Bommer, 2002). Therefore, the relationship between a leader's extraversion and his or her perceived transformational behaviors could be amplified by leader intelligence. Finally, researchers have shown that intelligence and creativity are closely related (Rushton, 1990). We argue that extraverted leaders who display high levels of creativity are in turn often likely to stimulate and encourage creativity in their followers. Promoting creativity and intelligence is a key characteristic of transformational behavior (Bass, 1990).

Another example of potential moderation is when a leader's gender interacts with his or her personality. For instance, a leader high in agreeableness will potentially act in a way that is characterized by mutual trust, respect, and high regard for his or her followers' feelings—actions closely related to consideration. If this leader is female, she will potentially show an even higher level of consideration than will a male counterpart, perhaps as a distancing mechanism or as a point of differentiation from a previous leader. In fact, research results indeed show that women tend to use more democratic and collaborative styles and less autocratic or directive styles than do men (Eagly & Johnson, 1990). Other possibilities include an agreeable female leader's attempt to alter negative attitudes toward her (Eagly & Johnson, 1990) or to improve low morale (O'Leary, 1974) by being more considerate than a man would be.

Follower Individual Differences

There are also reasons to expect follower individual differences to moderate the relationship in Figure 6.1. Research on social identification has shown that when the self is defined in collective terms (collective self-construal), collective interest is experienced as self-interest, and individuals experience intrinsic motivation when contributing toward collective goals and tasks (van Knippenberg, van Knippenberg, De Cremer, & Hogg, 2004). Moreover, collective self-construal has been proposed to be an important aspect in research on leader outcomes (Lord & Brown, 2004); and research by Conger, Kanungo, & Menon (2000) suggests that charismatic leadership and empowerment are both related to collective self-construal. Based on these predictions and findings and the assertion by Bass (1985) and others that a follower's conversion of interests from the self to the group is at the essence of transformational and charismatic leadership, we argue that collective self-construal moderates the relationship between leader behaviors and leader outcomes. Specifically, we posit that the benefits of transformational behaviors, from an effectiveness perspective, will be amplified for followers who identify with the group. Other followers high in collective self-construal will acknowledge this leader's effort as attending to group needs, because these followers identify more strongly with the group than with individuals. Leaders who attend to collective needs are therefore perceived to be more effective in group and team settings (Jung & Sosik, 2002).

Another follower individual difference that potentially moderates the relationship between leader states and styles and leader outcomes is follower job knowledge. Follower job knowledge varies in level, based on the individual or the complexity of the task (Kerr, Schriesheim, Murphy, & Stodgill, 1974). Kerr et al. summarized research that found that individuals with low job knowledge perceived structure as more important than consideration. Furthermore, these researchers highlighted other studies that showed that when job knowledge was at least adequate, followers preferred low structure (i.e., higher consideration). Additionally, House (1971) predicted that when a task is self-evident, structure is redundant and thus ineffective. Based on the research reported by Kerr and his colleagues and the speculation by House, we predict that the relationship between leader behavior and leader outcomes is neutralized by a higher level of individual job knowledge. To highlight an example, leaders high in conscientiousness should typically demonstrate a style that closely mirrors structure. If follower job knowledge level is high, then leader structuring decreases follower job satisfaction, thus weakening the relationship between leader behavior and the perceived effectiveness of that leader.

Contextual Differences

There are compelling and theoretical reasons to believe that culture can play a moderating role on the links in our model. As part of the GLOBE research program (see House, Hanges, Javidan, Dorfman, & Gupta, 2004), researchers investigated how national cultures differ on nine dimensions. One of these culture dimensions, uncertainty avoidance, describes the extent to which a society's members feel threatened by uncertain and unambiguous situations and try to avoid them. We argue that uncertainty avoidance potentially moderates the links to leader behaviors and outcomes. As an example, intelligent leaders are likely to understand that followers who belong to a culture high in uncertainty avoidance will potentially have high regard for morality. Therefore, these leaders may demonstrate higher levels of moral behavior as a signal of risk reduction to their followers. Furthermore, moral leaders will potentially be seen as more leader-like and thus have high levels of leader emergence and perceived effectiveness.

Research on a second GLOBE dimension, collectivism, suggests that it too plays an important moderating role in the relationship between leader traits and leader outcomes. Collectivism is a national culture attribute that describes a tightly knit social framework in which individuals in a group expect other group members to protect them and to look after them (House et al., 2004). As an example, agreeable leaders will potentially appear more transformational in a collective society. This occurs because collective group members are likely more inspired by leaders who are trusting, cooperative, and kind. Collectivism also potentially amplifies the relationship between transformational behavior and leader effectiveness. For instance, lab research has indicated that transformational leaders in a collective society stimulate higher levels of long-term planning and idea generation from their followers (Jung & Avolio, 1999). Additionally, Schaubroeck, Lam, and Cha (2007) conducted a field study and showed that collectivism strengthened the relationship between transformational leadership and team potency (i.e., collective efficacy).

In addition to culture, there are inter- and intraorganizational variables that also have the potential to moderate the linkages in our model. One example is organizational structure, as described by T. Burns and Stalker (1961). Mechanistic structures are centralized and machine-like, and are characterized by rigidity and procedural standardization. On the other extreme are organic structures, which are analogous to living organisms in that they are characterized by flexibility and adaptability to situations. These structure types have the potential to influence the relationships between traits and behaviors. For instance, open leaders, who have a natural tendency to be adaptable, may seem even more visionary in organic organizations, as their personalities mesh with their followers' desires for adaptability. Conversely, leaders high in Machiavellianism might appear somewhat transformational in mechanistic organizations as they use political skill to win over followers who are susceptible to cunning tactics.

Another likely contextual moderator is leader hierarchical level. For example, extraverted organizational leaders who are top managers might appear as less trustworthy and authentic to followers who perceive them as purely talkative or ingratiatory. Extraverted immediate supervisors, however, have the potential to be seen as more authentic and trustworthy. Research by Dirks and Ferrin (2002) has suggested that direct supervisors are important referents for follower trust and that trust is higher when leader–member exchange (LMX) is high.

Measurement Issues and Assumptions of Individual Differences in Leadership

Criticism of leadership research is certainly not a new phenomenon. Recent critics of leadership studies have focused attention not only on how leadership variables are measured but also on overall assumptions that are made about leaders and their environment. These critics, by suggesting remedies to their points, have ultimately strengthened the research on leadership. The following section elaborates on three of these critical points and touches on the possible remedies. The first criticism, measurement issues of traits, highlights points by some who feel that leadership is often undeservedly glorified in both research and the popular press. The second criticism, measurement issues of behaviors, discusses points raised by critics who feel that scholars are sometimes misguided in their efforts to capture valid leadership behavioral constructs. The third criticism, measurement issues of outcomes, touches on criticism that argues that leadership studies are weighted too heavily toward subjective or less important outcomes and not enough toward objective or more important outcomes.

Measurement Issues of Traits

Our first issue highlights an argument by some that researchers are typically influenced to measure leader traits to positive outcomes only, and they often forgo opportunities to study traits that might result in negative outcomes. This influence, we argue, is partially fueled by society's romanticism of leadership, which has channeled the views of many toward a perspective that leans in the direction of seeing leaders mostly as heroes (Meindl, Ehrlich, & Dukerich, 1985). This "rosy" view has likely led many to become enchanted with books and articles written by popular press authors who typify leaders as "extraordinary" or "inherent to us all" (Intrator & Scribner, 2007; Zenger & Folkman, 2002). These efforts, though enjoyable to read and arguably important, have left a void in our understanding of "other traits" that may have an impact on leaders, followers, and organizations. These "other traits" that should be included in studies are the narrow traits, dark side traits, and the trait paradox included in Figure 6.1. Additionally, further development of scales to capture the paradox and measure these other traits will allow us to develop a more comprehensive understanding of the influence of inherited traits (Arvey et al., 2006).

Measurement Issues of Behaviors

Critics of leadership studies have pointed to the typical study in leadership as one in which followers are asked to fill out surveys to assess the effectiveness of leader behaviors. These critics argue that this poses two potential problems. First, researchers often assume that the followers sampled in a study need or even desire leadership (Hunter, Bedell-Avers, & Mumford, 2007). To their point, it is not difficult to imagine (a) a scenario in which highly skilled or highly autonomous employees would be aloof or oblivious to a considerate leader or (b) another scenario in which employees in a high-justice climate might not need a leader who consistently reiterates his or her ethicality because all leaders in this climate are by association assumed ethical. Second, critics have pointed out that researchers assume leader behavior is always observed. This is not always the case. In some professions, such as outside sales or telecommuting, leader–follower interaction is rare. Furthermore, it is not difficult to imagine a scenario in which a leader spends an inordinate amount of time developing plans or crafting budgets, both of which potentially occur in isolation or behind closed doors and unobserved by followers. As a basic remedy to these two issues, critics argue that researchers should not rely too much on follower perception of behaviors (Hunter et al., 2007) and we should corroborate follower perceptions with other more pertinent performance measures. Additionally, we argue that studies should control for interaction time by measuring how often followers actually observe their leaders performing work tasks.

Measurement Issues of Outcomes

Many critics point out that leadership research often places too much emphasis on how leaders are perceived by followers and peers, and not enough emphasis on how organizations actually perform. In fact, many studies have used subjective measures of both effectiveness and emergence as criteria and have given little focus to objective measures (see Judge et al., 2002). These subjective measures, critics argue, are essentially another way of capturing how leaders "stand out in a crowd" (i.e., effectiveness) or how much "approval" (i.e., emergence) leaders warrant (Kaiser et al., 2008). Furthermore, these measures are susceptible to influence by rater affect because variables measured subjectively are often influenced by interpersonal liking (Tsui & Barry, 1986). The end result is that politics and socializing are potentially more influential of leader outcomes than is the actual impact that leaders have on group or organizational performance. Kaiser and his colleagues (2008) acknowledge that understanding the characteristics associated with how leaders are perceived is useful but typically more relevant to the careers of individual managers. Therefore, a more useful approach would be to study the actual impact that leaders have on group processes, team results, and ultimately the success of the organization. In fact, Figure 6.1 does include both subjective and objective leader outcomes to support this recommendation.

A second issue to which critics have pointed is that researchers who do measure leader effects on performance outcomes often fail to differentiate between group processes and goal accomplishment (Kaiser et al., 2008). Kaiser et al. define process outcomes as "how did the team play?" and goal achievement outcomes as "did the team win?" The majority of studies that include process and performance measures place more focus on how leaders influence individual followers (Bass, 1990) and less focus on actual performance. Three suggestions have been offered to researchers to alleviate the "play versus win" debate. First, they should investigate and incorporate comprehensive measures used by organizations (e.g., a balanced scorecard) to capture multiple leader outcomes (Kaiser et al., 2008). Second, utilizing external resources and perspectives, such as benchmarking, to measure performance offers a mechanism to mitigate an inward-looking focus that plagues many research studies. Finally, they should ensure proper time lags in studies as a best practice to measure objective leader outcomes.

Conclusion

Over time, scholarly focus has shifted between styles and traits of leaders and from surmising that leadership is malleable and teachable to concluding that it is hardwired into our genetic makeup. This ebb and flow has been fruitful, yielding rich and important theories, as researchers have incrementally advanced our understanding of leaders, their followers, and the surrounding context. As we move toward new understanding, it is important for us to keep three things in perspective, as we have argued in this chapter. First, individual differences do matter, and they provide a useful starting point to develop new models to test both subjective and objective outcomes in leadership research. Individual differences that matter include not only typical and expected leadership scenarios (i.e., positive trait equals positive action) but also paradoxical relationships (i.e., bad trait equals positive action). Second, leaders do demonstrate different states and styles based on their dispositions. These behaviors are affected not only by the leaders' traits but also by the individual differences of their followers. Third, leaders do not operate in silos. They must work with multiple personalities and with varying groups in diverse and complex organizations. Therefore, context matters and can play a significant role in leadership outcomes.

Future Research

As shown in Figure 6.1, our model includes multiple constructs. These constructs offer researchers several options for studies that link traits to behaviors to outcomes. The intentional broadness of our model should not be perceived as indeterminate, but instead should be viewed as flexible and therefore unconstrained by specificity. Our model should be used as a reference or a starting point to guide predictions in future studies. In addition to our model, we organize our suggestions for future research on leader individual differences around two themes. For the first theme, the saliency of different leader traits at different times, we suggest that the prominence of different traits that enhance (or compromise) leaders' emergence and effectiveness might vary over time and situation. For the second theme, leader–follower trait alignment, we recommend that researchers test scenarios in which there is a match (or mismatch) between leaders' and followers' traits.[3]

Trait Saliency Over Time

Researchers have suggested that over time and tenure, a leader's behavior and actions can change (Hambrick & Fukutomi, 1991). Based on this theorizing, we argue that the saliency of a leader's traits potentially changes over time and situation. We loosely argue that both leader and follower typically agree on which traits are most salient, although we do maintain that occasionally leaders might assume that they are demonstrating one trait (e.g., extraversion) while followers perceive another (e.g., dominance). This point aside and as an illustration of our main argument, a leader who is high in both extraversion and conscientiousness might show high exuberance to gain notice as he or she attempts to emerge as a leader. Over time, and after the leader is established in the role, conscientiousness might assume a more central position as he or she sets goals and structures tasks. Or, rather than being conscientious, this same extraverted leader might be Machiavellian as well. After emerging, this leader might use manipulation and cunning tactics for personal gain—a proverbial wolf in sheep's clothing.

Additionally, and also from a saliency and time perspective, we argue that researchers should consider trait clusters or configurations of multiple traits in predicting outcomes. In fact, longitudinal research by Foti and Hauenstein (2007) suggested that the same patterns of leader individual differences that were associated with emergence were also associated with effectiveness over time. Because many measures of emergence and effectives are subjective, perhaps the saliency of trait configurations could influence follower perceptions and ratings of leader outcomes.

Trait Alignment

We also suggest that researchers incorporate two different scenarios involving leader and follower traits into their studies. In the first scenario, trait matching, studies should be conducted in which a leader's traits coincide with the traits of his or her followers. For example, does placing an agreeable follower with an agreeable leader result in incremental performance gains in performance because of low conflict, or does this situation create an overly congenial and possibly detrimental work relationship? In the second scenario, trait mismatching, studies should be conducted in which a leader's traits do not match the traits of his or her followers. For example, what happens when hubristic followers low in conscientiousness work for leaders who are highly conscientious and who place great emphasis on details and task accuracy? Does this nonredundancy of traits actually enhance team performance, or does the trait mismatch create stressors that detract from team performance? Studies similar to these and others should be conducted to further our understanding of trait alignment and misalignment in work settings.

Discussion Questions

1. Make a compelling case for paths or variables that could be added (or deleted) from the model in Figure 6.1. What theory, previous finding, or speculation supports your case?

2. Why are certain traits perceived by some as "dark side," and others as "bright side?" In this context, how do you perceive leader hubris?

3. Do you think, as some (Robert Hogan) argue, that the dark side is simply an extreme score on a bright side trait? (In other words, conscientiousness is good in a leader, unless it is to the degree that the leader is excessively conscientiousness [exacting, punctilious, controlling].) Why or why not?

4. Do you agree that organizational or industry stability could be considered a "context" that might moderate the relationships between the variables in Figure 6.1? What other contexts could play a role in determining the strength of the relationships between a leader's traits, styles, behaviors, and outcomes?

5. Note—See Liden & Antonakis (2009) for a discussion of context and leadership.

6. Can you think of other mediating mechanisms that could potentially link transformational leaders to both subjective and objective outcomes?

Notes

1. House and Aditya (1997) themselves did not espouse this viewpoint. Rather, they were summarizing what they perceived to be the prevailing sentiment in the leadership community.

2. Figure 6.1 indicates that mediation could also occur for the trait paradox (e.g., bright side of dark traits). For example, research has shown that the dark side trait of narcissism leads to bold actions by leaders (Chatterjee & Hambrick, 2007). One could argue that this relationship is mediated by structure, because a narcissistic leader carries an intense need to have his or her superiority reaffirmed (Chatterjee & Hambrick, 2007), which can often be accomplished by asserting and defining roles or organizing tasks and goals for followers. For parsimony, we chose to leave out speculations of this trait paradox in this and subsequent sections.

3. We also refer readers to Roya Ayman's chapter in this book. Dr. Ayman offers a detailed exposition regarding the interactionist perspective, and our chapter can be viewed as complementary to her discussion on the influences of the relationships in leadership studies.

References

Allport, G. W. (1937). *Personality—A psychological interpretation.* New York: Holt Henry.

Altemeyer, B. (2004). Highly dominating, highly authoritarian personalities. *Journal of Social Psychology, 144,* 421–447.

Ames, D. R., & Flynn, F. J. (2007). What breaks a leader: The curvilinear relation between assertiveness and leadership. *Journal of Personality and Social Psychology, 92,* 307–324.

Andersen, J. A. (2006). Leadership, personality and effectiveness. *The Journal of Socio-Economics, 35,* 1078–1091.

Anderson, C., & Kilduff, G. J. (2009). Why do dominant personalities attain influence in face-to-face groups? The competence-signaling effects of trait dominance. *Journal of Personality and Social Psychology, 96,* 491–503.

Arvey, R. D., Rotundo, M., Johnson, W., Zhang, Z., & McGue, M. (2006). The determinants of leadership role occupancy: Genetic and personality factors. *The Leadership Quarterly, 17,* 1–20.

Avolio, B. J. (1999). *Full leadership development: Building the vital forces in organizations.* Thousand Oaks, CA: Sage.

Avolio, B. J., & Gardner, W. L. (2005). Authentic leadership development: Getting to the root of positive forms of leadership. *The Leadership Quarterly, 16,* 315–338.

Barrick, M. R., Mount, M. K., & Strauss, J. P. (1993). Conscientiousness and performance of sales representatives: Test of the mediating effects of goal setting. *Journal of Applied Psychology, 78,* 715–722.

Barrick, M. R., Stewart, G. L., & Piotrowski, M. (2002). Personality and job performance: Test of the mediating effects of motivation among sales representatives. *Journal of Applied Psychology, 87,* 43–51.

Bass, B. M. (1985). *Leadership and performance beyond expectations.* New York: Free Press.

Bass, B. M. (1990). *Bass and Stogdill's handbook of leadership.* New York: Free Press.

Baumeister, R. F., Campbell, J. D., Krueger, J. I., & Vohs, K. D. (2003). Does high self-esteem cause better performance, interpersonal success, happiness, or healthier lifestyles? *Psychological Science in the Public Interest, 4,* 1–44.

Beauducel, A., Brocke, B., & Leue, A. (2006). Energetical bases of extraversion: Effort, arousal, EEG, and performance. *International Journal of Psychophysiology, 85,* 232–236.

Becker, J. A. H., & O'Hair, H. D. (2007). Machiavellians' motives in organizational citizenship behavior. *Journal of Applied Communication Research, 35,* 246–267.

Benet-Martinez, V., & Waller, N. (1997). Further evidence for the cross-cultural generality of the Big Seven Model: Indigenous and imported Spanish personality constructs. *Journal of Personality, 65,* 567–598.

Bernardin, H. J., Cooke, D. K., & Villanova, P. (2000). Conscientiousness and agreeableness as predictors of rating leniency. *Journal of Applied Psychology, 85,* 232–236.

Block, J. (1995). A contrarian view of the five-factor approach to personality description. *Psychological Bulletin, 117,* 187–215.

Block, J. (2001). Millennial contrarianism: The five-factor approach to personality description 5 years later. *Journal of Research in Personality, 35,* 98–107.

Bono, J. E., Boles, T. L., Judge, T. A., & Lauver, K. J. (2002). The role of personality in task and relationship conflict. *Journal of Personality, 70,* 311–344.

Bono, J. E., & Judge, T. A. (2004). Personality and transformational and transactional leadership: A meta-analysis. *Journal of Applied Psychology, 89,* 901–910.

Brown, M. E., & Treviño, L. K. (2006). Ethical leadership: A review and future directions. *The Leadership Quarterly, 17,* 595–616.

Brown, M. E., Treviño, L. K., & Harrison, D. (2005). Ethical leadership: A social learning perspective for construct development and testing. *Organizational Behavior and Human Decision Processes, 97,* 117–134.

Brunell, A. M., Gentry, W. A., Campbell, W. K., Hoffman, B. J., Kuhnert, K. W., & DeMarree, K. G. (2008). Leader emergence: The case for the narcissistic leader. *Personality and Social Psychology Bulletin, 34,* 1663–1676.

Burns, J. M. (1978). *Leadership.* New York: Harper & Row.

Burns, T., & Stalker, G. M. (1961). *The management of innovation.* London: Tavistock.

Cable, D. M., & Judge, T. A. (2003). Managers' upward influence tactic strategies: The role of manager personality and supervisor leadership style. *Journal of Organizational Behavior, 24,* 197–214.

Cacioppo, J. T., Petty, R. E., Feinstein, J. A., & Jarvis, W. B. G. (1996). Dispositional differences in cognitive motivation: The life and times of individuals varying in need for cognition. *Psychological Bulletin, 119,* 197–253.

Carlyle, T. (1840/2008). *On heroes, hero-worship, and the heroic in history.* Retrieved from http://www.gutenberg.org

Chatterjee, A., & Hambrick, D. C. (2007). It's all about me: Narcissistic chief executive officers and their effects on company strategy and performance. *Administrative Science Quarterly, 52,* 351–386.

Conger, J. A. (1993). Max Weber's conceptualization of charismatic authority: Its influence on organizational research. *The Leadership Quarterly, 4,* 277–288.

Conger, J. A., & Kanungo, R. N. (1998). *Charismatic leadership in organizations.* Thousand Oaks, CA: Sage.

Conger, J. A., Kanungo, R. N., & Menon, S. T. (2000). Charismatic leadership and follower effects. *Journal of Organizational Behavior, 21,* 747–767.

Costa, P. T., & McCrae, R. R. (1992). *Revised NEO Personality Inventory (NEO-PI-R) and NEO Five Factor (NEO-FFI) Inventory Professional Manual.* Odessa, FL: PAR.

Cozzolino, P. J., & Snyder, M. (2008). Good times, bad times: How personal disadvantage moderates the relationship between social dominance and efforts to win. *Personality and Social Psychology Bulletin, 34,* 1420–1433.

Dasborough, M. T., & Ashkanasy, N. M. (2002). Emotion and attribution of intentionality in leader–member relationships. *The Leadership Quarterly, 13,* 615–634.

Deluga, R. J. (1997). Relationship among American presidential charismatic leadership, narcissism, and rated performance. *The Leadership Quarterly, 8,* 49–65.

DeYoung, C. G., Quilty, L. C., & Peterson, J. B. (2007). Between facets and domains: 10 aspects of the Big Five. *Journal of Personality and Social Psychology, 93,* 880–896.

Diamond, J. (2001). *Ernst Mayr: What evolution is.* Retrieved from http://www.edge.org/3rd_culture/mayr/mayr_print.html

Digman, J. M. (1990). Personality structure: Emergence of the five-factor model. *Annual Review of Psychology, 41,* 417–440.

Digman, J. M. (1997). Higher-order factors of the Big Five. *Journal of Personality and Social Psychology, 73,* 1246–1256.

Dingler-Duhon, M., & Brown, B. B. (1987). Self-disclosure as an influence strategy: Effects of Machiavellianism, androgyny, and sex. *Sex Roles, 16,* 109–123.

Dirks, K. T., & Ferrin, D. L. (2002). Trust in leadership: Meta-analytic findings and implications for research and practice. *Journal of Applied Psychology, 87,* 611–628.

Drory, A., & Gluskinos, U. M. (1980). Machiavellianism and leadership. *Journal of Applied Psychology, 65,* 81–86.

Eagly, A. H., & Johnson, B. T. (1990). Gender and leadership style: A meta-analysis. *Psychological Bulletin, 108,* 233–256.

Emmons, R. A. (1984). Factor analysis and construct validity of the Narcissistic Personality Inventory. *Journal of Personality Assessment, 48,* 291–300.

Erdheim, J., Wang, M., & Zickar, M. J. (2006). Linking the Big Five personality constructs to organizational commitment. *Personality and Individual Differences, 41,* 959–970.

Forret, M. L., & Dougherty, T. W. (2001). Correlates of networking behavior for managerial and professional employees. *Group & Organization Management, 26,* 283–311.

Foti, R. J., & Hauenstein, N. M. A. (2007). Pattern and variable approaches in leadership emergence and effectiveness. *Journal of Applied Psychology, 92,* 347–355.

Gardner, W. L., Avolio, B. J., Luthans, F., May, D. R., & Walumbwa, F. (2005). "Can you see the real me?" A self-based model of authentic leader and follower development. *The Leadership Quarterly, 16,* 343–372.

Goldberg, L. R. (1990). An alternative "description of personality": The Big-Five factor structure. *Journal of Personality and Social Psychology, 59,* 1216–1229.

Goldberg, L. R. (1999). A broad-bandwidth, public-domain, personality inventory measuring the lower-level facets of several five-factor models. In I. Mervielde, I. J. Deary, F. De Fruyt, & F. Ostendorf (Eds.), *Personality psychology in Europe* (pp. 7–28). Tilburg, Netherlands: Tilburg University Press.

Gosling, S. D. (2008). Personality in non-human animals. *Social and Personality Psychology Compass, 2,* 985–1001.

Graziano, W. G., & Eisenberg, N. H. (1997). Agreeableness: A dimension of personality. In R. Hogan, J. A. Johnson, & S. R. Briggs (Eds.), *Handbook of personality psychology* (pp. 767–793). San Diego, CA: Academic Press.

Guion, R. M., & Gottier, R. F. (1965). Validity of personality measures in personnel selection. *Personnel Psychology, 18,* 135–164.

Hambrick, D. C., & Fukutomi, G. D. S. (1991). The seasons of a CEO's tenure. *Academy of Management Review, 16,* 719–742.

Hare, A. P., Koenigs, R. J., & Hare, S. E. (1997). Perceptions of observed and model values of male and female managers. *Journal of Organizational Behavior, 18,* 437–447.

Hayward, M. L. A., & Hambrick, D. C. (1997). Explaining the premiums paid for large acquisitions: Evidence of CEO hubris. *Administrative Science Quarterly, 42,* 103–127.

Hiller, N. J., & Hambrick, D. C. (2005). Conceptualizing executive hubris: The role of (hyper-) core self-evaluations in strategic decision-making. *Strategic Management Journal, 26,* 297–319.

Hing, L. S., Bobocel, D. R., Zanna, M. P., & McBride, M. V. (2007). Authoritarian dynamics and unethical decision making: High social dominance orientation leaders and high right-wing authoritarianism followers. *Journal of Personality and Social Psychology, 92,* 67–81.

Hofstee, W. K. B., de Raad, B., & Goldberg, L. R. (1992). Integration of the Big Five and circumplex approaches to trait structure. *Journal of Personality and Social Psychology, 63,* 146–163.

Hogan, J., & Ones, D. S. (1997). Conscientiousness and integrity at work. In R. Hogan, J. A. Johnson, & S. R. Briggs (Eds.), *Handbook of personality psychology* (pp. 849–870). San Diego, CA: Academic Press.

Hogan, R. (1983). A socioanalytic theory of personality. In M. M. Page (Ed.). *1982 Nebraska symposium on motivation* (pp. 55–89). Lincoln, NE: University of Nebraska Press.

Hogan, R. (1986). A socioanalytic perspective on the five-factor model. In J. S. Wiggins (Ed.). *The five-factor model of personality* (pp. 163–179). New York: Guilford Press.

Hogan, R. (2005). In defense of personality measurement: New wine for old whiners. *Human Performance, 18,* 331–341.

Hogan, R., Curphy, G. J., & Hogan, J. (1994). What we know about leadership: Effectiveness and personality. *American Psychologist, 49,* 493–504.

Hogan, R., & Hogan, J. (2001). Assessing leadership: A view from the dark side. *International Journal of Selection and Assessment, 9,* 12–23.

Hogan, R., & Kaiser, R. (2005). What we know about leadership. *Review of General Psychology, 9,* 169–180.

Hogan, R., & Shelton, D. (1998). A socioanalytic perspective on job performance. *Human Performance, 11,* 129–144.

House, R. J. (1971). Path-goal theory of leadership effectiveness. *Administrative Science Quarterly, 16,* 321–339.

House, R. J. (1977). A 1976 theory of charismatic leadership. In J. G. Hunt & L. L. Larson (Eds.), *Leadership: The cutting edge* (pp. 189–207). Carbondale, IL: Southern Illinois University Press.

House, R. J., & Aditya, R. N. (1997). The social scientific study of leadership: Quo vadis? *Journal of Management, 23,* 409–473.

House, R. J., Hanges, P, J., Javidan, M., Dorfman, P., & Gupta, V. (2004). *Culture, leadership, and organizations: The GLOBE study of 62 societies.* Thousand Oaks, CA: Sage.

Hunter, S. T., Bedell-Avers, K. E., & Mumford, M. D. (2007). The typical leadership study: Assumptions, implications, and potential remedies. *The Leadership Quarterly, 18,* 435–446.

Hurtz, G. M., & Donovan, J. J. (2000). Personality and job performance: The Big Five revisited. *Journal of Applied Psychology, 85,* 869–879.

Ilies, R., Gerhardt, M. W., & Le, H. (2004). Individual differences in leadership emergence: Integrating meta-analytic findings and behavioral genetics estimates. *International Journal of Selection and Assessment, 12,* 207–219.

Intrator, S. M., & Scribner, M. (2007). *Leading from within: Poetry that sustains the courage to lead.* San Francisco: Jossey-Bass.

John, O. P., & Srivastava, S. (1999). The Big Five trait taxonomy: History, measurement, and theoretical perspectives. In E. Pervin & O. John (Eds.), *Handbook of personality* (pp. 102–138). New York: Guilford Press.

Johnson, A. M., Vernon, P. A., Harris, J. A., & Jang, K. L. (2004). A behavioral investigation of the relationship between leadership and personality. *Twin Research, 7,* 27–32.

Johnson, A. M., Vernon, P. A., McCarthy, J. M., Molso, M., Harris, J. A., & Jang, K. J. (1998). Nature vs. nurture: Are leaders born or made? A behavior genetic investigation of leadership style. *Twin Research, 1,* 216–223.

Johnson, D. D. P. (2004). *Overconfidence and war: The havoc and glory of positive illusions.* Cambridge, MA: Harvard University Press.

Judge, T. A. (2009). Core self-evaluations and work success. *Current Directions in Psychological Science, 18,* 58–62.

Judge, T. A., & Bono, J. E. (2000). Five-factor model of personality and transformational leadership. *Journal of Applied Psychology, 85,* 751–765.

Judge, T. A., Bono, J. E., Ilies, R., & Gerhardt, M. (2002). Personality and leadership: A qualitative and quantitative review. *Journal of Applied Psychology, 87,* 765–780.

Judge, T. A., & Cable, D. M. (2004). The effect of physical height on workplace success and income. *Journal of Applied Psychology, 89,* 428–441.

Judge, T. A., Colbert, A. E., & Ilies, R. (2004). Intelligence and leadership: A quantitative review and test of theoretical propositions. *Journal of Applied Psychology, 89,* 542–552.

Judge, T. A., & Ilies, R. (2002). Relationship of personality to performance motivation: A meta-analytic review. *Journal of Applied Psychology, 87,* 797–807.

Judge, T. A., & LePine, J. A. (2007). The bright and dark sides of personality: Implications for personnel selection in individual and team contexts. In J. Langan-Fox, C. Cooper, & R. Klimoski (Eds.), *Research companion to the dysfunctional workplace: Management challenges and* symptoms (pp. 332–355). Cheltenham, UK: Edward Elgar.

Judge, T. A., LePine, J. A., & Rich, B. L. (2006). The narcissistic personality: Relationship with inflated self-ratings of leadership and with task and contextual performance. *Journal of Applied Psychology, 91,* 762–776.

Judge, T. A., & Piccolo, R. F. (2004). Transformational and transactional leadership: A meta-analytic test of their relative validity. *Journal of Applied Psychology, 89,* 755–768.

Judge, T. A., Piccolo, R. F., & Ilies, R. (2004). The forgotten ones? The validity of consideration and initiating structure in leadership research. *Journal of Applied Psychology, 89,* 36–51.

Judge, T. A., Piccolo, R. F., & Kosalka, T. (2009). The bright and dark sides of leader traits: A review and theoretical extension of the leader trait paradigm. *The Leadership Quarterly, 20,* 855–875.

Jung, D. I., & Avolio, B. J. (1999). Effects of leadership style and followers' cultural orientation on performance in group and individual task conditions. *Academy of Management Journal, 42,* 208–218.

Jung, D. I., & Sosik, J. J. (2002). Transformational leadership in work groups: The role of empowerment, cohesiveness, and collective-efficacy on perceived group performance. *Small Group Research, 33,* 313–336.

Kaiser, R. B., Hogan, R., & Craig, S. B. (2008). Leadership and the fate of organizations. *American Psychologist, 63,* 96–110.

Kernis, M. H., & Sun, C. R. (1994). Narcissism and reactions to interpersonal feedback. *Journal of Research in Personality, 28,* 4–13.

Kerr, S., Schriesheim, C. A., Murphy, C. J., & Stogdill, R. M. (1974). Toward a contingency theory of leadership based upon the consideration and initiating structure literature. *Organizational Behavior and Human Performance, 12,* 62–82.

Khoo, H. S., & Burch, G. J. (2008). The "dark side" of leadership personality and transformational leadership: An exploratory study. *Personality and Individual Differences, 44,* 86–97.

Kirkpatrick, M., & Ryan, M. J. (1991). The evolution of mating preferences and the paradox of the lek. *Nature, 350,* 33–38.

Kirkpatrick, S. A., & Locke, E. A. (1991). Leadership: Do traits matter? *Academy of Management Executive, 5,* 48–60.

Kuhn, T. S. (1970). *The structure of scientific revolutions* (2nd ed.). Chicago: University of Chicago Press.

LePine, J. A., Colquitt, J. A., & Erez, A. (2000). Adaptability to changing task contexts: Effects of general cognitive ability, conscientiousness, and openness to experience. *Personnel Psychology, 53,* 563–593.

LePine, J. A., & Van Dyne, L. (2001). Voice and cooperative behavior as contrasting forms of contextual performance: Evidence of differential relationships with Big Five personality characteristics and cognitive ability. *Journal of Applied Psychology, 86,* 326–336.

Liden, R. C., & Antonakis, J. (2009). Considering context in psychological leadership research. *Human Relations, 62,* 1587–1605.

Liu, C. C. (2008). The relationship between Machiavellianism and knowledge sharing willingness. *Journal of Business and Psychology, 22,* 233–240.

Lord, R. G., & Brown, D. J. (2004). *Leadership processes and follower self-identity.* Mahwah, NJ: Lawrence Erlbaum.

Mael, F. A., Waldman, D. A., & Mulqueen, C. (2001). From scientific careers to organizational leadership: Predictors of the desire to enter management on the part of technical personnel. *Journal of Vocational Behavior, 59,* 132–148.

Mann, R. D. (1959). A review of the relationships between personality and performance in small groups. *Psychological Bulletin, 56,* 241–270.

Mayer, D., Nishii, L., Schneider, B., & Goldstein, H. (2007). The precursors and products of justice climates: Group leader antecedents and employee attitudinal consequences. *Personnel Psychology, 60,* 929–963.

Mayr, E. (2001). *What evolution is.* New York: Basic Books.

McAdams, D. P. (1992). The five-factor model in personality: A critical appraisal. *Journal of Personality, 60,* 329–361.

McCloskey, D. N. (2002). Other things equal: Samuelsonian economics. *Eastern Economic Journal, 28,* 425–430.

McCrae, R. R. (1996). Social consequences of experiential openness. *Psychological Bulletin, 120,* 323–337.

McCullough, M. E., Bellah, C. G., Kilpatrick, S. D., & Johnson, J. L. (2001). Vengefulness: Relationships with forgiveness, rumination, well-being, and the Big Five. *Personality and Social Psychology Bulletin, 27,* 601–610.

Meindl, J. R., Ehrlich, S. B., & Dukerich, J. M. (1985). The romance of leadership. *Administrative Science Quarterly, 30,* 78–102.

Mischel, W. (1968). *Personality and assessment.* New York: John Wiley.

Morf, C. C., & Rhodewait, F. (2001). Unraveling the paradoxes of narcissism: A dynamic self-regulatory processing model. *Psychological Inquiry, 12,* 177–196.

Morgeson, F. P., Campion, M. A., Dipboye, R. L., Hollenbeck, J. R., Murphy, K., & Schmitt, N. (2007). Are we getting fooled again? Coming to terms with limitations in the use of personality tests for personnel selection. *Personnel Psychology, 60,* 1029–1049.

Mount, M. K., & Barrick, M. R. (1998). Five reasons why the "Big Five" article has been frequently cited. *Personnel Psychology, 51,* 849–858.

Murphy, K. R., & Dzieweczynski, J. L. (2005). Why don't measures of broad dimensions of personality perform better as predictors of job performance? *Human Performance, 18,* 343–357.

Nettle, D. (2006). The evolution of personality variation in humans and other animals. *American Psychologist, 61,* 622–631.

Nicol, A. A. M. (2009). Social dominance orientation, right-wing authoritarianism, and their relation with leadership styles. *Personality and Individual Differences, 47,* 657–661.

Norman, W. T. (1963). Toward an adequate taxonomy of personality attributes: Replicated factor structure in peer nomination personality ratings. *Journal of Abnormal and Social Psychology, 66,* 574–583.

O'Leary, V. E. (1974). Some attitudinal barriers to occupational aspirations in women. *Psychological Bulletin, 81,* 809–826.

Ones, D. S., Dilchert, S., Viswesvaran, C., & Judge, T. A. (2007). In support of personality assessment in organizational settings. *Personnel Psychology, 60,* 995–1027.

Penke, L., Denissen, J. J. A., & Miller, G. F. (2007). The evolutionary genetics of personality. *European Journal of Personality, 21,* 549–587.

Reimers, J. M., & Barbuto, J. E. (2002). A framework exploring the effects of the Machiavellian disposition on the relationship between motivation and influence tactics. *Journal of Leadership & Organizational Studies, 9*(2), 29–41.

Resick, C. J., Whitman, D. S., Weingarden, S. M., & Hiller, N. J. (2009). The bright-side and the dark-side of CEO personality: Examining core self-evaluations, narcissism, transformational leadership, and strategic influence. *Journal of Applied Psychology, 94,* 1365–1381.

Rim, Y. (1982). Personality and risky shift in a passive audience. *Personality and Individual Differences, 3,* 465–467.

Roccas, S., Sagiv, L., Schwartz, S. H., & Knafo, A. (2002). The Big Five personality factors and personal values. *Personality and Social Psychology Bulletin, 28,* 789–801.

Rosenthal, S. A., & Pittinsky, T. L. (2006). Narcissistic leadership. *The Leadership Quarterly, 17,* 617–633.

Rubin, R. S., Bartels, L. K., & Bommer, W. H. (2002). Are leaders smarter or do they just seem that way? Exploring perceived intellectual competence and leadership emergence. *Social Behavior and Personality: An International Journal, 30,* 105–118.

Rushton, J. P. (1990). Creativity, intelligence, and psychoticism. *Personality and Individual Differences, 11,* 1291–1298.

Saucier, G. (1994). Mini-markers: A brief version of Goldberg's unipolar Big-Five markers. *Journal of Personality Assessment, 63,* 506–516.

Schmidt, F. L., & Hunter, J. E. (1998). The validity and utility of selection methods in personnel psychology: Practical and theoretical implications of 85 years of research findings. *Psychological Bulletin, 124,* 262-274.

Schaubroeck, J., Lam, S. S. K., & Cha, S. E. (2007). Embracing transformational leadership: Team values and the impact of leader behavior on team performance. *Journal of Applied Psychology, 92,* 1020–1030.

Simon, M., & Houghton, S. M. (2003). The relationship between overconfidence and the introduction of risky products: Evidence from a field study. *Academy of Management Journal, 46,* 139–149.

Simonton, D. K. (1986). Presidential personality: Biographical use of the Gough Adjective Check List. *Journal of Personality and Social Psychology, 51,* 149–160.

Sosik, J. J. (2005). The role of personal values in the charismatic leadership of corporate managers: A model and preliminary field study. *The Leadership Quarterly, 16,* 221–244.

Stogdill, R. M. (1948). Personal factors associated with leadership: A survey of the literature. *Journal of Psychology, 25,* 35–71.

Tett, R. P., & Burnett, D. D. (2003). A personality trait-based interactionist model of job performance. *Journal of Applied Psychology, 88,* 500–517.

Treviño, L. K., Brown, M., & Hartman, L. P. (2003). A qualitative investigation of perceived executive ethical leadership: Perceptions from inside and outside the executive suite. *Human Relations, 56,* 5–37.

Treviño, L. K., Hartman, L. P., & Brown, M. (2006). Moral person and moral manager: How executives develop a reputation for ethical leadership. In W. E. H. Rosenbach & R. L. Taylor (Eds.), *Contemporary issues in leadership* (pp. 45–62). Boulder, CO: Westview Press.

Tsui, A. S., & Barry, B. (1986). Interpersonal affect and rating errors. *Academy of Management Journal, 29,* 586–599.

Tupes, E. C., & Christal, R. E. (1961). *Recurrent personality factors based on trait ratings.* USAF ASD Tech. Rep. No. 61–97, Lackland Air Force Base, TX: U. S. Air Force.

Turkheimer, E. (2000). Three laws of behavior genetics and what they mean. *Current Directions in Psychological Science, 9,* 160–164.

Uhl-Bien, M., & Carsten, M. K. (2007). Being ethical when the boss is not. *Organizational Dynamics, 36,* 187–201.

Van Dijk, E., & De Cremer, D. (2006). Self-benefiting in the allocation of scarce resources: Leader-follower effects and the moderating role of social value orientations. *Personality and Social Psychology Bulletin, 32,* 1352–1361.

van Knippenberg, D., van Knippenberg, B., De Cremer, D., & Hogg, M. A. (2004). Leadership, self, and identity: A review and research agenda. *The Leadership Quarterly, 15,* 825–856.

Van Vugt, M. (2006). Evolutionary origins of leadership and followership. *Personality and Social Psychology Review, 10,* 354–371.

Van Vugt, M., Hogan, R., & Kaiser, R. B. (2008). Leadership, followership, and evolution: Some lessons from the past. *American Psychologist, 63,* 182–196.

Walumbwa, F. O., Avolio, B. J., Gardner, W. L., Wernsing, T. S., & Peterson, S. J. (2008). Authentic leadership: Development and validation of a theory-based measure. *Journal of Management, 34,* 89–126.

Willner, A. R. (1984). The *spellbinders: Charismatic political leadership.* New Haven, CT: Yale University Press.

Yukl, G. (1999). An evaluation of conceptual weaknesses in transformational and charismatic leadership theories. *The Leadership Quarterly, 10,* 285–305.

Yukl, G., & Tracey, J. B. (1992). Consequences of influence tactics used with subordinates, peers, and the boss. *Journal of Applied Psychology, 77,* 525–535.

Zenger, J., & Folkman, J. (2002). *The extraordinary leader: Turning managers into great leaders.* New York: McGraw-Hill.

Zibarras, L. D., Port, R. L., & Woods, S. A. (2008). Innovation and the "dark side" of personality: Dysfunctional traits and their relation to self-reported innovative characteristics. *Journal of Creative Behavior, 42,* 201–215.

7

Contingencies, Context, Situation, and Leadership

Roya Ayman

Illinois Institute of Technology

Susan Adams

Northeastern Illinois University

In leadership studies, we have observed two general lines of research proceeding in parallel. On one hand, many studies on the relationship between leader traits or behaviors and organizational outcomes find themselves invoking contingencies, context, and situation to explain their findings (e.g., Judge, Bono, Ilies, & Gerhardt, 2002; Judge & Piccolo, 2004). This demonstrates that despite efforts to find simple explanations for leadership, there is a more complex picture to consider. On the other hand, some scholars continue to focus on context and contingencies (e.g., Liden & Antonakis, 2009; Porter & McLaughlin, 2006), demonstrating the importance of these factors in the study of leadership. As Fiedler (1992) commented, life exists within a pretzel-shaped universe and therefore needs pretzel-shaped theories to explain it. This is especially the case in the field of leadership research.

Historically, the 20th-century psychological exploration of leadership research started with the "great man" theory, which focused on leadership as a quality within the individual (e.g., Ayman, 1993; Chemers, 1997; Zaccaro, Kemp, & Bader, 2004). This philosophical school dominated the majority of

AUTHORS' NOTE: Please address correspondence concerning this chapter to Roya Ayman, College of Psychology, Illinois Institute of Technology, 3105 South Dearborn, 2nd floor, Chicago, IL 60616, USA. Phone: 312–567–3516. e-mail: ayman@iit.edu.

the subsequent theoretical developments and empirical investigations and the practice of selection of leaders in organizations. On the other hand, Marx and Engels's Zeitgeist or "spirit of time" philosophical paradigm proposed that leadership is not within the person who becomes the leader, but rather in the situation and the time surrounding the person who becomes the leader. Thus, this approach focused more on the situational impact on leadership and leadership effectiveness (Ayman, 1993; Chemers, 1997) and was the backdrop of the contingency approaches to leadership in the 20th century. However, the dominant focus on the person of the leader within the leadership process is prevalent even after the introduction of contingency approaches. This is evident in the influential works of Big Five personality and leadership (Hogan, Curphy, & Hogan, 1994), full range of leadership theory (Antonakis, Avolio, & Sivasubramaniam, 2003), and leader–member exchange (Graen & Uhl-Bien, 1995). Despite this research, the empirical evidence attests that interest in contingencies and context persists (Porter & McLaughlin, 2006).

In this chapter, we first review the theories and models known within the contingency approaches of leadership. Subsequently, we analyze the definitions of contingencies, context, and situation present in leadership research, acknowledging the various variables and methodological approaches. In so doing, we present a conceptualization of these variables at the interpersonal and intrapersonal levels to assist model building regarding contingencies, context, and situation. In addition, methodological issues that facilitate the role of these concepts in understanding leadership will be discussed.

Contingency Models and Theories of Leadership

Historically, the models and theories of leadership developed in the late 1960s through the 1970s demonstrated that leadership effectiveness is a result of the interaction between the characteristics of the leader and the situation (Fiedler, 1978). Some models focused on the leader's internal state and traits, such as the contingency model of leadership effectiveness and the cognitive resource theory (Fiedler, 1978; Fiedler & Garcia, 1987). Others focused on the leader's perceived behaviors, such as the normative decision-making model (Vroom & Jago, 1978; Vroom & Yetton, 1973), path-goal theory (House, 1971; House & Mitchell, 1974), and situational leadership theory (Hersey & Blanchard, 1969). More recently, leadership categorization has been presented as another contingency theory. Its placement in our scheme of the trait and behavioral contingency approaches to leadership is not as transparent; however, it seems that the focus is on both leader traits (e.g., Offermann, Kennedy, & Wirtz, 1994) and leader behaviors (Lord, Foti, & DeVader, 1984). As we explain later, this approach demonstrates how expectations about leaders vary due to their role or the situation. In the following subsections, we briefly describe each of these models and present a matrix to compare the models and theories based on their approach to assessing the leader, the situation, and leadership effectiveness (see Table 7.1).

Table 7.1 A Matrix Comparing Contingency Models' Treatment of the Leader, the Situation, and Outcomes

	Contingency Model of Leadership Effectiveness	Cognitive Resource Theory	Normative Model of Leadership Decision Making	Path-Goal Theory	Situational Leadership Theory
The Leader					
Source	Leader	Leader	Mostly the leader; some from the subordinates	Subordinates	Subordinates
Characteristics	Trait (LPC scale): task and interpersonal orientation	Intelligence and experience	Decision strategies (five styles): autocratic I & II, consultative I & II, and group II	Supervisory behavior: participative, supportive, achievement-oriented, and directive	Supervisory behavior (LEAD): selling, telling, participating, and delegating
The Situation					
Source	The leader and experimenter	The leader	The leader and experimenter	The subordinate	The leader or experimenter
The Variables	Leader–member relationship Task structure Position power	Stress with boss Stress with coworkers Stress with task	Availability of information Team support and cohesion Time available (These are simplified representations of 11 conditions.)	Subordinates' needs, values and abilities Subordinates' task structure and difficulty	Subordinates' willingness and ability (follower maturity index)
Outcomes					
Group	Performance satisfaction (with leader and subordinates)	Actual performance	Performance satisfaction	General satisfaction	General satisfaction
Individuals	Leader's stress			Team member's stress	

Leader Trait Contingency Models

Contingency model of leadership effectiveness. Fiedler (1964) was the first to formulate a trait contingency model of leadership effectiveness, which became known as the contingency model of leadership effectiveness. In this model, Fiedler (1978) predicted leader or group success from the interaction of the leader's orientation with the leader's situation. A leader's orientation is an internal state and is not directly related to observed behaviors (Ayman, 2002). Thus, this orientation is fairly stable and comparable to other personality traits. The model uses the Least Preferred Coworker (LPC) scale (e.g., Ayman & Romano, 1998) to measure a leader's orientation toward the work setting. Most initial studies in this paradigm were experimental. Additionally, participants were chosen to act as leaders based on whether their LPC score was in the top one-third (relationship-oriented) or the bottom one-third (task-oriented). Using extreme categories allowed for an easier assessment of the effect of this trait on its interaction with the situation and the outcome of the group.

Many procedures were used to substantiate the task orientation of those with low LPC scores and the relationship orientation of those with high LPC scores. To clarify these labels further, two studies (Chemers & Ayman, 1985; Rice, Marwick, Chemers, & Bentley, 1982) examined the impact of LPC scores on the relationship between job satisfaction and performance evaluation. They found that when compared with leaders with high LPC scores, leaders with low LPC scores showed a significantly higher correlation between their satisfaction with work and their performance evaluation. This could be an indication that those with low scores seem to be task-focused individuals and those with high scores on the LPC scale could be considered relationship oriented. Based on these findings, the LPC scale was further substantiated as a measure of the individual's focus and self-worth based on accomplishment of the task.

The contingency model of leadership effectiveness, based on the leader-match concept, predicts that leaders who are more relationship oriented will be more effective in moderate situational control than will task-focused leaders, whereas leaders who are more focused on task than on interpersonal relationships will be more effective in both high- and low-control situations. When leaders are in the situation where the model predicts their greatest effectiveness, they are considered in-match leaders. When they are in situations where the model predicts they will be less effective, they are referred to as being out-of-match leaders (Ayman, 2002).

Based on this model, Fiedler and Chemers (1984) designed a leadership-training model, which was generally supported in subsequent research (Burke & Day, 1986). Furthermore, three separate meta-analyses (Peters, Hartke, & Pohlman, 1985; Schriesheim, Tepper, & Tetrault, 1994; Strube & Garcia, 1981) found support for the general predictions of the model and called for further development and extension (Ayman, 2002). A detailed review of this model and a discussion of its strengths and weaknesses are presented elsewhere (Ayman, 2002; Ayman, Chemers, & Fiedler, 1998).

The leader's situational control in this model refers to the leader's ability to predict group performance and is based on three aspects of the situation: team climate, leader-task structure, and leader-position power. The situation defines the leader's ability to influence the accomplishment of the group's task. The team's climate, better known as the leader–member relationship, assesses the cohesion of team members and their support of the leader. The task structure includes two aspects of the leader's task: the task-structure dimensions and the leader's background (i.e., the leader's experience and training). The final task-structure score is determined by adjusting the task's structure with the level of the leader's experience and training. Position power reflects the leader's legitimacy, as well as the authority for punishing and rewarding the team members (Ayman, 2002; Fiedler, 1978).The order of importance of the situational aspects is based on their contribution to the leader's sense of control and prediction in a situation. During decades of research, Fiedler (1978) concluded that leader–member relationship is twice as important as task structure. Furthermore, task structure is twice as important as position power (Ayman, Chemers, & Fiedler, 1995, 1998). Subsequently, Ayman (2002) argued that a sense of control in a situation gives a person power. The order of importance of situational control aspects, as proposed by Fiedler, are closely representative of the relative importance associated with French and Raven's (1959) sources of power (Podsakoff & Schriesheim, 1985).

Finally, the leader-effectiveness criterion in this model has been primarily defined as group performance (Fiedler, 1978). In response to some criticisms that the model predicts only performance, Rice (1981) suggested that the model could also predict team satisfaction, which was subsequently supported empirically (Ayman & Chemers, 1991). In addition, Chemers, Hays, Rhodewalt, and Wysocki (1985) found that if the leaders were out of match, they experienced high levels of stress and reported extreme clinical symptoms of illness.

The model has been validated mostly at the group level of analysis (Ayman et al., 1995, 1998). However, these authors noted that the design of the model allows for it to function at other levels, such as the individual and the dyadic levels of analysis. For example, in Chemers et al. (1985), the analysis was at the level of the individual leader. Results of two other studies, one laboratory (Chemers, Goza, & Plumer, 1978) and one field (Tobey-Garcia, Ayman, & Chemers, 2000), tentatively supported a dyadic level of analysis. These studies showed that in moderate situational-control conditions, relationship-oriented leaders with task-oriented subordinates yield the highest satisfaction and performance. But in these same situations, task-oriented leaders with task-oriented subordinates who have important but conflicting information seemed to do the worst. This could be partially due to the lack of match experienced in this situation by task-oriented leaders, who therefore may be stressed and not open to new ideas. In this situation, if the subordinate negates the task-oriented leader's structure and/or ideas, the leader by nature may feel further threatened and thus will likely reject the information that is vital and, potentially, lose the opportunity to succeed.

Cognitive resource theory. Cognitive resource theory (CRT) is the second contingency model based on leader traits and characteristics (Fiedler and Garcia, 1987) where the leader's effectiveness can be predicted based on the interaction of two individual, internal characteristics—intelligence and experience—with the situation. Intelligence has been one of the most frequently studied characteristics of leaders (Stogdill, 1974). However, the findings regarding its predictive validity have been somewhat inconsistent. Furthermore, although Lord, DeVader, and Alliger (1986) found intelligence to be strongly predictive of perceived leadership, it should be noted that the outcome variable was leadership emergence, not effectiveness.

In CRT, the core proposition states that situational factors will dictate whether leader intelligence or experience predicts leadership effectiveness. Fiedler (2002) incorporated Sternberg's (1995) explanations of (a) intelligence referring to "fluid" intelligence versus (b) experience being akin to "crystallized" intelligence. The first refers to cognitive ability to deal with novelty, and the second refers to automatization of responses reflective of experiences and mastery. The situation in this theory is defined by the leader's level of stress. A leader can experience job stress in various ways, such as role conflict and overload, as well as from various sources, such as coworkers, the task, or the leader's own superior (Fiedler, 1993). Empirical studies testing this theory have used stress with the leader's superior as the situational constraint (see Table 7.1 for a list of stress sources).

Fiedler (1993, 1995) summarized the findings of several studies in both the laboratory (e.g., Murphy, Blyth, & Fiedler, 1992) and the field (Potter & Fiedler, 1981) where, under stressful conditions, the leaders' performances were positively related to their experience and negatively related to their intelligence. In low-stress situations, conversely, a leader's intelligence was positively related to performance, and experience had less of an effect. Fiedler (2002) further concluded: "People can be experienced and bright or experienced and stupid. But the performance of a particular job requires the leader to give priority either to experience or to analytical or creative analysis in solving the particular problem" (p. 102).

A combination of the contingency model of leadership effectiveness with CRT could demonstrate that out-of-match leaders are stressed. These leaders then may need to rely more on their experience than their intelligence in order to perform well. Zaccaro (1995) considered CRT a promising starting point, and encouraged theorists to consider the roles of multiple traits, such as ego resilience and social intelligence. Recently, in their quantitative review, Judge, Colbert, and Ilies (2004) provided some support for this model.

Leader Behavioral Contingency Approaches

Normative model of leadership decision making. Vroom and Yetton (1973) and later Vroom and Jago (1988) proposed a contingency model of leader decision making. This prescriptive model of leader decision-making processes is narrower in focus than other leadership-contingency approaches (Vroom & Jago, 1998). The model goes by multiple names, such as the participative leadership model, Vroom and Yetton's normative model, and the Vroom-Jago model. Vroom acknowledged that the model is more focused on situations and how leaders respond (Sternberg & Vroom, 2002) than on leader characteristics and how they interact with the situation (e.g., Fiedler's contingency model). Although Vroom and colleagues do not use the term "contingency," they nevertheless propose that a leader's choice of decision style or strategy is guided by the situation.

Overall, the normative model focuses on the interaction between a leader's decision-making strategy choices and the decision situation. Vroom and Jago (1998) identified five leadership strategies for decision making (see Table 7.1). The strategies range from decision making by the leader, to the partial inclusion of the subordinates, to full involvement of the subordinates. The decision heuristics describe the situation based on four criteria: improve the quality of the decision, improve subordinate involvement, reduce the time spent, and develop the subordinates (Vroom & Jago, 1998). These criteria are also the basis for measuring the effectiveness of the decision. The leader is presented with a decision-making tree with yes/no responses reflecting the heuristics. The full representation of this decision-process flowchart is available for review in other sources (e.g., Vroom & Jago, 1998).

If decision quality is critical, the leader has to assess his or her knowledge level, the degree of problem structure, the degree of subordinate's agreeableness, and knowledge pertaining to the decision at hand. For example, group involvement is the advised strategy when subordinates are more knowledgeable on the issue than the leader. When time is of concern, the involvement of the group becomes less practical. In time-pressured situations, therefore, it seems most leaders use more autocratic decision-making strategies. Lastly, if development of subordinate interest, acceptance, and commitment are critical for the decision to be implemented favorably, then greater subordinate involvement is advised. In such situations, the leader may have to pay the cost of increased time and perhaps even sacrifice decision quality to ensure team support and cohesion. The goal of achieving a balance between quality, time, and maintenance of team support will affect whether the leader prioritizes the goal of reaching a high-quality decision over that of high acceptance by the team members, or vice versa.

Based on the normative model, one can assess a leader's decision-style tendencies by having the leader choose an appropriate behavior across 30 different situational conditions. The model is mostly prescriptive: helping a leader learn how to respond in a given situation. In descriptive studies, it appears the situation affects responses to a greater extent more strongly than does the leader's decision style (Vroom & Jago, 1998). As the authors of the model have stated, the situation drives the model more than the leader's characteristics do.

Research has shown that subordinates' involvement is critical in gaining their commitment to feeling ownership of and implementing the decision (Vroom & Jago, 1995). However, if the criterion is quality of the decision or efficiency in the decision-making process, then subordinates' involvement in the decision-making process may not be consistently appropriate, especially when the subordinates do not have the necessary information. Therefore, the styles that will be recommended to the leader will vary according to the criteria chosen for leadership effectiveness.

Some scholars have voiced that a concern about using some of the variations of the model is the extent to which the leader can comply with the prescriptive style (Jago & Vroom, 1980). Leaders with less skill in facilitation may need training in group problem solving and team facilitation. With such training, the leader can judge the appropriate decision-making strategy and determine the best method of implementing that strategy.

Two reports have supported that participative style was perceived positively for both genders (Heilman, Hornstein, Cage, & Herschlag, 1984; Jago & Vroom, 1983). However, Jago and Vroom (1983) also found that whereas male leaders perceived as autocratic were evaluated as modestly positive, female leaders seen as autocratic were rated negatively. Therefore, there seems to be a potential gender contingency in the relationship between the decision-making styles and outcomes.

Cross-cultural studies testing the model have shown that the cultural values in a social environment also affected the leaders' decision-making strategies. In one study, the findings were compared from before and after the fall of communism in Poland. The data show a trend for more participative practices after market economy reforms (Jago, Maczynski, & Reber, 1996). When the Polish managers were compared with Austrian and U.S. managers in another study, though, the results showed that the Polish managers had a harder time agreeing with the model's prescriptions. As the importance of the problem increased, they used a more autocratic style (Maczynski, Jago, Reber, & Boehnisch, 1994).

The effect of the perceiver's role and the perception of decision-making effectiveness were investigated across several studies (Field & House, 1990; Heilman et al., 1984). The results of these studies demonstrated that the description of the leader's decision-making style and the favorableness of the strategy vary depending on the role of the perceiver (i.e., leader or subordinate). For example, those assuming a leader role are more inclined to favor autocratic styles of decision making (Heilman et al., 1984). Field and House (1990) concluded that the model is supported when data were collected from a leader's perspective but not when collected from the subordinates' perspectives. Therefore, perceiver role appears to be a relevant contingency factor.

The participative leadership model or normative model of leadership decision making has received support. Based on the evidence, the model demonstrates that the level of participative decision making should be gauged based on the situation and the effectiveness criteria used. Additionally, there seem to be other contingencies (e.g., gender, cultural values) that appear to monitor the effectiveness of the leader's choice of decision-making style.

Path-goal theory. Inspired by Evans (1970), who further expanded the work of Georgopoulus, Mahoney, and Jones (1957), House (1971) proposed a path-goal theory of leader effectiveness (see House, 1996). The genesis of this theory was based in the Ohio State leader-behavior approach (Stogdill & Coons, 1957) and the expectancy theory of motivation (Vroom, 1964). In response to Korman (1966), House (1971) and House and Mitchell (1974) developed propositions in an attempt to reconcile inconsistent results from the leader-behavior studies. House (1971) identified directive, achievement-oriented, supportive, and participative leadership behaviors as the theory's independent variables (see Table 7.1). It should be noted that the first two are more task focused (e.g., assigning tasks, scheduling, emphasizing deadlines) and the latter two are more considerate (e.g., making people feel at ease, being open to suggestions, encouraging team members).

According to Evans (1996), the majority of the studies on path-goal theory included measures of instrumental/directive and supportive/considerate leadership styles. Schriesheim and Neider (1996) stated, "The need for such leadership [behavior] is moderated by characteristics of the environment as well as by characteristics of the subordinates" (p. 317). Schriesheim and Neider (1996) cited two meta-analyses that have been conducted to validate path-goal theory (Indvik, 1986; Wofford & Liska, 1993). Wofford and Liska (1993) included 120 studies covering the span of two and a half decades and stated: "The analysis indicated that much of the research testing path-goal theories has been flawed" (p. 857).

The most frequently studied work-environment moderator in this paradigm has been subordinates' task structure (Evans, 1996). Wofford and Liska (1993) did not find support for the moderating effect of task structure on the relationship between leader-initiated structure and subordinate satisfaction, performance, and role clarity. Also, across studies, the moderating effect of task structure on the relationship between considerate leader behavior and subordinates' satisfaction was not supported (Indvik, 1986; Wofford & Liska, 1993). However, subordinate task structure was found to have a positive effect on the relationship between considerate leader behavior and performance. When the task was unstructured, as compared with when the task was structured, a stronger relationship was found between considerate leader behavior and effectiveness.

Few studies have examined the personal characteristics of the subordinates as moderators (e.g., ability, locus of control). Schriesheim and Schriesheim (1980) demonstrated that the subordinates' need for affiliation, their authoritarianism, and their ability and experience moderated the relationship between leader behaviors and outcomes. A study demonstrated that subordinates with an external locus of control were more satisfied with participative

than with directive leaders, and they were more productive under these leaders (Algattan, 1985). However, subordinates with an internal locus of control
were more productive and happier when the leader's behavior was task oriented. Overall, the results of the Wofford and Liska (1993) meta-analysis
demonstrated that ability was the only subordinate characteristic that moderated the relationship between leader behavior and outcomes. Subordinates
with low ability, as compared with those with high ability, preferred leaders
who engaged in structuring and task-related behaviors.

Various authors have highlighted notable limitations of path-goal theory.
One issue seems to be related to the instruments used to measure leader
behavior (Fisher & Edwards, 1988; Schriesheim & Von Glinow, 1977).
Another is that most studies have examined either task or subordinate characteristics. Furthermore, Stinson and Johnson (1975) as well as Wofford and
Liska (1993) recommended testing of a multiple-moderator model. Finally,
Wofford and Liska (1993) also expressed concern that the majority of the
studies testing the theory suffered from same-source bias (i.e., common-
methods variance). To conclude, Evans (1996) stated, "In light of the
absence of studies testing the critical motivational hypothesis of the theory,
it is hard to argue that the theory has undergone reasonable testing. It has
not" (p. 307).

On a positive note, path-goal theory can be seen as an important development in leadership theory that encouraged the evolution of new leadership
conceptualizations. It was the basis of the development of theories of charismatic leadership and substitutes for leadership (House, 1996) and potentially
an impetus for the development of a vertical dyad linkage model (Dansereau,
Graen, & Haga, 1975). Although the empirical support for the model is
mixed, it helped drive new thinking about leadership.

Situational leadership theory. Hersey and Blanchard (1969) proposed that
the effectiveness of four leadership behaviors—selling, telling, participating,
and delegating—depends on whether they complement the subordinates'
task-related characteristics (e.g., ability, education, experience) and psychological maturity (e.g., willingness, self-esteem, motivation). Although the
theory does have a measure to assess the leader's style—the Leadership
Effectiveness and Adaptability Description (LEAD)—many of the empirical
studies on this model seem to use the Leader Behavior Description Questionnaire (LBDQ) in measuring the leader's behaviors (e.g., Case, 1987; Vecchio,
1987; Vecchio & Boatwright, 2002).

Based on the major tenets of the theory, the leader should "delegate" (i.e.,
exhibit low consideration and low-structuring behaviors) in situations where
subordinates are able and willing, having both the ability and the motivation
to perform effectively. When subordinates are willing and unable, the appropriate leader behavior is to "sell" (i.e., engage in high-consideration and high
structuring behaviors). In situations where the subordinates are unwilling but
able, the leader should engage in "participative decision-making" (i.e., show

high consideration but low-structuring behaviors). When the subordinates are unwilling and unable, the leader needs to "tell" them what to do (i.e., demonstrate low consideration but high-structuring behaviors). Although situational leadership theory has intuitive appeal, it has undergone only limited empirical examination. Unfortunately, most reviews have been very critical of the model and have not found much empirical support for it (e.g., Fernandez & Vecchio, 1997; Graeff, 1997; Vecchio, 1997; Vecchio & Boatwright, 2002; York, 1996).

The leadership contingency models and theories presented in this section have shown that while all are models of leadership effectiveness that acknowledge the role of the situation, they are distinctly different. The path-goal theory and situational leadership theory are different from the normative model of leadership decision making on the basis of the scope of the leader's behavior. In the normative model, the focus is on the leader's decision strategy, whereas in the path-goal and situational leadership theories, the leader's supervisory behaviors are key. The difference between the contingency model of leadership effectiveness and the path-goal theory is based on how the leader is assessed and how the situation is approached, among other factors. In path-goal theory, the perceived leader behavior is the focus, whereas in the contingency model of leadership effectiveness, the leader's traits and internal state are the focus. In the path-goal theory, the situation is assessed according to subordinates' perceptions, but in the contingency model of leadership effectiveness, the situation is described from the leader's point of view. Finally, Evans (1996) differentiated the theories according to how they were derived. He noted that Fiedler's model was empirically driven and that House "was led to the contingency aspects of his theory by both inconsistent empirical findings and theoretical insight" (p. 307).

Implicit leadership theory and leadership categorization. With the introduction of informational processing perspectives on leadership, a new paradigm grounded in implicit leadership theory (ILT) gained momentum (Eden & Leviantan, 1975). Initial research showed that expectations about a leader affect the perceptions of that leader's behavior (Lord & Emrich, 2001; Lord & Maher, 1991). The next phase of this research program focused on the content of expectations about a leader and that content's universality. Fischbein and Lord (2004) acknowledged that when examining factors that affect ILT, we need to consider the particular leadership context (e.g., political, business, military) as well as the perceiver's personal characteristics (e.g., gender, personality traits). Additionally, although some researchers believe that ideal images are the same as typical leader images (Epitropaki & Martin, 2004), others have suggested that people's image of an ideal and a typical leader have major distinctions. For example, Heilman, Block, Martell, and Simon (1989) found that when different groups of perceivers described their images of (a) the typical woman manager, (b) the typical male manager, and (c) the successful manager, the latter two descriptions shared many of the same characteristics. The image of the typical woman manager, however, did not share characteristics with either the image of the typical male manager or that of the successful manager. The gender difference disappeared, though, when the comparison was between a successful (ideal) woman manager and successful (ideal) man manager.

In cross-cultural studies, two main approaches are recognized (e.g., Ayman & Korabik, 2010): the imposed-etic approach, in which the measures and concepts of one culture are used in another, and the emic approach, in which the measures and concepts are developed from within the culture.

Two studies examining ILT across cultures used the imposed-etic approach (Epitropaki & Martin, 2004; Gerstner & Day, 1994). Gerstner and Day (1994) implemented a measure developed in the United States by Lord et al. (1984), and they examined the mean ratings of people from different cultures (e.g., China, France, Germany, Honduras, India, Japan, Taiwan) on their ideas of a typical leader. Differences were found that were consistent with the cultural values espoused in the various countries' cultures. On the other hand, Epitropaki and Martin (2004), who conducted their study in England, showed an overall similar factor structure to Offermann et al.'s (1994) original study.

In examining the effect of perceivers' characteristics on ILT, the factor analysis studies have shown some agreement on high-level structure of ILT across cultures, age, levels in the organization, and organization type (Den Hartog, House, Hanges, Ruiz-Quintanilla, & Dorfman, 1999; Epitropaki & Martin, 2004; Offermann et al., 1994). In all these studies, the differences across perceivers' categories were at the specifics that defined the factors. For example, Epitropaki and Martin (2004), using Offermann et al.'s (1994) measure, found universal structure for ILT among British participants regardless of age, organizational level, and type. However, they found that women described "their ideal leader as more understanding, sincere, and honest, and less domineering, pushy, and manipulative than did men" (p. 307). This shows the variance between British men and women on their ideal leader.

The above studies have used an imposed-etic approach when studying ILT across countries. When approaching the topic from an emic cross-cultural approach, we find a different result. Two lines of studies are presented here to make this point. One was a series of studies with children (Ayman-Nolley & Ayman, 2005), across gender and country, who were asked to draw a leader leading. The studies on children's ILT provided the opportunity to understand how early these ideas are formed, opening the way for potential interventions. The other series of studies replicated Offermann et al.'s (1994) methodology in China and Iran (Bassari & Ayman, 2009; W. Ling, Chia, & Fang, 2000).

The studies on children took place across three different countries: China (Liu, Ayman, & Ayman-Nolley, 2009), Costa Rica (Ayman-Nolley, Ayman, & Leone, 2006), and the United States (Leffler, Ayman, and Ayman-Nolley, 2006). The results showed that the majority of children had drawn a male image of the leader, with U.S. girls drawing more women as leaders compared with children in other countries.

Leffler et al. (2006) also showed that although the Caucasian children primarily left the leader's color blank (i.e., White, as the paper was white), the African American children tended to draw images representing shades of Brown and Black. The results for the African American girls favored neither the "similar to me" image of the leader nor the image of the leader as male. This finding needs further investigation to generalize the finding that the gender and the ethnicity of the perceiver can interact in affecting her or his image of a leader.

Also, one of the main roles that Chinese children drew for their leader leading was a manager (Liu et al., 2009), which was not present in the Costa Rican or U.S. drawings. Costa Rican children drew more military leaders as compared with U.S. children (Ayman-Nolley et al., 2006). This is interesting in light of the fact that Costa Rica does not have a military force. One explanation could be that joining mercenaries to fight in various militaries is an occupational choice, which may pay well, and the number of people who wear military fatigues in the streets is very noticeable. These findings depict the impact of culture on the content of ILT of children across countries when they are free to express themselves. Thus, not all children across countries have the same image of a leader.

Regarding adult's ILT, two studies applying a similar methodology to Offermann et al. (1994) found both similar and differing results (Bassari & Ayman, 2009; W. Ling et al., 2000). For example, in China the factors describing the leaders included morality, goal effectiveness, interpersonal competence, and versatility (W. Ling et al., 2000). This last factor was not present in previous studies of ILT and referred to the concept of a "renaissance man" or a person with wide knowledge and skills, well rounded and well read, someone who knows about the arts and sciences and is multilingual.

Bassari and Ayman (2009), with a preliminary factor analysis of data collected in Iran, showed the ILT structure for a leader and boss are somewhat different. The factors describing the leader were confident, goal oriented, considerate, and severe. The factors describing the boss were confident, goal oriented, considerate, and sensitive. Examining the factor loading for the boss showed that "severe," which was an independent factor in describing a leader, loaded on the confidence factor when describing the boss (Bassari & Ayman, 2009). These findings, while they showed some similarity to Offermann et al.'s (1994) ILT content (i.e., sensitivity, dedication, tyranny, charisma, attractiveness, masculinity, intelligence, and strength), also demonstrated differences unique to the various cultures and roles. Therefore, the concept of leadership exists in the eye of the beholder. Thus, the image of the leader is highly affected by the contingencies and situations defined from the perspective of both the leader and the perceiver, each influenced by his or her own characteristics (e.g., gender, ethnicity, culture).

_____ Contingencies, Context, and Situation Defined

In the previous section we presented traditional contingency leadership models and theories, which propose that leadership occurs in context. In most of those models, the operationalization of contingency is similar to Johns's (2006) concept of context. Johns stated that context, which can include constraints and opportunities for behavior, surrounds a phenomenon and is external to the individual. Scholars who have written about leadership contingencies have a similar conceptualization of these contingencies that is focused on context (Antonakis et al., 2003, 2004; Avolio, 2007; Chemers, 2000; Diedorff, Rubin, & Morgeson, 2009; Liden & Antonakis, 2009).

Some researchers have considered the gender of the leader as a contingency variable (Antonakis et al., 2003; Eagly, Johannesen-Schmidt, & van Engen, 2003). The gender of the leader is not an external situation or context, though, so the definition of contingency in this case seems to include a more intrapersonal level. At the intrapersonal level, contingencies could be aspects of the leader (traits or characteristics) that enhance or inhibit each other, as they relate to the behavior and effectiveness of the leader. In this section, we argue that contingencies in leadership can be at interpersonal and intrapersonal levels. Most research has focused on the interpersonal level, but we believe there is a place for future research additionally to consider intrapersonal-level contingencies.

Interpersonal Level

At the interpersonal level, the contingencies for leadership effectiveness have been defined as context assessed mainly through the subordinates' perspectives (e.g., path-goal, situational leadership, substitutes-for-leadership). Research has also assessed context using organizational level and type of industry, as well as subordinates' characteristics (e.g., Antonakis et al., 2003; Lowe, Kroeck, & Sivasubramaniam, 1996) and leader's distance from the followers (e.g., Antonakis & Atwater, 2002). Before we present the various factors that have gained recognition as contextual factors in leadership within the present framework, we will briefly review the substitutes-for-leadership theory. This theory expanded the classic work of the contingency models by developing a more inclusive list of contextual factors of leadership and by providing a framework for the contextual factors that hinder or enhance a leader's impact.

Substitutes-for-leadership theory. Based on Jermier and Kerr's (1997) discussion, a leader's behavior typically accounts for less variance in predicting relevant leadership outcomes than do situational factors (i.e., substitutes for leadership). Kerr and Jermier (1978) proposed a taxonomy of 14 situational contingencies divided into three classes: (a) characteristics of subordinates, (b) the nature of the subordinates' tasks, and (c) organizational characteristics. Podsakoff, Mackenzie, and Bommer (1996) also concluded "on average, the substitutes for leadership uniquely accounted for more of the variance in the criterion variables than did leader behaviors" (p. 380).

The key point to remember in this work is that the contingencies were originally conceived as substitutes for or neutralizers of a leader's behaviors. To further clarify these concepts, Schriesheim (1997) described *substitutes* as factors that were directly related to the employee's outcomes and that replaced the need for leader behavior. *Neutralizers* were those factors that inhibit the leader's behavioral influence on the outcome. The distinction between the two factors is based on the relationship the situational factor has with the leader's behavior. In the substitutes-for-leadership condition, the situational factors and the outcome variables are positively related regardless of the leader's behavior. However, neutralizers are correlated with neither the leader's behavior nor the outcome, but they will nullify the effect of the leader's behavior on the outcome.

As Podsakoff and Mackenzie (1997) have argued, research on the substitutes-for-leadership theory supports the notion that leader behavior does not have a universal effect on outcomes. The results of empirical tests of the substitutes-for-leadership theory are mixed. Podsakoff et al. (1996), through a meta-analysis, tested 22 studies and found support for this theory; whereas Dionne, Yammarino, Atwater, and James (2002) did not find similar support for this finding. Dionne et al. (2002) argued that the positive findings for the effects of substitutes for leadership on outcomes may be due to common-source ratings bias. Although the support for this model has been questioned, it has arguably contributed to a clearer conceptualization of the contingency variables from subordinates' perspectives. This model contributed to the study of moderators and mediators in leadership research.

Context in leadership. Since the 1970s, contextual factors have played a role in leadership research; however, the conceptualization of them has not been well developed. It has been argued (Sternberg & Vroom, 2002) that "We need a taxonomy of the situation, or at least dimensions on which the situations vary. Fiedler is one of the few psychologists to offer a language for describing both context and individual difference" (p. 317). Fiedler (1978) presented a taxonomy (Ayman, 2002; Sternberg & Vroom, 2002) focusing on the leader's situation. Through the level of clarity in the situation, a leader gains control and power in a small-group context. In path-goal and subsequently substitutes-for-leadership theories, the focus is on the subordinates' situation.

The early contingency theories focused primarily on leadership in the work group or in a small-group paradigm. Substitutes-for-leadership theory considered leadership in the context of a dynamic organizational and cultural milieu. Most authors seem to agree with the three main categories of context: characteristics of the subordinates, the nature of the subordinates' tasks, and organizational characteristics. This description focused more on the space surrounding the leadership process. However, in this space, most of the research primarily focused on face-to-face contact. With the evolution of information technology and virtual teams, the concept of space has expanded to include "leader distance." This concept includes both psychological and physical distance between the leader and his or her subordinates (Antonakis & Atwater, 2002).

Porter and McLaughlin (2006) argued that not only has the concept of space been expanded, but the concept of time and its impact on leadership has gained attention in leadership research. The theories that made reference to the concept of time include transactional leadership, transformational leadership, and leader–member exchange. Yet, the role of time in leadership needs further research support, both through cross-sectional studies and, more critically, through research examining development over time using longitudinal methods.

More recently, Ayman (2004) argued that culture and leadership have a symbiotic relationship, in which one cannot exist without the other; thus, leadership is culture bound. In this line of research, *culture* refers to both company and societal levels, incorporating values, policies, and norms (Liden & Antonakis, 2009). Some authors have further examined the concept of relationship and the social context of leadership. Historically, Fiedler (1978) was the first to highlight this concept through his group atmosphere or leader–member relationship construct. More recently, Liden and Antonakis (2009) expanded this notion to include social networks and demonstrated the role of the larger societal culture on the dynamics of group relationships. This opens the door for more research on the interaction among different contextual factors.

In the remainder of this section, we use a systems approach to groups—namely the input-process-output (I-P-O) model (Hackman & Morris, 1975)—as a heuristic for conceptualizing the contextual factors. We chose the model of team effectiveness proposed by West, Borrill, and Unsworth (1998) as a guide for this section, in part because they hold a dynamic process perspective, which allows for reciprocal effects between inputs and processes and between processes and outputs. For the purpose of our discussion, leadership process is the focus of interest. An additional reason we used the model by West and colleagues (1998) is their pronounced effort to incorporate the organizational context within the I-P-O framework of team effectiveness. As part of the inputs to the group, their definition of organization context includes reward structure, available support for the team in the form of feedback and training opportunities, location of group members, medium of communication, and time allotted to get the job done. This model also recognizes that output or outcomes can be either attitudinal (e.g., satisfaction, stress) or behavioral (e.g., turnover, performance, organizational citizenship), and can occur at leader, individual subordinate, or group levels. From a leadership perspective, both the input variables and outcomes have an important impact on the leader's characteristics and choice of action to achieve success. Each of the four input factors (cultural context, organizational context, group composition, and task features) within the West et al. (1998) team effectiveness model may be considered as moderators, and thereby, they establish the contingencies between leadership and organizational outcomes. We used this model of team effectiveness to stimulate consideration of a wide variety of interpersonal-level context variables for the study and model development of leadership and context. To further demonstrate the impact of these four input factors on leadership, the following section will highlight empirical examples for the role of organizational climate, group composition, and the nature of the task on leadership traits and behaviors.

Cultural context. Ayman and Korabik (2010) acknowledge the wide diversity of definitions provided for culture. However, for the operationalization of culture in leadership research, they identify two different categories: first, visible indices of culture as reflected by such differences between groups as country boundaries; and, second, invisible indices of culture as reflected by the values and norms that a social group has agreed on over time.

Scholars have argued that culture has more impact on individual behavior if it is strong (Mischel, 1977) or if it is tight (Pelto, 1968). Mischel (1977) stated that strong settings—such as in military organizations—where the latitude for self-expression is limited, as compared with weak settings—such as civilian organizations—have norms and demands that can control the individual's behavior. Similarly, Pelto (1968) defined cultures as being tight or loose. The more explicit the cultural norms, the tighter the culture and the less chance there is for the expression of individual differences in responses and behaviors.

Hall and Hall (1990) further explained that culture impacts communication. In some cultures, communication can either be high- or low-context. For example, in high-context cultures—such as Japan or the Middle East—where people interact with a very close social network, there is less need to provide detailed information when they interact. Thus, individuals rely on the common knowledge of the context they share. In contrast, in low-context cultures—such as Germany, Scandinavia, or the United States—individuals tend to compartmentalize their social interactions between work and personal life and thus have a greater need to explain background information when communicating. Such norms of conduct can have an impact on a leader's communication habits or expected style of social exchange with her or his team-members.

Such projects as the GLOBE studies have provided further evidence and popularity as to the impact of culture on leadership (House, Hanges, Javidan, Dorfman, & Gupta, 2004) by demonstrating similarities and differences across country boundaries and global regions on the manifestation of various leader behaviors. Additional scholars have recognized the impact of culture in understanding leadership through social cognition (Ayman, 1993; Chemers, 2000; Hanges, Lord, & Dickson, 2000).

Avolio (2007), Ayman (2004), and Chemers (2000) have offered ideas on how to integrate culture in theories and models of leadership. Three potential roles can be examined for culture in leadership: It can be considered (a) as an antecedent to leadership behavior, where leaders from different cultures may be perceived as acting differently; (b) as a moderating effect of culture on the relationship between leadership (trait or behavior) and outcomes, such as employee engagement or performance; and (c) in terms of the impact that the cultural diversity of the team and leader has on their relationship and effectiveness. In their review, Ayman and Korabik (2010) demonstrated how culture has been neglected in leadership research and theory development. They showed that most of our leadership models have not fully integrated culture in their design and conceptualization, though they have shown some validation across cultures. The complexity of the role of culture in leadership at multiple levels was further discussed in their article. Their final conclusion argues for a symbiotic relationship between leadership and culture, in which theories of leadership are evolving into a more inclusive cultural image of leadership.

Thus, it appears that the situation as a context plays an important role. For example, it is possible that in some cultures, leaders do not have the flexibility to express their personal values and beliefs because situational demands dictate their behavior. Cultural context provides restrictive norms that may not allow for a full representation of an individual leader's behavioral choices. The significance of this is that leadership needs to be considered within a cultural context because the context influences how individual leaders can behave (Rousseau & Fried, 2001).

Organizational context. Organizational context surrounds the work team and its leader. Organizational climate is reflective of organizational context, which includes normative social interactions and policies and procedures. Organizational climate can be defined objectively, such as a tall and flat hierarchy of the organization, as well as through its size. It can also be defined subjectively through shared beliefs and norms of interactions (Dennison, 1996).

The impact of organizational norms on leadership has been established across a number of studies. For example, Shartle (1951) illustrated the importance of workplace norms on how leaders behave in demonstrating that the best predictor of a leader's behavior in organizations is the behavior of his or her boss, not the leader's personality. Lowe et al. (1996) showed no effect associated with a leader's position in the hierarchy on their respective leadership styles or effectiveness. On the other hand, Lowe et al. did find that transformational leader behavior is more effective in public-sector organizations than in the private sector. This shows that although level in the organization did not affect the leader's behaviors, type of organization did.

Within the West et al. (1998) team effectiveness model, organizational context variables included, among others, physical conditions and affective reactions both to work groups and to the organization as a whole. In leadership research, though, only a few of these variables have been considered as moderators. To elaborate on the effect of space and physical conditions, earlier research on communication patterns (Leavitt, 1951) and seating arrangements (Howells & Becker, 1962) showed that these situational factors influenced leader identification and emergence. The main rationale behind such findings may be that greater eye contact gives more control and that, thereby, they are more likely to be identified as the leaders (Chemers, 1997; Shaw, 1981).

Contemporary leaders may not always engage in face-to-face interaction if work is conducted via computer-mediated environments. Along with the expansion of the virtual workplace, e-leadership has gained greater attention (Antonakis & Atwater, 2002; Avolio, Kahai, & Dodge, 2000). More recently, therefore, researchers are viewing the medium of communication as an organizational contextual factor relevant to e-leadership. Some research has shown there to be no major differences between face-to-face and computer-mediated conditions in terms of leadership emergence (e.g., Adams, Ayman, & Roch, 2010). Overall, where differences arise, they are in regard to leadership perceptions. For example, Puranova and Bono (2009) demonstrated that although transformational leaders were valuable in both face-to-face and computer-mediated conditions, the impact was stronger in virtual teams. Furthermore, Hoyt and Blascovich (2003) demonstrated that face-to-face conditions increased team members' satisfaction with a leader who was either transformational or transactional. More research is needed to better understand the impact of distance and modes of interaction on leadership and outcomes.

Group composition. The input variable of group composition (West et al., 1998) covers research that examines both the size of the work group and the effects of the heterogeneity of group membership on competitive group advantage. In today's diverse workforce, studies examining the role of group composition on leadership are of great value. Group composition can be examined at a group level or a dyadic level.

A small number of studies showed the effect of group size and composition on the relationship between leadership and outcomes. For example, to demonstrate the effect of organization or work group size on leadership and outcomes, Y. Ling, Simsek, Lubatkin, and Veiga (2008) found that the impact of transformational leadership on the objective performance of the organization was higher in smaller organizations than in larger ones. On the other hand, the cultural and gender composition of the group could affect group atmosphere and moderate the impact of a leader.

The following findings are examples across various leadership models on the role of group interaction and leadership effectiveness. At the group level, Fiedler (1978) reported poorer leader–member relationships, or group atmosphere, when the leader and group members were from different cultures, which impedes leader effectiveness. Similarly, Bass, Avolio, Jung, and Berson (2003) demonstrated that platoon potency and cohesion partially mediated the relationship between the leadership style of the superior officers and simulated platoon performance. To the extent that leader–member relationship and group cohesion may be related to group composition, these findings can be examples of how a group's social interaction may affect the relationship between the leader's behavior and group performance. At this point, there are not that many studies that have examined group composition as a context to leadership. However, Jung and Avolio (1999) demonstrated that transformational leaders were more effective in collectivist cultures and transactional leaders were more effective in individualistic cultures. Thus, the group's diversity and tension may affect how a particular leadership style relates to a given outcome.

At a dyadic level, Ayman, Korabik, and Morris (2009) demonstrated that dyad gender composition moderated the relationship between leaders' transformational leadership and their leadership performance. Male subordinates devalued female transformational leaders as compared with male transformational leaders. Ayman, Rinchiuso, and Korabik (2004) also found that men with female subordinates who had moderate leader–member exchange (LMX) relationships had the least satisfied subordinates. These findings show that the gender dyad of leaders and followers moderates the effect of the leadership behavior and outcomes. Additionally, Polyashuk, Ayman, and Roberts (2008) found that leader-subordinate dyads with ethnic similarities or differences showed different levels of LMX. Other than the African American dyads, where quality of relationship continued to strengthen, those who were in a relationship more than five years described a lower quality of LMX. These examples show how the composition of dyads or groups can significantly affect leadership and its relationship to outcomes.

Nature of the task. The nature of the group task holds implications for the process and outcome of the work completed. The nature of a task may be assessed in many ways (for more information on task typologies, refer to Hackman, 1968, and McGrath, 1984). For example, tasks may vary in type, difficulty, degree of dependence on communication for task completion (Hollingshead & McGrath, 1995), or even gender orientation (Wentworth & Anderson, 1984).

The nature of the task alone can influence leadership. As an example, the gender orientation of a task—i.e., whether it is feminine or masculine—has been found to influence whether a man or a woman emerged as a leader (e.g., Wentworth & Anderson, 1984), and some support (e.g., Gershenoff & Foti, 2003) has been found for the effect of the role of gender and intelligence on leader emergence being moderated by the nature of the task (e.g., initiating-structure task, consensus-building task). In their meta-analysis, Eagly and Karau (1991) found men tended to emerge as overall or task leaders and women were more likely to emerge as social leaders. However, the nature of the task and the length of time for leadership affected the role of leadership emergence in mixed-gender small groups. That is, when tasks required greater social interaction or allowed for longer time periods to identify the emergent leader, the tendency for males to emerge as leaders was reduced (Eagly & Karau, 1991). Lastly, Eagly, Karau, and Makhijani, (1995) demonstrated across studies that female leaders in masculine-task conditions were devalued. More specifically, Becker, Ayman, and Korabik (2002) found that female leaders who worked in educational organizations had more agreement with their subordinates on their leadership behaviors than did female leaders in business organizations. The task environment did not have as much impact for male leaders. Thus, gender congruency of the task affects the leader and how the leader can function and be effective.

The complexity of the task and its effect on leadership were examined in various contingency models from the leaders' and the subordinates' perspectives (e.g., contingency model of leadership effectiveness, path-goal theory). In addition, the complexity and certainty of the organization's task environment as perceived by top management moderated the impact of the charismatic leadership of CEOs on financial outcomes of (Waldman, Ramirez, House, & Puranam, 2001). Thus, we can see that regardless of how we define leadership, the nature of the goal at hand or the task can affect the success of that leader.

Organization and group outcomes. As previously mentioned at the start of this interpersonal subsection, the West et al. (1998) model of team effectiveness recognizes that outcomes can be either attitudinal (e.g., satisfaction) or behavioral (e.g., turnover), and can occur at leader, individual subordinate, or group levels. The importance of the relationship between the leadership and outcome may also be affected by the organizational outcome under investigation. As Table 7.1 shows, some of the contingency models use more subjective measures of outcomes, such as satisfaction, commitment, and stress (e.g., path-goal theory, normative model, contingency model of leadership effectiveness); others have used more objective measures, like meeting goals, hitting the target (e.g., contingency model of leadership effectiveness). Thus, the actual definition of the outcome may be considered a contingency for the leadership and effectiveness relationship.

Overall the team effectiveness model provides a theoretical group perspective to the potential substitutes or enhancers for leadership, in addition to stimulating researchers to consider other contingencies, such as cultural context. Additionally, researchers need to focus on the contextual factors that are most relevant today, such as the medium of communication, the effects of leadership behavior across hierarchical levels (e.g., Kane & Tremble, 2000), and the effects of distal (indirect) and proximal (direct) leadership (e.g., Avolio, Zhu, Koh, & Puja, 2004).

Intrapersonal Level

At the intrapersonal level, relevant contingencies include different leader characteristics that may affect each other and thereby influence the person's ability to lead. For example, in reviewing individual differences, we can consider sociodemographic and psychosocial characteristics. For a more detailed discussion on various traits and personal characteristics of the leader, please refer to Chapter 6 by Timothy Judge and David Long. However, as an example, we argue that a leader's gender and self-monitoring level are two characteristics that may act as contingencies within the leadership process.

Gender is a complex phenomenon. Korabik and Ayman (2007) showed how sociodemographic gender and sex role have demonstrated different effects on leadership processes. For example, Eagly and Carli (2007) provided evidence challenging the results of the Big Five for female and male leaders and their effectiveness. Ayman and Korabik (2010) presented an intrapersonal model of leadership, and they provided evidence of how gender and culture affect leadership behavior and can moderate the relationship of some traits with leadership behaviors or of some traits and behaviors with outcomes. Although men and women may not differ on various leadership styles, feminine and masculine individuals of both genders do differ in their leadership behaviors and effectiveness.

From a multitrait perspective, Zaccaro (2007) demonstrated that different aspects of a person's personality and competency might have reciprocal influence in shaping the resultant effectiveness of a leader. His proposed model has provided an enhancement to a traditional linear bivariate approach. Zaccaro's (2007) model addresses the role of such mediators as proximal skills and behavior but does not include moderators.

A trait that may play a moderating role in the intrapersonal characteristics of a leader is self-monitoring. Gangestad and Snyder (2000) have suggested, based on a deep program of research, that higher scores on an 18-item self-monitoring scale reflect a greater alignment of a person's attitude and behavior. This can have implications on the relationship between traits, leader behavior, and performance. Ayman and Chemers (1991) explored this concept by studying the moderating impact of self-monitoring on leader match and effectiveness. They demonstrated that leaders who were low self-monitors and in match did perform better than the high self-monitors who were in match. However, high self-monitor leaders compensated when they were out of match. For example, a high self-monitor and task-oriented leader with moderate situational control performed better than the low self-monitor leader. That is, the task-oriented leader who is a high self-monitor, when out of match, will be more attentive to situational cues and manage his or her responses so as to be more appropriate. More research exploring the role of self-monitoring in moderating the effect of personality and leader behavior would be informative.

Methodological Issues Within Contingency Research

Uncovering the patterns of relationship between leader characteristics, outcomes, and contingencies is challenging. Various complex designs and methods are needed to test for such relationships. Within this section, we caution researchers and consumers of such research on the potential impact of several issues, such as research design, data source, and levels of analysis.

Research Design

With regard to research design, we encourage researchers to seek opportunities for longitudinal research. The majority of research on leadership is cross-sectional in that the information about the leader, context, and outcomes are collected at the same time and often from the same source. Longitudinal designs and experimental studies allow for stronger causal inferences to be drawn but, unfortunately, are relatively uncommon in the leadership literature. Time has an enormous potential impact on leadership processes, yet the timing of effects in terms of when things occur remains theoretically underspecified (Mitchell & James, 2001). We consider time to include both the timing of when a leadership outcome is measured in relation to other variables and the length of the relationship between leader and follower. Next, the focus will be on the explanation of time as a critical contingency.

The timing of outcome measurement refers to the amount of time between the measurement of the leaders' trait and/or behavior and the measurement of the relevant leadership outcome. Such consideration can provide predictive validity of the relationship between leaders' characteristics and contingencies. The question then becomes: What is the appropriate time lag? This was evidenced by the work of Schneider and Hough (1995), who argued that when the task is simple, a short time is sufficient to yield the related outcome. However, if the task is complicated, then criterion measures may not be immediately predictable. Being a relational phenomenon, the impact of leadership may require extensive time before it is manifested in certain outcomes. For example, Waldman et al. (2001) argued that they needed to examine net profit margin across five years in order to establish the relationship between charismatic leadership, environmental uncertainty, and financial outcome of the organization. Day and Lord (1988) demonstrated that the relationship between CEO leadership as measured through succession and organizational performance was considerably stronger when a two-year time lag was considered as compared with no time lag.

As previously mentioned, though the number of leadership studies examining length of time or tenure in the leadership position is relatively small, some studies in the LMX paradigm have argued that the leadership relationship can only mature over time (Graen & Uhl-Bien, 1995). However, in a recent study on African American and Caucasian leaders and followers, Polyashuk et al. (2008) found that only African American leader–subordinate dyads showed an increase in trust and LMX beyond five years. Other ethnic combination dyads showed an increase in trust between the leader and follower until five years, beyond which the relationship quality decreased. From this data, the reason for this discrepancy is not clear at this point. Still, there are two important points: (a) the length of time and dyad composition may interact in moderating the effect of a leader's trustworthiness and (b) it is an oversimplification to assume that the longer a leader and subordinates are together, the more mature their relationship is. The impact of time on leadership clearly needs further investigation.

Data Source

Yukl and Van Fleet (1992) identified single-source bias as an endemic issue in leadership research. That is, information gathered about the leader, context, and outcome should not be collected from the same source (e.g., the subordinate), as this leads to artificial inflation of estimated relationships. Source of data seems to play a role in the relationship between trait and behavior or between behavior and outcome. Examples of the impact of this issue can be seen throughout leadership research. As mentioned, Field and House (1990) examined Vroom and Jago's model and found that the self-descriptions of the leader's decision strategy and the subordinates' description of the leader's decision strategy yielded differing results. This is a challenge facing all efforts in leadership research when the investigator is using survey methods as the sole tool for data collection. Thus, a more careful design of studies on leadership is warranted.

Levels of Analysis

Appropriate multilevel analysis is needed when leadership researchers include multilevel variables, such as organizational context (e.g., Porter & McLaughlin, 2006), in their research. The researchers must decide whether they are examining leadership at the individual, the dyadic, or the group level. This will affect the design of the study and the data collection strategy. Klein and Kozlowski (2000), expanding on this analytical approach, edited an influential volume that helps researchers both conceptualize and analyze multilevel data appropriately. Researchers pursuing a focus on context, situation, or contingencies need to be familiar with multilevel design and analyses issues to better examine the complexity of these relationships (Kozlowski & Klein, 2000; see also Rousseau, 2000).

Yammarino and Dansereau (2009) addressed multilevel issues pertaining to leadership and organizational behavior. There is evidence that leadership models function at multiple levels (Dansereau & Yammarino, 1998a; 1998b). They provided evidence in support of the presence and importance that levels of analysis hold in all approaches to leadership. The question remains: Is leadership best conceptualized as a group, dyad, or individual phenomenon? For example, Mumford, Dansereau, and Yammarino (2000) discussed how individualized consideration in leadership could be studied across levels. In the context of examining CEO leadership, Waldman and Yammarino (1999) argued that the inclusion of contingencies of organizational level and subordinates' perceptions call for cross-level analyses and model building. Similarly, Schyns and Van Veldhoven (2010) demonstrated that both level and strength of leadership climate affected employees' individual climate perceptions. After controlling for individual-level climate for leadership, the variability and level of leadership climate had an impact on employees' commitment. Their study showed that supportive leadership is not only dyadic but may be affected by the leaders' resources and the culture in which they are working.

In examining contingencies and context, levels of analysis become more important when a study examines the role of organizational climate on the relationship between leadership and outcomes, with each variable potentially occurring at differing levels of analysis. To examine such relationships, it is critical either to consider cross-level analysis or to align the analysis at one level. In leadership research, the relationship and nature of variables do not function at the same level. Recent promising methodological directions taken by researchers include cross-level moderation (e.g., Chen & Bliese, 2002; Chen, Kirkman, Kanfer, Allen, & Rosen, 2007) and moderated mediation models. For example, Chen et al. (2007) studied multilevel empowerment and found that leadership climate, as measured at the team level, positively moderated the relationship between LMX and individual empowerment. In addition, the use of moderated mediation techniques is becoming more accessible (e.g., Edwards & Lambert, 2007; Preacher, Rucker, & Hayes, 2007). As scholars unravel the complexity of leadership, methodologies are needed to test these assumptions and theories.

Summary and Conclusion

To address the contingency and contextual approach to leadership, this chapter has two main sections. The first part consists of a review of classical contingency models. The second part offers a conceptualization of the type of variables used to test contingencies in leadership research, as well as methodological issues related to this approach. In our review of classic contingency theories of leadership, we classified the theories into two types: (a) those based on the relationship between the leader's traits and the outcomes (i.e., contingency model of leadership effectiveness and cognitive resource theory) and (b) those that related the leader's behavior to the outcome (i.e., the normative decision-making model, situational leadership theory, and path-goal theory).

In most of the earlier research, the contingencies were generally conceptualized in terms of aspects of the situation that is the context for the leadership process. In this chapter, we recommended considering two different type of contingencies: intrapersonal (interaction of various aspects of the leader's traits and values) and interpersonal (interaction at dyad or group level within a social context). For intrapersonal contingencies, we proposed such concepts as leaders' gender, self-monitoring, and cultural values. For the interpersonal category of contingencies, we recommended considering the West et al. (1998) model of team effectiveness, advocating the consideration of group inputs and group outcomes as potential contextual factors.

In addition, we proposed that contingencies can also be discussed from a methodological perspective. The study's design as it relates to the role of time, source, and method of data collection was emphasized. Furthermore, we offered the analytical models that test patterns of relationship between contingencies and leadership through the use of such models as level of analysis, moderation, and mediation tests. Thus, we demonstrated the evolution of and maturity in understanding the role of contingencies in leadership. The various theoretical approaches reviewed and the new methodologies attest to the omnipresent complexity in leadership and its relationship with contingencies.

The key issue to consider when thinking of contingency approaches to leadership is to remember that this approach is based strongly in a person–situation fit concept. The models in this approach have demonstrated that effective leaders respond to the situation in multiple ways: by changing their behaviors, by being perceived as behaving differently, or by choosing and managing their situation. This position is similar to Sternberg's (1988) definition of intelligent functioning, which refers to the individual's "purposive adaptation to, selection of and shaping of real-world environment relevant to one's life and abilities" (p. 65).

Finding an optimal match is what Chemers (1997) referred to as *mettle*. As noted by Chemers, "Mettle captures the sense of a confident and optimistic leader whose perceptions, thoughts and mood provide a reservoir of enthusiasm and energy for meeting the challenges presented by the leadership task" (p. 166). This state is somewhat similar to Csikszentmihalyi's (1990) concept of "flow," referring to when an individual's skill and knowledge is neither more nor less than the situational needs. In this state, leaders manifest the height of their potential, expressing optimism and feeling efficacious (Chemers, 2002). Fiedler (1978) referred to this state as a leader being in-match. When the situation is congenial to the leader's characteristics, the leader functions optimally and with ease.

At first glance, some may perceive a contradiction in the concept of leaders being stable and consistent as well as being flexible to meet situational needs. In essence, however, there is no difference between the two. In either case, the leader's persona does not change. For example, a high self-monitoring leader does not become a low self-monitor; nor does a high LPC leader become a low LPC leader. Instead, leaders engage in behaviors and strategies that bring them closer to being in match with the situation and experience flow or mettle.

So for example, a low LPC leader in a moderate control situation (out of match) may realize that she or he needs to include other team members in the decision-making process, as recommended by Vroom's decision-making tree. The leader may then use a nominal group technique to have a structured method of managing the situation. The other alternative is to use a consultative style, rather than a group decision-making strategy, so as to still maintain some of the control over the outcome, which is demanded by the leader's personality trait. Thus, a simple matter of accepting drop-ins versus meeting only by appointment may seem a small issue, but it may have implications in the situational match of a leader. Therefore, when we talk about flexibility, it is in reference to behaviors that manage the situation, not to changing one's trait and personality.

In many of the previous works, the ability to adjust and be flexible is recognized as an important competency for a leader (e.g., Lord et al., 1986). This competency is also present in social/emotional intelligence (Van Rooy & Viswesvaran, 2004) and cultural intelligence (Triandis, 2006). Flexibility can be considered an intraperson contingency. Leaders facing a diverse workforce frequently find themselves in situations and contexts that need to be managed by adjusting their behaviors.

Future Research

With such strong and consistent evidence that situation, context, and contingencies matter in understanding and studying leadership, is there a place for direct impact of a leader's traits and behavior on organizational and personal outcomes related to leaders and followers? In the future, scholars may consider this issue when exploring new paradigms of leadership behaviors, such as authenticity or servant leadership. The trait researcher may want to consider the situational factors when examining the relationship between traits and outcomes to enhance the meaning of these findings.

Implication for Practitioners

Practitioners use leadership knowledge either for training and development or for evaluation processes in selection and in performance review. To consider the situation, job analysis prior to identification of competencies and abilities may clarify the nature of the job and the scope of the position, which are the contingencies. Thus, this procedure may allow for a more accurate prioritization of competencies, skills, and abilities (Dierdorff, Rubin, & Morgeson, 2009). Practitioners assessing leaders' performance may need to be mindful of other contingencies, such as gender or ethnicity. Results of some studies demonstrated that competencies considered for the manager's performance vary based on the gender of the leader (Frame, Roberto, Schwab, & Harris, 2010; Ostroff, Atwater, & Feinberg, 2004). The case offered at the end of this chapter offers the reader an opportunity to explore the practical implications of the approach on the daily life of leaders and practitioners in the workplace.

Overall, the contingency approach to leadership has alluded to the fact that leaders consciously or unconsciously try to reach their optimal level of performance by being aware of their situation and responding accordingly. Therefore, such leadership training programs as leader match (Fiedler & Chemers, 1984) and situational leadership (Hersey and Blanchard, 1982) facilitate leaders to become more sensitive, responsive, and flexible. Additionally, the practice of 360-degree feedback, as a means to develop leaders, gives leaders a chance to see themselves through the eyes of others (i.e., in an interpersonal context). Training outcomes can be attained either by the behavior adjustment of the leader, as described by the subordinates, or through the leader's description of how he or she managed the situation.

To conclude, contingencies, context, and the situation are important factors to consider when we train and select leaders. In our leadership theories, we need to integrate and conceptualize these factors more effectively. A combination of skills and competencies—such as sensitivity, responsiveness, and flexibility—may help a leader reach mettle (Chemers, 2002). These competencies can be manifested in various ways through particular traits, skills, or behaviors depending on the person, the method of assessment, and the leadership situation. Therefore, contingencies in leadership cannot be ignored, as they are inevitably connected to fully understanding leadership processes.

Discussion Questions

1. Knowing the role of contingencies and context, what should be considered when selecting leaders? Use both trait and behavioral approaches in your discussion.

2. How should leadership studies be designed so as to be attentive to contingencies? What are the options and strategies?

3. Consider a leader of your choice. Describe how her or his personality and behaviors in various situations could lead to success or failure.

Supplementary Readings

Hannah, S. T., Uhl-Bien, M., Avolio, B. J., & Cavarretta, F. L. (2009). A framework for examining leadership in extreme contexts. *The Leadership Quarterly, 20,* 897–919.

James, E. H., & Wooten, L. P. (2005). Leadership as (un)usual: How to display competence in times of crisis. *Organizational Dynamics, 34,* 141–152.

Kaplan, R. E., & Kaiser, R. B. (2003). Developing versatile leadership. *MIT Sloan Management Review, 44*(4), 19–26.

Sally, D. (2002). Co-leadership: Lessons from republican Rome. *California Management Review, 42*(4), 84–99.

Snowden, D., & Boone, M. (2007). A leader's framework for decision making. *Harvard Business Review, 85*(11), 68–76.

Case Study

Sims, H. P., Jr., Faraj, S., & Seokhwa, Y. (2009, March 15). When should a leader be directive or empowering? How to develop your own situational theory of leadership. *Harvard Business Review*. Available from http://www1.hbr.org/product/when-should-a-leader-be-directive-or-empowering-ho/an/BH318-PDF-ENG?N=516191%204294934782&Ntt=leadership

References

Adams, S., Ayman, R., & Roch, S. (2010, August). *Communication frequency and content on leader emergence: Does communication medium matter?* Paper presented at the annual Academy of Management Conference, Montreal, Canada.

Algattan, A. R. A. (1985, August). *Test of the path-goal theory of leadership in the multinational domain.* Paper presented at the annual Academy of Management Conference, San Diego, CA.

Antonakis, J., & Atwater, L. (2002). Leader distance: A review and a proposed theory. *The Leadership Quarterly, 13,* 673–704.

Antonakis, J., Avolio, B. J., & Sivasubramaniam, N. (2003). Context and leadership: An examination of the nine-factor full range leadership theory using the Multifactor Leadership Questionnaire. *The Leadership Quarterly, 14,* 261–295.

Antonakis, J., Schriesheim, C. A., Donovan, J. A., Gopalakrishna-Pillai, K., Pellegrini, E. K., & Rossomme, J. L. (2004). Methods for studying leadership. In J. Antonakis, A. T. Cianciolo, & R. S. Sternberg (Eds.), *The nature of leadership* (pp. 48–70). Thousand Oaks, CA: Sage.

Avolio, B. J. (2007). Promoting more integrative strategies for leadership theory building. *American Psychologist, 62,* 25–33.

Avolio, B. J., Kahai, S., & Dodge, G. E. (2000). E-leadership: Implications for theory, research, and practice. *The Leadership Quarterly, 11,* 615–668.

Avolio, B. J., Zhu, W., Koh, W., & Puja, B. (2004). Transformational leadership and organizational commitment: Mediating role of psychological empowerment and moderating role of structural distance. *Journal of Organizational Behavior, 25,* 951–968.

Ayman, R. (1993). Leadership perception: The role of gender and culture. In M. M. Chemers and R. Ayman (Eds.), *Leadership theory and research: Perspectives and directions* (pp. 137–166). New York: Academic Press.

Ayman, R. (2002). Contingency model of leadership effectiveness. In L. L. Neider & C. A. Schriesheim (Eds.), *Leadership* (pp. 197–228). Greenwich, CT: Information Age.

Ayman, R. (2004). Culture and leadership. In C. Spielberger (Ed.), *Encyclopedia of applied psychology* (Vol. 2, pp. 507–519). San Diego, CA: Elsevier.

Ayman, R., & Chemers, M. M. (1991). The effects of leadership match on subordinate satisfaction in Mexican organizations: Some moderating influences of self-monitoring. *Applied Psychology: An International Review, 44,* 299–314.

Ayman, R., Chemers, M. M., & Fiedler, F. (1995). The contingency model of leadership effectiveness and its levels of analysis. *The Leadership Quarterly, 6,* 147–168.

Ayman, R., Chemers, M. M., & Fiedler, F. (1998). The contingency model of leadership effectiveness and its levels of analysis. In F. Yammarino and F. Dansereau (Eds.), *Leadership: The multi-level approaches* (pp. 73–96). New York: JAI Press.

Ayman R., & Korabik, K. (2010). Leadership: Why gender and culture matter. *American Psychologist, 65,* 157–170.

Ayman, R., Korabik, K., & Morris, S. (2009). Is transformational leadership always perceived as effective? Male subordinates' devaluation of female transformational leaders. *Journal of Applied Social Psychology, 39,* 852–879.

Ayman, R., Rinchiuso, M., & Korabik, K. (2004, August). Organizational commitment and job satisfaction in relation to LMX and dyad gender composition. Paper presented at the International Congress of Psychology, Beijing, China.

Ayman, R., & Romano, R. (1998). Measures and assessments for the contingency model of leadership. In F. Yammarino and F. Dansereau (Eds.), *Leadership: The multi-level approaches* (pp. 97–114). New York: JAI Press.

Ayman-Nolley, S., & Ayman, R. (2005). Children's implicit theory of leadership. In J. R. Meindl and B. Schyns (Eds.), *Implicit leadership theories: Essays and explorations, A volume in the leadership horizons series* (pp. 189–233). Greenwich, CT: Information Age.

Ayman-Nolley, S., Ayman, R., & Leone, C. (2006, July). Gender differences in the children's implicit leadership theory: Costa Rican and American comparison. In R. Littrell (Convener*), Empirical studies: Qualitative and quantitative analyses of leadership and culture.* Symposium conducted at the International Congress of Cross-Cultural Psychology, Isle of Spetses, Greece.

Bass, B. M., Avolio, B. J., Jung, D. I., & Berson, Y. (2003). Predicting unit performance by assessing transformational and transactional leadership. *Journal of Applied Psychology, 88,* 207–218.

Bassari, A., & Ayman, R. (2009, May). Implicit leadership theory of Iranians. Paper presented at the meeting of the Leadership Trust Symposium, Ross-upon-Rye, UK.

Becker, J., Ayman, R., & Korabik, K. (2002). Discrepancies in self/subordinates' perceptions of leadership behavior: Leader's gender, organizational context, and leader's self- monitoring. *Group & Organizational Management, 27,* 226–244.

Burke, M. J., & Day, R. R. (1986). A cumulative study of the effectiveness of managerial training. *Journal of Applied Psychology, 71,* 242–245.

Case, B. (1987). Leadership behavior in sport: A field test of the situation leadership theory. *International Journal of Sport Psychology, 18,* 256–268.

Chemers, M. M. (1997). *An integrative theory of leadership.* Mahwah, NJ: Lawrence Erlbaum.

Chemers, M. M. (2000). Leadership research and theory: A functional integration. *Group Dynamics: Theory, Research, and Practice, 4,* 27–43.

Chemers, M. M. (2002). Efficacy and effectiveness: Integrating models of leadership and intelligence. In R. E. Riggio, S. E. Murphy, & F. J. Pirossolo (Eds.), *Multiple intelligences and leadership* (pp. 139–160). Mahwah, NJ: Lawrence Erlbaum.

Chemers, M. M., & Ayman, R. (1985). Leadership orientation as a moderator of the relationship between performance and satisfaction of Mexican managers. *Personality and Social Psychology Bulletin, 11,* 359–367.

Chemers, M. M., Goza, B., & Plumer, S. I. (1978, August). *Leadership style and communication process.* Paper presented at the annual meeting of the American Psychological Association, Toronto, Canada.

Chemers, M. M., Hays, R., Rhodewalt, F., & Wysocki, J. (1985). A person–environment analysis of job stress: A contingency model explanation. *Journal of Personality and Social Psychology, 49,* 628–635.

Chen, G., & Bliese, P. D. (2002). The role of different levels of leadership in predicting self and collective efficacy: Evidence for discontinuity. *Journal of Applied Psychology, 87,* 549–556.

Chen, G., Kirkman, B. L., Kanfer, R., Allen, D., & Rosen, B. (2007). A multilevel study of leadership, empowerment, and performance in teams. *Journal of Applied Psychology, 92,* 331–346.

Csikszentmihalyi, M. (1990). *Flow: The psychology of optimal experience.* New York: Harper Perennial.

Dansereau, F., Graen, G. B., & Haga, W. (1975). A vertical dyad linkage approach to leadership in formal organizations: A longitudinal investigation of the managerial role-making process. *Organizational Behavior and Human Performance, 13,* 46–78.

Dansereau, F., & Yammarino, F. J. (Eds.). (1998a). *Leadership: The multiple-level approaches—Classical and new wave.* Stamford, CT: JAI Press.

Dansereau, F., & Yammarino, F. J. (Eds.). (1998b). *Leadership: The multiple-level approaches—Contemporary and alternative.* Stamford, CT: JAI Press.

Day, D. V., & Lord, R. G. (1988). Executive leadership and organizational performance: Suggestions for a new theory and methodology. *Journal of Management, 14,* 453–464.

Den Hartog, D. N., House, R. J., Hanges, P. J., Ruiz-Quintanilla, S. A., & Dorfman, P. W. (1999). Culture specific and cross-culturally generalizable implicit leadership theories: Are attributes of charismatic/transformational leadership universally endorsed? *The Leadership Quarterly, 10,* 219–256.

Dennison, D. R. (1996). What is the difference between organizational culture and organizational climate? A native's point of view on a decade of paradigm wars. *Academy of Management Review, 21,* 619–654.

Dierdorff, E. C., Rubin, R. S., & Morgeson, F. P. (2009). The milieu of managerial work: An integrative framework linking work context to role requirements. *Journal of Applied Psychology, 94,* 972–988.

Dionne, S. D., Yammarino, F. J., Atwater, L. E., & James, L. R. (2002). Neutralizing substitutes for leadership theory: Leadership effects and common-source bias. *Journal of Applied Psychology, 87,* 454–464.

Eagly, A. H., & Carli, L. L. (2007). *Through the labyrinth: The truth about how women become leaders.* Boston, MA: Harvard Business School Press.

Eagly, A. H., Johannesen-Schmidt, M. C., & van Engen, M. L. (2003). Transformational, transactional, and laissez-faire leadership styles: A meta-analysis comparing women and men. *Psychological Bulletin, 129,* 569–591.

Eagly, A. H., & Karau, S. J. (1991). Gender and the emergence of leader: A meta-analysis. *Journal of Personality and Social Psychology, 60,* 685–710.

Eagly, A. H., Karau, S. J., & Makhijani, M. G. (1995). Gender and leader effectiveness: A meta-analysis. *Psychological Bulletin, 117,* 125–145.

Eden, D. & Leviantan, U. (1975). Implicit leadership theory as a determinant of the factor structure underlying supervisory behavior scales. *Journal of Applied Psychology, 60,* 736–741.

Edwards, J. R., & Lambert, L. S. (2007). Methods for integrating moderation and mediation: A general analytical framework using moderated path analysis. *Psychological Methods, 12,* 1–22.

Epitropaki, O., & Martin, R. (2004). Implicit leadership theories in applied settings: Factor structure, generalizability, and stability over time. *Journal of Applied Psychology, 89,* 293–310.

Evans, M. G. (1970). The effects of supervisory behavior on the path-goal relationship. *Organizational Behavior and Human Performance, 5,* 277–298.

Evans, M. G. (1996). R. J. House's "a path-goal theory of leader effectiveness." *The Leadership Quarterly, 7,* 305–309.

Fernandez, C. F., & Vecchio, R. P. (1997). Situational leadership theory revisited: A test of an across-jobs perspective. *The Leadership Quarterly, 8,* 67–84.

Fiedler, F. E. (1964). A contingency model of leadership effectiveness. In L. Berkowitz (Ed.), *Advances in experimental social psychology* (Vol. 1, pp. 149–190). New York: Academic Press.

Fiedler, F. E. (1978). The contingency model and the dynamics of the leadership process. In L. Berkowitz (Ed.), *Advances in experimental social psychology* (Vol. 11, pp. 59–112). New York: Academic Press.

Fiedler, F. E. (1992). Life in a pretzel-shaped universe. In A. Bedeian (Ed.), *Management laureates: A collection of autobiographical essays* (Vol. 1, pp. 301–334). Greenwich, CT: JAI Press.

Fiedler, F. E. (1993). The leadership situation and the black box in contingency theories. In M. Chemers and R. Ayman (Eds.), *Leadership theory and research: Perspectives and directions* (pp. 2–28). New York: Academic Press.

Fiedler, F. E. (1995). Cognitive resource and leadership performance. *Applied Psychology: An International Review, 44,* 5–28.

Fiedler, F. E. (2002). The curious role of cognitive resources in leadership. In R. Riggio, S. Murphy, & F. Pirozzolo (Eds.), *Multiple intelligences and leadership* (pp. 91–104). Mahwah, NJ: Lawrence Erlbaum.

Fiedler, F. E., & Chemers M. M. (1984). *Improving leadership effectiveness: The leader match concept* (2nd ed.). New York: John Wiley.

Fiedler F. E., & Garcia, J. E. (1987). *New approaches to effective leadership: Cognitive resources and organizational performance.* New York: John Wiley.

Field, R. H. G., & House, R. J. (1990). A test of the Vroom-Yetton model using manager and subordinate reports. *Journal of Applied Psychology, 75,* 362–366.

Fischbein, R. & Lord, R. G. (2004). Implicit leadership theory. In G. Goethale, G. Sorenson, & J. McGregor-Burns (Eds.), *Encyclopedia of Leadership* (Vol. 2, pp. 700–705). Thousand Oaks, CA: Sage.

Fisher, B. M., & Edwards, J. E. (1988). Consideration and initiating structure and their relationships with leader effectiveness: A meta-analysis. *Academy of Management Best Paper,* 201–205.

Frame, M. C., Roberto, K. J., Schwab, A. E., & Harris, C. T. (2010). What is important on the job? Differences across gender, perspective, and job level. *Journal of Applied Social Psychology, 40,* 36–56.

French, J. R., & Raven, B. (1959). The basis of social power. In D. Cartwright (Ed.), *Studies in social power* (pp. 150–167). Ann Arbor, MI: Institute for Social Research, University of Michigan.

Gangestad, S. W., & Snyder, M. (2000). Self-monitoring: Appraisal and reappraisal. *Psychological Bulletin, 126,* 530–555.

Georgopoulus, B. S., Mahoney, G. M., & Jones, N. W., Jr. (1957). A path-goal approach to productivity. *Journal of Applied Psychology, 41,* 345–353.

Gershenoff, A. B., & Foti, R. J. (2003). Leader emergence and gender roles in all female groups: A contextual examination. *Small Group Research, 34,* 170–196.

Gerstner, C. R., & Day, D. V. (1994). Cross-cultural comparison of leadership pro-
    totypes. *The Leadership Quarterly, 5,* 121–134.

Graeff, C. L. (1997). Evolution of situation leadership theory: A critical review. *The
    Leadership Quarterly, 8,* 153–170.

Graen, G. B., & Uhl-Bien, M. (1995). Relationship-based approach to leadership:
    Development of leader-member exchange (LMX) theory of leadership over
    25 years: Applying a multi-level multi-domain perspective. *The Leadership Quar-
    terly, 6,* 219–247.

Hackman, J. R. (1968). Effects of task characteristics on group products. *Journal of
    Experimental Social Psychology, 4,* 162–187.

Hackman, J. R., & Morris, C. G. (1975). Group task, group interaction process,
    and group performance effectiveness: A review and proposed integration. In
    L. Berkowitz (Ed.), *Advances in experimental social psychology* (Vol. 8).
    New York: Academic Press.

Hall, E. T., & Hall, M. R. (1990). *Understanding cultural differences.* Yarmouth,
    ME: Intercultural Press.

Hanges, P. J., Lord, R. G., & Dickson, M. W. (2000). An information-processing
    perspective on leadership and culture: A case for connectionist architecture.
    Applied Psychology: An International Review, 49, 133–161.

Heilman, M. E., Block, C. J., Martell, R. F., & Simon, M. (1989). Has anything
    changed? Current characterizations of men, women, and managers. *Journal of
    Applied Psychology, 74,* 935–942.

Heilman, M. E., Hornstein, H. A., Cage, J. H., & Herschlag, J. K. (1984). Reaction
    to prescribed leader behavior as a function of role perspective: The case of the
    Vroom-Yetton model. *Journal of Applied Psychology, 69,* 50–60.

Hersey, P., & Blanchard, K. (1969). Life cycle theory of leadership. *Training and
    Development Journal, 23,* 26–34.

Hersey, P., & Blanchard, K. (1982). *Management of organizational behavior* (4th ed.).
    Englewood Cliffs, NJ: Prentice Hall.

Hogan, R., Curphy, G. J., & Hogan, J. (1994). What we know about leadership:
    Effectiveness and personality. *American Psychologist, 49,* 493–504.

Hollingshead, A. B., & McGrath, J. E. (1995). Computer-assisted groups: A critical
    review of the empirical research. In R. A. Guzzo, E. Salas, & Associates (Eds.), *Team
    effectiveness and decision-making in organizations* (pp. 46–78). San Francisco:
    Jossey-Bass.

House, R. J. (1971). A path-goal theory of leadership effectiveness. *Administrative
    Quarterly, 16,* 312–338.

House, R. J. (1996). Path-goal theory of leadership: Lessons, legacy, and a reformu-
    lated theory. *The Leadership Quarterly, 7,* 323–352.

House, R. J., Hanges, P. M., Javidan, M., Dorfman, P., & Gupta, V. (2004). *Culture,
    leadership, and organizations: The GLOBE study of 62 societies.* Thousand
    Oaks, CA: Sage.

House, R. J., & Mitchell, T. R. (1974). Path-goal theory of leadership. *Journal of
    Contemporary Business, 9,* 81–97.

Howells, L. T., & Becker, S. W. (1962). Seating arrangement and leadership emer-
    gence. *Journal of Abnormal and Social Psychology, 64,* 148–150.

Hoyt, C. L., & Blascovich, J. (2003). Transformational and transactional leadership
    in virtual and physical environments. *Small Group Research, 34,* 678–715.

Indvik, J. (1986). Path-goal theory of leadership: A meta-analysis. *Proceedings of the Academy of Management Meeting, Chicago, IL* (pp. 189–192).

Jago, A. G., Maczynski, J., & Reber, G. (1996). Evolving leadership styles? A comparison of Polish managers before and after market economy reforms. *Polish Psychological Bulletin, 27*, 107–115.

Jago, A. G., & Vroom, V. H. (1980). An evaluation of two alternatives to the Vroom/Yetton normative model. *Academy of Management Journal, 23*, 347–355.

Jago, A. G., & Vroom, V. H. (1983). Sex differences in the incidence and evaluation of participative leader behavior. *Journal of Applied Psychology, 67*, 776–783.

Jermier, J. M., & Kerr, S. (1997). "Substitutes for leadership: Their meaning and measurement"—Contextual recollections and current observations. *The Leadership Quarterly, 8*, 95–102.

Johns, G. (2006). The essential impact of context on organizational behavior. *Academy of Management Review, 31*, 386–408.

Judge, T. A., Bono, J. E., Ilies, R., & Gerhardt, M. W. (2002). Personality and leadership: A qualitative and quantitative review. *Journal of Applied Psychology, 87*, 765–780.

Judge, T. A., Colbert, A. E., & Ilies, R. (2004). Intelligence and leadership: A quantitative review and test of theoretical propositions. *Journal of Applied Psychology, 89*, 542–552.

Judge, T. A., & Piccolo, R. F. (2004). Transformational and transactional leadership: A meta-analytic test of their relative validity. *Journal of Applied Psychology, 89*, 755–768.

Jung, D. I., & Avolio, B. J. (1999). Leadership style and followers' cultural orientation on performance in group and individual task conditions. *Academy of Management Journal, 42*, 208–218.

Kane, T. D., & Tremble, T. R. (2000). Transformational leadership effects at different levels of the Army. *Military Psychology, 12*, 137–160.

Kerr, S., & Jermier, J. M. (1978). Substitutes for leadership: Their meaning and measurement. *Organizational Behavior and Human Performance, 22*, 375–403.

Klein, K. J., & Kozlowski, S. W. J. (Eds.). (2000). *Multilevel theory, research, and methods in organizations: Foundations, extensions, and new directions.* San Francisco: Jossey-Bass.

Korabik, K., & Ayman, R. (2007). Gender and leadership in the corporate world: A multiperspective model. In J. C. Lau, B. Lott, J. Rice, and J. Sanchez-Hudes (Eds.). *Transforming leadership: Diverse visions and women's voices* (pp. 106–124). Malden, MA: Blackwell.

Korman, A. K. (1966). Consideration, initiating structure, and organizational criteria—A review. *Personnel Psychology, 19*, 349–361.

Kozlowski, S. W. J., & Klein, K. J. (2000). A multilevel approach to theory and research in organizations: Contextual, temporal, and emergent processes. In K. Klein & S. Kozlowski (Eds.), *Multilevel theory, research, and methods in organizations: Foundations, extensions, and new directions* (pp. 3–90). San Francisco: Jossey-Bass.

Leavitt, H. J. (1951). Some effects of certain communication patterns on group performance. *Journal of Abnormal and Social Psychology, 46*, 38–50.

Leffler, H., Ayman, R., & Ayman-Nolley, S. (2006, July). *Do children possess the same stereotypes as adults? An exploration of children's implicit leadership theories.* Poster session presented at the 26th International Congress of Applied Psychology, Athens, Greece.

Liden, R. C., & Antonakis, J. (2009). Considering context in psychological leadership research. *Human Relations, 62,* 1587–1605.

Ling, W., Chia, R. C., & Fang, L. (2000). Chinese implicit leadership theory. *Journal of Social Psychology, 140,* 729–739.

Ling, Y., Simsek, Z., Lubatkin, M. H., & Veiga, J. F. (2008). Impact of transformational CEOs on the performance of small to medium firms: Does organizational context matter? *Journal of Applied Psychology, 93,* 923–934.

Liu, L., Ayman, R., & Ayman-Nolley, S. (2009, May). *Children's implicit leadership in China.* Paper presented at the meeting of the Leadership Trust Symposium, Ross-upon-Rye, UK.

Lord, R. G., DeVader, C. L., & Alliger, G. M. (1986). A meta-analysis of the relation between personality traits and leadership: An application of validity generalization procedures. *Journal of Applied Psychology, 71,* 402–410.

Lord, R. G., & Emrich, C. G. (2001). Thinking outside the box by looking inside the box: Extending the cognitive revolution in leadership research. *The Leadership Quarterly, 11,* 551–579.

Lord, R. G., Foti, R. J., & DeVader, C. L. (1984). A test of leadership categorization theory: Internal structure, information processing, and leadership perceptions. *Organizational Behavior and Human Performance, 34,* 343–378.

Lord, R. G., & Maher, K. J. (1991). *Leadership and information processing: Linking perceptions and performance.* Boston: Routledge.

Lowe, K. B., Kroeck, G., & Sivasubramaniam, N. (1996). Effectiveness correlates of transformational and transactional leadership: A meta-analytic review of the MLQ literature. *The Leadership Quarterly, 7,* 385–425.

Maczynski, J., Jago, A. G., Reber, G., & Boehnisch, W. (1994). Culture and leadership styles: A comparison of Polish, Austrian, and U.S. managers. *Polish Psychological Bulletin, 25,* 303–315.

McGrath, J. E. (1984). A typology of tasks. *Groups, interaction and performance* (pp. 53–66). Englewood Cliffs, NJ: Prentice Hall.

Mischel, W. (1977). The interaction of person and situation. In D. Magnusson and D. Endler (Eds.), *Personality at the crossroads: Current issues in interactional psychology* (pp. 333–352). Hillsdale, NJ: Lawrence Erlbaum.

Mitchell, T. R., & James, L. R. (2001). Building better theory: Time and the specification of when things happen. *Academy of Management Review, 26,* 530–547.

Mumford, M. D., Dansereau, F., & Yammarino, F. Y. (2000). Followers, motivations, and levels of analysis: The case of individualized leadership. *The Leadership Quarterly, 11,* 313–340.

Murphy, S. E., Blyth, D., & Fiedler, F .E. (1992). Cognitive resource theory and the utilization of the leader's and group members' technical competence. *The Leadership Quarterly, 3,* 237–255.

Offermann, L. R., Kennedy, J. K., Jr., & Wirtz, P. W. (1994). Implicit leadership theories: Content, structure, and generalizability. *The Leadership Quarterly, 5,* 43–58.

Ostroff, C., Atwater, L. E., & Feinberg, B. J. (2004). Understanding self-other agreement: A look at rater and ratee characteristics, context, and outcomes. *Personnel Psychology, 57,* 333–375.

Pelto, P. J. (1968, April). The influence between "tight" and "loose" societies. *Transactions,* 37–40.

Peters, L. H., Hartke, D. D., & Pohlmann, J. F. (1985). Fiedler's contingency theory of leadership: An application of the meta-analysis procedures of Schmitt and Hunter. *Psychological Bulletin, 97,* 274–285.

Podsakoff, P. M., & Mackenzie, S. B. (1997). Kerr and Jermier's substitutes for leadership model: Background, empirical assessment, and suggestions for future research. *The Leadership Quarterly, 8,* 117–125.

Podsakoff, P. M., MacKenzie, S. B., & Bommer, W. H. (1996). Meta-analysis of the relationships between Kerr and Jermier's substitutes for leadership and employee job attitudes, role perceptions, and performance. *Journal of Applied Psychology, 81,* 380–399.

Podsakoff, P. M., & Schriesheim, C. A. (1985). Field studies of French and Raven's bases of power: Critique, reanalysis, and suggestions for future research. *Psychological Bulletin, 97,* 387–411.

Polyashuk, Y., Ayman, R., & Roberts, J. L. (2008, April). *Relationship quality: The effect of dyad composition diversity and time.* Poster session presented at the meeting of the Society of Industrial and Organizational Psychology, San Francisco, CA.

Porter, L. W., & McLaughlin, G. B. (2006). Leadership and the organizational context: Like the weather? *The Leadership Quarterly, 17,* 559–576.

Potter, E. H., III, & Fiedler, F. E. (1981). The utilization of staff members' intelligence and experience under high and low stress. *Academy of Management Journal, 24,* 361–376.

Preacher, K. J., Rucker, D. D., & Hayes, A. F. (2007). Addressing moderated mediation hypotheses: Theory, methods, and prescriptions. *Multivariate Behavioral Research, 42,* 185–227.

Puranova, R. K., & Bono, J. E. (2009). Transformational leadership in context: Face to face and virtual teams. *The Leadership Quarterly, 20,* 343, 357.

Rice, W. R. (1981). Leader LPC and follower satisfaction: A review. *Organizational Behavior and Human Performance, 28,* 1–25.

Rice, W. R., Marwick, N. J., Chemers, M. M., & Bentley, J. C. (1982). Task performance and satisfaction: Least Preferred Coworker (LPC) as a moderator. *Personality and Social Psychology Bulletin, 8,* 534–541.

Rousseau, D. (2000). Multilevel competencies and missing linkages. In K. Klein & S. Kozlowski (Eds.), *Multilevel theory, research, and methods in organizations: Foundations, extensions, and new directions* (pp. 557–571). San Francisco: Jossey-Bass.

Rousseau, D., & Fried, Y. (2001). Location, location, location: Conceptualizing organizational research. *Journal of Organizational Behavior, 22,* 1–13.

Schneider, R. J., & Hough, L. M. (1995). Personality and industrial/organizational psychology. In C. L. Cooper and I. T. Robertson (Eds.), *International review of industrial and organizational psychology* (Vol. 10). New York: John Wiley.

Schriesheim, C. A. (1997). Substitutes-for-leadership theory: Development and basic concepts. *The Leadership Quarterly, 8,* 103–108.

Schriesheim, C. A., & Neider, L. L. (1996). Path-goal leadership theory: The long and winding road. *The Leadership Quarterly, 7,* 317–321.

Schriesheim, C. A., & Schriesheim, J. F. (1980). A test of the path-goal theory of leadership and some suggested direction for future research. *Personnel Psychology, 33,* 349–370.

Schriesheim, C. A., Tepper, B. J., & Tetrault, L. A. (1994). Least preferred coworker score, situational control and leadership effectiveness: A meta-analysis of contingency model performance predictions. *Journal of Applied Psychology, 79,* 561–573.

Schriesheim C. A., & Von Glinow, M. A. (1977). The path-goal theory of leadership: A theoretical and empirical analysis. *Academy of Management Journal, 20,* 398–405.

Schyns, B., & Van Veldhoven, M. J. P. M. (2010). Group leadership climate and individual organizational commitment: A multilevel analysis. *Journal of Personnel Psychology, 9,* 57–68.

Shartle, C. L. (1951). Studies of naval leadership, part I. In H. Guetzkow (Ed.), *Groups, leadership and men: Research in human relations* (pp. 119–133). Pittsburgh, PA: Carnegie Press.

Shaw, M. E. (1981). *Group dynamics: The psychology of small group behavior* (3rd ed.) New York: McGraw-Hill.

Sternberg, R. J. (1988). *The triarchic mind: A new theory of human intelligence.* New York: Penguin Books.

Sternberg, R. J. (1995). A triarchic view of "cognitive resource and leadership performance." *Applied Psychology: An International Review, 44,* 29–32.

Sternberg, R. J., & Vroom, V. (2002). The person versus situation in leadership. *The Leadership Quarterly, 13,* 301–323.

Stinson, J. E., & Johnson, T. W. (1975). The path-goal theory of leadership: A partial test and suggested refinement. *Academy of Management Journal, 18,* 242–252.

Stogdill, R. M. (1974). *Handbook of leadership.* New York: Free Press.

Stogdill, R. M., & Coons, A. E. (1957). *Leader behavior: Its description and measurement.* Columbus, OH: Ohio State University, Bureau of Business Research.

Strube, M. J., & Garcia, J. E. (1981). A meta-analytical investigation of Fiedler's contingency model of leadership effectiveness. *Psychological Bulletin, 90,* 307–321.

Tobey-Garcia, A., Ayman, R., & Chemers, M. (2000, July). *Leader-subordinate trait dyad composition and subordinate satisfaction with supervision: Moderated by task structure.* Paper presented at the XXVII International Congress of Psychology, Stockholm, Sweden.

Triandis, H. C. (2006). Cultural intelligence in organizations. *Group & Organizational Management, 31,* 20–26.

Van Rooy, D. L., & Viswesvaran, C. (2004). Emotional intelligence: A meta-analytic investigation of predictive validity and nomological net. *Journal of Vocational Behavior, 65,* 71–95.

Vecchio, R. P. (1987). Situational leadership theory: An examination of a prescriptive theory. *Journal of Applied Psychology, 72,* 444–451.

Vecchio, R. P. (1997). Situational leadership theory: An examination of a prescriptive theory. In R. P. Vecchio (Ed.), *Leadership: Understanding the dynamics of power and influence in organizations* (pp. 334–350). Notre Dame, IN: University of Notre Dame Press.

Vecchio, R. P., & Boatwright, K. J. (2002). Preferences for idealized styles of supervision. *The Leadership Quarterly, 13,* 327–342.

Vroom, V. H. (1964). *Work and motivation.* New York: John Wiley.

Vroom V. H., & Jago, A. G. (1978). On the validity of the Vroom-Yetton model. *Journal of Applied Psychology, 63,* 151–162.

Vroom, V. H., & Jago, A. G. (1988). *The new leadership: Managing participation in organizations.* Englewood Cliffs, NJ: Prentice Hall.

Vroom, V. H. & Jago, A. G. (1995). Situation effects and levels of analysis in the study of leader participation. *The Leadership Quarterly, 6,* 169–181.

Vroom V. H., & Jago, A. G. (1998). Situation effects and levels of analysis in the study of leader participation. In F. Yammarino and F. Dansereau (Eds.), *Leadership: The multi-level approaches* (pp. 145–159). Stamford, CT: JAI Press.

Vroom, V. H., & Yetton, P. W. (1973). *Leadership and decision-making.* Pittsburgh, PA: University of Pittsburgh Press.

Waldman, D. A., Ramirez, G. G., House, R. J., & Puranam, P. (2001). Does leadership matter? CEO leadership attributes and profitability under conditions of perceived environmental uncertainty. *Academy of Management Journal, 44*(1), 134–143.

Waldman, D. A., & Yammarino, F. J. (1999). CEO charismatic leadership: Levels-of-management and levels-of-analysis effects. *Academy of Management Review, 24,* 266–285.

Wentworth, D. K., & Anderson, L. R. (1984). Emergent leadership as a function of sex and task type. *Sex Roles, 11,* 513–524.

West, M. A., Borrill, C. S., & Unsworth, K. L. (1998). Team effectiveness in organizations. In C. L. Cooper & I. T. Robertson (Eds.), *International review of industrial and organizational psychology* (pp. 1–48). Chichester, UK: Wiley.

Wofford, J. C., & Liska, L. Z. (1993). Path-goal theories of leadership: A meta-analysis. *Journal of Management, 19,* 857–876.

Yammarino, F. J., & Dansereau, F. (Eds.) (2009). *Multi-level issues in organizational behavior and leadership (Vol. 8 of Research in multi-level issues).* Bingley, UK: Emerald.

York, R. O. (1996). Adherence to situational leadership theory among social workers. *Clinical Supervisor, 14,* 5–26.

Yukl, G., & Van Fleet, D. D. (1992). Theory and research on leadership in organizations. In M. D. Dunnette and L. M. Hough (Eds.). *Handbook of industrial and organizational psychology* (2nd ed., Vol. 3, pp. 147–198). Palo Alto, CA: Consulting Psychologist Press.

Zaccaro, S. J. (1995). Leader resource and the nature of organizational problems. *Applied Psychology: An International Review, 44,* 32–36.

Zaccaro, S. J. (2007). Trait-based perspectives of leadership. *American Psychologist, 62,* 6–16.

Zaccaro, S. J., Kemp, C., & Bader, P. (2004). Leader traits and attributes. In J. Antonakis, A. T. Cianciolo, & R. J. Sternberg (Eds.) *The nature of leadership* (pp. 102–124). Thousand Oaks, CA: Sage.

Transformational and Charismatic Leadership

John Antonakis

University of Lausanne

Leaders have a significant role in creating the state of mind that is the society. They can serve as symbols of the moral unity of the society. They can express the values that hold the society together. Most important, they can conceive and articulate goals that lift people out of their petty preoccupations, carry them above the conflicts that tear a society apart, and unite them in the pursuit of objectives worthy of their best efforts.

—J. W. Gardner, 1965

The above quote, introduced in the preface, nicely sums up the importance we give to leadership; it also resonates with why charisma matters because of how leaders draw on morals and use symbolic influencing means to federate followers around collective goals. History has been marked by many men and women who have epitomized a potent force capable of doing great deeds but also of bringing about destruction on a grand scale. It would be hard to imagine what the field of leadership would have been like had transformational and charismatic[1] leadership theory not been developed to explain this leadership influencing tactic. Of course, transformational and charismatic leaders existed before the theories were proposed, and these leaders will continue to exist in the future. Such is the assumed impact of charismatic leaders on individuals, organizations, and societies that philosophers, historians, psychologists, and other social scientists have taken turns in attempting to provide a cohesive

AUTHOR'S NOTE: Please address correspondence concerning this chapter to John Antonakis, University of Lausanne, Internef 618, CH-1015 Lausanne-Dorigny, Switzerland. Phone: ++41 (0)21 692–3438; e-mail: john.antonakis@unil.ch.

explanation of what I think is probably one of the most interesting pieces of the leadership puzzle.

Transformational and charismatic leadership theory has had a massive impact on leadership as a scientific domain. This leadership approach was characterized by Bryman (1992) as the "new leadership," such was its break with existing leadership models. In a way, when transformational and charismatic leadership theory came along, it provided leadership researchers the "ah-ha" moment for which they had been waiting for many years; it is almost ironic to observe that in terms of its messianic explanations, the theory was to leadership research what charismatic leaders are to followers (cf. Hunt, 1999). That is, it delivered leadership researchers from their plight at a time where there was pessimism and no direction in leadership research; there even came a time when researchers made calls to abandon leadership as a research topic (Greene, 1977; Miner, 1975). It is almost surreal to imagine that leadership, as a discipline, was not taken seriously; so when transformational and charismatic leadership theory came along it was embraced in full earnest. As I argue later, perhaps the pendulum has swung too far on the side of transformational and charismatic leadership theories, which have eclipsed and possibly maybe stunted other important contributions to leadership.

Transformational and charismatic leadership has been the focus of a great many research inquiries (Yukl, 1999); these approaches have helped shift the leadership paradigm to what it is today (Antonakis, Cianciolo, & Sternberg, 2004; Conger, 1999; Hunt, 1999; Lowe & Gardner, 2000). This research stream dominates the leadership landscape—whether deservingly or not—at least in terms of published papers in the premier academic journal focused on leadership, *The Leadership Quarterly*, both in the last decade (Lowe & Gardner, 2000) and in the current one (W. L. Gardner, Lowe, Moss, Mahoney, & Cogliser, 2010).

How did transformational and charismatic leadership theory develop? Why is transformational and charismatic leadership so popular? Where is transformational and charismatic leadership theory heading? I will try to answer these questions and others in this chapter. First, I review some of the major historical works that provided the scaffolding for current theories of transformational and charismatic leadership. In terms of the contemporary theories, I focus in particular on Bass's (1985) theory—known also as the "full-range leadership theory" or the "transformational-transactional" leadership theory (Avolio & Bass, 1991)—because it is the flagship theory of the transformational and charismatic movement (Antonakis & House, 2002). Although a part of my work has focused on transformational and charismatic leadership (Antonakis, 2001; Antonakis & Atwater, 2002; Antonakis, Avolio, & Sivasubramaniam, 2003; Jacquart & Antonakis, 2010), I critically review this theoretical stream and in particular its forbearer, Bass's theory, highlighting some of its strengths and weaknesses. Given that I am "one of them"—that is, part of the charisma "leadership mafia" as Gemmill and Oakley (1992) would say—it is not easy for me to take this step back and review the theory with a critical eye. Although I pay my respects to the theory, my purposeful "friendly fire" highlights voids and inconsistencies in the full-range theory (Antonakis & House, 2002; Antonakis, House, Rowold, & Borgmann, 2010); a theory can only be improved if it can be challenged, and it is with this mindset that I am poking some holes in this model. Finally, I also briefly review competing transformational and charismatic paradigms and conclude with where transformational and charismatic leadership is heading, or rather should be heading.

Transformational and Charismatic Leadership: A Brief History

Most writers credit Weber (1947) for having coined the term "charisma" and having provided the first theoretical explanation of the impact of charismatic leadership on followers. I will get to Weber later to show how his ideas permeated leadership research. However, theoretical explanations of a phenomenon akin to charismatic leadership and the ways in which leaders should go about influencing followers using potent persuasive means goes back much further in time. In fact, the writings of Aristotle (trans., 1954), appearing in the fourth century BCE, first laid these foundations and, indeed, the foundations to the field of rhetoric, which is a key foundation of charismatic leadership.

In the *Rhetoric*, Aristotle argued that a leader must gain the confidence of her followers by using creative rhetorical means (i.e., charismatic and transformational), which include rousing follower emotions (the "pathos"), providing a moral perspective via her personal character ("ethos"), and using reasoned argument ("logos"). It will become evident that these three dimensions, as well as other means which Aristotle referred to as being non-artistic (i.e., transactional and aversive reinforcing)—including contracts, laws, tortures, witnesses, and oaths—can be seen as a parsimonious version of Bass's (1985) full-range leadership theory. To better understand the startling insights of Aristotle, which not only touch on charismatic leadership but also on affect and cognitive psychology, as well as other areas of science, I quote from Book I, Chapter II, where he refers to the three kinds of rhetorical influencing:

> The first kind [of persuasion] depends on the personal character of the speaker; the second on putting the audience into a certain frame of mind; the third on the proof, or apparent proof, provided by the words of the speech itself. Persuasion is achieved by the speaker's personal character when the speech is so spoken as to make us think him credible. We believe good men more fully and more readily than others: this is true generally whatever the question is, and absolutely true where exact certainty is impossible and opinions are divided. This kind of persuasion, like the others, should be achieved by what the speaker says, not by what people think of his character before he begins to speak. It is not true, as some writers assume in their treatises on rhetoric, that

the personal goodness revealed by the speaker contributes nothing to his power of persuasion; on the contrary, his character may almost be called the most effective means of persuasion he possesses. Secondly, persuasion may come through the hearers, when the speech stirs their emotions. Our judgments when we are pleased and friendly are not the same as when we are pained and hostile. It is towards producing these effects, as we maintain, that present-day writers on rhetoric direct the whole of their efforts. This subject shall be treated in detail when we come to speak of the emotions. Thirdly, persuasion is effected through the speech itself when we have proved a truth or an apparent truth by means of the persuasive arguments suitable to the case in question. (p. 7)

I encourage readers to go back and read the above passage (and indeed Aristotle's entire book) once they have read this chapter and the section on the "full-range leadership model" in particular. I find it a real eye-opener to read such classics and others like Plato's *Republic* (trans., 1901); these works provided important foundations for western thought on topics concerning leadership, ethics, and good government. What I also find troubling by reading these works is why humanity is not more sophisticated and responsible than it currently is, when so much was known so long ago. Why do countries still go to war? Why is corruption still rife? Why is there still large-scale poverty and disease? Why is our ecosystem under threat? and Why are people so easily duped by bad leaders?

In essence, many of these problems are problems of leadership. It is only recently that these problems of humanity have been scrutinized, after a particularly regressive period during the dark ages, when science and reason were sidelined; science and reason in all their forms must be brought to the fore and targeted toward better understanding the leadership process. Warren Bennis (this volume), who has over the decades demonstrated remarkable perspicacity about the problems of leadership, notes that "it is important to remember that the quality of all our lives is dependent on the quality of our leadership. The context in which we study leadership is very different from the context in which we study, say, astronomy. By definition, leaders wield power, and so we study them with the same self-interested intensity with which we study diabetes and other life-threatening diseases. Only when we understand leaders will we be able to control them."

Indeed, the most potent of leaders, charismatic and transformational leaders, are the ones who can bring about needed social change; although these types of leaders have also been capable of dreadful deeds, which explains Bennis's concern. Of course, my chapter does not provide a treatise on issues concerning the selection, development, and outcomes of leadership and related topics; this is the job of the entire volume. I focus on charismatic and transformational leadership, though I will touch on some of these other important issues where relevant. Next, I discuss the most important contributions to this research stream (chronologically).

The Weberian Perspective

Weber (1947) was the first to use the term "charisma" and describe the charismatic leader as one who could bring about social change. He identified these types of leaders who arise "in times of psychic, physical, economic, ethical, religious, [or] political distress" (Weber, 1968). For Weber (1968), charisma in leaders referred to "specific gifts of the body and spirit not accessible to everybody" (p. 19). These leaders were attributed "with supernatural, superhuman, or at least specifically exceptional powers or qualities" (Weber, 1947, p. 358), and could undertake great feats. Weber (1968) believed that followers of a charismatic leader willingly place their destiny in their leader's hands and support the leader's mission that may have arisen out of "enthusiasm, or of despair and hope" (p. 49). Weber (1968) argued that charismatic authority is different from bureaucratic authority and that at the core of charisma is an emotional appeal whose "attitude is revolutionary and transvalues everything; it makes a sovereign break with all traditional or rational norms" (p. 24). Finally, Weber (1968) stated that the charismatic effect and legacy of the leader may continue as artifacts of the organizational or societal culture, but then wane as the organization or society is enveloped in the rational and methodical processes of the bureaucracy.

What is interesting in the Weberian idea of the charismatic leader is the importance of context and the apparent salvationary qualities of the charismatic leader. Also important is the notion of charismatic authority as being distinct from other sources of authority. Weber was not very clear on what, specifically, charismatic leaders do, and he was more concerned with ends than with means. Other sociologists continued in this vein (e.g., Shils, 1965). Well-known is Etzioni's (1964) structuralist perspective, which focuses on the effect that formal leadership has on individuals and the source of power that is used to exert influence over followers. Etzioni (1964) differentiated three types of power bases that leaders may use, namely: (a) physical power, entailing the use of threats or coercion; (b) material power, entailing the use of rewards; and (c) symbolic power, entailing the use of normative or social power (see also French & Raven, 1968). Symbolic power is what Etzioni (1961) referred to as "charisma" (p. 203). According to Etzioni (1964), greater commitment and less alienation will be displayed in followers when their leaders are using symbolic over material or physical power, and material over physical power.

Downton's Rebel Leadership

In line with the Weberian notion of charisma, Downton (1973) proposed a theory of transactional, charismatic, and inspirational leadership in the context of the rebel political leader. After Aristotle's work, this was the first theory to pit contractual (transactional) principal-agent type influence processes against charismatic authority. Strangely, this work predates that of Bass (1985) by more than a decade, but it was not mentioned by Bass in his original work.

Burns (1978) refers to it indirectly (regarding revolutionary leadership) in his transformational-transactional leadership dichotomy. Bass, though, did pay his dues later (Hater & Bass, 1988).

Downton (1973) referred to the term transactional as being "a process of exchange that is analogous to contractual relations in economic life [and] contingent on the good faith of the participants" (p. 75). Downton believed that the fulfillment of mutual transactional commitments forms the basis of trust among leaders and their followers, strengthens their relationship, and results in a mutually beneficial climate for further transactions to occur. Downton distinguished between positive and negative transactions. Positive transactions occur when followers receive rewards contingent on achieving desired outcomes, whereas negative transactions refer to followers' noncompliance, resulting in punishment (as discussed later, this precise notion of positive and negative transactional is how Bass (1985), theorized contingent rewards and management-by-exception leader behavior).

Downton argued that charismatic leaders have potent effects on followers because of their transcendental ideals and authority that facilitate the followers' identification with the leader. In those conditions, trust is solidified as psychological exchanges occur. This commitment and trust is further augmented by inspirational leadership. The inspirational leader is persuasive, and he or she encourages followers to invest in and make sacrifices toward the identified ideals, gives followers a sense of purpose, and creates meaning for actions distinct from the charismatic appeal. Followers relate to these types of leaders, but they do not necessarily revere them. Thus, inspirational leadership is, apparently, independent of charismatic leadership; according to Downton (1973), inspirational leadership does not foster follower dependence in the leader. Rather, "inspirational commitment is always contingent on the leader's continuing symbolic presentation of the follower's world view" (p. 80).

Downton argued further that although charismatic relations between leaders and followers will ultimately lead to inspirational relations, not all inspirational relations lead to charismatic relations. Finally, Downton proposed that all sources of leadership, whether transactional, inspirational, or charismatic should be used in varying degrees (which is in line with the ideas of Bass, 1985). To conclude, according to Downton (1973), "A system of personal rule may derive its legitimacy from the manipulation of rewards as well as punishments [i.e., transactional leadership], from the manipulation of myths and symbols that give meaning to action and suffering [i.e., inspirational leadership], and from the presence of leaders who are able to provide security, a new identity, or cultural reinforcement for those whose psychological dispositions or socialization require that they obey orders [i.e., charismatic leadership]" (pp. 284–285). Although Downton set what were the foundations for transformational and charismatic leadership theory, the impact he had on the field was minimal—probably because his work was not picked up by psychologists studying leadership in the 1980s, by which time Bass's theory was firmly entrenched.

A Psychological Theory of Charismatic Theory

House (1977) was the first to present an integrated theoretical framework and testable proposition to explain the behavior of charismatic leaders; he also focused on the psychological impact of charismatic leaders on followers. Also very important was that House provided a theoretical explanation regarding the means charismatic leaders use to influence followers (and thus manage the perceptions of followers); importantly, he referred to charismatic leaders as having the necessary persuasive skills to influence others. He also described the personal characteristics of charismatic leaders and suggested that individual differences of charismatic leaders might be measurable. This theory was perhaps the most important theory that laid the foundations for how charisma is studied today; however, one regret that House did have, which he conveyed to me, was that he "undersold" it by publishing it as a book chapter and not a journal article (thus limiting its impact).

House (1977) proposed that the basis for the charismatic appeal is the emotional interaction that occurs between followers and their leader. Depending on mission requirements, charismatic leaders arouse followers' motives to accomplish the leader's ideals and values. Followers in turn display affection and admiration for the leader, in whom their sentiments and ideals are expressed. House believed that charismatic leaders are those "who by force of their personal abilities are capable of having profound and extra-ordinary effects on followers" (p. 189). According to House, these leaders display confidence in their own abilities and in their followers, set high expectations for themselves and their followers, and show confidence that these expectations can be achieved. As a result of these behaviors, House argued that these leaders become role models and objects of identification of followers, who in turn emulate their leader's ideals and values and are enthusiastically inspired and motivated to reach outstanding accomplishments. These types of leaders are seen as courageous, because they challenge a status quo that is seen as undesirable. Furthermore, "Because of other 'gifts' attributed to the leader, such as extraordinary competence, the followers believe that the leader will bring about social change and will thus deliver them from their plight" (House, 1977, p. 204).

House (1977) stated that "In actuality, the 'gift' is likely to be a complex interaction of personal characteristics, the behavior the leader employs, characteristics of followers, and certain situational factors prevailing at the time of the assumption of the leadership style" (p. 193). Finally, in focusing on the personal characteristics of charismatic leaders, House argued that they display a high degree of self-confidence, pro-social assertiveness (dominance), and moral conviction. These leaders model what they expect their followers to do, exemplify the struggle by self-sacrifice, and engage in image-building and self-promotion actions to come across as powerful and competent.

The insights of House (1977) were prescient. His theory was beautifully and clearly expressed and shook leadership scholars out of their current ideas of how leadership should be conceived at a time when leadership was not being taken very seriously (Antonakis et al., 2004).

Transforming-Transactional Leadership in Political Science

Burns (1978) published his opus magnum on leadership in political settings. His work laid the foundations for Bass (1985), particularly with respect to transformative effects of leaders on followers. Burns defined leadership as "inducing followers to act for certain goals that represent the values and the motivations—the wants and needs, the aspirations and expectations—*of both leaders and followers*" (p. 19). Although leaders are intricately tied in those goals with followers, they act as an independent force in steering followers toward those goals. The leader–follower interaction that could occur was defined as either: (a) transactional leadership, which entailed a relationship based on the exchange of valued items, whether political, economic, or emotional; or (b) transforming leadership, where the motivation, morality, and ethical aspirations of both the leader and followers are raised.

According to Burns, transforming leadership—focused on transcendent and far-reaching goals and ideals—has a greater effect on followers and collectives as compared to transactional leadership, which is focused on promoting self-interest and is thus limited in scope and impact. Transforming leaders theoretically raise the consciousness of followers for what is important, especially with regard to moral and ethical implications, and make them transcend their self-interest for that of the greater good. Although both transactional and transforming leadership can contribute to human purpose, Burns saw them as opposing ends of a spectrum. As stated by Burns, "The chief monitors of transactional leadership are modal values, that is, values of means. . . . Transformational leadership is more concerned with end-values" (p. 426). Burns saw these two leadership styles as a trade-off, a zero-sum game.

Bass (1985) essentially built his model on Burns's (1978) model. Bass extended the model to include subdimensions of what he termed "transformational" (instead of transforming) leadership. Also, although in Bass's original conceptualization of transformational leadership he was not concerned with moral and ethical overtones, he eventually came around to agreeing with Burns that the likes of Hitler were pseudotransformational and that at the core of authentic transformational leadership were "good" values (see Bass & Steidlmeier, 1999).

Bass's Transformational-Transactional Leadership Model

Bass's (1985) transformational-transactional theory includes both elements of the "new leadership" (i.e., charisma, vision, and the like) and elements of the "old leadership" (i.e., transactional leadership behavior focused on role and task requirements). I mention "some elements" here because the idea of this theory was to go beyond the behavioral two-factor theories of leadership (see Seltzer & Bass, 1990). These theories (see Fleishman, 1953, 1957; Halpin, 1954; Stogdill, 1963; Stogdill & Coons, 1957) conceptualized leadership as being focused on tasks (initiating structure) or people (consideration) and were the dominant leadership paradigm in the 1950s and 1960s. As I mention below, however, the Bass model misses out on task-related leader behavior.

Antonakis and House (2002) encouraged researchers to use the full-range theory of Bass (1985) as a platform from which to build more complete leadership theories; however, they also suggested that the theory does not include instrumental leadership (initiating structure), although Bass had suggested otherwise. Antonakis and House came to this conclusion by comparing and contrasting the Bass theory with other "new" theories, which I discuss below, too. Their suggestion was recently tested, and there is strong evidence to suggest that the full-range theory is not as "full" as first purported (Antonakis & House, 2004; Antonakis, House, et al., 2010), particularly with respect to strategic as well as work-facilitation aspects of instrumental leader behavior (Hunt, 2004; Yukl, 1999). That is, it appears that a major class of leader behavior is missing regarding aspects that may affect both organizational as well as follower effectiveness. I will touch on these points later, particularly concerning the strategic aspects of instrumental behavior, when I review some competing charismatic-transformational leadership theories.

I first present the Bass theory in its current form (Avolio & Bass, 1991; Bass & Avolio, 1997), which has a long history of research emanating from the work of Bass, Avolio, and their colleagues (Avolio & Bass, 1995; Avolio, Bass, & Jung, 1999; Bass & Avolio, 1993, 1994; Bass, Avolio, & Atwater, 1996; Bass, Waldman, Avolio, & Bebb, 1987; Hater & Bass, 1988; Waldman, Bass, & Yammarino, 1990; Yammarino & Bass, 1990). This theory has been operationalized and can be reliably measured by the Multifactor Leadership Questionnaire (MLQ), as demonstrated in very large-scale studies that have modeled sample heterogeneity (Antonakis et al., 2003; Antonakis, House, et al., 2010). Important to note here, particularly because there has been much controversy about the validity of the MLQ factor structure, is that sample heterogeneity is an overlooked aspect of construct validation. For instance, if two factors covary positively in one context and negatively in another context, then mixing the samples will perturb the stability of the factor structure (Antonakis et al., 2003). Substantial work has been done in this area of psychometrics (Muthén, 1989); however, understanding sample heterogeneity and modeling it is only slowly seeping through into applied psychology and leadership research. For instance, in the most recent large-scale validation study of the MLQ and an extension of the model (to which instrumental leadership was added), Antonakis, House, et al. (2010) showed that using a MIMIC model (multiple indicator, multiple causes) essentially partialed out the effects of contextual factors that were causally related to the variables of the MLQ model, thereby improving the fit of the model. Moreover, they showed that with a very large sample size, the unique effects of the factors can be estimated, despite the strong correlations between factors; that is, the simplest solution to mitigate the effects of collinearity is to increase sample size (Kennedy, 2003). I am stating this latter point expressly because some researchers have suggested that even though the factors constituting the theory are theoretically distinct, their high correlations make them redundant in a regression model. In fact, the ordinary least squares or maximum likelihood estimators have no problem estimating models with highly correlated independent variables as long as the sample size is large enough—and what is "large enough" can be established only through Monte Carlo analysis (Antonakis, House, et al., 2010).

Although there has been much debate about the factor structure of the MLQ model, there is little or no controversy about the predictive (concurrent) validity of this MLQ, which has been supported by numerous meta-analyses (DeGroot, Kiker, & Cross, 2001; Dumdum, Lowe, & Avolio, 2001; Gasper, 1992; Judge & Piccolo, 2004; Lowe, Kroeck, & Sivasubramaniam, 1996). In its current form, the MLQ measures nine leadership factors. The first five (idealized influence attributes, idealized influence behaviors, inspirational motivation, intellectual stimulation, and individualized consideration) measure transformational leadership; the next three (contingent rewards, management-by-exception active, and management-by-exception passive) measure transactional leadership; the last factor is concerned with nonleadership (i.e., laissez-faire leadership). Following below is a description of the transformational factors.

Charisma—Attributed and Behavioral Idealized Influence

Idealized influence, or charisma, as Bass (1985) originally defined it, is the emotional component of leadership, which is "used to describe leaders who by the power of their person have profound and extraordinary effects on their followers" (p. 35). Theoretically, these leaders are revered by followers who show loyalty and devotion to the leader's cause, as they shed their self-interest. As noted by Bass (1998), "transformational leaders shift goals [of followers] away from personal safety and security toward achievement, self-actualization, and the greater good" (p. 41). Followers idealize these leaders, who are role models and who provide them with a vision and purpose, seem powerful and confident, and consider the moral and ethical implications of their decisions. Theoretically, these leaders focus followers on the mission of the group by arousing their need for achievement, affiliation, or power motives. Charismatic leaders communicate symbolically, use imagery, and are persuasive in communicating a vision that promises a better future. In this way, they create an intense emotional attachment with their followers.

Initially, idealized influence was named charisma. However, as mentioned to me by Bruce Avolio, because charisma may connote idolization of the leader, a more neutral term was sought. Hence, the factor was renamed idealized influence (i.e., connoting idealization) in subsequent publications (Avolio, Waldman, & Yammarino, 1991; Bass & Avolio, 1994). Idealized influence was later split into behavioral and attributional components, to answer previous criticisms (Hunt, 1991; Yukl, 1998, 1999), because the scale did not account for "charismatic leadership that was behaviorally-based . . . versus an attribution or impact on followers referred to as idealized influence" (Avolio, Bass, & Jung, 1995, p. 7). Attributional idealized influence refers to attributions of the leader made by followers as a result of how they perceive the leader. Behavioral idealized influence refers to specific behaviors of the leader that followers can observe directly. Although both factors are essentially concerned with a leader's charismatic appeal, they are enacted and measured differently. Researchers sometimes bundle these factors together; oftentimes, all five of the transformational leadership scales are aggregated, given that they have similar effects and because they are highly correlated (Judge & Piccolo, 2004). However, as mentioned above with a large-enough sample size, their differential effects can be estimated (Antonakis, House, et al., 2010).

One problem with the MLQ charisma items is that some are written in very general ways: For example, for the idealized influence attributes scale, how can one go about objectively measuring a leader who seems to be "powerful and confident?" More specific behavioral indicators should be considered for the attribute scale in future versions of the MLQ (refer to the discussion regarding future leadership research).

Inspirational Motivation

Inspirational motivation is leadership that inspires and motivates followers to reach ambitious goals that may have previously seemed unreachable. This factor, which is distinct from the idealized charismatic effect, "employs or adds nonintellectual, emotional qualities to the influence process" (Bass, 1985, p. 63). Here, the leader raises followers' expectations and inspires action by communicating confidence that they can achieve these ambitious goals—described as the *Pygmalion effect* by Bass (see also Eden, 1988; Eden et al., 2000). By predicting that followers are able to reach ambitious goals, and showing absolute confidence and resolve that this outcome will occur, followers are inspired to reach the requisite level of performance beyond normal expectations, and a self-fulfilling prophecy occurs.

Intellectual Stimulation

This is mostly a "rational" and "nonemotional" component of transformational leadership, distinct from the other transformational components. Here, the leader appeals to followers' intellects by creating "problem awareness and problem solving, of thought and imagination, and of beliefs and values" (Bass, 1985, p. 99). Bass noted further that as a result of intellectual stimulation, "followers' conceptualization, comprehension, and discernment of the nature of the problems they face, and their solutions" are radically altered (Bass, 1985, p. 99). Because individuals are included in the problem-solving process, they are motivated and committed to achieving the goals at hand. Intellectual stimulation involves challenging follower assumptions, generalizations, and stereotypes and stimulating followers to seek ways of improving current performance.

Individualized Consideration

Bass (1985) stated that a leader using individualized consideration provides socio-emotional support to followers and is concerned with developing followers to their highest level of potential and empowering them. The leader in this instance gives "individualized attention and a developmental or mentoring orientation" toward followers (p. 83). This outcome is achieved by coaching and counseling followers, maintaining frequent contact with them, and helping them to self-actualize. According to Bass and Avolio (1993) and Seltzer and Bass (1990), individualized consideration should not be confused with the scale "leader consideration" of the Ohio State leader behavioral studies (Stogdill & Coons, 1957), which labeled the leader as being friendly and approachable. However, the data show that this scale probably measures mostly consideration, which is not a bad thing per se (though to avoid construct proliferation, scientists should not give new names to existing constructs). Beyond Seltzer and Bass (1990), whose study was very limited, there have not been any studies estimating the strength of correlation between leader consideration and individualized consideration. The correlation between the two constructs was .60 in the study by Seltzer and Bass (1990); however, this correlation was uncorrected for measurement error, and the sample size of this study was relatively small ($n = 138$). Next, individualized consideration did not predict outcomes beyond initiating structure and consideration, though when Bass and Seltzer used a split-sample design, which reduced the sample size and hence reliability, they found results that did not make sense (e.g., intellectual stimulation was negatively related to outcomes, which was probably due to multicollinearity in the presence of a small sample size).

I present the three transactional factors next.

Contingent Reward

Bass (1985) argued that contingent reward leadership is based on economic and emotional exchanges by clarifying role requirements and rewarding desired outcomes. In this way, Bass proposed that contingent reward leadership functions in a similar manner to the path-goal theory proposed by House (1971). Contingent reward is a constructive transaction (Bass, 1998), and it is reasonably effective in motivating followers, but to a lesser degree than the transformational leadership behaviors. Here, the leader assigns tasks to followers, provides assistance for their efforts, and praises and recognizes followers for goal achievement (Bass & Avolio, 1997).

Again, however, although Bass suggested that this factor functions in a way that is similar to initiating structure (which is one of the factors subsumed in path-goal theory), contingent reward is more concerned with role requirements and rewards and less about structuring. Indeed, the instrumental leader factors go beyond (and have a stronger effect than do) contingent rewards, as recently shown by Antonakis, House, et al. (2010).

Management-by-Exception (Active) and Management-by-Exception (Passive)

Management-by-exception is by definition a negative transaction, because the leader monitors deviations from norms (Bass, 1998). It is similar to contingent reward in terms of focusing on outcomes, but here, the leader acts on mistakes or errors. Based on empirical research by Hater and Bass (1988), management-by-exception was carved into an active and passive component. According to Bass (1998), a leader employing active management-by-exception watches for deviations from norms, whereas a leader employing passive management-by-exception waits until deviations occur before intervening. Thus, the passive form of management-by-exception is often correlated with the last factor of the model, laissez-faire leadership (and researchers often refer to these two forms as passive-avoidant leadership).

Again, as part of transactional leadership, management-by-exception is purported to cover aspects of initiating structure. Some conceptualizations of initiating structure, for example, Fleishman's (1953) SBDQ (Supervisory Behavior Description Questionnaire) contain aspects of contingent aversive reinforcements (see Schriesheim, House, & Kerr, 1976). So it is good that this corrective transactional element is measured separately from contingent rewards. However, the positive aspect of task-related developmental feedback, which is based on prevention of mistakes (e.g., providing information about how mistakes can be corrected, providing learning feedback, and having a continuous improvement orientation), is not measured in this factor (Antonakis, House, et al., 2010).

Laissez-Faire Leadership

To fully account for all potential full-range leadership behaviors, a scale of nonleadership was added to indicate an absence of leadership (i.e. a nontransaction; Bass 1998; Bass & Avolio, 1994; 1997). These types of leaders avoid taking positions or making decisions, and they abdicate their authority. After management-by-exception passive, this factor is the most inactive form of leadership.

As mentioned, several meta-analyses have established that these factors predict outcomes. The latest meta-analysis indicates that transformational leadership, contingent reward leadership, and management-by-exception active correlate positively with leader outcomes, whereas management-by-exception passive and laissez-faire leadership correlate negatively with outcomes (Judge & Piccolo, 2004); similar multivariate regression effects are evident, too.

_____ Competing Charismatic-Transformational Models

Here, I am including multivariable models that have a transformational-charismatic or visionary component. Some of these are theoretical exposés that are integrative and propositional in nature (e.g., Shamir, House, & Arthur, 1993). As for the empirical ones, at this time, only the model of Podsakoff and associates (Podsakoff, MacKenzie, & Bommer, 1996; Podsakoff, MacKenzie, Moorman, & Fetter, 1990) has generated substantial research interest. Although the Podsakoff questionnaire measure, the Transformational Leadership Inventory, has not been as closely scrutinized as the MLQ, it is particularly well appreciated by the research community because it is not a propriety instrument (as is the MLQ).

Attribution Theory of Charisma

Conger and Kanungo (1988, 1998) proposed a theory of charismatic leadership whereby a leader is legitimized through an attributional process based on the perceptions that followers have of the leader's behaviors. Leadership is thus "both a relational and attributional phenomenon" and exists in the process of a leader's interaction with followers (Conger & Kanungo, 1998, p. 38). Conger and Kanungo (1998) proposed that individuals are validated as leaders by their followers through a three-stage behavioral process. This process is not necessarily linear, and the stages can occur in any order and may exist concomitantly.

First, effective charismatic leaders assess the status quo to determine the needs of followers, evaluate the resources that are available within the constituency, and articulate a compelling argument to arouse follower interest. Second, leaders articulate a vision of the future that will inspire follower action to achieve objectives that are instrumental in fulfilling the vision. The idealized vision creates follower identification and affection for the leader, because the vision embodies a future state of affairs that is valued by followers. Third, leaders create an aura of confidence and competence by demonstrating conviction that the mission is achievable. Leaders use unconventional means and expertise to inspire action and display how objectives can be achieved. In this way, they serve as powerful role models to promote follower action. This three-stage process is hypothesized to engender high trust in the leader, and follower performance that enables the organization to reach its goals.

According to Conger and Kanungo (1998), the aforementioned processes can be captured by a behavioral scale, the CKS (Conger Kanungo Scale) comprising the following five factors: (a) formulation and articulation of a strategic vision, (b) sensitivity to the environment, (c) sensitivity to member needs, (d) personal risk, and (e) unconventional behavior. Compared to the full-range leadership theory, it appears that the MLQ scale does not directly capture sensitivity to the environment, personal risk, and unconventional behavior. Theoretically, personal risk and unconventional behavior appear to overlap with the idealized influence (attributed) scale of the full-range leadership theory (FRLT) and, thus, should not account for further variation in leadership outcomes beyond this scale. Indeed, recent research indicates that the CKS correlates very highly with transformational leadership ($r = .88$, uncorrected for measurement error). More importantly, the CKS failed to predict incremental variance beyond transformational and transactional leadership in objective performance outcomes (Rowold & Heinitz, 2007). Also, although Conger and Kanungo do provide some evidence in support of their five-factor model, their evidence is not very convincing and there has not been a great deal of validation studies from independent research groups.

Self-Concept and Charisma

House and Shamir (1993) proposed an integrative theory of leadership based on what they termed the "new genre" of charismatic theories. House and Shamir's integrative framework is largely based on how leaders engage the self-concepts of follower. This theory was based on Shamir, House, and Arthur's (1993) propositions that charismatic leaders use their vision and mission as a platform to implicate the self-concept of followers. In this way, leaders have exceptional effects on followers, who are motivated by increased levels of self-esteem, self-worth, self-efficacy, collective efficacy, identification with the leader, social identification, and value internalization. Shamir et al. stated that these exceptional leaders affect followers as a result of motivational mechanisms that are induced by the leaders' behaviors. These behaviors include providing an ideological explanation for action, emphasizing a collective purpose, referring to historical accounts related to ideals, referring to the self-worth and efficacy of followers, and expressing confidence in followers that they are capable of fulfilling the mission. As a result of the leader's behavior, the motivational mechanisms trigger the self-concept effects that lead to personal commitment to the leader's mission, self-sacrificial behavior, organizational citizenship, and task meaningfulness. These effects are further enhanced by the generation of self-expression and consistency on the part of the followers. As an example of the intricateness of these effects, Shamir et al. stated that "Charismatic leaders . . . increase followers' self-worth through emphasizing the relationships between efforts and important values. A general sense of self-worth increases general self-efficacy; a sense of moral correctness is a source of strength and confidence. Having complete faith in the moral correctness of one's convictions gives one the strength and confidence to behave accordingly" (p. 582).

Based on decades of work by McClelland (1975, 1985), House and Shamir (1993) argued further that in addition to follower self-concept arousal, leaders selectively arouse follower achievement, affiliation, and power motives, depending on situational factors. For example, in task-intensive environments, leaders arouse achievement motives. In situations requiring competitiveness in followers, leaders arouse the power motive. House and Shamir state that this arousal process occurs nonconsciously in followers, and "As a consequence of motive arousal, individuals become further self-engaged, and their feelings of self-worth and self-efficacy become contingent on satisfying the aroused motives" (p. 92). House and Shamir's theory further proposes that as the leader sets examples of desired behaviors in terms of achievement, affiliation, or power, followers learn vicariously from the leader and emulate these behaviors. In this way, House and Shamir argued that the leader "helps define for the followers just what kinds of traits, values, beliefs, and behaviors it is good and legitimate to develop" (p. 95).

As a result of the above, and in identifying patterns and gaps in the theoretical frameworks they reviewed, House and Shamir (1993) proposed a seven-factor model of leadership including (a) visionary behavior, (b) positive self-presentation, (c) empowering behaviors, (d) calculated risk taking and self-sacrificial behavior, (e) intellectual stimulation, (f) supportive leader behavior, and (g) adaptive behavior. These factors overlap somewhat with the MLQ factors, with the possible exceptions of positive self-presentation, calculated risk taking and self-sacrificial behavior, and adaptive behavior. Risk taking and self-sacrificial behavior is evident in the attributions followers' make of the leader's idealized influence, because the leader displays a high ethical and moral code, is a risk-taker, and has a strong sense of mission (Bass, 1998). The leader, thus by definition, takes calculated risks and makes personal sacrifices. Adaptive behavior is borrowed from Conger and Kanungo's (1998) theory, and reflects the environmental-monitoring factor that we discussed earlier. Positive self-presentation may be evident in indicators of the MLQ (e.g., the power and confidence that a leader displays), and may be gauged in terms of whether followers respect their leader and are proud to be associated with him or her (Bass & Avolio, 1995). In other words, the degree to which a leader uses positive self-presentation will be evident in the charismatic attributions followers make of the leader. House and Shamir also argued that positive self-presentation is concerned with building credibility. Followers who respect and are proud of their leader and see that leader as powerful and confident—elements that are captured directly by the MLQ—must by definition see the leader as being credible and legitimate. The leader therefore must have cultivated an appropriate image for that process to occur.

The Visionary Leader

Sashkin's (1988) theoretical framework focused on the key components of visionary leadership in top-level leaders. Sashkin proposed that leaders display sensitivity to situational constraints and operate more on intuition than intellect. Visionary leaders have a high need for socialized power (McClelland, 1985) and domain-specific knowledge of what vision to project as a function of environmental conditions. That is, by virtue of their cognitive skills, they are able to take advantage of situational conditions and are "attuned to the construction of opportunities; they create the future as much as they adapt to it" (p. 128). Sashkin stated that visionary leaders are able to initially express their vision, explain it to others, extend the vision in other situations, and finally expand the vision in a broader context, thus widening the vision's temporal and spatial sphere of influence. They are able to deal heuristically with uncertain conditions and offer some flexibility in their visions to anticipate and account for unfamiliar situations. Sashkin also noted that visionary leaders use their insight to adapt the organization to environmental change, and they promote values and ideals that allow for the realization of the vision. Furthermore, they use their vision as a social glue with which to bind followers into a team that collectively pursues a common purpose.

Visionary leaders know how to carve the vision into operational components that translate into action for all organizational levels. These components involve actions that affect the strategic and tactical levels of the organization and its players. Furthermore, through personal and consistent actions, visionary leaders focus the attention of followers on key issues and ensure that followers understand these issues. Finally, these leaders are respectful to themselves and others, increase follower self-worth, and take calculated risks to draw followers into their mission. These actionable behaviors are mutually reinforcing and interrelated.

Sashkin's (1988) propositions overlap substantially with what the MLQ model espouses, focus more on ideals than ethical or moral overtones, and are strategically oriented, much like Westley and Mintzberg's (1988) strategic vision theory. Although Sashkin provided a thorough explanation of how vision "functions," his model generally overlaps with environmental sensitivity and with a combination of factors espoused in the FRLT (e.g., idealized influence, inspirational motivation, and individualized consideration). His propositions regarding the strategic functions of the leader do not appear to be addressed by the other approaches, and they may fill a deficiency in the MLQ model. The rest of his propositions, though, together with Conger and

Kanungo's (1998) sensitivity to the environment factor and House and Shamir's (1993) adaptive behavior factor, could serve as a useful basis from which to generate manifest indicators for a behavioral scale of environmental monitoring, as proposed by Antonakis and House (2002).

The Podsakoff Transformational-Transactional Leadership Model

This model is conceptually similar to the original Bass (1985) model. After the Bass model, the Podsakoff model is the most widely used transformational-transactional leadership model (Bass & Riggio, 2006). The model that Podsakoff and colleagues (Podsakoff et al., 1990, 1996) proposed includes both transformational and transactional leadership factors. The transformational factors include (a) identifying and articulating a vision—looking for new opportunities, projecting a vision for the future, knowing the direction that will be taken, being inspiring, and getting others behind the mission; (b) providing an appropriate model—setting an example, leading by doing (rather than telling), being a good role model; (c) fostering the acceptance of group goals—promoting group cooperation and teamwork, gets the team behind the same goal, develops a team spirit; (d) high performance expectations—setting challenging goals and giving articulating high-performance expectations, expecting top performance; (e) providing individualized support—considering others' feelings, respecting others, being thoughtful about others; and (f) intellectual stimulation—challenging followers to think differently, making followers rethink their ideas, looking at old problems in new way.

The Podsakoff model also includes a transactional leader factor: contingent reward—giving frequent and positive feedback, gives special recognition for good work, complimenting others for exceptional performance. These factors essentially map on the Bass transformational-transactional model, except for the fact that the Podsakoff model does not include management-by-exception active and passive as well as laissez-faire leadership. For those wishing to include similar factors to these omitted styles, contingent and noncontingent punishment scales, also developed by Podsakoff and colleagues, could be useful (see Podsakoff, Todor, Grover, & Huber, 1984; Podsakoff, Todor, & Skov, 1982); these constructs have shown relatively good validities (Podsakoff, Bommer, Podsakoff, & MacKenzie, 2006).

Other Models

Beyond the models that I have reviewed, there are other lesser-known models that are being used. Rafferty and Griffin (2004) recently proposed a five-factor model of transformational leadership, which looks like it might have some potential; however, this instrument has not been extensively studied by independent research groups, and it omits important correlates of leader outcomes. The Transformational Leadership Questionnaire (TLQ) has been recently proposed as an alternative to the United States–centered MLQ-type models (Alimo-Metcalfe & Alban-Metcalfe, 2001); I cannot, however, identify much evidence for the validity of the TLQ. There are not many studies that have used it, and there are no large-scale strong psychometric tests to support its construct validity.

There are several other measures that I could have mentioned; however, they simply have not had much of an impact on research or practice. One measure, which seems to have had an important impact on practice, is the Leadership Practices Inventory (LPI) by Kouzes and Posner (1987). Although intuitively appealing and driven by the popularity of their book, I am not very impressed with the validation results of the LPI (and there has been very little research on the psychometric properties of this model).

Future Research

Research in transformational and charismatic leadership appears to be in a mature stage (cf. Hunt, 1999). Informal discussions that I have had with leading scholars in the field make me wonder who of the established researchers will lead the transformational-charismatic movement in this current decade, in the way that Robert House and Bernard Bass did. Bass's long-time collaborator Bruce Avolio has been advancing other lines of research (e.g., authentic leadership, leadership development), as has Francis Yammarino (who has been focusing more on methodological issues and levels-of-analysis issues). Perhaps the top contender for this spot is Boas Shamir; he is probably the most established scholar of charisma, a creative and deep thinker (Howell & Shamir, 2005; Shamir, 1995; Shamir et al., 1993), who has published extensively on transformational leadership, too (Dvir, Eden, Avolio, & Shamir, 2002; Kark, Shamir, & Chen, 2003). However, because he is much broader in his outlook than House and Bass were and he moved into the field once it was already established, he might not ever have the "cult" status of a Bass or House.

Collectively speaking, though—and this is good news—work in this area continues at a brisk pace, not only in the traditional spheres of management, applied psychology, business, and general and social psychology, but also in other disciplines—including, nursing, education, political science, public health, public administration, sociology, ethics, operations research, computer sciences, industrial engineering, and others. As shown in Figure 8.1, both the number of papers and the number of citations in the field have been growing at an increasing rate. Perhaps this "distributed leadership" setup is good, in the sense that there are many research groups dispersed around the globe in various fields reflecting the "distant" leadership of the trailblazers!

Figure 8.1   Biliometrics of charismatic and transformational leadership theory

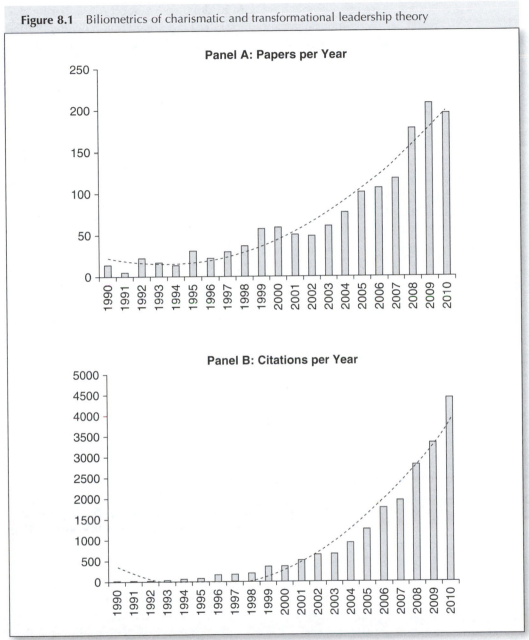

NOTE: Searches were conducted using the exact terms "transformational leader*" or "charismatic leader*" in the ISI Web of Knowledge topic field (for the time period 1990-2010). Panel A refers to the number of published papers or proceedings indexed in ISI with regression fitted trend line. (Using 1990 as the baseline year, i.e., 1, the number of citations per year was predicted by the following regression model: $y_{papers} = 27.15 - 5.63*time + 0.66*time^2$.) Panel B refers to citations received in ISI papers and proceedings with regression fitted trend line. (Using 1990 as the baseline year, i.e., 1, the number of citations per year was predicted by the following regression model: $y_{citations} = 560.80 - 216.58*time + 17.56*time^2$.) Note, I estimated the regression models simultaneously using maximum likelihood multivariate regression with robust standard errors; coefficients of the quadric terms were significant in both models, both individually and simultaneously ($p < .001$). Data retrieved 1 March 2011.

Still, there remains much work to be done with respect to measuring charisma, correctly modeling leadership styles (and identifying individual difference predictors of the model), and developing process leadership models in process theories, as I discuss next.

What Makes Leaders Charismatic?

We still do not have a good idea about what makes a leader seem powerful, confident, and charismatic (reflecting the idealized influence attributes of the MLQ scale). In fact, one of the oft-leveled criticisms at the MLQ reflects the fact that some of the factors might actually reflect outcomes (Yukl, 1999)—that is, they are endogenous, which is not a desirable state of affairs when the factor is modeled as an independent variable (see discussion below on the "correct modeling issue"). Of course, charismatic leaders must use some kinds of communication and image-building strategies to seem powerful and confident (House, 1977). Researchers have identified some of these strategies with respect to the content of the speech, its framing, and the delivery mode (Den Hartog & Verburg, 1997; Shamir et al., 1993). Essentially, charismatic leaders engage followers' self-concepts (Shamir, Arthur, & House, 1994; Shamir et al., 1993) by using a number of "tricks." I like to refer these tricks as charismatic leadership tactics, which researchers have been able to manipulate in laboratory experiments (Antonakis, Angerfelt, & Liechti, 2010; Awamleh & Gardner, 1999; Howell & Frost, 1989).

Charismatic leaders are risk-takers and are unconventional (Conger & Kanungo, 1998; House, 1977). They set high goals (House, 1977) and make sacrifices for the greater good (Shamir et al., 1993). Most important, charismatic leaders know how to communicate in appropriate (e.g., emotionally charged) ways so that they can package their message to be easily understood (Frese, Beimel, & Schoenborn, 2003; Wasielewski, 1985); they use positive (Bono & Ilies, 2006) and negative emotions (Wasielewski, 1985) and various nonverbal strategies (Cherulnik, Donley, Wiewel, & Miller, 2001). They are good storytellers; they know how to use their voice as well as body gestures (Frese et al., 2003; Towler, 2003). In particular, these leaders are masters in rhetoric and make use of contrasts, lists, repetition, as well as alliteration and rhetorical questions (Den Hartog & Verburg, 1997; Willner, 1984). They also use metaphors extensively. These communication devices simplify the message and render it highly understandable and visible (Charteris-Black, 2005; Emrich, Brower, Feldman, & Garland, 2001; Mio, 1997; Mio, Riggio, Levin, & Reese, 2005).

These charismatic leadership tactics render the elusive charisma factor more tangible, which can be used as a basis to measure a more pure form of charisma (instead of attributions) either directly via others' reports, using trained coders, or machine coding, which can reliably code certain text themes (Hart, 2000), even semantic meanings in text (Landauer, 1999; Landauer,

Foltz, & Laham, 1998; Landauer, Laham, & Derr, 2004); there are also automated technologies to measure emotions (Sorci et al., 2010). Research in using objective means to measure charisma is sorely needed; it is time to go beyond MLQ-style questionnaire measures.

Correctly Modeling Leadership Style

The discussion here is not only leveled to transformational and charismatic leadership theory; it is relevant to all theories of leadership, particularly the leader-member exchange construct, which is more of an outcome of leadership than it is a leadership style (House & Aditya, 1997). Briefly, the problem that researchers have when undertaking cross-sectional or longitudinal research is that the modeled independent variable, say transformational leadership (x), is not exogenously manipulated. As I show below, it is important to use stable individual differences or other contextual factors to estimate the causal effect of leadership style on outcomes. I discuss this problem in more detail below, because it is important not only for correct empirical estimation but also for correct theorizing regarding the nature of the leadership effect.

In experimental research, the experimenter is assured that the effect of x on y is due to the manipulation and nothing else. By randomly assigning the treatment, the error term in the regression model captures no systematic variation that is correlated with the treatment or with y (for a detailed exposé refer to Antonakis, Bendahan, Jacquart, & Lalive, 2010). However, with nonexperimental research, the modeler has a problem, in the sense that x may correlate with unobserved variation affecting y (this problem is referred to as one of endogeneity) or that y might simultaneously cause x. Thus, the case of x being modeled as an independent variable, when it is in fact endogenous, creates the condition for a biased estimate of the effect of x on y. That is, the coefficient could be higher, lower, or of a different sign. Many researchers do not understand that the problem of endogeneity renders estimates that are fatally flawed: They often note, for instance, that the relation could be due to y causing x, and thus assume that the coefficient is correctly estimated (but that they are unsure of the direction of causality). That is precisely where the problem is: The coefficient is *not* correctly estimated and is not even worth reporting, not even as a mere correlation or association. The relation could be zero, negative, or positive.

I will briefly run through two examples to show the problem of endogeneity. First, if individuals rating leadership style know of the leader outcomes (e.g., how well the leaders' company has performed), they will be biased when rating the leader due to attribution processes (Lord, Binning, Rush, & Thomas, 1978; Rush, Thomas, & Lord, 1977). That is, good performance will be associated with prototypically good leadership, and thus raters will "see" the leader being better on aspects of leadership that are implicitly associated with good (or bad) outcomes. Given this biasing effect, leadership is operationalized in terms of follower perceptions and attributions, which may have little to do with how the leader acts! Such findings make for a sorry state of affairs in leadership research; however, theoretically, this attribution mechanism will be more prevalent in situations of high leader-follower distance (Antonakis, 2011; Antonakis & Atwater, 2002; Shamir, 1995). In distant contexts, followers have to "go on" something when rating leaders and will use whatever information is available, including performance cues, to help them correctly categorize the leader (Jacquart & Antonakis, 2010). There are many clear biasing mechanisms at play, including other factors like facial appearance, gender, height, and the like (Antonakis, 2011; Antonakis & Dalgas, 2009). Furthermore, once an individual is classified in a certain way, it is difficult for the perceiver to change the classification (Cantor & Mischel, 1977).

Of course, leaders can affect leader outcomes, too. Yet, failure to correctly model this reciprocal relationship (i.e., a dual-causal model where leadership causes outcomes and outcomes "cause" leadership) or to "lock-in" the causal direction in one of the directions can render estimates suspect. I cannot stress enough the importance of understanding the limitations of leadership questionnaire measures (like the MLQ, and others) and then using the correct design conditions and statistical methods to overcome these limitations.

To better understand this simultaneous causation problem, here is a very well-known example in economics (see Levitt, 1997, 2002). One would reasonably assume that hiring more police should reduce crime. However, regressing crime on police produced a positive coefficient (because when crime goes up, more police are hired); such results really baffled researchers. However, correct estimation of this model, where an exogenous source of variance is used to "purge" x of endogeneity, reverses the sign of the estimated coefficient. Thus, in this case, the model that is estimated is $z \rightarrow x \rightarrow y$ (where z in this case is referred to as an instrumental variable, one that varies independently of the residual variance in predicting y and x). In this case, Levitt used timing of elections (which led to more police hirings; the predicted value of x did not correlate with the error term in the y equation, thus producing the correct coefficient). There is also the case where x and y depend on a common omitted cause (e.g., affect for the leader). As shown by Antonakis, Bendahan, et al. (2010) this problem of omitted variance bias, of which common method variance is a case, can inflate or deflate coefficients (see also Podsakoff, MacKenzie, Lee, & Podsakoff, 2003); furthermore, the common method variance problem is not an urban legend, as suggested by Spector (2006).

These problems of endogeneity can be solved by modeling exogenous sources of variance that first predict x and that affect y only via x. Examples could include genetically determined individual differences that can be reliably (and ideally objectively) measured (e.g., IQ, personality), fixed-effects of leaders (i.e., obtaining repeated measures over time or from many raters), contextual factors (country, industry, firm), or exogenous shocks (for ideas, see Antonakis, Bendahan, et al., 2010). Although some research has been undertaken in this area of individual differences (Bono & Judge, 2004; Judge & Bono, 2000), not enough has been done to predict the factors of the full-range model, and this considering contextual factors, too (Lim & Ployhart, 2004). There is hardly any research linking cognitive ability to transformational leadership. This factor should be one "usual suspect" in a correct model specification (Antonakis, 2011). There is not much research on the ethical development of transformational and charismatic leaders (e.g., Turner, Barling, Epitropaki, Butcher, & Milner, 2002), not to mention biological correlates (Antonakis, 2011).

Finally, another problem that I often see is models being estimated that have blatantly obvious omitted causes, for example, regressing y only on charismatic leadership (e.g., Keller, 1992; Koene, Vogelaar, & Soeters, 2002). If variables are omitted from the regression equation that correlate with y as well as with other predictors in the regression equation, then omitting them will produce biased estimates (Antonakis, Bendahan, et al., 2010; Cameron & Trivedi, 2005). Thus, it is important to control for all theoretical causes of y (e.g., task-oriented leadership, transactional leadership) that may correlate with the modeled independent variables. The full-range leadership theory that is estimated must be truly a "full" one, though not to the point of bringing in redundant factors.

Leadership Process Model

As many researchers have suggested, to fully understand the leadership phenomenon, it is important to model the full leadership process that produces leadership outcomes (Antonakis et al., 2004; Antonakis, House, et al., 2010; Lim & Ployhart, 2004; Zaccaro, Kemp, & Bader, 2004). That is, we must link together leader individual differences, leader styles, and leader outcomes, while also considering level-of-analysis issues (Antonakis & Atwater, 2002; Waldman & Yammarino, 1999) as well as contextual affects, both as moderator and predictors (Liden & Antonakis, 2009). Doing so will ensure not only correct estimation of endogenous variables, but also provide us with a better understanding concerning the importance of leadership. More research should move in this direction to provide truly new and important discoveries.

Conclusion

It is clear from this review that transformational and charismatic leadership has become an integral part of leadership theory; this leadership approach is here to stay. However, I must admit that the field has been a bit carried away by the theory. Some cold showers are in order, and they have been coming, albeit sporadically (Antonakis, House, et al., 2010; Hunt, 2004; Judge,

Piccolo, & Ilies, 2004; Yukl, 1999). Although called a "full-range theory," it misses out on good old task leadership (Hunt, 2004) as well as strategic leadership aspects inherent to transformational and charismatic leadership approaches (Antonakis, House, et al., 2010).

On another note, House and I threw out a challenge to transformational-charismatic leadership scholars about a decade ago, though we still have not had any takers. After paying tribute to Bernard Bass for significantly advancing the field's understanding of leadership theory—and this in an edited book emanating from his Festschrift—we noted the following in our conclusions (Antonakis & House, 2002):

> We hope to see longitudinal research that establishes that transformational leaders have the ability to actually transform individuals and organizations. This notion implicitly pervades the theories and assumptions of leadership scholars of the new paradigm (Beyer, 1999; House, 1999). We have evidence that behaviors of transformational leaders are associated with improved organizational effectiveness, follower satisfaction, and follower motive arousal, but this evidence does not imply that transformational leaders caused transformations in organizations and followers. Although causal links could be theorized, up to this point, we have seen no empirical evidence to make that deduction. (p. 27)

We are still waiting. To conclude, I trust that the concluding section does not give readers the impression that I am disillusioned by the state-of-research in this aspect of the leadership field. I am not. In fact, I am very impressed by how much research has been done and how much our understanding of the phenomenon has improved due to the efforts of hundreds of researchers. I am also optimistic that we will learn much more about this research stream in the future. What is clear from my review is that even though research in transformational and charismatic leadership is mature, there is still much to be done; just like in the medical sciences, where researchers constantly update treatments for diseases, so too must we find better measures and better interventions. To recap, there is a need for (a) more longitudinal and multilevel research, (b) the development of more inclusive and less biased questionnaire measures, (c) the development of objective leadership measures, and (d) a fuller understanding of process models that also consider contextual effects and individual difference antecedents.

Leadership, particularly its transformational and charismatic form, is simply too important to leave to random processes or to weak institutions. Once societies, companies, or teams appoint leaders who have charismatic influence, they will be stuck with them for some time, so it is best to get this appointment right the first time. We must better understand the processes that produce these leaders because history will, again and again, toss up leaders who will wield charismatic power.

Note

1. As will become evident later, I consider charisma as part of transformational leadership. However, I also use the terms "charisma" and "transformational" separately to refer to different research streams that treat the terms differently or that focus mostly on charisma.

Discussion Questions

1. Using the full-range leadership styles, compare and contrast the leadership styles of an effective and ineffective leader.

2. Is transformational leadership moral leadership? That is, is it morally good for collectives to fall in behind a leader who has them cast under a "spell" of sorts? Discuss.

3. Compile an in-depth profile of Jean-Marie Messier, former CEO of Vivendi. Why was his charismatic leadership style a possible contributor to the massive losses incurred by Vivendi under his tenure?

Supplementary Readings

Antonakis, J. (2006). Leadership: What is it and how it is implicated in strategic change? *International Journal of Management Cases, 8*(4), 4–20.

Antonakis, J., & Hooijberg, R. (2008). Cascading a new vision: Three steps for real commitment. *Perspectives for Managers, 157,* 1–4

Bass, B. M. (1985). Leadership: Good, better, best. *Organizational Dynamics, 13*(3), 26–40.

Bass, B. M. (1990). From transactional to transformational leadership: Learning to share the vision. *Organizational Dynamics, 18*(3), 19–31.

Berlew, D. E. (1974). Leadership and organizational excitement. *California Management Review, 17*(2), 21–30.

Nadler, D. A., & Tushman, M. L. (1990). Beyond the charismatic leader: Leadership and organizational change. *California Management Review, 32*(2), 77–97.

Case Studies

Film Case: *12 Angry Men,* starring Henry Fonda.

Case: Gavetti, G., & Canato, A. (2008). Universita' Bocconi: Transformation in the New Millennium. *Harvard Business School Case 709406-PDF-ENG.*

Case: Ichijo, K. (2007). Creating, growing and protecting knowledge-based competence: The case of Sharp's LCD business. In R. Hooijberg, J. G. Hunt, J. Antonakis, K. B. Boal, & N. Lane (Eds.), *Being there even when you are not: Leading through strategy, structures, and systems* (pp. 87–102). Amsterdam: Elsevier Science.

Case: Mark, K., & Konrad, A. (2005). Anita Jairam at Metropole Services. *Richard Ivey School of Business Case.*

Case: Podsakoff, N. P., Podsakoff, P. M., & Valentina Kuskova. (2010). Dispelling misconceptions and providing guidelines for leader reward and punishment behavior. *Harvard Business School Case BH388-PDF-ENG.*

References

Alimo-Metcalfe, B., & Alban-Metcalfe, R. J. (2001). The development of a new Transformational Leadership Questionnaire. *Journal of Occupational and Organizational Psychology, 74,* 1–27.

Antonakis, J. (2001). The validity of the transformational, transactional, and laissez-faire leadership model as measured by the Multifactor Leadership Questionnaire (MLQ5X). *Dissertation Abstracts International, 62* (01), 233. (UMI No. 3000380)

Antonakis, J. (2011). Predictors of leadership: The usual suspects and the suspect traits. In A. Bryman, D. Collinson, K. Grint, B. Jackson, & M. Uhl-Bien (Eds.), *Sage Handbook of Leadership* (pp. 269–285). Thousand Oaks, CA: Sage.

Antonakis, J., Angerfelt, M., & Liechti, S. (2010, August). *Testing if charisma can be taught: Evidence from a laboratory and field study.* Paper presented at the annual meeting of the Academy of Management, Organizational Behavior Division, Montréal, Canada.

Antonakis, J., & Atwater, L. (2002). Leader distance: A review and a proposed theory. *The Leadership Quarterly, 13,* 673–704.

Antonakis, J., Avolio, B. J., & Sivasubramaniam, N. (2003). Context and leadership: An examination of the nine-factor full-range leadership theory using the Multifactor Leadership Questionnaire. *The Leadership Quarterly, 14,* 261–295.

Antonakis, J., Bendahan, S., Jacquart, P., & Lalive, R. (2010). On making causal claims: A review and recommendations. *The Leadership Quarterly, 21,* 1086–1120.

Antonakis, J., Cianciolo, A. T., & Sternberg, R. J. (2004). Leadership: Past, present, future. In J. Antonakis, A. T. Cianciolo, & R. J. Sternberg (Eds.), *The nature of leadership* (pp. 3–15). Thousand Oaks, CA: Sage.

Antonakis, J., & Dalgas, O. (2009). Predicting Elections: Child's Play! *Science, 323*(5918), 1183.

Antonakis, J., & House, R. J. (2002). An analysis of the full-range leadership theory: The way forward. In B. J. Avolio & F. J. Yammarino (Eds.), *Transformational and charismatic leadership: The road ahead* (pp. 3–34). Amsterdam: JAI.

Antonakis, J., & House, R. J. (2004, June). *On instrumental leadership: Beyond transactions and transformations.* Paper presented at the Gallup Leadership Institute, University of Nebraska, Omaha.

Antonakis, J., House, R. J., Rowold, J., & Borgmann, L. (2010). *A fuller full-range leadership theory: Instrumental, transformational, and transactional leadership.* Manuscript submitted for publication.

Aristotle. (trans. 1954). *Rhetoric* (W. R. Roberts & I. Bywater, Trans., 1st Modern Library ed.). New York: Modern Library.

Avolio, B. J., & Bass, B. M. (1991). *The full range leadership development programs: Basic and advanced manuals.* Binghamton, NY: Bass, Avolio & Associates.

Avolio, B. J., & Bass, B. M. (1995). Individual consideration viewed at multiple levels of analysis: A multi-level framework for examining the diffusion of transformational leadership. *The Leadership Quarterly, 6,* 199–218.

Avolio, B. J., Bass, B. M., & Jung, D. I. (1995). *MLQ Multifactor leadership questionnaire: Technical report.* Redwood City, CA: Mindgarden.

Avolio, B. J., Bass, B. M., & Jung, D. I. (1999). Re-examining the components of transformational and transactional leadership using the MLQ. *Journal of Occupational and Organizational Psychology, 72,* 441–462.

Avolio, B. J., Waldman, D. W., & Yammarino, F. J. (1991). Leading in the 1990s: The four I's of transformational leadership. *Journal of European Industrial Training, 15*(4), 9–16.

Awamleh, R., & Gardner, W. L. (1999). Perceptions of leader charisma and effectiveness: The effects of vision content, delivery, and organizational performance. *The Leadership Quarterly, 10,* 345–373.

Bass, B. M. (1985). *Leadership and performance beyond expectations.* New York: Free Press.

Bass, B. M. (1998). *Transformational leadership: Industrial, military, and educational impact.* Mahwah, NJ: Lawrence Erlbaum.

Bass, B. M., & Avolio, B. J. (1993). Transformational leadership: A response to critiques. In M. M. Chemers & R. Ayman (Eds.), *Leadership theory and research: Perspectives and directions* (pp. 49–80). San Diego: Academic Press.

Bass, B. M., & Avolio, B. J. (Eds.). (1994). *Improving organizational effectiveness through transformational leadership.* Thousand Oaks, CA: Sage.

Bass, B. M., & Avolio, B. J. (1995). *MLQ Multifactor Leadership Questionnaire for research: Permission set.* Redwood City, CA: Mindgarden.

Bass, B. M., & Avolio, B. J. (1997). *Full range leadership development: Manual for the multifactor leadership questionnaire.* Palo Alto, CA: Mindgarden.

Bass, B. M., Avolio, B. J., & Atwater, L. (1996). The transformational and transactional leadership of men and women. *Applied Psychology: An International Review, 45,* 5–34.

Bass, B. M., & Riggio, R. E. (2006). *Transformational leadership* (2nd ed.). Mahwah, N.J.: Lawrence Erlbaum.

Bass, B. M., & Steidlmeier, P. (1999). Ethics, character, and authentic transformational leadership behavior. *The Leadership Quarterly, 10,* 181–217.

Bass, B. M., Waldman, D. A., Avolio, B. J., & Bebb, M. (1987). Transformational leadership and the falling dominoes effect. *Group & Organization Studies, 12*(1), 73–87.

Bono, J. E., & Ilies, R. (2006). Charisma, positive emotions and mood contagion. *The Leadership Quarterly, 17,* 317–334.

Bono, J. E., & Judge, T. A. (2004). Personality and transformational and transactional leadership: A meta-analysis. *Journal of Applied Psychology, 89,* 901–910.

Bryman, A. (1992). *Charisma and leadership in organizations.* London: Sage.

Burns, J. M. (1978). *Leadership.* New York: Harper & Row.

Cameron, A. C., & Trivedi, P. K. (2005). *Microeconometrics: Methods and applications.* New York: Cambridge University Press.

Cantor, N., & Mischel, W. (1977). Traits as prototypes: Effects on recognition memory. *Journal of Personality and Social Psychology, 35,* 38–48.

Charteris-Black, J. (2005). *Politicians and rhetoric: The persuasive power of metaphor.* Basingstoke, UK: Palgrave-MacMillan.

Cherulnik, P. D., Donley, K. A., Wiewel, T. S. R., & Miller, S. R. (2001). Charisma is contagious: The effect of leaders' charisma on observers' affect. *Journal of Applied Social Psychology, 31,* 2149–2159.

Conger, J. A. (1999). Charismatic and transformational leadership in organizations: An insider's perspective on these developing streams of research. *The Leadership Quarterly, 10,* 145–179.

Conger, J. A., & Kanungo, R. N. (1988). *Charismatic leadership: The elusive factor in organizational effectiveness.* San Francisco: Jossey-Bass.

Conger, J. A., & Kanungo, R. N. (1998). *Charismatic leadership in organizations.* Thousand Oaks, CA: Sage.

DeGroot, T., Kiker, D. S., & Cross, T. C. (2001). A meta-analysis to review organizational outcomes related charismatic leadership. *Canadian Journal of Administrative Sciences, 17,* 356–371.

Den Hartog, D. N., & Verburg, R. M. (1997). Charisma and rhetoric: Communicative techniques of international business leaders. *The Leadership Quarterly, 8,* 355–391.

Downton, J. V. (1973). *Rebel leadership: Commitment and charisma in the revolutionary process.* New York: Free Press.

Dumdum, U. R., Lowe, K. B., & Avolio, B. J. (2001). A meta-analysis of transformational and transactional leadership correlates of effectiveness and satisfaction: An update and extension. In B. J. Avolio & F. J. Yammarino (Eds.), *Transformational and charismatic leadership: The road ahead* (pp. 35–66). Amsterdam: JAI.

Dvir, T., Eden, D., Avolio, B. J., & Shamir, B. (2002). Impact of transformational leadership on follower development and performance: A field experiment. *Academy of Management Journal, 45,* 735–744.

Eden, D. (1988). Pygmalion, goal setting, and expectancy: Compatible ways to boost productivity. *Academy of Management Review, 13,* 639–652.

Eden, D., Geller, D., Gewirtz, D., Gordon-Terner, R., Inbar, I., Liberman, M., et al. (2000). Implanting Pygmalion leadership style through workshop training: Seven field experiments. *The Leadership Quarterly, 11,* 171–210.

Emrich, C. G., Brower, H. H., Feldman, J. M., & Garland, H. (2001). Images in words: Presidential rhetoric, charisma, and greatness. *Administrative Science Quarterly, 46,* 527–557.

Etzioni, A. (1961). *A comparative analysis of complex organizations.* New York: Free Press.

Etzioni, A. (1964). *Modern organizations.* Englewood Cliffs, NJ: Prentice Hall.

Fleishman, E. A. (1953). The description of supervisory behavior. *Journal of Applied Psychology, 37,* 1–6.

Fleishman, E. A. (1957). A leader behavior description for industry. In R. M. Stogdill & A. E. Coons (Eds.), *Leader behavior: Its description and measurement* (Research Monograph No. 88, pp. 103–119). Columbus: Ohio State University Bureau of Business Research.

French, J. R. P., & Raven, B. H. (1968). The bases of social power. In D. Cartwright & A. F. Zander (Eds.), *Group dynamics: Research and theory* (3rd ed., pp. 259–269). New York: Harper & Row.

Frese, M., Beimel, S., & Schoenborn, S. (2003). Action training for charismatic leadership: Two evaluations of studies of a commercial training module on inspirational communication of a vision. *Personnel Psychology, 56,* 671–697.

Gardner, J. W. (1965). The antileadership vaccine. *Annual report for the fiscal year, Carnegie Corporation of New York* (pp. 3–12).

Gardner, W. L., Lowe, K. B., Moss, T. W., Mahoney, K. T., & Cogliser, C. C. (2010). Scholarly leadership of the study of leadership: A review of *The Leadership Quarterly's* second decade, 2000–2009. *The Leadership Quarterly, 12,* 922–958.

Gasper, J. M. (1992). *Transformational leadership: An integrative review of the literature.* Kalamazoo: Western Michigan University.

Gemmill, G., & Oakley, J. (1992). Leadership: An alienating social myth? *Human Relations, 45,* 113–129.

Greene, C. N. (1977). Disenchantment with leadership research: Some causes, recommendations, and alternative directions. In J. G. Hunt & L. L. Larson (Eds.), *Leadership: The cutting edge* (pp. 57–67). Carbondale: Southern Illinois University Press.

Halpin, A. W. (1954). The leadership behavior and combat performance of airplane commanders. *Journal of Abnormal and Social Psychology* [now named *Journal of Abnormal Psychology*], *49,* 19–22.

Hart, R. P. (2000). *DICTION 5.0: The text analysis program.* Thousand Oaks, CA: Sage-Scolari.

Hater, J. J., & Bass, B. M. (1988). Superiors' evaluations and subordinates' perceptions of transformational and transactional leadership. *Journal of Applied Psychology, 73,* 695–702.

House, R. J. (1971). Path-goal theory of leadership effectiveness. *Adminstrative Science Quarterly, 16,* 321-339.

House, R. J. (1977). A 1976 theory of charismatic leadership. In J. G. Hunt & L. L. Larson (Eds.), *Leadership: The Cutting Edge* (pp. 189–207). Carbondale: Southern Illinois: University Press.

House, R. J., & Aditya, R. N. (1997). The social scientific study of leadership: Quo vadis? *Journal of Management, 23,* 409–473.

House, R. J., & Shamir, B. (1993). Toward the integration of transformational, charismatic, and visionary thories. In M. M. Chemers & R. Ayman (Eds.), *Leadership theory and research: Perspectives and directions* (pp. 81-108). San Diego: Academic Press.

Howell, J. M., & Frost, P. J. (1989). A laboratory study of charismatic leadership. *Organizational Behavior and Human Decision Processes, 43,* 243–269.

Howell, J. M., & Shamir, B. (2005). The role of followers in the charismatic leadership process: Relationships and their consequences. *Academy of Management Review, 30,* 96–112.

Hunt, J. G. (1991). *Leadership: A new synthesis.* Newbury Park, CA: Sage.

Hunt, J. G. (1999). Tranformational/charismatic leadership's transformation of the field: An historical essay. *The Leadership Quarterly, 10,* 129–144.

Hunt, J. G. (2004). Task leadership. In G. R. Goethels, G. J. Sorensen, & J. M. Burns (Eds.), *Encyclopedia of leadership* (Vol. IV, pp. 1524–1529). Thousand Oaks, CA: Sage.

Jacquart, P., & Antonakis, J. (2010, August). *"It's the economy stupid," but charisma matters too: A dual-process model of presidential election outcomes.* Paper presented at the annual meeting of the Academy of Management, Organizational Behavior Division, Montréal, Canada.

Judge, T. A., & Bono, J. E. (2000). Five-factor model of personality and transformational leadership. *Journal of Applied Psychology, 85,* 751–765.

Judge, T. A., & Piccolo, R. F. (2004). Transformational and transactional leadership: A meta-analytic test of their relative validity. *Journal of Applied Psychology, 89,* 755–768.

Judge, T. A., Piccolo, R. F., & Ilies, R. (2004). The forgotten ones? The validity of consideration and initiating structure in leadership research. *Journal of Applied Psychology, 89,* 36–51.

Kark, R., Shamir, B., & Chen, G. (2003). The two faces of transformational leadership: Empowerment and dependency. *Journal of Applied Psychology, 88,* 246–255.

Keller, R. T. (1992). Transformational leadership and the performance of research-and-development project groups. *Journal of Management, 18,* 489–501.

Kennedy, P. (2003). *A guide to econometrics* (5th ed.). Cambridge, MA: MIT Press.

Koene, B. A. S., Vogelaar, A. L. W., & Soeters, J. L. (2002). Leadership effects on organizational climate and financial performance: Local leadership effect in chain organizations. *The Leadership Quarterly, 13,* 193–215.

Kouzes, J. M., & Posner, B. Z. (1987). *The leadership challenge: How to get extraordinary things done in organizations.* San Francisco: Jossey-Bass.

Landauer, T. K. (1999). Latent semantic analysis: A theory of the psychology of language and mind. *Discourse Processes, 27,* 303–310.

Landauer, T. K., Foltz, P. W., & Laham, D. (1998). An introduction to latent semantic analysis. *Discourse Processes, 25,* 259–284.

Landauer, T. K., Laham, D., & Derr, M. (2004). From paragraph to graph: Latent semantic analysis for information visualization. *Proceedings of the National Academy of Sciences of the United States of America, 101,* 5214–5219.

Levitt, S. D. (1997). Using electoral cycles in police hiring to estimate the effects of police on crime. *American Economic Review, 87,* 270–290.

Levitt, S. D. (2002). Using electoral cycles in police hiring to estimate the effects of police on crime: Reply. *American Economic Review, 92,* 1244–1250.

Liden, R. C., & Antonakis, J. (2009). Considering context in psychological leadership research. *Human Relations, 62,* 1587–1605.

Lim, B. C., & Ployhart, R. E. (2004). Transformational leadership: Relations to the five-factor model and team performance in typical and maximum contexts. *Journal of Applied Psychology, 89,* 610–621.

Lord, R. G., Binning, J. F., Rush, M. C., & Thomas, J. C. (1978). The effect of performance cues and leader behavior on questionnaire ratings of leadership behavior. *Organizational Behavior and Human Performance, 21,* 27–39.

Lowe, K. B., & Gardner, W. L. (2000). Ten years of *The Leadership Quarterly*: Contributions and challenges for the future. *The Leadership Quarterly, 11,* 459–514.

Lowe, K. B., Kroeck, K. G., & Sivasubramaniam, N. (1996). Effectiveness correlates of transformational and transactional leadership: A meta-analytic review of the MLQ literature. *The Leadership Quarterly, 7,* 385–425.

McClelland, D. C. (1975). *Power: The inner experience.* New York: Irvington, distributed by Halsted Press.

McClelland, D. C. (1985). *How motives interact with values and skills to determine what people do.* Glenview, IL: Scott, Foresman.

Miner, J. B. (1975). The uncertain future of the leadership concept. An overview. In J. G. Hunt & L. L. Larson (Eds.), *Leadership frontiers* (pp. 197–208). Kent, OH: Kent State University Press.

Mio, J. S. (1997). Metaphor and politics. *Metaphor and Symbol, 12,* 113–133.

Mio, J. S., Riggio, R. E., Levin, S., & Reese, R. (2005). Presidential leadership and charisma: The effects of metaphor. *The Leadership Quarterly, 16,* 287–294.

Muthén, B. O. (1989). Latent variable modeling in heterogenous populations. *Psychometrika, 54*, 557–585.

Plato (trans. 1901). *The republic of Plato: An ideal commonwealth* (B. Jowett, Trans., Rev. ed.). New York: Colonial Press.

Podsakoff, P. M., Bommer, W. H., Podsakoff, N. P., & MacKenzie, S. B. (2006). Relationships between leader reward and punishment behavior and subordinate attitudes, perceptions, and behaviors: A meta-analytic review of existing and new research. *Organizational Behavior and Human Decision Processes, 99*, 113–142.

Podsakoff, P. M., MacKenzie, S. B., & Bommer, W. H. (1996). Tranformational leader behaviors and substitutes for leadership as determinants of employee satisfaction, commitment, trust, and organizational citizenship behaviors. *Journal of Management, 22*, 259–298.

Podsakoff, P. M., MacKenzie, S. B., Lee, J.-Y., & Podsakoff, N. P. (2003). Common method biases in behavioral research: A critical review of the literature and recommended remedies. *Journal of Applied Psychology, 89*, 879–903.

Podsakoff, P. M., MacKenzie, S. B., Moorman, R. H., & Fetter, R. (1990). Transformational leader behaviors and their effects on follower's trust in leader, satisfaction, and organizational citizenship behaviors. *The Leadership Quarterly, 1*, 107–142.

Podsakoff, P. M., Todor, W. D., Grover, R. A., & Huber, V. L. (1984). Situational moderators of leader reward and punishment behaviors: Fact or fiction? *Organizational Behavior and Human Performance, 34*, 21–63.

Podsakoff, P. M., Todor, W. D., & Skov, R. (1982). Effects of leader contingent and noncontingent reward and punishment behaviors on subordinate performance and satisfaction. *Academy of Management Journal, 25*, 810–821.

Rafferty, A. E., & Griffin, M. A. (2004). Dimensions of transformational leadership: Conceptual and empirical extensions. *The Leadership Quarterly, 15*, 329–354.

Rowold, J., & Heinitz, K. (2007). Transformational and charismatic leadership: Assessing the convergent, divergent and criterion validity of the MLQ and the CKS. *The Leadership Quarterly, 18*, 121–133.

Rush, M. C., Thomas, J. C., & Lord, R. G. (1977). Implicit leadership theory: A potential threat to the internal validity of leader behavior questionnaires. *Organizational Behavior and Human Performance, 20*, 93–110.

Sashkin, M. (1988). The visionary leader. In J. A. Conger & R. N. Kanungo (Eds.), *Charismatic leadership: The elusive factor in organizational effectiveness* (pp. 122–160). San Francisco: Jossey-Bass.

Schriesheim, C. A., House, R. J., & Kerr, S. (1976). Leader initiating structure: A reconciliation of discrepant research results and some empirical tests. *Organizational Behavior and Human Performance, 15*, 297–321.

Seltzer, J., & Bass, B. M. (1990). Transformational leadership: Beyond initiation and consideration. *Journal of Management, 16*, 693–703.

Shamir, B. (1995). Social distance and charisma: Theoretical notes and an exploratory study. *The Leadership Quarterly, 6*, 19–47.

Shamir, B., Arthur, M. B., & House, R. J. (1994). The rhetoric of charismatic leadership: A theoretical extenson, a case study, and implications for research. *The Leadership Quarterly, 5*, 25–42.

Shamir, B., House, R. J., & Arthur, M. B. (1993). The motivational effects of charismatic leadership: A self-concept based theory. *Organization Science, 4*, 577–594.

Shils, E. (1965). Charisma, order, and status. *American Sociological Review, 30,* 199–213.

Sorci, M., Antonini, G., Cruz, J., Robin, T., Bierlaire, M., & Thiran, J. P. (2010). Modelling human perception of static facial expressions. *Image and Vision Computing, 28,* 790–806.

Spector, P. E. (2006). Method variance in organizational research: Truth or urban legend? *Organizational Research Methods, 9,* 221–232.

Stogdill, R. M. (1963). *Manual for the Leader Behavior Description Questionnaire.* Columbus: Ohio State University Bureau of Business Research.

Stogdill, R. M., & Coons, A. E. (Eds.). (1957). *Leader behavior: Its description and measurement* (Research Monograph No. 88). Columbus: Ohio State University Bureau of Business Research.

Towler, A. J. (2003). Effects of charismatic influence training on attitudes, behavior, and performance. *Personnel Psychology, 56,* 363—381.

Turner, N., Barling, J., Epitropaki, O., Butcher, V., & Milner, C. (2002). Transformational leadership and moral reasoning, *Journal of Applied Psychology, 2,* 304–311.

Waldman, D. A., Bass, B. M., & Yammarino, F. J. (1990). Adding to contingent reward behavior: The augmenting effect of charismatic leadership. *Group & Organization Studies, 15,* 381–394.

Waldman, D. A., & Yammarino, F. J. (1999). CEO charismatic leadership: Levels-of-management and levels-of-analysis effects. *Academy of Management Review, 24,* 266–285.

Wasielewski. (1985). The emotional basis of charisma. *Symbolic Interaction, 8,* 207–222.

Weber, M. (1947). *The theory of social and economic organization* (T. Parsons, Trans.). New York: Free Press.

Weber, M. (1968). *Max Weber on charisma and institutional building* (S. N. Eisenstadt, Ed.). Chicago: The University of Chicago Press.

Westley, F. R., & Mintzberg, H. (1988). Profiles of strategic vision: Levesque and Iacocca. In J. A. Conger & R. N. Kanungo (Eds.), *Charismatic leadership: The elusive factor in organizational effectiveness* (pp. 161–212). San Francisco: Jossey-Bass.

Willner, A. R. (1984). *The spellbinders: Charismatic political leadership.* New Haven, CT: Yale University Press.

Yammarino, F. J., & Bass, B. M. (1990). Transformational leadership and multiple levels of analysis. *Human Relations, 43,* 975–995.

Yukl, G. A. (1998). *Leadership in organizations* (4th ed.). Englewood Cliffs, NJ: Prentice Hall.

Yukl, G. A. (1999). An evaluation of conceptual weaknesses in transformational and charismatic leadership theories. *The Leadership Quarterly, 10,* 285–305.

Zaccaro, S. J., Kemp, C., & Bader, P. (2004). Leader traits and attributes. In J. Antonakis, A. T. Cianciolo, & R. J. Sternberg (Eds.), *The nature of leadership* (pp. 101–124). Thousand Oaks, CA: Sage.

9

The Nature of Relational Leadership

A Multitheoretical Lens on Leadership Relationships and Processes

Virtually every study of human happiness reveals that satisfying close relationships constitute the very best thing in life; there is nothing people consider more meaningful and essential to their mental and physical well-being than their close relationships with other people.

AUTHORS' NOTE: Please address correspondence concerning this chapter to Mary Uhl-Bien, Department of Management, College of Business, University of Nebraska, P.O. Box 880491, Lincoln, NE 68588–0491, USA. Phone: 402–472–2314; e-mail: mbien2@unl.edu.

The suspicion is growing that our understanding of many social phenomena not only is incomplete but actually may be misleading in terms of its generalizability to behavior in the very situations to which we wish to predict: to naturalistic situations where people are almost always enmeshed in a web of ongoing relationships with others. The suspicion . . . is that the omnipresent relationship context of human behavior makes a difference—that the properties of individuals do not exert simple and sovereign effects independent of context and that, in fact, the influence of the relationship context on behavior is often so powerful that it overturns what we think we know about behavior.

The opening quotes are from Ellen Berscheid's (1999) article in *American Psychologist* based on her acceptance speech for the Distinguished Scientific Contribution Award from the American Psychological Association. Berscheid, who spent her career studying interpersonal relationships, reflects her sense of excitement regarding the significance and meaning of relationships in human life—combined with a sense of dismay that research on relationships is largely missing the mark in terms of generalizability. This dismay comes from the individualistic orientation that has pervaded the fields of psychology and social psychology. As she describes, the "individualistic soul of our discipline" has generated a body of work that tells us little about how relationships operate in context (p. 265).

She is not alone in this sentiment. In her book *Organizing Relationships*, Patricia Sias (2009) describes the study of work relationships as limited by its uni-theoretical positioning in a postpositivist paradigm. As described by Sias (2009), postpositivism is an approach to research in which assumptions are rooted in the scientific method; it is primarily concerned with the search for causal relationships among variables in ways that assume ability to predict and control our environments. In relational research, the effect of postpositivist approaches is that they have primarily focused on identifying relationships among variables to predict effectiveness in specific contexts, rather than adopting lenses that allow for consideration of relational dynamics, contexts, and processes (Sias, 2009). "Relying on a single theoretical lens and conceptualization of a subject narrows our vision . . . much like using only a zoom lens on a camera limits our view . . . by focusing on only one aspect of [a] subject" (p. 2). To begin to redress this problem, in her treatment of workplace relationships, she considers not only postpositivism but also perspectives from social constructionism (Berger & Luckmann, 1966; Fairhurst & Grant, 2010), critical theory (Deetz, 2005), and structuration theory (Giddens, 1984).

Similar sentiments were expressed by Dian Marie Hosking, in her calls for paradigm diversity and a *"post-modern discourse of leadership as a process"* (2007, p. 243), and Gail Fairhurst (2007), who renounced the overriding concern in leadership for the individual and the psychological at the expense of the social and cultural. As described by Fairhurst, "both sets of concerns [individual/psychological and social/cultural] must be entertained in equal strengths in order to understand a socially constructed world" (p. viii). Fairhurst offers discursive leadership—the study of the social, linguistic, and cultural aspects of leadership—as a way to help shed light on what leadership psychologists see as the "elusive, unwieldy, mutable, and maddening error variance in leadership" (2007, p. ix).

The issue can be summarized as follows: We are fascinated by relationships because they are central to social and organizational life. However, studying them requires multiple and interconnected frameworks that can together provide a rich and complex context for understanding relational reality. By restricting the study of relationships to individualistic ontologies and epistemologies, we are limiting our ability to advance understanding of the interactional and relational contexts, processes, and collective practices through which relationships operate. As a result, the leadership and workplace relationship literature is comparatively underdeveloped (Sias, 2009; Uhl-Bien, 2006). It can be enriched by adopting theoretical lenses and methodologies that acknowledge relationality—the interrelated, interdependent, and intersubjective nature of social/organizational phenomena (Bradbury & Lichtenstein, 2000).

This is not to say that we do not have an extensive body of evidence. Manager–subordinate relationships are one of the most studied phenomena in the organizational literature (Sias, 2009). We know a lot about them from the standpoint of leader–member exchange (LMX) theory, more specifically, and leadership theory more broadly. What we know from this literature is that when managers and subordinates have good, trusting, open, and supportive relationships, they report more positive attitudinal and behavioral outcomes, and workplace and leadership dynamics are more effective. In other words, when people report "feeling good" about one another, they also report more satisfaction and productivity in the workplace.

What we know less about are the intricacies of these relationships and relational processes. The vast majority of research on leader–member exchange is cross-sectional and survey based. Most LMX research is based on a 7- or 12-item measure (Graen & Uhl-Bien, 1995; Liden & Maslyn, 1998) that predefines the topics to be addressed, restricting people's ability to tell us more about the nature of the exchanges. These measures assess individual perceptions and cognitions, "tunnel[ing] into the minds of individuals" (Berscheid, 1999, p. 262), rather than informing us about the relational interaction patterns in which relationships and leadership are constructed (Fairhurst, 2007; Fairhurst & Grant, 2010). Moreover, this work has missed discussion of the local-cultural-historical contexts and processes in which leadership relationships function (Berscheid, 1999; Hosking, 2007). In sum, although we know a lot about how people respond to a measure of LMX quality, we know much less about relational leadership processes and practices in the workplace.

The differences can be described as the distinction between positivistic, or *postpositive* (Sias, 2009), and *constructionist* orientations in research. Postpositive approaches assume there is a reality (i.e., a "realist" view) of which people are conscious, and that people act on this reality as self-contained individuals. Postpositivists believe individuals develop accurate mental images and understandings of the world, and by studying these understandings, we can identify the "laws" of human behavior (Cunliffe, 2008). Accordingly, good knowledge is that which "accurately and objectively captures and represents the processes, systems and laws underlying the way the world works, which, when theorized and/or modeled, can be used to improve the way things are done" (Cunliffe, 2008, p. 123). Therefore, these approaches focus on "entities"—individuals and their traits, roles, identities, individual communication abilities—using primarily survey research and psychometrically established measures of variables that they test in statistical (e.g., regression) modeling.

Constructionism assumes that social reality is not separate from individuals but that both are intimately interwoven and shaped by each other in everyday interactions (Cunliffe, 2008). From this perspective, knowledge is socially constructed: Social reality, identities, and knowledge are culturally, socially, historically, and linguistically influenced. As a result, these approaches focus on intersubjective social reality. They use methods such as narrative inquiry (Ospina & Foldy, 2010; Ospina & Su, 2009), semiotics, discourse analysis, conversation analysis (Fairhurst, 2007), documentary and oral history (Gronn, 1999), social poetics, autoethnography, and ethnography (Tierney, 1987, 1988).

Each has its strengths and weaknesses (Fairhurst, 2007; Sias, 2009), and neither can claim superiority. What can be claimed, however, is that effective study of relational leadership requires *both* lenses (Fairhurst, 2007; Hosking, 2007; Uhl-Bien, 2006). Postpositive perspectives help us learn about the "what" of relational leadership; constructionism helps us learn about the "how."

In this spirit, this chapter adopts a multiple-theory lens to relational leadership. We draw from findings regarding relationships across a variety of literature and perspectives to provide a review of relational leadership from the standpoint of leader–follower relationships (e.g., leader–follower relationship quality) and leadership relationality (e.g., relational leadership processes and practices). The former represents the postpositivist perspective, and the latter the constructionist view.

We begin by discussing relational leadership at the dyadic level and from a postpositivist perspective, addressing leader–member exchange (LMX) and Hollander's relational leadership research (Hollander, 2009). LMX focuses primarily on leadership in manager–subordinate dyads, though it has implications and applications for other relational dyads (e.g., coworker exchange, or CWX, Sherony & Green, 2002; LMX social comparison, Vidyarthi, Liden, Anand, Erdogan, & Ghosh, 2010) and networks (Sparrowe & Liden, 2005). Hollander's relational research began with the idiosyncrasy credit model (Hollander, 1958, 1960), and has more recently evolved into a framework for "inclusive leadership" (Hollander, 2009). Because much has been written about both of these approaches, and excellent and detailed reviews are available elsewhere (Anand, Hu, Liden, & Vidyarthi, 2011; Graen & Uhl-Bien, 1995; Hollander, 2009; Liden, Sparrowe, & Wayne, 1997; Stone & Cooper, 2009), our focus here is on the antecedents of leader–follower relationships and stages of relationship development to identify what they can tell us about relational processes and contexts. In our discussion, we pay attention to views from both sides of the dyad—leader and follower—and consider relationships that develop both well (high-quality relationships) and poorly (low-quality relationships).

We then address leadership relationships from a constructionist perspective. Social construction approaches focus on *relationality,* or leadership as it is constructed "in relation." From this perspective, leadership relationships are emergent and co-constructed in interactive dynamics. They get at what Berscheid (1999) describes as the *dynamic oscillating rhythm of influence and interaction patterns observed in the interactions of people.* In this section, we focus on leadership processes and practices at dyadic and collective levels and discuss how these approaches differ from postpositivist orientations. We describe how constructionist approaches are theorized and operationalized and what we can learn from research using this approach. Given that this area of relational leadership research is emerging compared to the postpositivist paradigm, this portion of the chapter is less a review and more a discussion of how these perspectives can enrich relational leadership research.

We conclude by providing a suggested research agenda that adopts a multitheoretical perspective. This agenda recognizes the value that multiple perspectives can bring to the study of relational leadership. It challenges researchers to move beyond studies showing the benefits of high-quality relationships to begin exploring in earnest how relationships emerge and function in organizations and how they engage the processes of relational organizing in the workplace.

Leader–Follower Relationships: Postpositive View

For decades, the study of leadership relationships and relationship development in organizations has focused on the nature of exchanges between formal leaders (i.e., managers) and their followers (i.e., subordinates), with leader–member exchange being one of the most studied relationship-oriented theories. Initially proposed in the mid-1970s (Dansereau, Graen, & Haga, 1975; Graen, 1976; Graen & Cashman, 1975), LMX draws from role theory (Katz & Kahn, 1978) and social exchange theory (Blau, 1964) as explanatory mechanisms for the development and maintenance of dyadic leader–follower relationships. Research has shown extensive support for the basic premise that leaders differentiate in the quality and nature of their relationships with immediate followers and that such differentiation is associated with numerous important outcomes for both members of the relationship dyad and their organizations (Gerstner & Day, 1997; Ilies, Nahrgang, & Morgeson, 2007).

Relational leadership at the dyadic level has also been extensively studied by Hollander, first with the idiosyncrasy credit model (1958, 1960, 2006) and more recently with his work on inclusive leadership (2009). Inclusive leadership advocates the importance of departing from the long-standing focus on the leader to recognize the relational context in which leadership occurs (Hollander, 2009). It is an interpersonal process in which leaders provide resources in terms of "adequate role behavior" directed toward group goal attainment, and followers determine whether leaders are accorded legitimacy to lead through their provision to the leader of status, recognition, and esteem (Hollander & Julian, 1969). As such, followers are vital in this process—"an active role of followers is essential for attaining group, organizational, and societal goals" (Hollander, 2009, p. 4)—and leaders engage inclusive process by building and bolstering leadership practices through climates that encourage loyalty and trust.

Relationship Quality

The primary interest of both approaches is in high-quality relationships, where high-quality relationships are characterized by mutual trust and support. Factors associated with high-quality LMX relationships are increased communication between members, higher levels of dyadic loyalty and trust, higher levels of subordinate in-role and extra-role behavior, and more positive job attitudes (Dienesch & Liden, 1986; Gerstner & Day, 1997; Liden et al., 1997). Dimensions associated with effective relational processes in Hollander's model are respect, recognition, responsiveness, and responsibility (Hollander, 2009). Extensive research has confirmed the value of such relationships in the workplace, with the positive benefits of high LMX and inclusive leadership one of the most robust findings in leadership research.

Both approaches also recognize the limits and problems of low-quality relational exchanges. In LMX, lower quality relationships are characterized by more traditional supervision, lower levels of interaction, and reduced trust and support (Dansereau et al., 1975; Graen & Cashman, 1975; Ilies et al., 2007; Uhl-Bien, Graen, & Scandura, 2000). In Hollander's approach, low-quality (ineffective) leadership occurs when followers withhold attributions of leadership (e.g., status, esteem, recognition), thereby inhibiting leaders' ability to accomplish goals. Although research on low-quality exchanges lags behind investigation of the positive aspects of relationships, recent LMX research suggests that lower quality relationships have important consequences for both managers and their followers (Bolino & Turnley, 2009; Henderson, Wayne, Shore, Bommer, & Tetrick, 2008; Uhl-Bien & Maslyn, 2003; Vidyarthi et al., 2010).

For example, in their study of forms of reciprocity, Uhl-Bien and Maslyn (2003) found that negative reciprocity by followers was associated with lower performance ratings from managers. Bolino and Turnley (2009) argued that employees with lower quality LMX exchange relationships experience feelings of relative deprivation in comparison to their higher quality relationship colleagues, with attendant negative reactions such as stress and counterproductive work behavior. Consistent with this, Henderson et al. (2008) coined the term RLMX (relative leader–member exchange) to describe and test the importance of relationship quality in relative terms, and Vidyarthi et al. (2010) similarly examined LMX as a social comparison (LMXSC). Each of these studies found negative outcomes of poor relationship quality, even when low quality was defined only in relation to others in the work group.

Relationship Development

Although discussed and examined since the inception of the theory, research has been less successful in enhancing the details in our understanding of how these high- and low-quality relationships develop; the majority of research on antecedents has been cross-sectional, providing valuable but limited insight into the development process. One reason for this is the relative difficulty in capturing relationships as they develop, as it requires both longitudinal research and the availability of newly formed dyad pairs.

However, we can glean some insight regarding the nature of factors that contribute to relationship development from the few longitudinal studies that have investigated developing relationships. Liden, Wayne and Stilwell (1993) found that supervisors' and subordinates' expectations of the other's work competence and the degree of similarity between leader and member were significant predictors of LMX at both the initial stages of the relationship and in subsequent weeks. Additionally, liking and perceived similarity predicted LMX, although demographic similarity did not. Just as noteworthy, Liden et al. (1993) concluded that relationships tend to form relatively quickly (within a few days) and remain stable over time.

Similarly, Nahrgang, Morgeson, and Ilies (2009) focused on the development and maintenance of high-quality relationships. They proposed a two-phase process: (1) initial development based on personality that impacts initiation and interaction (exchange) and (2) performance as an outgrowth and extension of initial phases of development. A key finding of their study is that after the initial interaction, performance is a key predictor of quality. In other words, they found support for an approach consistent with the prior models of LMX development: Certain characteristics promote initiation, followed by actions that enable and reinforce development.

Below we examine more closely the recent research on antecedents and development of dyadic leadership relationships with an eye toward identifying patterns in the literature relative to the basic processes outlined by the theory. We do not intend our discussion to be an exhaustive review, but a basis for areas for future study—the "what's missing"—to develop a broader understanding of the processes of relational leadership. We begin with discussion of the stage models of relationship development and then review research on antecedents to leader–follower relationship quality.

Stage models of relationship development. Based on role theory (Katz & Kahn, 1978), LMX relationships are proposed to develop through a process of role-making, role-taking, and role routinization behaviors exhibited by both supervisor and subordinate in the early stages of their relationship (Graen, 1976; Graen & Cashman, 1975; Graen & Scandura, 1987; Uhl-Bien et al., 2000). Specifically, roles are established through a process that involves the interaction and performance of leaders and their subordinates. During role clarification episodes, leaders provide subordinates with an opportunity to perform an assigned task. The leader evaluates each subordinate's performance on these tasks and determines whether or not future opportunities will be offered. Subordinates whose performance impresses the leader begin to develop an exchange with the leader that is of higher "quality" than subordinates who have either resisted or not performed as well according to the leader. The exchange is developed and maintained over time through a process of reciprocal reinforcement, inasmuch as each rewarding contribution by one member (e.g., good performance) tends to result in a positive contribution (e.g., favorable task assignment) by the other (Graen & Cashman, 1975).

In an expansion of this model, Liden and colleagues (Dienesch & Liden, 1986; Liden et al., 1997) describe leader–member relationship development as a series of steps that begins with the initial interaction between the members of the dyad, followed by a series of exchanges in which individuals determine the extent to which a positive or beneficial relationship may develop. These exchanges are not limited to job task and performance but may include socially based currencies of exchange as well. If receipt of one member's offer or opportunity is positive and the party initiating the exchange is satisfied with the response, the individuals continue to exchange. If the response to an exchange is not positive (e.g., not reciprocated, or fails to meet the expectations of the member), or if exchanges never occur, opportunities to develop high-quality exchanges are limited, and relationships will likely remain at lower levels of LMX development (Blau, 1964; Dienesch & Liden, 1986).

To facilitate the exchange, members must have valued resources to offer one another. If a leader's resources for exchange are limited, including the amount of time available to develop and maintain high-quality relationships, high levels of exchange tend to be focused on a limited number of supervisor-subordinate dyads (Dienesch & Liden, 1986; Graen, 1976). Additionally, dyad members must perceive effort exerted toward relationship development on the part of the potential partner, either in terms of initiation (i.e., a first step) or reciprocation (i.e., response to offers) for relationship development to proceed (Maslyn & Uhl-Bien, 2001).

The initiation/reciprocation of valued currencies of exchange process continues to serve as the foundation of LMX development research. In their multidimensional model of work relationships, Ferris et al. (2009) provide an updated description of the relationship development process. Though not all members will proceed through all stages, these authors identify a four-step process: initial interaction, development and expansion of roles, expansion and commitment, and increased interpersonal commitment. They further note that factors such as prior history between the parties, other information or reputation, as well as the personal characteristics, backgrounds, experiences, and styles of each member has the potential to impact relationship development. Although recent literature on LMX development has not been as broad as described in the Ferris et al. model, it has generally supported this process while drawing heavily from the early theoretical work (e.g., Dienesch & Liden, 1986; Graen & Scandura, 1987). For example, Nahrgang et al. (2009) classified factors associated with relationship development into two broad categories: variables such as personality characteristics that affect initial interaction and behavioral influences such as testing processes that follow initial interaction.

From an alternative theoretical perspective, Hollander (2009) describes leadership relationship development from the standpoint of inclusive leadership (Hollander, 2009). Consistent with LMX approaches, an inclusive leadership process is one in which both dyad members are truly involved, acting as partners making inputs to the process based on persuasion rather than coercion. The paramount values of inclusive leadership are respecting and involving others, with listening. The process starts with respect for others, recognition of their input, and responsiveness to the other. Central to this process is responsibility in both directions, which acts as an enduring basis for leader–follower relations and which engenders approval among dyad partners (Hollander, 2009).

Effort and reciprocity. As identified in the LMX literature, a key element of relationship development testing processes is assessments of both effort and reciprocity (Uhl-Bien et al., 2000). The assumption is that exchanges are based on effort exerted by the parties to the relationship (e.g., individuals exert effort to initiate exchanges, reciprocate exchanges). In support of this, Maslyn and Uhl-Bien (2001) found that when each member of an LMX dyad perceived that the potential dyad partner was making an effort, higher quality relationship resulted.

Dienesch and Liden (1986) describe the process of reciprocation as contingent on attributions regarding the responses to offers made by the other member of the dyad. Recent study in this area has laid the groundwork for research into motivation for or the enabling of reciprocity. The accuracy of one's attributions and the perceived intentions of the actors have been shown to impact the exchange process (Harvey, Martinko, & Douglas, 2006; Lam, Huang, & Snape, 2007). For example, as discussed above, certain behaviors or subordinate characteristics can reflect expected value or competence, thus contributing to the desire to engage in relationship development. Feedback seeking by subordinates is one of these behaviors (Ashford & Cummings, 1983). However, attributions regarding the intentions behind feedback seeking have been shown to moderate the relationship between feedback seeking behavior and LMX quality, such that if managers interpreted the subordinate's feedback-seeking as a step toward subordinate performance enhancement rather than impression management, LMX quality was higher (Lam et al., 2007).

Attribution processes also play a central role in the idiosyncrasy credit model of relational leadership (Hollander, 1958, 1960, 2006). This model describes a dynamic process of interpersonal evaluation in which followers, not leaders, determine the effects of leader authority (Hollander, 2009). This process is based on attributions made by individuals about the influence source (i.e., leader). It begins by followers attributing credits to leaders based on perceptions of important characteristics, such as competence (e.g., a needed knowledge or skill), conformity to group norms, favorable reputation, or high status (e.g., group status, socioeconomic status). Leaders can then draw on these credits to take innovative actions (e.g., lead change) in accordance with their leader role. Leaders continue to have authority and influence as long as they do not "bankrupt" their account. If credits are low, leaders must work to rebuild them before they can begin expending again. Hence, in the idiosyncrasy credit model, relationships operate through the building and expending of "credits" that come from attributions of leaders by followers (cf. reciprocity processes in social exchange, Blau, 1964).

Once attributions of leadership are made, a number of factors have been found to enable or facilitate the process of exchange. In many cases, the same variables that lead to initiation of exchange serve also in the facilitating function. For example, similarity builds affect, eases communication, and increases interaction between the parties (Bhal, Ansari, & Aafaqi, 2007; Goodwin, Bowler, & Whittington, 2009; Liden et al., 1993). Personality characteristics such as the subordinate's agreeableness are helpful in making subordinates easy to approach by managers (Bernerth, Armenakis, Feild, Giles, & Walker, 2008). Goal interdependence and congruence, particularly cooperative goals, also positively influence interaction and resulting LMX quality (Hui, Law, Chen, & Tjosvold, 2008).

Uhl-Bien (2003) notes that some relationships are easier to develop than others (i.e., the conditions are favorable), saying people sometimes just "hit it off" with others. From this perspective, the higher the relationship favorability the easier it is for a high-quality relationship. Factors such as dissimilarity between manager and subordinate can be overcome, but it will require extra effort. The skills needed to do this include an understanding of the testing/reciprocity process, self-presentation, and communication.

Factors that enable the reciprocity process, even in light of possible barriers to initiation or interaction, have also been the subject of recent study. Masterson, Lewis, Goldman, and Taylor (2000) studied judgments of fairness as a mechanism that helps engage the norm of reciprocity and found that LMX mediated the effects of interactional justice on subordinate outcomes. Drawing from social exchange theory explicitly, Murphy, Wayne, Liden, and Erdogan (2003) proposed and found that perceptions of the manager's interactional justice were positively associated with subordinate reported LMX quality, whereas LMX was negatively associated with social loafing.

Antecedents to Relationship Quality

In addition to the stage models of relationship development, which describe the process of relationship development, research has investigated variables that act as antecedents to LMX quality. These antecedents include factors such as personality of dyad members, political skill, and similarity, or congruence, variables.

Personality. The personality of the members of the exchange has been found to contribute to both the willingness or ability to engage in LMX relationship development generally and the likelihood that effort will be made to establish positive relationships. Early work in this area found support for a positive association between LMX and subordinates' internal locus of control (Kinicki & Vecchio, 1994) and extraversion (Phillips & Bedeian, 1994). Phillips and Bedeian concluded that extraversion might enable subordinates to engage in actions that make their skills obvious to leaders. This is consistent with previous findings showing that higher quality LMX relationships are characterized by more frequent interaction than low-quality relationships (e.g., Graen & Schiemann, 1978; Liden & Graen, 1980).

More recently, certain personality characteristics have been proposed to play a role in motivating LMX development because they are expected to affect interaction between managers and subordinates (Bono & Judge, 2004). That is, some researchers suggest that individuals may have a predisposition to engage in relationship development.

For example, recent research on attachment style, where individuals have a preferred style in the degree and manner in which they develop interpersonal relationships, has been proposed to affect leader–follower relationships (Keller & Cacioppe, 2001; Manning, 2003; Popper, Mayseless, & Castelnovo, 2000). According to Hazan and Shaver (1990), some individuals have an avoidant attachment style and do not look for relationships but rather try to avoid establishing relationships, preferring to work alone. In the workplace, managers with this style are likely to be inattentive, manipulative, and provide little interpersonal support to subordinates (Keller & Cacioppe, 2001). Therefore, managers with this attachment style would not be expected to be willing or able to initiate and maintain high-quality relationships. Conversely, leaders with a secure attachment style feel comfortable about interdependence with others and have been shown to recognize and balance the needs of the parties to the relationship (Hazan & Shaver, 1990). Past research has linked a secure attachment style to relational competence (Manning, 2003) and to transformational leadership behavior, such as individualized consideration and intellectual stimulation (Popper & Mayseless, 2003; Popper et al. 2000).

Ng, Koh, and Goh (2008) proposed that leader propensity toward serving others may also act as an antecedent of LMX. Drawing from social exchange theory, these authors propose that the supportive and developmental behavior associated with a service orientation by leaders will result in higher LMX because attributions of leader's motives are other-serving instead of self-serving, leading subordinates to reciprocate. They developed a construct of leader's motivation to serve, and found it to be positively related to LMX quality. Similar proposals were made by Henderson, Liden, Glibkowski, and Chaudhry (2009) who suggest that transformational and servant leadership approaches will lead managers to engage larger numbers of subordinates in attempts to develop high-quality relationships.

Several other personality characteristics have been found to relate to relationship development. In their review, Liden et al. (1997) related the influence of affectivity, locus of control, and extraversion. This earlier work has been supplemented by research on the Big Five, proposing that higher levels of certain characteristics will be associated with LMX quality. Nahrgang et al. (2009) found support for the agreeableness of the leader and the extraversion of the follower as predictors of interaction and initial judgments. Bernerth, Armenakis, Feild, Giles, and Walker (2007) proposed that each of the Big Five were associated with initiation, attractiveness of the other member, or reciprocity. The mechanism for each dimension was unique. For example, conscientiousness by subordinates is valuable to managers, leading to reciprocation; a manager's conscientiousness will show concern and result in effort put forth toward relationship development; and a subordinate's openness or intellect and curiosity will please managers and yield greater acceptance of various currencies of exchange from the dyad partner. The same mechanism holds for managers.

As noted, Bernerth et al.'s (2007) study includes the personality of the dyad partner as an indicator of potential value of that partner. In Harris, Harris, and Eplion (2007), personality characteristics of locus of control, need for power, and self-esteem were proposed to lead to subordinate behavior valued by managers, thus activating an exchange between parties. Specifically, subordinates with these characteristics are expected to show higher initiative, be more competent and confident, and be more motivated and desirable partners to managers. These propositions were supported (Harris et al., 2007).

Huang, Wright, Chiu, and Wang (2008) followed this line of thinking in their examination of managers' and subordinates' relational schemas about the roles of dyad partners. Their basic premise is that leaders and followers have different schemas that result in expectancies of relationship quality. Usually leaders look for competence (team player, reliability, self-directedness, and commitment to work), and subordinates look for interpersonal elements (mutual understanding, development, friendly attitudes, and manager's ability to influence or inspire the subordinate). Greater matches between the expectancy and the behavior of the partner (e.g., leaders' expectation that the follower will be proactive combined with proactive behavior by follower) were found to facilitate relationship development. The authors suggested that perceptions of matches lead to greater liking (cf. Wayne & Ferris, 1990) and positive evaluation of the dyad partner as elements of initiation and reciprocation. Similar to the mechanisms discussed by Liden et al. (1993) regarding expectations of competence, the personality match and associated need satisfaction are proposed to be the drivers behind LMX development.

Perceptions of relational match are also an important part of the idiosyncrasy credit model (Hollander, 2009). As described earlier, Hollander's model is based on a perceptual process. Evaluations are made based on followers' perceptions regarding the legitimacy of the leader with respect to competence, conformity to group norms, and loyalty (Hollander, 1964). When there is a match, leaders earn credit; when there is a gap, leaders lose credit (Hollander, 2009). In a series of studies examining this process using critical incident techniques, Hollander and colleagues found that respondents were found to distinguish good from bad leaders mostly by relational qualities. The four relational qualities that most frequently differentiated good from bad leadership were perceptiveness, involvement, trustworthiness, and rewardingness (Hollander, 2007).

Finally, although personality is a useful predictor of LMX relationship quality, the perceived value of the relationship has been found to moderate effects of personality. Goodwin et al. (2009) found that LMX quality as reported by managers was based on personality and competence similarity with followers, but only when followers had high advice centrality, meaning they were individuals others go to often for advice. This suggests that similarity is not a straightforward predictor, but its role in relationship development is contingent on other variables.

Political skill. Another factor that helps enable relationship development may be political skill: the ability to understand others at work and to use such knowledge to influence others to enhance one's personal and/or organizational objectives (Ahern, Ferris, Hochwarter, Douglas, & Ammeter, 2004). Ferris et al. (2005) identified four key dimensions to political skill: social astuteness, interpersonal influence, networking ability, and apparent sincerity. In an application of political skill to the development of LMX, Treadway, Breland, Williams, Wang, and Yang (2008) posited that possessing political skill allows dyad members to accurately understand their partners and thus be able to determine if the formation of an LMX relationship is appropriate. Further, leaders with higher political skill will be more likely to instill feelings of affect in followers, which then leads the follower to be motivated and able to engage in LMX development.

Similarly, Brouer, Duke, Treadway, and Ferris (2009) argue that political skill (social astuteness, in particular) increases understanding of the workplace and a need to develop effective work relationships. It increases the ability of potential partners to properly participate in the testing process, including recognition of when supervisors are initiating testing, and the ability to use influence effectively and to adjust behavior accordingly. As such, Brouer et al. (2009) proposed that political skill would help moderate the negative impact of demographic dissimilarity between potential dyad partners. Their study found that subordinates with high political skill established comparable quality relationships regardless of demographic similarity/dissimilarity, although this was not true for those with lower levels of political skill. However, political skill was not important to LMX quality if manager and subordinate were similar. This finding suggests the importance of awareness of the process of development in light of contextual factors that might inhibit initiation of relationship development.

In addition to the elements that help drive the initiation and the reciprocity process, most approaches to LMX development rely on the continued exchange of valued currencies to firmly establish and maintain high-quality relationships. Although often assessed as tangible currencies, such as subordinate work performance (Nahrgang et al., 2009), Ferris et al. (2009) also discussed exchanges in established relationships in terms of less-economic forms of exchange such as trust, respect, affect, and support between parties (expansion of roles). This represents a new view of the relationship as an end in itself, and the willingness to be flexible in one's interactions (expansion and commitment) along with the willing expression of loyalty and commitment and accountability (increased interpersonal commitment). This is consistent with findings from Maslyn and Uhl-Bien (2001) regarding expectations of future effort in relationship development on the part of subordinates. Their findings showed that employees in higher quality relationships report a higher degree of intended future effort to keep up the relationship, whereas those who were less successful in establishing a positive relationship report lower intentions of applying future effort into relationship development.

Congruence. Goodwin et al. (2009) illustrated the important role of similarity or congruence between dyad members, examined in many studies as predictors of LMX. Based on Byrne's (1971) attraction-similarity hypothesis, Liden et al. (1993) showed the importance of perceived similarity between manager and subordinate in LMX development. Subsequent research has worked to identify the extent to which similarity manifests itself in higher quality LMX. Phillips and Bedeian (1994) also tested attitude similarity, along with introversion/extraversion, locus of control, growth need strength, performance, and various demographic measures as predictors of LMX. Results indicated the greatest support for attitude similarity.

Bernerth et al. (2008) extended their previous work with the Big 5 and proposed that congruence of personality dimensions between dyad members will result in higher LMX because compatible members can and will communicate better and be more motivated to work together. They found that the greater the difference between leader and member on the dimensions, the lower the quality of LMX. This was true for each of the Big Five dimensions, except for extraversion. The authors explained that extraverts could engage in relationships with anyone; congruence was not necessary to facilitate the process.

Leader–follower agreement. Despite the depth of study on the process of development, and the consistencies in attributions and behavior proposed to be exhibited by both leader and follower, actual agreement between leaders and followers regarding the quality of their relationship remains generally low (Schriesheim, Neider, & Scandura, 1998; Zhou & Schriesheim, 2009). Gerstner and Day (1997) reported a meta-analytic average correlation of .29, although ranges of .16 to .50 have been reported (Schriesheim et al., 1998).

In this regard, Zhou and Schriesheim (2009) note that "according to Graen and Uhl-Bien (1995) the exchange relationship is a separate entity from the individuals involved in the relationship, and it is objective, not perceptive. Based on these arguments, SLMX and LMX should be seen as two measures of the same construct and one would expect that both reports should converge at least moderately well" (p. 921). Zhou and Schriesheim offer several explanations for the low convergence. These include a lack of measurement invariance or equivalence, different expectations and assumptions regarding effective relationships on the part of leaders and followers, different foci between leaders (task-based) and followers (relationship-based), frequency of interaction, task interdependence between leader and member, and relationship tenure.

Summary

In sum, the groundwork established by Graen and Scandura (1987) and Dienesch and Liden (1986) has served as the template for research into the antecedents and development of LMX relationships. To this day, a process whereby initial offers are made, responses generated, and new relational roles established drives our study of the development of LMX. We have theories about the basis for offers to engage in relationship development, the importance of perceived or expected value in exchanges, and how attributions and reciprocity contribute to development and maintenance of high-quality relationships. We have details about what impacts each of these (e.g., personality, skills) and ways process can overcome barriers to initiation of relationship development.

We also see strong convergence in findings between the LMX and Hollander's idiosyncrasy credit models. These two streams of research developed separately across the same time period, and each has demonstrated the nature and importance of relational exchanges in leadership processes.

Together, they confirm the validity and robustness of a relational approach to leadership. They also lead to the same conclusions: Effective leadership is that in which leaders and followers have strong, partnership relationships. The role of leaders in these processes is to provide environments that are inclusive, trusting, and supportive to followers; the role of the followers is to be active partners in the leadership process.

Relationality in Leadership: Constructionist Views _____

Although LMX and idiosyncrasy credit theorists (Hollander, 2009) have considerably advanced a perspective of leader–follower relationships as the focal point of leadership research, other scholars are calling for a different kind of understanding—a *relational* understanding—of leadership (Hosking, 2007; Uhl-Bien, 2006; Uhl-Bien & Ospina, in press). A relational understanding focuses on the rich interconnections among people acting in contexts that allow leadership to be "co-produced" in "the space between" (Bradbury & Lichtenstein, 2000). Applying such an understanding to the study of relational leadership is consistent with Sias's (2009) call to broaden our theoretical lenses by incorporating perspectives not traditionally considered in relationship research (cf. Fairhurst, 2007).

This view differs from that of LMX in several ways. First, it uses a different theory of knowledge, social constructionism, to consider the meaning of leadership relationships. Constructionist approaches challenge the privileging of a researcher-imposed view of leadership in favor of participants' constructions of the concept (Cunliffe, 2008; Fairhurst & Grant, 2010). Rather than starting with predefined theoretical models and variables, they use methodologies that allow the data to drive the findings. This means they often use approaches that are more qualitative and inductive (Fairhurst, 2007; Ospina & Sorenson, 2006), gathering data that are not variable-based but language-based (e.g., narratives, text, stories, interviews) or observational.

Second, they offer an alternative to the individual and cognitive lens of most psychological approaches to leadership, opting instead for a lens that is more social and cultural. As described by Fairhurst and Grant (2010), constructionism sees leadership as "co-constructed, a product of socio-historical and collective meaning making, and negotiated on an ongoing basis through a complex interplay among leadership actors, be they designated or emergent leaders, managers, and/or followers" (p. 172). Thus, rather than examining the perceptions, cognitions, behavioral intentions, and personality traits of leaders and followers, they investigate the patterns of interaction and communicative processes associated with the creation of leadership (Drath et al., 2008; Hosking, 2007). In this view, understandings and practices of leadership are constructed over time, as individuals interact with one another (Drath, 2001; Ospina & Sorenson, 2006), rather than being embodied in leaders and followers, or being something they "possess."

Third, they use different methodologies, with the biggest difference being their movement away from objectivist scientific inquiry methods of proposition testing. With some exceptions (e.g., Fiol, Harris, & House, 1999, who use content analysis), these studies tend to use qualitative methodologies (Ospina, 2004), such as narrative inquiry (Fairhurst, 2007; Ospina & Foldy, 2010; Ospina & Su, 2009), ethnography (Tierney, 1987, 1988), documentary and oral history (Gronn, 1999), or a combined approach (e.g., phenomenology, grounded theory, and action research in the case of Huxham & Vangen, 2000; narrative, ethnography, and action research in the case of Schall, Ospina, Godsoe, & Dodge, 2004). These methodologies generate data that are more sensitive to context and capture meaning from the inside-out (Evered & Louis, 1981), that is, considering the perspective of the individuals involved and seeing how they relate to the whole (Bryman, Stephens, & à Campo, 1996; Tierney, 1996). Qualitative research addresses questions that cannot be answered by way of quantification and are better off explored with research that is "interpretive, historical, language sensitive, local, open and non-authoritative" (Alvesson 1996, p. 468), so as to capture the multiple levels at which leadership happens, its character dynamic, and its symbolic components (Conger, 1998; Parry, 1998).

Fourth, relational leadership scholars are beginning to shift attention from a single dyad as the point of interest to *fields* of relationships, or structures of relationships within which individuals and groups reside (Hosking, 1997; Ospina & Sorenson, 2006). This moves the focus from the individual to the collective (e.g., the study of leadership practices, shared leadership processes). Leadership is seen as a collective achievement, the result of generative processes of interaction among participants working jointly for a given purpose that requires organizing (Drath, 2001; Drath & Palus, 1994; Hosking, Dachler, & Gergen, 1995; Ospina & Sorenson 2006; Pearce & Conger, 2003). Scholars are adopting this shift, in part, because the individual dimension has been extensively studied while the collective processes have been ignored. However, they also recognize that any type of leadership relationship among individuals cannot be understood in isolation from the organizational and social forces that help to shape it (Fairhurst, 2007; Fletcher, 2004; Hosking, 1997; Osborn, Hunt, & Jauch, 2002; Ospina & Sorenson, 2006; Smircich & Morgan, 1982).

To illustrate the value of constructionist approaches for the study of relational leadership, in the section below we provide additional background on social constructionism and examples of how these approaches are and can be studied in leadership.

Social Construction Approaches to Leadership

As described by Fairhurst and Grant (2010) and Ospina and Sorenson (2006), social constructionism has roots in symbolic interactionism (Mead, 1934) and phenomenology (Schutz, 1970), though its acknowledged origin is

Berger and Luckmann's influential book, *The Social Construction of Reality* (1966; Cunliffe, 2008). Its basic tenet is that people make their cultural and social worlds at the same time as the worlds make them. In social constructionist terms, "taken-for-granted realities are produced from interactions between and among social agents" (Fairhurst & Grant, 2010, p. 174). Reality is not an objectifiable truth waiting to be uncovered through positivistic scientific inquiry; rather, multiple realities compete for the truth, and this is played out as meanings are negotiated, consensus formed, and contestations occur.

Although there are many approaches to studying the social construction of leadership, and the field has grown dramatically during the past 15 years (Fairhurst & Grant, 2010; Ospina & Sorenson, 2006), one distinction that has relevance for our discussion here is the difference in approaches that stress the *construction of social reality* from those approaches that stress the *social construction of reality*:

> The former drives theorizing around the cognitive products of social interaction—constructions of social reality involving categories, implicit theories, attributions, and sense-making accounts—whereas the latter emphasizes sociality or the interactions themselves, be they implicitly, explicitly, or sociohistorically interactional. At a more basic level, the theorizing of cognitive products emphasizes leadership actors' inner motors, whereas the theorizing of sociality focuses on actors as cultural products, among other things (Fairhurst & Grant, 2010, p. 196).

This is a useful distinction in that we can see evidence of each in our literature. The focus on cognitive products from a construction of social reality orientation is seen in the work of Meindl (1993, 1995; Meindl, Erlich, & Dukerich, 1985), Lord's implicit theories (Engle & Lord, 1997; Lord & Brown, 2004), and more recently, in Carsten and colleagues work on the social construction of followership (Carsten, Uhl-Bien, West, Patera, & MacGregor, 2010). We also see attributions and sensemaking in Calder (1977) and Weick (1995). The theorizing on sociality (social construction of reality) can be seen in work of Drath and colleagues (Drath, 2001; Drath et al., 2008), Hosking (Hosking et al., 1995; Hosking & Morley, 1988) and Ospina and colleagues (Foldy, Goldman, & Ospina, 2008; Ospina & Foldy, 2010).

The two differ, however, in their treatment of relationality. The former, with a focus on the individual and perception and cognition, remains more in the "entity" perspective of leadership (Uhl-Bien, 2006). Although it recognizes social reality, it approaches it from the standpoint of how individuals see and interact with that reality. The latter, with its focus on the interaction patterns of social dynamics, brings to the foreground "sociality." In this way, it captures the intersubjective experiences of relationality, as described next.

Relationality in leadership research. Relationality addresses the "space between" people—It assumes that the self and other are not separable but are coevolving in ways that need to be accounted for in organizational research (Bradbury & Lichtenstein, 2000). Consistent with this, in a constructionist theory of knowledge, relationships are not formed from individual minds coming together but the reverse: Individual functioning results from being in relation (Gergen, 2009). Rather than placing primacy on the individual, constructionist theories begin with the social. Constructionist scholars approach leadership not as a phenomenon embodied in persons but as an organizing process grounded in task accomplishment (Fairhurst, 2007). They consider the actual behaviors and interactions of individuals as part of this broader organizing process, where patterned interactions and networks of relationships contribute to define the outcomes. They are interested in illuminating the mechanisms through which leadership emerges or happens within this broader social context. To study this, they use more qualitative (e.g., in-depth interview, participant and unobtrusive observation) or narrative techniques (examination of language, text, or stories) rather than surveys. Moreover, instead of individual perception and cognition, they focus on ontological units that are more consistent with their interest in "sociality," such as intersubjectivity, identities, relationships, cultures and linguistic communities, and organizations as macro-actors (Fairhurst, 2007). For these scholars, the leader–follower relationship is not just (or primarily) an interpersonal relationship, but a *social* relationship, that is, something that carries within it understandings that both parties take for granted and use to inform their interaction and make sense of it.

Through this focus on relationality, constructionism offers to relational leadership a more dynamic view of relational processes and contexts. For example, constructionism offers an alternative to the strict stage models of relationship development processes previously suggested in LMX theory (Graen & Uhl-Bien, 1995; Uhl-Bien et al., 2000):

> The LMX literature assumes that successful relationships progress on a path that is unidirectional and cumulative, moving toward increasing levels of closeness or fusion, and transformation beyond self-interests (Fairhurst, 2001). The three stage process of the leadership-making model (Graen & Uhl-Bien, 1995 . . .) is a case in point. . . . In the leadership-making model, participants progress through an initial "stranger" stage of role-finding, which is formal and contractual. If both want to improve the relationship, they progress to a second, "acquaintance" stage of role-making where there is a lot of secret testing and feeling out of one another. If test results are mutually satisfactory, a select few make it to the "mature partnership" stage where there is an in-kind exchange of resources. . . . Thus, in successful relationships, there is a putatively simple progression to an increasingly close, stable, and mutually satisfying relationship (Fairhurst, 2007, pp. 121–122).

Constructionist approaches do not see relational processes as stable and linear. They view relationships as sensemaking processes involving tension, dynamism, contradiction, and flux. Fairhurst and Hamlett (2004), drawing from work on dialectical communication, discuss how most relationships, even healthy ones, possess tension in the form of dialectical oppositions. These oppositions create simultaneous pulls to fuse with and differentiate from the other: "Relational bonding not only implies fusion, closeness and interdependence, but also separation, distance and independence" (Fairhurst & Hamlett, 2004, p. 123). Similarly, work from team relationships literature shows that relationships are full of paradox that can alternately paralyze and energize those within them (Smith & Berg, 1987).

Constructionist approaches consider relationships as dynamic and interactive contexts and processes of meaning making. In a constructionist view of leadership, meaning is something constructed from the world, not something discovered in the world. Meaning is not simply created in the mind of an individual acting absent context. Instead, it emerges—is constructed—when human beings engage with objects and with other humans in the world. Because people draw from prior agreed-on meanings in their culture, and because culture in turn is historically bounded, constructing meaning can be understood as a social process as much as an individual mental operation (Ospina & Sorenson, 2006).

Thus, rather than viewing relationship as the consequence of independent beings coming together and examining the antecedents that help understand LMX exchanges and relationship quality, constructionist relational researchers focus on relationships as the generative source of leadership. Leadership relationships are not an outcome to be explained or an antecedent of performance (another outcome to be explained; Fairhurst, 2007; Sias, 2009), but they constitute the leadership process itself. Constructionist relational leadership researchers (Hosking, 2007; Ospina & Su, 2009) are interested in understanding the means by which relationships produce a particular type of social experience—that of leadership.

Here the interest falls on the processes that constitute leadership as the outcome of particular types of social relationships and interactions (Uhl-Bien, 2006). This distinction helps to illuminate the shift in interest from explaining the who (leader or follower) to the how (the processes and practices). It focuses on *how* leadership is developed in and emerges from relationships oriented toward organizing purposes. It also shifts the meaning of the "what" of leadership from the leader–follower relationship to the patterns of relations and interactions that produce leadership in a given context.

Constructionist approaches are therefore contextual theories of leadership (Osborn et al., 2002). They shift attention in leadership research from the leader–follower dyadic relationship to the constructs of people in relationship (Gergen, 2009; Ospina & Foldy, 2010), communities of practice (Drath, 2001; Drath & Palus, 1994), and fields or networks of relationships (Fletcher, 2004; Mayo & Pastor, 2007). By focusing on social mechanisms (Davis &

Marquis, 2005; Hedström & Swedberg, 1998), constructionism is interested in finding out the interpretive meaning of patterns (that is, what patterns say about how people understand each other and their lives in relational contexts). They consider that social interactions emerge from repeated contacts among participants engaged in other-regarded behaviors with meaning, purpose, and the expectation of a response by another—and that these social interactions operate in contexts regulated by law, custom, or tradition over time (Ospina & Sorenson, 2006). This perspective, therefore, highlights the collective dimensions of personal experience, without necessarily disregarding its individual dimensions. Because these scholars are more interested in exploring collective rather than individual aspects of leadership, attention shifts from the *interpersonal* nature of dyadic relationships, and the associated behaviors, to the *social* nature of relations, and the associated patterns of interaction and the coproduction of shared assumptions and agreements that support them. This social nature can manifest at the dyadic, group, or collective levels of action.

Collective leadership. This does not dismiss the dyadic dimension of leadership as a relational phenomenon, but it places it within a broader structure of relationships organized for collective purposes. Raelin (2003) clarifies this distinction when he uses the term community to define the "unit that receives or conducts leadership" (p. 11), and defines it as any setting where a group of participants assemble to accomplish joint work, allowing for a variety of settings, from group to organization to system and from private to public sectors. He argues: "The community is a unit in which members already have or may establish human contact with others. In this sense, it is a social structure that extends beyond the self, that links people together for some common purpose" (p. 12). This social structure cannot be ignored when understanding leadership as a collective process.

The foundations for this view have a rich underpinning in leadership scholarship. For example, Burns's seminal work starts with the premise that leadership, like power, is "relational, collective and purposeful" (Burns, 1978, p. 18). Pastor (1998) defines leadership as "a collective social consciousness that emerges in the organization" as individuals interact with one another (p. 5). As this process of social construction goes on, as people develop a shared understanding of the work and the roles assigned to members in pursuing it, leadership takes on an independent life that continues to be enacted over time. In this sense, as it emerges, leadership becomes the property of the social system, rather than being just a shared idea in people's minds, or a quality located in a single individual, the leader.

Although fewer scholars in the organizational behavior and psychology-dominated leadership field have been drawn to the collective approach to relational leadership, scholars in other disciplines and fields have been more enthusiastic. For example, advocating the idea that leadership emerges from the constructions and actions of people in organizations, three decades ago sociologists Smircich and Morgan (1982) invited researchers to look deeper into the collective leadership phenomenon and to "focus on the way meaning in organized settings is created, sustained, and changed [to] provide a powerful means of understanding the fundamental nature of leadership as a social process" (p. 261). In education, Lambert et al. (1995) defined leadership as "the reciprocal process that enables participants in [a] community to construct meanings that lead toward a common purpose" (p. 32). More recently, in management, Fletcher and Kaeufer (2003) highlighted the micro-processes of shared leadership that occur in and through the relational interactions that make up networks of influence in the context of moving organizational agendas. Moreover, Gergen (2009) proposes to focus on the process of "relational leading," which he describes as "the ability of persons *in relationship* to move with engagement and efficacy into the future" (p. 333).

Following this line of thinking, sociological perspectives on constructionism have been helpful in beginning to identify dynamics of structured social relations among group participants engaged in action together (be it in a team, an organization, a network, or a larger system) and to ask in what ways these illuminate how collective leadership happens. Shifting the phenomena one step up the level of analysis, this work focuses analytical attention to enduring and relatively stable patterns of social actions and social interactions (Drath, 2001; Drath et al., 2008). The focus is on exploring the "arenas" where leadership participants interact and relate to pursue a collective purpose (Ospina & Sorenson, 2006).

The work of Ospina and colleagues (Foldy et al., 2008; Ospina & Foldy, 2010; Ospina & Saz-Carranza, 2010; Ospina & Su, 2009) offers an example. Their in-depth, multiyear study examined collective leadership practices in 92 nonprofit organizations working to advance an agenda of social change in the United States during the course of six years. Drawing from a relational constructionist approach, they captured the meaning-making process of social change leaders by engaging them and their constituents in sustained conversations around the work that brought them together (i.e., social change work). Using ethnographic, narrative, and action-based methodologies, they elicited individual and group stories where participants described the work when it was happening at its best. They then triangulated the data gathered with these three methodologies and analyzed the stories interpretively. They identified as the analytical unit the *practices* developed over time and in context. These represented embodiments of the collective understandings of what participants believed they ought to do to attain their social change agendas.

Through multiple iterations of data analysis, three key mechanisms were identified that illuminate how collective leadership happened in these organizations: reframing discourse (Foldy et al., 2008; Ospina & Su, 2009), bridging difference (Ospina & Foldy, 2010; Ospina & Saz-Carranza, 2010), and unleashing human energies (El Hadidy, Ospina, & Hofmann-Pinilla, 2010). These mechanisms help us to understand how leadership emerged in these social change organizations to help participants leverage the power they needed to influence their external targets. In support of a constructionist orientation, the data collected in this research project reveal a worldview composed of implicit assumptions about the nature of power, knowledge, change, humans, and the world, anchored in core values of social justice, which guided decisions and actions. Moreover, the researchers uncovered articulations of the expected outcomes of change, mediated through levers of personal empowerment and organizational capacity development. The recurrent collective leadership practices through which this work was done were in alignment with the group's worldview and visions of the future. They also gave meaning and substance to the technologies of management (strategic planning, budget management, etc.) and to the core tasks of social change (organizing, advocacy, and service delivery) through which these nonprofit organizations became sustainable and resourceful.

Huxham and Vangen (2000) offer another example of research that explores the collective relational perspective based on the social construction of reality. They report that the notion of the "decentering of leadership" in their study of collaboration in service delivery networks was directly inspired by this perspective (in particular by Hosking's conception of leadership as the process in which flexible social order is negotiated, by research about self-managing work teams, and by studies based on cultural perspectives of leadership). Based on a 10-year program of action research with practitioners involved in a number of public and community partnerships in the United Kingdom, and following a phenomenological approach, their goal was to develop practice-oriented theory on the management of collaboration. Using a conception of collective leadership as involving mechanisms that "make things happen" in a collaboration, they identify three media through which agendas are created and driven forward, that is, through which collective leadership happened in these networks: structures (e.g., collaborative governance structures), processes (e.g., committees, workshops, seminars through which the collaboration's communication takes place), and participants (e.g., positional leading roles, such as a steering group, with a chair). They also identify a set of activities that participants used to carry out their collaborative agendas: finding ways to control the collaboration's agenda, representing and mobilizing member organizations, and creating enthusiasm and empowering those who could deliver the collaboration aims.

Summary

In sum, as a developing field, constructionist approaches to leadership offer a rich additional lens for relational leadership theory. They allow us to operationalize studies of leadership from the standpoint of relational and communicative processes in a manner that systematically considers the dynamic and collective dimensions of leadership. By shedding light on the co-constructed relational processes and practices of leadership, they can help add to our current body of knowledge and enrich our understanding of the interactive and interconnected nature of relational leadership.

In our discussion of constructionism, we identify two types of agendas for relational research (though there are clearly many more possibilities). The first is to adopt more constructionist approaches to the study of relationships. Consistent with Berscheid (1999), Fairhurst (2007), and Sias (2009), this means adopting methods and research designs that allow us to better capture the social reality of work relationships. The second is to focus on relational organizing and collective leadership. Consistent with the *social construction of reality*, these approaches emphasize the interactions themselves as well as the shared patterns of meaning-making, conjoint agency, and coordinated behavior through which collective leadership is enacted.

Relational Leadership: A Research Agenda _____

Using the two types of approaches identified above, in this section we focus on outlining an initial research program that addresses the study of relational leadership. Given that clear directions for LMX research are identified elsewhere in the literature, here we describe a research agenda for relational leadership more broadly: We view the study of relational leadership as not just LMX (and its more limited set of measures) but the wider examination of leadership relationships (dyadic and collective) and relational processes (and practices) in organizations that contribute to the generation of leadership. We believe these relationships and processes are so central to the establishment of healthy and effective workplace functioning that studying them warrants a broad, cross-disciplinary and multiple method research program. Moreover, contrary to the "paradigm wars" of the past, we believe relational leadership can be most effectively studied by both paradigms (and many varieties of methods), and that by dialoguing with one another, scholars can advance richer understandings of relational leadership.

We propose a different type of research agenda—one driven not by a measure or a method but by research questions that are pursued across multiple theoretical perspectives. These questions should build on what we have already learned. For example, we could explore questions such as: Do the attributes of effective (and ineffective) leadership relationships vary in the workplace, and how? What is the nature of interactive dynamics in these relationships? How do effective leadership relationships develop, and what inhibits effective leadership relationship development? What are the relational processes that comprise effective collective relational leadership practice? How and why can relational leadership help to address the challenges of organizing in contemporary contexts? Under what conditions, and how, do systems and networks of relations produce different forms of leadership? What leadership practices reflect collective aspirations, and how do they contribute to realize them? To more fully advance understanding,

researchers across perspectives (e.g., psychology, management, communication, sociology, public policy) should engage in dialogue with one
another about what they are uncovering and learning and use these findings to enrich their subsequent research efforts. In the sections below, we
offer an initial outline for such an agenda.

Nature of Relationship

From the review above, we see that effective leadership is that in which
leaders and followers have strong, partnership relationships with one another.
What we know less about, however, is what constitutes these relationships
and how they are developed. Fairhurst and Hamlett (2004), for example,
question the use of a 7- (or 12-) item measure that predefines the components
of a high-quality relationship because it restricts respondents' ability to comment on the nature of this relationship. This issue was also raised more than
a decade ago by House and Aditya (1997), who pointed out that although
LMX theory states that high-quality relationships are characterized by
mutual trust, respect, and loyalty (Graen & Uhl-Bien, 1995), it is not clear
that these are universal attributes of high-quality relationships. "It may well
be that what is considered a high-quality relationship varies among individuals" (House & Aditya, 1997, p. 431). As described by Liden (2007):

> It appears that researchers working within LMX have made the ques-
> tionable assumption that all high (or low) LMX relationships can be
> characterized in the same way. However, I argue that substantial differ-
> ences within each LMX status group may exist. Specifically, the same
> leader may form dramatically different high LMX relationships with a
> corresponding difference in the nature of communications. For example,
> the leader may simply empower and "set loose" one high LMX member,
> whereas with another high LMX member, the leader may provide sub-
> stantial guidance and mentoring. Similarly, communication patterns
> within high LMX may vary considerably. Some may be characterized by
> polite, respectful interactions whereas others may involve off-color jokes
> and teasing. In sum, . . . the psychological approaches need to consider
> the many forms that good (or bad) relationships can take. (p. 179)

Addressing this is difficult if we stick with only survey methods that use
established LMX measures. Given that the basis for this work was established more than three decades ago, it seems fitting that research should again
examine the nature and variety of ways in which leadership relationships can
be of higher and lower quality in the workplace. Constructionist scholars,
and more qualitative and mixed methods approaches, can help in this regard.

For example, Fairhurst (2007) describes how narrative analysis has been,
and can continue to be, helpful in informing such understanding. The use of
interviews gives leadership actors a chance to discursively reflect on their

relational leadership experiences (Fairhurst, 1993; Fairhurst, 2001; Fairhurst & Chandler, 1989; Lee & Jablin, 1995; Sias, 1996). A form of this method was used in early research on LMX, in which stories (qualitative data) were gathered from managers and subordinates about what life was like in the in-group and out-group. It was these stories that then led to initial LMX scale development (Fairhurst, 2007).

A discursive approach can also be found in Prebles (2002), who used a mixed methods design of survey and interviews of leaders and members in a medium-sized manufacturing firm who were asked to report on their LMX relationship. Participants completed the LMX-7, and researchers then used the items as prompts in ensuing interviews to elicit narrative experiences behind the ratings judgment. Findings reveal a variety of ways in which LMX relationships are constructed. Similarly, Fairhurst (2001), examining narrative data, showed that LMX is not just relational but also significantly impacted by cultural forces (i.e., a contextual approach to leadership, Osborn et al., 2002). She suggests that discursive (narrative) approaches can allow us to further enhance understanding of the interactive input of both culture and dyad in relational leadership processes (Fairhurst, 2007).

Although these examples focus primarily on LMX, which has typically been associated with manager–subordinate relationships, leadership relationships do not have to be restricted to managerial dyads (Uhl-Bien et al., 2000). For example, as in the case of informal or shared leadership (Pearce & Conger, 2003), leadership relationships can be with coworkers (Sherony & Green, 2002; Tse, Dasborough, & Ashkanasy, 2008). They can also be mentoring relationships (Scandura & Schriesheim, 1994).

Given that the LMX measure is currently designed to assess a subordinate's view of the relationship, simply mirroring these items for other types of relationships is likely not appropriate. Strict adherence to LMX items as currently defined may lead to skewed understandings of the nature of these relationships (i.e., findings regarding what items ask about rather than what is primarily important in the relationship). When viewed from a manager's (and likely a coworker's) perspective, the characteristics that are important in the relationship are different (Huang et al., 2008; Maslyn, Uhl-Bien, & Mitchell, 2007; Zhou & Schriesheim, 2009). Hence, we need to adopt more thoughtful and open approaches in our studies of leadership relationships.

Relationship Development

Another key challenge in LMX research has been the study of relationship development. Compared to the amount of LMX research overall, the number of studies examining relationship development are extremely limited. Yet one could argue that after identifying the importance of effective relationships—which has by now been clearly established—the major need in relational leadership research is to understand how leadership relationships develop: why some relationships develop well and other relationships develop poorly.

Addressing this question can be accomplished in a variety of ways. This is an area that could benefit greatly from exploratory methods, including qualitative, inductive studies that allow respondents, rather than researchers, to identify the processes and patterns involved in relationship development. As mentioned earlier, relationships often involve dialectical tensions (Fairhurst & Hamlett, 2004), which lend themselves well to discursive techniques (Fairhurst, 2007). An example of a combination of qualitative methods that lend themselves to exploring these processes and patterns of relationship development include narrative analysis of journal entries over time from both participants of the supervisory relationship under study, combined with recurrent in-depth individual and paired interviews where stories associated with critical incidents identified in the journal entries at key developmental moments could be further explored jointly. This could then be complemented with what Gubrium and Holstein (2009) call ongoing "narrative ethnographies," where the researcher uses naturalistic observations as well as ethnomethodological and conversational analytical approaches to capture the everyday narrative activity that unfolds within the situated interaction defining and contextualizing the experience of the study participants.

Developing relationships could also be examined using more quantitative or mixed methods approaches. For example, longitudinal network analysis (Lubbers et al., 2010) offers a potentially rich way to understand individual perceptions of relationship development over time. With longitudinal network analysis, respondents could be given a set of "predictor" measures at Time 1, and then relationship quality measures could be collected during subsequent time periods to identify variables associated with higher and lower quality relationship development. This method could also be combined with experience sampling techniques (Bono, Foldes, Vinson, & Muros, 2007), which would allow respondents to provide narrative descriptors regarding the nature of the relationship as it is developing.

Another promising quantitative approach is growth curve analysis (Day & Sin, in press; Nagin, 1999), which allows for examination of developmental trajectories in relationship development. Rather than assuming that all relationships start at the same level and change in the same way, analyses that combine techniques of random coefficient modeling and growth mixture modeling of longitudinal relationship development data can help uncover differences in developmental paths of relationships over time and identify whether there are patterns among these different types of paths (Day & Sin, in press).

A method that is not so promising is attempts to model dynamic relationship development using longitudinal studies with very limited measures during a couple of time periods. As described by Shamir (in press):

Such studies seldom tell us anything about reciprocal relational processes and dynamics. Even multiwave longitudinal studies are at best a series of time-spaced sequential snapshots, which don't tell us much about *how* the process of leadership unfolds. Similarly, qualitative studies of leadership which are carried out over lengthy periods often do not provide a better understanding of leadership processes because such an understanding is not an automatic result of spending a long time in the field and collecting many interviews and observations (e.g., Maitlis & Lawrence, 2007). It requires deliberate attention to the dynamic, mutual and reciprocal aspects of leadership relations.

Investigation of relational leadership means taking seriously the need to study dynamic processes and identifying approaches to research that truly capture these processes.

Level of Analysis

In a special issue of *The Leadership Quarterly* on levels of analysis, Graen and Uhl-Bien (1995) identified the level of LMX as the dyad. This position has subsequently been criticized, as actual LMX research is primarily conducted at the individual level: LMX research is conducted by asking individuals to report on their perceptions regarding the relationship (i.e., an individual level approach; Schriesheim, Castro, Zhou, & Yammarino, 2001).

This issue of inconsistency between a dyadic theory (Graen & Uhl-Bien, 1995) and an individual level of analysis has been clearly and repeatedly identified in the literature (Dansereau, 1995; Krasikova & LeBreton, 2010; Schriesheim, Castro, & Cogliser, 1999; Schriesheim et al., 2001; Yammarino & Dansereau, 2007). Seers and Chopin (in press) similarly identify the problem: "The entity of primary interest within the LMX approach has been the subordinate role, . . . with less attention to the relationship as an entity." The individual level of analysis can be seen in the lack of congruence between manager and subordinate measures of LMX (Gerstner & Day, 1997; Maslyn et al., 2007), as well as in the work on balance in leader and follower perceptions of LMX (Cogliser, Schriesheim, Scandura, & Gardner, 2009), which shows that individual perceptions of the relationship do not always agree (e.g., an individual, rather than dyadic, level of analysis).

Capturing a dyadic level of analysis is challenging when we consider traditional survey approaches to LMX study. The question is: How can we capture a dyad with a survey? The answer is, we probably cannot; what we capture with surveys is individual perceptions of the relationship. What we can do, however, is try to align our *analyses* with a dyad level (Krasikova & LeBreton, 2010; Schriesheim et al., 2001). For example, Krasikova and LeBreton (2010), drawing from work by Kenny, Kashy, Cook, and colleagues (e.g., Cook & Kenny, 2005; Kenny, Kashy, & Cook, 2006) on dyadic analysis, offer a detailed and thorough explanation of how LMX can be more appropriately analyzed at a dyadic level.

The issue becomes more complicated when we consider that the levels-of-analysis literature has developed in the postpositivist paradigm, and according to Yammarino (2009, 2010), there is no level for dyadic "relationality"

(Bradbury & Lichtenstein, 2000). In the levels literature, the dyad is a combination of individual perceptions; it does not lie *between* individuals, which is the essence of a dyadic phenomenon. As described by Berscheid (1999), however, a relationship does not reside in the individual; it lies in individuals' interactions with one another—in the influence that each person exerts on the other's behavior.

For relationship scholars, the "tissue of a relationship, and the object of study, is the oscillating rhythm of influence observed in the interactions of . . . people. . . . It is displayed . . . in their interaction pattern" (Berscheid, 1999, p. 261). Moreover, this rhythm is revealed only over time, and like other great forces of nature (e.g., gravity, wind, electricity), it is invisible; its existence can only be discerned by observing its effects (Berscheid, 1999). This type of relational thinking—about recurring interconnections between individuals rather than properties within individuals—is foreign to some psychologists, but according to Berscheid (1999), it doesn't have to be:

> Just one example of why it shouldn't is provided by subatomic physics, the exemplar of the study of matter, or of material "things." Physicists long ago were forced to recognize that the properties of isolated material particles are, as Niels Bohr observed, "definable and observable only through their interaction with other systems" (Bohr, 1934, p. 37). As one contemporary physicist elaborated, "Subatomic particles . . . are not 'things' but are interconnections between 'things,' and these 'things' in turn, are interconnections between other 'things,' and so on. In quantum theory you never end up with 'things'; you always deal with interconnections" (Capra, 1982, p. 80). Thus, the growing attempt by the social and behavioral sciences to transcend the study of individuals—our material "things"—to the study of interconnections between individuals, as exemplified by relationship science, is neither without precedent nor revolutionary. (p. 261)

This, again, is where constructionist approaches can be helpful in aligning a relational theory with a *relationality* level of analysis. When constructionists think about studying leadership, they are by the very nature of their ontological and epistemological assumptions thinking about leadership as a social phenomenon and thus will place their interest on its relational and collective (including dyadic) dimensions. Indeed, the comparative advantage of a constructionist approach lies in concentrating on exploring questions associated with relational organizing (e.g., exploring shared patterns of meaning making, conjoint agency, and coordinated behavior through which leadership is enacted). They direct attention to questions about the relational processes that comprise effective, collective, relational leadership practice, that link relational leadership to the challenges of organizing in contemporary contexts, and that illuminate the conditions and mechanisms by which systems and networks of relations produce different forms of leadership in different contexts.

Relational Contexts

Leadership scholars have been concerned with the interconnections between the leadership relationship and the circumstances and conditions where it emerges (Biggart & Hamilton, 1987). Yet context continues to be marginalized or unsuccessfully integrated (Beyer, 1999; Bryman et al., 1996) in leadership studies and remains an "under-researched area" (Porter & McLaughlin, 2006, p. 573). Thinking of context in relational terms offers a novel view, and here, again, constructionism can make an important contribution: Rather than juxtaposing "leadership" and "organizational context" in a foreground-background manner, constructionists understand leadership as a process embedded in the organizational dynamics of which it is a part (Hosking, 1997; Ospina & Hittleman, in press). And these processes are, as Hosking (2007) suggests, always local-cultural and local-historical, "about what works in some 'here and now' performance" (p. 250).

The study of relational leadership means taking seriously the issue of relational context. Returning to the Berscheid (1999) quote at the beginning of the chapter, people are enmeshed in a web of ongoing relationships with others, such that the influence of the relationship context on behavior is often so powerful that it overturns what we think we know about behavior. Studying relational context means findings ways to shine light on the social milieu within which relationships, interactions, and processes are negotiated and constituted.

From a research perspective, these ideas point to the primacy of *local, situated contexts* as the adequate locus for illuminating how and why emergent dynamics and patterns of organizing, embedded in systems and networks of relations, are, or are not, transformed into leadership relationships, processes, and practices. Answering this query empirically is not an easy task and can take different forms, but all choices give primacy to the idea of the situated reality. Examples of constructionist strategies to address this include (a) the detailed investigation of the contextual organizing forces that create functional demands for leadership in an organization and from which leadership processes emerge as an organizational response (Drath, 2001; Drath et al., 2008; Hosking, 1997); (b) the search for leadership practices, that is, the patterned interactions and repeated activities developed over time, which reflect the shared, negotiated assumptions and understandings of what constitutes effective work in a given context, and exploring how these are used to generate collective achievements in that particular context (Foldy et al., 2008; Ospina & Foldy, 2010; Ospina & Saz-Carranza, 2010; Ospina & Su, 2009); and (c) investigating the discursive and communicative patterns official leaders use with followers to negotiate and frame the situation (Fairhurst, 2007; Fairhurst & Grant, 2010).

These research strategies have in common researchers' willingness to stop thinking of context as the background environment where leaders relate to followers, act, and make decisions. Constructionists challenge the notion that context exists prior to leadership or to the leadership relationship, because actions and interactions of social agents are both generative of situated social reality as much as they are influenced by it. People construct and name the emergent space that we call "context," drawing on and negotiating shared agreements as events unfold and as they define the situation to make sense and frame their experience. Precisely because people make sense of the world only through interactions with their environment and others in it, it is the emerging, mutually constituted relationships between leaders, followers, and situation that provide the conditions for leadership to happen. As Hosking has argued, "the study of leadership, properly conceived, is the study of the process in which flexible social order is negotiated and practiced so as to protect and promote the values and interests in which it is grounded" (Hosking, 1997, p. 315). In other words, it is the study of the context within which leadership contributes to negotiate social order in a given setting.

In sum, this conceptualization of relational contexts helps explain why constructionists tend to favor interpretive, narrative-oriented, and inductive studies, where the researcher's interpretations stem from the data, and where the data reflect the interpretations of the actors in relationship, which facilitate theorizing about these intertwined realities. It also points to the benefit of research designs and studies that allow researchers to consider multiple perspectives—perspectives from key organizational actors, in addition to formal leaders, and those whom they supervise—and to ensure multiple entries into the intersubjective experience of organizational life. This exploration can take multiple interpretive methodological pathways, depending on the researcher's interest, theoretical orientation, and specific research questions. Methods include, but are not limited to, narrative studies and discourse analysis; ethnography and its variations (e.g., narrative, critical, participatory ethnography); phenomenological studies; interpretive case studies; action research and its variations (e.g., participatory action research, cooperative inquiry, community-based participatory research); historical and hermeneutical studies; and so on (see Denzin & Lincoln, 2000; Yanow & Schwartz-Shea, 2006). All of these allow the researcher to shift back and forth between the organizational gestalt and particular situations, and from intersubjective experiences to the broader patterns of interaction and networks of relationship that help shape and understand these experiences.

Conclusion

It is an exciting time to be in leadership research. As Hunt and Dodge (2000) predicted, the relational perspective—a view of leadership that goes beyond unidirectional or even reciprocal leader/follower relations to a focus on leadership wherever it occurs, that is not restricted to a single or even small set of formal or informal leaders, and that is a dynamic system embedding leadership, environmental, and organizational aspects—is now the zeitgeist of the times. We see in leadership a movement toward leadership approaches that are shared, distributed, complex, and relational (Bryman, Collinson, Grint, Jackson, & Uhl-Bien, 2011). These all comprise the relational perspective— the *relationality* movement in leadership.

The opportunities for research in this area have never been greater, but they come with challenges. To address these challenges, we need to focus less on why relationships are important and how they are associated with organizational variables (e.g., mediators and moderators), and more on how they emerge and function in organizational contexts. The issue of the importance and value of effective work relationships has been extensively and convincingly established (e.g., LMX, idiosyncrasy credit theory, transformational research, work on trust)—we *know* this. What practitioners want to understand, and what researchers need to investigate, is relational dynamics: relational processes, practices (collective leadership, patterns or social mechanisms of relational organizing), and contexts. These are issues of relationality more than of typologies and frameworks of relationships (e.g., high-, medium-, low-LMX).

If we look at recent writings from the pioneers of relational research (Graen's book series, *LMX Leadership: The Series;* Hollander's 2009 *Inclusive Leadership* book), we can see these issues are clearly recognized. Both Graen and Hollander advocate the need to focus on relational organizing. Hollander's work, as described in this chapter and in his book (2009), even sounds constructionist in its description of how leaders and followers interact with and intersubjectively interrelate with one another. What is holding this work back is the use of lenses that capture only the individual without capturing the relational. As Fairhust and Hamlett (2004) describe:

> Graen (personal communication) has consistently eschewed an individualistic focus calling the path of individualism "a failed paradigm" to draw attention to the inherently social nature of leadership. However, how can such a position be taken seriously when the social is *equated* with the study of individuals and their summary judgments of a relational history captured in seven point scales? (p. 119)

The challenge to relational scholars, as described by Berscheid (1999), is to broaden our paradigms and perspectives to capture relationality:

> The emergence of relationship science represents the flag of a higher truth that has now been planted in the individualistic soul of our discipline. Whether that flag will continue to stand or even someday wave over a new synthesis in psychology depends on whether future generations of scholars can conquer the daunting problems relationship science presents. (p. 265)

To meet these challenges, we are calling for a broad research agenda on relational leadership that is driven by research questions rather than methods. The intent is to stimulate a multitheoretical lens on relational leadership.

Meeting this agenda would engage dialogue among scholars from other fields—communication, social psychology, and sociology are obvious candidates—and multiple ontological traditions (e.g., colleagues from Europe and Australasia who have been rapidly advancing the field of social construction of leadership; Fairhurst & Grant, 2010). We emphasize this must be in the form of relational dialogue—as Hosking (2007) says, "We need a 'thinking space' in which 'new kinds of questions can be asked' and 'new kinds of possible futures . . . articulated and debated'" (p. 245).

In sum, in this chapter, we have demonstrated the value both postpositive and constructionist perspectives bring to the study of relationships in organizations. We hope that by presenting a multitheoretical agenda for relational leadership, we have helped open up a "thinking space" that motivates new kinds of questions and raises new kinds of possible futures for relational leadership research.

Discussion Questions

1. What do you see as the strengths and weaknesses of relational leadership research?

2. How well are researchers capturing issues of relationality, and why is this an issue in relational leadership research?

3. What are, in your view, shared areas and areas of difference between the postpositivist and constructionist approaches to relational leadership? Are there ways to reconcile the differences? How would you go about generating a dialogue across paradigms?

4. If you had to design the ideal study on dyadic leadership relationship development, what would it be? What factors influence your choice of research questions and methods?

5. What items would you add to the multiparadigmatic research agenda for the study of relational leadership? What do you see as the most important avenues for future research in this area?

References

Ahern, K. K., Ferris, G. R., Hochwarter, W. A., Douglas, C., & Ammeter, A. P. (2004). Leader political skill and team performance. *Journal of Management, 30,* 309–327.

Alvesson, M. (1996). Leadership studies: From procedure and abstraction to reflexivity and situation. *The Leadership Quarterly, 7,* 455–485.

Anand, S., Hu, J., Liden, R. C., & Vidyarthi, P. R. (2011). Leader–member exchange: Recent research findings and prospects for the future. In A. Bryman, D. Collinson, K. Grint, B. Jackson, & M. Uhl-Bien (Eds.), *The Sage handbook of leadership* (pp. 311–325). London: Sage.

Ashford, S. J., & Cummings, L. L. (1983). Feedback as an individual resource: Personal strategies of creating information. *Organizational Behavior and Human Performance, 32,* 370–398.

Berger, P. L., & Luckmann, T. (1966). *The social construction of reality: A treatise in the sociology of knowledge.* New York: Doubleday.

Bernerth, J. B., Armenakis, A. A., Feild, H. S., Giles, W. F., & Walker, H. J. (2007). Is personality associated with perceptions of LMX? An empirical study. *Leadership & Organization Development Journal, 28,* 613–631.

Bernerth, J. B., Armenakis, A. A., Feild, H. S., Giles, W. F., & Walker, H. J. (2008). The influence of personality differences between subordinates and supervisors on perceptions of LMX: An empirical investigation. *Group & Organization Management, 33,* 216–240.

Berscheid, E. (1999). The greening of relationship science. *American Psychologist, 54,* 260–266.

Beyer, J. M. (1999). Taming and promoting charisma to change organizations. *The Leadership Quarterly, 10,* 307–330.

Bhal, K. T., Ansari, M. A., & Aafaqi, R. (2007). The role of gender match, LMX tenure, and support in leader–member exchange. *Journal of Business and Society, 8,* 63–80.

Biggart, G., & Hamilton, N. (1987). An institutional theory of leadership. *Journal of Applied Behavioral Science, 23,* 429–441.

Blau, P. (1964*). Exchange and power in social life.* New York: John Wiley.

Bohr, N. (1934). *Atomic physics and the description of nature.* Cambridge, UK: Cambridge University Press.

Bolino, M. C., & Turnley, W. H. (2009). Relative deprivation among employees in lower-quality leader–member exchange relationships. *The Leadership Quarterly, 20,* 276–286.

Bono, J. E., & Judge, T. A. (2004). Personality and transformational and transactional leadership: A meta-analysis. *Journal of Applied Psychology, 89,* 901–910.

Bono, J. E., Foldes, H. J., Vinson, G., & Muros, J. P. (2007). Workplace emotions: The role of supervision and leadership. *Journal of Applied Psychology, 92,* 1357–1367.

Bradbury, H., & Lichtenstein, B. (2000). Relationality in organizational research: Exploring the "space between." *Organization Science, 11,* 551–564.

Brouer, R., Duke, A., Treadway, D., & Ferris, G. (2009). The moderating effect of political skill on the demographic dissimilarity—leader–member exchange quality relationship. *The Leadership Quarterly, 20,* 61–69.

Bryman, A., Collinson, D., Grint, K., Jackson, B., & Uhl-Bien, M. (Eds.). (2011). *The Sage handbook of leadership.* London: Sage.

Bryman, A., Stephens, M., & à Campo, C. (1996). The importance of context: Qualitative research and the study of leadership. *The Leadership Quarterly, 7,* 353–370.

Burns, J. M. (1978). *Leadership.* New York: Harper & Row.

Byrne, D. (1971). *The attraction paradigm.* New York: Academic Press.

Calder, B. J. (1977). An attribution theory of leadership. In B. M. Staw & G. R. Salancik (Eds.), *New directions in organizational behavior* (pp. 179–202). Chicago: St. Clair Press.

Capra, F. (1982). *The turning point: Science, society, and the rising culture.* New York: Simon & Schuster.

Carsten, M. K., Uhl-Bien, M., West, B. J., Patera, J., & McGregor, R. (2010). Exploring social constructions of followership: A qualitative study. *The Leadership Quarterly, 21*, 543–562.

Cogliser, C., Schriesheim, C., Scandura, T., & Gardner, W. (2009). Balance in leader and follower perceptions of leader–member exchange: Relationships with performance and work attitudes. *The Leadership Quarterly, 20*, 452–465.

Conger, J. (1998). Qualitative research as the cornerstone methodology for understanding leadership. *The Leadership Quarterly, 9*, 107–121.

Cook, W. L., & Kenny, D. A. (2005). The actor–partner interdependence model: A model of bidirectional effects in development studies. *International Journal of Behavioral Development, 29*, 101-109.

Cunliffe, A. (2008). Orientations to social constructionism: Relationally responsive social constructionism and its implications for knowledge and learning. *Management Learning, 39*, 123–139.

Dansereau, F. (1995). A dyadic approach to leadership: Creating and nurturing this approach under fire. *The Leadership Quarterly, 6*, 479–490.

Dansereau, F., Jr., Graen, G., & Haga, W. J. (1975). A vertical dyad linkage approach to leadership within formal organizations: A longitudinal investigation of the role-making process. *Organizational Behavior and Human Performance, 13*, 46–78.

Davis, G. F., & Marquis, C. (2005). Prospects for organization theory in the early twenty-first century: Institutional fields and mechanisms. *Organization Science, 16*, 332–343.

Day, D., & Sin, H. (in press). Longitudinal tests of an integrative model of leader development: Charting and understanding developmental trajectories. *The Leadership Quarterly.*

Deetz, S. (2005). Critical theory. In S. May and D. K. Mumby (Eds.), *Engaging organizational communication theory and research: Multiple perspectives* (pp. 85–112). Thousand Oaks, CA: Sage.

Denzin, N. K., & Y. S. Lincoln (Eds.). (2000). *The Sage handbook of qualitative research* (2nd ed.). Thousand Oaks, CA: Sage.

Dienesch, R. M., & Liden, R. C. (1986). Leader–member exchange model of leadership: A critique and further development. *Academy of Management Review, 11*, 618–634.

Drath, W. (2001). *The deep blue sea: Rethinking the source of leadership.* San Francisco: Jossey-Bass & Center for Creative Leadership.

Drath, W., McCauley, C., Palus, J., Van Velsor, E., O'Connor, P., & McGuire, J. (2008). Direction, alignment, commitment: Toward a more integrative ontology of leadership. *The Leadership Quarterly, 19*, 635–653.

Drath, W., & Palus, C. (1994). *Making common sense: Leadership as meaning-making in a community of practice.* Greensboro, NC: Center for Creative Leadership.

El Hadidy, W., Ospina, S., & Hofmann-Pinilla, A. (2010). Popular education. In R. A. Couto (Ed.), *Political and civic leadership* (Vol. 2, pp. 857–865). Thousand Oaks, CA: Sage.

Engle, E. M., & Lord, R. G. (1997). Implicit theories, self-schemas, and leader-member exchange. *Academy of Management Journal, 40*, 988–1010.

Evered, R., & Louis, M. (1981). Alternative perspectives in organizational sciences: "Inquiry from the inside" and "inquiry from the outside." *Academy of Management Review, 6*, 385–95.

Fairhurst, G. (1993). The leader–member exchange patterns of women leaders in industry: A discourse analysis. *Communication Monographs, 60,* 321–351.

Fairhurst, G. (2001). Dualisms in leadership research. In F. M. Jablin & L. L. Putnam (Eds.), *The new handbook of organizational communication: Advances in theory, research and methods* (pp. 379–439). Thousand Oaks, CA: Sage.

Fairhurst, G. (2007). *Discursive leadership: In conversation with leadership psychology.* Thousand Oaks, CA: Sage.

Fairhurst, G., & Chandler, T. (1989). Social structure in leader–member interaction. *Communication Monographs, 56,* 215–239.

Fairhurst, G., & Grant, D. (2010). The social construction of leadership: A sailing guide. *Management Communication Quarterly, 24,* 171–210.

Fairhurst, G., & Hamlett, S. (2004). The narrative basis of leader–member exchange. In G. Graen (Ed.), *Dealing with diversity* (pp. 117–144). Greenwich, CT: Information Age.

Ferris, G. R., Liden, R. C., Munyon, T. P., Summers, J. K., Basik K. J., & Buckley, M. R. (2009). Relationships at work: Toward a multidimensional conceptualization of dyadic work relationships. *Journal of Management, 35,* 1379–1403.

Ferris, G. R., Treadway, D. C., Kolodinsky, R. W., Hochwarter, W. A., Kacmar, C. J., & Douglas, C. (2005). Development and validation of the political skill inventory. *Journal of Management, 31,* 1–28.

Fiol, C., Harris, D., & House, R. (1999). Charismatic leadership: Strategies for effecting social change. *The Leadership Quarterly, 10,* 449–482.

Fletcher, J. K. (2004). The paradox of post heroic leadership: An essay on gender, power and transformational change. *The Leadership Quarterly, 15,* 647–661.

Fletcher, J. K., & Kaeufer, K. (2003). Shared leadership: Paradox and possibility. In C. Pearce & J. Conger (Eds.), *Shared leadership: Reframing the hows and whys of leadership* (pp. 21–47). London: Sage.

Foldy, E., Goldman, G., & Ospina, S. (2008). Sensegiving and the role of cognitive shifts in the work of leadership. *The Leadership Quarterly, 19,* 514–529.

Gergen, K. (2009). *Relational being: Beyond self and community.* Oxford, UK: Oxford University Press.

Gerstner, C. R., & Day, D. V. (1997). Meta-analytic review of leader–member exchange theory: Correlates and construct issues. *Journal of Applied Psychology, 82,* 827–844.

Giddens, A. (1984). *The constitution of society.* Berkeley: University of California Press.

Goodwin, V. L., Bowler, W. M., & Whittington J. L. (2009). A social network perspective on LMX relationships: Accounting for the instrumental value of leader and follower networks. *Journal of Management, 35,* 954–980.

Graen, G. B. (1976). Role making processes within complex organizations. In M. D. Dunnette (Ed.), *Handbook of industrial and organizational psychology* (pp. 1201–1245). Chicago: Rand McNally.

Graen, G., & Cashman, J. (1975). A role-making model of leadership in formal organizations: A developmental approach. In J. G. Hunt & L. L. Lawson (Eds.), *Leadership frontiers.* Kent, Ohio: Kent State University Press.

Graen, G. B., & Scandura, T. A. (1987). Toward a psychology of dyadic organizing. In B. M. Staw & L. L. Cummings (Eds.), *Research in organizational behavior* (Vol. 9, pp. 175–208). Greenwich, CT: JAI.

Graen, G. B., & Schiemann, W. (1978). Leader–member agreement: A vertical dyad linkage approach. *Journal of Applied Psychology, 63,* 206–212.

Graen, G. B., & Uhl-Bien, M. (1995). Relationship-based approach to leadership: Development of leader-member exchange (LMX) theory of leadership over 25 years: Applying a multi-level multi-domain perspective. *The Leadership Quarterly, 6,* 219–247.

Gronn, P. (1999, August). *A realist view of leadership.* Paper presented at the Australian Council for Educational Administration, Educational Leadership Online (ELO)–AusAsia Online Conference on Leadership for the New Millenium: Leaders With Soul.

Gubrium, J. F., & Holstein, J. A. (2009). *Analyzing narrative reality.* Thousand Oaks, CA: Sage.

Harris, K. J., Harris, R. B., & Eplion, D. M. (2007). Personality, leader–member exchanges, and work outcomes. *Journal of Behavioral and Applied Management, 8,* 92–107.

Harvey, P., Martinko, M. J., & Douglas, S. C. (2006). Causal reasoning in dysfunctional leader–member interactions. *Journal of Managerial Psychology, 21,* 747–762

Hazan, C., & Shaver, P. R. (1990). Love and work: An attachment-theoretical perspective. *Journal of Personality and Social Psychology, 59,* 270–280.

Hedström, P., & Swedberg, R. (1998). *Social mechanisms: An analytical approach to social theory.* Cambridge, UK: Cambridge University Press.

Henderson, D. J., Liden, R. C., Glibkowski, B. C., & Chaudhry, A. (2009). Within-group LMX differentiation: A multilevel review and examination of its antecedents and outcomes. *The Leadership Quarterly, 20,* 517–534.

Henderson, D. J., Wayne, S. J., Shore, L. M., Bommer, W. H., & Tetrick, L. E. (2008). Leader–member exchange, differentiation, and psychological contract fulfillment: A multilevel examination. *Journal of Applied Psychology, 93,* 1208–1219.

Hollander, E. P. (1958). Conformity, status, and idiosyncrasy credit. *Psychological Review, 65,* 117–127.

Hollander, E. (1960). Competence and conformity in the acceptance of influence. *Journal of Abnormal and Social Psychology, 61,* 361–365.

Hollander, E. P. (1964). *Leaders, groups, and influence.* New York: Oxford University Press.

Hollander, E. (2006). Influence processes in leadership-followership: Inclusion and the idiosyncrasy credit model. In D. A. Hantula (Ed.), *Advances in social and organizational psychology: A tribute to Ralph Rosnow.* Mahwah, NJ: Lawrence Erlbaum.

Hollander, E. (2007). Relating leadership to active followership. In Richard A. Couto (Ed.), *Reflections on leadership: Essays honoring James MacGregor Burns* (pp. 57–64). Lanham, MD: University Press of America.

Hollander, E. (2009). *Inclusive leadership: The essential leader–follower relationship.* New York: Routledge.

Hollander, E. P., & Julian, J. W. (1969). Contemporary trends in the analysis of leadership processes. *Psychological Bulletin, 71,* 387.

Hosking, D. M. (1997). Organizing, leadership and skillful processes. In K. Grint (Ed.), *Leadership: Classical, contemporary and critical approaches* (pp. 293–318). Oxford, UK: Oxford University Press.

Hosking, D. M. (2007). Not leaders, not followers: A post-modern discourse of leadership processes. In B. Shamir, R. Pillai, M. Bligh, & M. Uhl-Bien (Eds.), *Follower-centered perspectives on leadership: A tribute to the memory of James R. Meindl* (pp. 243–263). Greenwich, CT: Information Age.

Hosking, D. M., Dachler, H. P., & Gergen, K. J. (Eds.). (1995). *Management and organization: Relational alternatives to individualism.* Brookfield, VT: Avebury.

Hosking, D. M., & Morley, I. E. (1988). The skills of leadership. In J. G. Hunt, B. R. Baliga, H. P. Dachler, & C. A. Schriesheim (Eds.), *Emerging leadership vistas* (pp. 80–106). Lexington, MA: Lexington Books/D. C. Heath.

House, R. J., & Aditya, R. (1997). The social scientific study of leadership: Quo vadis? *Journal of Management, 23,* 409–474.

Huang, X., Wright, R. P., Chiu, W., & Wang, C. (2008). Relational schemes as sources of evaluation and misevaluation of leader–member exchanges: Some initial evidence. *The Leadership Quarterly, 19,* 266–282.

Hui, C., Law, K. S., Chen, N., & Tjosvold, D. (2008). The role of co-operation and competition on leader–member exchange and extra-role performance in China. *Asia Pacific Journal of Human Resources, 46,* 133–152.

Hunt, J. G., & Dodge, G. E. (2000). Leadership déjà vu all over again. *The Leadership Quarterly, 11,* 435–458.

Huxham, C., & Vangen, S. (2000). Leadership in the shaping and implementation of collaboration agendas: How things happen in a (not quite) joined up world. *Academy of Management Journal, 43,* 159–175.

Ilies, R., Nahrgang, J. D., & Morgeson, F. P. (2007). Leader–member exchange and citizenship behaviors: A meta-analysis. *Journal of Applied Psychology, 92,* 269–277.

Katz, D., & Kahn, R. L. (1978). *The social psychology of organizations* (2nd ed.). New York: John Wiley.

Keller, T., & Cacioppe, R. (2001). Leader–follower attachments: Understanding parental images at work. *Leadership & Organizational Development Journal, 22,* 70–75.

Kenny, D. A., Kashy, D. A., & Cook, W. L. (2006). *Dyadic data analysis.* New York: Guilford.

Kinicki, A. J., & Vecchio, R. P. (1994). Influences on the quality of supervisor-subordinate relations: The role of time-pressure, organizational commitment, and locus of control. *Journal of Organizational Behavior, 15,* 75–82.

Krasikova, D., & LeBreton, J. (2010, August). *Misalignment of theory and method in leader–member exchange (LMX) research: Reciprocal dyadic designs as a recommended remedy.* Paper presented at the annual meeting of the Academy of Management, Montréal, Canada.

Lam, W., Huang, X., & Snape, E. (2007). Feedback-seeking behavior and leader–member exchange: Do supervisor-attributed motives matter? *Academy of Management Journal, 50,* 348–363.

Lambert, L., Walker, D., Zimmerman, D., Cooper, J., Lambert, M., Gardner, M., et al. (1995). *The constructivist leader.* New York: Teachers College Press.

Lee, J., & Jablin, F. (1995). Maintenance communication in superior–subordinate work relationships. *Human Communication Research, 22,* 220–257.

Liden, R. C. (2007) Letter. In G. Fairhurst (Ed.), *Discursive leadership: In conversation with leadership psychology* (pp. 178–180). Thousand Oaks, CA: Sage.

Liden, R. C., & Graen, G. B. (1980). Generalizability of the vertical dyad linkage model of leadership. *Academy of Management Journal, 23,* 451–465.

Liden, R. C., & Maslyn, J. M. (1998). Multi-dimensionality of leader–member exchange: An empirical assessment through scale development. *Journal of Management, 24,* 43–72.

Liden, R. C., Sparrowe, R. T., & Wayne, S. J. (1997). Leader–member exchange theory: The past and potential for the future. In G. R. Ferris (Ed.), *Research in personnel and human resources management* (Vol. 15, pp. 47–119). Greenwich, CT: JAI.

Liden, R. C., Wayne, S. J., & Stilwell, D. (1993). A longitudinal study on the early development of leader–member exchanges. *Journal of Applied Psychology, 78,* 662–674.

Lord, R., & Brown, D. (2004). *Leadership processes and follower self-identity.* Mahwah, NJ: Lawrence Erlbaum.

Lubbers, M., Molina, J., Lerner, J., Brandes, U., Avila, J., & McCarty, C. (2010). Longitudinal analysis of personal networks: The case of Argentinean migrants in Spain. *Social Networks, 32,* 91–104.

Maitlis, S., & Lawrence, T. B. (2007). Triggers and enablers of sensegiving in organizations. *Academy of Management Journal, 50,* 57–84.

Manning, T. (2003). Leadership across cultures: Attachment style influences. *Journal of Leadership and Organizational Studies, 9,* 20–30.

Maslyn, J. M., & Uhl-Bien, M. (2001). Leader–member exchange and its dimensions: Effects of self-effort and other's effort on relationship quality. *Journal of Applied Psychology, 86,* 697–708.

Maslyn, J., Uhl-Bien, M., & Mitchell, M. (2007, April). *Exploring leader–member exchange (LMX) from the manager's perspective: Development of a supervisor LMX measure.* Symposium presentation at the national meeting of the Society for Industrial/Organizational Psychology (SIOP), New York, NY.

Masterson, S., Lewis, K., Goldman, B., & Taylor, M. (2000). Integrating justice and social exchange: The differing effects of fair procedures and treatment on work relationships. *Academy of Management Journal, 43,* 738–749.

Mayo, M., & Pastor, J. C. (2007). Leadership embedded in social networks: Looking at inter-follower processes. In B. Shamir, R. Pillai, M. Bligh, and M. Uhl-Bien (Eds.), *Follower-centered perspectives on leadership: A tribute to the memory of James R. Meindl* (pp. 93–113). Greenwich, CT: Information Age.

Mead, G. H. (1934). *Mind, self and society.* Chicago: University of Chicago Press.

Meindl, J. (1993). Reinventing leadership: A radical, social psychological approach. In J. Murnigan (Ed.), *Social psychology in organizations: Advances in theory and research* (pp. 89–118). Englewood Cliffs, NJ: Prentice Hall.

Meindl, J. (1995). The romance of leadership as a follower-centric theory: A social constructionist approach. *The Leadership Quarterly, 6,* 329–341.

Meindl, J., Ehrlich, S., & Dukerich, J. (1985). The romance of leadership. *Administrative Science Quarterly, 30,* 78–102.

Murphy, S. M., Wayne, S. J., Liden, R. C., & Erdogan, B. (2003). Understanding social loafing: The role of justice perceptions and exchange relationships. *Human Relations, 56,* 61–84.

Nagin, D. (1999). Analyzing developmental trajectories: A semiparametric group-based approach. *Psychological Methods, 4,* 139–157.

Nahrgang, J. D., Morgeson, F. P., & Ilies, R. (2009). The development of leader–member exchanges: Exploring how personality and performance influence leader and member relationships over time. *Organizational Behavior and Human Decision Processes, 108,* 256–266.

Ng, K., Koh, C., & Goh, H. (2008). The heart of the servant leader: Leader's motivation-to-serve and its impact on LMX and subordinates' extra-role behaviors. In G. B. Graen & J. A. Graen (Eds.), *Knowledge-driven corporation: Complex creative destruction* (pp. 125–144). Greenwich, CT: Information Age.

Osborn, R. N., Hunt, J. G., & Jauch, L. R. (2002). Toward a contextual theory of leadership. *The Leadership Quarterly, 13*, 797–837.

Ospina, S. (2004). Qualitative research. In G. R. Goethals, G. J. Sorenson, & J. MacGregor Burns (Eds.), *Encyclopedia of leadership* (pp. 1279–1284). London: Sage.

Ospina, S., & Foldy, E. (2010). Building bridges from the margins: The work of leadership in social change organizations. *The Leadership Quarterly, 21*, 292–307.

Ospina, S., & Hittleman, M. (in press) Thinking sociologically about leadership. In M. Harvey & R. Riggio (Eds.), *Research companion to leadership studies: The dialogue of disciplines*. Cheltenham, UK: Edward Elgar.

Ospina, S., & Saz-Carranza, A. (2010). Leadership and collaboration in coalition work. In Z. van Zwanenberg (Ed.), *Leadership in social care* (pp. 103–128). London: Jessica Kingsley, Publishers.

Ospina, S., & Sorensen, G. (2006). A constructionist lens on leadership: Charting new territory. In G. Goethals & G. Sorenson (Eds.), *In quest of a general theory of leadership* (pp. 188–204). Cheltenham, UK: Edward Elgar.

Ospina, S., & Su, C. (2009). Weaving color lines: Race, ethnicity, and the work of leadership in social change organizations. *Leadership, 5*, 131–170.

Parry, K. (1998). Grounded theory and social process: A new direction for leadership research. *The Leadership Quarterly, 9*, 85–105.

Pastor, J. C. (1998). *The social construction of leadership: A semantic and social network analysis of social representations of leadership*. Ann Arbor, MI: University of Michigan Dissertation Services.

Pearce, C. L., & Conger, J. A. (2003). *Shared leadership: Reframing the hows and whys of leadership*. Thousand Oaks, CA: Sage.

Phillips, A. S., & Bedeian, A.G. (1994). Leader–follower exchange quality: The role of personal and interpersonal attributes. *Academy of Management Journal, 37*, 990–1001.

Popper, M., & Mayseless, O. (2003). Back to basics: Applying a parent perspective to transformational leadership. *The Leadership Quarterly, 14*, 41–65.

Popper, M., Mayseless, O., & Castelnovo, O. (2000). Transformational leadership and attachment. *The Leadership Quarterly, 11*, 267–289.

Porter, L. W., & McLaughlin, G. B. (2006). Leadership and the organizational context: Like the weather? *The Leadership Quarterly, 17*, 559–576.

Prebles, E. (2002). Sensemaking in narratives and the uniqueness paradox in leader–member exchange. Unpublished master's thesis, University of Cincinnati.

Raelin, J. A. (2003). *Creating leaderful organizations: How to bring out leadership in everyone*. San Francisco: Berrett-Koehler.

Scandura, T., & Schriesheim, C. (1994). Leader–member exchange and supervisory career mentoring as complementary constructs in leadership research. *Academy of Management Journal, 37*, 1588–1602.

Schall, E., Ospina, S., Godsoe, B., & Dodge, J. (2004). Appreciative narratives as leadership research: Matching method to lens. In D. L. Cooperrider & M. Avital (Eds.), *Advances in appreciative inquiry* (Vol. 2, pp. 147–170). Oxford, UK: Elsevier Science.

Schriesheim, C., Castro, S., & Coglister, C. (1999). Leader–member exchange (LMX) research: A comprehensive review of theory, measurement, and data-analytic practices. *The Leadership Quarterly, 10,* 62–113.

Schriesheim, C., Castro, S., Zhou, X., & Yammarino, F. (2001). The folly of theorizing "A" by testing "B": A selective level-of-analysis review of the field and a detailed leader–member exchange illustration. *The Leadership Quarterly, 12,* 515–551.

Schriesheim, C. A., Neider, L. L., & Scandura, T. A. (1998). A within- and between-groups analysis of leader–member exchange as a correlate of delegation and as a moderator of delegation relationships with performance and satisfaction. *Academy of Management Journal, 41,* 298–318.

Schutz, A. (1970). *On phenomenology and social relations.* Chicago: University of Chicago Press.

Seers, A., & Chopin, S. (in press). The social production of leadership: From supervisor–subordinate linkages to relational organizing. In M. Uhl-Bien & S. Ospina (Eds.), *Advancing relational leadership theory: A dialogue among perspectives.* Charlotte, NC: Information Age.

Shamir, B. (in press). Leadership research or post-leadership research: Advancing leadership research versus throwing out the baby with the bath water. In M. Uhl-Bien & S. Ospina (Eds.), *Advancing relational leadership theory: A dialogue among perspectives.* Charlotte, NC: Information Age.

Sherony, K. M., & Green, S. G. (2002). Co-worker exchange: Relationships between co-workers, leader–member exchange, and work attitudes. *Journal of Applied Psychology, 87,* 542–548.

Sias, P. M. (1996). Constructing perceptions of differential treatment: An analysis of coworker discourse. *Communication Monographs, 63,* 171–187.

Sias, P. M. (2009). *Organizing relationships: Traditional and emerging perspectives on workplace relationships.* London: Sage.

Smircich, L., & Morgan, G. (1982). Leadership: The management of meaning. *Journal of Applied Behavioral Science, 18,* 257–273.

Smith, K. K., & Berg, D. N. (1987). *Paradoxes of group life understanding conflict, paralysis, and movement in group dynamics.* San Francisco: Jossey-Bass.

Sparrowe, R., & Liden, R. C. (2005). Two routes to influence: Integrating leader–member exchange and social network perspectives. *Administrative Science Quarterly, 50,* 505–535.

Stone, T. H., & Cooper, W. H. (2009). Emerging credits. *The Leadership Quarterly, 20,* 785–798.

Tierney, W. (1987). The semiotic aspects of leadership: An ethnographic perspective. *American Journal of Semiotics, 5,* 223–250.

Tierney, W. G. (1988). *The web of leadership: The presidency in higher education.* Greenwich, CT: JAI.

Tierney, W. G. (1996). Leadership and postmodernism: On voice and the qualitative method. *The Leadership Quarterly, 7,* 371–383.

Treadway, D. C., Breland, J. W., Williams, L. A., Wang, L., & Yang, J. (2008). The role of politics and political behavior the development and performance of LMX relationships: A multilevel approach. In G. B. Graen & J. A. Graen (Eds.), *Knowledge-driven corporation: Complex creative destruction* (pp. 145–180). Greenwich, CT: Information Age.

Tse, H., Dasborough, M., & Ashkanasy, M. (2008). A multi-level analysis of team climate and interpersonal exchange relationships at work. *The Leadership Quarterly, 19,* 195–211.

Uhl-Bien, M. (2003). Relationship development as a key ingredient for leadership development. In S. Murphy & R. Riggio (Eds.), *The future of leadership development* (pp. 129–147). Mahwah, NJ: Lawrence Erlbaum.

Uhl-Bien, M. (2006). Relational leadership theory: Exploring the social processes of leadership and organizing *The Leadership Quarterly, 17,* 654–676.

Uhl-Bien, M., Graen, G., & Scandura, T. (2000). Implications of leader–member exchange (LMX) for strategic human resource management systems: Relationships as social capital for competitive advantage. In G. R. Ferris (Ed.), *Research in personnel and human resources management* (Vol. 18, pp. 137–185). Greenwich, CT: JAI.

Uhl-Bien, M., & Maslyn, J. M. (2003). Reciprocity in manager–subordinate relationship: Components, configurations, and outcomes. *Journal of Management, 29,* 511–532.

Uhl-Bien, M., & Ospina, S. (Eds.). (in press). *Advancing relational leadership theory: A dialogue among perspectives.* Charlotte, NC: Information Age.

Vidyarthi, P. R., Liden, R. C., Anand, S., Erdogan, B., & Ghosh, S. (2010). Where do I stand? Examining the effects of leader–member exchange social comparison on employee work behaviors. *Journal of Applied Psychology, 95,* 849–861.

Wayne, S. J., & Ferris, G. R. (1990). Influence tactics, affect, and exchange quality in supervisor–subordinate interactions: A laboratory experiment and field study. *Journal of Applied Psychology, 75,* 487–499.

Weick, K. (1995). *Sensemaking in organizations.* Thousand Oaks, CA: Sage.

Yammarino, F. (2009, July). *Levels of analysis.* Presentation at Collective Leadership Workshop, Army Research Institute, Fort Leavenworth, Kansas.

Yammarino, F. (2010, August). *Acceptance speech for Distinguished Scholar Award in Leadership.* Annual meeting of the Academy of Management, Montréal, Canada.

Yammarino, F., & Dansereau, F. (2007). *Leadership: The multiple level approaches.* Greenwich, CT: JAI.

Yanow, D., & Schwartz-Shea, P. (Eds.). (2006). *Interpretation and method: Empirical research methods and the interpretive turn.* New York: M.E. Sharp.

Zhou, X., & Schriesheim, C.A. (2009). Supervisor–subordinate convergence in descriptions of leader–member exchange (LMX) quality: Review and testable propositions. *The Leadership Quarterly, 20,* 920–932.

10

In the Minds of Followers

Follower-Centric
Approaches to Leadership

Douglas J. Brown

University of Waterloo

But, as Yertle, the Turtle King, lifted his hand

And started to order and give the command,

That plain little turtle below in the stack,

That plain little turtle whose name was just Mack,

Decided he'd taken enough. And he had.

And that plain little lad got a bit mad.

And that plain little Mack did a plain little thing.

He burped!

And his burp shook the throne of the king!

—Dr. Seuss

AUTHOR'S NOTE: Please address correspondence concerning this chapter to Douglas J. Brown, Department of Psychology, University of Waterloo, 200 University Avenue West, Waterloo, Ontario, Canada, N2L 3G1. e-mail: djbrown@ uwaterloo.ca.

Anyone who has read *Yertle the Turtle* knows what happens following Mack's burp, Yertle the Turtle King is hurtled from his turtle throne into the mud, seemingly never to lead the turtles of Sala-ma-Sond again. When approached from the perspective of a parent, this is simply another delightful Seuss story, one that brings great joy to my 4-year-old daughter when we read it together, typically repeatedly because she, like Yertle, is ruler of all that she can see. However, in those rare moments, typically during our fourth consecutive reading, when my identity wanders to that of a leadership researcher, the story takes on a wholly different meaning. No longer is Yertle the Turtle simply the best tale ever written on the subject of turtle stacking, it is an allegory about leaders and followers and the pivotal importance of followers to leaders. In contrast with many of the other chapters in this book, which concern themselves with understanding Yertle the Turtle King, this chapter is different. It is about that plain little turtle named Mack—as well as the other follower turtles who live in the pond on Sala-ma-Sond—and it is motivated by a pressing question that is frequently posed to me by a quizzical 4-year-old, "Why did Mack burp?"

There is substantial debate among scholars regarding the definition of leadership. Although it is generally agreed that at its core, leadership is the investigation of influence and the outcomes that arise from this influence process within a given context (Antonakis, Cianciolo, & Sternberg, 2004), scholars have scrutinized and dissected this phenomenon in diverse ways. Simultaneously, leadership has been approached from a leader-centric position, as an outcome, and as an interaction between leaders and the led (Bass, 2008). Despite such apparent diversity, in practice and publication, the normative approach has been leader centric, emphasizing the variance in the influence process which can be explained by the dispositional characteristics, behaviors, and cognitions of leaders. Although a leader-centric approach is important, it can deliver only partial answers. Fundamentally, leaders simultaneously affect and are affected by their subordinates and achieve relevant group goals indirectly through their ability to influence others (Graen & Scandura, 1987; Hollander & Offerman, 1990). Research shows that followers engage in upward influence (e.g., Kipnis, Schmidt, & Wilkinson, 1980) and provide feedback to leaders (Walker & Smither, 1999) and that these activities are among the most important antecedents of leadership performance (McEvoy & Beatty, 1989). Leadership is not simply about leader characteristics and actions; it is also about recognition of leadership by followers, follower attributions for group outcomes, and the extent to which followers identify with a leader (Bass, 2008).

To highlight the relevance of followers, consider that despite widespread belief that Hitler is personally responsible for the genocide of six million Jews during World War II, not a single individual died at his hands (Goldhagen, 2009). Similarly, it is commonly understood that Pol Pot exterminated 1.7 million Cambodians, Jean Kambanda is responsible for butchering 800,000 Tutsis in Rwanda, Saddam Hussein is responsible for the

deaths of an estimated 600,000 Kurds, and Slobodan Milosevic is responsible for the ethnic cleansing of Bosnians (Goldhagen, 2009). Although each
of these examples certainly speaks to the depravity of individual leaders,
each instance simultaneously highlights the limits of a strict leader-centric
model and highlights the relevance of followers. Without the obedience,
fanaticism, fervor, or support of followers, each of these genocidal directives
would have been ineffectual. Ultimately, it is followers who legitimize leaders, empower them, and provide them with the means to attain their visions
and goals. In addition, outstanding leadership depends on good followers—
individuals who are proactive, competent, self-managing, high in integrity,
and who willingly contribute to the success of their groups and organizations (Bass, 2008). Good followers help drive outstanding outcomes by
pushing their leaders to be better, whereas bad followers do the opposite. In
sum, as Yertle the Turtle King learned the hard way, there is no leadership
without followers and followership (Hollander, 1993).

Given the centrality of followers for understanding leadership, historical
mainstream scholarly indifference to the topic of followers and followership is
rather curious (Bennis, 2008). In recent years, however, there seemingly has
been a shift in scholars' thinking, attitudes, and behavior that has brought
followers and followership into the foreground and has generated several
interesting and stimulating tomes for the consumption of the general public,
scholars, and business leaders: *The Art of Followership: How Great Followers
Create Great Leaders and Organizations* (Riggio, Chaleff, & Lipman-Blumen,
2008); *The Power of Followership* (Kelley, 1992); *The Courageous Follower:
Standing Up to and for Our Leaders* (Chaleff, 1995); and *Followership: How
Followers Are Creating Change and Changing Leaders* (Kellerman, 2008).
Despite the position advanced in several of these books that followers matter
and that researchers have been largely silent on the topic, in actuality there is
a long and rich history of follower-centric research that has been ignored, gone
unnoticed, or altogether forgotten by many commentators (Lord, 2008). This
is not to say that the leadership field is not largely leader centric (Meindl,
1995) or that followers do not "remain an under-explored source of variance"
in leadership models (Lord, Brown, & Freiberg, 1999, p. 167), but rather that
something is known about followers and followership and that the state of our
understanding is not as bleak as we might be led to believe.

In this chapter, I begin with broad brush strokes, considering key assumptions about followers and the role that followers have played in much previous
leadership literature. Next, I focus on the dominant follower-centric perspective. Although recent discussions of followership have attempted to develop
behavioral typologies, understand how followers influence leaders, and highlight the characteristics that make for good, bad, and indifferent followers,
follower-centric theory and research itself has primarily dealt with the likely
precursor to these activities—information processing. If we are to understand
why followers behave as they do, a necessary first step is understanding their
thought processes. Hence, my emphasis herein lies in examining two issues

surrounding follower thought. First, why is it that we understand the world through leaders? Second, what is the nature of our mental category leader, and how does it influence our perceptions of leaders?

What Is Followership?

The suggestion that followers are a relevant consideration in leadership models is not novel, as many leader-centric leadership frameworks do account for followers (Howell & Shamir, 2005). For the most part, however, prior leader-centric work has characterized followers and subordinates as passive elements of the situation or context that necessarily should be considered when attempting to understand when various leader styles will be and will not be effective (Avolio, 2007). The passivity of followers in such works is not particularly surprising, as the primary underlying motivation guiding this literature has been leader centric. For instance, contingency frameworks, such as Fiedler's leader-match theory (1967) have suggested that the alignment of a leader's behavioral style and the context, which includes aspects of followers such as their loyalty and cooperation, is an important precursor to effectiveness. Situational leadership models, such as Hersey and Blanchard's model (1977), propose that the appropriate leadership style depends in part on the developmental level of subordinates. House's path-goal theory (1971) indicates that the skills and experience of followers is an important antecedent of which leadership style will be most motivating. Kerr and Jermier (1978) argue in their leadership substitutes theory that characteristics of followers can both make leadership unnecessary (i.e., act as a substitute) or nullify a leader's actions (i.e., neutralize). Finally, thinking in the areas of charismatic and transformational leadership has likened followers to necessary flammable material who are set ablaze by leaders (Klein & House, 1995).

The implicit assumption of passivity that characterizes prior leader-centric work is at odds with our common understanding of human nature. Followers are not simply a passive part of the environment to be acted on by leaders, or in the case of poor Mack to be sat on by Yertle, but rather possess an innate drive to act in a self-determining fashion (Grant & Ashford, 2008). Although it is certainly true that at times, followers choose to behave as passive bystanders, neither participating nor objecting to their leaders' actions and directives, it is also true that in other instances, they are diehard zealots who are deeply devoted or opposed to their leaders and their leader's causes (Kellerman, 2008). In organizations, employees range from those who narrowly define their roles in terms of their formal job requirements and who will simply do their jobs, to others who will choose to enthusiastically embrace their leader's vision and goals, oftentimes at a significant personal cost to their future freedom, health, family life, values, and well-being. Yet in other instances, followers proactively engage in upward influence tactics and sell issues (Dutton & Ashford, 1993), voice their opinions (LePine & Van Dyne, 2001), psychologically or physically withdraw from their work, blow the whistle (Near & Miceli, 1987), or attempt to directly undermine or deviate against their superiors (Mitchell & Ambrose, 2007). In the end, our understanding of followers must be premised on the assumption that they are agentic, intelligent beings who actively attempt to understand and shape their environments in order to bring about self-relevant goals and outcomes (Bandura, 1986).

Research also demonstrates that different followers (Yammarino & Dubinsky, 1994), as well as followers and leaders (Bass & Yammarino, 1991; McCauley & Lombardo, 1990; van Velsor, Taylor, & Leslie, 1993), differ considerably in terms of their views of how much leadership an individual has exhibited. For instance, behavioral ratings of transformational leadership indicate that there is such profound individual variability in ratings that rather than reflecting the leader, transformational leadership may exist solely in the "eye of the beholder" (Yammarino & Dubinsky, 1994, p. 792). Re-analyses of archival data suggest that roughly 20% of the variance in leadership ratings is idiosyncratic and, hence, is dependent on who is rating whom (Livi, Kenny, Albright, & Pierro, 2008). Such individual variability in perceptions is important, insofar as characteristics of the world are not given to observers and social actors but rather are constructed (Salancik & Pfeffer, 1978), and it is those constructions that are most relevant for understanding human activity (Fiske, 1998). As such, the influence afforded to an individual leader does not reside solely in his or her behavioral repertoire or skill set, but rather resides in part in the mind's eye of relevant observers (Hollander, 1958). As such, it should not surprise us that perceived intelligence predicts leader emergence (Judge, Colbert, & Ilies, 2004) or that it is perceived competence and not actual competence that predicts who is and is not influential in a group setting (Anderson & Kilduff, 2009). Such findings should not be taken as evidence that actual intelligence or competence are unimportant, but rather that the relationship between these characteristics and effectiveness are mediated through the perceptions of observers. Fundamentally, perception is reality, and it is our perceptions that propel us through life.

Premised on the notions that individuals are proactive rather than passive and that perceptions rather than objective reality are most relevant for understanding human behavior, follower-centric researchers have busied themselves for the past 40 years trying to comprehend follower sensemaking activities (Lord & Maher, 1993; Meindl, 1995). The emphasis of followership research has been on understanding how followers make sense out of the vast quantities of information that flow unceasingly each day. Human information-processing capacity is finite, and the information-processing demands confronted each day exceed our very limited information-processing abilities. To circumvent this information-processing bottleneck and facilitate our interaction with the external world, humans lean heavily on stable internal mental representations that allow us to "comprehend, understand, explain, attribute, extrapolate, and predict" (Starbuck & Milliken, 1988, p. 51). The mental categories that we use guide what we pay attention to, what we encode, and how we form judgments. Thus, rather than simply conceptualize followers as passive recipients of leader behaviors, follower-centric researchers propose that followers are active causal agents who construct leadership through the application of relevant categories (Lord & Maher, 1993; Meindl, 1995).

Although it is implicit in the preceding text, it is important to emphasize that follower sensemaking activities are not the consequence of the random firing of neurons, nor are followers dispassionate recorders of leadership information. Human information processing is a goal-directed activity that is based on discrepancy creation or reduction (Kruglanski, 1996). Effectively, followers are compelled to understand the world in terms of leadership because it serves some overarching conscious or unconscious purpose. For instance, as we shall see subsequently, in part, followers are driven to understand organizational events in terms of leadership because it alleviates negative emotional states such as anxiety and uncertainty. As motivated thinkers, our attention, encoding, and memory for events are guided by preexisting conclusions, goals, or expectations (Kunda, 1990). Hence, we should not be particularly surprised to learn that party identification colors what Republicans and Democrats "see" in their political leaders (Pillai, Kohles, & Bligh, 2007) or that the extent to which we like our leaders colors our judgments and memory for their behavior (D. J. Brown & Keeping, 2005). By seeing the world as we expect to see it, we avoid the discomfort of discrepancies.

Follower-centric researchers further contend that categorization processes are not insignificant. Subordinate information processing serves as the most proximal determinant of who will emerge and remain as leaders in groups, how much leeway subordinates will provide them, as well as how enthusiastically they will be followed. Effectively, the impact of leaders is mediated through the information processing of subordinates (Lord & Emrich, 2000). How subordinates make sense of the leadership context is important, insofar as this symbolic activity defines one's role in the social context and serves as a proximal antecedent to how one defines the self and the self-in-relation to significant others (Howell & Shamir, 2005; Lord & Brown, 2004). To define our role as that of a follower or subordinate should automatically trigger relevant behavioral norms and scripts in observers (Baumeister & Newman, 1995). Research, for instance, suggests that humans typically behave submissively when confronted with a dominant partner and that such complementarity in interpersonal relations is preferred (Tiedens & Fragale, 2003; Tiedens, Unzueta, & Young, 2007). Although there are, no doubt, universally shared followership scripts that exist and that need to be better understood, it is also likely that researchers need to uncover systematic idiosyncratic and dyadic script variability. For some individuals, to define one member of the group as a leader suggests that one is dependent, obedient, and powerless, whereas for others, the adopted identity might be that of the courageous follower who voices opinions and questions authority (Uhl-Bien & Pillai, 2007). Finally, as shown in the context of the charismatic leadership literature, the nature of the relationship form that results from followers' sensemaking efforts (Howell & Shamir, 2005) reverberates, influencing one's overall sense of self (Kark, Shamir, & Chen, 2003).

Beyond the fact that follower sensemaking of leaders is an important mechanism through which leadership influence flows, from a practical standpoint, follower sensemaking is pivotal to the advancement of a psychometrically sound discipline. The preponderance of our understanding of leadership depends on surveys in which subordinates are asked to report how frequently their immediate supervisors engage in various behaviors (Hunter, Bedell-Avers, & Mumford, 2007). To operationalize leadership in such a way makes the disentanglement of leader behavior and follower sensemaking difficult, if not impossible. It also raises serious questions regarding the construct validity of our most cherished behavioral taxonomies and, ultimately, what it is we have accumulated with our mountains of behaviorally oriented data. As follower-centric researchers repeatedly have documented, follower conceptualizations of leadership play a pivotal role in terms of how subordinates respond to behavioral questionnaires (e.g., Eden & Leviatan, 1975; Lord, Foti, & De Vader, 1984). As such, one might reasonably ask whether the dominant behavioral paradigm and methodology have actually addressed what it is leaders do or how followers encode, store, retrieve, and integrate information to render behavioral judgments (Eden & Leviatan, 1975; Rush, Thomas, & Lord, 1977; Weiss & Adler, 1981). If, as a discipline, we are going to continue to lean on subordinate reports it seems only reasonable that we should think more carefully about how those perceptions are formed and judgments are rendered.

To summarize, followers are proactive sensemakers and their sensemaking is pivotal to the advancement of leadership knowledge. Below, I delve deeper into the cognitively oriented follower-centric literature, which for sake of clarity I have bifurcated. In the first section, I address the overarching question of why humans are leader-centric thinkers and examine those factors that influence our inclination to comprehend the world through leaders. Much of the work reviewed in this section traces its roots to social constructionist observations made by Jeffrey Pfeffer (1977) and Bobby Calder (1977) and empirical work conducted by James Meindl (1995). Building from this literature, I next dig deeper and address how it is we come to understand and label particular individuals as leaders. Here, I probe the content of the leader category and address the underlying social-cognitive processes that dictate our use of this category. Much of the literature in this second section originates from the theoretical and empirical work conducted by Robert Lord and his colleagues (e.g., Lord & Maher, 1993).

Why and When Are We Leader-Centric Thinkers?

An enigma that has beguiled observers for some time is the tendency for humans to construe the world through the prism of leaders and leadership. A key to unlocking this mystery lies in developing an appreciation for the tendency for humans to romanticize leadership. The *romance of leadership* perspective suggests that "as observers of and as participants in organizations, we have developed highly romanticized, heroic views of leadership, what leaders do, what they are able to accomplish, and the general effects that they have on our lives" (Meindl, Ehrlich, & Dukerich, 1985, p. 79). At its core, the romance of leadership is an implicit theory that observers hold and utilize when they are attempting to comprehend the "causes, nature, and consequences of organizational activities" (Meindl & Ehrlich, 1987).

Building from the radical perspective advanced by several authors who have argued that leadership is simply an explanatory category (Calder, 1977; Pfeffer, 1977), Meindl proposed that the leader category has "achieved a heroic, larger-than-life value." Social actors have immense faith in the efficacy of leaders who are perceived to be the "premier force" underlying all organizational events, regardless of whether they are positive or negative (Meindl et al., 1985, p. 79). As naïve scientists (Heider, 1958), perceivers utilize the leader category to organize, understand, and predict the world. Functionally, the leader category reduces our uncertainty and anxiety and allows us to "come to grips with the cognitive and moral complexities of understanding the myriad interactions among the causal forces that create and maintain organized activity" (Meindl & Ehrlich, 1987, p. 92).

In their initial work, Meindl and his colleagues (1985) sought evidence for the romance of leadership through a series of archival and experimental investigations. In two initial archival studies, Meindl et al. found that during times of extreme performance, interest in leadership soared—as indexed by the number of articles written in *The Wall Street Journal* about leadership and dissertations completed on the topic. Seemingly, in extreme situations, people turn to leadership. To directly test this idea, Meindl et al. completed a series of vignette studies in which participants read about companies that had performed positively or negatively to varying degrees (e.g., high, medium, small). After reading the vignettes, participants were asked to account for company performance by evaluating the causal significance of several factors. Relative to the alternative explanations (e.g., economy), extreme performance, regardless of valence, led individuals to accentuate leadership. Such findings underscore the romanticized view held by observers who see leaders as capable of controlling and influencing the fate of organizations and people.

Subsequently, Meindl and Ehrlich (1987) tested whether individual's reactions to organizational performance might depend on whether outcomes are attributable to other factors (e.g., workforce) or leadership. To these ends, they completed a series of vignette studies in which they had their participants read descriptions of an organization that included a general organizational description, a summary of operating strengths, and a summary of selected performance indicators. Importantly, they manipulated the operating strengths paragraph to emphasize either leadership or other factors (e.g., regulatory policies). In line with the romance of leadership perspective, when outcomes were attributable to leadership, participants were generally more optimistic about the profitability of the organization and perceived it to be less risky. Such findings suggest that we are comforted when performance is linked to leadership.

Further work has refined our knowledge by examining the contexts that increase our propensity to generate heroic, charismatic leadership images. Perhaps most notably, researchers have explored the role of crises. Seemingly, crises propel even the most charismatically challenged individuals to act charismatically (Bligh, Kohles, & Meindl, 2004), can serve to whet perceivers' appetites for charisma (Bass, 2008), increase susceptibility to charismatic influence (Shamir & Howell, 1999), and unconsciously activate our search for leadership (Emrich, 1999). In a study of U.S. presidents, House, Spangler, and Woycke (1991) found a correlation between crisis measures and measures of presidential charisma. McCann (1997) found that threatening times were associated with the appeal of charismatic presidents. Pillai (1996) found that in student work groups, crisis situations fostered the emergence of charismatic leadership perceptions but, interestingly, not transactional leadership perceptions. These findings unambiguously suggest that charismatic perceptions and crises are related.

Why crises intensify perceivers' thirst for leadership can be understood by the reactions they elicit. Crises generate intense unpleasant feelings of ambiguity and uncertainty (Pearson & Clair, 1998), a state that conflicts with powerful motives to view the world as predictable and controllable (Pittman, 1998). Because direct control is oftentimes impossible during crises, individuals attempt to reassert control indirectly through secondary means (Skinner, 2007), such as projecting charismatic qualities onto their leaders, who are viewed as a source of meaning, salvation, and distress relief (Shamir & Howell, 1999). In line with this motivational explanation, findings reveal that crisis-induced charismatic leadership perceptions fade rapidly once a crisis has passed (Hunt, Boal, & Dodge, 1999).

Although such research suggests that crises are unique, in actuality, any situation that heightens a perceiver's psycho-physiological state propels us to romanticize leaders (Meindl, 1995). For instance, Pastor, Mayo, & Shamir (2007) heightened arousal by having participants ride a stationary bike, whereas others have manipulated psycho-physiological states by reminding participants of their own mortality (Cohen, Solomon, Maxfield, Pyszczynski, & Greenberg, 2004; Gordijn & Stapel, 2008; Landau, Greenberg, & Sullivan, 2009; Pittinsky & Welle, 2008). Regardless of the manipulation utilized, heightened arousal accentuated charismatic leadership perceptions (Cohen et al., 2004; Pastor et al., 2007), and the perceptions were stronger when the target already possessed some semblance of charisma (Pastor et al., 2007). Moving beyond simple perception, research further documents that heightened arousal increases support for incumbents (Landau et al., 2009), compliance (Landau et al., 2009), and receptivity to counterattitudinal visions (Gordijn & Stapel, 2008). Why cycling, thoughts of death, and experiencing a crisis function similarly requires further consideration from scholars.

Beyond crises, researchers have also demonstrated a link between charismatic leadership images and perceived distance to a target. Although perceptions of charisma are distributed across all organizational levels, it is widely recognized that there is a fundamental difference between proximal leadership and leadership at a distance (Shamir, 1995). As distance increases between leaders and the led, observers are more prone to base their leadership impressions on simplified heuristics, such as the performance of the organization or their general stereotyped impression of leaders (Antonakis & Atwater, 2002). Better understanding of this perceptual bias may lie in a better appreciation of the principles of construal level theory (CLT; see Trope & Liberman, 2003), which suggests that with increasing distance, regardless of type, our conceptualizations of events and objects become more abstract and simpler. Seemingly, CLT may provide us with a promising overarching framework and important insights into the characteristics of leadership judgments that predispose perceivers to generate overly ideal, prototypic, and charismatic leadership evaluations.

A further contextual consideration that has received some attention is the social environment within which observers find themselves. Individual perceivers are interconnected into larger social networks, which raise the possibility that leadership perceptions are susceptible to social contagion (Meindl, 1990). Rather than simply resulting from individual sensemaking, leadership perceptions can spread like a common cold throughout a social network (Mayo & Pastor, 2007; Pastor, Meindl, & Mayo, 2002). Such findings undermine a common misperception regarding the wisdom of crowds and proposals that group-level analyses reflect the actual behavior of the target (Mount & Scullen, 2001). Instead, contagion research suggests that the social construction of leadership can, and does, span all levels of analysis (i.e., individual, dyadic, group).

Interestingly, communication along social pathways need not be explicit, but rather, it can spread subtly through seemingly irrelevant derogatory remarks (Goodman, Schell, Alexander, & Eidelman, 2008) or nonverbal displays. Nonverbal facial expressions represent a particularly intriguing investigative angle, not only because they are widely recognized to serve as clues to a fellow social actor's attitudes and behavioral intentions (Ekman & Oster, 1979) but also because their spread can be insidious and, therefore, unpreventable. Functionally, the nonverbal displays of fellow social actors assist us in making sense of a leader's activities. Once perceived, nonverbal information is spontaneously mimicked by observers, and the afferent feedback that results generates corresponding emotions, which can color subsequent information processing (Halberstadt, Winkielman, Niedenthal, & Dalle, 2009). Coinciding with this thinking, research shows that observers judge leaders to be more effective when they are surrounded by positive, versus negative, nonverbal displays from group members (V. Brown & Geis, 1984) and that negative attitudes toward a female leader may stem in part from the nonverbal disapproval on the faces of fellow subordinates (Butler &

Geis, 1990). Interestingly, susceptibility to nonverbal leadership influences may depend on individual differences, such as one's interest in affiliating with others (Lakin & Chartrand, 2003), self-monitoring (Cheng & Chartrand, 2003), or information-processing style (van Baaren, Horgan, Chartrand, & Dijkmans, 2004).

To summarize, research indicates that humans are leader-centric thinkers who use the leader category to explain their worlds. What remains unclear is the very concept of leadership itself—what it looks like, how it develops, and the information processing that lies behind its application. I turn to these questions below.

The Social-Cognitive Approach

To delve deeper into how followers generate leadership perceptions, it is necessary to underscore the fact that human cognition is premised on symbolic structures that are stored in long-term memory and that serve as a stable, internal, mental model. Instead of processing each instance of an object, event, person, or animal as novel, people transform their "transient experiences into internal models" (Bandura, 1986, p. 18). In categorizing instances, social actors are able to bring to bear enormous quantities of stored conceptual knowledge, which in turn allows them to know what to anticipate and how to behave (G. L. Murphy, 2002). Furthermore, concepts and categories are the bedrock of efficient, effective communication, which is premised on a common mental map of the world. In the end, the application of the leader category to a target such as Yertle the Turtle allows us to infer a tremendous amount of information, to understand his actions, to coordinate our actions in relation to him, and comprehend the activities of our fellow pond dwellers.

Given the centrality of categories for information processing, the content, creation, and deployment of the leader category are central to the follower-centric approach (D. J. Brown, Scott, & Lewis, 2004). In the sections that follow, I address these issues. First, I consider what is known about the content of the leader category. Second, I address issues surrounding the variability and stability of the category. Third, I consider the development of the category. Fourth, I address how the category influences information processing and comes to be applied. Finally, I briefly discuss how the application of relevant leader categories can free or constrain a leader's behavior.

The Content and Nature of the Leader Category

As with other elements of the world, perceivers hold in memory a well-elaborated category that includes the features that distinguish leaders from nonleaders (Lord et al., 1984; Lord, Foti, & Phillips, 1982). Following the probabilistic view (Rosch, 1978), the leader category is conceptualized as a

fuzzy and ill-defined knowledge structure composed of properties that individually, are neither necessary nor sufficient to warrant inclusion in the category. As with other concepts, the application of the leader category follows
the family resemblance principle, whereby potential category members vary
along a prototypic fit gradient. As one example, consider that although
"birds" typically fly, the fact that a particular animal does not fly (e.g., a
chicken) does not preclude it from membership as a "bird," but rather simply
suggests that the target is less bird-like than other exemplars (e.g., robin).
Ultimately, the higher the proportion of attributes a target shares with other
category members, the more prototypical it is deemed to be.

Based on previous work (Cantor & Mischel, 1979), Lord and his colleagues have suggested that the leader category is structured around traits
(Lord, De Vader, & Alliger, 1986). Traits are central to human thinking and
memory processes (Srull & Wyer, 1989) and are automatically and spontaneously applied when perceivers are confronted with others' behavior (e.g.,
Uleman, Newman, & Moskowitz, 1996). In fact, traits are so hardwired
into our thinking that we perceive much of the inanimate and animal world
in trait terms (Epley, Waytz, & Cacioppo, 2007). Given the centrality of
traits, it makes considerable sense that they are the foundation of leadership
perception.

Several authors have attempted to document the precise trait content of
the leader category (Epitropaki & Martin, 2004; Lord et al., 1984;
Offermann, Kennedy, & Wirtz, 1994). In an initial investigation utilizing a
free recall methodology, Lord et al. (1984) found that 59 traits were uniquely
generated by their participants (e.g., honest, intelligent, dedicated) and that
these traits varied in terms of their prototypicality. Subsequent investigations
have replicated this initial work, shortened the measure, and identified the
second-order factor structure (Epitopaki & Martin, 2004; Offerman et al.,
1994). Despite these noteworthy gains, one oddity with this recent literature
has been its failure to keep pace with personality science. Research shows that
the Big Five personality structure is elicited universally when rating both
oneself and others (Goldberg, 1990) and has been linked to leadership emergence and effectiveness (Judge, Bono, Ilies, & Gerhardt, 2002). Moving forward, modeling the leader category with the Big Five would seem to offer the
significant advantage of providing leader-centric and follower-centric
researchers with a common construct space.

In the end, individuals do not extract a single leader category from the
world, but rather a nested three-level structure: superordinate, basic, and
subordinate (Rosch, 1978). At the most inclusive level, referred to as superordinate, the broadest and most abstract representation of the category
exists. This level of representation contains those features that are generally
common to most leaders and that overlap very little with contrasting categories (e.g., nonleaders). Immediately embedded beneath this level is the basic
level, which incorporates context. Lord et al. (1984) have argued that individuals distinguish 11 different basic level leaders: business, finance, minority,

education, religion, sports, national politics, world politics, labor, media, and military. Although Lord et al.'s work is seminal, it is worth noting that this structure is based on a single study and that alternative basic level categories may exist (see Den Hartog & Koopman, 2005). Finally, at the subordinate level, leader categories are further differentiated, providing a highly nuanced understanding of leadership. As but one example, some research indicates that the leader category may differ for male and female leaders (Johnson, Murphy, Zewdie, & Reichard, 2008).

Before continuing, it is worth mentioning that in recent years, there has been growing interest in the role that group categories play in terms of our information processing about leadership (see Chapter 14 this volume; D. van Knippenberg, van Knippenberg, & Giessner, 2007). In everyday situations, leadership is enacted in group settings, and fit with a group is germane to understanding how followers react to potential leaders (Hogg, 2001; van Knippenberg & Hogg, 2003). On the basis of social identity theory, Hogg and his colleagues have proposed that in addition to our general leader stereotype, discussed above, the group prototype that encapsulates the prototypical values, attitudes, and norms of a group also serves as a relevant yardstick against which potential leaders can be evaluated. As with the general leader category, potential leader targets vary along a group prototypicality gradient and followers' endorsement of leaders depends on the target's fit with the shared social identity of a group. Fit with a group's shared identity is relevant to leadership perceptions because it serves to reassure followers that a leader is trustworthy and that he or she will behave in a manner that is consistent with the collective interest (D. van Knippenberg et al., 2007). Coinciding with this thinking, a substantial and ever-growing body of work indicates that leader fit to a group category relates to perceived leader effectiveness (Hains, Hogg, & Duck, 1997; Hogg, Hains, & Mason, 1998; Platow & van Knippenberg, 2001) and charisma (Platow, Haslam, Foddy, & Grace, 2003; B. van Knippenberg & van Knippenberg, 2005). At this point, I simply acknowledge the relevance of the group category; subsequently, I discuss how perceivers reconcile and integrate information about a given target's fit with the general leader category and the group category.

Variability and Stability of the Leader Category

Despite attempts to demonstrate otherwise, research findings indicate that the cumulative lifetime leadership observations and experiences of groups within a society are largely shared. Sensibly, just as most groups within a society share a common conceptual understanding of other concepts, they also share a common understanding of leadership. Findings indicate that university students and employees possess similar mental models of leadership, as do employees who differ in terms of age, organizational tenure, organizational position (Epitropaki & Martin, 2004; Offermann et al., 1994), and organizational identification (Martin & Epitropaki, 2001). If we are to find group level differences, it seems likely that we will need to find groups who may have had significant, early, repeated exposure to different role models, group structures, and leadership experiences. Consistent with this idea, some evidence suggests that males and females exhibit slight differences in their leader categories (Deal & Stevenson, 1998; Den Hartog & Koopman, 2005; Epitropaki & Martin, 2004). In this regard, some findings suggest that males, relative to females, may hold ideal leader categories that are more forgiving of antiprototypical characteristics, such as domineering and pushy, whereas females' ideal prototypes emphasize interpersonal sensitivity (Deal & Stevenson, 1998). Thus, despite some limited evidence for gender differences, the leader category appears to be highly robust, at least within a culture.

Increased globalization has motivated numerous scholars to investigate how culture can taint the leader category. Cultural differences exist in what individuals expect from, and how they perceive and react to different leader behaviors (Ensari & Murphy, 2003; for a review, see Tsui, Nifadkar, & Ou, 2007). For instance, research suggests that individuals vary cross-culturally in how they react to abusive leaders (Bond, Wan, Leung, & Giacalone, 1985) or violations of justice principles (Gelfand, Erez, & Aycan, 2007; Tsui et al., 2007). Such findings underscore the possibility that Western leadership conceptualizations may not be universally endorsed (Den Hartog, House, Hanges, Ruiz-Quintanilla, & Dorfman, 1999; Gerstner & Day, 1994; Javidan, Dorfman, de Luque, & House, 2006).

To assess cross-cultural variability in the leader category, Robert House and his colleagues (Javidan et al., 2006) questioned 15,022 middle managers from 62 different societies (average per society $n = 250$), who were organized into 10 cultural clusters of nations. They asked the managers to rate 112 leadership items, which composed 21 primary and 6 underlying dimensions, in terms of each item's ability to impede or facilitate effective leadership. Research from this herculean effort has provided us with an initial glimpse into the cultural universality and divergence of the leader category. In terms of the second-order factors, significant differences emerged between the 10 cultural clusters along all six dimensions. For instance, results at this level of analysis suggest that the 10 clusters of nations differ significantly in terms of the extent to which they emphasize charismatic/value-based leadership, a form of leadership that focuses on motivating and expecting high outcomes from individuals. Thus, whereas Anglo countries, such as the United States, score high on the charismatic/value-based dimension, Middle Eastern countries, such as Egypt, place less emphasis on this dimension; countries in the Confucian Asia cluster (e.g., China) fall between these two extremes (Javidan et al., 2006).

Although results along the six dimensions suggest that cultures differ profoundly in terms of their understanding of what it means to be a leader, item-level analyses suggest that such conclusions should be tempered and that a significant universally shared understanding of leadership exists. On this front, 22 attributes investigated by the GLOBE researchers emerged as universally desirable (e.g., honest, decisive, motivational, dynamic), whereas eight were widely regarded as undesirable (e.g., loner, irritable, egocentric, ruthless). Such similarity suggests that there may be a common universal leadership experience. In this regard, evolutionary thinkers propose that leadership is a group adaptation and that ideal leaders fulfill common group functions, such as initiating group activity, maintaining cohesion, and planning for the future (see chapter 5, this volume; Van Vugt, Hogan, & Kaiser, 2008).

Moving beyond group differences, our understanding of the leader category has also been enhanced by work that has assessed individual stability (Epitropaki & Martin, 2004). In one such examination, Epitropaki and Martin asked respondents to indicate how descriptive a series of traits were of a business leader in general, assessed on two occasions, one year apart. Overall, they concluded that the business leader category is not particularly ephemeral. To understand why stability emerged in their research, it is necessary that readers first recognize that although humans are capable of careful, conscious, serial thought, more often than not the world is experienced through a nonconscious system (Macrae & Bodenhausen, 2000; McClelland, McNaughton, & O'Reilly, 1995). Knowledge in this system includes our generic beliefs about the world, which are gradually accumulated through repeated associations. Beginning early in childhood (see below), we are repeatedly exposed to leaders who possess particular traits, such as dedicated, intelligent, and sensitive. These repeated associations become interconnected, forming a generic leader knowledge structure (i.e., a leader category). Once formed, this generic category is highly resistant to change and provides us with a stable backdrop on which to experience the world. Devoid of context, Epitropaki and Martin's procedures likely resulted in participants simply recovering and utilizing their generic, static, stable mental representation (Macrae & Bodenhausen, 2000; McClelland et al., 1995; Smith & DeCoster, 2000). Their findings show us that the generic leader category possesses the same stability as other generic concepts, such as turtle, cow, mule, blueberry bush, and cat, which we would anticipate to remain highly stable over a one-year period.

Notwithstanding these findings, cognitive research does unequivocally suggest that categories can be quite dynamic and can be generated *in the moment*. The cognitive architecture of the nonconscious system is generally regarded to be connectionist. It is a system that is subsymbolic, meaning that knowledge is represented by patterns of activation of neuron-like units (Smith & DeCoster, 2000). As information is input into this system, connectionist architectures settle into (i.e., recognize) the best interpretation through a process of parallel constraint satisfaction, finding the pattern of activation that maximally accommodates the stored associations and the momentary pattern of external (e.g., gender, behavior) and internal (e.g., motives) constraints. Thus, for instance, whereas our generic concept of a bird might remain highly stable over time, our image of the category bird might shift slightly when standing on a ship gazing out over the vast expanse of Antarctica (see Barsalou, 1982).

Based on connectionist principles, Lord and his colleagues have laid out in very general terms how such a system might operate to generate dynamic, *momentary,* leader categories (Hanges, Lord, & Dickson, 2000; Lord, Brown, & Harvey, 2001). In one of the few studies to directly test their ideas, Foti, Knee, and Backert (2008) found evidence that suggested that the leader category shifted depending on the internal goals of an observer. Despite such encouraging findings, empirical data into the dynamic generation of the leader category remains limited, and this area remains ripe for research. It is worth noting that to effectively proceed with such investigations, it is likely that applied leadership researchers will need to forsake their preference for field data and conduct laboratory studies that allow them to momentarily manipulate constraints, such as observer goals, in a controlled manner.

The Development of the Leader Category

As noted above, beginning early in life, the leader category is unconsciously and slowly acquired as individuals soak up co-occurring leadership features. For instance, as children, we begin to associate business leaders with such characteristics as intelligent, competent, male, and White, and we mindlessly tether these together and lock them away in memory (Rosette, Leonardelli, & Phillips, 2008). Given that the bedrock of most leadership perception is the category stored in the slow learning, slow changing neocortical system, one may wonder whether there is a discernable developmental trajectory and age at which our generic leader category solidifies in memory. Simply put, leadership scholars largely have ignored this important basic scientific question. In one of the few studies to directly address this topic, Matthews, Lord, and Walker (1990) examined the development of the leader category among 159 children in the 1st, 3rd, 6th, 9th, and 12th grades. Coinciding with our understanding of the neocortical system, they found, relative to older children (i.e., 6th, 9th, and 12th grades), younger children (1st and 3rd grades) felt leadership was exemplified by specific actions, outcomes, and exemplars (e.g., parents), whereas older children based their judgments on a highly elaborated leader category. More recent work by Antonakis and Dalgas (2009) found that young children and naïve adults were similarly capable, and quite successful, at predicting election results on the basis of photographs. Seemingly, their findings suggest that very early on, children associate facial features with personality characteristics (i.e., competent), which are used to make leadership decisions similar to those generated by adults. Together, these two studies indicate that the standards utilized to form leadership perceptions consolidate at a very early age. An important practical implication of this work is that it suggests that interventions intended to

undermine biased leadership categories (e.g., emphasis on masculine characteristics) may be most efficacious at a very early age.

If the leader category takes shape early in our development, one might
anticipate that the world as seen through the eyes of children would play a
pivotal role in the nature of the leader category. As one obvious example,
because children are generally shorter than leadership figures in their lives
(e.g., teachers or parents), height (Judge & Cable, 2004) and the vertical
dimension of space (Schubert, 2005) should be tightly coupled to leadership,
which they are. Beyond such universal childhood experiences, idiosyncratic
childhood experiences with leadership figures should also be pivotal antecedents of category content (Hunt, Boal, & Sorenson, 1990). In one investigation, Keller (1999) asked participants to rate the extent to which a series of
characteristics were descriptive of their mother, their father, and an ideal
leader. Overall, her findings indicate that maternal and paternal characteristics influenced the ideal leader image. Although linkages between childhood
experiences and the leader category are sensible, the topic remains poorly
understood. This is unfortunate as associations with early childhood experience are provocative and may possibly underlie cultural variability or gender
bias in the category.

Category Use and Application

Prior research indicates that categories, such as stereotypes, are an important determinant of the impressions that are formed about a target. When
confronted with ambiguous or incomplete data, perceivers utilize categories
in a top-down manner, filling in gaps and generating stereotypic judgments.
Perhaps most famously, research shows that the factor structure of behavioral
questionnaires can be extracted, even when raters are asked to rate imaginary
leaders (Eden & Leviatan, 1975; Rush et al., 1977; Weiss & Adler, 1981). In
line with these findings, research also indicates that subordinate evaluations
on behavioral leadership questionnaires are strongly related to the leader
category (Avolio & Bass, 1989) and that raters who share a common leader
category generate similar behavioral ratings, even when they are rating different targets (Rush & Russell, 1988). Categorical thinking also leads individuals to misremember what it is an observed target has done (Sherman &
Hamilton, 1994; Srull & Wyer, 1989). For instance, several studies have
documented that perceivers confuse unobserved category-consistent behavior
with behaviors that were actually observed (Binning, Zaba, & Whattam,
1986; Phillips, 1984; Phillips & Lord, 1982). Practically, these findings have
important implications for leadership practice and, in particular, the amount
of faith we should place in behavioral questionnaires (Hunter et al., 2007).
Although behavioral leadership instruments are presumed to capture the
behavior of the target being scrutinized, categorical thinking processes can
color memory, encoding, and the retrieval of behavior (Shondrick, Dinh, &

Lord, 2010). Hence, what may be extracted from behavioral assessments may say more about the information processing of observers than the actual behavior of leaders.

One question that remains is how it is that perceivers decide to apply the label leader to a given target. In their categorization theory of leadership perceptions, Lord and his colleagues have argued that the assignment of the leader label to a target is contingent on the degree to which a target's features overlap with a perceiver's leadership category (Lord et al., 1984). The greater the overlap that exists between a target's perceived features and the category held in long term memory, the more strongly the category label leader will be applied to a target. In their seminal work, Lord and his associates (1984; Study 3) randomly assigned 95 undergraduate participants to read one of three vignettes that described a target, John Perry, as displaying either prototypical, neutral, or antiprototypical leadership behaviors. Their results indicated that this manipulation accounted for significant variation in perceivers' expectations that John Perry would engage in prototypical, antiprototypical, and neutral behaviors, as well as in his perceived accountability and responsibility for the success of a new product. Overall, these findings provided strong causal evidence for the operation of the recognition system and suggested that the application of the leader label also generated expectations for a target's future behavior.

Since this initial investigation, further refinements have documented that leader categorization mediates the relationship between observable target behaviors and leadership ratings (Fraser & Lord, 1988), biases memory retrieval (Rush & Russell, 1988), and is not dependent on the availability of a perceiver's cognitive resources (Maurer & Lord, 1991). Although relatively underinvestigated, some research has also documented the applicability of categorization theory to real-world settings, thus documenting the theory's external validity and applied utility. Such fieldwork has demonstrated that fit to the leader category not only influences leadership perceptions (Fielding & Hogg, 1997; Foti, Fraser, & Lord, 1982) but also serves as an antecedent of relevant employee outcomes (Engle & Lord, 1997; Epitropaki & Martin, 2005). On this latter point, in a longitudinal survey investigation, Epitropaki and Martin demonstrated that perceived supervisory fit to the leader category impacted the quality of the leader–member exchange (LMX) and, indirectly through LMX, influenced employee organizational commitment, job satisfaction, and well-being. Beyond demonstrating the applicability of the categorization approach, this research also highlights a way in which interested researchers might operationalize leader categorization. Although Lord's categorization theory has been highly regarded and cited, there has been little effort to understand how categorization mediates the impact of leader behavior, despite previous literature that has directly linked common behavioral measures with the leader category (Avolio & Bass, 1989).

Research also shows that seemingly irrelevant characteristics may lead to the perception that a target is leader like. For instance, data indicates that leadership is ascribed to targets based on their talkativeness (Stein & Heller, 1979), attractiveness (Cherulnik, Turns, & Wilderman, 1990), masculine appearance (Sczesny & Kühnen, 2004), or their perceptual salience (Phillips & Lord, 1981). Recently, it has been suggested that thinking does not simply occur in the head and our conceptual knowledge is grounded in our sensory and motor systems (Barsalou, Simmons, Barbey, & Wilson, 2003). Our conceptual representations are not simply stored as abstract symbols in memory but are also known through the way in which we directly experience the phenomenon in question. Motivational systems are intertwined with specific motor movements, emotions are linked to facial expressions, loneliness is linked to coldness (Zhong & Leonardelli, 2008), virtue is tied to clean smells (Liljenquist, Zhong, & Galinsky, 2010), and leadership is related to height (Judge & Cable, 2004). Dominant individuals lord over us, we look up to them, they are high in the food chain, they are at the top of the organizational chart, and like Yertle, they look down on us from high upon their thrones. The bodily experience of looking up, versus down, relates to leadership, power, and dominance and, hence, data indicate that we are more fluent in processing status information when it is presented in the appropriate spatial location (Schubert, 2005) and that vertical information conveyed through an organizational chart colors our leadership perceptions (Giessner & Schubert, 2007). Unraveling the links between bottom-up perceptual processes, embodied cognition, and the leader category promises to be an exciting research opportunity moving forward (see Lord & Shondrick, in press).

Although the recognition of leadership based on a match to the leader category deepens our understanding, it draws back the curtain only part way. Followers defer to leaders, not simply because they fit leadership images or because they occupy the appropriate spatial location, but also because they are relevant for meeting our goals. As Barsalou (1985) noted many years ago, target categorization depends not only on fit to the central tendency of a category, but also on the end-state or goal toward which a perceiver is striving. Although there is some speculation regarding the focal functions of leaders for groups and their members, it seems clear that the ultimate reason we forego our freedom is because leaders promote group survival and success (see chapter 5, this volume; Van Vugt et al., 2008). Findings stretching back more than 40 years have unequivocally demonstrated a link between leadership and group outcomes (e.g., Binning & Lord, 1980; Larson, 1982; Larson, Lingle, & Scerbo, 1984; Lord, Binning, Rush, & Thomas, 1978; Phillips & Lord, 1982). This research has shown that the attribution of group performance to leaders is robust and is not dependent on when the outcome information is delivered to the perceiver (Larson, 1982) or whether or not an individual has personal experience with a leader (Binning & Lord, 1980). Moreover, in line with Barsalou's findings, comparative studies that have contrasted recognition processes with performance information indicates that both sources are combined additively to render a judgment (Lord et al., 1978), although the relative weighting may depend on observer characteristics, such as culture (Ensari & Murphy, 2003).

As many readers may already have deduced, targets elicit the activation of numerous, sometimes competing, categories. At a minimum, followers can think about targets in terms of their compatibility with the leader category (Lord & Maher, 1993), the group category (B. van Knippenberg & van Knippenberg, 2005), racial categories (Rosette et al., 2008), previous leaders (Ritter & Lord, 2007), group performance (Phillips & Lord, 1981), and gender categories (Scott & Brown, 2006). The competition and interaction among these sources of information ricochets throughout the observer's mind, marking information processing in a multitude of ways. For example, Scott and Brown (2006) demonstrated that gender categories interacted with the processing of prototypical leadership behavior to impact behavioral encoding. Martell and DeSmet (2001) demonstrated that gender information influenced the decision criteria used by raters in forming judgments. Other research has shown that the sources of information interact to influence our evaluations of leaders. In this regard, prototypical leaders are viewed more favorably than nonprototypical leaders following success (Ensari & Murphy, 2003)—an effect that is particularly pronounced for Whites, as opposed to ethnic minorities (Rosette et al., 2008). Finally, some research has shown that the relative influence of various pieces of information may depend on characteristics of the perceiver. Here, a growing body of work has demonstrated that whereas fit to the leader category is generally important, it diminishes in importance, relative to the group category, as a function of individual identification with the group (Fielding & Hogg, 1997; Hains et al., 1997; Hogg et al., 1998). Clearly, the sensemaking of observers is highly complex and dependent on multiple pieces of data. The nuances of how perceivers integrate these sources still require further attention.

Follower Perceptions and Leader Action

To this point, I have highlighted some of the nuances that underlie leadership perceptions. Ultimately, leadership is about bidirectional influence, and the nature of follower's categorizations can serve as an important constraint on leader actions. For instance, although their perceived ability to deliver success is critical and failure is typically not an option for leaders, not all failures are equal and, at times, leaders may be granted a license to fail by subordinates (Giessner & van Knippenberg, 2008; Giessner, van Knippenberg, & Sleebos, 2009). In those two recent articles, Giessner and his colleagues manipulated a leader's fit to a group category, which was discussed previously, and the nature of the type of goal that the leader failed to achieve. Findings from this research indicated that although failure to meet minimal goals dampened the positive perceptions that subordinates had of leaders who fit a group category, the same was not true when leaders failed to reach maximal goals. In maximal goal contexts, group prototypical leaders were seemingly given the benefit of the doubt, and their failure did not undermine the benefits that they incurred from fitting the group category. Such findings reflect the wider literature that highlights the fact that performance and leadership inferences are not direct; rather, they are sensitive to the nature of the causal accounts offered for performance (Phillips & Lord, 1981) as well as to the processing schema utilized by observers (Foti & Lord, 1987; M. R. Murphy & Jones, 1993).

The research mentioned above suggests that follower leadership standards are potentially flexible and that at times, followers will free up leaders to behave in an idiosyncratic and nonnormative fashion (Hollander, 1992). For instance, research has demonstrated that self-sacrificial behavior, relative to self-beneficial behavior, is related to follower perceptions of a leader's legitimacy (Choi & Mai-Dalton, 1999; B. van Knippenberg & van Knippenberg, 2005; Yorges, Weiss, & Stickland, 1999). Although generally true, the relationship between leader self-sacrificial behavior and leader endorsement is contingent on whether or not a leader is categorized by observers to be a typical group member (B. van Knippenberg & van Knippenberg, 2005). Individuals categorized as typical of a group seemingly are not held to the same self-sacrificial standards as their less typical counterparts. Similarly, procedural fairness (Ullrich, Christ, & van Dick, 2009) and distributive justice (Platow & van Knippenberg, 2001) appear to be standards that are less important for leaders who are typical of the group than atypical. Finally, Platow and his colleagues (Platow, van Knippenberg, Haslam, van Knippenberg, & Spears, 2006) found that whereas leaders who were prototypical of the group could flexibly employ either transactional or group-oriented rhetoric, leaders who were atypical were seemingly tolerated only when they utilized group-oriented rhetoric. According to Hollander's idiosyncrasy credit model (1958), leaders accumulate subordinate trust from their contributions to groups. Findings such as those discussed above indicate that credit and leadership need not be hard fought, but instead can flow simply from followers' categorizations.

Conclusion

This chapter began with a question from a quizzical four-year-old who was befuddled by the curious, if not somewhat rude, behavior of an insolent turtle named Mack. In this chapter, I have presented literature, data, theory, and thoughts that I hope serve the reader well should he or she ever be similarly interrogated by an unrelenting preschooler—or a deposed politician, coach, business leader, or academic advisor—who wants to know why Yertle, the king of all turtles, received such shoddy treatment. Although traditionally leadership has been approached as a leader-centric phenomenon, the past 40 years of follower-centric research have demonstrated that leadership is bidirectional and is highly dependent on followers. Yertle failed as a leader not simply because of his behavioral shortcomings, but because Mack no longer categorized him as a leader. As I have highlighted in this chapter, researchers have made substantial strides in our understanding of the information processing behind these leadership perceptions.

Discussion Questions

1. Using what you know about follower information processing, create a leadership training intervention that is likely to maximize the extent to which a manager is assigned the label leader by his or her subordinates.

2. Before beginning, choose a specific setting and generate a list of the characteristics that are most likely to be deemed to be prototypical of leaders in that setting.

3. Following this, consider the nature of the behaviors that you would need to train.

4. Also, based on your understanding of observer information processing, in your training consider some of the challenges that a manager might confront in being deemed to be leader-like and how your training would help him or her offset these challenges.

5. Research discussed in this chapter indicates that the business leader category is associated with being White (see Rosette, Leonardelli, & Phillips, 2008). Develop a training intervention that might be used with children to offset this source of bias.

Supplementary Readings

Javidan, M., Dorfman, P. W., de Luque, M. S., & House, R. J. (2006). In the eye of the beholder: Cross cultural lessons in leadership from project GLOBE. *Academy of Management Perspectives, 20,* 67–90.

Kellerman, B. (2007). What every leader needs to know about followers. *Harvard Business Review, 85,* 84–91.

Kelley, R. E. (1988). In praise of followers. *Harvard Business Review, 66,* 142–148.

References

Anderson, C., & Kilduff, G. J. (2009). Why do dominant personalities attain influence in face-to-face groups? The competence-signaling effects of trait dominance. *Journal of Personality and Social Psychology, 96,* 491–503.

Antonakis, J., & Atwater, L. (2002). Leader distance: A review and a proposed theory. *The Leadership Quarterly, 13,* 673–704.

Antonakis, J., Cianciolo, A. T., & Sternberg, R. J. (2004). Leadership: Past, present, and future. In: J. Antonakis, A. T. Cianciolo, & R. J. Sternberg (Eds.), *The nature of leadership* (pp. 3–15). Thousand Oaks, CA: Sage.

Antonakis, J., & Dalgas, O. (2009). Predicting elections: Child's play! *Science, 323*(5918), 1183.

Avolio, B. J. (2007). Promoting more integrative strategies for leadership theory-building. *American Psychologist, 62,* 25–33.

Avolio, B. J., & Bass, B. M. (1989). Transformational leadership, charisma, and beyond. In J. G. Hunt, B. R. Baliga, H. P. Dachler, & C. A. Schreisheim (Eds.), *Emerging leadership vistas. International leadership symposia series* (pp. 29–49). Lexington, MA: Lexington Books.

Bandura, A. (1986). *Social foundations of thought and action: A social cognitive theory.* Englewood Cliffs, NJ: Prentice-Hall.

Barsalou, L. W. (1982). Context-independent and context-dependent information in concepts. *Memory & Cognition, 10,* 82–93.

Barsalou, L. W. (1985). Ideals, central tendency, and frequency of instantiation as determinants of graded structure in categories. *Journal of Experimental Psychology: Learning, Memory, and Cognition, 11,* 629–654.

Barsalou, L. W., Simmons, W. K., Barbey, A., & Wilson, C. D. (2003). Grounding conceptual knowledge in modality-specific systems. *Trends in Cognitive Sciences, 7,* 84–91.

Bass, B. M. (2008). *The Bass handbook of leadership: Theory, research, and managerial applications* (4th ed.). New York: Free Press.

Bass, B. M., & Yammarino, F. J. (1991). Congruence of self and others' leadership ratings of naval officers for understanding successful performance. *Applied Psychology: An International* Review, *40,* 437–454.

Baumeister, R. F., & Newman, L. S. (1995). The primacy of stories, the primacy of roles, and the polarizing effects of interpretive motives: Some propositions about narratives. In R. S. Wyer (Ed.), *Advances in social cognition* (Vol. 8, pp. 97–108). Hillsdale, NJ: Lawrence Erlbaum.

Bennis, W. (2008). Introduction. In R. E. Riggio, I. Chaleff, & J. Lipman-Blumen (Eds.), *The art of followership: How great followers create great leaders and organizations* (pp. xxiii–xxvii). San Francisco: Jossey-Bass.

Binning, J. F., & Lord, R. G. (1980). Boundary conditions for performance cue effects on group process ratings: Familiarity versus type of feedback. *Organizational Behavior and Human Decision Processes, 26,* 115–130.

Binning, J. F., Zaba, A. J., & Whattam, J. C. (1986). Explaining the biasing effects of performance cues in terms of cognitive categorization. *Academy of Management Journal, 29,* 521–535.

Bligh, M. C., Kohles, J. C., & Meindl, J. R. (2004). Charisma under crisis: Presidential leadership, rhetoric, and media responses before and after the September 11th terrorist attacks. *The Leadership Quarterly, 15,* 211–239.

Bond, M. H., Wan, W. C., Leung, K., & Giacalone, R. (1985). How are responses to verbal insult related to cultural collectivism and power distance? *Journal of Cross-Cultural Psychology, 16,* 111–127.

Brown, D. J., & Keeping, L. M. (2005). Elaborating the construct of transformational leadership: The role of affect. *The Leadership Quarterly, 16,* 245–272.

Brown, D. J., Scott, K. A., & Lewis, H. (2004). *Information processing and leadership.* In J. Antonakis, A. T. Cianciolo, & R. J. Sternberg (Eds.), *The nature of leadership* (pp. 125–147). Thousand Oaks, CA: Sage.

Brown, V., & Geis, F. L. (1984). Turning lead into gold. Evaluations of men and women leaders and the alchemy of social consensus. *Journal of Personality and Social Psychology, 46,* 811–824.

Butler, D., & Geis, F. L. (1990). Nonverbal affect responses to male and female leaders: Implications for leadership evaluations. *Journal of Personality and Social Psychology, 58,* 48–59.

Calder, B. J. (1977). An attribution theory of leadership. In B. M. Staw & G. R. Salancik (Eds.), *New directions in organizational behavior* (pp. 179–204). Chicago: St. Clair.

Cantor, N. W., & Mischel, W. (1979). Prototypes in person perception. In L. Berkowitz (Ed), *Advances in experimental social psychology* (Vol. 12, pp. 3–52). New York: Academic Press.

Chaleff, I. (1995). *The courageous follower: Standing up to and for our leaders.* San Francisco, CA: Berrett-Koehler.

Cheng, C. M., & Chartrand, T. L. (2003). Self-monitoring without awareness: Using mimicry as a nonconscious affiliation strategy. *Journal of Personality and Social Psychology, 85,* 1170–1179.

Cherulnik, P. D., Turns, L. C., & Wilderman, S. K. (1990). Physical appearance and leadership: Exploring the role of appearance-based attribution in leader emergence. *Journal of Applied Social Psychology, 20,* 1530–1539.

Choi, Y., & Mai-Dalton, R. R. (1999). The model of followers' responses to self-sacrificial leadership: An empirical test. *The Leadership Quarterly, 10,* 397–421.

Cohen, F., Solomon, S., Maxfield, M., Pyszczynski, T., & Greenberg, J. (2004). Fatal attraction: The effects of mortality salience on evaluations of charismatic, task-oriented, and relationship-oriented leaders. *Psychological Science, 15,* 846–851.

Deal, J. J., & Stevenson, M. A. (1998). Perceptions of female and male managers in the 1990s: Plus ca change. *Sex Roles, 38,* 287–300.

Den Hartog, D. N., House, R. J., Hanges, P. J., Ruiz-Quintanilla, S. A., & Dorfman, P. W. (1999). Culture specific and cross-culturally generalizable implicit leadership theories: Are attributes of charismatic/transformational leadership universally endorsed? *The Leadership Quarterly, 10,* 219–256.

Den Hartog, D. N., & Koopman, P. L. (2005). Implicit theories of leadership at different hierarchical levels. In B. Schyns & J. R. Meindl (Eds.), *Implicit leadership theories: Essays and explorations* (pp.135–148). Greenwich, CT: Information Age.

Dutton, J. E., & Ashford, S. J. (1993). Selling issues to top management. *Academy of Management Review, 18,* 397–428.

Eden, D., & Leviatan, U. (1975). Implicit leadership theories as determinant of the factor structure underlying supervisory behavior scales. *Journal of Applied Psychology, 60,* 736–741.

Ekman, P., & Oster, H. (1979). Facial expressions of emotion. *Annual Review of Psychology, 20,* 527–554.

Emrich, C. D. (1999). Context effects in leadership perception. *Personality and Social Psychology Bulletin, 25,* 991–1006.

Engle, E. M., & Lord, R. G. (1997). Implicit theories, self-schemas, and leader-member exchange. *Academy of Management Journal, 40,* 988–1010.

Ensari, N., & Murphy, S. E. (2003). Cross-cultural variations in leadership perceptions and attribution of charisma to the leader. *Organizational Behavior and Human Decision Processes, 92,* 52–66.

Epitropaki, O., & Martin, R. (2004). Implicit leadership theories in applied settings: Factor structure, generalizability and stability over time. *Journal of Applied Psychology, 89,* 293–310.

Epitropaki, O., & Martin, R. (2005). The moderating role of individual differences in the relation between transformational/transactional leadership perceptions and organizational identification. *The Leadership Quarterly, 16,* 569–589.

Epley, N., Waytz, A., & Cacioppo, J. T. (2007). On seeing human: A three-factor theory of anthropomorphism. *Psychological Review, 114,* 864–886.

Fiedler, F. E. (1967). *A theory of leadership effectiveness.* New York: McGraw-Hill.

Fielding, K. S., & Hogg, M. A. (1997). Social identity, self-categorization, and leadership: A field study of small interactive groups. *Group Dynamics: Theory, Research, and Practice, 1,* 39–51.

Fiske, S. T. (1998). Stereotyping, prejudice, and discrimination. In D. T. Gilbert, S. T. Fiske, & G. Lindzey (Eds.), *Handbook of social psychology* (4th ed., Vol. 2, pp. 357–411). Boston: McGraw-Hill.

Foti, R. J., Fraser, S. L., & Lord, R. G. (1982). Effects of leadership labels and prototypes on perceptions of political leaders. *Journal of Applied Psychology, 67,* 326–333.

Foti, R. J., Knee, R. E., & Backert, S. G. (2008). Multi-level implications of framing leadership perceptions as a dynamic process. *The Leadership Quarterly, 19,* 178–194.

Foti, R. J., & Lord, R. G. (1987). Prototypes and scripts: The effects of alternative methods of processing information on rating accuracy. *Organizational Behavior and Human Decision Processes, 39,* 318–340.

Fraser, S. L., & Lord, R. G. (1988). Stimulus prototypicality and general leadership impressions: Their role in leadership and behavioral ratings. *Journal of Psychology, 122,* 291–303.

Gelfand, M. J., Erez, M., & Aycan, Z. 2007. Cross-cultural organizational behavior. *Annual Review of Psychology, 58,* 479–514.

Gerstner, C. R., & Day, D. V. (1994). Cross-cultural comparison of leadership prototypes. *The Leadership Quarterly, 5,* 121–134.

Giessner, S. R., & Schubert, T. (2007). High in the hierarchy: How vertical location and judgments of leaders' power are interrelated. *Organizational Behavior and Human Decision Processes, 104,* 30–44.

Giessner, S. R., & van Knippenberg, D. (2008). "License to fail": Goal definition, leader group prototypicality, and perceptions of leadership effectiveness after leader failure. *Organizational Behavior and Human Decision Processes, 105,* 14–35.

Giessner, S. R., van Knippenberg, D., & Sleebos, E. (2009). License to fail? How leader group prototypicality moderates the effects of leader performance on perceptions of leadership effectiveness. *The Leadership Quarterly, 45,* 434–451.

Goldberg, L. R. (1990). An alternative "description of personality": The Big-Five factor structure. *Journal of Personality and Social Psychology, 59,* 1216–1229.

Goldhagen, D. J. (2009). *Worse than war: Genocide, eliminationism, and the ongoing assault on humanity.* New York: PublicAffairs.

Goodman, J. A., Schell, J., Alexander, M. G., & Eidelman, S. (2008). The impact of a derogatory remark on prejudice toward a gay male leader. *Journal of Applied Social Psychology, 38,* 542–555.

Gordijn, E. H., & Stapel, D. A. (2008). When controversial leaders with charisma are effective: The influence of terror on the need for vision and impact of mixed attitudinal messages. *European Journal of Social Psychology, 38,* 389–411.

Graen, G. B., & Scandura, T. A. (1987). Toward a psychology of dyadic organizing. In B. M. Staw & L. L. Cummings (Eds.), *Research in organizational behavior* (Vol. 9, pp.175–208). Greenwich, CT: JAI.

Grant, A. M., & Ashford, S. J. (2008). The dynamics of proactivity at work. *Research in Organizational Behavior, 28,* 3–34.

Hains, S. C., Hogg, M. A., & Duck, J. M. (1997). Self-categorization and leadership: Effects of group prototypicality and leader stereotypicality. *Personality and Social Psychology Bulletin, 23,* 1087–1100.

Halberstadt, J., Winkielman, P., Niedenthal, P. M., & Dalle, N. (2009). Emotional conception: How embodied emotion concepts guide perception and facial action. *Psychological Science, 20,* 1254–1261.

Hanges, P., Lord, R. G., & Dickson, M. W. (2000). An information-processing perspective on leadership and culture: A case for a connectionist architecture. *Applied Psychology: An International Review, 49,* 133–161.

Heider, F. (1958). *The psychology of interpersonal relations.* NY: John Wiley.

Hersey, P., & Blanchard, K. H. (1977). *The management of organizational behavior* (3rd ed.). Upper Saddle River, NJ: Prentice Hall.

Hogg, M. A. (2001). A social identity theory of leadership. *Personality and Social Psychology Review, 5,* 184–200.

Hogg, M. A., Hains, S. C. & Mason, I. (1998). Identification and leadership in small groups: Salience, frame of reference, and leader stereotypicality effects on leader evaluations. *Journal of Personality and Social Psychology, 75,* 1248–1263.

Hollander, E. P. (1958). Conformity, status, and idiosyncrasy credit. *Psychological Review, 65,* 117–127.

Hollander, E. P. (1992). Leadership, followership, self, and others. *The Leadership Quarterly, 3,* 43–54.

Hollander, E. P. (1993). Legitimacy, power and influence: A perspective on relational features of leadership. In M. M. Chemers & R. Ayman (Eds.), *Leadership theory and research: Perspectives and directions* (pp. 29–47). San Diego, CA: Academic Press.

Hollander, E. P., & Offermann, L. R. (1990). Power and leadership in organizations: Relationships in transition. *American Psychologist, 45,* 179–189.

House, R. J. (1971). A path-goal theory of leader effectiveness. *Administrative Science Quarterly, 16,* 321–339.

House, R. J., Spangler, W. D., & Woycke, J. (1991). Personality and charisma in the U.S. presidency: A psychological theory of leader effectiveness. *Administrative Science Quarterly, 36,* 364–396.

Howell, J. M., & Shamir, B. (2005). The role of followers in the charismatic leadership process: Relationships and their consequences. *Academy of Management Review 30,* 96–112.

Hunt, J. G., Boal, K. B., & Dodge, G. E. (1999). The effects of visionary and crisis-responsive charisma on followers: An experimental examination of two kinds of charismatic leadership. *The Leadership Quarterly, 10,* 423–448.

Hunt, J. G, Boal, K. B., & Sorenson, R. L. (1990). Top management leadership: Inside the black box. *The Leadership Quarterly, 1,* 41–65.

Hunter, S. T., Bedell-Avers, K. E., & Mumford, M. D. (2007). The typical leadership study: Assumptions, implications, and potential remedies. *The Leadership Quarterly, 18,* 435–446.

Javidan, M., Dorfman, P. W., de Luque, M. S., & House, R. J. (2006). In the eye of the beholder: Cross cultural lessons in leadership from project GLOBE. *Academy of Management Perspectives, 20,* 67–90.

Johnson, S. J., Murphy, S. E, Zewdie, S., & Reichard, R. J. (2008). The strong, sensitive type: Effects of gender stereotypes and leadership prototypes on the evaluation of male and female leaders. *Organizational Behavior and Human Decision Processes, 106,* 39–60.

Judge, T. A., Bono, J. E., Ilies, R., & Gerhardt, M. W. (2002). Personality and leadership: A qualitative and quantitative review. *Journal of Applied Psychology, 87,* 765–780.

Judge, T. A., & Cable, D. M. (2004). The effect of physical height on workplace success and income: Preliminary test of a theoretical model. *Journal of Applied Psychology, 89,* 428–441.

Judge, T. A., Colbert, A. E., & Ilies, R. (2004). Intelligence and leadership: A quantitative review and test of theoretical propositions. *Journal of Applied Psychology, 89,* 542–552.

Kark, R., Shamir, B., & Chen, G. (2003). The two faces of transformational leadership: Empowerment and dependency. *Journal of Applied Psychology, 88,* 246–255.

Keller, T. (1999). Images of the familiar: Individual differences and implicit leadership theories. *The Leadership Quarterly, 10,* 589–607.

Kellerman, B. (2008). *Followership: How followers are creating change and changing leaders.* Boston: Harvard Business School Publishing.

Kelley, R. E. (1992). *The power of followership.* New York: Doubleday.

Kerr, S., & Jermier, J. M. (1978). Substitutes for leadership: Their meaning and measurement. *Organizational Behavior and Human Performance, 22,* 375–403.

Kipnis, D., Schmidt, S. M., & Wilkinson, I. (1980). Intraorganizational influence tactics: Explorations in getting one's way. *Journal of Applied Psychology, 65,* 440–452.

Klein, K. J., & House, R. J. (1995). On fire: Charismatic leadership and levels of analysis. *The Leadership Quarterly, 6,* 183–198.

Kruglanski, A.W. (1996). Motivated social cognition: Principles of the interface. In E. T. Higgins & A. W. Kruglanski (Eds.), *Social psychology: Handbook of basic principles* (pp. 493–520), New York: Guilford.

Kunda, Z. (1990). The case for motivated reasoning. *Psychological Bulletin, 108,* 480–498.

Lakin, J. L., & Chartrand, T. L. (2003). Using nonconcious behavioral mimicry to create affiliation and rapport. *Psychological Science, 14,* 334–339.

Landau, M. J., Greenberg, J., & Sullivan, D. (2009). Managing terror when self-worth and worldviews collide: Evidence that mortality salience increases reluctance to self-enhance beyond authorities. *Journal of Experimental Social Psychology, 45,* 68–79.

Larson, J. R. (1982). Cognitive mechanisms mediating the impact of implicit theories of leader behavior on leader behavior ratings. *Organizational Behavior and Human Decision Processes, 29,* 129–140.

Larson, J. R., Lingle, J. H., & Scerbo, M. M. (1984). The impact of performance cues on leader-behavior ratings: The role of selective information availability and probabilistic response bias. *Organizational Behavior and Human Decision Processes, 33,* 323–349.

LePine, J. A., & Van Dyne, L. (2001). Voice and cooperative behavior as contrasting forms of contextual performance: Evidence of differential relationships with Big Five personality characteristics and cognitive ability. *Journal of Applied Psychology, 86,* 326–336.

Liljenquist, K., Zhong, C. B., & Galinsky, A. D. (2010). The smell of virtue: Clean scents promote reciprocity and charity. *Psychological Science, 21*, 381–383.

Livi, S., Kenny, D. A., Albright, L., & Pierro, A. (2008). A social relations analysis of leadership. *The Leadership Quarterly, 19*, 235–248.

Lord, R. G. (2008). Followers' cognitive and affective structures and leadership processes. In R. E. Riggio, I. Chaleff, & J. Lipman-Blumen (Eds.), *The art of followership: How great followers create great leaders and organizations* (pp. 255–266). San Francisco: Jossey-Bass.

Lord, R. G., Binning, J. F., Rush, M. C., & Thomas, J. C. (1978). The effect of performance cues and leader behavior on questionnaire ratings of leadership behavior. *Organizational Behavior and Human Decision Processes, 21*, 27–39.

Lord, R. G., & Brown, D. J. (2004). *Leadership processes and follower self-identity.* Mahwah, NJ: Lawrence Erlbaum.

Lord, R. G., Brown, D. J., & Freiberg, S. J. (1999). Understanding the dynamics of leadership: The role of follower self-concepts in the leader/follower relationship. *Organizational Behavior and Human Decision Processes, 78*, 167–203.

Lord, R. G., Brown, D. J., & Harvey, J. L. (2001). System constraints on leadership perceptions, behavior, and influence: An example of connectionist level processes. In M. A. Hogg & R. S. Tindale (Eds.), *Blackwell handbook of social psychology: Vol. 3. Group processes* (pp. 283–310.). Oxford, UK: Blackwell.

Lord, R. G., De Vader, C. L., & Alliger, G. M. (1986). A meta-analysis of the relation between personality traits and leadership perceptions: An application of validity generalization procedures. *Journal of Applied Psychology, 71*, 402–410.

Lord, R. G., & Emrich, C. G. (2000). Thinking outside the box by looking inside the box: Extending the cognitive revolution in leadership research. *The Leadership Quarterly, 11*, 551–579.

Lord, R. G., Foti, R. J., & De Vader, C. L. (1984). A test of leadership categorization theory: Internal structure, information processing, and leadership perceptions. *Organizational Behavior and Human Performance, 34*, 343–378.

Lord, R. G., Foti, R. J., & Philips, J. S. (1982). A theory of leadership categorization. In J. G. Hunt, U. Sekaran, & C. Schriesheim (Eds.), *Leadership: Beyond establishment views* (pp. 104–121). Carbondale: Southern Illinois University Press.

Lord, R. G., & Maher, K. J. (1993). *Leadership and information processing: Linking perceptions and performance.* New York: Routledge.

Lord, R. G., & Shondrick, S. J. (in press). Leadership and knowledge: Symbolic, connectionist, and embodied perspectives. *The Leadership Quarterly.*

Macrae, C. N., & Bodenhausen, G. V. (2000). Social cognition: Thinking categorically about others. *Annual Review of Psychology, 51*, 93–120.

Martell, R. F., & DeSmet, A. L. (2001). A diagnostic-ration approach to measuring beliefs about the leadership abilities of male and female managers. *Journal of Applied Psychology, 86*, 1223–1231.

Martin, R., & Epitropaki, O. (2001). Role of organizational identification on implicit leadership theories (ILTs), transformational leadership and work attitudes. *Group Processes and Intergroup Relations, 4*, 247–262.

Matthews, A. M., Lord, R. G., & Walker, J. B. (1990). *The development of leadership perceptions in children.* Unpublished manuscript, University of Akron.

Maurer, T. J., & Lord, R. G. (1991). An exploration of cognitive demands in group interaction as a moderator of information processing variables in perception of leadership. *Journal of Applied Social Psychology, 21*, 821–840.

Mayo, M., & Pastor, J. C. (2007). Leadership embedded in social networks: Looking at inter-follower processes. In B. Shamir, R. Pillai, M. C. Bligh, & M. Uhl-Bien (Eds.), *Follower-centered perspectives on leadership: A tribute to the memory of James R. Meindl* (pp. 93–114). Greenwich, CT: Information Age.

McCann, S. J. H. (1997). Threatening times and the election of charismatic U.S. presidents: With and without FDR. *The Journal of Psychology, 131*, 393–400.

McCauley, C. D., & Lombardo, M. M. (1990). BENCHMARKS®: An instrument for diagnosing managerial strengths and weaknesses. In K. E. Clark & M. B. Clark (Eds.), *Measures of leadership* (pp. 535–545). West Orange, NJ: Library of America.

McClelland, J. L., McNaughton, B. L., & O'Reilly, R. C. (1995). Why there are complementary learning systems in the hippocampus and neocortex: Insights from the successes and failures of connectionist models of learning and memory. *Psychological Review, 102*, 419–457.

McEvoy, G. M., & Beatty, R. (1989). Assessment centers and subordinate appraisals of managers: A seven year examination of predictive validity. *Personnel Psychology, 42*, 37–52.

Meindl, J. R. (1990). On leadership: An alternative to the conventional wisdom. In B. A. Staw (Ed.), *Research in organizational behavior* (Vol. 12, pp. 159–203). New York: JAI.

Meindl, J. R. (1995). The romance of leadership as a follower-centric theory: A social constructionist approach. *The Leadership Quarterly, 6*, 329–341.

Meindl, J. R., & Ehrlich, S. B. (1987). The romance of leadership and the evaluation of organizational performance. *Academy of Management Journal, 30*, 91–109.

Meindl, J. R., Ehrlich, S. B., & Dukerich, J. M. (1985). The romance of leadership. *Administrative Science Quarterly, 30*, 78–102.

Mitchell, M. S., & Ambrose, M. L. (2007). Abusive supervision and workplace deviance and the moderating effects of negative reciprocity beliefs. *Journal of Applied Psychology, 92*, 1159–1168.

Mount, M. K., & Scullen, S. E. (2001). Multisource feedback ratings: What do they really measure? In M. London (Ed.), *How people evaluate others in organizations* (pp. 155–176). Mahwah, NJ: Lawrence Erlbaum.

Murphy, G. L. (2002). *The big book of concepts.* Cambridge, MA: MIT Press.

Murphy, M. R., & Jones, A. P. (1993). The influences of performance cues and observational focus on performance rating accuracy. *Journal of Applied Social Psychology, 23*, 1523–1545.

Near, J. P., & Miceli, M. P. (1987) Whistle-blowers in organizations: Dissidents or reformers? In M. S. Barry & L. L. Cummings (Eds.), *Research in organizational behavior* (Vol. 9, pp. 321–368). Greenwich, CT: JAI.

Offerman, L. R., Kennedy, J. K., & Wirtz, P. W. (1994). Implicit leadership theories: Content, structure and generalizability. *The Leadership Quarterly, 5*, 43–58.

Pastor, J. C., Mayo, M., & Shamir, B. (2007). Adding fuel to fire: The impact of followers' arousal on ratings of charisma. *Journal of Applied Psychology, 92*, 1584–1596.

Pastor, J. C., Meindl, J. R., & Mayo, M. C. (2002). A network effects model of charisma attributes. *Academy of Management Journal, 2*, 410–420.

Pearson, C. M., & Clair, J. A. (1998). Reframing crisis management. *The Academy of Management Review, 23*, 59–76.

Pfeffer, J. (1977). The ambiguity of leadership. *Academy of Management, 2,* 104–112.

Phillips, J. S. (1984). The accuracy of leadership ratings: A cognitive categorization perspective. *Organization Behavior and Human Performance, 33,* 125–138.

Phillips, J. S., & Lord, R. G. (1981). Causal attributions and perceptions of leadership. *Organizational Behavior and Human Performance, 28,* 143–163.

Phillips, J. S., & Lord, R. G. (1982). Schematic information processing and perceptions of leadership in problem-solving groups. *Journal of Applied Psychology, 67,* 486–492.

Pillai, R. (1996). Crisis and the emergence of charismatic leadership in groups: An experimental investigation. *Journal of Applied Social Psychology, 26,* 543–562.

Pillai, R., Kohles, J. C., & Bligh, M. C. (2007). Through thick and thin? Follower constructions of presidential leadership amidst crisis, 2001–2005. In B. Shamir, R. Pillai, M. C. Bligh, & M. Uhl-Bien, M. (Eds.), *Follower-centered perspectives on leadership: A tribute to the memory of James R. Meindl* (pp. 135–166). Greenwich, CT: Information Age.

Pittinsky, T. L., & Welle, B. (2008). Negative outgroup leader actions increase liking for ingroup leaders: An experimental test of intergroup leader-enhancement effects. *Group Processes & Intergroup Relations, 11,* 513–523.

Pittman, T. S. (1998). Motivation. In D. Gilbert, S. Fiske, & G. Lindsay (Eds.), *Handbook of social psychology* (4th ed., pp. 549–590). Boston: McGraw-Hill.

Platow, M. J., Haslam, S. A., Foddy, M., & Grace, D. M. (2003). Leadership as the outcome of self-categorization processes. In D. van Knippenberg & M. A. Hogg (Eds.), *Identity, leadership and power* (pp. 34–47). London: Sage.

Platow, M. J., & van Knippenberg, D. (2001). A social identity analysis of leadership endorsement: The effects of leader ingroup prototypicality and distributive intergroup fairness. *Personality and Social Psychology Bulletin, 27,* 1508–1519.

Platow, M. J., van Knippenberg, D., Haslam, S. A., van Knippenberg, B., & Spears, R. (2006). A special gift we bestow on you for being representative of us: Considering leader charisma from a self-categorization perspective. *British Journal of Social Psychology, 45,* 303–320.

Riggio, R. E., Chaleff, I., & Lipman-Blumen, J. (2008) *The art of followership: How great followers create great leaders and organizations.* San Francisco: Jossey-Bass.

Ritter, B. A., & Lord, R. G. (2007). The impact of previous leaders on the evaluation of new leaders: An alternative to prototype matching. *Journal of Applied Psychology, 92,* 1683–1695.

Rosch, E. (1978). Principles of categorization. In E. Rosch & B. B. Lloyd (Eds.), *Cognition and categorization* (pp 27–48). Hillsdale, NJ: Lawrence Erlbaum.

Rosette, A., Leonardelli, G. J., & Phillips, K. W. (2008). The White standard: Racial bias in leader categorization. *Journal of Applied Psychology, 93,* 758–777.

Rush, M. C., & Russell, J. E. (1988). Leader prototypes and prototype-contingent consensus in leader behavior descriptions. *Journal of Experimental Social Psychology, 24,* 88–104.

Rush, M. C., Thomas, J. C., & Lord, R. G. (1977). Implicit leadership theory: A potential threat to the internal validity of leader behavior questionnaires. *Organizational Behavior and Human Performance, 20,* 93–110.

Salancik, G. R., & Pfeffer, J. (1978). A social information processing approach to job attitudes and task design. *Administrative Science Quarterly, 23,* 224–253.

Schubert, T. W. (2005). Your highness: Vertical positions as perceptual symbols of power. *Journal of Personality and Social Psychology, 89,* 1–21.

Scott, K. A., & Brown, D. J. (2006). Female first, leader second? Gender bias in the encoding of leadership behavior. *Organizational Behavior and Human Decision Processes, 101,* 230–242.

Sczesny, S., & Kühnen, U. (2004). Meta-cognition about biological sex and gender-stereotypic physical appearance: Consequences for the assessment of leadership competence. *Personality and Social Psychology Bulletin, 30,* 13–21.

Seuss, Dr. [Theodore Geisel]. (1958). *Yertle the Turtle and other stories.* New York: Random House.

Shamir, B. (1995). Social distance and charisma: Theoretical notes and an exploratory study. *The Leadership Quarterly, 6,* 19–47.

Shamir, B., & Howell, J. M. (1999). Organizational and contextual influences on the emergence and effectiveness of charismatic leadership. *The Leadership Quarterly, 10,* 257–283.

Sherman, J. W., & Hamilton, D. L. (1994). On the formation of interitem associative links in person memory. *Journal of Experimental Social Psychology, 30,* 203–217.

Shondrick, S. J., Dinh, J. E., & Lord, R. G. (2010). Developments in implicit leadership theory and cognitive science: Applications to improving measurement and understanding alternatives to hierarchical leadership. *The Leadership Quarterly, 21,* 959–978.

Skinner, E. A. (2007). Secondary control critiqued: Is it secondary? Is it control? Comment on Morling and Evered (2006). *Psychological Bulletin, 133,* 911–916.

Smith, E. R., & DeCoster, J. (2000). Dual-process models in social and cognitive psychology: Conceptual integration and links to underlying memory systems. *Personality and Social Psychology Review, 4,* 108–131.

Srull, T. K., & Wyer, R. S. (1989). Person memory and judgment. *Psychological Review, 96,* 58–83.

Starbuck, W. H., & Milliken, F. J. (1988). Executive perceptual filters: What they notice and how they make sense. In D. Hambrick (Ed.), *The executive effect: Concepts and methods for studying top managers* (pp. 35–65). Greenwich, CT: JAI.

Stein, R. T., & Heller, T. (1979). An empirical analysis of the correlation between leadership status and participation rates reported in the literature. *Journal of Personality and Social Psychology, 37,* 1993–2002.

Tiedens, L. Z., & Fragale, A. R. (2003). Power moves: Complementarity in submissive and dominant nonverbal behavior. *Journal of Personality and Social Psychology, 84,* 558–568.

Tiedens, L. Z., Unzueta, M. M., & Young, M. J. (2007). The desire for hierarchy? The motivated perception of dominance complementarity in task partners. *Journal of Personality and Social Psychology, 93,* 402–414.

Trope, Y., & Liberman, N. (2003). Temporal construal. *Psychological Review, 110,* 403–421.

Tsui, A. S., Nifadkar, S. S., & Ou, A. Y. (2007). Cross-national, cross-cultural organizational behavior research: Advances, gaps, and recommendations, *Journal of Management, 33,* 426–478.

Uhl-Bien, M., & Pillai, R. (2007). The romance of leadership and the social construction of followership. In B. Shamir, R. Pillai, M. Bligh, & M. Uhl-Bien (Eds.), *Follower-centered perspectives on leadership: A tribute to the memory of James R. Meindl* (pp. 187–209). Greenwich, CT: Information Age.

Uleman, J. S., Newman, L. S., & Moskowitz, G. B. (1996). People as flexible interpreters: Evidence and issues form spontaneous trait inference. In M. P. Zanna (Ed.), *Advances in experimental social psychology* (Vol. 28, pp. 211–279). New York: Academic Press.

Ullrich, J., Christ, O., & van Dick, R. (2009). Substitutes for procedural fairness: Prototypical leaders are endorsed whether they are fair or not. *Journal of Applied Psychology, 94,* 235–244.

van Baaren, R., Horgan, T., Chartrand, T. L., & Dijkmans, M. (2004). The forest, the trees, and the chameleon: Context dependency and nonconscious mimicry. *Journal of Personality and Social Psychology, 86,* 453–459.

van Knippenberg, B., & van Knippenberg, D. (2005). Leader self-sacrifice and leadership effectiveness: The moderating role of leader prototypicality. *Journal of Applied Psychology, 90,* 25–37.

van Knippenberg, D., & Hogg, M. A. (2003). A social identity model of leadership effectiveness in organizations. *Research in Organizational Behavior, 25,* 243–295.

van Knippenberg, D., van Knippenberg, B., & Giessner, S. R. (2007). Extending the follower-centered perspective on leadership: Leadership as an outcome of shared social identity. In B. Shamir, R. Pillai, M. Bligh, & M. Uhl-Bien (Eds.), *Follower-centered perspectives on leadership: A tribute to the memory of James R. Meindl* (pp. 51–70). Greenwich, CT: Information Age.

van Velsor, E., Taylor, S., & Leslie, J. B. (1993). An examination of the relationships among self-perception accuracy, self-awareness, gender, and leader effectiveness. *Human Resource Management, 32,* 249–255.

Van Vugt, M., Hogan, R., & Kaiser, R. B. (2008). Leadership, followership, and evolution: Some lessons from the past. *American Psychologist, 63,* 182–196.

Walker, A. G., & Smither, J. W. (1999). A five-year study of upward feedback: What managers do with their results matters. *Personnel Psychology, 52,* 393–423.

Weiss, H. M., & Adler, S. (1981). Cognitive complexity and the structure of implicit leadership theories. *Journal of Applied Psychology, 66,* 69–78.

Yammarino, F., & Dubinsky, A. (1994). Transformational leadership theory: Using levels of analysis to determine boundary conditions. *Personnel Psychology, 47,* 787–811.

Yorges, S. L., Weiss, H. M., & Strickland, O. J. (1999). The effect of leader outcomes on influence, attributions, and perceptions of charisma. *Journal of Applied Psychology, 84,* 428–436.

Zhong, C. B., & Leonardelli, G. J. (2008). Cold and lonely: Does social exclusion literally feel cold? *Psychological Science, 19,* 838–842.

11

The Nature of
Shared Leadership

Christina L. Wassenaar

Claremont Graduate University

Craig L. Pearce

University of Nebraska

It is amazing how much people get done if they do not worry about who gets the credit.

Swahili proverb

When we consider the nature of leadership, it conjures deep and profound considerations (Antonakis, Cianciolo & Sternberg, 2004). In this regard, shared leadership theory moves us from a perspective on leadership as a hierarchical role to that of leadership as a dynamic social process (Pearce & Conger, 2003). The notion of nature in human social behavior implies that the activities that are engaged in are inherent or characterological, that our instinct takes over our decisions, or that certain attributes or behaviors are innate. It implies that the actions that we take in our daily lives are part of a predetermined character that is formed through our environment, upbringing, and cultural history. As members of a community, as parents, children, employees, and finally as leaders, our nature—the foundation of who we are—is integral to how we interact with those around us.

But is that enough? Can we rely on our personal and traditional understanding of societal rules in a world that is clearly moving in new directions, driven primarily by technology but also by demography, the rise and fall of various

AUTHORS' NOTE: Please address correspondence concerning this chapter to Christina L. Wassenaar, e-mail christina.l.wassenaar@gmail.com, or Craig L. Pearce, e-mail craig.l.pearce@gmail.com.

embedded norms, and by new geopolitical paradigms? At some level, we are part of a brave new world—but how many times have our ancestors wrestled with change? Even more relevant to the topic at hand, *who* led this change?

Accordingly, the purpose of this chapter is to offer a foundational view of the theory of shared leadership. In the past few decades, this particular form of leadership—which has been present in our society for ages—has gained relevance both in its practical application through the workplace and in scientific research. Shared leadership is defined as "a dynamic, interactive influence process among individuals in groups for which the objective is to lead one another to the achievement of group or organizational goals or both" (Pearce & Conger, 2003, p. 1). In other words, shared leadership occurs when group members actively and intentionally shift the role of leader to one another as needed by the environment or circumstances in which the group operates. Although this is markedly different from the more traditional models of leadership where the influence and decision making travels downstream from the vertical leader to the followers (Day, Gronn, & Salas, 2004, 2006; Day & O'Connor, 2003; Pearce & Sims, 2000, 2002; Riggio, Chaleff, & Lipman-Blumen, 2008), it is *not* our intention to promote the idea that studying shared leadership supersede or replace the study of hierarchical leader or the more traditionally understood forms of leadership (Pearce, Conger, & Locke, 2008). Rather, with shared leadership, the role of leadership does not reside in one person's hands, but rather, in the group's arms as they move together toward common objectives.

Clearly, this type of leadership is a departure from the traditional understanding of the hierarchical leader. Our typical notion is that of a single person around whom the rest of the group circles and who is the arbiter of decisions and purpose. Throughout history, we have read about these celebrated souls (Bass & Bass, 2008; Carlyle, 1841/1894; Figueira, Brennan, & Sternberg, 2009)—and yes, we do celebrate them, for better or for worse. We aspire to achieve their status or at least, their acceptance. Because of this, the primary focus in the study of leadership has been on the attitudes, behaviors, and activities of these leaders with the hope of understanding, demystifying and, perhaps, even emulating them (Bass & Bass, 2008).

Pearce and Conger (2003) suggest that lately some in the scholarly community have divested themselves from this norm and have taken to the notion that leadership is actually a *process* that can be taught, shared, distributed, and collectively enacted. These scholars have also begun to popularize the view that leadership can be a shared influence process and that the role of leadership does *not* have to originate solely from a hierarchical leader. Rather, leadership can derive from any member of a group or social system who can offer the skills and talent that are needed by the project or system at the time (Hunt, 2004; Ropo, Eriksson, & Hunt, 1997). Of course, at this point, there exists far less empirical study in this area than in the older, more established leadership theories, but in the past two decades, momentum in the study of shared leadership has grown and taken great strides.

Therefore, in this chapter we will cover five main areas regarding shared leadership. First, we will identify the historical theoretical precursors to the development of shared leadership theory. Then we review studies of shared leadership that have begun to document its antecedents and outcomes. We then discuss some of the techniques that can be used to measure shared leadership, some of which have been used to great effect and some of which we would suggest using, based on the results of some of the more recent empirical study. Our fourth section will focus on the future of shared leadership research and some ideas for theory building and empirical research that can further expand our knowledge about this area of leadership. Finally, we will close with a view toward the future of leadership in organizations.

Sometimes, in order to go forward, we first need to go back. In the case of leadership study, Bass and Avolio (1993) point out that "new" theories related to the field of leadership are often re-pioneered versions of older theories (Yukl, 2002). In order to not fall into the selective memory trap, we will spend just a little time reviewing some of the historical underpinnings of shared leadership and how our current understanding of the shared leadership experience has been influenced by offerings from the fields of organizational behavior, psychology, teamwork, sociology, and leadership.

Historical Bases of Shared Leadership

It generally appears that prior to the Industrial Revolution, very little thought was given to the scientific study of leading others, or leadership. It was during this period, especially toward the 1830s and on, that the impact from the changes that were occurring at an increasingly rapid pace began to be studied in any scientific manner (Nardinelli, 2008). Of course, there were many people, from manufacturers to philosophers, who were writing about the phenomena that were affecting the global stage, but the main focus of their work centered on the transfer and movement of knowledge about technological advances (Stewart, 1998, 2003). However, Stewart (2003) noted that as late as the end of the 18th century, many of those who were considered scientists also began to address the scientific measurement of the social and managerial occurrences of the day. It was at the beginning of the 19th century when economists such as Jean Baptiste Say (1803/1964) wrote that entrepreneurs "must possess the art of superintendence and administration" (p. 330). The main interests of economists prior to his writing this were land and labor, and to some extent, capital. Eventually, the idea that leadership did have a role in business began to be more understood; however, this idea of leading others still focused mainly on the command and control activities that would be generated from the hierarchical leader. It was only later in that century that slight hints of shared leadership can be detected in management writing as another form of leading others (Pearce & Conger, 2003).

One of the earliest management thinkers in the area of systemic organizational and leadership approaches was Daniel C. McCallum. He developed one of the first groupings of principles related to management that could span various industries and were mainly focused on leadership. One of these principles was unity of command, where orders came from the top, and work was carried out by those down subsequent levels of the hierarchy (Wren, 1994). The overwhelming majority of the Industrial Revolution writing on leadership was focused on a top-down, command-and-control perspective (e.g., Montgomery, 1836, 1840; Wren, 1994). This perspective became firmly ensconced by the turn of the 20th century and was captured in what came to be known as "scientific management" (Gantt, 1916; Gilbreth, 1912; Gilbreth & Gilbreth, 1917; Taylor, 1903, 1911).

If we simply rested on the writing of the aforementioned authors and social philosophers, we could easily draw the conclusion that the absolute control of employee behavior by the employers is the only way our forebearers knew. However, if we step outside of these scholars, we notice small leadership nudges in another direction. One of the people who noticed and then wrote about her dissonant observations was a management consultant and community activist named Mary Parker Follett. She wrote about a concept called the *law of the situation* (Follett, 1924). She thought that instead of following the articulated leader in any and all situations, it sometimes made more sense to follow the person in the group who had the most knowledge about the situation in which the group was operating. Clearly, her ideas were a sharp departure from the normally accepted, hierarchical leadership model of the day—yet, they also appear to be quite closely associated with the idea of shared leadership theory.

Although Follett was a popular management consultant and speaker during the 1920s, the majority of the business community of the time discounted many of her ideas and writings. Some of this was a result of the economic reality of the time; things were so uncertain, especially during the 1930s and 1940s that the idea of losing control to anyone was anathema to the organizational leadership of the time (Drucker, 1954). However, Peter Drucker calls her "the brightest star in the management firmament" for that era (Drucker, 1995, p. 2).

Another pivotal pillar to the development of shared leadership in our historical review was the writing done by Hollander (1961) and quickly followed by others, which dealt with the idea that a leader can emerge or be selected by members of a leaderless group (e.g., Bartol & Martin, 1986; Hollander, 1978; Stein & Heller, 1979). It is clear that this type of theory building is integral to our deeper understanding of the psychological underpinnings for the emergence of a leader who has not been "chosen" by the upper management. The difference between shared leadership and emergent leadership is that whereas emergent leadership deals mainly with the choosing of an ultimate leader, the concept of shared leadership deals more with the idea that multiple leaders can and will emerge over time, based on the needs and situation in which the group finds itself (Pearce, 1997; Pearce & Sims, 2002).

An additional component that allows us a foundational look at the development of shared leadership theory is the literature on substitutes for leadership (e.g., Kerr & Jermier, 1978). Those writings suggest that there are possible substitutes for a hierarchical leader that can manifest themselves under certain circumstances. For example, in work that is highly routinized, the need for a leader or supervisor to oversee all facets of each individual's work is unnecessary. Taking this idea a step further, shared leadership can also serve as a substitute for a more formally designated leader.

The concept of self-leadership (Manz, 1986) can also be seen as emergent from the theory of leadership substitutes. Manz and Sims (1980) identified self-management, or self-leadership, as a possible substitute for a more traditionally appointed, vertical leader. They believed that (1) the more individual group members knew and understood about the organization's needs, the more highly skilled they were, and (2) the more motivated they were to engage in activities that were productive, the more likely their ability to lead themselves would mitigate the need for proximal control, direction, and supervision. Taking this idea just a little further, we can draw the conclusion that this could also work well at the group level and lead to the development of shared leadership in a group as each individual displayed his or her abilities, skills, organizational understanding, and motivation to achieve (Pearce & Conger, 2003).

Finally, the theory of empowerment should be briefly explored as a foundational component to shared leadership. This is a topic that has interested many in the field of leadership (e.g., Blau & Alba, 1982; Conger & Kanungo, 1988; Cox, Pearce, & Sims, 2003; Manz, 1986: Manz & Sims, 1989, 1990; Mohrman, Cohen, & Mohrman, 1995; Pearce & Sims, 2000, 2002) and deals mainly with the issue of power (e.g., Conger & Kanungo, 1988). Often, the primary focus in management research is on those at the top of the organization and their activities. Empowerment, however, focuses on the devolvement of power from those central power sources to those who are dealing with circumstances on a daily basis about which they might have higher levels of decision-making qualifications than those at the top.

Most of the literature and research in empowerment is focused on the individual (e.g., Conger & Kanungo, 1988), although there are some who are researching this phenomenon at the group level (e.g., Mohrman et al., 1995). It must be clearly noted that although empowering leadership or empowerment is definitely the act of sharing leadership, it is also not the equivalent of the shared leadership that can be created by a group. In order for shared leadership to fully exist in a group, members must be actively engaged and participative in the leadership process (Conger & Pearce, 2009). Because of this, it is evident that empowerment is a critical and necessary component for the development of shared leadership in a group.

In this section, we have very briefly discussed some of the most important historical underpinnings to the development of shared leadership theory—from the Industrial Revolution, which began in Great Britain but which quickly spread to the rest of the globe, to the pioneers in the area of "scientific management," to several interesting and valuable streams of research that allow us more clarity when beginning our own exploration of shared leadership theory. In the following section, we will delve further into the literature on shared leadership, exploring both the antecedents and outcomes of this important leadership concept.

Recent Evidence on the Antecedents and Outcomes of Shared Leadership

Recently, shared leadership has been receiving increasing attention in both the practitioner (e.g., Pearce, Manz & Sims, in press) and academic literature (e.g., Carson, Tesluk, & Marrone, 2007; Wassenaar & Pearce, in press). Although the vast majority of the writing on shared leadership has been conceptual in nature, a modicum of empirical advance is worth noting. This empirical work has identified both antecedents and outcomes of shared leadership in a wide variety of contexts—ranging from hospitals, to research and development, to the blue-collar world of manufacturing, to the white-collar world virtual teams of knowledge workers, and even to the c-suite ranks of top management teams. Below, we briefly review the empirical evidence on shared leadership to date. That said, there is still a large amount of work that needs to be done to further understand the role of shared leadership in organizational systems.

Some of the Antecedents of Shared Leadership

One of the most fascinating angles when studying any phenomenon in organizational behavior is to investigate its antecedents, or more simply put, what potential activities or behaviors result in an outcome. Lately, researchers have been focusing their efforts on developing a richer and deeper understanding of the precursors to the evolution of shared leadership in groups and organizations. In this vein, they have discovered three main groups of antecedents to shared leadership, which we will briefly explain in the following paragraphs.

Hierarchical/vertical leaders. Not surprisingly, hierarchical or vertical leaders have been found to have a considerable influence on the development and occurrence of shared leadership. For example, the actions or behaviors of the vertical leader are directly related to the development of group members' satisfaction with their work and activities (George et al., 2002; Shamir & Lapidot, 2003). Additionally, trust in the hierarchical leader is directly correlated to the shared leadership formation in groups (George et al., 2002; Olson-Sanders, 2006), and it serves as a facilitating force for smooth social interactions (Dirks & Ferrin, 2002), which in turn directly affect the group's ability to share leadership effectively. Shamir and Lapidot (2003) were able, in their study of the Israeli Defense Forces, clearly to conclude that leader and follower goal alignment contribute to the development of shared leadership. They also confirmed that group members' trust in, and satisfaction with, their leaders is directly related to the degree to which shared leadership exists in those groups. Similarly, Elloy (2008) discovered that when the vertical leader allows group members latitude in decision-making, the incidence of shared leadership increased.

The gender of the vertical leader has been found to be important when considering the development of shared leadership (Konu & Viitanen, 2008). In their study that was conducted in several major Finnish healthcare organizations, Konu and Viitanen (2008) uncovered that teams who have a female vertical leader are more likely to share leadership among group members. Their research also suggests that the reason for this higher incidence of shared leadership in these female-led groups is that these leaders are more likely to be inclined to nurture those around them than are their male counterparts (Paris, Howell, Dorfman, & Hanges, 2009).

Finally, the behavior of the vertical leader has been found to be integrally important to the development of shared leadership in a group (Hooker & Csikszentmihalyi, 2003). In the qualitative work done by Hooker and Csikszentmihalyi (2003), six vertical leader behaviors were found to support the development of shared leadership: (1) valuing excellence, (2) providing clear goals, (3) giving timely feedback, (4) matching challenges and skills, (5) diminishing distractions, and (6) creating freedom. Taken together, these studies identify the important role that vertical leadership has in the display and development of shared leadership.

Support structures. Another important group of antecedents that have been studied in the past few years are those that enhance our understanding of the support structures that are in place or can be developed to aid in a group's development of shared leadership. For example, technology has been, is, and will continue to be a foundational underpinning to the development of shared leadership in groups (Wassenaar et al., 2010). Cordery, Soo, Kirkman, Rosen and Mathieu (2009) realized that critical components in the development and sustainability of shared leadership in virtual teams are the support structures, both social and technological, that enable group members to communicate more easily, fluidly transporting information across time and geography. These support mechanisms can be constituted of the technical infrastructure that is in place, which supports communication between members of a group or others, and training (employee training, orientations, or other organized learning environments) that augments the skills of the group.

Elloy (2008) discovered that when an organization provided team training, and when it encouraged and facilitated communication between employees within a paper mill that the development of shared leadership was greatly facilitated. Another line of research that has been gaining momentum in both the academic and practitioner literatures is specifically related to executive coaching (Bono, Purvanova, Towler, & Peterson, 2009; Elmhirst, 2008; Leonard & Goff, 2003). The incidence of coaching in organizations has been extolled as essential in leader and team development, yet very little empirical research has, as of yet, been done—particularly as it relates to groups. However, Carson et al. (2007), as well as Cordery et al. (2009), did uncover that coaching was positively related to the demonstration of shared leadership.

Culture and empowerment. Context of leadership has been gaining increasing attention in the literature (e.g., Antonakis, Avolio & Sivasubramaniam, 2003). Clearly, there must be more ways that cause or lead to an environment in which leadership is shared than just the activities of the vertical leader or how much support a group or its members receive. One of these is culture (Pearce, 2008). For example, Konu and Viitanen (2008) learned that a group's values are an important predictor of shared leadership. Moreover, in the same study in which they explored coaching and its contribution to sharing leadership, Carson et al. (2007) found that internal environment—a concept similar to cultural values—was also a contributor to shared leadership, thus further providing confirmation for our belief that organizational culture or context is a contributing factor in the development of shared leadership.

Wood (2005) also discovered that if a team and its members perceive that they are empowered, they are more likely to behave in a way that shares leadership. He was exploring the question of whether members of top management teams in church organizations could even occur in what is normally considered a highly developed hierarchical organization. It was a revealing outcome, especially when taking into account our previous explorations of the incidence of shared leadership throughout history and how, against our initial expectations or knowledge, it also did occur in many religious denominations, particularly through the Middle Ages (Coss, 1996).

Other antecedents. There are three other interesting and valuable antecedents that have been explored in the research literature as precursors to shared leadership. The first is relationship longevity. Ropo and Sauer (2003) conducted a longitudinal qualitative study of orchestras, uncovering the fact that the length of relationships, also called relationship longevity, between various members, such as orchestra leaders, sponsors, members, or other possible group members is an important foreshadowing to sharing leadership between the various orchestral constituents. Hooker and Csikszentmihalyi (2003), in their study of university research teams, discovered that flow (Csikszentmihalyi, 1990) and the development of a state of flow was a foundational link in the development of shared leadership in the creative group. Our final antecedent is proximity. It was studied by Balthazard, Waldman,

Howell, and Atwater (2004), who found that face-to-face teams are more likely to develop shared leadership than virtual teams, which builds on the work of Antonakis and Atwater (2002).

Summary. As we can clearly observe from the varied possible antecedents that we have just examined, there are many precursors, or causes that enable shared leadership to occur in groups. We, as researchers, are merely at the beginning of the exploration of these antecedents, and there is enormous opportunity for further research in this area. Developing a more complete understanding of these causes will only further enable organizations and groups to capitalize on the benefits or outcomes of sharing leadership, which we will explore in some detail in the next section.

Outcomes Associated With Shared Leadership

Broadly speaking, there are three levels of analysis regarding outcomes in organizational behavior and leadership research—individual-, group-, and organization-level outcomes—and outcome variables span from intermediate-type outcomes, such as attitudes, behaviors, and cognitions, to effectiveness or performance outcomes (Luthans, 2010). Below we review the extant literature on the outcomes empirically associated with shared leadership.

Individual-level outcomes. At least six individual-level outcomes have been associated with shared leadership. Individual satisfaction is one of the most widely researched individual-level variables in organizational behavior (e.g., Cranny, Smith, & Stone, 1992), and two of studies have specifically examined the effects of shared leadership on satisfaction. First, Avolio, Jung, Murray, and Sivasubramaniam (1996), in a study of undergraduate project teams, found team member satisfaction to be positively related to shared leadership. Next, Shamir and Lapidot (2003), in a study of Israeli military officer training, found that shared leadership was positively related to satisfaction with, as well as trust in, hierarchical leaders. Thus, shared leadership has been linked to satisfaction with both team members as well as team leaders.

Building on the work of Bandura (1986), George et al. (2002), in a nursing study, found shared leadership to be directly related to follower self-efficacy. Also in the hospital environment, Klein, Zeigert, Knight, and Xiao (2006), found shared leadership to be positively associated with the skill development of junior medical staff. Finally, Hooker and Csikszentmihalyi (2003), in a study of R&D laboratories, found mimetic effects of shared leadership. That is, as followers learned shared leadership from the lead scientist in their original PhD training laboratory, they mimicked those lead scientist behaviors to develop shared leadership in their own laboratories. This is similar to what Bass, Waldman, Avolio, and Bebb (1987) called the "falling dominoes effect," noted for transformational leadership mimetic effects. Accordingly, shared leadership has been empirically associated with multiple individual level outcomes.

Group-/team-level outcomes. At least 15 group-/team-level, intermediate-type outcomes have been associated with shared leadership. Moreover, at least six studies have identified group effectiveness/performance outcomes of shared leadership.

Group confidence or potency (e.g., Gully, Incalcaterra, Joshi, & Beaubien, 2002) has received considerable attention in recent years. In this vein, Pearce (1997); Hooker and Csikszentmahalyi (2003); and Pearce, Yoo, and Alavi (2004) all found shared leadership to be positively associated with team confidence or potency. Similarly, Solansky (2008), in a laboratory study, found that shared leadership was associated with higher levels of motivation and cognitive advantage, whereas Pearce et al. (2004) found shared leadership predictive of social integration, and Balthazard et al. (2004) found shared leadership to positively predict group cohesion (e.g., Evans & Dion, 1991). It is important to note that Hooker and Csikszentmahalyi (2003) also linked shared leadership with group empowerment (Conger & Pearce, 2009) and sense of flow (Csikszentmahalyi, 1990). Together these studies suggest that shared leadership is a useful predictor of cognitive outcomes in groups.

An important group-level behavioral variable in organizational behavior research is organizational citizenship behavior (OCB; e.g., Organ, 1988), and leadership has been found to be an important predictor of OCB (e.g., Pearce & Herbik, 2004). Moving to the shared leadership level of analysis, Pearce (1997) found shared leadership to be predictive of team citizenship behavior and team networking behavior. Relatedly, Balthazard et al. (2004) found shared leadership was positively predictive of a constructive interaction style and negatively associated with a defensive interaction style. Klein et al. (2006) also found shared leadership to be positively related to swift coordination of activities, as well as reliability. Khourey-Bowers, Dinko, and Hart (2005), in a study of 216 educators in 17 school districts who were part of a change management plan, found that shared leadership facilitated information exchange among teachers. Finally, in a study of 32 United States and Mexico strategic alliances, Rodríguez (2005) found that shared leadership can facilitate the development of intercultural fit. As such, shared leadership appears to be an important predictor of group-level behavioral outcomes.

Six studies have specifically linked shared leadership to group/team effectiveness and performance. For example, Pearce and Sims (2002) found that shared leadership, relative to vertical leadership, was a more useful predictor of team effectiveness in 71 change management teams from the point of view of managers, internal customers, and team members. Similarly, Olson-Sanders (2006) found that shared leadership was positively linked with new product development performance orientation and team effectiveness. In the same vein, Carson et al. (2007) found that shared leadership predicted consulting team performance, and Avolio et al. (1996) found shared leadership to be appreciably related to group members' self-ratings of effectiveness. Moving to the virtual team arena, Carte, Chidambaram, and Becker (2006), in a study of 22 virtual teams, also found shared leadership to be a significant predictor of team performance. Moreover, Pearce et al. (2004) found that, controlling for team size and vertical leadership, shared leadership was positively related to problem-solving quality and an increased perception of task effectiveness. Taken together, these studies clearly suggest a shared leadership to group performance link.

Organization-level outcomes. Although the effects of shared leadership on individuals and groups are important, perhaps most importantly one should consider the effects of shared leadership at the organizational level of analysis. In this regard, four studies help to shed some light. First, O'Toole, Galbraith, and Lawler (2003), in a qualitative study of shared leadership at the top of organizations of 25 firms, concluded that 17 firms experienced positive effects, whereas 8 experienced negative effects. Potentially more significantly, using multiple regression analysis, Ensley, Hmieleski, and Pearce (2006) conducted a two-sample study of shared leadership in entrepreneurial firms. Their first sample of 66 firms was drawn from the inc. 500, which are the fastest growing, privately held firms in the United States. Their second sample was a random national sample of United States-based firms, drawn from Dun & Bradstreet's market identifiers database. In both samples, they found that, controlling for CEO leader behavior, shared leadership predicted the financial performance of the firms.

Furthermore, Manz, Shipper, and Stewart (2009) conducted a qualitative study of shared leadership at W. L. Gore & Associates. As an organization, Gore has consciously decided not to implement an articulated hierarchical structure but rather to advocate a system called "natural leadership." Here are some examples: Associates move into a leadership role once they have gained enough credibility with their peers to gain influence, or if they have demonstrated their expertise in a given situation, which Gore also calls knowledge-based decision making. By creating this type of environment, Gore has been able to minimize employee turnover to approximately 5%, and in 2007, they received 34,585 applications for only 272 jobs. Just as telling, Gore's team and their work together yielded revenues of more than $2 billion in 2007, which placed them near the top of Forbes annual ranking of privately held companies (Manz et al., 2009). As such, the initial evidence on shared leadership indicates that it can have a potential powerful effect on organizational performance outcomes.

Summary. In sum, shared leadership appears to be an important predictor of several outcome variables that span attitudinal, behavioral, cognitive, and effectiveness outcomes, at the individual, group, and organizational levels of analysis. In the following section, we explore the measurement of shared leadership.

The Measurement of Shared Leadership _____

To date, there has been little research that examines the various methods by which to measure shared leadership. This is not surprising, especially since this field is still quite new and the complexity in its measurement can be, on the surface, daunting. However, as the field continues to grow, it will become ever more critical for a more clear understanding of the most effective methods that can be used to measure shared leadership as we search for more answers about this theory. Pearce and Conger (2003) noted five methods that can be and are currently the most commonly used to measure shared leadership; of these five, three are quantitative and survey based and two are qualitative and observation based.

In order to study shared leadership at the group level, whether (1) as whole, (b) the individual or "sum of its parts," or even (2) the social network of the group, a revised traditional leadership items list can be used for the three quantitative survey approaches. As an example, when examining the entire team, or the whole group, the approach that uses items where (1) the group is the entity and is the source of influence and (2) the group as a whole is the target of influence has proven to yield valuable insights. When using variables that have been conceived at the group level of analysis, researchers are able to perform analyses comparable to those that are conducted at the individual leader level of data (e.g., regression, SEM; Antonakis, Bendahan, Jacquart, & Lalive, in press; Mundlak, 1978; Yammarino, 1990). There are several examples of this approach in Pearce and Conger (2003), Avolio et al. (1996), Pearce (1997), Ensley et al. (2006), and Pearce and Sims (2002). This method is particularly attractive in that the collection of data is fairly innocuous to the participants in the study, especially as it relates to individual group member anonymity. However, a potential shortcoming of this method is that important variance in contributions by individual members of the group could potentially be smoothed. It is also important to note that there is some debate whether simply measuring constructs at the group level of analysis is sufficient to determine outcomes of group-level variables (James, Demaree, & Wolf, 1984, 1993; Kozlowski & Klein, 2000; Yammarino, 1990; Yammarino & Bass, 1990; Yammarino, Dansereau, & Kennedy, 2001).

The second method, which measures the "group as a sum of its parts," utilizes items that measure individual group members as the basis for influence and the total group as the target of influence. There are three options when using this method that can be used to create group-level variables. One of these options is that the level of shared leadership can be evaluated using the dominant member's results. This means using the highest rated individual's scores. The second option involves doing the opposite of the first and measuring shared leadership by using the scores of the individual rated lowest on leadership, also known as the "weakest link." The third option assesses shared leadership by using what is called the "behavioral average option." This method is similar to the method mentioned in the previous paragraph, the group as a whole approach.

Some research has been begun by Pearce and colleagues (Pearce & Conger, 2003), but additional data should be collected to further explore these methods before truly meaningful results can be discussed. Ideally, once this has occurred, these group-level variables can then be utilized in research in a similar vein as those variables that are used at the individual leader level. The main strength of this research is that it allows the researcher to explore the influence of single group members on the overall leadership of the group. However, unlike the previous method of research where the effort involved for the respondent in data collection was relatively minimal, a key weakness of this method is that it requires a considerable investment of time from each participant because each respondent must answer the same item multiple times, thus increasing the possibility of respondent fatigue.

The final quantitative method, which studies the group as a social network, focuses on items that measure individual group members as both sources of influence and also the targets of influence. The primary variable that is measured at the group level by using this method is the degree to which leadership behaviors are centralized and/or directed by one or a few or, alternatively, if these same leadership behaviors are dispersed and/or shared by a wider group of team members. A primary component of this line of research, the investigation of social networks, has been eventually to be able to predict who, in a group, will become a central, or controlling member. It seems possible that this method can be used in a similar manner as those that use individual leader data to predict shared leadership, primarily by taking into account the opposite of the centrality score as a predictor of shared leadership. However, another interesting and valuable direction of research is using the compliment of the centrality score to carry out analyses that uncover the density of leadership in groups. For example, a potential avenue for research would be to examine whether or not shared leadership behaviors can be predicted by locating the density.

The positive strengths of this approach are that it allows for the following areas of examination: (1) the extent that each member is involved in group or team leadership; (2) how dispersed the leadership really is on the team; and (3) what patterns of interaction exist between individuals, primarily those who are the sources of influence in the group, and how influence moves within and through the group. However, as with the previous method of analysis, the weaknesses of this method also are both that it is taxing to the participants, primarily with regard to the time required to fill out the instrument, and that the methods ultimately used to analyze the collected data are usually quite complex. Finally, it is important to note that this particular method does not measure influence that emerges from the group as a whole or influence that is aimed at the whole group.

As we mentioned earlier in this section, there are also two qualitative methods that have lately been used to measure shared leadership. They are (1) leadership sociograms (Pearce, 2002) and (2) ethnographic methods (e.g., Manz et al., 2009). A primary focus in the leadership sociogram method is the documentation of individual and group patterns of interactions and the observation of group meetings. There are two primary strengths to this method. The first is that it allows a far more comprehensive understanding of group dynamics to be developed than the questionnaire-based methods. The second is that the data collected can be quantified and used as a source of data for a social network analysis. The main weaknesses of this approach are that it is time intensive, as it requires a researcher to be located in the same place as the group for what can be extended periods of time, and also that even with this co-location, key interactions between group members may be missed, as they might occur outside of the observed meetings.

The fifth method, our second qualitative approach, involves utilizing ethnography as a tool for analysis. This method requires the researcher to invest immersive time in the organization or group, observing the interactions and interplay between members in their natural setting(s). This observation does not focus only on the group that is being studied and their meeting(s), but rather it focuses on the group and its members in the context of their daily activities and interactions. The strength of this approach is that it allows the researcher the most holistic understanding of the group and its dynamics. The weakness is similar to that of the previous qualitative method, leadership sociograms, in that it requires an even more extensive investment of time commitment on the part of the researcher.

Although we have highlighted the basic characteristics, strengths, and weaknesses of five of the most prevalent and promising methodological avenues for the further research of shared leadership theory, by no means does this suggest our list is exhaustive. We also do not believe that each of these methods is perfect or cannot be developed. For example, adding an element of contextual research, especially in situations where qualitative data is collected, can add another valuable facet to our understanding of both the antecedents and the outcomes of shared leadership (Liden & Antonakis, 2009). Further research should be done to compare the efficacy of each of these methods in various contexts. Additionally, we do not suggest that this methodological list is complete, but rather, we look forward to the additional research methods that might be attempted in the future as the research of shared leadership theory evolves.

The Future of Shared Leadership

Although much of this chapter is devoted to exploring the development of shared leadership theory, especially as it relates to the empirical research that has already been conducted to examine the antecedents and outcomes of this phenomenon, the reality is that there is still a tremendous amount of interesting and valuable work that must be done on shared leadership. In order to aid this endeavor, we would like to take time to highlight some of the gaps in our knowledge about shared leadership, in the hope that by doing so we will broaden the field for research rather than restrict it. Thus, the following section will describe some possible directions for research in the area of shared leadership. Several important categories for future research include (1) the relationships that exist between shared and vertical leadership; (2) which dynamics (or fundamental factors) are present when leadership is shared in groups and/or organizational settings? (3) what steps are necessary to implement shared leadership? (4) what outcomes are linked to shared leadership? (5) how should shared leadership be assessed and codified? (6) how does culture—organizational, ethnic, and national—affect or influence shared leadership? and (7) what are the possible limits or liabilities of shared leadership? Below we draw attention to the more specific research questions and ideas that could advance leadership dialogue in the area of shared leadership. The possibilities are seemingly endless. They are exciting, and as we discover more about shared leadership theory, the implications for practice are even more profound.

The Relationship Between Shared and Vertical Leadership

Typically, researchers focus their studies on the behavior or attributes of a single leader, the person who either is the appointed or formal leader or the person who appears to be the most influential in a group. We call the relationship between this person and the group members around them a "vertical" relationship, implying that there exists a hierarchy and followers. We call this relationship "vertical leadership" (Gerstner & Day, 1997). Although some researchers have suggested that shared and vertical leadership are mutually exclusive, there are a number in the academic community who believe that shared and vertical leadership are actually intertwined and interdependent (Pearce & Conger, 2003).

Obviously, just these questions open up the opportunity for extensive research. However, in order to simplify the dialogue, we can summarize three primary areas that should be examined: (a) what are the activities and roles in which vertical leaders should engage that will facilitate or catalyze the evolution of shared leadership in groups or organizations? (b) in what ways can the vertical leader become an obstacle to the development or display of shared leadership? and (c) how would, or even can, the two forms of leadership work together to elevate the effectiveness of an organization or a group?

Context, or the environment in which the group or organization finds itself, is another important issue when considering the relationship between vertical and shared leadership. We assume that there are some settings that would be more hospitable or conducive to the parallel incidence of these two leadership forms—but what are they? Would there be some situations that simply, by their nature, make the coexistence of vertical and shared leadership impossible? Are there circumstances in which strong direction, in the guise of vertical leadership, is needed? Or conversely, if a group or organization is in need of increased levels of group consent, harmony, or engagement, is shared leadership the more valuable form of organization?

Another cadre of research questions are those that relate to the life cycle of the group. Does vertical leadership occur more often at the inception or creation of a new group? So then, does shared leadership occur more frequently in more established groups or groups that are at the later stages of a project? What about internal or external events, such as crisis? Can these events cause the form of leadership to shift from one to the other? More subtly, will shared leadership shift in form or "strength" based on the life stage of the group? These are all important questions for future research.

The Fundamentals (or Dynamics) of Shared Leadership

One of the main areas relating to shared leadership process that poses considerable interest to researchers are the roles or bases of leadership. Pearce and Conger (2003) found it apparent that most of the authors who contributed their thoughts on shared leadership believed that shared leadership, as a process, was dependent on demonstrable and conclusive bases of leadership ranging on a continuum from vertical to shared. Shifts in leadership forms take place as they are needed and are primarily driven by things like the group's or organization's environment, challenges facing the group or organization, or skills that are ascending or descending in primacy at a certain point in time (Gerstner & Day, 1997). Pearce and Conger (2003) point out that because of this, shared leadership is then a powerful solution to a foundational organizational problem: that not one person in any organization is able to function effectively in all of the possible leadership aspects that are needed in either a group or an organizational context.

One of the areas of interest, in this regard, in the exploration of shared leadership theory is the roles that are most effective or even relevant when sharing leadership in groups. Clearly, not all leadership roles are consistently present or even necessary in shared leadership environments. Rather some of them, in various permutations, can either facilitate or hinder the development and outcomes of shared leadership in groups or organizations. Additionally, some of these leadership roles can become more or less critical at certain times in the life cycle of the team. What has become evident through the initial research in shared leadership theory is that in order to move forward in a thorough way, a comprehensive and clearly defined set of leadership roles would be extremely helpful when exploring and testing our hypotheses about the shared leadership phenomenon.

And what about how influence works in a shared leadership environment? Both Locke (2003) and Seibert, Sparrowe, and Liden (2003) discuss the idea that some influence strategies are more appropriate than others in a situation where shared leadership is present. Pearce and Sims (2002) provide some valuable insights on the subject of influence creation, the five types of leadership, and some outcomes of shared leadership. As an example, aversive leadership is negatively related to team self-ratings of their team's effectiveness. They also discovered that directive leadership was negatively related to both internal customer and manager ratings of the team's effectiveness. Finally, they found that shared empowering, transactional and transformational leadership were positively related to team self-ratings of team effectiveness.

Causes or Antecedents of Shared Leadership

One of the most fundamentally interesting areas for research in shared leadership theory is the investigation into the causes, or antecedents of shared leadership. Pearce (1997) raised the question of whether or not there is a process of "serial emergence." Although this seems a simplistic model for what is a more complex process of leading groups, it does allow the research community to begin to question how this process of sharing leadership starts.

Based on the potential avenues for research into the causes of shared leadership, we can suggest the following four overarching research areas: (a) what are the most standard causes that enable shared leadership? (b) which of these causes are more significant than others? (c) how does the situation assist or detract from some of these causes? and (d) can certain leadership typologies or roles, or which external factors, or the group life cycle help to classify certain causal agents for shared leadership?

Enabling or Facilitating Factors

There are many possible factors that facilitate shared leadership that were proposed through the work of Pearce and Conger (2003), but not many have been explored in any great detail. For example, here are a few factors that appear to be important facilitating factors: (1) the competence of group members; (2) the complexity of the task itself; (3) the mental models and shared knowledge of members in the group; (4) the leadership prototypes of the group; (5) the status, influence, and power of each group member; (6) the diversity of the group; (7) the proximity of the group members; (8) the familiarity or personal attraction for group members to one another; (9) the amount, extent, and timing of group member turnover; (10) the life-cycle of the group or project; and (11) the size of the group.

Is it possible for a group to move from a vertical leadership model to one of shared leadership? Or can a group develop shared leadership from its inception? How best to achieve that goal? What are some of the "best practices" and/or interventions that can best enable the development of sharing leadership in a group or organization? So far, very little research has been done in the area of implementing shared leadership, especially at the organizational level of analysis.

How does organizational design affect shared leadership? What types of rewards, performance measurement, or other processes are important to encourage shared leadership? Do these rewards work best at the individual or the group level, or perhaps a combination of both?

Clearly, this is just a small array of the possible questions that can be asked about the implementation of shared leadership in groups, but even more so, about the study of shared leadership theory in a larger sense. In the following section, we will briefly explore the influence that cross-cultural values might also play in the development of shared leadership.

Culture and Shared Leadership

As mentioned in the previous section, it makes sense, especially due to the wide array of cultures, to wonder how these differences in values and norms affect the possibility of sharing leadership in organizations and groups. There are many factors that form culture, and they shape how cognitions and perceptions occur in groups all over the world. For example, power distance, or the degree to which group members of a specific culture expect that power in the group, organization, or society be distributed unequally (Hofstede, 1980; House et al., 1999; Pearce, 2008; Pearce & Osmond, 1999), can greatly influence the behavior of individuals or groups toward a leader in organizations. Research (Pearce, 2008) has also demonstrated that countries with cultures that are nurturing or aggressive have fascinating implications for how leaders lead and develop those around them. For example, societies that are more nurturing are interested in developing the potential of the people around them, rather than competing. They are concerned with growing the totality of their society and community rather than simply focusing on their own little piece. Contrast this to societies in which aggressive behavior is the norm. These groups are more likely to be materialistic, aggressive, and competitive. They are far more interested in goal achievement, but this achievement can often occur at the expense of those around them. These societies are particularly at a disadvantage when it comes to sharing leadership. They cause people to jockey for control and power, and once they have it, they are far less likely to relinquish that control to anyone around them, regardless of the other's skills (Pearce, 2008).

Another aspect to study when examining culture and shared leadership is whether the society is collectivist or individualist. People who live in a more collectivist society will be more inclined to work in groups, even those made up of relatives or other groups and organized communities, and will expect that in return for their loyalty to the group, they will be taken care of by the community or group in which they are a member. We can compare this to the individualistic societies where this is completely the opposite. People who are in individualistic societies are far more self-reliant and independent. They do not gravitate toward working in teams and find that they are more interested in personal freedom than working with others (Pearce, 2008).

Our overall knowledge of how organizational culture, politics, and design affect or influence shared leadership is still quite scant. A good example of this is the question of whether shared leadership can occur in an organization where the cultural norm values a vertical or top-down form of leadership. Another example of an organization in which the development of shared leadership might be difficult would be one that does not articulate clear goals or vision or where there is not an emphasis on excellence. Would shared leadership still be able to develop under these circumstances, perhaps under the aegis of an organizational maverick or perhaps in a remote location that is not as affected by the organization's norms and culture? These are many of the other questions that comprise a rich, varied, and valuable dialogue in shared leadership study for many years to come, particularly as our organizations continue to evolve along with the knowledge economy.

The Future of Organizational Leadership

As we forge further into the knowledge era, our models of leadership will continue to evolve to embrace the paradigmatic shift away from leadership as merely a hierarchical role to leadership as an unfolding social process, that is, a shared leadership-type perspective (Wassenaar et al., 2010). This evolutionary process, as with many others, brings to light several questions beginning with the most simple: Can leadership be shared effectively? Yes. Pearce, Manz, and Sims (2009) have uncovered numerous organizations where shared leadership is affecting real outcomes. Examples include how the medical team at a trauma center treats patients more quickly and safely; how sharing leadership in Alcoholics Anonymous helps people who are struggling to heal their addictions more effectively; or how Southwest Airlines attributes their success not to how they structure their costs, but rather to how their corporate culture of feedback from all points of the hierarchy can enable leadership to originate from any level.

Is developing shared leadership challenging? Yes. Having said that, we firmly believe that most people are capable of being both followers *and* leaders and that shared leadership is an organizational imperative for the age of knowledge work (Pearce, 2010). Although there are circumstances where shared leadership approaches might not work, the research evidence demonstrates that shared leadership can positively affect individual, group, and organizational level outcomes, including organizational performance.

Does this mean that shared leadership is a panacea? No. There will nearly always be a need for hierarchical leadership in our modern organizations (Leavitt, 2005). As documented by several studies (e.g., Ensley et al., 2006;

Hooker & Csikszentmihalyi, 2003; Pearce & Sims, 2002; Shamir & Lapidot, 2003) shared and hierarchical leadership work in tandem to effect individual, group, and organizational outcomes.

Are there circumstances where we do not advocate shared leadership? Yes. For example, shared leadership is applicable only to tasks where there is inter-dependency between the individuals involved. To force fit any particular potential organizational process simply does not seem wise. We might further speculate that certain other preconditions are necessary for shared leadership to flourish. For instance, it seems important that the individuals involved should have well-developed knowledge, skills, and abilities—not only for the technical aspects of their tasks but also for how to engage effectively as both followers and leaders if shared leadership is to be effective. These are but a few caveats regarding shared leadership: Shared leadership, and related approaches, require far more research, not only on their outcomes but also on their ante-cedents and moderators. As research continues to delve deeper into leadership processes, we will yield more insights for the organizations of the future.

CASE STUDIES

The following cases are two examples where leadership is shared. One is a scenario where the employees of United Baggage Claims service are given the ability to make decisions based on each passenger's situation. The other is an example drawn from the famous Napa restaurant The French Laundry and its Chef, Thomas Keller.

Lost Bag on United

You never want United Airlines to lose your bag. In order to get it back, you will have to wade through a convoluted maze of 800 numbers, claim forms, and airline schedules—all while they survey you to find out how well they are servicing your claim. The main number to the people who are supposed to help you takes you to a call center in India where ostensibly helpful people attempt to locate a bag on the other side of the world. They are extremely concerned with get-ting you to fill out a survey at the end of the call on how they did and how well they helped you. However, after three days with a missing bag and calls from an airport telling me my bag was in one place, when in reality, it had never left the airport where I had asked *for it not to be delivered,* a United employee honestly said: "We get this all the time. A lot of our call centers are in India. They're in a different country; a different world; a world away. People call and are told all the time that their bag is in one place, but when I check, I find that they are really in a different place. They don't understand, and they don't care." Quote 11:05 p.m., Friday, August 6, 2010, Montreal.

The reason this is happening is that many companies judge their call center employees solely on how long they spend on their service calls, which in essence, turns the concept of service into a disservice. In addition, when they don't understand what you are saying, they just give up, or tell you what they think you want to hear in order to get the call completed. They are obsequious in order to get you to feel as if they have helped, yet no actual help or resolution has actually occurred. The actual ability or desire to help and resolve, although on the surface appears to be genuine, is in reality only a cover in order to increase customer service ratings at the moment of the call, when the customer is hoping that the diffident United call center employee actually did resolve the lost bag. Yet these survey results are what is portrayed to the public as how wonderfully United treats its "valuable" customers.

This is one example of how leadership is ostensibly shared, by giving the call center employees the power to appear to resolve problems through their own initiative and abilities. However, when the capacity for them to actually truly execute their jobs is hampered by systems, bureaucracy, or other rules, they are potentially even more unempowered than if they simply had to pass along the problems to their supervisors for solving.

Sharing the Menu—Thomas Keller and The French Laundry

Typical chefs rule their kitchens. They design the menu and the theme, the style of cuisine. They select the vendors, the ingredients, and how they are presented to the customers in their final preparation. Traditionally, it is the job of the chef de cuisine, the sous chef, or any of the rest of the kitchen and wait staff to simply *repeat* the vision of the head chef, but never to interpret or improvise and never, ever to create.

This is not the case in the land of Chef Thomas Keller. In his kitchens, each part of a growing group of restaurants scattered around the United States, he takes a different tack, one of vision and empowerment. He sets the vision: that of extremely high quality ingredients and preparations, based on seasonal and local organic ingredients, served in both traditional and innovative ways in memorable settings. Then he hires people who can execute that vision with little hands-on guidance from him. He states, "Cooking is a simple equation: product and execution. If you have quality product and people who are going to execute it; bringing the two together, a strong team with a common goal and building relationships with suppliers, you've got great food."

He goes on to say, "Chefs have a new responsibility. No longer is there just one restaurant, one menu. This means we have to hand down to our younger chefs the opportunities that we have. That can mean writing a book, or creating a menu, or sourcing a new sort of supply. They have a determination to, every day, evolve their work a little better than the day before." June, 2010.

By managing his kitchen in this way, he is able to immediately accomplish several things. First, he is able to hire some of the most talented, up-and-coming people who want to learn from him yet who are also interested in developing their own flavors in their cooking. Second, these people will understand very clearly how the environment that Chef Keller creates is different. Because they recognize this difference, they are more committed to the overall vision and success of the French Laundry Group because, at the end of the day, they are a foundational part of their overall success.

Favorite meal, roasted chicken.

These two small vignettes are excerpted from the upcoming book *Share the Lead* by Craig L. Pearce, Charles C. Manz, and Henry P. Sims Jr., reproduced with permission from Stanford University Press.

Discussion Questions

1. Where have you experienced shared leadership? What were some of the positive aspects? Why? Were there some things about shared leadership that you felt could work better?

2. Are there some situations in which shared leadership might work better than others?

3. In addition to some of the future areas for research in the area of shared leadership mentioned in the chapter, what other possible directions do you think that research in this area could go?

Supplementary Reading

Pearce, C. L. (2008, July 7). Follow the leaders. *Wall Street Journal*, pp. R8.

References

Antonakis, J., & Atwater, L. (2002). Leader distance: A review and a proposed theory. *The Leadership Quarterly, 13*, 673–704.

Antonakis, J., Avolio, B. J., & Sivasubramaniam, N., (2003). Context and leadership: An examination of the nine-factor full-range leadership theory using the Multifactor Leadership Questionnaire. *The Leadership Quarterly, 14*, 261–295.

Antonakis, J., Bendahan, S., Jacquart, P., & Lalive, R. (in press). On making causal claims: A review and recommendations. *The Leadership Quarterly*.

Antonakis, J., Cianciolo, A. T., & Sternberg, R. J. (2004). *The nature of leadership*. Thousand Oaks, CA: Sage.

Avolio, B. J., Jung, D., Murray, W., & Sivasubramaniam, N. (1996). Building highly developed teams: Focusing on shared leadership process, efficacy, trust, and performance. In M. M. Beyerlein, D. A. Johnson, & S. T. Beyerlein (Eds.), *Advances in interdisciplinary studies of work teams* (pp. 173–209). Greenwich, CT: JAI.

Balthazard, P., Waldman, D., Howell, J., & Atwater, L. (2004, January). Shared leadership and group interaction styles in problem-solving virtual teams. *Proceedings of the 37th annual Hawaii international conference on system sciences* 43(HICSS, Vol. 1, p. 10043b).

Bandura, A. (1986). *Social foundations of thought and action: A social cognitive theory*. Englewood Cliffs, NJ: Prentice Hall.

Bartol, K. M., & Martin, D. C. (1986). Women and men in task groups. In R. D. Ashmore & F. K. Del Boca (Eds.), *The social psychology of female-male relations.* (pp. 259–310). New York: Academic Press.

Bass, B. M., & Avolio, B. J. (1993). Transformational leadership: A response to critiques. In J. G. Hunt, B. R. Baliga, H. P. Dachler, & C. A. Schriesheim (Eds.), *Emerging leadership vistas* (pp. 29–40). Lexington, MA: D. C. Heath.

Bass, B. M., & Bass, R. (2008). *The Bass handbook of leadership: Theory, research, and managerial applications*. New York: Simon & Schuster.

Bass, B. M., Waldman, D. A., Avolio, B. J., & Bebb, M. (1987). Transformational leadership and the falling dominoes effect. *Group & Organization Studies* [now named *Group & Organization Management*], *12*, 73–87.

Blau, J. R., & Alba, R. D. (1982). Empowering nets of participation. *Administrative Science Quarterly, 27*, 363–379.

Bono, J., Purvanova, R., Towler, A., & Peterson, D. (2009). A survey of executive coaching practices. *Personnel Psychology, 62*, 361–404.

Carlyle, T. (1894). *On heroes and hero worship and the heroic in history.* London, UK: Chapman and Hall, Ltd. (Original work published 1841)

Carson, J., Tesluk, P., & Marrone, J. (2007). Shared leadership in teams: An investigation of antecedent conditions and performance. *Academy of Management Journal, 50*, 1217–1234.

Carte, T. A., Chidambaram, L., & Becker, A. (2006). Emergent leadership in self-managed virtual teams: A longitudinal study of concentrated and shared leadership behaviors. *Group Decision and Negotiation, 15*, 323–343.

Conger, J. A., & Kanungo, R. N. (1988). The empowerment process: Integrating theory and practice. *Academy of Management Review, 13*, 639–652.

Conger, J. A., & Pearce, C. L. (2009) Using empowerment to motivate people to engage in effective self- and shared leadership. In E. A. Locke (Ed.), *Principles of organizational behavior* (pp. 201–216). New York: John Wiley.

Cordery, J., Soo, C., Kirkman, B., Rosen, B., & Mathieu, J. (2009). Leading parallel global virtual teams: Lessons from Alcoa. *Organizational Dynamics, 38*, 204–216.

Coss, P. R. (1996). *The knight in medieval England.* Conshohocken, PA: Combined Books.

Cox, J. F., Pearce, C. L., & Sims, H. P., Jr. (2003). Toward a broader agenda for leadership development: Extending the traditional transactional–transformational duality by developing directive, empowering and shared leadership skills. In S. E. Murphy & R. E. Riggio (Eds.). *The future of leadership development* (pp. 161–180). Mahwah, NJ: Lawrence Erlbaum.

Cranny, C. J., Smith, P. C., & Stone, E. F. (1992). *Job satisfaction: How people feel about their jobs and how it affects their performance.* Lexington, MA: Lexington Books.

Csikszentmihalyi, M. (1990). *Flow: The psychology of optimal experience.* New York: Harper & Row.

Day, D. V., Gronn, P., & Salas, E. (2004). Leadership capacity in teams. *The Leadership Quarterly, 15*, 857–880.

Day, D. V., Gronn, P., & Salas, E. (2006). Leadership in team-based organizations: On the threshold of a new era. *The Leadership Quarterly, 17*, 211–216.

Day, D. V., & O'Connor, P. M. G. (2003). Leadership development: Understanding the process. In S. E. Murphy & R. E. Riggio (Eds.). *The future of leadership development* (pp. 11–28). Mahwah, NJ: Lawrence Erlbaum.

Dirks, K. T., & Ferrin, D. L. (2002). Trust in leadership: Meta-analytic findings and implications for research and practice. *Journal of Applied Psychology, 87*, 611–628.

Drucker, P. F. (1954). *The practice of management.* New York: Harper & Row.

Drucker, P. F. (1995). *Management in time of great change.* New York: Penguin Putnam.

Elloy, D. F. (2008). The relationship between self-leadership behaviors and organization variables in a self-managed work team environment. *Management Research News, 31*, 801–810.

Elmhirst, K. (2008). Executive coaching. *Leadership Excellence, 25*(1), 11.

Ensley, M. D., Hmieleski, K. M., & Pearce, C. L. (2006). The importance of vertical and shared leadership within new venture top management teams: Implications for the performance of startups. *The Leadership Quarterly, 17*, 217–231.

Evans, C. R., & Dion, K. L. (1991). Group cohesion and performance: A meta-analysis. *Small Group Research, 22,* 175–186.

Figueira, T. J., Brennan, T. C., & Sternberg, R. H. (2009). *Wisdom from the ancients: Leadership lessons from Alexander the Great to Julius Caesar.* New York: Fall River Press.

Follett, M. P. (1924). *Creative experience.* New York: Longmans Green.

Gantt, H. L. (1916). *Industrial leadership.* New Haven, CT: Yale University Press.

George, V., Burke, L. J., Rodgers, B., Duthie, N., Hoffmann, M. L., Koceja, V., et al. (2002). Developing staff nurse shared leadership behavior in professional nursing practice. *Nursing Administration Quarterly, 26*(3), 44–59.

Gerstner, C. R., & Day, D. V. (1997). Meta-analytic review of leader–member exchange theory: Correlates and construct issues. *Journal of Applied Psychology, 82,* 827–844.

Gilbreth, F. B. (1912). *Primer of scientific management.* New York: Van Nostrand Reinhold.

Gilbreth, F. B., & Gilbreth, L. M. (1917). *Applied motion study.* New York: Sturgis & Walton.

Gully, S. M., Incalcaterra, K. A., Joshi, A., & Beaubien, J. M. (2002). A meta-analysis of team-efficacy, potency, and performance: Interdependence and level of analysis as moderators of observed relationship. *Journal of Applied Psychology, 87,* 819–832.

Hofstede, G. H. (1980). *Culture consequences: International differences in work-related values.* London: Sage.

Hollander, E. P. (1961). Some effects of perceived status on responses to innovative behavior. *Journal of Abnormal and Social Psychology, 63,* 247–250.

Hollander, E. P. (1978). *Leadership dynamics: A practical guide to effective relationships.* New York: Free Press.

Hooker, C., & Csikszentmihalyi, M. (2003). Flow, creativity, and shared leadership: Rethinking the motivation and structuring of knowledge work. In C. L. Pearce & J. A. Conger (Eds.), *Shared leadership: Reframing the hows and whys of leadership* (pp. 217–234). Thousand Oaks, CA: Sage.

House, R. J., Hanges, P. J., Ruiz-Quintanilla, S. A., Dorfman, P. W., Javidan, M., Dickson, M., et al. (1999). Cultural influences on leadership in organizations: Project GLOBE. In W. H. Mobley, M. J. Gessner, & V. Arnold (Eds.), *Advances in global leadership* (Vol. 1, pp. 171–234). Stamford, CT: JAI.

Hunt, J. G. (2004). What is leadership? In J. Antonakis, A. T. Cianciolo, & R. J. Sternberg (Eds.), *The nature of leadership* (pp. 19–47). Thousand Oaks: Sage.

James, L. R., Demaree, R. G., & Wolf, G. (1984). Estimating within-group interrater reliability with and without response bias. *Journal of Applied Psychology, 69,* pp. 85–99.

James, L. R., Demaree, R. G., & Wolf, G. (1993). rwg: An assessment of interrater agreement. *Journal of Applied Psychology, 78,* 306–310.

Kerr, S., & Jermier, J. (1978). Substitutes for leadership: Their meaning and measurement. *Organizational Behavior and Human Performance, 22,* 374–403.

Khourey-Bowers, C., Dinko, R. L., & Hart, R. G. (2005). Influence of a shared leadership model in creating a school culture of inquiry and collegiality. *Journal of Research in Science Teaching, 42,* 3–24.

Klein, K. J., Ziegert, J. C., Knight, A. P., & Xiao, Y. (2006). Dynamic delegation: Shared, hierarchical, and deindividualized leadership in extreme action teams. *Administrative Science Quarterly, 51,* 590–621.

Konu, A., & Viitanen, E. (2008). Shared leadership in Finnish social and health care. *Leadership in Health Services, 21,* 28–40.

Kozlowski, S. W. J., & Klein, K. J. (2000). A multilevel approach to theory and research in organizations: Contextual, temporal, and emergent processes. In K. J. Klein & S. W. J. Kozlowski (Eds.), *Multilevel theory, research, and methods in organizations* (pp. 3–90. San Francisco: Jossey-Bass.

Leavitt, H. J. (2005). *Top down: Why hierarchies are here to stay and how to manage them more effectively.* Boston: Harvard Business School Press.

Leonard, H. S., & Goff, M. (2003). Leadership development as an intervention for organizational transformation. *Consulting Psychology Journal, 55,* 58–67.

Liden, R. C., & Antonakis, J. (2009). Considering context in psychological leadership research. *Human Relations, 62,* 1587–1605.

Locke, E. A. (2003). Leadership: Starting at the top. In C. L. Pearce & J. A. Conger (Eds.), *Shared leadership: Reframing the hows and whys of leadership* (pp. 271–284). Thousand Oaks, CA: Sage.

Luthans, F. (2010). *Organizational behavior.* New York: McGraw-Hill.

Manz, C. C. (1986). Self-leadership: Toward an expanded theory of self-influence processes in organizations. *Academy of Management Review, 11,* 585–600.

Manz, C. C., Shipper, F., & Stewart, G. L. (2009). Everyone a team leader: Shared influence at W. L. Gore & Associates. *Organizational Dynamics, 38,* 239–244.

Manz, C. C., & Sims, H. P., Jr. (1980). Self-management as a substitute for leadership: A social learning theory perspective. *Academy of Management Review, 5,* 361–367.

Manz, C. C., & Sims, H. P., Jr. (1989). *Super leadership: Leading others to lead themselves.* New York: Prentice Hall.

Manz, C. C., & Sims, H. P., Jr. (1990). *Super leadership: Leading others to lead themselves.* New York: Berkley Books.

Mohrman, S. A., Cohen, S. G., & Mohrman, A. M. (1995). *Designing team-based organizations: New forms for knowledge work.* San Francisco: Jossey-Bass.

Montgomery, J. (1836). *The theory and practice of cotton spinning; or the carding and spinning master's assistant.* Glasgow, Scotland: John Niven, Trongate.

Montgomery, J. (1840). *The cotton manufacture of the United States of America contrasted and compared with that of Great Britain.* London: John N. Van.

Mundlak, Y. (1978). Pooling of time-series and cross-section data. *Econometrica, 46*(1), 69–85.

Nardinelli, C., (2008). *Industrial revolution and the standard of living.* Library of Economics and Liberty. Available at http://www.econlib.org/library/Enc/IndustrialRevolutionandtheStandardofLiving.html

Olson-Sanders, T. (2006). Collectivity and influence: The nature of shared leadership and its relationship with team learning orientation, vertical leadership and team effectiveness (Doctoral dissertation, George Washington University, 2006). Retrieved from ABI/INFORM Global (Publication No. AAT 3237041).

Organ, D. W. (1988). *Organizational citizenship behavior: The good soldier syndrome.* Lexington, MA: Lexington Books.

O'Toole, J., Galbraith, J., & Lawler, E. E., III. (2003). The promise and pitfalls of shared leadership: When two (or more) heads are better than one. In C. L. Pearce & J. A. Conger (Eds.), *Shared leadership: Reframing the hows and whys of leadership* (pp. 250–268). Thousand Oaks, CA: Sage.

Paris, L., Howell, J., Dorfman, P., & Hanges, P. (2009). Preferred leadership prototypes of male and female leaders in 27 countries. *Journal of International Business Studies, 40,* 1396–1405.

Pearce, C. L. (1997). *The determinants of change management team (CMT) effectiveness: A longitudinal investigation.* Unpublished doctoral dissertation, University of Maryland, College Park.

Pearce, C. L., (2002, August). Quantitative and qualitative approaches to the study of shared leadership. In C. L. Pearce (symposium chair), *Shared leadership: Reframing the hows and whys of leadership.* Presented at the annual conference of the Academy of Management, Denver, CO.

Pearce, C. L. (2008, July 7). Follow the leaders. *The Wall Street Journal,* p. R8.

Pearce, C. L. (2010). Leading knowledge workers: Beyond the era of command and control. In C. L. Pearce, J. A. Maciariello, & H. Yamawaki (Eds.), *The Drucker difference* (pp. 35–46). New York: McGraw-Hill.

Pearce, C. L., & Conger, J. A. (Eds.). (2003). *Shared leadership: Reframing the hows and whys of leadership.* Thousand Oaks, CA: Sage.

Pearce, C. L., Conger, J. A., & Locke, E. (2008). Shared leadership theory. *The Leadership Quarterly, 19,* 622–628.

Pearce, C. L., & Herbick, P. A. (2004). Citizenship behavior at the team level of analysis: The role of team leader behavior, team dynamics, the team's environment, and team demography. *Journal of Social Psychology, 144,* 293–310.

Pearce, C. L., Manz, C. C., & Sims, H. P., Jr. (2009). Where do we go from here? Is shared leadership the key to team success? *Organizational Dynamics, 38,* 234–238.

Pearce, C. L., Manz, C. C., & Sims, H. P., Jr. (in press). *Share the lead.* Palo Alto, CA: Stanford University Press.

Pearce, C. L., & Osmond, C. P., (1999). From workplace attitudes and values to a global pattern of nations: An application of latent class modeling. *Journal of Management, 25,* 759–778.

Pearce, C. L., & Sims, H. P., Jr. (2000). Shared leadership: Toward a multi-level theory of leadership. In M. M. Beyerlein, D. A. Johnson, & S. T. Beyerlein (Eds.), *Advances in interdisciplinary studies of work teams* (pp. 115–139). Greenwich, CT: JAI.

Pearce, C. L., & Sims, H. P., Jr. (2002). Vertical versus shared leadership as predictors of the effectiveness of change management teams: An examination of aversive, directive, transactional, transformational, and empowering leader behaviors. *Group Dynamics, Theory, Research, and Practice, 6,* 172–197.

Pearce, C. L., Yoo, Y., & Alavi, M. (2004). Leadership, social work, and virtual teams: The relative influence of vertical versus shared leadership in the nonprofit sector. In R. E. Riggio & S. Smith Orr (Eds.), *Improving leadership in nonprofit organizations* (pp. 160–203). San Francisco: Jossey-Bass.

Riggio, R. E., Chaleff, I., & Lipman-Blumen, J. (Eds.). (2008). *The art of followership: How great followers create great leaders and organizations.* San Francisco: Jossey-Bass.

Rodríguez, C. (2005). Emergence of a third culture: Shared leadership in international strategic alliances. *International Marketing Review, 22,* 67–95.

Ropo, A., Eriksson, P., & Hunt, J. G. (1997). Reflections on conducting processual research on management and organizations. *Scandinavian Journal of Management, 13,* 331–335.

Ropo, A., & Sauer, E. (2003). Partnerships of orchestras: Towards shared leadership. *International Journal of Arts Management, 5*(2), 44–55.

Say, J. B. (1964). *A treatise on political economy.* New York: Augustus M. Kelley. (Original work published 1803)

Seibert, S. E., Sparrowe, R. T., & Liden, R. C. (2003). A group exchange structure approach to leadership in groups. In C. L. Pearce & J. A. Conger (Eds.), *Shared leadership: Reframing the hows and whys of leadership* (pp. 173–192). Thousand Oaks, CA: Sage.

Shamir, B., & Lapidot, Y. (2003). Shared leadership in the management of group boundaries: A study of expulsions from officers' training courses. In C. L. Pearce & J. A. Conger (Eds.), *Shared leadership: Reframing the hows and whys of leadership* (pp. 235–249). Thousand Oaks, CA: Sage.

Solansky, S. (2008). Leadership style and team processes in self-managed teams. *Journal of Leadership & Organizational Studies, 14,* 332–341.

Stein, R. T., & Heller, T. (1979). An empirical analysis of the correlations between leadership status and participation rates reported in the literature. *Journal of Personality and Social Psychology, 37,* 1993–2002.

Stewart, L. (1998). A meaning for machines: Modernity, utility, and the eighteenth century British public. *Journal of Modern History, 70,* 259–294.

Stewart, L., (2003). Science and the eighteenth-century public: Scientific revolutions and the changing format of scientific investigation. In M. Fitzpatrick, P. Jones, C. Knelworf, & I. McAlmon (Eds.), *The Enlightenment world* (pp. 234–246). London: Routledge.

Taylor, F. W. (1903). *Shop management.* New York: Harper & Row.

Taylor, F. W. (1911). *Principles of scientific management.* New York: Harper & Brothers.

Wassenaar, C. L., & Pearce, C. L. (in press). Shared leadership 2.0: A 2010 glimpse into the state of the field. In M. Uhl-Bien & S. Ospina, (Eds.), *Relational leadership theory.* Charlotte, NC: Information Age.

Wassenaar, C. L., Pearce, C. L., Hoch, J., & Wegge, J. (2010). Shared leadership meets virtual teams: A match made in cyberspace. In P. Yoong (Ed.), *Leadership in the digital enterprise: Issues and challenges* (pp. 15–27). Hersey, PA: IGI Global.

Wood, M. S. (2005). Determinants of shared leadership in management teams. *International Journal of Leadership Studies, 1*(1) 64–85.

Wren, D. A. (1994). *The evolution of management thought* (4th ed.). New York: John Wiley.

Yammarino, F. J. (1990). Individual- and group-directed leader behavior descriptions. *Educational and Psychological Measurement, 50,* 739–759.

Yammarino, F. J., & Bass, B. M. (1990). Transformational leadership and multiple levels of analysis. *Human Relations, 43,* 975–996.

Yammarino, F. J., Dansereau, F., & Kennedy, C. J. (2001). A multiple-level multidimensional approach to leadership: Viewing leadership through an elephant's eye. *Organizational Dynamics, 29,* 149–163.

Yukl, G. A. (2002). *Leadership in organizations* (5th ed.). Englewood Cliffs, NJ: Prentice Hall.

PART IV

Leadership and Special Domains

12

Leadership and Culture

Deanne N. Den Hartog

University of Amsterdam

Marcus W. Dickson

Wayne State University

Although business is done all over the globe, differences exist in what is seen as acceptable or effective behavior in organizations. Similarly, one does not have to look far to see cultural differences in what is considered effective leadership. Think of some of the political leaders who are immensely popular in their home countries for reasons that people in other areas of the world just do not understand (see, e.g., poll of the Pew Research Center, 2007). What leaders and managers do and why they do it is influenced by what is customary in their organization, industry, or country. Whether managers typically seek to "expand their business rapidly, to undercut their competitors, to misrepresent their products, or to put customer satisfaction before economic production will . . . at least partly depend on the prevailing mores" (Stewart, 1997, p.129). Similarly, what people from different backgrounds see as effective leadership will reflect the values held in their groups. *Cultural values* are defined as a set of beliefs and norms—often anchored in the morals, laws, customs, and practices of a society—that define what is right and wrong and specify general preferences (e.g., Adler, 2002).

AUTHORS' NOTE: Please address correspondence concerning this chapter to Deanne N. Den Hartog, Faculty of Economics and Business, University of Amsterdam, Plantage Muidergracht 12, 1015 LL Amsterdam, The Netherlands. Phone: +31205255287. e-mail: d.n.denhartog@uva.nl.

Leaders increasingly need to deal with people from different cultures (e.g., Javidan, Dorfman, de Luque, & House, 2006). The question for organizations is no longer whether they are in a global industry and operate internationally; rather, it is a matter of degree (e.g., Czinkota & Ronkainen, 2005). In addition, in many countries, the workforce is growing more culturally diverse. Thus, people from different cultures increasingly come into contact in work situations, and leaders are faced with the difficult task of convincingly presenting the organization's vision to a multicultural and diverse workforce in an uncertain and unpredictable environment. In such roles, leaders need the knowledge and skills to act and decide in a culturally sensitive manner. Thus, more insight into leadership in different cultural contexts can be both interesting and useful for managers doing business in another culture or working with people from abroad.

Stories emphasizing the importance of leadership are found throughout history, and leadership as a function in human groups is found all over the world (e.g., Bass & Bass, 2008). Leadership everywhere has to do with disproportionate influence, and the leadership role is associated with power and status. For example, Pickenpaugh (1997) assessed symbols of leadership in traditional cultures from the Pacific Islands, sub-Saharan Africa, and lowland South America and found that the leaders (kings, chiefs, headmen) in such cultures often wear necklaces of large canine teeth from the most powerful and ferocious animals in their respective environments. Elsewhere in the world, power and status may be conveyed through such things as job titles, business cards, office size, or other symbols recognizable as status and power related by those witnessing them (e.g., Gupta, de Luque, & House, 2004).

In this chapter, we are interested in organizational leadership in different countries and cultures. However, when looking at leadership cross-culturally, it is important to remember that such fundamental organizational concepts as leadership, participation, control, and cooperation do not necessarily mean the same in every cultural context. As cultures vary, so vary the institutions within those cultures, and leadership as a central component of institutional functioning varies as well (Dickson, Den Hartog, & Castaño, 2009). For instance, in the "West," participation usually refers to having influence on the outcome of a decision by taking part in it in one form or another, whereas in Japan it refers to the consensus-oriented approach through the bottom-up procedures and lobby consultations of the ringi system (Heller, Drenth, Koopman, & Rus, 1988; Heller & Misumi, 1987; Steers, Nardon, & Sanchez-Runde, 2009). Thus, different connotations, perceptions, and attitudes can lie hidden behind the same term.

These differences in meaning occur for leadership as well, and even the term "leadership" itself can be interpreted somewhat differently across cultures. *Leader* and *leadership* have a positive connotation in Anglo-Saxon countries, conjuring up heroic images of outstanding individuals. Meindl's classic work on the "romance of leadership" shows the American romantic attachment to—and in some cases overestimation of—the importance of the leadership role (Meindl, Ehrlich, & Dukerich, 1985; see Meindl, 1990). However, this does not hold globally for all direct translations. The direct translation of "leader" to German is "Führer." Obviously, the historically laden connotation here is rather negative. Similarly, in some other countries, literal translations of "leader" conjure up images of recent dictatorship. There, the term "manager" may have the more positive connotations that "leader" has in English (Den Hartog & Koopman, 2001). Other translation issues abound. For example, in some egalitarian societies literally translating *follower* or *subordinate* may be less appropriate: In the Netherlands, subordinates are typically referred to as "medewerkers," which literally translates as coworkers, not subordinates (Dickson et al., 2009). Such examples show that even with careful attention to translation, there may be unrecognized subtle shadings and nuances of meaning that vary across languages and cultures. Problems of meaning and language such as these pose obvious measurement problems—How can we be sure we are even measuring the same construct? If we are not, to what should found differences be attributed? This issue remains an area of concern in all cross-cultural research, including cross-cultural research on leadership.

An attempt to define leadership cross-culturally comes from the Global Leadership and Organizational Behavior Effectiveness (GLOBE) Project, which is a large-scale research project that is described in more detail below, designed to assess both similarities and differences in the cultural semantic definition of leadership in the 60 participating countries. GLOBE researchers defined leadership as *"the ability of an individual to influence, motivate, and enable others to contribute toward the effectiveness and success of the organizations of which they are members."* The definition was based on an extensive discussion among 84 social scientists and management scholars representing 56 countries, which took place at an international meeting in 1994. This rather abstract definition of leadership was acceptable to these representatives of a wide range of cultures. Thus, some agreement about what leadership entails can be found. Still, the evaluative and semantic interpretation of the term "leadership," the cognitive prototypes characterizing leadership, and the culture-specific enactments of leadership also vary by culture (e.g., Den Hartog et al., 1999; Hanges, Lord, & Dickson, 2000; House et al., 2004; Javidan, Dorfman, et al., 2006).

Thus, what is seen as effective leader behavior may vary in different societies, resulting in different leader behaviors and leadership-related practices. A study showing differences between two countries in the way people are typically prepared for future leadership roles can illustrate this. Stewart, Barsoux, Kieser, Ganter, and Walgenbach (1994) compared the education and careers of German and British middle managers. They showed that Britain has a tradition of recruiting talented graduates of any discipline for management careers. In Germany, the management task is perceived in more functional terms, and a direct relationship between the content of vocational training and the job to be done was more common. In career development, the British placed more emphasis on mobility. Large companies prepare their future leaders through frequent changes of jobs, tasks, and functions. Variety and generalized knowledge and skills are valued. In contrast, in Germany, they saw less emphasis on mobility and development through exposure to different situations. Managers spent more time in a single job, and development of specialized expertise was valued. These different approaches in developing leaders reflect differences in ideas on what makes leaders at this level effective in these two cultures.

In the sections that follow, we present some examples of studies on leader behavior in different countries. As we will show below, to date, the ways in which researchers study and think about leadership have been strongly influenced by North American values. However, the assumptions underlying these values are not necessarily shared in other cultures. Thus, we describe different dimensions of societal cultures and the ways in which they might lead to differences in approaching leadership. Next, we turn to the developing world and highlight some elements that are specific to this group of nations. We then turn to leadership perceptions around the world and show similarities and differences in the way people view effective leadership across many different cultures. Finally, we briefly discuss organizational culture in relation to societal culture and leadership.

Leadership Research in Different Countries

Overviews show that most leadership research of the past half century was conducted in the United States, Canada, and Western Europe (e.g., Dickson, Den Hartog, & Mitchelson, 2003). Whereas the early North American leadership studies tended to focus on leader–group interaction, older European studies tended to place leadership in a broader social, legal, and political context, for example, comparing participative management systems in different countries (e.g., Heller et al., 1988). During the last decade, leadership has also more widely been investigated by social scientists in other regions of the world that traditionally did not study leadership that much. To mention only a few examples: Pasa (2000) studied influence behaviors, and Pellegrini and Scandura (2006) focused on leader–member exchange (LMX) and delegation in Turkey; Kahtri, Ng, and Lee (2001) assessed leader charisma and vision in Singapore; and Silverthorne (2001) looked at the applicability of the path-goal model in Taiwan. Like these examples, many of the leadership studies to date in non-Western regions of the world are carried out in a single country.

Comparative leadership research is still less common, and the available studies often take only small numbers of groups into account. Some comparative studies assess differences between groups with a different cultural background within a certain country. The idea is that even if they live in the same sociocultural context, managers from different cultural backgrounds may demonstrate or appreciate different leader behaviors. For example, Xin and Tsui (1996) compared the influence styles of Asian American and Caucasian American managers. They found only minor differences between the two groups, and ethnic background accounted for only little variance in their measures. This highlights that we should not take for granted that people will behave differently in leadership roles solely based on their ethnicity or country of origin. Also, although cultural values that are shared in a given group are expected to influence individual behavior, large individual differences may also exist.

Other such comparisons between different cultural groups within a single country can focus on managers from different backgrounds in joint ventures or local versus international managers working in a given country. For instance, Quang, Swierczek, and Chi (1998) compared Vietnamese managers to foreign managers working in Vietnam. They showed that the Vietnamese nationals did not differ from other international managers on factors such as the importance of having a strategic vision and adaptability to environmental demands. However, the Vietnamese managers placed more importance on responding to deadlines and time management than did the international managers. The Vietnamese managers also placed less emphasis on performance and productivity, which may reflect the heritage from the command economy. Finally, Vietnamese managers in the sample also wanted less sharing of power and delegation than did their international counterparts.

Other comparative studies focus on leadership in a few different countries. For example, Den Hartog et al. (1997) compared the characteristics that Polish and Dutch managers considered important for outstanding leadership. Visionary qualities scored high for both. Dutch managers valued attributes associated with integrity and inspirational leader behavior more strongly than did Polish managers. Diplomacy and administrative skills (e.g., orderly, well-organized) were more important in Poland. Such differences may be related to the transition from communist rule and a command economy toward a market economy. Similarly, Abdalla and Al-Homoud (2001) compared Kuwaitis' and Qataris' views of outstanding leadership and found these groups stress similar characteristics—namely, integrity, visionary, inspirational, administrative skills, diplomatic, and performance orientation. There are many other examples of smaller comparative studies in the literature (e.g., Bu, Craig, & Peng, 2001; Fu & Yukl, 2000; Keating, Martin, Resick, & Dickson, 2007; Osland, Snyder, & Hunter, 1998). Most such studies take only a few cultures into account, and these are often convenience samples rather than sampling cultures based on a theoretical framework.

An example of studying cross-cultural aspects of leadership in a more elaborate project involving more than 40 countries is the research on event management that analyzes role relationships, putting the role of leaders in the context of other sources of meaning (see e.g., Smith & Peterson, 1988; Smith, Peterson, & Misumi, 1994; Smith, Peterson, & Schwartz, 2002). In handling events, managers can use different sources of information and meaning (e.g., rules and regulations; national norms; widespread beliefs; information from superiors, peers, or subordinates; unwritten rules). Preferences are found to differ across nations. For example, participation-oriented sources of guidance such as relying on subordinates were found mostly in Western Europe. Managers from other regions such as Africa tended to rely on more hierarchically oriented sources of information such as superiors and rules. Also, managers in countries such as China and Romania relied more strongly on widespread beliefs as a source of guidance than did managers elsewhere (Smith et al., 2002).

North American Bias

Although the discussion above shows that leadership studies are now conducted in many countries and some comparative work is done, there is still a strong North American bias in the leadership theories, models, and measures that are used and published in mainstream social science literature. Research conducted elsewhere often directly applies leadership models and measures developed in North America. However, it has long been noted that the applicability of theories and concepts developed in one part of the world, such as the United States, should not be taken for granted when applied in substantially different cultures (Boyacigiller & Adler, 1991).

Hofstede (1993) stated that U.S. management theories contain idiosyncrasies not necessarily shared elsewhere (e.g., a stress on market processes and on the individual; focus on managers rather than workers). Similarly, House (1995) noted that most theories and empirical evidence on leadership is rather North American in character, that is, "individualistic rather than collectivistic; emphasizing assumptions of rationality rather than ascetics, religion, or superstition; stated in terms of individual rather than group incentives; stressing follower responsibilities rather than rights; assuming hedonistic rather than altruistic motivation and assuming centrality of work and democratic value orientation" (p. 443). Such assumptions affect what is modeled as effective leadership. However, many cultures do not share these assumptions. Thus, a better understanding is needed of the ways in which leadership is enacted in various cultures, and an empirically grounded theory to explain differential leader behavior and effectiveness across cultures is needed (House, 1995). When applying models in a cultural context that were developed in a different one, we need to carefully consider the role that cultural differences might play and how such differences may affect the meaning, enactment, and effectiveness of leader behaviors. Thus, Leung (2007) called for Asian researchers to enhance their efforts in investigating indigenous constructs and developing indigenous theoretical explanations for phenomena—and this is also needed in other regions.

An example of a widely used measure of U.S. origin is Bernard Bass and colleagues' Multifactor Leadership Questionnaire (MLQ), tapping transactional and transformational leadership (see, e.g., Antonakis, Avolio, &

Sivasubramaniam, 2003; Bass, 1985). This questionnaire has been used in many different countries. Among these are European countries such as Austria, Germany, the UK, the Netherlands, and Belgium; Anglo-Saxon countries such as the UK and Australia; and Asian countries such as Taiwan and Japan (e.g., Bass, 1997; Den Hartog, Van Muijen, & Koopman, 1997; Geyer & Steyrer, 1998; Koh, Steers, & Terborg, 1995; Lievens, van Geit, & Coetsier, 1997; Rowold & Heinitz, 2007). There is evidence that a preference for transformational leadership exists in most cultures. Also, virtually everywhere, transformational leadership correlates more positively with positive outcomes than transactional leadership (Bass, 1997). For example, a study among bank employees in the United States, China, and India showed that transformational leadership related positively to follower self-efficacy, commitment, and satisfaction in all three samples (Walumbwa, Lawler, Avolio, Wang, & Shi, 2005).

Thus, a preference for and positive effects of transformational leadership are found in many places. However, the questions in the MLQ are phrased in somewhat abstract ways. Thus, such leadership does not necessarily look exactly the same in different cultures. It could be enacted in different ways (e.g., House, Wright, & Aditya, 1997). For example, charismatic leaders articulate an ideological message, set a personal example, and convey self-confidence—resulting in being trusted and respected by their followers. However, charisma can be enacted in a highly assertive manner (e.g., John F. Kennedy, Winston Churchill) or in a quiet, nonaggressive manner (e.g., Aung San Suu Kyi, Mahatma Gandhi). Bass also provided such examples and stated that although concepts such as "transactional leadership" and "transformational leadership" may be universally valid, specific behaviors representing these styles may vary profoundly. For instance, Bass (1997) stated, "Indonesian inspirational leaders need to persuade their followers about the leaders' own competence, a behavior that would appear unseemly in Japan" (p. 132). Bass also noted that contingent rewarding is more implicit in Japan than in the United States.

Transformational leadership may also take more as well as less participative forms (Bass & Bass, 2008), which seems likely to be linked to societal norms and values regarding the distribution of power. In the Netherlands, for instance, transformational leader behaviors were highly correlated with participation in decision making (Den Hartog et al., 1999); that also holds in Australia (Ashkanasy, 2007; Feather, 1994). Both these countries have egalitarian cultures. Thus, in highly egalitarian societies, to be seen as transformational, leaders may need to be more participative than they would need to be in high power distance societies. In such societies, transformational leadership may take a more directive form (Den Hartog et al., 1999). Testing these and other propositions could yield more insight into what it means to be transformational in different cultures.

Finally, it is important to recognize the one major study to date that has assessed leadership and leadership preferences in a large number of cultures, at both the societal and organizational levels. The GLOBE Project, mentioned earlier, is a long-term study directed toward the development of systematic knowledge concerning how societal and organizational cultures affect leadership and organizational practices (House et al., 2004). Approximately 60 countries from all major regions of the world participate in GLOBE, making it the most extensive investigation of cross-cultural aspects of leadership to date. The project was originated by Robert J. House, who has led the project's *coordinating team,* which includes representatives from several different cultures. Besides the coordinating team, some 150 social scientists from around the world are responsible for managing the project and collecting data in their respective countries.

After developing measures of culture using a dimension-based approach as described below, data were collected on leadership preferences, organizational culture, and societal culture. More than 15,000 middle managers from more than 800 organizations in three industries in more than 60 countries were asked to describe leader attributes and behavior that they perceived to enhance or impede outstanding leadership. The measures of both societal and organizational culture consisted of two parts. GLOBE views culture as consisting of both (a) values; that is, what is considered desirable in society, as well as (b) practices; that is, actual ways in which members of a culture go about dealing with their collective challenges (e.g., Javidan, House, Dorfman, Hanges, & de Luque, 2006). This is in line with the broad definition of national culture as "values, beliefs, norms, and behavioral patterns of a national group" (Leung, Bhagat, Buchan, Erez, & Gibson, 2005, p. 357). The results of the GLOBE project were reported in journal articles (e.g., Javidan, Dorfman, et al., 2006) and a book (House et al., 2004). A second book based on this project provides an in-depth analysis of leadership in 25 different individual countries (Chhokar, Brodbeck, & House, 2007). At various points throughout the remainder of this chapter, GLOBE study results will be presented. However, we will first go into societal culture and the impact that different dimensions of culture are likely to have on leadership.

Dimensions of Societal Culture Related to Leadership

Culture can be seen as a set of relatively stable, basic, and shared practices and values that help human social groups or societies find solutions to fundamental problems. Schein (1992) focused on two such fundamental challenges. The first is how to survive, grow, and adapt to the environment (i.e., external adaptation). The second is how to achieve sufficient internal integration, which permits daily functioning and ensures the capacity or ability to adapt and survive. When people come together as a group, they develop shared beliefs and assumptions about the world and the people in it. These beliefs help them survive as a group. Such value orientations, beliefs, and assumptions refer to the basic nature of people, human relationships, as well as relationships with nature, time, and activity (e.g., Adler, 2002; Hofstede, 2001; Kluckhohn & Strodtbeck, 1961; Nardon & Steers, 2009; Parsons & Shils, 1951; Schwartz, 1999).

One way to approach the study of culture is through the identification and measurement of dimensions of culture. Several different typologies of societal cultural value orientations or culture dimensions have been developed. The most widely recognized, as well as strongly criticized, is probably Hofstede's framework (1980, 2001). Hofstede's (1980) original study was based on a survey among IBM managers and employees in more than 40 countries. He found four culture dimensions: individualism-collectivism, masculinity-femininity, uncertainty avoidance, and power distance. In later work, a fifth dimension—future orientation—was added.

Hofstede's work has been the target of substantial criticism, including arguments that it presents an overly simplistic four- or five-dimension conceptualization of culture, that the original sample came from a single multinational corporation (IBM), that culture is malleable over time, that his measures are not sufficiently well-developed, and that his work ignores within-country cultural heterogeneity (see Sivakumar & Nakata, 2001; see also McSweeney, 2002; Schwartz, 1994; Smith, 2002; Smith & Bond, 1993/1999, for recent overviews and critiques; see Kirkman, Lowe, & Gibson, 2006, for an extensive overview of research using Hofstede's dimensions in different ways). Rather than providing an in-depth discussion or critique of Hofstede's research, we will discuss Hofstede's dimensions alongside other, sometimes similar, dimensions that have been proposed and studied, for example in the aforementioned GLOBE study. We do not purport to present an exhaustive discussion of culture dimensions here—other dimensions have also been proposed and studied.

Like Hofstede's work, the GLOBE study has received some criticism (see e.g., Hofstede, 2006, and their rejoinder by Javidan, House, et al., 2006). For example, as mentioned, GLOBE measures both cultural practices and values, and Hofstede (2006) criticizes the measurement. Although theoretically cultural values are often proposed to drive cultural practices (e.g., Hofstede, 2001), previous research had not yet directly tested that assumption. GLOBE aimed to construct measures that would allow for that. Societal cultural practices and values were operationalized through isomorphic items. For example, a cultural practice item of the power distance dimension is: In this society, power is . . . . On a reverse-coded, Likert-type scale, responses ranged from 1 (*concentrated at the top*) through 7 (*shared throughout the society*). The related (reverse-coded) cultural value question is: In this society, power should be: 1 (*concentrated at the top*) through 7 (*shared throughout the society*). (Similar questions assessed organizational culture, described later on in this chapter.) Unexpectedly, for six of the nine culture dimensions, the correlations between values and practices dimensions were negative. The relationship is dimension specific, and the most notable relationship between values and practices is seen in societies with practice scores in the extreme regions, either high or low. For example, societies with the lowest future orientation practices scores show the highest upward move in their aspirations. In contrast, societies with the highest assertiveness orientation practices show the largest downward move in their aspirations. Javidan, House, et al. (2006) thus concluded that these findings suggest that the assumption of a simple linear relationship between values and practices does not seem to hold.

Javidan, House, et al. (2006) also caution that the negative correlations between the practices and values scores do not mean that a score above the midpoint (i.e., 4) on one scale (e.g., practices) is associated with a score below the midpoint (i.e., 4) on the other scale (e.g., values). For example, respondents from virtually all societies report a higher value score on performance orientation than their practices scores. The average values score on this dimension is 5.94 and the average practice score is 4.10, yet there is a -0.28 correlation between them. The negative correlation occurs because for societies with higher practices scores the *increment desired* is smaller than for those with low practices scores. This holds for four dimensions: performance orientation, future orientation, humane orientation, and in a reverse sense for power distance (societies prefer less power distance). Javidan, House, et al. (2006) discuss these issues in more detail. Clearly, when it comes to the GLOBE measures, the interpretation of the cultural practices scales is easier than that of the values scales. Measurement remains a difficult issue when it comes to culture.

The researchers developing the specific culture dimensions, described in more detail below, have mostly studied culture at a societal level, and a wide range of research shows that societies do indeed differ on these value orientations. In addition to the societal level, Kirkman, Chen, Fahr, Chen, and Lowe (2009) suggested that cultural differences can also meaningfully affect leadership processes at the individual level of analysis. In line with this, several reviews of the cross-cultural literature suggest that the level at which cultural influences operate—individual, or country, or both—remains an open research question in many substantive areas in the organizational behaviour and management field (e.g., Gelfand, Erez, & Aycan, 2007; Kirkman et al., 2006).

Masculinity

Having an aggressive attitude in the Western business world seems to have a relatively positive connotation. Aggressive, then, implies being tough, fast, and forceful, as opposed to weak and vulnerable (Den Hartog, 2004). According to Hofstede (1980; 2001), the word "aggressive" carries a positive connotation only in what he calls "masculine" countries. Hofstede described differences between societies in the desirability of assertive and tough behavior versus modest and tender behavior. He labeled this dimension "masculinity" versus "femininity." Masculinity implies dominant societal values stressing assertiveness and toughness, the acquisition of money and things, and not caring for others or their quality of life. In feminine cultures, values such as warm social relationships, quality of life, and care of the weak are stressed. Doney, Cannon, and Mullen (1998) contrasted masculinity versus femininity in terms of valuing individual achievement versus norms for solidarity and service, having a norm for confrontation versus a norm for cooperation, and having social norms stressing independent thought and action versus social norms honoring moral obligations.

Hofstede also explicitly linked this dimension to gender differences. High cultural masculinity characterizes societies in which men are expected to be assertive and tough and women are expected to be modest and tender. In contrast, low masculinity (or high femininity) characterizes societies where both men and women are expected to be modest and tender. Achievement motivation and an acceptance of "machismo style" management should be higher in countries high on masculinity than in those low on masculinity (Triandis, 1994). Hofstede (2001) holds that masculine and feminine cultures create different leader hero types. The masculine manager is assertive, aggressive, and decisive. Survival of the fittest is the credo. Conversely, the hero in feminine cultures seeks consensus, is less visible, and is intuitive rather than tough and decisive. Here, business is a cooperative venture. Japan, Austria, Italy, Mexico, Germany, the UK, and the United States are examples of more masculine cultures, and Sweden, Norway, the Netherlands, and Costa Rica are examples of more feminine countries (Hofstede, 2001).

Critique of the masculinity–femininity dimension includes that it is not well measured and that it includes too many very different topics (e.g., gender role division, assertiveness in social relationships, being humane or focused on quality of life, being performance- or achievement-oriented). In the afore-mentioned GLOBE study (e.g., House et al., 1999, 2004), these aspects are measured separately. The GLOBE dimensions related to this are labeled assertiveness, gender egalitarianism, performance orientation, and humane orientation (two aspects of collectivism, power distance, uncertainty avoid-ance, and future orientation are also culture dimensions measured in GLOBE). For instance, GLOBE assertiveness is defined as the degree to which individuals in organizations or societies are assertive, tough, dominant, and aggressive in social relationships (Den Hartog, 2004).

Among other things, assertiveness is linked to the preferred use of lan-guage in society. Assertiveness can be seen as a style of responding that implies making one's wants known to others, which is why in many "west-ern" cultures, being direct and unambiguous is acceptable. Indeed a negative relationship between assertiveness and indirect language use was found in the United States. Also, conversational indirectness was found to correlate nega-tively with social desirability. Thus, saying what one means in a direct man-ner is valued in the United States (Holtgraves, 1997). In other cultures, however, a less direct manner of responding may be valued. In assertive societies, people will tend to use what is also referred to as "low-context" language, emphasizing the need to be direct, clear, and explicit. In contrast, less assertive cultures tend to use "high-context" languages that are less direct and more ambiguous and subtle (Hall, 1959; S. C. Schneider & Barsoux, 1997). High-context language or being indirect in communication can be linked to "face management" (Brown & Levinson, 1987). People are motivated to collectively manage each other's face or public identity, and they do this by phrasing remarks politely and indirectly (Holtgraves, 1997). Although face management in some form or another is important in any culture, people from so-called collectivist cultures are usually assumed to be more concerned with face management than are people from individualistic countries (Ting-Toomey, 1988).

There is some support for the idea of cultural differences in this area. In Holtgraves' (1997) research, for example, Koreans were found to be more indirect than were Americans. Societal norms can also influence the amount of emotion one typically shows in public within a certain society. Trompenaars and Hampden-Turner (1997) contrast "neutral" with "affective" cultures. In affective cultures, showing one's emotions in laughter or gesture, as well as in heated debate, is the norm. In more neutral cultures, people tend to keep their emotions in check. In such cultures, a subdued manner, self-possessed conduct, and repression of emotional expression is the norm. Such differences in acceptable communication styles and patterns impact the way in which leaders present themselves in order to effectively influence others.

Uncertainty Avoidance

Uncertainty avoidance is another dimension Hofstede (1980, 2001) distinguishes. It describes a society's reliance on social norms and procedures to alleviate the unpredictability of the future. Hofstede defined uncertainty avoidance as the extent to which a society feels threatened by uncertain and ambiguous situations and tries to avoid these situations by providing greater (career) stability, establishing formal rules, rejecting deviant ideas and behaviors, and believing in absolute truths and the attainment of expertise. It refers to the degree to which members in a society feel uncomfortable with ambiguous and uncertain situations.

In high uncertainty avoidance societies, people tend to prefer career stability and formal rules, whereas people from low uncertainty avoidance cultures tend to prefer more flexibility in roles and jobs and are more mobile when it comes to jobs. High uncertainty avoidant countries also foster a belief in experts (Hofstede, 2001). The aforementioned study by Stewart et al. (1994) comparing the career management activities of German and UK managers illustrates this point. German culture shows a far stronger antipathy toward uncertainty than does the British culture (Hofstede, 1980, 2001). This difference was reflected in the managers' typical career patterns and behaviors. Recall that the British typically placed more emphasis on career mobility, whereas the German managers spent more time in a single job and valued the development of task-related expertise. Also, whereas British managers emphasized the importance of resourcefulness and improvisation in behavior, German managers expected reliability and punctuality. Strict planning and sticking to previously agreed plans were very important for the German managers. Not doing so was seen as a sign of weakness, much more so than in the United Kingdom.

The results of the Stewart et al. (1994) study are congruent with those from other studies. For example, one such study compares German and Irish entrepreneurs running small companies (Rauch, Frese, & Sonnentag, 2000). Germany and Ireland are similar on all of Hofstede's culture dimensions except uncertainty avoidance, where Germany ranks high and Ireland low. Thus, in Germany, business plans are highly detailed. Customers prefer such planning and expect transactions to be adhered to by the letter, on time, and as agreed. Meeting customer expectations in such an environment is linked to careful and detailed planning. In contrast, in Ireland planning is seen as less necessary. Customers have less respect for plans, show unplanned behavior themselves, and expect high flexibility. It is believed that planning too much renders business owners inflexible and makes it harder to meet customer demands. In line with this, Rauch and colleagues found that detailed planning had a positive influence on small business success in Germany and a negative influence on small business success in Ireland.

Several other studies provide similar evidence. Shane (1993) found that uncertainty-accepting societies are more innovative than are uncertainty-avoiding societies. In a later study, Shane (1995) found *lower* preferences for innovation-championing roles (including the transformational leader role) in uncertainty-avoidant societies. Shane, Venkataraman, and MacMillan (1995) examined the relationship between culture dimensions and preferences for innovation championing strategies in 30 countries. They found that the higher the level of uncertainty avoidance in a society, the more people preferred champions to work through organizational norms, rules, and procedures to promote innovation. In other words, the more *uncertainty accepting* the society, the more people endorsed champions' efforts to overcome organizational inertia to innovation by violating organizational rules and regulations.

Relationships With Others: Collectivism

Another well-known culture dimension is individualism versus collectivism. Hofstede (1980, 2001) described cultures characterized by *individualism* as loosely knit social frameworks in which people are supposed to take care of themselves and look after their own interests and those of their close families only. In contrast, a tight social framework in which people distinguish between in-groups and out-groups is the key characteristic of cultures high on collectivism. In-groups are cohesive and strong. People expect their in-group to look after them throughout life and, in exchange, feel they owe the in-group absolute loyalty.

Similarly, Schwartz (1999) noted that a society has to decide to what extent people are autonomous versus embedded in the group. In cultures high on embeddedness, people are perceived as part of the collective, and they find meaning and direction in life through participating in the group and identifying with its goals. Organizations tend to take responsibility for members in all domains of life and, in return, expect members to identify with and work toward organizational goals. In contrast, individuals in autonomous cultures are perceived as autonomous entities who find meaning in life through their uniqueness.

Schwartz (1999) further distinguished between intellectual autonomy (i.e., individuals are encouraged to follow their own ideas and intellect) and affective autonomy (i.e., people are encouraged to independently find positive experiences for themselves). In cultures that emphasize intellectual autonomy, organizations are likely to treat their members as independent actors with their own interests, preferences, abilities, and allegiances. Employees are typically granted (some) autonomy and are encouraged to generate their own ideas and act on them (Brannen et al., 2004; Sagiv & Schwartz, 2000). In a 47-nation study, Schwartz and Sagie (2000) found that socioeconomic development as well as democratization increased the importance of independent thought and action, openness to change, concern for the welfare of others, self-indulgence, and pleasure and decreased the importance of conformity, tradition, and security.

Hierarchy, Status, and Power Distance

Within all societies, there are status and power differentials. These are obviously related to conceptions of leadership. Hofstede (1980) defined *power distance* as the extent to which a society accepts and embraces the fact that power in institutions and organizations is distributed unequally. In cultures with large differences in power between individuals, organizations will typically have many layers, and the chain of command is very important. In line with this definition, the relationship between job satisfaction and job level was found to be weaker in low power distance than in high power distance cultures (Robie, Ryan, Schmieder, Parra, & Smith, 1998). Power distance is also related to concentration of authority (Hofstede, 2001). In high power distance countries such as China, Mexico, and the Philippines, subordinates are typically more reluctant to challenge their supervisors than are employees in low power distance countries like Finland, the Netherlands, Israel, and the United States. Employees in high power distance cultures have also been found to be more fearful in expressing disagreement with their managers (Adsit, London, Crom, & Jones, 2001).

Not only are people in high power distance countries less likely to provide negative feedback to superiors, but the idea that subordinates would be allowed to provide such ratings is also likely to be rejected in high power distance countries, as such upward feedback may be perceived as threatening status positions (Kirkman & Den Hartog, 2004). Power distance is also found to be an important predictor in the aforementioned studies on event management. The way in which managers typically handle events is related to power distance in society. Smith et al. (1994; 2002) show that managers in countries characterized by high power distance report more use of rules and procedures. They also report less reliance on subordinates and their own experience in dealing with everyday events than do managers from low power distance countries.

Authoritarian leadership and more autocratic decision making are likely to be accepted and expected in high power distance cultures. In egalitarian cultures, employees expect to have a say in decisions affecting their work. For instance, France scores much higher on power distance than does Denmark. In studies comparing French and Danish managers, French respondents indicated that the boss almost always had to be consulted simply because he or she was the boss, whereas the Danish indicated the boss had to be consulted only when the boss was likely to know the answer to their problem. In France, bosses were highly respected by virtue of their position, whereas in Denmark, respect relationships were found to be independent of rank. A Danish boss could do the work of a subordinate without loss of prestige, but a French manager could not. Finally, the Danish firms were characterized by delegation of authority and flatter hierarchical structures (e.g., Sondergaard, 1988, as cited in Hofstede, 2001).

Hofstede (2001) reported that subordinates in high power distance countries saw their managers primarily as well-meaning autocrats, whereas subordinates in low power distance countries saw them primarily as resourceful democrats. Shane et al. (1995) found that the greater the power distance in a society, the more people preferred innovation champions to focus on gaining the support of those in authority before other actions are taken on an innovation (rather than on building a broad base of support for new ideas among organization members).

Similarly, Schwartz (1999) noted that an issue confronting any society is how to guarantee the necessary responsible behavior of its members. One solution to this challenge is found in hierarchical cultures, which rely on hierarchical systems of ascribed roles and perceive the unequal distribution of power as legitimate. This conception of culture has elements of both power distance and collectivism, in that individuals are socialized to comply with the roles and obligations attached to their position in society. Organizations emphasize the chain of authority, assign well-defined roles in a hierarchical structure, and demand compliance in the service of goals set from the top. Organizational members are expected to put the interests of the organization before their own interests. In contrast, egalitarian cultures encourage people to view each other as moral equals. Individuals are socialized to internalize a voluntary commitment toward others. Organizations emphasize cooperative negotiation, and employees flexibly enact roles as they try to attain organizational goals. Leaders motivate others by enabling them to share in goal-setting activities and by appealing to others to act on behalf of the joint welfare of all (Sagiv & Schwartz, 2000; Schwartz, 1999).

Related to this is research focused on willingness to accept and responsiveness to supervisory direction. For example, Bu et al. (2001) compared the tendency to accept a supervisor's direction among Chinese, Taiwanese, and U.S. employees using their responses to several vignettes. Overall, the Chinese employees in their sample demonstrated the strongest tendency to accept direction and the U.S. employees the least. Peer consensus had more influence on the tendency to accept in the United States than in Taiwan or the People's Republic of China (PRC). Also, Chinese employees were more sensitive to the consistency between the supervisory direction and company policies and were less responsive to their own assessment of the merit of the directions they were given. These differences seem to reflect differences in power distance. Also, the aforementioned study by Den Hartog et al. (1997) showed that Dutch managers had a much more negative attitude toward autocratic leader behavior and status consciousness than did Polish managers, which may reflect the egalitarian (i.e., low power distance) values found in the Netherlands.

In a larger study conducted by Dorfman et al. (1997), the researchers compared leader behavior in five Western and Asian countries, namely the United States, Mexico, Japan, Taiwan, and South Korea. They found that some leader behaviors were positively related to outcomes (e.g., satisfaction with supervision, organizational commitment) in all these nations, but other leader behaviors were not universally endorsed.

Dorfman et al. (1997) related the differences they found to culture and especially to differences in the way power is typically distributed in society. For instance, supportive leadership was positively related to satisfaction with the supervisor (and in some cases, other outcomes) in all five samples, but directive leadership was positively related to commitment only in Mexico and Taiwan. Charismatic leadership also had positive effects on one or more outcomes in all five samples. For instance, in Japan, charisma was related to subordinates' experiencing less role ambiguity; in Mexico, the United States, and South Korea, it was related to satisfaction with the supervisor; whereas in Taiwan, charisma was related to both of these outcomes, as well as to satisfaction with work. Contingent rewarding also had a positive effect on one or more of the outcomes in all samples. Participative leadership had positive effects only in the United States and South Korea. In Mexico and the United States, they were able to collect similar job performance data from company records. They found that in Mexico only supportive and directive leadership were directly and positively related to performance, whereas in the United States, only participative leadership had a direct and positive relationship with performance, and charismatic leadership did not affect performance.

Thus, out of the six tested behaviors, three (i.e., supportive, contingent reward, and charismatic leadership) had positive effects in all five countries. Three others (i.e., participative, directive, and contingent punishment) had positive impacts in only one or two cultures and equivocal or negative impacts in the other countries. These results confirm the idea that the impact of some behaviors may, to some extent, be cross-culturally generalizable, whereas for others it may be much more culture specific. To use the terminology presented by Bass (1997, building on Lonner, 1980), this study was testing for the presence of "functional universals," which are relationships between variables that are consistent across cultures.

Another issue related to power and status arises from the question of whether status is based on achievement or ascription (Parsons & Shils, 1951). Whereas some societies accord status to people on the basis of their achievements, others ascribe it to people based on age, gender, social class, profession, or other criteria. Achieved status is based on what one has done or accomplished, and ascribed status is based on who one "is." Achievement-oriented societies tend to accord status based on their members' accomplishments. Evaluations are based on how people perform. Ascribing cultures confer status on the individual and not on the task or the individual's accomplishments. In ascribing societies where seniority and age are major requirements, for example, it will usually be unacceptable to have people report to bosses who are younger than they are. In the United States, the idea that anyone can become president is a strong reflection of achievement orientation, whereas, in France, becoming president without attending the right *grande ecole* and without the right connections seems impossible. In Japan, promotion to higher positions has historically been based on seniority, gender, and age (Javidan, 2004; S. C. Schneider & Barsoux, 1997), and employees recognize these practices and shape their expectations accordingly.

In a recent study among leaders and their followers in the PRC and the United States, Kirkman et al. (2009) take a different approach and focus on individual-level differences in power distance orientation. Country differences did not significantly affect findings. They found that both individual follower's power distance orientation and their group's shared perceptions of transformational leadership were positively related to procedural justice perceptions. Power distance orientation also moderated the relationship between transformational leadership and procedural justice (it was stronger when power distance orientation was lower). Procedural justice, in turn, linked the unique and interactive relationships of transformational leadership and power distance orientation with followers' organizational citizenship behavior. This study highlights that besides the role of societal culture in leadership, we also need to start taking individual-level culture orientation effects into account in studying leadership.

Assumptions About Human Nature

One basic value orientation on which cultures differ, and which was not explicitly addressed by Hofstede (1980), is their assumptions on the nature of human beings: Are people generally neutral, good, or evil? Kluckhohn and Strodtbeck (1961) presented this distinction in terms of their dimension ranging from "human nature is good" to "human nature is bad." Within groups viewing humans as basically good, people will tend to trust others' intentions. In leadership terms, one might, for example, expect less emphasis on control and direct supervision of employees if a basic belief exists that people have good intentions. In contrast, distrust prevails in cultures where people are believed to be evil, and as such, more monitoring and closer supervision of employees can be expected (e.g., Brannen et al., 2004).

Whereas Hofstede (1980) did not explicitly incorporate this dimension into his taxonomy, it seems that there is at least some degree of conceptual overlap with the power distance dimension. Specifically, when power distance is high, there may be an accompanying lack of trust among the various social players. When power distance is low, there may be an accompanying high level of trust between social players. Certainly there are exceptions to this—high power distance societies are not always low on interpersonal trust, and the dimension of "human nature is good" versus "human nature is bad" is certainly broader than simply the degree of interpersonal trust. Nonetheless, cultural dimensions are never purely orthogonal, and there is at least some degree of potential overlap between this dimension and power distance. Whether a culture views humans as changeable or not is also of interest. In cultures where people are viewed as changeable, organizations and their managers are more likely to invest in training their employees. In cultures where people are considered to be less changeable, the emphasis would more likely be on selecting the correct person for the job (e.g., Brannen et al., 2004).

Control Orientation

An interesting element of culture pertains to the perceived nature of relationship with the outside world (Kluckhohn & Strodtbeck, 1961). Some societies view this relationship as one of subjugation, others as one of harmony, and still others as one of dominance. This latter view reflects the assumption that nature can be controlled and manipulated, a pragmatic orientation toward the nature of reality, and a belief in human perfectibility. It is thus also related to the dimension mentioned above, of whether humans are able to change or not. In societies holding a dominance view, "It is taken for granted that the proper thing to do for people is to take charge and actively control their environment" (Schein, 1992, p. 127).

At the other extreme, the assumption is that nature is powerful and humanity subservient to nature. This implies a kind of fatalism, as one cannot influence nature and must therefore accept one's destiny and enjoy what one has. The Moslem phrase, "Insh'allah" (God willing), is reflective of a culture characterized by a subjugation view. In contrast, the phrase "may the best person win" is an example of the value of control, dominance, and competitiveness (Javidan, 2004; S. C. Schneider & Barsoux, 1997). As noted above, Hofstede's cultural dimensions are not orthogonal, and this appears to be similar to the masculinity–femininity dimension. Similarly, Schwartz (1999) described mastery cultures, in which people are encouraged to master, change, and exploit the environment in order to attain goals.

In these cultures, it is believed that organizations and their leaders need to be dynamic, competitive, and strongly oriented toward achievement and success. Cultures at the opposing pole are labeled harmony cultures. In these cultures, people are encouraged to understand and integrate with their natural environment, rather than to change or exploit it. Leaders tend to take a holistic view and try to understand the social and environmental implications of organizational actions and to seek nonexploitative ways to work toward organizational goals (Sagiv & Swartz, 2000).

In line with the above, Trompenaars and Hampden-Turner (1997) hold that societies that conduct business "either believe they can and should control nature by imposing their will upon it, as in the ancient biblical injunction 'multiply and subdue the earth'; or they believe that man is part of nature and must go along with its laws, directions and forces" (p. 141). Trompenaars and Hampden-Turner identified these as internal and external cultures (in line with Rotter's 1966 classic work on internal versus external locus of control). Culture-related differences exist in the degree to which people feel they have control over (i.e., internal control) or are controlled by external forces (i.e., external control). For instance, when asked to choose between the statements "What happens to them is their own doing" or "Sometimes I feel that I do not have enough control over the directions my life is taking," more than 80% of U.S. managers choose the former (belief in control over own destiny) versus some 40% of Russian and Chinese managers.

Internal cultures have a dominating and controlling attitude toward nature. Conflict and resistance are taken to mean that one has strong convictions. In contrast, in external cultures, being at ease with the natural shifts and cycles of nature, willingness to compromise, seeking harmony, and responsiveness are seen as sensible and desirable characteristics for leaders. In internal cultures, the focus is on the self and one's own group or organization, and playing "hard ball" is legitimate to test the resilience of an opponent. In contrast, in external cultures, the focus is on the "other" (customer, partner, colleague), and softness, persistence, politeness, and patience are needed to succeed (Den Hartog, 2004). In internal societies, a strong belief in the value of competition and competitiveness exists. In the United States, for instance, competition is seen as "a fundamental aspect of human nature; people live in a dog-eat-dog world; people need to compete to survive and prosper" (Bonta, 1997, p. 299). Bonta showed that in most nonviolent or peaceful societies, an opposition to competition and support for cooperation constitute basic cultural beliefs. Such societies de-emphasize individual achievement, as it is too closely linked to competitiveness and aggressiveness.

These, and possibly other, dimensions of culture provide one approach to differentiating between societal cultures and the leadership styles that societies prefer. Certainly, other factors also come into play, including the degree of economic development of the society. To address this issue, we now turn more specifically to culture and leadership in the developing world.

Culture and Leadership in the Developing World _____

Models and research on leadership and culture were developed in and thus mostly focus on the "developed world" or, in other words, the Western or industrialized countries as opposed to the "developing" countries (Aycan, 2004; Sinha, 2003; Sinha et al., 2004). However, the developing countries represent almost 80% of the world population. This 80% comprises a large, growing market and labor force, spread among countries that are extremely diverse and produce a wide array of products and services (Punnett, 2004). Although there is no generally acceptable way to refer to these societies as a group, given that terms such as "developing" and "third world" are value-laden and originate in the "developed" societies, we use the term "developed world" to refer to the OECD countries and the rest of Western Europe, and the term "developing world" to refer to the rest of the world. The major distinctions between the *developed* and *developing* world are that on average, the developed world countries have significantly higher *per capita* income than do the developing world countries and that developed world countries rank higher on the Human Development Index (United Nations Development Program, 2002)—a composite index, which indicates the presence of good education, health care, and quality of life.

Increasingly, businesspeople recognize the vast potential of the growing markets and young labor force in developing countries. Specific developing countries also offer other strengths. Some are physically large and offer access to substantial reserves of natural resources (e.g., Brazil). Some have large numbers of highly trained and qualified people (e.g., India), good infrastructures (e.g., Zimbabwe), or good medical facilities (e.g., Cuba), and some achieve high scores on the Human Development Index (e.g., Barbados). These are all characteristics that may provide a good environment for both inward and outward business opportunities (Punnett, 2004).

The group of developing countries is diverse, and presenting a single unified and detailed portrayal of the cultural characteristics representing the whole group is thus impossible. However, as Aycan (2004) and others have noted, many developing countries share key elements in historical background (e.g., autocratic rule, colonialism), subsistence systems (e.g., reliance on agriculture), political environments (e.g., volatility and instability, improper law and enforcement system), economic conditions (e.g., resource scarcity, insufficient technological infrastructure), and/or demographic makeup (e.g., young work-force, unequal opportunity to access high quality education). Such economic and political environments as well as historical events are among the forces that shape cultures. Thus, it is reasonable to expect that at least some aspects of the cultures of these countries are similar. However, as we discuss these similarities, it is important to keep two things in mind. First, substantial differences exist between developing countries. Second, many differences may exist within developing countries. Such differences in values may, for instance, be regional or reflect differences between religions or ethnic groupings.

Differences in values and behavior can also be related to the organizations people work for or can be based on individuals' education, socioeconomic status, or age. For example, the values and behavior of a highly educated Indian manager, trained abroad and working for an American multinational corporation in an urban area, may resemble the values of other U.S. managers more than the values of an Indian manager with less education working for a small family business in a rural area. Such subcultural variations exist in every country, but the magnitude of such differences may well be larger in developing countries (Aycan, 2004).

Similarities in Cultural Dimensions Among Developing Countries

Cultures of developing countries *tend* to be somewhat more collectivistic and somewhat higher on power distance. They also tend to be externally oriented. As Aycan et al. (2000) noted, feelings of helplessness and fatalism are common cultural traits in these societies. Again, though, it is important to emphasize that the nature and degree to which these cultural traits are manifested can vary widely between developing countries, and there may be significant within-country variation on these dimensions, as well.

Having said the above, it is still generally the case that relationships and the networking that sustains them tend to be very important in the cultures of developing countries. Relationships and networks are more important than rules and procedures in virtually every aspect of social, political, and economic life of these countries, which sometimes leads to favoritism among in-group members—including relatives, friends, and members of one's own ethnic or religious group—and to discrimination against and alienation of out-group members. Within-group loyalty and harmony are central concepts. Because interdependence is fostered as a cultural value, self-reliance has a negative connotation, as it is seen as deserting the group. Thus, personal achievement is stressed less, and getting along is more important than getting ahead (Abdalla & Al-Homoud, 2001). These values, focused on maintaining harmony, tend to ensure smoothly running work processes, though not necessarily the most objectively efficient ones.

For example, a study on human resource management in China showed that very few companies have implemented individual-based rewards, because these types of rewards are believed to lead to so-called "red eye disease" among workers, an expression used in China to refer to jealousy (Verburg, 1996). Jealousy emanating from individual-based pay could constitute a disruption of harmony and, as such, have a negative impact on working relationships and performance (Verburg, Drenth, Koopman, Van Muijen, & Wang, 1999). Such patterns may, of course, change over time. Zhou (2002) reports on groups of employees in a Chinese factory recently acquired by a foreign investor. These employees overcame their cultural hesitancy to confront management and formally requested of their manager that the individual-based reward system that had been implemented be replaced by a seniority-based system.

In the developing world, the pattern of communication in organizations is often indirect, nonassertive, nonconfrontational, and usually downward. Negative feedback is often avoided or given very indirectly as it is quickly seen as destructive and disruptive to group harmony. In Eastern cultures such as China, Japan, and the Philippines, the loss of face, or public humiliation can result from receiving negative feedback (Earley, 1997). Because personal and work lives are intertwined, negative feedback can easily be interpreted as an attack on the person, tarnishing one's reputation and honor, rather than as an observation on behavior with a constructive aim (Aycan, 2004). Also, much of people's lives revolves around the nuclear and extended family, and work and family spheres tend to be closely interrelated. Thus, a loss of face at work can have substantial ramifications in the family, as well.

Similarities in Preferred Leadership Style in Developing Countries

As we have noted above, there are substantial variations between cultures in the developing world. However, one relatively common theme across these societies appears to be a preference for a leadership style that is high on status orientation, high on involvement in nonwork lives, and highly directive. This is often referred to as a "paternalistic" style of leadership (e.g., Aycan, 2004; Dorfman et al., 1997; Kanungo & Mendonca, 1996; Pellegrini & Scandura, 2008), and given the relationship that currently exists between differentiated gender roles and societal economic development (Emrich, Denmark, & Den Hartog, 2004), this masculine term (rather than the more gender neutral "parentalistic") seems appropriate. In many of these societies, there is a clear distinction in gender expectations, and the expected role of the leader is much more similar to that of the prototypical father, rather than that of the proto-typical mother or of a generic "parent."

In general, in these societies, organizations are expected to take care of their workers as well as the workers' families. Leaders in organizations tend to establish close interpersonal relationships with subordinates, as well as with people in higher authority. Subordinates expect personalized relationships, protection, close guidance, and supervision. Leaders are willing to assume responsibility for their followers and, in return, demand followers' loyalty.

The paternalistic relationship is strongly hierarchical. As noted above, the superior assumes the role of a father who protects and provides for the subordinate, whereas the subordinate voluntarily submits to the superior, showing loyalty and deference. The leader is assumed to "know what is best" for subordinates, and is expected to guide them in different aspects of life including nonwork-related issues. Such a leader typically shows a strong concern for the well-being of the subordinate as well as his or her family (Aycan, 2004; Pellegrini & Scandura, 2006, 2008).

Paternalistic leadership is, for instance, strong in Mexico (Dorfman et al., 1997). An example described by Martinez and Dorfman (1998) involved an inspirational Mexican entrepreneur who received many positive reactions from subordinates. He was seen as humorous, enthusiastic, and a good speaker, who had brought the company through a severe crisis. An example of his paternalistic behavior was that he involved himself in the private lives of his employees and that he felt that this was required of him because of the employees' personal needs and expectations of him. He was described as taking care of employees in a manner that would be uncharacteristic of a high-level manager in the United States or many other countries. For example, when a secretary remarked to the leader that her husband was going into the hospital for an operation, this leader then called the doctor and discussed the matter with the doctor to make sure that the operation was legitimate (see also Den Hartog et al., 1999).

Other examples of paternalistic behaviors given by Aycan (2004) include attending congratulatory and condolence ceremonies of employees as well as their immediate family members (e.g., weddings, funerals); providing financial assistance (e.g., donations, loans) to employees when in need for expenses such as housing, health-care, and children's education expenses, and acting as a mediator in interpersonal conflicts among employees. As stated, in return, employees display high levels of loyalty and deference and are often more willing to perform personal favors for superiors. A problem that can be seen with paternalistic leaders is the differential treatment among workers and the aforementioned related problems such as rivalry and jealousy (e.g., Sinha, 1995).

Pellegrini and Scandura (2008) note that authors disagree on the extent to which benevolent paternalistic acts are conducted with genuinely benevolent intentions and suggest that this construct might be culture bound. Aycan (2004) holds that paternalism is a leadership style that is not well understood in Western industrialized countries. Individualist values endorsed in many of the more industrialized nations imply a striving for autonomy and self-reliance, which is at odds with the guiding role of the paternalistic leader. The high levels of involvement in subordinates' personal lives would be perceived as intrusive in the Western(ized) countries, and the highly personal nature of the relationship might be interpreted as unprofessional—even potentially leading to litigation. However, in many developing countries, reciprocal consent for these paternalistic relationships between superior and subordinate is often found. Employees may sometimes even feel resentment if their managers are not involved in their personal lives and leave them to make important decisions by themselves. Again, such patterns and preferences may change over time.

In the previous section, we discussed how culture might impact leader behavior. Research has shown that being perceived as a leader is a prerequisite for being able to go beyond a formal role in influencing others (Lord & Maher, 1991). In other words, in order to be successful, leaders first need to have characteristics or show behavior that people in a given context recognize as "leadership." Thus, perceptual processes on the part of followers play a crucial role in the leadership process, as well as in researching leadership. But, what characteristics and behavior does one need to show? As is clear from the discussion of culture, attributes and behaviors that are seen as characteristic for effective leaders may also strongly vary in different cultures. In the following section we will explore this topic in more depth.

Leadership Perceptions Across Cultures _____

People in many societies frequently interact with formal leaders at work and are exposed to others through the media. As a result, people form ideas about what makes a leader effective. These ideas are influenced by culture. When thinking of a prototypical leader, a bold, autonomous, and decisive hero may typically come to mind in some cultures, whereas different images of ideal leaders may prevail in other cultures. For instance, an ideal leader may be a mature person whose experience and wisdom, rather than speed and boldness, are admired and valued. The evaluation and meaning of leader behaviors and characteristics may also vary across cultures. Relatively few studies have focused explicitly on culture-based differences in leadership prototypes or so-called implicit theories of leadership.

Both Hunt, Boal, and Sorenson (1990) and Lord and Maher (1991) proposed that societal culture has an important impact on the content and development of leadership prototypes and implicit leadership theories. Values and ideologies are expected to act as a determinant of culture-specific leadership prototypes. In strong or uniform cultures, prototypes will be widely shared, whereas in a country with a weak culture or multiple subcultures, a wider variance among individual prototypes is expected (Hunt et al., 1990). In other words, one would expect that shared beliefs exist within cultures about what an effective leader is like and that in strong cultures, individuals' beliefs are more similar than in weak ones. House et al. (1999) refer to these shared beliefs as culturally endorsed implicit leadership theories (CLTs).

Gerstner and Day (1994) were among the first to focus on cross-cultural comparisons of leadership prototypes. Respondents to their survey assigned prototypicality ratings to 59 leadership attributes. Comparing ratings from American students ($n = 35$) to small samples (n = between 10 and 22) of foreign students from seven countries, they found that the traits considered to be most, moderately, or least characteristic of business leaders varied by respondents' country or culture of origin. The study has obvious limitations that would lead to conservative biases (e.g., small sample sizes, student samples, only foreign students currently in the United States to represent other cultures in the sample, employing an English-language trait-rating instrument that was not cross-culturally validated). However, reliable differences in leadership perceptions of members of various countries were found that warranted further examination.

Hanges et al. (2000) have recently presented a model suggesting that the influences of societal culture and of leadership are enacted on individuals in very similar ways, through the development of "connectionist schemas." An analogy helps to explain this concept. Imagine a field with grass and weeds that are wildly overgrown. Crossing through the field would be quite a challenge, and after having gone through it once, there is likely to be very little evidence of a path. But if you cross through the field a second time, and then a third time, each time using the same path, eventually that path becomes more worn, and it becomes substantially easier to cross the field using that path than it would be to cross the field using any other path. Analogously, Hanges et al. argue that leadership and culture both serve to give initial guidance to people about how to perceive and how to act in novel situations, and over time, these patterns of perception and behavior become well established. It requires less cognitive energy to act and perceive according to the established pattern than it does to venture into new ways of perceiving and acting. This model suggests that this approach can be used to understand the relationship between culture, leadership, follower perceptions, and behavior. The focus is on the importance of the self-concept, arguing that this variable plays a critical role in the relationship between culture and leadership.

An interesting question in this area is whether we can distinguish leader behaviors and characteristics that are universally accepted and effective across cultures as well as behaviors and characteristics that are differentially accepted and effective across cultures. As was seen above, a preference for transformational rather than transactional leadership has been found in many countries (Bass, 1997). Thus, one might ask whether characteristics associated with this kind of leadership are seen as effective across many different cultures.

Universally Endorsed Leader Characteristics

As noted above, the GLOBE Project is the largest cross-cultural study of leadership and culture carried out to date (Dorfman, 1996). One of the early results of the GLOBE study is a report on which various leadership attributes were (a) found to be universally endorsed as contributing to outstanding leadership, (b) seen as undesirable, or (c) are culturally contingent. For instance, in all participating countries, an outstanding leader is expected to be encouraging, positive, motivational, a confidence builder, dynamic, and to have foresight. Such a leader is excellence oriented, decisive, and intelligent. Outstanding leaders need to be good at team building, communicating, and coordinating. Integrity is valued, as such leaders are trustworthy, just, and honest. Several other attributes were universally viewed as ineffective or, in other words, as impediments to outstanding leadership. These include being noncooperative, ruthless, nonexplicit, a loner, irritable, and dictatorial (Den Hartog et al., 1999; Dorfman, Hanges, & Brodbeck, 2004).

Culturally Contingent Leader Characteristics

The importance of many other leader attributes was found to vary across cultures. These culturally contingent attributes had high means in some cultures, indicating this characteristic is seen in this context as facilitating outstanding leadership, and low means in other cultures, indicating this characteristic is seen in this context as impeding outstanding leadership. For instance, country means for the attribute "risk taking" ranged from 2.14 to 5.96 on a 7-point scale, for "sensitive" from 1.96 to 6.35, for "class-conscious" from 2.53 to 6.09, and for "autonomous" from 1.63 to 5.17 (see Den Hartog et al., 1999, for the complete list).

Cultural differences clearly play a role here. For instance, differences that were found in appreciation of characteristics such as "subdued" and "enthusiastic" reflect differences in cultural rules regarding the appropriate expression of emotion. In many—predominantly Asian—cultures, displaying emotion is interpreted as a lack of self-control and thus as a sign of weakness. Not showing one's emotions is the norm. In other cultures, such as Latin and Mediterranean cultures, it is hard to be seen as an effective communicator and leader without expressing emotions in a vivid manner. Also, several of the leader attributes that were found to vary across cultures reflect preferences for high power distance versus egalitarianism in society. For example, "status-conscious," "class-conscious," "elitist," and "domineering" are all leader attributes that are appreciated in high power distance, but not in low power distance, cultures.

Other leader characteristics that varied strongly across cultures in the GLOBE results seem to reflect uncertainty avoidance, which as a culture dimension refers to the tolerance for ambiguity in society. Being risk taking, habitual, procedural, able to anticipate, formal, cautious, and orderly impede outstanding leadership in some countries and enhance it in others. Finally, being autonomous, unique, and independent are found to contribute to outstanding leadership in some but to be undesirable in other cultures. These attributes seem to reflect different cultural preferences for individualism. These differences show that although images of outstanding leaders around the world share some characteristics, there are also vast differences in what is seen as desirable for leaders (Den Hartog et al., 1999; Dorfman et al., 2004).

Variations in the Enactment of Universal Leader Characteristics

The characteristics described above show a "universal" appreciation of certain leadership attributes and a more varied appreciation of others. However, as was stressed before, even when attributes are universally valued, this does not mean such attributes will necessarily be enacted in the same way across cultures. The behavior that reflects an attribute may vary in different contexts. Dickson, Hanges, and Lord (2001) address this point in their discussion of the advancements in the understanding of the various meanings of "universal" findings. Of most relevance to the present discussion is the distinction made by Lonner (1980) between simple universals, in which the principle and enactment are the same across contexts, and variform universals, in which the principle is consistent across contexts but the enactment differs.

A specific example of a variform universal is that *visionary* is seen as a positive leader attribute in most cultures, but what one needs to do to be seen as visionary varies from one culture to another. For instance, as was mentioned before, effective styles of communicating visions may differ. Whereas macho-oratory is linked to effective communication of visions in some cultures, Fu, Wu, Yang, and Ye (2007) hold that a vision in China is normally expressed in a nonaggressive manner. Confucian values (e.g., kindness, benevolence) may play a role in making people wary of leaders giving pompous talks without engaging in specific action, and lead the people to dislike leaders who are arrogant and distant. Chhokar (2007) holds that although Indian leaders must be flexible in this regard, bold, assertive styles are generally preferred to quiet and nurturing styles (Den Hartog et al., 1999).

Another example is that some authors hold that a certain amount of risk taking is part of transformational leadership. The GLOBE results suggest that risk taking is not universally valued as contributing to outstanding leadership. Moreover, what is considered risk taking in one context may not be in another. The Mexican entrepreneur described by Martinez and Dorfman (1998), for instance, appointed someone from the Mexican lower class as a member of the administrative staff, despite the objections of stockholders. He did this on the basis of her hard work, education, and expertise. Whereas in the United States or many other countries, one would not find anything particularly strange about this, a person's social status is extremely important in Mexico. Thus, this behavior by the Mexican entrepreneur was seen as quite risky, illustrating that the same behavior can take on a very different meaning in cultures that differ in their core shared values.

Leadership Profiles and Culture Clusters

The GLOBE findings demonstrate that members of cultures share a common frame of reference regarding effective leadership. Above, we showed leader attributes that were universally appreciated and attributes that were endorsed in some, but not other, cultures. However, the GLOBE data were not only analyzed at the attribute (i.e., item) level, but the leadership attributes were statistically grouped into 21 "first-order" basic factors or dimensions that were then consolidated into 6 "second-order" global leadership dimensions (see Hanges & Dickson, 2004, 2006). These six dimensions were: (a) charismatic/value-based leadership (e.g., visionary, inspirational, integrity, decisive), (b) team-oriented leadership (e.g., collaborating, integrating, diplomatic), (c) participative leadership (e.g., nonautocratic, allowing participation in decision making, (d) autonomous leadership (e.g., individualistic, independent, unique), (e) humane leadership (e.g., modesty, tolerance, sensitivity), and (f) self-protective leadership (e.g., self-centered, status conscious, a face-saver).

Does the endorsement of these dimensions differ in different parts of the worlds? Scholars have used different forces in grouping countries into similar clusters, including geographical proximity, mass migrations and ethnic social capital, religious and linguistic communality, social variables such as attitudes and values, and economic or sociopolitical development (Gupta, Hanges, & Dorfman, 2002). GLOBE results indicate the presence of 10 meaningful clusters of cultures, based on the GLOBE culture dimensions described earlier. The meta-Western region consisted of the Nordic Europe, Germanic Europe, Anglo, Latin America, and Latin Europe clusters; the meta-Eastern region consisted of Southern Asia, Confucian Asia, Central/Eastern Europe, sub-Saharan Africa, and the Middle East (Arabic) clusters (see also the "GLOBE," 2002, special issue in the *Journal of World Business*). Leadership profiles were developed for these 10 culture clusters using the six leadership dimensions. These culturally endorsed leadership profiles highlight elements of leadership perceived to be culturally common, as well as those which are culturally unique (see Dorfman et al., 2004).

Charismatic and team-oriented leadership dimensions were strongly positively perceived in all 10 clusters. Looking at the absolute scores, this was most strongly so in the Anglo, Southern Asian, and Latin American clusters and somewhat less so in the Middle Eastern cluster. Humane leadership contributed somewhat to effective leadership, but it was not nearly as strongly endorsed as charismatic or team-oriented leadership. Southern Asia, Anglo, and sub-Saharan Africa score somewhat higher and Latin and Nordic Europe somewhat lower on the humane leadership dimension. Autonomous leadership was often reported among the 10 clusters to be about neutral regarding its contribution to effective leadership, but for some of the 62 cultures (and 10 clusters) it was reported to be a factor that contributed slightly (e.g., Eastern and Germanic Europe), and for some others a factor that inhibited slightly (e.g., Latin Europe, Middle East). Much greater variation among cultures and culture clusters was found for the two remaining CLT dimensions. The self-protective CLT dimension was perceived to be an inhibitor of effective leadership everywhere. However, it was seen as more inhibiting in the Nordic, Germanic, and Anglo clusters and less so in the Middle Eastern, Confucian, and Southern Asian clusters. Participative leadership was reported to contribute to effective leadership for all culture clusters; however, considerable variation exists. The GLOBE results suggest that the Germanic, Anglo, and Nordic clusters were particularly attuned to participative leadership, whereas the Middle Eastern, East European, Confucian, and Southern Asian clusters were not (see, e.g., Dorfman et al., 2004).

Whereas the results show that values characterizing a society clearly have a major impact on the shared perceptions of effective leader behaviors, the

GLOBE Project is one of the first studies to allow large-scale assessment of the relative impact of *societal* culture as well as *organizational* culture on these perceptions. For example, the performance orientation of culture was related to charismatic/value-based leadership and participative leadership at both the organizational and societal levels of culture. In other words, societies as well as organizations valuing a strong performance orientation seem to look to charismatic leaders with the ability to paint the picture of an ambitious and exciting future. They also value a leader who involves others in building this future in a participative manner (Javidan, 2004). In many cases the impact of organizational culture on the leadership belief system, or CLT, was at least as strong as that of societal culture (Dorfman et al., 2004). Thus, we include here a brief discussion of the relationship of organizational culture and leadership.

Organizational Culture

As noted before, "culture" refers to a set of shared values that are held by members of a collectivity, and this is not limited to the societal level. Where leadership in organizations is concerned, organizational culture is also relevant. Denison (1996) described organizational culture as follows: "*Culture* refers to the deep structure of organizations, which is rooted in the values, beliefs, and assumptions held by organization members. Meaning is established through socialization to a variety of identity groups that converge in the workplace. Interaction produces a symbolic world that gives culture both a great stability and a certain precarious and fragile nature rooted in the dependence of the system on individual cognition and action" (p. 624).

Clearly, values that characterize a society are likely to be reflected in the values held by members of organizations. Dickson, BeShears, and Gupta (2004) described mechanisms by which this influence is likely to occur. These include: The simple fact that people who make up organizations come from some societal culture and are likely to hold the values that characterize that society; the pressures placed on organizations to conform to the values of the society, either through subtle rewards or perceived advantages for conformity and punishments for nonconformity (i.e., coercive, normative, and mimetic isomorphic pressures); resource dependency pressures, in which conformity is required in order to acquire and retain necessary physical and human resources; and social network pressures, through which the patterns of interactions and dependence relationships compel organizations toward adopting and/or reflecting societal values.

Several authors have argued that congruence between societal culture and organizational culture is desirable and important for strong organizational performance (e.g., Newman & Nollen, 1996). However, it is important to note that there is substantial variation in the organizational cultures of even successful organizations within any given society.

Organizational Culture and Leadership

Leaders of organizations embed and transmit culture in the thinking, feeling, and behavior of the group. Schein (1992) holds that a decisive function of leadership is the creation, management, and sometimes the destruction of organizational culture. However, in line with the debate on the measurement of culture, "most anthropologists would find the idea that leaders create culture preposterous: leaders do not create culture; it emerges from the collective social interaction of groups and communities" (Meek, 1988, p. 459). We disagree with this position, at least regarding organizational culture. At the societal level, most people indeed do not choose their societal culture; most remain part of the culture into which they were born. However, people do actively seek out organizations to which they belong. Members are not randomly assigned to organizations—they choose the organizations to which they apply and organizations choose the applicants whom they wish to hire. These decisions are, at least to some degree, based on the perception of "fit," or the perceived congruence between the organization's values and the values of the employee (e.g., Kristof, 1996). Thus, the leader initially creates something, which is differentially attractive to outsiders, who then choose whether to attempt to join. Eventually, interactions of the individuals in the organization refine and modify the initial culture established by the founder, but the founder nonetheless establishes the initial culture (Giberson, Resick, & Dickson, 2002; B. Schneider, Goldstein, & Smith, 1995).

We thus focus more on the view taken by Schein (1992), who stated that "leadership is originally the source of the beliefs and values that get a group moving to deal with its internal and external problems. If what a leader proposes works and continues to work, what once was only the leader's assumption gradually comes to be a shared assumption" (pp. 26–27). This view highlights the impact of the founder of the organization on its culture. Dickson, Smith, Grojean, and Ehrhart (2001) also argued that the ethical climate in a firm is linked to the personal values and motives of founders and early leaders. The founder plays a crucial role in culture formation by choosing the basic mission, the group members, the environmental context in which to operate, and the initial responses of the group to succeed and integrate within this environment.

Culture can spring from three sources: the beliefs, values, and assumptions of founders of organizations; the learning experiences of group members as their organization evolves; and new beliefs, values, and assumptions brought by new members and leaders. Schein (1992) suggests leaders have several primary culture embedding mechanisms, including what leaders regularly pay attention to, measure, and control; how they react to crises and critical incidents; their role modeling and coaching; and the observed criteria by which they both allocate resources, rewards, and status and recruit, select, promote, or excommunicate organizational members. Secondary culture articulation and reinforcement mechanisms work only when they are in line with the primary mechanisms. These include: organizational design, structure, systems and procedures; stories, legends, and myths about people and events; rites and rituals; design of physical space (e.g., buildings); and formal statements of organizational values, philosophy, or creed.

Charismatic leaders have a special impact on organizational culture: "The simplest explanation of how leaders get their message across is through charisma, in that one of the main elements of that mysterious quality undoubtedly is a leader's ability to communicate major assumptions and values in a vivid and clear manner" (Schein, 1992, p. 229). According to Bass (1985), charismatic leaders create new cultures for their subordinates by creating new meaning for them. Leadership as management of meaning is an important notion where the relationship between leadership and culture is concerned (e.g., Smith & Peterson, 1988). The process of meaning making is enhanced by the use of *framing* or *frame alignment* (cf. Goffman, 1974). Frame alignment refers to the linkage of individual and leader interpretative orientations in such a way that some set of followers' interests, values, and beliefs and the leader's activities, goals, and ideology become congruent and complementary (e.g., House & Podsakoff, 1994).

Frames themselves are symbolic structures people use to make sense of personal and social experiences and to guide action (Conger, 1989). Frames or "schemata of interpretation" enable individuals to locate, perceive, and label occurrences within their life and the world at large. By rendering events or occurrences meaningful, frames function to organize experience and guide individual or collective action (Goffman, 1974; House & Podsakoff, 1994). By formulating a vision, a charismatic leader engages in framing, thereby placing the vision in a certain context and interpreting reality for listeners and giving meaning to events. Pfeffer (1981) viewed organizations as systems of completely or partly shared meanings. Meanings can be attached to the organization's purposes and to its goals, ideologies, and values, as well as to its beliefs about the ways in which the organization is to accomplish these purposes. It is more difficult for people to change goals and values than to change beliefs about the best way to accomplish goals. The role of leaders in organizations includes influencing the meanings and values placed on particular ways of approaching goals, which is highly symbolic in this view.

Trice and Beyer (1991, 1993) presented a model of cultural leadership. They suggested that literature on cultural leadership emphasizes cultural innovation, either founding an organization and creating a new culture or drastically changing the existing one. In the literature, culture initiation and change are often associated with charismatic leadership. However, they also call into attention cultural maintenance leadership, which is important for effectiveness of organizations in more stable environments. Cultural innovation and maintenance leaders have some features in common. Both create an impression of competence, articulate ideologies, communicate strong convictions, show confidence in and high expectations of followers, serve as role models, and strengthen follower commitment. However, they differ, too. Cultural maintenance leaders aim to reinforce existing values and traditions that are effective for reaching organizational goals. Change is incremental. Cultural innovation leaders aim to create a new culture or drastically change the existing one. These leaders articulate a radical ideology with new values and strategies, often dealing with crises. Cultural innovation leaders need to be more dramatic and expressive than maintenance leaders, and they must show more extraordinary qualities in dealing with crises. The attributions of charisma that such qualities may enhance form an extra power base in implementing new strategies and dealing with opponents of change.

Bass and Bass (2008) suggest leaders can function as founders of cultures or countercultures, as culture builders, and as agents of change in the dominant culture. Trice and Beyer (1991, 1993) add the leader's role in maintaining culture. However, precisely *how* the content or nature of cultures is related to leadership is not immediately clear from these roles. Kerr and Slocum (1987), for instance, described two types of corporate reward systems that give rise to different cultures (so-called *clan* and *market* cultures) and, thus, characteristically lead to different leadership experiences. This example demonstrates that besides their role in creating, changing, or maintaining culture, the content of culture also shapes how followers experience leaders and which types of leaders are effective. Schein (1992) ironically suggested that often culture may manage management more than management manages culture.

Dickson, Resick, and Hanges (2006) focus on the strength of organizational culture or climate and show, based on GLOBE data, that unambiguous climates tend to be stronger. Strong cultures can inhibit or promote the effects of leaders' efforts, depending on whether the influence attempts are in line with the dominant values in that culture. Rubin and Berlew (1984), for example, report that a strong organizational culture with values and internal guidelines for more autonomy at lower levels in the organization can prevent top management from increasing personal power at the expense of middle management.

Whereas some theorists focused on identifying levels of organizational cultures, others focused on developing categorical taxonomies of organizational cultures. An example of the latter comes from a group of researchers from 14 countries, who developed an organizational culture questionnaire (Van Muijen et al., 1999). Four culture orientations are distinguished that are based on two dimensions: internal versus external focus, and flexibility versus control. *Support* (internal/flexible) is characterized by mutual trust, cooperation, team spirit, commitment, and individual growth. A person- or relationship-oriented leadership style fits here. *Rules* (internal/control) is characterized by respect for authority, procedures, division of work, and hierarchical communication. Leadership is primarily procedure oriented. *Goals* (external/control) emphasizes rationality, performance indicators, accomplishment, accountability, and contingent reward. A task-oriented style of leadership fits. *Innovation* (external/flexible) emphasizes creativity, openness to change, searching for new information, anticipation, and experimentation. Change-oriented leadership fits (Van Muijen et al., 1999).

Den Hartog, Van Muijen, and Koopman (1996) linked this model to transformational and transactional leadership in five organizations. They built on Bass's (1985) speculations that transactional leadership would fit better in more well-ordered and stable environments—such as in bureaucratic organizations—than in adhocracies and organic organizations. In contrast, Bass speculated that transformational leadership would be preferred in more innovative, flexible, and supportive environments. They found (a) that the relationship between transformational leadership and the innovative and supportive orientations was higher than that between transactional leadership and those orientations and (b) that the relationship between transactional leadership and the goal and rules orientations was higher than that for transformational leadership.

Conclusions

In this chapter on leadership and culture, we aimed to show that we should not take for granted that models and theories developed in one place will work similarly in another. We described culture at the societal and organizational levels and showed how culture can affect implicit leadership theories and behavior. We showed that even when preferred and effective leader characteristics and behaviors are similar, their enactment might differ across cultures. As Smith and Bond (1999) noted, if we wish to make statements about "universal" aspects of social behavior, they need to be phrased in highly abstract ways. Conversely, if we wish to highlight the meaning of these generalizations in cultural specific ways, then we need to refer to more precisely specified events or behaviors. Similarly, we showed that leadership could be conceived in culturally universal or specific terms. We also highlighted the developing world, because most theories presented in the literature to date have more bearing on the developed, or Western, world.

Clearly, more research on leadership in different cultures is needed. Several types of studies would be useful. Large-scale comparative studies involving comparable samples from many different countries are of interest. Preferably, such studies can be repeated over time to gain more insight in the changing nature of leadership. However, at the other extreme, more indigenous, local, and rich studies, yielding more culture-specific models, are also of interest.

We did not describe in detail the many potential problems and methodological pitfalls that need to be addressed in any cross-cultural research endeavor, because a full review of this topic is beyond the scope of this chapter. Measured invariance is one such issue. Another potential obstacle is the problem of translation in measurement. How do we ensure that respondents interpret questions similarly? How do we know constructs have the same meaning? How are results influenced in cases where respondents complete questionnaires in a language that is not their native language? Sampling provides another interesting challenge in cross-cultural research. When interested in societal culture, using national borders as cultural boundaries may not be appropriate in countries that have large subcultures. In large, multicultural countries such as India, the United States, and China, it is not even clear which sample would be most representative. Nevertheless, the samples from all countries need to be relatively homogeneous within countries to be able to interpret differences that are found.

Also, many studies run the risk of committing the "ecological fallacy." This occurs if we assume isomorphic relationships between variables across differing levels of analysis, such as assuming characteristics and/or relationships existing at the cultural level will automatically apply to other levels of analysis, such as the individual. What applies for individuals may or may not apply for groups, and vice versa (e.g., Dorfman et al., 2004). The ecological fallacy problem can be minimized by paying careful attention to the level of analysis issue in theory building and in collecting and analyzing data. For instance, in questionnaire research aimed at the culture level, culture items can be phrased to explicitly refer to groups, organizations, or societies, rather than to individuals. Whether individual responses can then be aggregated to group levels can then be tested statistically.

These examples of methodological challenges show that studying leadership in different cultures is not easy. However, well-designed studies will help develop a better understanding of the differences and similarities in what is acceptable and effective organizational leadership around the world. Clearly, enhanced understanding in this area is crucial in the increasingly international world of work.

Discussion Questions

1. What do you see as the major findings in cross-cultural studies of leadership and what do you consider the major research questions that remain?

2. What types of dilemmas and problems does this type of research face?

3. How can this type of research help inform managers who need to work with people from diverse cultural backgrounds?

4. What does this research suggest about the common practice of sending expatriate managers or executives to work in countries other than their own? What barriers are likely to emerge related to cultural differences? What sort of person might be effective in that role?

5. How can organizations be proactive to try to prevent problems arising from people of different cultural backgrounds having different expectations of leaders and different understandings of what leadership is?

How can cultural values, which are generally implicit, be made explicit so that they can be discussed and addressed to increase effectiveness and reduce misunderstandings?

6. Are there particular dimensions of culture where differences between managers on that dimension would be more likely to lead to organizational problems, misunderstandings, or ineffectiveness? Why do you think differences on those dimensions would be particularly problematic?

7. If you were to be placed in the role of leader of a multicultural team that has never worked together, how would you begin your interactions together? Are there things you would do to specifically address your cultural background and its impact on you as the leader? Are there things you would do to address the multicultural background of the team members? How would you move forward to ensure the best performance from the talented but different people who are now working for you?

Supplemental Readings

Javidan, M., Dorfman, P., de Luque, M. S., & House, R. J. (2006). In the eye of the beholder: Cross-cultural lessons in leadership from Project GLOBE. *Academy of Management Perspectives, 20*(1), 67–90.

Javidan, M., & House, R. J. (2001). Cultural acumen for the global manager: Lessons from Project GLOBE. *Organizational Dynamics, 29,* 289–305.

Javidan, M., Teagarden, M., & Bowen, D. (2010). Making it overseas. *Harvard Business Review, 88*(4), 109–113.

Case Studies

1. IMD case: Learning to Lead in China: Antonio Scarsi Takes Command

   Reference: IMD-3–1696

   Authors: Fischer, William A.; Chung, Rebecca

   Copyright: © IMD 2006

2. IMD case: Petter Eiken at Skanska: Leading Change

   Reference: IMD-3–1823

   Authors: Maznevski, Martha; Leger, Katarina

   Copyright: © IMD 2008

3. INSEAD Mini-Case Series. (Although these are a bit older, they are very short and provide opportunities for undergraduates or others less familiar with case methodology to begin to use the approach and to apply them to the cross-cultural domain. The titles mentioned are two of the eight cases, though most of them are appropriate for this topic.)

3(a). Title: Blowing in the Wind

  Reference: 495–028–1

  Product type: Case

  Author(s):   de Bettignies, H.; Butler, C.

  Publisher: INSEAD

  Settings: Indonesia; Pulp and paper; US$6 billion; 1994–1995

  Topics: Team building; Ethical dilemmas; Cross-cultural conflict; Leadership styles; The expatriate process; Communications

  Date: 1995

  Length: 3 pages

  Data source: Field research

  Status: Active

3(b). Title: Leading Across Cultures at Michelin (A; prize winner)

  Reference: 409–008–1

  Product type: Case

  Authors: Meyer, E.; Gupta, S.

  Publisher: INSEAD

  Settings: United States; Tires

  Topics: Cross-cultural; Intercultural/inter-cultural; Multicultural/multi-cultural; Performance feedback; National culture; Leadership; Global leadership; International human resources

  Date: 2009

  Version date: 03.2010

  Length: 7 pages

  Data source: Field research

  Status: Active

References

Abdalla, I. A., & Al-Homoud, M. A. (2001). Exploring the implicit leadership theory in the Arabian Gulf States. *Applied Psychology: An International Review, 50,* 506–531.

Adler, N. J. (2002). *International dimensions of organizational behavior* (4th ed.). Cincinnati, OH: South-Western College Publishing.

Adsit, D. J., London, M., Crom, S., & Jones, D. (2001). Cross-cultural differences in upward ratings in a multinational company. *The International Journal of Human Resource Management, 8,* 385–401.

Antonakis J., Avolio B. J., & Sivasubramaniam, N. (2003). Context and leadership: An examination of the nine-factor full-range leadership theory using the Multifactor Leadership Questionnaire. *The Leadership Quarterly, 14,* 261–295.

Ashkanasy, N. M. (2007). The Australian enigma. In J. S. Chhokar, F. C. Brodbeck, & R. J. House (Eds.), *Culture and leadership across the world: The GLOBE book of in-depth studies of 25 societies* (pp. 299–333) New York: Lawrence Erlbaum.

Aycan, Z. (2004). Managing inequalities: Leadership and teamwork in the developing country context. In: H. W. Lane, M. L. Maznevski, M. E. Mendenhall, & J. McNett (Eds.). *The Blackwell handbook of global management: A guide to managing complexity* (pp. 406–423). Malden, MA: Blackwell.

Aycan, Z., Kanungo, R., Mendonca, M., Yu, K., Deller, J., Stahl, G., et al. (2000). Impact of culture on human resource management practices: A 10-country comparison. *Applied Psychology: An International Review, 49,* 192–221.

Bass, B. M. (1985). *Leadership and performance beyond expectations.* New York: Free Press.

Bass, B. M. (1997). Does the transactional–transformational leadership paradigm transcend organizational and national boundaries? *American Psychologist, 52,* 130–139.

Bass, B. M., & Bass, R. (2008). *The Bass handbook of leadership: Theory, research, and managerial applications* (4th ed.). New York: Free Press.

Bonta, B. D. (1997). Cooperation and competition in peaceful societies. *Psychological Bulletin, 121,* 299–320.

Boyacigiller, N. A., & Adler, N. J. (1991). The parochial dinosaur: Organizational science in a global context. *Academy of Management Review, 16,* 262–290.

Brannen, M. Y., Gomez, C., Peterson, M. F., Romani, L., Sagiv, L., & Wu, P. C. (2004). People in global organizations: Culture, personality, and social dynamics. In H. W. Lane, M. L. Maznevski, M. E. Mendenhall, & J. McNett (Eds.). *The Blackwell handbook of global management: A guide to managing complexity* (pp. 26–54). Malden, MA: Blackwell.

Brown, P., & Levinson, S. (1987). *Politeness: Some universals in language usage.* Cambridge, UK: Cambridge University Press.

Bu, N., Craig, T. J., & Peng, T. K. (2001). Acceptance of supervisory direction in typical workplace situations: A comparison of US, Taiwanese and PRC employees. *International Journal of Cross-Cultural Management, 1,* 131–152.

Chhokar, J. S. (2007) India: Diversity and complexity in action. In J. S. Chhokar, F. C. Brodbeck, & R. J. House (Eds.), *Culture and leadership across the world: The GLOBE book of in-depth studies of 25 societies* (pp. 971–1019) New York: Lawrence Erlbaum.

Chhokar, J. S., Brodbeck F. C., & House, R. J. (Eds.). (2007). *Culture and leadership across the world: The GLOBE book of in-depth studies of 25 societies.* New York: Lawrence Erlbaum.

Conger, J. A. (1989). *The charismatic leader: Behind the mystique of exceptional leadership.* San Francisco: Jossey-Bass.

Czinkota, M. R., & Ronkainen, I. A. (2005). A forecast of globalization, international business and trade: Report from a Delphi study. *Journal of World Business, 40,* 111–123.

Den Hartog, D. N. (2004). Assertiveness. In R. J. House, P. J. Hanges, M. Javidan, P. W. Dorfman, V. Gupta, & GLOBE Associates (Eds.), *Culture, leadership, and organizations: The GLOBE study of 62 societies* (pp. 395–436). Thousand Oaks, CA: Sage.

Den Hartog, D. N., House, R. J., Hanges, P., Dorfman, P., Ruiz-Quintanilla, A., & 159 co-authors (1999). Culture specific and cross-culturally endorsed implicit leadership theories: Are attributes of charismatic/transformational leadership universally endorsed? *The Leadership Quarterly, 10,* 219–256.

Den Hartog, D. N., & Koopman, P. L. (2001). Leadership in organizations. In N. Anderson, D. S. Ones, H. Kepir Sinangil, & C. Viswesvaran (Eds.). *Handbook of industrial, work and organizational psychology: Volume 2. Organizational psychology* (pp. 166–187). London: Sage.

Den Hartog, D. N., Koopman, P. L., Thierry, H., Wilderom, C. P. M., Maczynski, J., & Jarmuz, S. (1997). Dutch and Polish perceptions of leadership and national culture: The GLOBE project. *European Journal of Work and Organizational Psychology, 6,* 389–415.

Den Hartog, D. N., Van Muijen, J. J., & Koopman, P. L. (1996). Linking transformational leadership and organizational culture. *Journal of Leadership Studies, 3,* 68–83.

Den Hartog, D. N., Van Muijen, J. J., & Koopman, P. L. (1997). Transactional versus transformational leadership: An analysis of the MLQ. *Journal of Occupational and Organizational Psychology, 70*(1), 19–34.

Denison, D. R. (1996). What *is* the difference between organizational culture and organizational climate? A native's point of view on a decade of paradigm wars. *Academy of Management Review, 21,* 619–654.

Dickson, M. W., BeShears, R. S., & Gupta, V. (2004). The impact of societal culture and industry on organizational culture: Theoretical explanations. In R. J. House, P. J. Hanges, M. Javidan, P. W. Dorfman, V. Gupta, & GLOBE Associates (Eds.), *Culture, leadership, and organizations: The GLOBE study of 62 societies* (pp. 74–90). Thousand Oaks, CA: Sage.

Dickson, M. W., Den Hartog, D. N., & Castaño, N. (2009). Understanding leadership across cultures. In R. S. Bhagat & R. M. Steers (Eds.), *Cambridge handbook of culture, organizations, and work* (pp. 219–244). Cambridge, UK: Cambridge University Press.

Dickson, M. W., Den Hartog, D. N., & Mitchelson, J. K. (2003). Research on leadership in a cross-cultural context: Making progress, and raising new questions. *The Leadership Quarterly, 14,* 729–768.

Dickson, M. W., Hanges, P. J., & Lord, R. M. (2001). Trends, developments, and gaps in cross-cultural research on leadership. In W. Mobley & M. McCall (Eds.), *Advances in global leadership,* (Vol. 2, pp. 75–100). Stamford, CT: JAI.

Dickson, M. W., Resick, C. J., & Hanges, P. J. (2006). When organizational climate is unambiguous, it is also strong. *Journal of Applied Psychology, 91,* 351–364.

Dickson, M. W., Smith, D. B., Grojean, M. W., & Ehrhart, M. (2001). An organizational climate regarding ethics: The outcome of leader values and the practices that reflect them. *The Leadership Quarterly, 12,* 197–217.

Doney, P. M., Cannon, J. P., & Mullen, M. R. (1998). Understanding the influence of national culture on the development of trust. *Academy of Management Review, 23,* 601–620.

Dorfman, P. W., (1996). International and cross-cultural leadership. In J. Punnitt and O. Shanker (Eds.), *Handbook for international management research* (pp. 267–349). Cambridge, MA: Blackwell.

Dorfman, P. W., Hanges, P. J., & Brodbeck, F. C. (2004). Leadership and cultural variation: The identification of culturally endorsed leadership profiles. In R. J. House, P. J. Hanges, M. Javidan, P. W. Dorfman, V. Gupta, & GLOBE Associates (Eds.), *Culture, leadership, and organizations: The GLOBE study of 62 societies* (pp. 669–720). Thousand Oaks, CA: Sage.

Dorfman, P. W., Howell, J. P., Hibino, S., Lee, J. K., Tate, U., & Bautista, A. (1997). Leadership in Western and Asian countries: Commonalities and differences in effective leadership processes across cultures. *The Leadership Quarterly, 8,* 233–274.

Earley, P. C. (1997). *Face, harmony, and social structure: An analysis of organizational behavior across cultures.* New York: Oxford University Press.

Emrich, C. G., Denmark, F. L., & Den Hartog, D. N. (2004). Cross-cultural differences in gender egalitarianism: Implications for societies, organizations, and leaders. In R. J. House, P. J. Hanges, M. Javidan, P. W. Dorfman, V. Gupta, & GLOBE Associates (Eds.), *Culture, leadership, and organizations: The GLOBE study of 62 societies* (pp. 343–394). Thousand Oaks, CA: Sage.

Feather, N. T. (1994). Attitudes towards high achievers and reactions to their fall: Theory and research concerning tall poppies. In M. P. Zanna (Ed.), *Advances in social psychology* (Vol. 26, pp. 1–73). New York: Academic Press.

Fu, P. P. Wu, R., Yang, Y., & Ye, J. (2007). Chinese culture and leadership in China. In J. S. Chhokar, F. C. Brodbeck, & R. J. House (Eds.), *Culture and leadership across the world: The GLOBE book of in-depth studies of 25 societies* (pp. 877–907). New York: Lawrence Erlbaum.

Fu, P. P., & Yukl, G. (2000). Perceived effectiveness of influence tactics in the United States and China. *The Leadership Quarterly, 11,* 251–266.

Gelfand, M. J., Erez, M., & Aycan, Z. (2007). Cross-cultural organizational behavior. *Annual Review of Psychology, 58,* 479–514.

Gerstner, C. R., & Day, D. V. (1994). Cross-cultural comparison of leadership prototypes. *The Leadership Quarterly, 5,* 121–134.

Geyer, A. L. J., & Steyrer, J. M. (1998). Transformational leadership and objective performance in banks. *Applied Psychology: An International Review, 47,* 397–420.

Giberson, T. R., Resick, C. J., & Dickson, M. W. (2002, August). Examining the relationship between organizational homogeneity and organizational outcomes. In C. J. Resick & M. W. Dickson (Chairs), *Person-organization fit: Balancing its constructive and destructive forces.* Paper presented at the annual meeting of the Academy of Management, Denver, CO.

GLOBE [Special issue]. *Journal of World Business, 37*(1).

Goffman, E. (1974). *Frame analysis.* Cambridge, MA: Harvard University Press.

Gupta, V., de Luque, M. S., & House, R. J. (2004). Multisource construct validity of GLOBE Scales. In R. J. House, P. J. Hanges, M. Javidan, P. W. Dorfman, V. Gupta, & GLOBE Associates (Eds.), *Culture, leadership, and organizations: The GLOBE study of 62 societies* (pp. 152–177). Thousand Oaks, CA: Sage.

Gupta, V., Hanges, P. J., & Dorfman, P. (2002). Cultural clusters: Methodology and findings. *Journal of World Business, 37,* 11–15.

Hall, E. T. (1959). *The silent language.* New York: Anchor Press.

Hanges, P. J., & Dickson, M. W. (2004). The development and validation of the GLOBE Culture and Leadership Scales. In R. J. House, P. J. Hanges, M. Javidan, P. W. Dorfman, V. Gupta, & GLOBE Associates (Eds.), *Culture, leadership, and organizations: The GLOBE study of 62 societies* (pp. 122–151). Thousand Oaks, CA: Sage.

Hanges, P. J., & Dickson, M. W. (2006). Agitation over aggregation: Clarifying the development of and the nature of the GLOBE scales. *The Leadership Quarterly, 17,* 522–536.

Hanges, P. J., Lord, R. G., & Dickson, M. W. (2000). An information processing perspective on leadership and culture: A case for connectionist architecture. *Applied Psychology: An International Review, 49,* 133–161.

Heller, F. A., Drenth, P. J. D., Koopman P. L., & Rus, V. (1988). *Decisions in organisations: A three country comparative study.* London: Sage.

Heller, F. A., & Misumi, J. (1987). Decision making. In B. M. Bass, P. J. D. Drenth, & P. Weissenberg (Eds.), *Advances in organizational psychology* (Vol. 1, pp. 207–219). Newbury Park, CA: Sage.

Hofstede, G. (1980). *Culture's consequences: International differences in work-related values.* Beverly Hills, CA: Sage.

Hofstede, G. (1993). Cultural constraints in management theories. *Academy of Management Executive, 7,* 81–94.

Hofstede, G. (2001). *Culture's consequences: Comparing values, behaviors, institutions, and organizations across nations* (2nd ed.). Thousand Oaks, CA: Sage.

Hofstede, G. (2006). What did GLOBE really measure? Researchers' minds versus respondents' minds. *Journal of International Business Studies, 37,* 882–896.

Holtgraves, T. (1997). Styles of language use: Individual and cultural variability in conversational indirectness. *Journal of Personality and Social Psychology, 73,* 624–637.

House, R. J. (1995). Leadership in the twenty-first century: A speculative enquiry. In A. Howard (Ed.), *The changing nature of work* (pp. 411–450). San Francisco: Jossey Bass.

House, R. J., Hanges, P. J., Javidan, M., Dorfman, P.W., Gupta, V., & GLOBE Associates (Eds.). (2004). *Culture, leadership, and organizations: The GLOBE study of 62 societies.* Thousand Oaks, CA: Sage.

House, R. J., Hanges, P. J., Ruiz-Quintanilla, S. A., Dorfman, P. W., Javidan, M., Dickson, M., Gupta, V., & 170 coauthors (1999). Cultural influences on leadership and organizations: Project GLOBE. In W. Mobley, M. J. Gessner, & V. Arnold (Eds.), *Advances in global leadership* (Vol. 1, pp. 171–233). Stamford, CT: JAI Press.

House, R. J., & Podsakoff, P. M. (1994). Leadership effectiveness: Past perspectives and future directions for research. In J. Greenberg (Ed.), *Organizational behavior: The state of the science* (pp. 45–82). Hillsdale, NJ: Lawrence Erlbaum.

House, R. J., Wright, N. S., & Aditya, R. N. (1997). Cross-cultural research on organizational leadership: A critical analysis and a proposed theory. In P. C. Earley & M. Erez (Eds.), *New perspectives on international industrial/organizational psychology* (pp. 535–625). San Francisco: New Lexington Press.

Hunt, J. G., Boal, K. B., & Sorenson, R. L. (1990). Top management leadership: Inside the black box. *The Leadership Quarterly, 1,* 41–65.

Javidan M. (2004). Performance orientation. In R. J. House, P. J. Hanges, M. Javidan, P. W. Dorfman, V. Gupta, & GLOBE Associates (Eds.), *Culture, leadership, and organizations: The GLOBE study of 62 societies* (pp. 239–281). Thousand Oaks, CA: Sage.

Javidan, M., Dorfman, P. W., de Luque, M. S., & House, R. J. (2006). In the eye of the beholder: Cross cultural lessons in leadership from Project GLOBE. *Academy of Management Perspectives, 20,* 67–90.

Javidan, M., House, R. J., Dorfman, P. W., Hanges, P. J., & de Luque, M. S. (2006). Conceptualizing and measuring cultures and their consequences: A comparative review of GLOBE's and Hofstede's approaches. *Journal of International Business Studies, 37,* 897–914.

Kahtri, N., Ng, H. A., & Lee, T. H (2001). The distinction between charisma and vision: An empirical study. *Asia Pacific Journal of Management, 18,* 373–393.

Kanungo, R. N., & Mendonca, M. (1996). Cultural contingencies and leadership in developing countries. *Research in the Sociology of Organizations, 14*, 263–295.

Keating, M., Martin, G. S., Resick, C. J., & Dickson, M. W. (2007). A comparative study of the endorsement of ethical leadership in Ireland and the United States. *Irish Journal of Management, 28*, 5–30.

Kerr, S., & Slocum, J. W. (1987). Managing corporate culture through reward systems. *Academy of Management Executive, 1*, 99–108.

Kirkman, B. L., Chen, G., Fahr, J. L., Chen, Z. X., & Lowe, K. B. (2009). Individual power distance orientation and follower reactions to transformational leaders: A cross-level, cross-cultural examination. *Academy of Management Journal, 52*, 744–764.

Kirkman, B. L., & Den Hartog, D. N. (2004). Performance management in global teams. In H. W. Lane, M. L. Maznevski, M. E. Mendenhall, & J. McNett (Eds.). *The Blackwell handbook of global management: A guide to managing complexity* (pp. 250–272). Malden, MA: Blackwell.

Kirkman, B. L., Lowe, K. B., & Gibson, C. B. (2006). A quarter century of *Culture's Consequences*: A review of empirical research incorporating Hofstede's cultural values framework. *Journal of International Business Studies, 37*, 285–320.

Kluckhohn, F., & Strodtbeck, F. L. (1961). *Variations in value orientations*. Westport, CT: Greenwood Press.

Koh, W. L., Steers, R. M., & Terborg. J. R. (1995). The effects of transformational leadership on teacher attitudes and student performance in Singapore. *Journal of Organizational Behavior, 16*, 319–333.

Kristof, A. L. (1996). Person-organization fit: An integrative review of its conceptualizations, measurement, and implications. *Personnel Psychology, 49*, 1–49.

Leung, K. (2007). Asian social psychology: Achievements, threats, and opportunities. *Asian Journal of Social Psychology, 10*, 8–15.

Leung, K., Bhagat, R. S., Buchan, N. R., Erez, M., & Gibson, C. B. (2005). Culture and international business: Recent advances and their implications for future research. *Journal of International Business Studies, 36*, 357–378.

Lievens, F., Van Geit, P., & Coetsier, P. (1997). Identification of transformational leadership qualities: An examination of potential biases. *European Journal of Work and Organizational Psychology, 6*, 415–430.

Lonner, W. J. (1980). The search for psychological universals. In H. C. Triandis & W. W. Lambert (Eds.), *Handbook of cross-cultural psychology: Perspectives* (Vol. 1, pp. 143–204.). Boston, MA: Allyn & Bacon.

Lord, R. G., & Maher, K. J. (1991*). Leadership and information processing*. London: Routledge.

Martinez, S. M., & Dorfman, P. W. (1998). The Mexican entrepreneur: An ethnographic study of the Mexican empressario. *International Studies of Management & Organization, 28*, 97–123.

McSweeney, B. (2002). Hofstede's model of national cultural differences and their consequences: A triumph of faith—A failure of analysis. *Human Relations, 55*, 89–118.

Meek, V. L. (1988). Organizational culture: Origins and weaknesses. *Organization Studies, 9*, 453–473.

Meindl, J. R. (1990). On leadership: An alternative to the conventional wisdom. In B. M. Staw & L. L. Cummings (Eds.), *Research in organizational behavior* (Vol. 12, pp. 159–203). Greenwich, CT: JAI.

Meindl, J. R., Ehrlich, S. B., & Dukerich, J. M. (1985). The romance of leadership. *Administrative Science Quarterly, 30,* 78–102.

Nardon, L., & Steers, R. M. (2009). The culture theory jungle: Divergence and convergence in models of national culture. In R. S. Bhagat & R. M. Steers (Eds.), *Cambridge handbook of culture, organizations, and work* (pp. 3–22). Cambridge, UK: Cambridge University Press.

Newman, K. L., & Nollen, S. D. (1996). Culture and congruence: The fit between management practices and national culture. *Journal of International Business Studies, 27,* 753–779.

Osland, J. S., Snyder, M. M., & Hunter, L. (1998). A comparative study of managerial styles among female executives in Nicaragua and Costa Rica. *International Studies of Management and Organization, 2,* 54–73.

Parsons, T., & Shils, E. A., (1951). *Toward a general theory of action.* Cambridge, MA: Harvard University Press.

Pasa, S. F. (2000). Leadership influence in a high power distance and collectivist culture. *Leadership & Organization Development Journal, 21,* 414–426.

Pellegrini, E. K., & Scandura, T. A. (2006). Leader–member exchange (LMX), paternalism, and delegation in the Turkish business culture: An empirical investigation. *Journal of International Business Studies, 37,* 264–279.

Pellegrini, E. K., & Scandura, T. A. (2008). Paternalistic leadership: A review and agenda for future research. *Journal of Management, 34,* 566–593.

Pew Research Center. (2007, June 27). *Rising environmental concern in 47-nation survey: Global unease with major world powers.* Retrieved from http://pewglobal .org/2007/06/27/global-unease-with-major-world-powers/

Pfeffer, J. (1981). Management as symbolic action: The creation and maintenance of organizational paradigms. *Research in Organizational Behavior, 3,* 1–52.

Pickenpaugh, T. E. (1997). Symbols of rank, leadership and power in traditional cultures. *International Journal of Osteoarcheaology, 7,* 525–541.

Punnett, B. J. (2004). The developing world: Toward a managerial understanding. In H. W. Lane, M. L. Maznevski, M. E. Mendenhall, & J. McNett (Eds.). *The Blackwell handbook of global management: A guide to managing complexity* (pp. 387–405). Malden, MA: Blackwell.

Quang, T., Swierczek, F. W., & Chi, D. T. K. (1998). Effective leadership in joint ventures in Vietnam: A cross-cultural perspective. *Journal of Organizational Change Management, 11,* 357–372.

Rauch A., Frese, M., & Sonnentag, S. (2000). Cultural differences in planning/ success relationships: A comparison of small enterprises in Ireland, West Germany, and East Germany. *Journal of Small Business Management, 38,* 28–41.

Robie, C., Ryan, A. M., Schmieder, R. A., Parra, L. F., & Smith, P. C. (1998). The relation between job level and job satisfaction. *Group & Organization Management, 23,* 470–495.

Rotter, J. (1966). Generalized expectancies for internal versus external control of reinforcement. *Psychological Monographs, 80*(Whole No. 609).

Rowold, J., & Heinitz, K. (2007). Transformational and charismatic leadership: Assessing the convergent, divergent and criterion validity of the MLQ and the CKS. *The Leadership Quarterly, 18,* 121–133.

Rubin, I. M., & Berlew, D. E. (1984). The power failure in organizations. *Training and Development Journal, 38,* 35–38.

Sagiv, L., & Schwartz, S. H. (2000). Value priorities and subjective well-being: Direct relations and congruity effects. *European Journal of Social Psychology, 30,* 177–198.

Schein, E. H. (1992). *Organizational culture and leadership* (2nd ed.). San Francisco: Jossey-Bass.

Schneider, B., Goldstein, H. W., & Smith, D. B. (1995). The ASA framework: An update. *Personnel Psychology, 48,* 747–773.

Schneider, S. C., & Barsoux, J. L. (1997). *Managing across cultures.* London: Prentice Hall Europe.

Schwartz, S. H. (1994). Beyond individualism/collectivism: New cultural dimensions of values. In U. Kim, H. C. Triandis, C. Kagitcibasi, S. C. Choi, & G. Yoon (Eds.), *Individualism and collectivism: Theory, method, and applications* (pp. 85–119). Thousand Oaks, CA: Sage.

Schwartz, S. H. (1999). Cultural value differences: Some implications for work. *Applied Psychology: An International Review, 48,* 23–48.

Schwartz, S. H., & Sagie, G. (2000). Value consensus and importance: A cross-national study. *Journal of cross-cultural psychology, 31,* 465-497.

Shane, S. (1993). Cultural influences on national rates of innovation. *Journal of Business Venturing, 8,* 59–73.

Shane, S. (1995). Uncertainty avoidance and the preference for innovation championing roles. *Journal of International Business Studies, 26,* 47–68.

Shane, S., Venkataraman, S., & MacMillan, I. (1995). Cultural differences in innovation championing strategies. *Journal of Management, 21,* 931–952.

Silverthorne, C. (2001). A test of the path-goal leadership theory in Taiwan. *Leadership & Organization Development Journal 22,* 151–158.

Sinha, J. B. P. (1995). *The cultural context of leadership and power.* New Delhi, India: Sage.

Sinha, J. B. P. (2003). Trends toward indigenization of psychology in India. In K.-S. Yang, K.-K. Hwang, P. B. Pedersen, & I. Daibo (Eds.), Progress in Asian social psychology: Conceptual and empirical contributions (pp. 11-28). Westport, CT: Praeger.

Sinha, J. B. P., Sinha, R. B. N., Bhupatkar, A. P., Sukumaran, A., Gupta, P., Gupta, R., et al. (2004). Facets of societal and organisational cultures and managers' work related thoughts and feelings. *Psychology and Developing Societies, 16,* 1–25.

Sivakumar, K., & Nakata, C. (2001). The stampede toward Hofstede's framework: Avoiding the sample design pit in cross-cultural research. *Journal of International Business Studies, 32,* 555–574.

Smith, P. B. (2002). Culture's consequences: Something old and something new. *Human Relations, 55,* 119–135.

Smith, P. B., & Bond, M. H. (1999). *Social psychology across cultures: Analysis and perspectives* (2nd ed.). London, UK: Harvester Wheatsheaf. (First edition published 1993)

Smith, P. B., & Peterson, M. F. (1988). *Leadership, organizations and culture.* London: Sage.

Smith, P. B., Peterson M. F., & Misumi, J. (1994). Event management and work team effectiveness in Japan, Britain and the USA. *Journal of Occupational and Organizational Psychology, 67,* 33–43.

Smith, P. B., Peterson, M. F., Schwartz, S. H. (2002). Cultural values, sources of guidance, and their relevance to managerial behavior: A 47-nation study. *Journal of Cross-Cultural Psychology, 33,* 188–208.

Steers, R. M., Nardon, L., & Sanchez-Runde, C. (2009). Culture and organization design: Strategy, structure, and decision-making. In R. S. Bhagat and R. M Steers (Eds.), *Cambridge handbook of culture, organizations, and work* (pp. 71–117). Cambridge, UK: Cambridge University Press.

Stewart, R. (1997). *The reality of management.* Oxford, UK: Butterworth-Heinemann.

Stewart, R., Barsoux, J. L., Kieser, A., Ganter, H. D., & Walgenbach, P. (1994). *Managing in Britain and Germany.* London: St. Martin's Press/MacMillan Press.

Ting-Toomey, S. (1988). Intercultural conflict styles. In Y. Kim & W. Gudykunst (Eds.), *Theories in intercultural communication* (pp. 213–235). Newbury Park, CA: Sage.

Triandis, H. C. (1994). Cross-cultural industrial and organizational psychology. In H. C. Triandis, M. D. Dunnette, & L. M. Hough (Eds.), *Handbook of industrial and organizational psychology* (Vol. 4, 2nd ed., pp 103–172). Palo Alto, CA: Consulting Psychologists Press.

Trice, H. M., & Beyer, J. M. (1991). Cultural leadership in organizations. *Organization Science, 2,* 149–169.

Trice, H. M., & Beyer, J. M. (1993). *The culture of work organizations.* Englewood Cliffs, NJ: Prentice Hall.

Trompenaars, F., & Hampden-Turner, C. (1997). *Riding the waves of culture: Understanding cultural diversity in business* (2nd ed.). London: Nicholas-Brealey.

United Nations Development Program. (2002). *Human development report: Deepening democracy in a fragmented world.* New York: Oxford University Press. Retrieved from http://hdr.undp.org/en/reports/global/hdr2002/

Van Muijen, J. J., Koopman, P. L., De Witte, K., et al. (1999) Organizational culture: The Focus questionnaire. *European Journal of Work and Organizational Psychology, 8,* 551–568.

Verburg, R. M. (1996). Developing HRM in foreign Chinese joint ventures. *European Management Journal, 14,* 518–525.

Verburg, R. M., Drenth, P. J. D., Koopman, P. L., Van Muijen, J. J., & Wang, Z. M. (1999). Managing human resources across cultures: A comparative analysis of practices in industrial enterprises of China and the Netherlands. *International Journal of Human Resource Management, 10,* 391–410.

Walumbwa, F. O., Lawler, J. J., Avolio, B. J., Wang, P., & Shi, K. (2005). Transformational leadership and work-related attitudes: The moderating effects of collective and self-efficacy across cultures. *Journal of Leadership and Organizational Studies, 11,* 2–16.

Xin, K. R., & Tsui, A. S. (1996). Different strokes for different folks? Influence tactics by Asian-American and Caucasian-American managers, *The Leadership Quarterly, 7,* 109–132.

Zhou, J. (2002, September). *Work group creativity in China: A paternalistic organizational control perspective.* Paper presented at the Human Resource Management: Global Perspectives conference, Oak Brook, IL.

13

Leadership
and Gender

Linda L. Carli

Wellesley College

Alice H. Eagly

Northwestern University

A profound divide in power and authority separates women from men. Although women have made progress as leaders, men remain in charge of the most consequential activities of most organizations and governments. In the hierarchical structures of contemporary nations, the proportion of women decreases at higher levels, until at the highest level women are unusual. Patriarchy prevails in world societies. Although power is often evenly divided between women and men in societies with simple socioeconomic structures, even in these nonpatriarchal societies, men still monopolize public leadership (Whyte, 1978; Wood & Eagly, 2002).

In our chapter, we document the current status of women leaders and explore five explanations for women's lesser occupancy of high-level leadership positions. We first examine whether women's lesser investments in human capital (e.g., education, work experience) account for leadership differentials. The second explanation considers whether women's style of leading is different from men's. Any such differences might advantage or disadvantage women, depending on their implications for leaders' effectiveness. The third explanation considers the evolutionary psychology argument that it is in the

AUTHORS' NOTE: Please address correspondence concerning this chapter to Linda L. Carli, Department of Psychology, Wellesley College, Wellesley, MA 02481, USA. Phone: 781–283–3351; e-mail: lcarli@wellesley.edu.

nature of men but not women to be motivated to lead and dominate others. Our fourth explanation focuses on prejudice and discrimination, and our fifth explanation considers the contribution of structural barriers within organizations. Before evaluating these potential causes of women's rarity in positions of power and authority, we present information on the distribution of women and men in leadership roles.

Representation of Women and Men in Leadership Roles

Even in postindustrial societies, political, corporate, and other leadership at the highest levels has remained largely a male prerogative. Although women have gained considerable access to supervisory and middle management positions and are well represented as leaders in U.S. philanthropic organizations and foundations, where women hold 55% of chief executive and chief giving officer positions (Council on Foundations, 2009), they remain scarce as elite leaders and top executives in most domains. Women are particularly underrepresented at higher levels of leadership; the percentage of female executives declines with increasing organizational rank (Helfat, Harris, & Wolfson, 2006). For example, across all organizations in the United States, women constitute 52% of the professional and managerial positions, but only 26% of chief executives (U.S. Bureau of Labor Statistics, 2011, Table 11). In the most capitalized companies, constituting the Fortune 500, only 16% of all corporate officers, 16% of board members (Catalyst, 2010c), and less than 3% of chief executive officers are women (Catalyst, 2010a). Statistics for women among corporate executives are similar in Canada, Australia (Catalyst, 2010b), and Europe (Desvaux, Devillard-Hoellinger, & Baumgarten, 2007). And less than 3% of chief executive officers of the Global Fortune 500 are women (*Fortune*, 2009b).

Women's political leadership is increasing in the United States and other nations, but women remain underrepresented in government leadership roles (UNIFEM, 2008), especially in the more powerful elected positions. In the United States, women are 17% of the members of the U.S. Senate, 17% of the members of the U.S. House of Representatives, 12% of state governors, and 24% of state legislators (Center for American Women and Politics, 2010). Women also comprise 28% of the Senior Executive Service of the federal government (U.S. Office of Personnel Management, 2007).

Women are especially underrepresented in leadership roles that provide substantial authority over other people. It is not that women lack prestige, because women are well represented in many moderately prestigious professional roles (e.g., teacher, registered nurse, social worker). However, men more often occupy positions conferring decision-making authority and the ability to influence others' pay or promotions (Smith, 2002). Female managers have less authority than male managers, even when rank and tenure in organizations are held constant (Lyness & Thompson, 2000; Reskin & Ross, 1995). Among male and female managers at the same level, women also have less access to the demanding responsibilities and complex challenges that may lead to positions of greater authority (Lyness & Thompson, 1997; Ohlott, Ruderman, & McCauley, 1994). Even in female-dominated organizations and professions, men ascend to leadership faster than women—a phenomenon known as the "glass escalator" (e.g., Maume, 1999; C. L. Williams, 1995).

Clearly, women still confront obstacles as leaders, but times have changed, and women leaders have emerged in very high places. More women lead nations (de Zárate, 2010) and large corporations (e.g. *Fortune*, 2009a) than ever before. Thus, there no longer is an impenetrable barrier for women at the highest levels of leadership. Instead, women face a variety of complex challenges, some subtle and some more obvious. Overcoming them is difficult, but not impossible. To reflect the convoluted and obstructed path to leadership that women leaders and aspiring leaders face, we use the metaphor of the labyrinth (Eagly & Carli, 2007). Some women make it to the center of the labyrinth and attain leadership, but compared with the relatively straight path taken by men, women require more careful navigation to overcome the obstacles. We now consider what forms the labyrinth. Why do women remain underrepresented as leaders?

Gender Differences in Human Capital Investments and Family Responsibilities

Gender Differences in Human Capital

One explanation for the gender gap in leadership is that women's human capital investment in education, training, and work experience is lower than men's. According to *human capital theory* of economics, women's greater domestic responsibilities undermine their investment in their careers in terms of hours worked, breaks in employment, training, or effort (see Kunze, 2008). However, with respect to education, this argument has little force. Beginning in 1981–1982 in the United States, women earned more bachelor's degrees than men did; in 2009, women received 57% of bachelor's degrees, 60% of master's degrees, and 50% of PhDs and first professional degrees (U.S. National Center for Education Statistics, 2010). Similar results of women's greater education are found in many industrialized countries (United Nations Development Programme, 2009).

Considerable evidence, moreover, argues against the proposition that family and domestic responsibilities cause employed women to avoid leadership responsibility (Corrigall & Konrad, 2006; Galinsky, Aumann, & Bond, 2008; Smith, 2002). Specifically, an assumption of self-selection predicts that the marriage, the presence of children, and inegalitarian household arrangements depress women's workplace authority relative to that of men. However, such findings are not usually obtained. For example, a large cross-national study of the United States, Canada, the United Kingdom, Australia, Sweden, Norway, and Japan did not support this self-selection hypothesis, except to some degree in Canada (Wright, Baxter, & Birkelund, 1995).

There is little evidence that women avoid challenging work more than men do. A large meta-analytic review of gender differences in career preferences revealed that on average, women and girls preferred jobs that provided creativity, a sense of accomplishment, opportunities to grow and develop, and the ability to work with and help others, whereas men and boys preferred jobs that provided good pay, and opportunities for promotion, leadership, and leisure (Konrad, Ritchie, Lieb, & Corrigall, 2000). Given that the desire for promotion is a function of having promotion opportunities, women and men should be more similar in preference for promotion and leadership when in positions with more comparable advancement opportunities (Cassirer & Reskin, 2000). And indeed, in the meta-analysis, adult men and women in similar occupations had the same desire for leadership and promotions; moreover, women actually expressed a greater desire for high earnings than men did (Konrad et al., 2000).

Research on career commitment has likewise shown few differences between men and women. Men and women feel equally committed to their organizations (Aven, Parker, & McEvoy, 1993). Moreover, in the United States, the majority of both women and men would prefer to have a job rather than stay home (Saad, 2007) and report a greater commitment to family than to career (Families and Work Institute, 2005). Still, women report a greater commitment to family than men do (Families and Work Institute, 2005), and a higher percentage of women than men would prefer to stay home than have a job (Saad, 2007).

Women's and Men's Family Responsibilities

Although women and men differ little in career preferences or commitment, human capital explanations for gender differences in leadership predict that compared with men, women devote relatively more time to family than career. Men, in fact, spend more time in child care than they did in the past, but so do women (Bianchi, Robinson, & Milkie, 2006; Bond, Thompson, Galinsky, & Prottas, 2002). Even with smaller families, both men and women now spend more time interacting with children than they did in 1965 (Aguiar & Hurst, 2007; Bianchi et al., 2006). Nevertheless, there is little doubt that women spend more time than men on housework and child care (U.S. Bureau of Labor Statistics, 2010a, Table 1). Because the custodial care aspect of domestic work (e.g., laundry, cooking) is typically obligatory and routine, women cannot readily opt out of such responsibilities because of time constraints or employment obligations. Rather than reduce time spent with children, women sacrifice personal time and, as a result, experience less leisure than men do (see U.S. Bureau of Labor Statistics, 2010a, Table 1). Family responsibilities also reduce women's job experience. Having a spouse or children is associated with a reduction in paid work hours for women, but with an increase for men (Corrigall & Konrad, 2006). This division of labor reflects the cultural association of the father role with being a good provider and the mother role with nurturing and custodial care.

A common presumption is that women have less job experience because they quit their jobs more often than men do (e.g., Almer, Hopper, & Kaplan, 1998). However, a study of more than 26,000 full-time managers for a multinational financial services organization revealed that the women quit somewhat less than men, both with and without the introduction of controls for human capital variables (Lyness & Judiesch, 2001). Similar results were found in another study of a large firm with more than 25,000 employees, where men quit slightly more than women when controlling for human capital variables (Petersen & Saporta, 2004). Moreover, a meta-analysis by Griffeth, Hom, and Gaertner (2000) found that overall, men quit slightly more often than women do (P. W. Hom, personal communication, February 24, 2003). Still, one study of 20 firms, predominantly of the Fortune 500, revealed that the rate of quitting in 2003 among professional and managerial employees was 5% for women and 3% for men; the study controlled for the firm's size, seniority levels of the workforce, and proportion of female employees, but not individual human capital variables (Hom, Roberson, & Ellis, 2008). And research on managers and highly qualified MBAs has shown that women do quit somewhat more than men do because of family responsibilities (Bertrand, Goldin, & Katz, 2010; Lyness & Judiesch, 2001).

Still, employed women do suffer income loss as a result of breaks for motherhood, which are more costly than breaks taken for other reasons (Arun, Arun, & Borooah, 2004). Women experience long-term cumulative losses in income not only from time away from work, but also from part-time employment (Rose & Hartmann, 2004), and women work part-time more often than men do. In 2010, 27% of employed women worked part-time compared with 13% of men (U.S. Bureau of Labor Statistics, 2011, Table 8). Even women in traditionally male-dominated, high status professions are more likely than their male counterparts to reduce their work hours to accommodate child care and family responsibilities (Boulis, 2004; Noonan & Corcoran, 2004).

To explore loss of income associated with motherhood, Budig and England (2001) used data from the National Longitudinal Survey of Youth to examine the contribution of job characteristics and human capital variables to this income loss, which amounted to 7% per child. Although two thirds of the income loss could not be explained with human capital variables, about one third of it was attributable to the lesser experience of mothers, who more often worked part-time, took breaks from employment, and had less seniority. Other studies have shown that wage penalties can be reduced by limiting time away from work after having children (Bond et al., 2002; Lundberg & Rose, 2000).

Overall, one human capital explanation for the gender wage gap has received clear support, namely, that women have less job experience and consistency of employment than men. Nevertheless, the inability of human capital variables to account for the majority of the gender wage gap leaves ample room for other causal factors. The overriding importance of other factors is further suggested by evidence that women receive substantially smaller gains in authority than men for similar human capital investments (see Smith, 2002). These findings raise questions about the adequacy of women's performance in leadership roles as well as about possible resistance to women's rise in organizational hierarchies.

The Leadership Styles of Women and Men_____

If women lack adequacy as leaders, perhaps they have a different style of leadership than men. Although leaders vary their behavior in response to situational contingencies, they still have typical modes of interacting with their superiors and subordinates. Because styles are one determinant of leaders' effectiveness, any sex difference in style could affect people's views about whether women should advance to higher positions in organizational hierarchies.

Research on Comparing
Leadership Styles of Women and Men

Most research on leadership style conducted prior to 1990 derived from Bales's (1950) classification of leadership behavior that distinguished *task-oriented style*, defined as behavior related to accomplishing assigned tasks, and *interpersonally oriented* style, defined as behavior related to maintaining interpersonal relationships. A somewhat less popular distinction, deriving from experimental research by Lewin and Lippitt (1938), was between (a) *democratic* or *participative* leaders who behave democratically and allow subordinates to participate in decision making and (b) *autocratic* or *directive* leaders who behave autocratically and discourage subordinates from such participation. To assess sex differences and similarities in these styles, Eagly and Johnson (1990) reviewed 162 studies that provided quantitative comparisons of women and men on relevant measures.

This meta-analysis (Eagly & Johnson, 1990) of studies from the period 1961 to 1987 found that leadership styles were somewhat gender-stereotypic in laboratory experiments using student participants and in other assessments using participants not selected for occupancy of leadership roles (e.g., samples of employees or students in university business programs). In this research, women, more than men, manifested relatively interpersonally oriented and democratic styles, and men, more than women, manifested relatively task-oriented and autocratic styles. In contrast, sex differences were more limited in organizational studies, which assessed managers' styles. The only difference obtained between female and male managers was that women adopted a somewhat more democratic (or participative) style and a less autocratic (or directive) style than men did. This finding, which was based on 23 data sets and a heterogeneous set of measuring instruments, produced a relatively small mean effect size ($d = 0.22$). In contrast, male and female managers did not differ in their tendencies to use interpersonally oriented and task-oriented styles. Similar results were found in a subsequent meta-analysis, which focused on studies published between 1987 and 2000 (van Engen & Willemsen, 2004).

In the 1980s and 1990s, many researchers began to make new distinctions about leadership styles in order to identify the types of leadership that are attuned to the conditions faced by contemporary organizations. Their emphasis was on leadership that is future oriented rather than present oriented and that strengthens organizations by inspiring followers' commitment and ability to contribute creatively to organizations. This approach initially emerged in Burns's (1978) delineation of a type of leadership that he labeled *transformational*. As subsequently elaborated by Bass (1985, 1998), transformational leadership involves establishing oneself as a role model by gaining followers' trust and confidence. Transformational leaders state future goals, develop plans to achieve those goals, and innovate, even when their organization is generally successful. By mentoring and empowering followers, such leaders encourage them to develop their full potential and thus to contribute more effectively to their organization.

Burns (1978) and other researchers (e.g., Avolio, 1999; Bass, 1998) contrasted transformational leaders to *transactional* leaders, who appeal to subordinates' self-interest by establishing exchange relationships with them. This type of leadership involves managing in the conventional sense of clarifying subordinates' responsibilities, rewarding them for meeting objectives, and correcting them for failing to meet objectives. Although empirically separable, transformational and transactional leadership styles can both contribute to effective leadership. In addition to these two styles, these researchers distinguished a *laissez-faire* style that is marked by a general failure to take responsibility for managing. The components of transformational and transactional leadership as well as laissez-faire leadership are most commonly assessed by the Multifactor Leadership Questionnaire, known as the MLQ (Avolio, Bass, & Jung, 1999). As shown in Table 13.1, this instrument generally represents transformational leadership by five subscales, transactional leadership by three subscales, and laissez-faire leadership by one scale.

A meta-analysis of 45 studies compared male and female managers on measures of transformational, transactional, and laissez-faire leadership styles (Eagly, Johannesen-Schmidt, & van Engen, 2003). Although many

Table 13.1   Definitions of Transformational, Transactional, and Laissez-Faire Leadership Styles in the Multifactor Leadership Questionnaire

Type of Scale and Subscale	Description of Leadership Style
Transformational	
Idealized influence (attribute)	Demonstrates qualities that motivate respect and pride from association with him or her
Idealized influence (behavior)	Communicates values, purpose, and importance of organization's mission
Inspirational motivation	Exhibits optimism and excitement about goals and future states
Intellectual stimulation	Examines new perspectives for solving problems and completing tasks
Individualized consideration	Focuses on development and mentoring of followers and attends to their individual needs
Transactional	
Contingent reward	Provides rewards for satisfactory performance by followers
Active management-by-exception	Attends to followers' mistakes and failures to meet standards
Passive management-by-exception	Waits until problems become severe before attending to them and intervening
Laissez-faire	Exhibits frequent absence and lack of involvement during critical junctures

NOTE. From "Transformational, transactional, and laissez-faire leadership styles: A meta-analysis comparing women and men," by A. H. Eagly, M. C. Johannesen-Schmidt, & M. van Engen, 2003. *Psychological Bulletin, 129,* p. 571.

types of organizations were represented, the majority were either business or educational organizations. This meta-analysis also included a large study conducted to provide norms and psychometric standards for the MLQ as well as many studies conducted within specific organizations or groups of organizations. The measures of leadership style were completed by the leaders themselves or by their subordinates, peers, or superiors.

In general, Eagly et al.'s (2003) meta-analysis revealed that female leaders were more transformational than male leaders and also engaged in more of the contingent reward behaviors that are one component of transactional leadership. Among the five subscales of transformational leadership, women most exceeded men on the individualized consideration subscale that identifies supportive, encouraging treatment of subordinates. Also, male leaders were more likely to manifest two other aspects of transactional leadership (active and passive management-by-exception) and laissez-faire leadership, although fewer studies had assessed these aspects of style. These differences between male and female leaders were small. However, they prevailed in the meta-analysis as a whole, as well as in auxiliary analyses of (a) the large MLQ norming study, (b) a heterogeneous group of other studies that used the MLQ measures, and (c) a smaller group of studies that used a variety of other measures of the styles. Another large-scale study consisting primarily of business managers, which was published around the same time as the meta-analysis, produced quite similar results (Antonakis, Avolio, & Sivasubramaniam, 2003).

In summary, meta-analyses of leadership styles found that gender-stereotypic sex differences tended to prevail among leaders who were somewhat arbitrarily thrust into leader roles in laboratory experiments. Under these conditions, women attended somewhat more to interpersonal considerations and men more narrowly to task-relevant considerations. Without selection or preparation for a longer term leadership role, leaders rely to some extent on gender roles to guide their behavior. Nonetheless, among managers, some small sex differences have been detected, but in a narrower range of leadership behaviors. Women's style tends to be more democratic and participative, compared with men's more autocratic and directive style—again a pattern of differences that is consistent with gender-stereotypic roles.

Female managers tend to adopt a transformational style somewhat more than men do, especially the individualized consideration aspect of this style. Transactionally, female managers use more rewards than men do to encourage appropriate subordinate behavior. In contrast, men, more than women, attend to subordinates' failures to meet standards, and they display the more problematic styles that involve avoiding solving problems until they become acute and being absent or uninvolved at critical times. This pattern of sex-related differences in transformational and transactional behavior also emerged in a study of stereotypes about female and male leaders, suggesting that people are generally aware of these relatively subtle behavioral differences (Vinkenburg, van Engen, Eagly, & Johannesen-Schmidt, 2011).

Transformational leadership incorporates feminine, communal qualities, especially in its individualized consideration dimension, and therefore represents a blend of feminine and masculine qualities (Hackman, Furniss, Hills, & Paterson, 1992). Despite this blend, participants in the stereotype study indicated that the more agentic, inspirational motivation aspects of transformational leadership are especially important for male managers and that the more communal, individualized consideration aspects are especially important for female managers (Vinkenburg et al., 2011). Thus, although transformational leadership is quite androgynous, female managers remain pressured to be especially communal. Nonetheless, the alignment of transformational leadership with the female as well as the male gender role should make the style more attractive to female leaders than more traditional and masculine styles (Eagly & Carli, 2007).

Leadership Style and Leaders' Effectiveness

Do the gender differences in leadership style give an advantage to either male or female leaders? The implications of female managers' relatively democratic and participative style are not clear-cut because this style's effectiveness is contingent on various features of group and organizational environments (Foels, Driskell, Mullen, & Salas, 2000; Gastil, 1994). Under some circumstances, democratic and participative styles are effective, and under other circumstances, autocratic and directive styles are effective.

In contrast to democratic versus autocratic leadership, the implications of transformational and transactional leadership are much clearer. A meta-analytic review of 87 studies was conducted to assess the effectiveness of transformational, transactional, and laissez-faire leadership (Judge & Piccolo, 2004). Results revealed moderate to large correlations between transformational leadership and a variety of measures reflecting effectiveness: leader effectiveness, group or organizational performance, leader performance, follower satisfaction, and follower motivation. One component of transactional leadership, the use of contingent rewards by leaders, showed comparable correlations with the same measures of effectiveness. The other two components of transactional leadership were much less effective: Leaders' use of negative, punishing behavior (active management-by-exception) was only weakly related to effectiveness, and delaying action until problems become severe (passive management-by-exception) was negatively correlated with effectiveness. Finally, laissez-faire leadership also decreased leaders' effectiveness. Thus, the leadership styles that women adopt more often than men have higher levels of effectiveness, whereas the styles adopted more often by men than women are only slightly beneficial or actually ineffective.

Women's use of effective styles of leadership suggests that women might be more effective as leaders than men are. One way to test whether this is true is to examine the relation between the percentage of women in executive positions in organizations and how well those organizations perform financially. Such studies have been conducted examining Fortune 1000 and other large U.S. companies. Results show that the higher the percentage of women in executive positions or on boards of directors, the better financial outcome for the companies (Carter, Simkins, & Simpson, 2003; Erhardt, Werbel, & Shrader, 2003; Krishnan & Park, 2005). A similar study on European-based companies compared the financial performance of organizations having the greatest gender diversity in top management with the average performance of companies in their economic sector; companies with greater gender diversity performed better (Desvaux et al., 2007). These results are ambiguous because companies with better financial performance might appoint more women to positions of authority. Yet, despite the ambiguity of this correlational association between financial performance and women's representation in corporate leadership, these data suggest that women are a corporate asset.

A final method of assessing the effectiveness of male and female leaders consists of having research participants rate the effectiveness of individual male and female leaders. These effectiveness ratings may be contaminated by gender bias, but have some validity because leaders can be effective only if their leadership is endorsed and accepted by others. In a meta-analysis of 96 studies comparing the effectiveness of male and female leaders holding comparable leadership roles, no overall gender differences were found (Eagly, Karau, & Makhijani, 1995). However, some contexts favored men, and some favored women: In masculine settings, such as the military, men received higher ratings of effectiveness than women, whereas in less masculine settings, such as in education, women received somewhat higher effectiveness ratings than men (Eagly et al., 1995). These findings suggest that effectiveness may well be affected by gender stereotypes. In male-dominated settings, people are most likely to equate good leadership with stereotypically masculine behaviors, creating doubt about women's effectiveness as leaders and greater challenges in becoming effective.

In conclusion, research on leadership style shows that the sex differences substantiated by empirical research are unlikely to hinder women's performance as leaders but instead should promote their performance. Thus, the relative absence of female leaders cannot be due to their ineffective style.

The Nature Arguments: Men as Naturally Dominant

The Evolutionary Psychology Argument

According to scholars who endorse evolutionary psychology, men have the most powerful leadership roles because they possess biologically based attributes that ideally suit them for leadership (e.g., Browne, 1999; Goldberg, 1993). According to this argument, these attributes evolved through genetically mediated adaptation to primeval conditions (e.g., Buss & Kenrick, 1998) and disqualify women from substantial participation as leaders: As Browne (1999) wrote, "if high-status roles are found exclusively in the extra-domestic sphere—a sphere in which men's temperament gives them an advantage—then women will be forever consigned to lower status" (p. 57). Outside of the kitchen and nursery, women are thus doomed to cede power and status to men.

Evolutionary psychologists link current sex differences in behavior to the differing reproductive pressures experienced by males and females in the early history of the human species (Buss & Kenrick, 1998). These sexual selection pressures presumably shaped psychological sex differences, with the ultimate source being an asymmetry in the sexes' parental investment (Trivers, 1972). Specifically, women, the sex that invested more in offspring (e.g., through gestation and nursing), became choosier about potential mates than men, the sex that invested less. Ancestral women presumably developed a proclivity to choose mates who could provide resources to support them and their children. As a result, ancestral men competed with other men to obtain sexual access to women and resources, and the winners in these competitions were more likely to procreate and thus have their genes carried on to the next generation. According to this logic, men who fared better in these competitions were aggressive, risk taking, competitive, and status seeking, passing on these traits to their male progeny. In short, a tendency for men to seek leadership could have evolved because more dominant men would have controlled more resources and had higher status and these qualities were associated with reproductive success.

In summary, for evolutionary psychologists, men's efforts to dominate one another and to control women emerge from these evolved psychological dispositions that are "fossils" of the selection pressures that shaped the human species (Buss & Kenrick, 1998, p. 983). These arguments rest on a skein of assumptions about relations between the sexes in primeval times. The contentious scientific debates about these assumptions cannot be easily summarized here. Nonetheless, we note in particular one effort to test these assumptions by examining cross-cultural data from nonindustrial societies (Wood & Eagly, 2002). This review failed to find evidence to support the predictions of evolutionary psychology. Crucially, the assumption that male dominance is universal (e.g., Buss, 1995) is inconsistent with evidence that patriarchy instead emerged along with a variety of economic and social developments, including warfare and intensive agriculture. Thus, the majority of foraging societies organized as bands are nonhierarchical and nonpatriarchal (e.g., Boehm, 1999; Salzman, 1999), a finding that would not be obtained were male dominance inherent in men's nature. As new roles developed in more socioeconomically complex societies, the roles in the nondomestic economies increasingly required training, intensive energy expenditure, and travel away from the home. Because of their freedom from the reproductive responsibility of gestation and nursing of infants, men were better positioned to occupy these roles and to reap the economic and social capital that these roles yielded.

Wood and Eagly (2002) also failed to find support for the assumption that women uniquely depended on men to provide resources to support women and their children. On the contrary, women not only contributed substantially to subsistence activities in most nonindustrial societies but also were the primary food providers in gathering societies. It is therefore likely that ancestral men and women were mutually dependent for their subsistence, with the balance of dependence determined by their society's environment and ecology. Both sexes would have reaped advantages from pair bonds with effective resource providers (see also Wrangham, Jones, Laden, Pilbeam, & Conklin-Brittain, 1999). Yet, as societies moved away from the simpler socioeconomic structures in which humans evolved, men came to disproportionally occupy roles that entailed primary responsibility for providing resources for family units.

Gender Differences in Leadership Traits

Because modern industrialized societies are moderately patriarchal, some psychological sex differences should result from socialization, if not from evolved dispositions. Of special interest are the traits that are thought to be relevant to leadership. According to some scholars of evolutionary psychology (e.g., Browne, 1999), these traits include competitiveness, dominance, and aggressiveness, usually defined in terms of behavior intended to harm others. Indeed, meta-analyses of workplace aggression (Hershcovis et al., 2007) and general aggression have found greater aggressiveness in men than women, especially for physical rather than verbal aggression (Archer, 2004; Bettencourt & Miller, 1996; Eagly & Steffen, 1986). Men also score higher on self-report and personality measures of overall assertiveness than women do (Costa, Terracciano, & McCrae, 2001; Feingold, 1994). In particular, men more often use negative assertion, a forceful and controlling form of self-expression, whereas women use greater positive assertion, expressing their views in a way that acknowledges the rights of others as well as their own rights (Carli, 2001a). And, as shown in a meta-analysis of studies of managers' motivation to manage in a traditional, hierarchic manner (Eagly, Karau, Miner, & Johnson, 1994), women tend to be less motivated than men to impose their authority in a command-and-control style. And finally, in a meta-analytic review of gender differences in competitiveness in bargaining and mixed-motive games, a very small gender effect was revealed, with men behaving only slightly more competitively than women (Walters, Stuhlmacher, & Meyer, 1998). Overall, then, these findings show a consistent pattern for men to exhibit greater aggression and dominance than women.

But what effect, if any, do these behaviors have on leadership? First, there is little reason to believe that aggression facilitates effective leadership. Physical aggression may be useful to advance in contact sports or in criminal groups, but it is hardly a means of advancement in modern professional organizations. Furthermore, verbal aggression, negative assertion, dominance, and unilateral competition may be useful in certain contexts, but in general, they appear to provide little benefit to leaders (see Van Vugt, 2006). The success of contemporary organizations depends on responsiveness to customers and clients and to fast-changing technological developments. Successful leadership in such contexts requires the ability to form effective relationships with others and to work within teams of people offering differing skills and knowledge. Successful leaders influence others and motivate them to contribute enthusiastically and creatively to organizational goals (e.g., Bass, 1998). Although many management experts have emphasized social skills compatible with a traditionally feminine behavioral repertoire (Fondas, 1997), effective leadership requires both masculine and feminine skills.

What are the specific traits associated with becoming a leader and leading effectively? A meta-analysis of studies assessing the Big Five personality traits has shown that extraversion, openness to experience, and conscientiousness show small to moderate associations with leader emergence, and along with agreeableness, with performing effectively as a leader; on the other hand, neuroticism is negatively correlated with leader emergence and effectiveness (Judge, Bono, Ilies, & Gerhardt, 2002). Based on a multiple regression analysis, the strongest Big Five predictor of leadership overall is extraversion, followed by conscientiousness and openness; neuroticism and agreeableness are of least importance. A second meta-analysis has also found evidence that general intelligence is associated in a small to moderate degree with emerging as a leader and with leadership effectiveness (Judge, Colbert, & Ilies, 2004).

And how do men and women compare in these traits? Neither gender has a clear overall advantage in the Big Five traits or intelligence. A large cross-cultural study found that women show higher levels of neuroticism, extraversion, agreeableness, and conscientiousness, with differences ranging from moderate in the case of neuroticism, to small for the other traits (Schmitt, Realo, Voracek, & Allik, 2008). No gender differences exist for overall intelligence (Halpern, 2001; Halpern & LaMay, 2000). Thus, women have a disadvantage in neuroticism and an advantage in agreeableness, neither of which has much relevance to leadership, and women show more conscientiousness and extraversion, which predict leadership more strongly. A second large-scale study that examined gender differences within various components of each of the five personality traits (Costa et al., 2001) revealed that women surpassed men in warmth, positive emotions, gregariousness, and activity, but men surpassed women in assertiveness and excitement seeking. Overall then, neither gender has an advantage in personality traits clearly linked to leadership.

Integrity, of special concern in the wake of contemporary corporate scandals, generally favors women, who show more disapproval than men of questionable business practices such as the use of insider information—although this sex difference becomes smaller with more years of labor force participation (Franke, Crown, & Spake, 1997). To the extent that risk taking is important, perhaps especially to entrepreneurial leadership, it is notable that the sex difference in the male direction is also very small and has decreased in magnitude over time (Byrnes, Miller, & Schafer, 1999). Effective leadership thus reflects a wide range of traits and skills, none of which empirical research has placed strongly in the domain of one sex.

Given the preponderance of men in leadership positions, it might be expected that men would possess more natural leadership ability, at least to some degree. Yet, research has not shown evidence of an inherent male advantage in leadership. In fact, studies comparing the leadership roles of fraternal and identical twins suggest that genetic factors have comparable effects on men's and women's attainment of leadership (see Arvey, Rotundo, Johnson, Zhang, & McGue, 2006; Arvey, Zhang, Avolio, & Krueger, 2007). Moreover, although some psychological sex differences may indeed be influenced by evolved dispositions, scientific evidence does not support the claims of evolutionary psychology that masculine traits such as aggressiveness and dominance facilitate effective leadership. On the contrary, most managerial experts advocate more feminine and androgynous skills of negotiation, cooperation, diplomacy, team building, and inspiring and nurturing others. It is these qualities that are represented in theories about effective leadership taking the form of transformational and contingent reward behaviors. Moreover, some of the characteristics that are known to derail leaders, such as arrogance, coldness, or having an intimidating or abrasive style (Nahavandi, 2008), are stereotypically masculine (Diekman & Eagly, 2000). So it is implausible that effective leadership in contemporary organizations mainly consists of traditionally masculine command-and-control behaviors or that men's ascendance to elite leadership roles reflects their natural dominance. Therefore, in view of the insufficiency of human capital explanations of women's lesser occupancy of such roles and the failure of explanations based on leadership styles and men's natural dominance, we turn to the possibility of prejudice and discrimination.

Prejudice and Discrimination Against Female Leaders

Gender Discrimination

One way to explore the effects of discrimination on the gender gaps in pay and advancement is to conduct studies examining whether the gaps can be explained by human capital variables, such as education, job experience, marital and parental status, part-time or full-time status, and number of breaks in employment. As we noted earlier, such studies by economists and sociologists, often with representative samples of participants, have shown that the different employment patterns of men and women do account for some of the wage gap. Still, nearly all studies show that human capital accounts for only a portion of the gender gaps in pay and advancement, leading to the conclusion that discrimination contributes to at least a portion of the unexplained gaps (see reviews by Blau & Kahn, 2006; Smith, 2002). Moreover, most U.S. studies show a constant level of discrimination that operates at all organizational levels (e.g., Baxter & Wright, 2000; Elliot & Smith, 2004; Wright et al., 1995). Thus, women do not face increasing discrimination at higher levels of leadership, but rather a steady attrition of women leaders creates a greater scarcity of women at higher levels.

Evidence of discrimination comes not just from the unexplained gender gaps in wages and promotions but also from experiments that compare the evaluation of male and female job applicants, where the characteristics of the applicants are held constant except for their gender. Some of these experiments involve actual hiring situations, in which employers evaluate applicants or job applications. These studies show that men are favored for jobs providing higher status and wages and for male-dominated positions, whereas women are favored only for female-dominated jobs (see review by Riach & Rich, 2002). Other experiments involve simulated hiring decisions, in which students, managers, or other participants evaluate applicants based on resumes. A meta-analysis of 49 such studies (Davison & Burke, 2000) revealed that men were preferred over identically qualified women for male-dominated jobs (e.g., auto salesperson) and gender-neutral jobs (e.g., psychologist; Davison, 2005, personal communication). Only in female-dominated jobs (e.g., secretary) were women preferred over identically qualified men. And other experiments show that mothers are especially likely to be targets of workplace discrimination (Correll, Benard, & Paik, 2007; Heilman & Okimoto, 2008).

Stereotypes About Women, Men, and Leaders and the Double Bind

Discrimination against female leaders occurs because people believe that women lack the capacity to be effective leaders. From a social psychological perspective, bias against female leaders is best regarded as one instance of more general processes of stereotyping and prejudice (Eagly & Diekman, 2005). Prejudice is a common outcome when social perceivers stereotype others, holding beliefs about them on the basis of their group membership. Stereotypes can be elicited automatically and tend to be resistant to change because people seek out and attend to information that confirms their stereotypes and disregard contradictory information. The potential for prejudice exists when social perceivers hold a stereotype about a group that is incongruent with the attributes that they think are required for success in certain classes of social roles. When a group member and an incongruent social role become joined in the mind of a perceiver, this inconsistency generally lowers the evaluation of the group member as an occupant of the role. The person is considered less qualified for the role because members of his or her social group are thought to lack the qualifications that are requisite for the role.

Consistent with this idea that prejudice emerges at the intersection of a group's stereotype and the requirements of a social role, Eagly and Karau (2002) proposed a role incongruity theory of prejudice toward female leaders, which is an extension of Eagly's social role theory of sex differences and similarities in social behavior (Eagly, 1987). This analysis emphasizes gender roles, defined as consensual beliefs about the attributes of women and men. These beliefs comprise two kinds of expectations, or norms: *descriptive norms,* which are consensual expectations about what members of a social group actually do, and *injunctive norms,* which are consensual expectations about what group members ought to do or ideally would do (Cialdini & Trost, 1998). The term *gender role* thus refers to the descriptive and injunctive expectations associated with women and men. Other researchers have used different labels for this distinction between descriptive and injunctive expectations, including descriptive and prescriptive stereotypes (e.g., Burgess & Borgida, 1999; Fiske & Stevens, 1993). Prejudice against women as leaders flows from the incongruity that people often perceive between the characteristics typical of women and the requirements of leader roles.

According to research in the United States and other nations, people expect men to be agentic—assertive, dominant, competent, and authoritative—and women to be communal—warm, supportive, kind, and helpful (Newport, 2001; J. E. Williams & Best, 1990). The inconsistency follows from the predominantly agentic qualities that people believe are necessary to succeed as a leader. Beliefs about leaders are more similar to beliefs about men than about women, as Schein (1973) demonstrated in her "think manager, think male" studies. In Schein's studies, participants rate a man, a woman, or a successful leader on gender-stereotypical traits; correlational analyses are then conducted on the ratings to determine whether the leader traits are more similar to the traits of men or of women. In a related paradigm (Powell & Butterfield, 1979), participants rate leaders on agentic and communal traits, and the ratings are analyzed to test whether leaders are seen as communal or agentic. Similarly, researchers have sometimes assessed gender stereotypes about leaders by having participants rate leaders on bipolar scales measuring masculinity versus femininity (Shinar, 1975).

A meta-analytic review of studies in the three paradigms revealed that although the association of leadership and masculine characteristics has weakened over time, leaders continue to be perceived as stereotypically masculine (Koenig, Eagly, Mitchell, & Ristikari, 2010). The association of leadership with masculine traits emerged more strongly for more highly male-dominated and higher status leadership roles. Thus, women do not always experience prejudice in relation to leader roles. Because the relevant incongruity is either between the descriptive contents of the female gender role and the leader role or between a leader's behavior and the injunctive content of the female gender role, when the incongruity is weaker, such as in less male-dominated settings or in leadership roles that place a premium on socially skilled rather than controlling behavior, there is less prejudice.

One of the consequences of stereotypes is that they can be self-fulfilling. Thinking about negative stereotypic portrayals of one's group can cause group members to become concerned about fulfilling the stereotype, and this concern can derail their performance in the stereotypic domain. In a demonstration of such processes, experiments in the "stereotype threat" paradigm made the female stereotype accessible to students by having them view television commercials featuring female-stereotypic (vs. neutral) content (Davies, Spencer, & Steele, 2005). Women, but not men, who had been exposed to the female-stereotypic portrayals, expressed less preference for a leadership role versus a nonleadership role.

In addition to the potential for self-fulfilling prophecies, women face other unique challenges as leaders. On one hand, they are perceived as lacking the agency to be effective leaders. On the other hand, because of injunctive norms about female communion, female leaders are perceived as lacking sufficient warmth if they behave too agentically. The challenge for women leaders is to balance the demand for agency required of the leader role and the demand for communion required of the female role. This need to balance both demands creates a double bind: Female leaders who show their warm communal side may be criticized for not being agentic enough, but female leaders who take charge and act tough may be criticized for lacking communion (Eagly & Carli, 2007).

As a result of the double bind, female leaders are typically held to a higher standard of competence than male leaders. A meta-analysis of studies comparing the evaluations of male and female leaders has shown that for comparable levels of performance, female leaders overall receive somewhat lower evaluations than male leaders (Eagly, Makhijani, & Klonsky, 1992). The tendency to evaluate female leaders less favorably was especially pronounced in male-dominated settings. In studies of military cadets (Boldry, Wood, & Kashy, 2001) and managers (Heilman, Block, & Martell, 1995), men received higher evaluations than women who performed equally well. In a study of college students participating in a group survival exercise, group members were better able to identify the most expert member of their group when that member was a man, rather than a woman (Thomas-Hunt & Phillips, 2004). And in another group decision-making study, group members discussing a child custody case were much more likely to attend to and use information presented by a male member of the group than the identical information presented by a female member (Propp, 1995). Except in feminine settings, women must display greater evidence of skill than men to be considered equally competent (Biernat & Kobrynowicz, 1997; Carli, 1990, 2006; Foschi, 2000). As a result, women have more difficulty influencing others (Carli, 2001b).

These challenges that gender stereotypes produce for women leaders are often compounded by cultural stereotypes about other group memberships, especially race and ethnicity. These other stereotypes also contain some attributes disadvantageous for leadership—For example, African Americans have been stereotyped as less competent, Hispanics as less ambitious, and Asian Americans as less assertive (e.g., Madon et al., 2001; Niemann, Jennings, Rozelle, Baxter, & Sullivan, 1994). Therefore, women who are members of racial and ethnic minorities may face more complex challenges than White women in exerting leadership (e.g., Eagly & Chin, 2010; Sanchez-Hucles & Davis, 2010).

Restrictions on Women's Agency

Paradoxically, becoming prototypical of desirable leadership in a group or organization does not ordinarily protect women from prejudiced evaluations. Women who are effective leaders tend to violate standards for their gender because they are perceived to manifest male-stereotypic, agentic attributes more than female-stereotypic, communal attributes. Unlike traditional women who are considered warm and nice but not especially instrumentally competent, women who excel and display leadership are considered instrumentally competent but not particularly warm (Glick, Diebold, Bailey-Werner, & Zhu, 1997). This perceived gender-role violation can, in turn, lower evaluations of women in leadership roles.

Compared with men, women's ability to lead is more dependent on their adherence to a constricted range of behavior (Carli, 1999). In particular, behaviors that convey dominance, negative assertion, self-promotion, or a lack of warmth conflict with the communal demands of the female gender role and therefore interfere with female influence. Women who disagree or behave dominantly or selfishly exert less influence over their audience than comparable men or more communal women (Burgoon, Birk, & Hall, 1991; Carli, 2006; Copeland, Driskell, & Salas, 1995; Mehta et al., 1989, cited in Ellyson, Dovidio, & Brown, 1992). People likewise express more negative reactions when a woman attempts to lead or direct them than when a man does (e.g., Butler & Geis, 1990). In addition, women, more than men, receive greater recognition when they are modest, rather than self-promoting (Carli, 2006; Giacalone & Riordan, 1990; Wosinska, Dabul, Whetstone-Dion, & Cialdini, 1996). Demonstrating this effect, Rudman (1998) had participants evaluate the job-interviewing skills of a target individual who behaved in a self-promoting or self-effacing manner. Female participants gave the female target lower evaluations when she was self-promoting compared with self-effacing, and male participants gave more favorable evaluations to a self-promoting woman only if they had something to gain from her. Yet, in no condition, were male self-promoters evaluated less favorably than self-effacing men.

Similar effects have been reported in organizational studies. In such studies men, but not women, who communicated in a more competent or assertive manner were rated as more desirable to hire (Buttner & McEnally, 1996) and received more support and mentoring (Tepper, Brown, & Hunt, 1993). Other research has demonstrated that people respond more negatively when receiving criticism from female than male leaders (see Atwater, Carey, & Waldman, 2001; Sinclair & Kunda, 2000). Thus, agentic behavior is less acceptable in women than in men.

Studies have also shown that because women are expected to be communal, they reap fewer benefits from helpful supportive behavior than men do. For example, one study found that men who were described as particularly helpful to their work colleagues were evaluated more favorably than unhelpful men, who were evaluated as favorably as particularly helpful women; unhelpful women received the lowest evaluations (Heilman & Chen, 2005). Organizational studies confirm these findings. In one such study, helpfulness increased men's promotions but had no effect on women's (Allen, 2006). In another, subordinates' irritation and stress levels dropped when their male leaders were especially considerate but were unaffected by female leaders' consideration (Mohr & Wolfram, 2008).

The double bind operates especially strongly in male-dominated domains. In experiments, women who are described as highly successful in male-dominated occupations are judged to have less desirable characteristics than men who are highly successful in the same occupation or than women with comparable success in a typically feminine career (e.g., Heilman et al., 1995; Heilman, Wallen, Fuchs, & Tamkins, 2004; Yoder & Schleicher, 1996). These penalties occurred because people judged women who succeeded in masculine domains to be especially lacking in communion (Heilman & Okimoto, 2008).

Although both men and women have been found to be more critical of female than male leaders, this tendency is stronger among men than women. Men, more than women, associate leadership with masculine traits (Koenig et al., 2010) and give less favorable evaluations to female than to male leaders (Eagly et al., 1992). Also, a meta-analysis of actual leaders (Eagly et al., 1995) showed that women tended to be perceived as less effective than men to the extent that men served as their evaluators or that they had male subordinates. Men also react more negatively to agentic behavior in women. For example, Geller and Hobfoll (1993) found that although male and female participants gave similar evaluations to men who expressed disagreement, women received less favorable evaluations by male than female participants for the same behavior. Likewise, displays of competence alone can, at times, reduce women's appeal to men. Studies have revealed that women can exert more influence with men when their behavior conveys lower levels of competence, but incompetent behavior has not been found to be influential with women (e.g., Carli, 1990; Carli, LaFleur, & Loeber, 1995; Matschiner & Murnen, 1999; Reid, Palomares, Anderson, & Bondad-Brown, 2009).

When the context of the interaction is a job application, men's greater resistance to women's influence affects women's chances of being hired. For example, in Buttner and McEnally's (1996) study assessing managers' reactions to job applicants, male applicants increased their chances of being hired by exhibiting direct and dominant behavior, whereas female applicants who did the same reduced their chances. In other studies, men also preferred to hire male over female job applicants, even when the female applicants had equal or superior qualifications (Foschi, Lai, & Sigerson, 1994; Uhlmann & Cohen, 2005).

One way that women can increase their likableness and thereby increase their influence with men is to "feminize" their behavior by increasing their interpersonal warmth. Warm women are better liked, especially by men, and this increased likableness results in increased influence (Carli, 2001b). Female leaders may therefore display an amalgam of agentic and communal qualities in order to gain influence and lead effectively. For example, in one experiment, female leaders had to show both communion and agency to be seen as effective, whereas male leaders needed to show only agency (Johnson, Murphy, Zewdie, & Reichard, 2008). Pressures on women leaders to conform to injunctive gender roles likely contribute to women's motivation to avoid autocratic forms of leadership and their reliance on more democratic and transformational leadership styles. In addition, although as we have shown, women and men differ little in the intrinsic qualities that facilitate leadership, women's reliance on transformational leadership, a more effective leadership style, may reflect a double standard that produces higher quality female than male leaders.

In summary, gender roles lead people to expect and prefer women to be communal, creating a double bind for female leaders, who must demonstrate exceptional competence to be seen as equal in ability to men and must also avoid threatening others with their competence and lack of warmth. Conversely, there is generally no incongruity between the male gender role and leadership roles. Men are not penalized for dominance, competence, or assertion and, at the same time, are generally not penalized for exhibiting communality. This situation creates an advantage for male leaders, who can display a wider range of behaviors, tailoring their leadership style to the demands of the situation. Moreover, men's greater resistance to female leadership also slows women's advancement to higher levels of leadership, where men currently reside in much higher proportions than women. Research thus makes a strong case that prejudicial barriers against female leaders are a major factor accounting for their rarity in elite leadership roles.

_____ Organizational Barriers to Women's Leadership

Because men have traditionally held positions of authority, organizations have developed in a way that best suits the needs and experiences of men. As a result, organizations often present impediments to women's advancement, impediments that may appear on the surface to be gender-neutral, not favoring men or women, but that inherently advantage men (e.g., Acker, 1990; Martin, 2003). For example, organizations have become increasingly demanding of their professional workforce, requiring long work hours and personal sacrifices for the organization. As a result, modern organizational culture has created an implicit model of an ideal employee, one who has few outside responsibilities and can be totally devoted to the organization (Acker, 1990; J. Williams, 2000). Demands for such commitment are especially pronounced for those in high-status executive positions, where advancement and pay are contingent on long hours of work (Judge, Cable, Boudreau, & Bretz, 1995). As a result, people employed in management and related fields usually work longer than average hours (Brett & Stroh, 2003; Jacobs & Gerson, 2004). Compared with other employees, professionals and managers are also more likely to have work-extending technology such as laptops and Blackberries, which are used to continue paid work in the evenings, on weekends, and during vacations; the most commonly reported effect of these technologies is to make the employee always available to the organization (Towers, Duxbury, Higgins, & Thomas, 2006).

Rewarding employees for long hours seems fair and equitable, yet it presents a particular challenge to families and especially to women, who have the bulk of domestic responsibilities. Because men have fewer domestic duties and more leisure time than women, men find it easier to commit to extreme hours on the job and experience fewer family–career time conflicts. One study revealed, for example, that male executives more often reported handing over domestic responsibilities to their spouses and were less likely to forgo or delay having children than their female counterparts; the female executives more often sacrificed personal interests and made efforts to manage domestic duties by finding outside help (Catalyst, 2004). In addition, a study of senior executives revealed that 75% of the men had stay-at-home wives, whereas 74% of the women had employed spouses (Galinsky et al., 2003). Thus, even at very high levels, female leaders have more home responsibilities and are less likely to fit the model of ideal employee.

Women's family and work responsibilities also undermine their ability to network and thereby create social capital in the workplace. Studies indicate that women have less access to powerful career networks than men do (Burt, 1998; Dreher & Cox, 1996). As revealed in a meta-analysis, having networks and mentors is associated with increased salary and promotions (Ng, Eby, Sorensen, & Feldman, 2005). And a longitudinal study demonstrated that networking both within and outside one's organization contributes to future career gains (Wolff & Moser, 2009). Thus, women's relative lack of social capital impedes their leadership opportunities (see Timberlake, 2005).

Women's lack of social capital is not merely a function of their limited free time. Studies have found that men benefit more than women do from having connections with colleagues and mentors (Dreher & Cox, 1996; Forret & Dougherty, 2004). Networks generally are gender-segregated because people tend to affiliate with others who are similar to themselves (McPherson, Smith-Lovin, & Cook, 2001). Men hold the bulk of leadership positions, and as a result, the most powerful networks tend to be dominated by men. Consistent with Campbell's (1965) realistic group conflict theory and Kanter's (1977) notion of homosocial reproduction, men and women are to some extent in competition for power and influence, perhaps especially at the tops of hierarchies where men have more to lose from women's advancement. In support of this idea, Maume (1999) found that working in male-dominated professions increased men's, but not women's, chances of promotion. Such professions may particularly benefit men because they have greater access than women to the more extensive male network that such organizations provide. Thus, even though connections with men can be helpful to women's careers (Burt, 1998; Dreher & Cox, 1996; Huffman & Torres, 2002), such connections are difficult to form.

In addition to lack of access to important networks, women face other challenges in traditional male corporate cultures. Female executives and professionals have reported that they have difficulty fitting in with the culture of their organizations and obtaining developmental work assignments and international travel opportunities (e.g., Lyness & Thompson, 2000; Ohlott et al., 1994). Women also receive fewer line management positions than their male counterparts (Catalyst, 2004; Galinsky et al., 2003). Similarly, in an experiment, pairs of men and women negotiated to determine whether they would work on challenging or easy assignments; although there were no differences in interest in these assignments or in self-reported negotiation style, men ultimately received more of the challenging assignments than women did (De Pater et al., 2009). On the other hand, women are more likely to be given highly risky assignments that are likely to fail, a phenomenon known as the *glass cliff* (see Haslam & Ryan, 2008; Ryan & Haslam, 2007). Based on archival research on firms in the United Kingdom (Ryan & Haslam, 2005), although not replicated in a study of U.S. firms (Adams, Gupta, & Leeth, 2009), women had a higher probability of being appointed to a leadership position than men did when the companies were experiencing downturns in financial performance. Consequently, women are denied achievable challenging assignments that are likely to lead to advancement, but they receive more ill-fated assignments that are unlikely to advance their careers.

In conclusion, organizational structure and culture implicitly favor men. Because men lack the domestic duties of women, men can more easily satisfy the corporate demand that professional and managerial employees provide long work hours and continuous availability. Corporate cultures and male networks are also often unwelcoming to women, undermining their ability to create valuable social capital on the job. And women have difficulty obtaining desirable assignments with advancement potential. These obstacles discriminate against women and contribute to their relative absence from leadership positions.

The Rise of Female Leaders

Despite the discriminatory barriers that we have documented, women are rising into leadership roles in many nations. In the United States, the occupational category for which women's share of employment has shown the greatest increase in recent decades is "executive, administrative, and manage-rial occupations"; these gains far outstrip women's gains in any other group-ing (Wootton, 1997). Specifically, in management, business, and financial operations occupations, women have increased from 18% in the early 1970s to 43% in 2010 (U.S. Bureau of Labor Statistics, 1982, 2011). In some catego-ries of management, women now predominate—for example, in medical and health services, education administration, and financial managers (U.S. Bureau of Labor Statistics, 2011, Table 11). Women are also increasingly pres-ent at higher levels of leadership. Political leadership provides evidence of women's rise in power and authority. In fact, of the 89 women who have ever served as presidents or prime ministers of nations, 69 first came into office since 1990, and 36 of those since 2000 (de Zárate, 2010). These 89 women are only a tiny fraction compared to the number of men who have served in these roles, but notably most of the women attained their positions quite recently. The idea of a woman as president or prime minister is no longer as unthinkable as it was in earlier years.

Other powerful political roles show similar shifts. In the United States, the 2010 percentages of women in the U.S. Congress and state legislatures are the highest in American history (Center for American Women and Politics, 2010). Within the Senior Executive Service of the federal government, con-sisting of the highest nonelective positions, the percentage of women has risen from 11% in 1990 (U.S. Office of Personnel Management, 1997) to 28% in 2007 (U.S. Office of Personnel Management, 2007).

Large business organizations have been especially slow to accept women in elite executive roles. Only a small percentage of CEOs in the Fortune 500 are women (Catalyst, 2010b), yet a record number of women held this posi-tion in 2010 (*Fortune,* 2009a). Also, more women now occupy posts as presidents of universities in the United States, even high-status universities such as Princeton, University of Pennsylvania, University of Michigan, and University of Illinois. In universities and colleges in the United States, the percentage of presidencies held by women increased from 10% in 1986 to 23% in 2006 (American Council on Education, 2007). It is thus unmistak-able that women are rising, not merely into lower and midlevel managerial roles but more slowly into leadership roles at the tops of organizations and governments.

What changes have enabled at least some women to rise into leadership roles that women have very rarely occupied in the past? We suggest several causes. Related to our discussion of women's human capital investments, we note changes toward increased investment, especially in work experi-ence. Also, as a product of underlying shifts in women's roles, women have changed their personal attributes in a masculine direction toward greater consistency with stereotypic definitions of leaders. In addition, many leader roles have changed to incorporate a greater measure of traditionally femi-nine qualities. Finally, successful women leaders find ways to lead that finesse the still remaining incongruity between leader roles and the female gender role. We discuss each of these causes of women's rise and point to relevant research support.

Changes in Women's Human Capital Investments

One important factor in women's rise is their increasing educational advantage relative to men. As we noted earlier, currently more women receive bachelor's and advanced degrees than men, a trend that can found be in nations around the world.

Earlier in this chapter, we reported that because of women's greater domestic responsibilities, women have less work experience, which in turn contributes to the gender gaps in workplace advancement and pay. The domestic division of labor has changed, however, in recent years. Diary studies with representative samples of Americans demonstrate that housework and child care are now shared more equally by women and men than ever before. In 1965, married women performed 34 hours of housework per week, and married men performed 5 hours (Bianchi et al., 2006). By 2009, married women's housework declined to 19 hours, and married men's housework had increased to 11 hours (U.S. Bureau of Labor Statistics, 2010a, Table 3). In addition, the amount of time spent on child care as a primary activity has increased for both men and women, but especially for men: From 1965 to 2000, child care rose from 11 to 13 hours weekly for women and from 3 to 7 hours for men (Bianchi et al., 2006).

Changes in the domestic division of labor reflect changing attitudes about family and employment roles. In the United States, most adults now believe that child care responsibilities should be shared equally by men and women (e.g., Milkie, Bianchi, Mattingly, & Robinson, 2002). Endorsement of traditional gender roles in the United States is at an all-time low, a change that has occurred across all generations, but is especially pronounced among younger Americans (Galinsky et al., 2008). Men's commitment to family has also increased (Families and Work Institute, 2005). In general, men and women are more becoming more alike in desire for workplace authority and in commitment to family (Galinsky et al., 2008). There has been a drop in the percentage of women who report preferring to stay home rather than have a job and an increase in the percentage of men—with 29% of men, the highest percentage ever, preferring to stay home (Saad, 2007). This convergence has also occurred in employment and income. Whereas in 1973, the labor force participation was 79% for men and 45% for women, by 2010, 71% of men and 59% of women were in the labor force (U.S. Bureau of Labor Statistics, 2011, Table 2). Furthermore, among an increasing percentage of married couples in the United States—now 35%—women are the primary or sole wage earners (U.S. Bureau of Labor Statistics, 2010b, Table 25).

The increased sharing of family responsibilities is beneficial, not only to women's careers but also to the well-being of both men and women (e.g., Barnett & Hyde, 2001; Greenhaus & Powell, 2006). For example, a review of longitudinal and cross-sectional studies on the effects of employment on women's health revealed that regardless of marital and parental status, employment is associated with better mental and physical health in women (Klumb & Lampert, 2004).

Masculine Changes in Women

As women shift more of their time from domestic labor to paid labor, they assume the personal characteristics required to succeed in these new roles (Eagly, Wood, & Diekman, 2000). These changes in the division of labor are associated with a redefinition of the patterns of behavior that are appropriate to women. People therefore readily acknowledge that women are becoming more masculine, particularly in agentic attributes, and will continue to change in this direction (Diekman & Eagly, 2000). Moreover, it is not surprising that research tracking sex differences across recent time periods reveals that women have become more agentic in concert with their entry into formerly male-dominated roles.

Research conducted primarily in the United States has documented changes in the sex differences of a wide range of attributes over time, beginning as early as the 1930s and extending to the present. Among these changes are the following: (a) the value that women place on job attributes such as freedom, challenge, leadership, prestige, and power has increased to be more similar to that of men (Konrad et al., 2000), and women's vocational interests have changed so that they are now indistinguishable from men's on the *enterprising* dimension, which encompasses leading, persuading, managing, and influencing (Su, Rounds, & Armstrong, 2009); (b) the amount of risky behavior in which women engage has become more similar to that of men (Byrnes et al., 1999); (c) women's self-reports of assertiveness, dominance, and masculinity have increased to become more similar to men's (Twenge, 1997, 2001); and (d) a higher proportion of science, math, and engineering degrees are being awarded to women than in the past (U.S. National Center for Education Statistics, 2008). Such findings suggest some convergence in the psychological attributes of women and men in traditionally masculine domains.

Feminine Changes in Leadership Roles

The qualities that now are seen as characteristic of good leadership have become more androgynous with the incorporation of a greater measure of feminine, communal qualities. This generalization emerged in the meta-analysis on the cultural masculinity of leadership roles that we noted earlier (Koenig et al., 2010). These new themes reflect changing organizational environments marked by accelerated technological growth, rapid social change, increasing workforce diversity, and a weakening of geopolitical boundaries. In these environments, traditional command-and-control style leadership may undermine leaders' ability to negotiate, manage relationships, and motivate high-level performance in subordinates. Thus, leadership scholars and experts now recommend that leaders seek new modes of managing in modern organizational environments, emphasizing democratic relationships, participatory decision making, delegation of responsibility, developing subordinates, and relying on team-based skills (see Avolio, 1999; Garvin, 1993; Kanter, 1997; Lipman-Blumen, 2000).

The changes in beliefs about what constitutes good leadership can be found not only among experts but also in popular sources and in the mind of the public. Evidence of these trends emerged in Fondas's (1997) textual analysis of mass-market books on management, which found many traditionally feminine, communal themes in authors' advice. Further evidence comes from people's increasing support for female leaders. For example, attitudes toward women leaders have become more positive (Inglehart & Norris, 2003). In polls, people increasingly indicate that they would vote for a woman for president (CBS News/New York Times, 2006) or prefer to work for a female boss (Carroll, 2006).

Given that humans evolved in foraging societies organized into small, nonhierarchical, nonpatriarchal bands (e.g., Boehm, 1999), it is possible that the emerging cultural model of good organizational leadership is moving toward ancestral patterns. Moreover, the more equal participation of women in leadership would also match the sharing of power and influence between the sexes in simply organized foraging societies, where women had influence in some domains and men in other domains (Whyte, 1978; Wood & Eagly, 2002). Relevant to these considerations is Van Vugt, Hogan, and Kaiser's (2008) argument that relatively collaborative modes of leadership, involving a good measure of teaching and mentoring, match humans' evolved preferences more than top-down modes of leadership. However, the hypothesis of evolved preferences for certain forms of leadership remains highly speculative. We suspect that people's preferences for differing types of leadership reflect the exigencies of their contemporaneous organizational environments far more than those of ancestral environments. Changes in cultural preferences for leadership styles likely follow from people's beliefs about whether particular styles, given current conditions, would be expected to produce favorable outcomes for individuals or organizations.

Finessing Role Incongruity With Competent, Androgynous Leadership Style

If women have become more masculine and leader roles more feminine, could we be reaching a middle ground where the characteristics ascribed to women match leadership roles as well as those ascribed to men? At such a point, prejudice against female leaders should have disappeared. This resolution is not near at hand, however, because as we have shown, gender prejudice and discrimination have not been eliminated. Women's masculine behaviors are still met with resistance, particularly in male-dominated and traditionally masculine settings. The domestic division of labor remains unequal, women continue to earn less and advance more slowly, and people still associate leadership more strongly with male than female traits. Moreover, consistent with traditional contingency theories of leadership (see House & Aditya, 1997), effective leadership in some situations no doubt requires an authoritative, directive approach. In addition, the degree of incongruence between female and leader roles may depend on national culture, including the extent to which it can be characterized as feminine versus masculine (see Hofstede, 1998; House, Hanges, Javidan, Dorfman, & Gupta, 2004). Thus, cultural differences may magnify or minimize resistance to female leadership.

Easing this dilemma of continuing role incongruity requires that women in leader roles behave very competently while reassuring others that they, to some degree, conform to expectations concerning appropriate female behavior. Given these constraints on women's behavior, transformational leadership may be especially advantageous for them, although it is an effective style for men as well (Yoder, 2001). The reason that this style may be a special asset for women is that it encompasses some behaviors that are consistent with the female gender role's demand for caring, supportive, and considerate behaviors. Especially communal are the individualized consideration behaviors, which are marked by developing and mentoring followers and attending to their individual needs. Other aspects of transformational leadership do not seem to be aligned with the gender role of either sex (e.g., demonstrating attributes that instill respect and pride by association with a leader). Few, if any, transformational behaviors have distinctively masculine connotations. This transformational repertoire, along with the contingent reward aspect of transactional leadership, may help resolve some of the incongruity between the demands of leadership roles and the female gender role and so allow women to excel as leaders.

The rise of women into elite leadership roles has gained momentum in very recent years. In this time of change, in many contexts female leaders have come to symbolize modernity and the potential for better leadership (Adler, 1999). Moreover, ensuring women equal access to leadership roles is unlikely to disadvantage organizations and, in fact, should benefit them—not only because the pool of managerial talent will be greatly increased but also because women lead in ways that are effective under contemporary conditions. Therefore, both the economic rationality of bureaucratic organizations in capitalist societies and the fundamental fairness that is highly valued in democratic societies should facilitate women's entry into the ranks of leaders in the future.

Discussion Questions

1. What things can employers do to reduce conflicts between family obligations and workplace responsibilities? How can male and female employees be encouraged to participate equally in family-friendly benefits?

2. What popular images are there in the media of male and female leaders? Are there more images of male than female leaders? Are women leaders found in different domains? Have these images changed over time?

3. How can the double-bind be addressed beyond encouraging women to lead with a mix of masculine and feminine qualities? Can people be educated about gender stereotypes and the challenges that women leaders face?

4. What are the advantages and disadvantages of men as leaders? Of women?

5. Imagine that you had to make the case for more women in positions of authority to organizational leaders and male coworkers. What arguments would you make?

Supplementary Readings

Eagly, A. H., & Carli, L. L. (2007). Women and the labyrinth of leadership. *Harvard Business Review, 85,* 62–71.

Hewlett, A., & Luce, C. B. (2005). Off-ramps and on-ramps: Keeping talented women on the road to success. *Harvard Business Review, 83,* 43–52.

Konrad, A., Kramer, V., & Erkut, S. (2008). Critical mass: The impact of three or more women on corporate boards. *Organizational Dynamics, 37,* 145–164.

Perrewé, P., & Nelson, D. (2004). Gender and career success: The facilitative role of political skill. *Organizational Dynamics, 33,* 366–378.

Case Studies

Bersoff, D. (1988). Brief for Amicus Curiae American Psychological Association in Support of Respondent. Price Waterhouse v. Ann B. Hopkins, Respondent. Available at http://www.apa.org/about/offices/ogc/amicus/hopkins.pdf.

Gentile, M. (1994). *Ann Livingston and Power Max Systems.* Harvard Business School Publishing.

References

Acker, J. (1990). Hierarchies, jobs, bodies: A theory of gendered organizations. *Gender & Society, 4,* 139–158.

Adams, S. M., Gupta, A., & Leeth, J. D. (2009). Are female executives over-represented in precarious leadership positions? *British Journal of Management, 20,* 1–12.

Adler, N. J. (1999). Global leaders: Women of influence. In G. N. Powell (Ed.), *Handbook of gender & work* (pp. 239–261). Thousand Oaks, CA: Sage.

Aguiar, M., & Hurst, E. (2007). Measuring trends in leisure: The allocation of time over five decades. *The Quarterly Journal of Economics, 122*, 969–1006.

Allen, T. D. (2006). Rewarding good citizens: The relationship between citizenship behavior, gender, and organizational rewards. *Journal of Applied Psychology, 36*, 120–143.

Almer, E. D., Hopper, J. R., & Kaplan, S. E. (1998). The effect of diversity-related attributes on hiring, advancement and voluntary turnover judgments. *Accounting Horizons, 12*, 1–17.

American Council on Education. (2007). *The American college president: 2007 edition.* Washington, DC: American Council on Education.

Antonakis, J., Avolio, B. J., & Sivasubramaniam, N. (2003). Context and leadership: An examination of the nine-factor full-range leadership theory using the Multifactor Leadership Questionnaire., *The Leadership Quarterly, 14*, 261–295.

Archer, J. (2004). Sex differences in aggression in real-world settings: A meta-analytic review. *Review of General Psychology, 8*, 291–322.

Arun, S. V., Arun, T. G., & Borooah, V. K. (2004). The effect of career breaks on the working lives of women. *Feminist Economics, 10*, 65–84.

Arvey, R., Rotundo, M., Johnson, W., Zhang, Z., & McGue, M. (2006). The determinants of leadership role occupancy: Genetic and personality factors. *The Leadership Quarterly, 17*, 1–20.

Arvey, R., Zhang, Z., Avolio, B., & Krueger, R. (2007). Developmental and genetic determinants of leadership role occupancy among women. *Journal of Applied Psychology, 92*, 693–706.

Atwater, L. E., Carey, J. A., & Waldman, D. A. (2001). Gender and discipline in the workplace: Wait until your father gets home. *Journal of Management, 27*, 537–561.

Aven, F. F., Jr., Parker, B., & McEvoy, G. M. (1993). Gender and attitudinal commitment to organizations: A meta-analysis. *Journal of Business Research, 26*, 63–73.

Avolio, B. J. (1999). *Full leadership development: Building the vital forces in organizations.* Thousands Oaks, CA: Sage.

Avolio, B. J., Bass, B. M., & Jung, D. I. (1999). Re-examining the components of transformational and transactional leadership using the Multifactor Leadership Questionnaire. *Journal of Occupational and Organizational Psychology, 72*, 441–462.

Bales, R. F. (1950). *Interaction process analysis: A method for the study of small groups.* Cambridge, MA: Addison-Wesley.

Barnett, R. C., & Hyde. J. S. (2001). Women, men, work, and family: An expansionist theory. *American Psychologist, 56*, 781–796.

Bass, B. M. (1985). *Leadership and performance beyond expectations.* New York: Free Press.

Bass, B. M. (1998). *Transformational leadership: Industry, military, and educational impact.* Mahwah, NJ: Lawrence Erlbaum.

Baxter, J., & Wright, E. O. (2000). The glass ceiling hypothesis: A comparative study of the United States, Sweden, and Australia. *Gender & Society, 14*, 275–294.

Bertrand, M., Goldin, C., & Katz, L. F. (2010). Dynamics of the gender gap for young professionals in the financial and corporate sectors. *American Economic Journal: Applied Economics, 2*, 228–255.

Bettencourt, B. A., & Miller, N. (1996). Gender differences in aggression as a function of provocation: A meta-analysis. *Psychological Bulletin, 119*, 422–447.

Bianchi, S. M., Robinson, J. P., & Milkie, M. A. (2006). *Changing rhythms of American family life.* New York: Russell Sage.

Biernat, M., & Kobrynowicz, D. (1997). Gender- and race-based standards of competence: Lower minimum standards but higher ability standards for devalued groups. *Journal of Personality and Social Psychology, 72*, 544–557.

Blau, F. D., & Kahn, L. M. (2006). The U.S. gender pay gap in the 1990s: Slow convergence. *Industrial and Labor Relations Review, 60*, 45–66.

Boehm, C. (1999). *Hierarchy in the forest.* London: Harvard University Press.

Boldry, J., Wood, W., & Kashy, D. A. (2001). Gender stereotypes and the evaluation of men and women in military training. *Journal of Social Issues, 57*, 689–705.

Bond, J., Thompson, T. C., Galinsky, E., & Prottas. D. (2002). *Highlights of the national study of the changing workforce.* New York: Families and Work Institute.

Boulis, A. (2004). The evolution of gender and motherhood in contemporary medicine. *Annals of the American Academy of Political and Social Science, 596*, 172–206.

Brett, J. M., & Stroh, L. K. (2003). Working 61 hours a week: Why do managers do it? *Journal of Applied Psychology, 88*, 67–78.

Browne, K. R. (1999). *Divided labours: An evolutionary view of women at work.* New Haven, CT: Yale University Press.

Budig, M. J., & England, P. (2001). The wage penalty for motherhood. *American Sociological Review, 66*, 204–225.

Burgess, D., & Borgida, E. (1999). Who women are, who women should be: Descriptive and prescriptive gender stereotyping in sex discrimination. *Psychology, Public Policy, and Law, 5*, 665–692.

Burgoon, M., Birk, T. S., & Hall, J. R. (1991). Compliance and satisfaction with physician-patient communication: An expectancy theory interpretation of gender differences. *Human Communication Research, 18*, 177–208.

Burns, J. M. (1978). *Leadership.* New York: Harper & Row.

Burt, R. S. (1998). The gender of social capital. *Rationality and Society, 10*, 5–46.

Buss, D. M. (1995). Evolutionary psychology: A new paradigm for psychological science. *Psychological Inquiry, 6*, 1–30.

Buss, D. M., & Kenrick, D. T. (1998). Evolutionary social psychology. In D. T. Gilbert, S. T. Fiske, & G. Lindzey (Eds.), *The handbook of social psychology* (4th ed., Vol. 2, pp. 982–1026). Boston: McGraw-Hill.

Butler, D., & Geis, F. L. (1990). Nonverbal affect responses to male and female leaders: Implications for leadership evaluations. *Journal of Personality and Social Psychology, 58*, 48–59.

Buttner, E. H., & McEnally, M. (1996). The interactive effect of influence tactic, applicant gender, and type of job on hiring recommendations. *Sex Roles, 34*, 581–591.

Byrnes, J. P., Miller, D. C., & Schafer, W. D. (1999). Gender differences in risk taking: A meta-analysis. *Psychological Bulletin, 125*, 367–383.

Campbell, D. T. (1965). Ethnocentric and other altruistic motives. In D. Levine (Ed.), *Nebraska symposium on motivation* (Vol. 13, pp. 283–311). Lincoln: University of Nebraska Press.

Carli, L. L. (1990). Gender, language, and influence. *Journal of Personality and Social Psychology, 59*, 941–951.

Carli, L. L. (1999). Gender, interpersonal power, and social influence. *Journal of Social Issues, 55,* 81–99.

Carli, L. L. (2001a). Assertiveness. In J. Worell (Ed.), *Encyclopedia of women and gender: Sex similarities and differences and the impact of society on gender* (pp. 157–168). San Diego, CA: Academic Press.

Carli, L. L. (2001b). Gender and social influence. *Journal of Social Issues, 57,* 725–741.

Carli, L. L. (2006, July). *Gender and social influence: Women confront the double bind.* Paper presented at the 26th International Conference of Applied Psychology, Athens, Greece.

Carli, L. L., LaFleur, S. J., & Loeber, C. C. (1995). Nonverbal behavior, gender, and influence. *Journal of Personality and Social Psychology, 68,* 1030–1041.

Carroll, J. (2006, September 1). *Americans prefer male boss to a female boss.* Retrieved from http://www.gallup.com/poll/24346/americans-prefer-male-boss-female-boss.aspx.

Carter, D. A., Simkins, B. J., & Simpson, W. G. (2003). Corporate governance, board diversity, and firm value. *Financial Review, 38,* 33–53.

Cassirer, N., & Reskin, B. F. (2000). High hopes: Organizational positions, employment experiences, and women's and men's promotion aspirations. *Work and Occupations, 27,* 438–463.

Catalyst. (2004). *Women and men in U.S. corporate leadership: Same workplace, different realities?* Retrieved from http://catalyst.org/file/74/women%20and%20men%20in%20u.s.%20corporate%20leadership%20same%20workplace,%20different%20realities.pdf.

Catalyst. (2010a). *Pyramids: Women CEOs of the Fortune 1000.* Retrieved from http://catalyst.org/publication/322/women-ceos-of-the-fortune-1000.

Catalyst. (2010b). *Quick takes: Australia, Canada, South Africa and the United States.* Retrieved from http://catalyst.org/publication/239/australia-canada-south-africa-united-states.

Catalyst. (2010c). *Quick takes: Women in U.S. management.* Retrieved from http://catalyst.org/publication/206/women-in-us-management.

CBS News/New York Times. (2006, February 5). *A woman for president.* Retrieved from http://www.cbsnews.com/htdocs/pdf/020306woman.pdf#search=%. 22a%20woman%20for%20president%20CBS%20News%2FNew%20York %20Times%20Poll%22.

Center for American Women and Politics. (2010). *Women in elective office 2010.* Retrieved from http://www.cawp.rutgers.edu/fast_facts/levels_of_office/documents/elective.pdf.

Cialdini, R. B., & Trost, M. R. (1998). Social influence: Social norms, conformity and compliance. In D. T. Gilbert, S. T. Fiske, & G. Lindzey (Eds.), *The handbook of social psychology* (4th ed., Vol. 2, pp. 151–192). Boston: McGraw-Hill.

Copeland, C. L., Driskell, J. E., & Salas, E. (1995). Gender and reactions to dominance. *Journal of Social Behavior and Personality, 10,* 53–68.

Correll, S. J., Benard, S., & Paik, I. (2007). Getting a job: Is there a motherhood penalty? *American Journal of Sociology, 112,* 1297–1338.

Corrigall, E. A., & Konrad, A. M., (2006). The relationship of job attribute preferences to employment, hours of paid work, and family responsibilities: An analysis comparing women and men. *Sex Roles, 54,* 95–111.

Costa, P. T., Jr., Terracciano, A., & McCrae, R. R. (2001). Gender differences in personality traits across cultures: Robust and surprising findings. *Journal of Personality and Social Psychology, 81,* 322–331.

Council on Foundations. (2009). *2008 Grantmakers salary and benefits report: Executive summary.* Washington, DC: Council on Foundations. Retrieved from http://www.cof.org/files/Bamboo/programsandservices/research/documents/08 salarybenefitsexecsum.pdf.

Davies, P. G., Spencer, S. J., & Steele, C. M. (2005). Clearing the air: Identity safety moderates the effects of stereotype threat on women's leadership aspirations. *Journal of Personality and Social Psychology, 88,* 276–287.

Davison, H. K., & Burke, M. J. (2000). Sex discrimination in simulated employment contexts: A meta-analytic investigation. *Journal of Vocational Behavior, 56,* 225–248.

De Pater, I., Van Vianen, A., Humphrey, R., Sleeth, R., Hartman, N., & Fischer, A. (2009). Individual task choice and the division of challenging tasks between men and women. *Group & Organization Management, 34,* 563–589.

Desvaux, G., Devillard-Hoellinger, S., & Baumgarten, P. (2007). *Women matter: Gender diversity, a corporate performance driver.* Paris: McKinsey & Company.

de Zárate, R. O. (2010). *Women world leaders: 1945–2007.* Retrieved from http://www.terra.es/persona12/monolith/00women.htm.

Diekman, A. B., & Eagly, A. H. (2000). Stereotypes as dynamic constructs: Women and men of the past, present, and future. *Personality and Social Psychology Bulletin, 26,* 1171–1188.

Dreher, G. F., & Cox, T. H., Jr. (1996). Race, gender, and opportunity: A study of compensation attainment and establishment of mentoring relationships. *Journal of Applied Psychology, 81,* 297–308.

Eagly, A. H. (1987). *Sex differences in social behavior: A social-role interpretation.* Hillsdale, NJ: Lawrence Erlbaum.

Eagly, A. H., & Carli, L. L. (2007). *Through the labyrinth: The truth about how women become leaders.* Cambridge, MA: Harvard Business School Press.

Eagly, A. H., & Chin, J. L. (2010). Diversity and leadership in a changing world. *American Psychologist, 65,* 216–224.

Eagly, A. H., & Diekman, A. B. (2005). What is the problem? Prejudice as an attitude-in-context. In J. F. Dovidio, P. Glick, & L. Rudman (Eds.). *On the nature of prejudice: Fifty years after Allport* (pp. 19–35). Malden, MA: Blackwell.

Eagly, A. H., Johannesen-Schmidt, M. C., & van Engen, M. (2003). Transformational, transactional, and laissez-faire leadership styles: A meta-analysis comparing women and men. *Psychological Bulletin, 129,* 569–591.

Eagly, A. H., & Johnson, B. T. (1990). Gender and leadership style: A meta-analysis. *Psychological Bulletin, 108,* 233–256.

Eagly, A. H., & Karau, S. J. (2002). Role congruity theory of prejudice toward female leaders. *Psychological Review, 109,* 573–598.

Eagly, A. H., Karau, S. J., & Makhijani, M. G. (1995). Gender and the effectiveness of leaders: A meta-analysis. *Psychological Bulletin, 117,* 125–145.

Eagly, A. H., Karau, S. J., Miner, J. B., & Johnson, B. T. (1994). Gender and motivation to manage in hierarchic organizations: A meta-analysis. *The Leadership Quarterly, 5,* 135–159.

Eagly, A. H., Makhijani, M. G., & Klonsky, B. G. (1992). Gender and the evaluation of leaders: A meta-analysis. *Psychological Bulletin, 111,* 3–22.

Eagly, A.H., & Steffen, V. J. (1986). Gender and aggressive behavior: A meta-analytic review of the social psychological literature. *Psychological Bulletin, 100,* 309–330.

Eagly, A. H., Wood, W., & Diekman, A. B. (2000). Social role theory of sex differences and similarities: A current appraisal. In T. Eckes & H. M. Trautner (Eds.), *The developmental social psychology of gender* (pp. 123–174). Mahwah, NJ: Lawrence Erlbaum.

Elliott, J. R., & Smith, R. A. (2004). Race, gender, and workplace power. *American Sociological Review, 69,* 365–386.

Ellyson, S. L., Dovidio, J. F., & Brown, C. E. (1992). The look of power: Gender differences in visual dominance behavior. In C. L. Ridgeway (Ed.), *Gender, interaction, and inequality* (pp. 50–80). New York: Springer-Verlag.

Erhardt, M. L., Werbel, J. D., & Shrader, C. B. (2003). Board of director diversity and firm financial performance. *Corporate Governance, 11,* 102–111.

Families and Work Institute. (2005). *Generation and gender in the workplace.* New York: Families and Work Institute. Retrieved from http://familiesandwork.org/site/research/reports/genandgender.pdf.

Feingold, A. (1994). Gender differences in personality: A meta-analysis. *Psychological Bulletin, 116,* 429–456.

Fiske, S. T., & Stevens, L. E. (1993). What's so special about sex? Gender stereotyping and discrimination. In S. Oskamp & M. Costanzo (Eds.), *Gender issues in contemporary society: Claremont symposium on applied social psychology* (Vol. 6, pp. 173–196). Newbury Park, CA: Sage.

Foels, R., Driskell, J. E., Mullen, B., & Salas, E. (2000). The effects of democratic leadership on group member satisfaction: An integration. *Small Group Research, 31,* 676–701.

Fondas, N. (1997). Feminization unveiled: Management qualities in contemporary writings. *Academy of Management Review, 22,* 257–282.

Forret, M., & Dougherty, T. (2004). Networking behaviors and career outcomes: Differences for men and women? *Journal of Organizational Behavior, 25,* 419–437.

Fortune. (2009a). *Fortune 500 CEOs: Women on the rise.* Retrieved from the Fortune Magazine website at http://postcards.blogs.fortune.cnn.com/2009/04/20/fortune-500-ceos-women-on-the-rise/.

Fortune. (2009b). *Global 500: Women CEOs.* Retrieved from the Fortune Magazine website at http://money.cnn.com/magazines/fortune/globa1500/2009/womenceos/.

Foschi, M. (2000). Double standards for competence. *Annual Review of Sociology, 26,* 21–42.

Foschi, M., Lai, L., & Sigerson, K. (1994). Gender and double standards in the assessment of job applicants. *Social Psychology Quarterly, 57,* 326–339.

Franke, G. R., Crown, D. F., & Spake, D. F. (1997). Gender differences in ethical perceptions of business practices: A social role theory perspective. *Journal of Applied Psychology, 82,* 920–934.

Galinsky, E., Aumann, K., & Bond, J. T. (2008). *Times are changing: Gender and generation at work and at home.* New York: Families and Work Institute. Retrieved from http://familiesandwork.org/site/research/reports/Times_Are_Changing.pdf.

Galinsky, E., Salmond, K., Bond, J. T., Kropf, M. B., Moore, M., & Harrington, B. (2003). *Leaders in a global economy: A study of executive women and men.* New York: Families and Work Institute.

Garvin, D. A. (1993). Building a learning organization. *Harvard Business Review, 71*(4), 78–91.

Gastil, J. (1994). A meta-analytic review of the productivity and satisfaction of democratic and autocratic leadership. *Small Group Research, 25,* 384–410.

Geller, P. A., & Hobfoll, S. E. (1993). Gender differences in preference to offer social support to assertive men and women. *Sex Roles, 28,* 419–432.

Giacalone, R. A., & Riordan, C. A. (1990). Effect of self-presentation on perceptions and recognition in an organization. *Journal of Psychology, 124,* 25–38.

Glick, P., Diebold, J., Bailey-Werner, B., & Zhu, L. (1997). The two faces of Adam: Ambivalent sexism and polarized attitudes toward women. *Personality and Social Psychology Bulletin, 23,* 1323–1334.

Goldberg, S. (1993). *Why men rule: A theory of male dominance.* Chicago: Open Court.

Greenhaus, J. H., & Powell, G. N. (2006). When work and family are allies: A theory of work-family enrichment. *Academy of Management Review, 31,* 72–92.

Griffeth, R. W., Hom, P. W., & Gaertner, S. (2000). A meta-analysis of antecedents and correlates of employee turnover: Update, moderator tests, and research implications for the next millennium. *Journal of Management, 26,* 463–488.

Hackman, M. Z., Furniss, A. H., Hills, M. J., & Paterson, T. J. (1992). Perceptions of gender-role characteristics and transformational and transactional leadership behaviours. *Perceptual and Motor Skills, 75,* 311–319.

Halpern, D. F. (2001). Sex difference research: Cognitive abilities. In J. Worrell (Ed.), *Encyclopedia of women and gender: Sex similarities and differences and the impact of society on gender* (Vol. 2, pp. 963–971). San Diego: Academic Press.

Halpern, D. F., & LaMay, M. L. (2000). The smarter sex: A critical review of sex differences in intelligence. *Educational Psychology Review, 12,* 229–246.

Haslam, S. A., & Ryan, M. K. (2008). The road to the glass cliff: Differences in the perceived suitability of men and women for leadership positions in succeeding and failing organizations. *The Leadership Quarterly, 19,* 530–546.

Heilman, M. E., Block, C. J., & Martell, R. F. (1995). Sex stereotypes: Do they influence perceptions of managers? *Journal of Social Behavior and Personality, 10* [No. 6: Special issue: Gender in the workplace], 237–252.

Heilman, M. E., & Chen, J. J. (2005). Same behavior, different consequences: Reactions to men's and women's altruistic citizenship behavior. *Journal of Applied Psychology, 90,* 431–441.

Heilman, M. E., & Okimoto, T. G. (2008). Motherhood: A potential source of bias in employment decisions. *Journal of Applied Psychology, 93,* 189–198.

Heilman, M. E., Wallen, A. S., Fuchs, D., & Tamkins, M. M. (2004). Penalties for success: Reactions to women who succeed in male gender-typed tasks. *Journal of Applied Psychology, 89,* 416–427.

Helfat, C. E., Harris, D., & Wolfson, J. P. (2006). The pipeline to the top: Women and men in the top executive ranks of U.S. corporations. *Academy of Management Perspectives, 20,* 42–64.

Hershcovis, M. S., Turner, N., Barling, J., Arnold, K. A., Dupré, K. E., Inness, M., et al. (2007). Predicting workplace aggression: A meta-analysis. *Journal of Applied Psychology, 92,* 228–238.

Hofstede, G. (1998). A case for comparing apples with oranges: International differences in value. *International Journal of Comparative Sociology, 39,* 16–31.

Hom, P. W., Roberson, L., & Ellis, A. D. (2008). Challenging conventional wisdom about who quits: Revelations from corporate America. *Journal of Applied Psychology, 93,* 1–34.

House, R. J., & Aditya, R. N. (1997). The social scientific study of leadership: Quo vadis? *Journal of Management, 23,* 409–473.

House, R. J., Hanges, P. J., Javidan, M., Dorfman, P. W., & Gupta, V. (Eds.). (2004). *Culture, leadership, and organizations: The GLOBE study of 62 societies.* Thousand Oaks, CA: Sage.

Huffman, M. L., & Torres, L. (2002). It's not only "who you know" that matters: Gender, personal contacts, and job lead quality. *Gender & Society, 16,* 793–813.

Inglehart, R., & Norris, P. (2003). *Rising tide: Gender equality and cultural change around the world.* New York: Cambridge University Press.

Jacobs, J. A., & Gerson, G. (2004). *The time divide: Work, family, and gender inequality.* Cambridge, MA: Harvard University Press.

Johnson, S., Murphy, S., Zewdie, S., & Reichard, R. (2008). The strong, sensitive type: Effects of gender stereotypes and leadership prototypes on the evaluation of male and female leaders. *Organizational Behavior and Human Decision Processes, 106,* 39–60.

Judge, T. A., Bono, J. E., Ilies, R., & Gerhardt, M. W. (2002). Personality and leadership: A qualitative and quantitative review. *Journal of Applied Psychology, 87,* 765–780.

Judge, T. A., Cable, D. M., Boudreau, J. W., & Bretz, R. D., Jr. (1995). An empirical investigation of the predictors of executive career success. *Personnel Psychology, 48,* 485–519.

Judge, T. A., Colbert, A. E., & Ilies, R. (2004). Intelligence and leadership: A quantitative review and test of theoretical propositions. *Journal of Applied Psychology, 89,* 542–552.

Judge, T. A., & Piccolo, R. F. (2004). Transformational and transactional leadership: A meta-analytic test of their relative validity. *Journal of Applied Psychology, 89,* 901–910.

Kanter, R. M. (1977). *Men and women of the corporation.* New York: Basic Books.

Kanter, R. M. (1997). *On the frontiers of management.* Boston: Harvard Business School Press.

Klumb, P. L., & Lampert, T. (2004). Women, work, and well-being 1950–2000: A review and methodological critique. *Social Science & Medicine, 58,* 1007–1024.

Koenig, A. M., Eagly, A. H., Mitchell, A. A., & Ristikari, T. (2010). *Are leader stereotypes masculine? A meta-analysis of three research paradigms.* Unpublished manuscript, University of San Diego.

Konrad, A. M., Ritchie, J. E., Jr., Lieb, P., & Corrigall, E. (2000). Sex differences and similarities in job attribute preferences: A meta-analysis. *Psychological Bulletin, 126,* 593–641.

Krishnan, H. A., & Park, D. (2005). A few good women—on top management teams. *Journal of Business Research, 58,* 1712–1720.

Kunze, A. (2008). Gender wage gap studies: Consistency and decomposition. *Empirical Economics, 35,* 63–76.

Lewin, K., & Lippitt, R. (1938). An experimental approach to the study of autocracy and democracy: A preliminary note. *Sociometry, 1,* 292–300.

Lipman-Blumen, J. (2000). *Connective leadership: Managing in a changing world.* New York: Oxford University Press.

Lundberg, S., & Rose, E. (2000). Parenthood and the earnings of married men and women. *Labour Economics, 7,* 689–710.

Lyness, K. S., & Judiesch, M. K. (2001). Are female managers quitters? The relationships of gender, promotions, and family leaves of absence to voluntary turnover. *Journal of Applied Psychology, 86,* 1167–1178.

Lyness, K. S., & Thompson, D. E. (1997). Above the glass ceiling? A comparison of matched samples of female and male executives. *Journal of Applied Psychology, 82,* 359–375.

Lyness, K. S., & Thompson, D. E. (2000). Climbing the corporate ladder: Do female and male executives follow the same route? *Journal of Applied Psychology, 85,* 86–101.

Madon, S., Guyll, M., Aboufadel, K., Montiel, E., Smith, A., Palumbo, et al. (2001). Ethnic and national stereotypes: The Princeton trilogy revisited and revised. *Personality and Social Psychology Bulletin, 27,* 996–1010.

Martin, P. Y. (2003). "Said and done" versus "saying and doing": Gender practices, practicing gender at work. *Gender & Society, 17,* 342–366.

Matschiner, M., & Murnen, S. K. (1999). Hyperfemininity and influence. *Psychology of Women Quarterly, 23,* 631–642.

Maume, D. J., Jr. (1999). Occupational segregation and the career mobility of White men and women. *Social Forces, 77,* 1433–1459.

McPherson, M., Smith-Lovin, L., & Cook, J. M. (2001). Birds of a feather: Homophily in social networks. *Annual Review of Sociology, 27,* 415–444.

Milkie, M. A., Bianchi, S. M., Mattingly, M. J., & Robinson, J. P. (2002). Gendered division of childrearing: Ideals, realities, and the relationship to parental well-being. *Sex Roles, 47,* 21–38.

Mohr, G., & Wolfram, H. (2008). Leadership and effectiveness in the context of gender: The role of leaders' verbal behaviour. *British Journal of Management, 19,* 4–16.

Nahavandi, A. (2008). *The art and science of leadership.* Upper Saddle River, NJ: Prentice Hall.

Newport, F. (2001, February 21). *Americans see women as emotional and affectionate, men as more aggressive.* Gallup Poll News Service. Retrieved from http://www.gallup.com/poll/1978/Americans-See-Women-Emotional-Affectionate-Men-More-Aggressive.aspx.

Ng, T. W. H., Eby, L. T., Sorensen, K. L., & Feldman, D. C. (2005). Predictors of objective and subjective career success: A meta-analysis. *Personnel Psychology, 58,* 367–408.

Niemann, Y. F., Jennings, L., Rozelle, R. M., Baxter, J. C., & Sullivan, E. (1994). Use of free responses and cluster analysis to determine stereotypes of eight groups. *Personality and Social Psychology Bulletin, 20,* 379–390.

Noonan, M. C., & Corcoran, M. E. (2004). The mommy track and partnership: Temporary delay or dead end? *Annals of the American Academy of Political and Social Science, 596,* 130–150.

Ohlott, P. J., Ruderman, M. N., & McCauley, C. D. (1994). Gender differences in managers' developmental job experiences. *Academy of Management Journal, 37,* 46–67.

Petersen, T., & Saporta, I. (2004). The opportunity structure for discrimination. *American Journal of Sociology, 109,* 852–901.

Powell, G. N., & Butterfield, D. A. (1979). The "good manager": Masculine or androgynous? *Academy of Management Journal, 22,* 395–403.

Propp, K. M. (1995). An experimental examination of biological sex as a status cue in decision-making groups and its influence on information use. *Small Group Research, 26,* 451–474.

Reid, S. A., Palomares, N. A., Anderson, G. L., & Bondad-Brown, B. (2009). Gender language and social influence: A test of expectation states, role congruity, and self-categorization theories. *Human Communication Research, 35,* 465–490.

Reskin, B. F., & Ross, C. E. (1995). Jobs, authority, and earnings among managers: The continuing significance of sex. In J. A. Jacobs (Ed.), *Gender inequality at work* (pp. 127–151). Thousand Oaks, CA: Sage.

Riach, P. A., & Rich, J. (2002). Field experiments of discrimination in the market place. *Economic Journal, 112,* F480–F518.

Rose, S. J., & Hartmann, H. I. (2004). *Still a man's labor market: The long-term earnings gap.* Washington, DC: Institute for Women's Policy Research. Retrieved from http://www.iwpr.org/pdf/C355.pdf.

Rudman, L. A. (1998). Self-promotion as a risk factor for women: The costs and benefits of counterstereotypical impression management. *Journal of Personality and Social Psychology, 74,* 629–645.

Ryan, M. K., & Haslam, S. A. (2005). The glass cliff: Evidence that women are over-represented in precarious leadership positions. *British Journal of Management, 16,* 81–90.

Ryan, M. K., & Haslam, S. A. (2007). The glass cliff: Exploring the dynamics surrounding women's appointment to precarious leadership positions. *Academy of Management Review, 32,* 549–572.

Saad, L. (2007, August 31). *Women slightly more likely to prefer working to homemaking.* Gallup Poll News Service. Retrieved from http://www.gallup.com/poll/28567/Women-Slightly-More-Likely-Prefer-Working-Homemaking.aspx.

Salzman, P. C. (1999). Is inequality universal? *Current Anthropology, 40,* 31–44.

Sanchez-Hucles, J. V., & Davis, D. D. (2010). Women and women of color in leadership: Complexity, identity, and intersectionality. *American Psychologist, 65,* 171–181.

Schein, V. E. (1973). The relationship between sex role stereotypes and requisite management characteristics. *Journal of Applied Psychology, 57,* 95–100.

Schmitt, D. P., Realo, A., Voracek, M., & Allik, J. (2008). Why can't a man be more like a woman? Sex differences in Big Five personality traits across 55 cultures. *Journal of Personality and Social Psychology, 94,* 168–182.

Shinar, E. H. (1975). Sexual stereotypes of occupations. *Journal of Vocational Behavior, 7,* 99–111.

Sinclair, L., & Kunda, Z. (2000). Motivated stereotyping of women: She's fine if she praised me but incompetent if she criticized me. *Personality and Social Psychology Bulletin, 26,* 1329–1342.

Smith, R. A. (2002). Race, gender, and authority in the workplace: Theory and research. *Annual Review of Sociology, 28,* 509–542.

Su, R., Rounds, J., & Armstrong, P. I. (2009). Men and things, women and people: A meta-analysis of sex differences in interests. *Psychological Bulletin, 135,* 859–884.

Tepper, B. J., Brown, S. J., & Hunt, M. D. (1993). Strength of subordinates' upward influence tactics and gender congruency effects. *Journal of Applied Social Psychology, 23,* 1903–1919.

Thomas-Hunt, M. C., & Phillips, K. W. (2004). When what you know is not enough: Expertise and gender dynamics in task groups. *Personality and Social Psychology Bulletin, 30,* 1585–1598.

Timberlake, S. (2005). Social capital and gender in the workplace. *Journal of Management Development, 24,* 34–44.

Towers, I., Duxbury, L., Higgins, C., & Thomas, J. (2006). Time thieves and space invaders: Technology, work and the organization. *Journal of Organizational Change Management, 19,* 593–618.

Trivers, R. L. (1972). Parental investment and sexual selection. In B. Campbell (Ed.), *Sexual selection and the descent of man: 1871–1971* (pp. 136–179). Chicago: Aldine.

Twenge, J. M. (1997). Changes in masculine and feminine traits over time: A meta-analysis. *Sex Roles, 36,* 305–325.

Twenge, J. M. (2001). Changes in women's assertiveness in response to status and roles: A cross-temporal meta-analysis, 1931–1993. *Journal of Personality and Social Psychology, 81,* 133–145.

Uhlmann, E. L., & Cohen, G. L. (2005). Constructed criteria: Redefining merit to justify discrimination. *Psychological Science, 16,* 474–480.

UNIFEM. (2008). *Progress of the world's women 2008–2009: Who answers to women? Gender and accountability.* Retrieved from http://www.unifem.org/progress/2008/media/POWW08_Report_Full_Text.pdf.

United Nations Development Programme. (2009). *Human development report 2009.* Retrieved from http://hdr.undp.org/en/media/HDR_2009_EN_Complete.pdf.

U.S. Bureau of Labor Statistics. (1982). *Labor force statistics derived from the current population survey: A databook* (Vol. 1: Bulletin 2096). Washington, DC: U.S. Department of Labor.

U.S. Bureau of Labor Statistics. (2010a). *News: American time-use survey—2009 results.* Retrieved from http://www.bls.gov/news.release/pdf/atus.pdf.

U.S. Bureau of Labor Statistics. (2010b). *Women in the labor force: A databook (2010 edition).* Retrieved from http://www.bls.gov/cps/wlf-databook2010.htm.

U.S. Bureau of Labor Statistics. (2011). *Labor force statistics from the current population survey.* Retrieved from http://www.bls.gov/cps/tables.htm.

U.S. National Center for Education Statistics. (2010). *Digest of education statistics, 2008.* Retrieved from http://nces.ed.gov/programs/d10/tables/dt10_279.asp.

U.S. Office of Personnel Management. (1997). *The fact book, 1997 edition: Federal civilian workforce statistics.* Retrieved from http://www.opm.gov/feddata/factbook/97factbk.pdf.

U.S. Office of Personnel Management. (2007). *Senior executive service: Facts and figures.* Retrieved from http://www.opm.gov/ses/facts_and_figures/demographics.asp.

van Engen, M. L., & Willemsen, T. M. (2004). Sex and leadership styles: A meta-analysis of research published in the 1990s. *Psychological Reports, 94,* 3–18.

Van Vugt, M. (2006). Evolutionary origins of leadership and followership. *Personality and Social Psychology Review, 10,* 354–371.

Van Vugt, M., Hogan, R., & Kaiser, R. B. (2008). Leadership, followership, and evolution: Some lessons from the past. *American Psychologist, 63,* 182–196.

Vinkenburg, C. J., van Engen, M. L., Eagly, A. H., & Johannesen-Schmidt, M. C. (2011). An exploration of stereotypical beliefs about leadership styles: Is transformational leadership a route to women's promotion? *The Leadership Quarterly.*

Walters, A. E., Stuhlmacher, A. F., & Meyer, L. L.. (1998). Gender and negotiator competitiveness: A meta-analysis. *Organizational Behavior and Human Decision Processes, 76*, 1–29.

Whyte, M. K. (1978). *The status of women in preindustrial societies.* Princeton, NJ: Princeton University Press.

Williams, C. L. (1995). *Still a man's world: Men who do "women's" work.* Berkeley: University of California Press.

Williams, J. (2000). *Unbending gender: Why family and work conflict and what to do about it.* New York: Oxford University Press.

Williams, J. E., & Best, D. L. (1990). *Measuring sex stereotypes: A multination study.* Newbury Park, CA: Sage.

Wolff, H., & Moser, K. (2009). Effects of networking on career success: A longitudinal study. *Journal of Applied Psychology, 94*, 196–206.

Wood, W., & Eagly, A. H. (2002). A cross-cultural analysis of the behavior of women and men: Implications for the origins of sex differences. *Psychological Bulletin, 128*, 699–727.

Wootton, B. H. (1997). Gender differences in occupational employment. *Monthly Labor Review, 120*, 14–24.

Wosinska, W., Dabul, A. J., Whetstone-Dion, R., & Cialdini, R. B. (1996). Self-presentational responses to success in the organization: The costs and benefits of modesty. *Basic and Applied Social Psychology, 18*, 229–242.

Wrangham, R. W., Jones, J. H., Laden, G., Pilbeam, D., & Conklin-Brittain, N. (1999). The raw and the stolen: Cooking and the ecology of human origins. *Current Anthropology, 40*, 567–577.

Wright, E. O., Baxter, J., & Birkelund, G. E. (1995). The gender gap in workplace authority: A cross-national study. *American Sociological Review, 60*, 407–435.

Yoder, J. D. (2001). Making leadership work more effectively for women. *Journal of Social Issues, 57*, 815–828.

Yoder, J. D., & Schleicher, T. L. (1996). Undergraduates regard deviation from occupational gender stereotypes as costly for women. *Sex Roles, 34*, 171–188.

14

Leadership and Identity

Daan van Knippenberg

Erasmus University Rotterdam

Leadership is a core and integral aspect of human groups, organizations, and societies. Indeed, it is hard to think of social groupings without some sort of leadership structure, even if only informal. Leadership also has the potential to be a major influence on the functioning and performance of groups, organizations, and societies. Not surprisingly, then, leadership has been high on the agenda of behavioral research in management, psychology, and the social sciences for more than a century (cf. chapter 6). What is surprising, however, is that leadership research for a long time paid little attention to the fact that leaders, too, are members of the groups (teams, organizations, nations) they lead and that leadership is a process that takes place in the context of a group membership shared by leader and followers (cf. D. van Knippenberg, in press). What this means is that the effects of leadership are influenced by processes related to the psychology of group membership. This is the issue that is highlighted in this chapter.

Central to the psychology of group membership is *identity*—the perception of self and others in terms of a shared group membership. Identity plays an important role in the leadership process (or the self-concept; self and identity are constructs that can be used interchangeably; Leary & Tangney, 2003). Follower identity both influences responses to leadership and is influenced by leadership (Hogg, 2001; Hogg & van Knippenberg, 2003; Lord & Brown, 2004; Lord, Brown, & Freiberg, 1999; Shamir,

AUTHOR'S NOTE: Please address correspondence concerning this chapter to Daan van Knippenberg, Rotterdam School of Management, Erasmus University Rotterdam, PO Box 1738, 3000 DR Rotterdam, Netherlands. e-mail: dvanknippenberg@rsm.nl.

House, & Arthur, 1993; D. van Knippenberg & Hogg, 2003a, 2003b; D. van Knippenberg, van Knippenberg, De Cremer, & Hogg, 2004). Although this analysis puts a premium on understanding the role of group identity—the shared social identity of leaders and followers—it can easily be extended to cover two other core aspects of identity and self-conception that are not necessarily specifically tied to a shared group membership (but can be): self-evaluations and conceptions of identity change and continuity over time. These issues, too, are addressed in the current chapter. The same identity principles can also be extended to include the influence of leader identity on leadership—not only in terms of the shared group membership but also in terms of the role identity as a leader (i.e., in group identity terms, the membership in an abstracted leader category. This issue, too, is addressed, albeit more briefly, given the more limited empirical evidence as well as some overlap with chapter 4 in this respect.

Although leadership research has been slow to connect with the role of self and identity, during the past 15 years or so, this has changed dramatically. The aim of the current chapter is to capture this development and to provide a state of the science overview of research in leadership, self, and identity. To do so, I first address what is arguably the core of research in leadership, self, and identity: the notion of social (group) identity and the social identity perspective on leadership. This core aspect captures both the ways in which follower social identity informs responses to leadership and leadership's influence on follower social identity. The discussion then moves on to the roles of self-evaluation, identity change and continuity, and leader identity.

Social Identity and Leadership

If we think about ourselves, one of the things that come to mind in capturing who we are is our belongingness to social groups. Whether it is our nationality, ethnicity, organizational membership, profession, or yet other group memberships, we tend to take our membership in social groups (i.e., teams, organizations, nations, demographic categories) as describing, to a greater or lesser extent, important aspects of ourselves. This self-defining quality of social group memberships is captured by theories of social identity, self-categorization, and self-construal (Hogg, 2003; Sedikides & Brewer, 2001; Tajfel & Turner, 1986; Turner, Hogg, Oakes, Reicher, & Wetherell, 1987), more recently increasingly grouped under the heading social identity approach (Haslam, 2004). The social identity approach describes how individuals see themselves not only in individual terms (i.e., characteristics that identify the self as a unique individual, the individual self or identity, "I") but also in terms of group or organizational memberships (i.e., characteristics that identify the self as a group member, the collective self or social identity, "we").

The social identity approach was developed as a perspective on intergroup relations to explain why people tend to be biased in favor of their membership groups ("in-group"; Brewer & Brown, 1998; Tajfel & Turner, 1986; D. van Knippenberg, 2003). However, the essence of the approach—social self-definition—captures what is perhaps the core aspect of the psychology of group membership and has far broader implications for our understanding of social attitudes and behavior than just intergroup relations, as more recent developments in social identity research show (for reviews, see e.g., Haslam, 2004; Hogg, 2003). Self-definition as a group member (social identity) exerts an important influence on perceptions, attitudes, and behavior. Because it implies seeing the self through the lens of group membership, social identity entails taking the group's best interest to heart—indeed, experiencing the group interest as the self-interest (i.e., the interest of an inclusive "we"; D. van Knippenberg, 2000a)—and experiencing the group identity as both self-describing and self-guiding (Turner et al., 1987). These two processes are of particular importance to the social identity analysis of leadership. In a nutshell, follower social identity leads followers to favor leaders who are perceived to be *group prototypical* (i.e., embodying the group identity and, thus, the social reality shared by the group) and to be serving the group's best interest. Moreover, effective leadership may derive from leaders' ability to build follower identification with the collective and to change followers' understanding of this collective identity.

Group Prototypicality and Group-Orientedness

The social identity approach describes how social groups are mentally represented as group prototypes—fuzzy sets of characteristics that capture what defines the group, what group members have in common, and what distinguishes the group from other groups (Hogg, 2001; Turner et al., 1987; cf. Rosch, 1978). Such group prototypes are subjective representations and capture not so much the group average as an idealized image of the group—what is judged to be truly group defining. Group prototypes capture the socially shared reality of the group. They describe what the group values, believes, and considers important and what are seen as appropriate and desirable behaviors and courses of action. In effect, group prototypes capture what is group-normative. Thus, the group prototype is a source of influence on those who identify with the group (i.e., self-define in terms of the group membership; Ashforth & Mael, 1989; Tajfel & Turner, 1986; D. van Knippenberg & Sleebos, 2006), as identification leads one to ascribe group-defining characteristics to self and motivates the individual to conform to group norms (Abrams & Hogg, 1990; Turner et al., 1987; D. van Knippenberg, 2000b).

Core to the social identity analysis of leadership is the fact that group members, and therefore also group leaders, may differ in the extent to which they represent or embody the group prototype—are group prototypical. To the extent that a leader of a collective (i.e., group, team, organization, nation) is perceived to be group prototypical (i.e., to embody the collective identity), the leader derives influence from the (implicit) perception that he or she represents what is group-normative (Hogg, 2001; Hogg & van Knippenberg, 2003; D. van Knippenberg & Hogg, 2003a; cf. D. van Knippenberg, Lossie, & Wilke, 1994). Moreover, group prototypicality also induces trust in the leader's intentions. Because they embody the group identity, group prototypical leaders are trusted to pursue the group's best interests (B. van Knippenberg & van Knippenberg, 2005; D. van Knippenberg & Hogg, 2003a). Because identification results in the internalization of group interests, serving the group is a quality that individuals who identify highly with their group prioritize in their leaders (Haslam & Platow, 2001; Platow & van Knippenberg, 2001). Accordingly, the trust in leaders' group-orientedness elicited by leader group prototypicality feeds into leadership effectiveness (Giessner & van Knippenberg, 2008; Giessner, van Knippenberg, & Sleebos, 2009).

Evidence for the role of leader group prototypicality is found in lab experiments (e.g., Hains, Hogg, & Duck, 1997) as well as field research (e.g., B. van Knippenberg & van Knippenberg, 2005), as is evidence for the effectiveness of individuals in formal leadership positions (e.g., Pierro, Cicero, Bonaiuto, van Knippenberg, & Kruglanski, 2005; Platow & van Knippenberg, 2001) and for emergent leaders (Fielding & Hogg, 1997; D. van Knippenberg, van Knippenberg, & van Dijk, 2000). Indicators of effectiveness include follower perceptions and attitudes such as perceived leadership effectiveness and job satisfaction (e.g., Giessner & van Knippenberg, 2008; Hogg, Hains, & Mason, 1998; Pierro et al., 2005) as well as more objective indicators of leadership effectiveness such as task performance (B. van Knippenberg & van Knippenberg, 2005) and creativity (Hirst, van Dick, & van Knippenberg, 2009). Moreover, support derives from studies from a range of countries (Australia, Germany, Italy, the Netherlands, Sweden, United Kingdom, United States; e.g., Hirst et al., 2009; Ullrich, Christ, & van Dick, 2009) testifying to the robustness of this analysis (at least within "western" or "individualistic" cultures).

More anecdotally, too, the notion of leader group prototypicality seems instrumental in explaining the effectiveness of business and political leaders. Reicher and Hopkins (2001, 2003), for instance, discuss how national leaders like Thatcher, Sukharno, and Ghandi derived influence from their followers' perception that they were the embodiment of the nation (see also below for the active role that leaders may play in fostering such perceptions). Business leaders, too, may in part base their influence and appeal on their perceived group prototypicality—for example, because as the business founder, he or she has become the embodiment of the company (e.g., Steve Jobs at Apple) or because his or her personal history is closely linked to the company (e.g., Philips CEO Gerard Kleisterlee).

One question that this emphasis on leader group prototypicality may give rise to is, what about group diversity? Can group prototypicality still play a role in leadership when group members differ widely in terms of their demographic characteristics (age, gender, ethnicity) and/or job-related characteristics (functional and educational background)? This is no trivial question, as organizations and societies are growing increasingly diverse and diversity clearly is not without consequence for group process and performance (D. van Knippenberg & Schippers, 2007). In this respect, it is important to realize that group prototypicality does not revolve around being as similar as possible to the group on as many attributes as possible. Rather, it concerns the extent to which the leader represents the ideal type of the group in terms of *group-defining* characteristics. For instance, the fact that a research and development team has male as well as female members may be irrelevant to team members' sense of identity derived from the team membership. In contrast, the sense that the team is deeply committed to breakthrough innovations and undertakes whatever risky or unconventional way is required to get there may be an important part of team identity. The issue then would not be whether the leader represents the team's composition in terms of gender but, rather, whether the leader embodies the do-or-die commitment of the team to realizing innovative products. Diversity should not be mistaken for an absence of shared identity (cf. D. van Knippenberg, Haslam, & Platow, 2007), and group prototypicality may play a similar role in leadership effectiveness for more diverse and more homogeneous groups. Demographic attributes may indeed play a role in leader group prototypicality, but a high degree of group member diversity does not necessarily preclude the possibility of a leader's embodying the group identity. In fact, demographics may be more likely to play a role in leader group prototypicality the more they are shared. Even when demographics are not core to how the team sees itself, a leader deviating from the team in demographic attributes shared by the team (e.g., the male leader of an all-female team or the female leader of an all-male team) may be faced with at least the initial impression that the leader is different from the team and unlikely to embody what the group stands for. In such situations, the leader's active role in managing perceptions of the team's identity and the leader's representativeness of that team identity become all the more important—More on this below.

The proposition that group members favor leaders whom they perceive to serve the group and act in the group's best interest (i.e., to which part of leader group prototypicality's link with effectiveness is attributed) also implies that acts that are (or can be interpreted as) indicative of the leader's group-oriented motivation feed into leadership effectiveness (Haslam & Platow, 2001; D. van Knippenberg & Hogg, 2003a). Consistent with this analysis, leadership effectiveness has been linked to such behavior as leader self-sacrifice on behalf of the group (Yorges, Weiss, & Strickland, 1999), leader allocation decisions that favor the group over other groups (Platow, Hoar, Reid, Harley, & Morrison, 1997), and leader expressions of commitment to the group (De Cremer & Van Vugt, 2002). Interestingly and importantly, such leadership that flags the leader's commitment to the group's plight is also quoted as an important part of charismatic leadership (Choi & Mai-Dalton, 1998; Conger & Kanungo, 1987; Shamir et al., 1993)—an issue that will be explored further below. Indeed, a classic example of such leader group-oriented behavior is also quoted as an example of charismatic leadership: Lee Iacocca's decision as CEO of Chrysler in the 1970s to reduce his annual salary to one U.S. dollar to flag his commitment to Chrysler as well as the need to make personal sacrifices to help the company survive a life-threatening crisis (cf. Conger & Kanungo, 1987).

The social identity analysis advanced both leader group prototypicality and leader group-oriented behavior as key elements of effective leadership. Leader group prototypicality engenders trust in leaders' group-orientedness (B. van Knippenberg & van Knippenberg, 2005) and, in part, derives its effectiveness from this trust (Giessner & van Knippenberg, 2008). Leader group prototypicality and leader group-oriented behavior, thus in part, derive their effectiveness from the same mechanism—the perception of leader group-orientedness. Accordingly, leader group prototypicality and leader group-oriented behavior may be expected to have an interactive influence on leadership effectiveness, such that one in a sense compensates for the other. Given one element, the other's relationship with leadership effectiveness becomes weaker (D. van Knippenberg & Hogg, 2003a). This is indeed what is found across a number of different operationalizations of leader group-orientedness, such as allocation decisions (Platow & van Knippenberg, 2001), self-sacrifice (B. van Knippenberg & van Knippenberg, 2005), and appeals to the collective interest (vs. the self-interest; Platow, van Knippenberg, Haslam, van Knippenberg, & Spears, 2006): Group prototypical leaders are effective regardless of whether or not they engage in group-oriented behavior, but nonprototypical leaders are more effective when they engage in group-oriented acts than when they do not.

All other things being equal, the effectiveness of leader group prototypicality, leader group-oriented behavior, and their interaction should hold. Core to the social identity analysis, however, is of course that these leadership influences are rooted in follower identification with the collective. Accordingly, these influences are expected to be stronger with higher follower identification and social identity salience (Hogg, 2001).[1] Thus, if follower social identity lies at the root of group prototypical leaders' effectiveness, the relationship between prototypicality and effectiveness should be moderated by identification. This has indeed been shown to be the case (Fielding & Hogg, 1997; Hains et al., 1997; Hogg et al., 1998). In a similar vein, research has shown that followers respond more positively to leader group-oriented behavior the more they identify with the collective (De Cremer, van Knippenberg, van Dijke, & Bos, 2006; De Cremer & Van Vugt, 2002; Platow et al., 1997). Further validating this analysis, the interactive influence of leader group prototypicality and leader group-oriented behavior was also shown to be contingent on follower identification (Platow & van Knippenberg, 2001).

The social identity model of leadership advances prototypicality and group-orientedness as two core aspects of effective leadership—aspects that directly follow from an analysis of the psychology of group membership in terms of social identity and self-categorization. More recently, this analysis has been extended with insights that have a shorter tradition in the social identity approach but are, nevertheless, well grounded in this approach: the role of uncertainty and change in leadership, and leader fairness. Moreover, throughout its development, cross-links and integrations with other approaches to leadership have been established that may provide the building blocks for more integrative and broad-ranging theories of leadership (cf. D. van Knippenberg & Hogg, 2003a). These issues are addressed in the following sections.

Extension and Integration

Prototypicality, uncertainty, and change. An important leadership function—some would argue the core of leadership—lies in bringing about change and managing uncertainty. (Note that although change and uncertainty are not the same, one is often associated with the other, and there are communalities in the implications of the identity approach to leadership for leadership of change and uncertainty.) It is not self-evident that what makes leaders effective as change agents or in managing and reducing uncertainty is the same as what makes leaders effective in more stable times (cf. Conger & Kanungo, 1987). The relationship between leadership, change, and uncertainty is, thus, an issue to consider in and of itself.

Uncertainty plays an important role in the social identity approach. Indeed, Hogg (2007) has advanced a desire for uncertainty reduction as a key motive underlying affiliation with social groups. From a psychological perspective, uncertainty is an aversive psychological state that individuals will desire to resolve or at least reduce. Social identity may be important in this respect because it captures a shared social reality that may help reduce uncertainty. Social identity helps define what is important, valued, and even what is "real," and it may provide guidance as to appropriate responses to uncertain situations. Accordingly, a desire to reduce uncertainty may lead individuals to rely on their group memberships and to think and act more on the basis of their social identity (Hogg, 2007). Uncertainty also invites a desire for leadership. When people are uncertain, they look to leadership to reduce this uncertainty (D. van Knippenberg et al., 2000). In combination, these propositions suggest that individuals desiring to reduce subjective uncertainty will be particularly sensitive to leader group prototypicality—leadership that is perceived to embody a shared social reality.

In support of this proposition, D. van Knippenberg et al. (2000) show that prototypical group members are more likely to emerge as leaders when task uncertainty is higher, and a line of research by Pierro and colleagues suggests that individual-level influences on the desire for uncertainty reduction moderate the relationship between leader group prototypicality and leadership effectiveness. Pierro et al. (2005) focused on individual differences in the need for closure (the desire to avoid uncertainty, ambiguity, and unresolved issues) and proposed and found that leader group prototypicality was more strongly related to leadership effectiveness for followers with a greater need for closure. Extending this analysis to more situational (i.e., rather than dispositional) indicators of a desire to reduce uncertainty, Cicero, Pierro, and van Knippenberg (2007, in press) obtained similar moderated relationships for follower job stress and role ambiguity (i.e., both are associated with a greater need for closure). Providing further support for the social identity basis of these relationships, Pierro, Cicero, Bonaiuto, van Knippenberg, and Kruglanski (2007) showed that the interactive effect of prototypicality and need for closure was moderated by follower identification.

These findings may also have important implications for leadership of change, as change is typically associated with uncertainty. As a case in point, Pierro et al. (2007) conducted their study in the context of organizational change and found that leader prototypicality predicted follower openness to change as a function of follower need for closure and identification (see B. van Knippenberg & van Knippenberg, 2005, for evidence that leader group-oriented behavior may also be important in overcoming resistance to change). Change—be it organizational or societal—also puts another issue on the agenda, however: potential changes to the collective identity. In the course of their lives, people change and develop, and so does their identity. The same holds for social identities: In the course of time, group, organizational, and national identities may change. This, in and of itself, is unproblematic—as, indeed, it should be. Importantly, however, people value a sense of continuity of identity—individual identity as well as social identity (Sani, 2008). This may render people resistant to collectives changes, because these can be perceived as a threat to the continuity of a valued identity (Rousseau, 1998; D. van Knippenberg, van Knippenberg, Monden, & de Lima, 2002). Because collective changes rely heavily on the active cooperation of the members of the collective, such resistance to change is a major challenge for leadership of change (Conner, 1995).

From an identity perspective, then, an important role for leadership of change is to act not only as agents of change, but also as agents of continuity of identity to remove resistance to change (D. van Knippenberg & Hogg, 2003a; cf. Shamir, 1999). Leadership of change is more effective if it conveys the message that despite all changes, the core aspects of the collective identity are maintained—The message of change should also convey that "we will still be us" (cf. Rousseau, 1998). As a case in point, Reicher and Hopkins (2003) even argue that successful leadership of change may actually convey the message that as a consequence of change, the collective will become *more* true to its "real" identity. As an illustrative corporate example in this respect, D. van Knippenberg and Hogg (2003a) point to Apple founder Steve Jobs's return to the company after years of absence. Originally, Jobs had helped create an organizational identity as an unconventional and creative company, but after Jobs's departure, these aspects of identity gradually faded. On returning to Apple, Jobs's strategy to change matters at Apple appears to have included advocating a return to Apple's roots of being unconventional and creative, in a sense, advocating that the company return to its "true identity" from which it had strayed. Framed like this, Jobs's message of change was not just a message of continuity of identity—It was a call to *increase* continuity of identity *through* the change.

D. van Knippenberg, van Knippenberg, and Bobbio (2008) discuss evidence that leader group prototypicality may be particularly effective in instilling such a sense of continuity of identity in times of change. Prototypical leader's representativeness of the shared identity engenders trust that the leader will act as an agent of continuity—Group prototypical leaders are trusted to ensure that treasured aspects of the collective identity will survive the change. In support of this prediction, D. van Knippenberg et al. discussed evidence from two experimental studies focusing on organizational change in the form of a merger, showing that a group prototypical leader was more effective in engendering willingness to contribute to the change than a non-prototypical leader, because the group prototypical leader was seen more as an agent of continuity of the organizational identity (i.e., a mediation model). In addition, the second study provided further evidence for the role of continuity of identity by manipulating the size of the discontinuity threat (i.e., the extent to which the change could potentially change the organization's identity) and showing that the effect of leader group prototypicality was stronger with greater threat to the continuity of the organizational identity.

Leadership of change is an understudied issue (cf. Yukl, 2002), and these studies, too, in a sense, only scratch the surface of the issues at stake in leadership of change. Even so, they do testify to the promise and broader applicability of the social identity approach to leadership. As such, they invite further exploration of the issue from an identity angle.

Social identity and leader fairness. There is a long-running tradition in the study of the psychology of justice (Lind & Tyler, 1988; Thibaut & Walker, 1975). This research has identified the perceived fairness of the outcomes one receives (distributive justice), the procedures used to arrive at these outcomes (procedural justice), and the fairness of interpersonal treatment (interactional justice) as important determinants of people's responses to treatment by and relationships with authorities (Colquitt, Conlon, Wesson, Porter, & Ng, 2001). Only relatively recently, however, has research started to engage with the implications of the fact that in organizational contexts, these authorities, as often as not, are leaders. The analysis of organizational justice, thus, is very much also an analysis of leader fairness (D. van Knippenberg, De Cremer, & van Knippenberg, 2007). Indeed, many of the outcomes studied in this area of research, such as follower satisfaction, motivation, cooperation, and performance, can be understood in terms of leadership effectiveness.

Analyses of the psychology of justice have also recognized that there is an important social identity function to fairness, in particular to procedural and interactional fairness (Lind & Tyler, 1988; Tyler, 1999; Tyler & Blader, 2000). The way an authority (e.g., one's leader) chooses to treat one (i.e., procedural and interactional fairness) conveys one's standing with the authority (Koper, van Knippenberg, Bouhuijs, Vermunt, & Wilke, 1993). Recent social identity analyses of fairness have proposed that identification with the group or organization leads one to be more sensitive to procedural fairness because of a greater concern with such social evaluations from one's identity group. In support of this proposition, these studies have shown that the impact of leader procedural fairness is stronger for followers with higher levels of identification (Lind, Kray, & Thompson, 2001; Tyler & De Cremer, 2005).

More firmly integrating research on leader fairness into the social identity analysis of leadership, research also suggests that the trust in group prototypical leaders extends to trust in the leader's fairness (Janson, Levy, Sitkin, & Lind, 2008; van Dijke & De Cremer, 2008). What this also implies is that analogously to the prototypicality group-oriented behavior interactions proposed in the social identity analysis of leadership, leader group prototypicality and leader fairness interact in predicting leadership effectiveness. This is exactly what Janson et al. proposed and found for leader interactional fairness. Ullrich et al. (2009) obtained similar findings for procedural fairness and, moreover, showed that this interaction was moderated by follower identification, as one would expect if the effect is rooted in social identity.

Janson et al. (2008) also extended this logic to leader group-oriented behavior (self-sacrificial leadership) and showed that self-sacrifice and interactional fairness interacted in such a way that the positive influence of one was attenuated under high levels of the other. De Cremer and van Knippenberg (2002) reported similar findings for the interactive effects of leader self-sacrifice and leader procedural fairness, albeit that their analysis emphasized leadership's role in building follower collective identification (more on this below). In sum, then, a social identity approach to leader fairness seems to offer a viable perspective to advance our understanding of this important aspect of leadership and to more firmly integrate it into other perspectives on leadership (for a review of the literature on leader fairness, see D. van Knippenberg et al., 2007).

Group versus leader prototypicality. The concept of leader group prototypicality, which is central to the social identity analysis of leadership, can be traced back to categorization theory in cognitive psychology (Rosch, 1978). There is another perspective in leadership that also revolves around the notion of prototypicality and also traces its roots back to the same work in cognitive psychology: leadership categorization theory (Lord & Maher, 1991; chapter 10). The important difference, however, is that leadership categorization theory does not refer to group prototypicality but, rather, to prototypicality of an abstracted category of leaders (cf. the leader role)—mental representations capturing the ideal type of a leader. Although leadership categorization theory is the only other leadership theory that explicitly uses the concept of prototypicality, there are a number of similar approaches revolving around individuals' mental representations of leadership that there-fore, may be grouped under the heading of leadership categorization theories (D. van Knippenberg & Hogg, 2003a). This includes work on implicit leader-ship theories (Eden & Leviatan, 1975), the romance of leadership (Meindl, Ehrlich, & Dukerich, 1985), role congruity theory of gender and leadership (Eagly & Karau, 2002; chapter 13), and cross-cultural differences in leader-ship perceptions (chapter 12).

What all these approaches share is that they are *follower-centric* (chapter 10; Meindl, 1995; Shamir, Pillai, Bligh, & Uhl-Bien, 2007)—They put the notion center stage that leadership is in the eye of the beholder. That is, all these approaches, in one way or another, advance the notion that one's understand-ing of leadership (i.e., one's leadership prototype) is an implicit standard against which (potential) leaders are judged. Individuals with characteristics more prototypical of leaders (i.e., as per the perceiver's implicit understanding of leadership) are more likely to be judged as effective leaders. Eagly and Karau's (2002) role congruity theory, for instance, applies this principle to explain gender biases in leadership perceptions: For many individuals, their implicit leader prototypes emphasize male over female characteristics, which biases their perceptions to see more leadership qualities in male than in female (potential) leaders—even when objectively such differential percep-tions are unjustified (see also chapter 13).

The social identity analysis of leadership advances a highly similar process. Only the implicit standard differs: Leaders are proposed to be implicitly judged in terms of their group prototypicality rather than their leader proto-typicality. Although these propositions seem to be at odds, they are in fact easily reconciled (Lord & Hall, 2003; D. van Knippenberg & Hogg, 2003a). A line of research by Hogg and colleagues (Fielding & Hogg, 1997; Hains et al., 1997; Hogg et al., 1998; see also Platow & van Knippenberg, 2001) identifies follower identification as the key moderator of the relative impor-tance of group prototypicality versus leader prototypicality in responses to leadership. With higher follower identification, group prototypicality becomes a more important basis for leadership effectiveness compared to leader pro-totypicality. More recently, Hogg et al. (2006) showed that this analysis also applies specifically to gender and leadership. When follower identification was high, it was leader group prototypicality, which was experimentally induced to be either higher for female leaders or for male leaders, that drove perceptions of leadership effectiveness, not leader gender.

Giessner and colleagues extended this integration to the study of responses to leader performance (Giessner et al., 2009; Giessner & van Knippenberg, 2008). Leadership categorization theories have established a tendency to overattribute performance to leadership. That is, people have a tendency to see success as an indicator of good leadership and failure as an indicator of bad leadership and to discount nonleadership influences on these outcomes

(Lord, Binning, Rush, & Thomas, 1978; Meindl et al., 1985). Part of what this means is that leaders will be held responsible for negative outcomes and will, in effect, be judged as poor leaders after failure to achieve collective goals. Giessner and colleagues argued that leader group prototypicality attenuates this tendency. Specifically, they proposed that the greater trust in group prototypical leaders extends to perceptions of the leader's performance, so that group prototypical leaders would suffer less negative leadership evaluations after failure. Their studies supported this proposition. They showed that the attenuating effect of group prototypicality was stronger with higher follower identification and was contingent on the extent to which the performance goal allowed leeway in interpreting leader failure (i.e., when the failure was more ambiguous, group prototypicality was more able to protect the leader against negative evaluations).

Leadership categorization processes are important both because they introduce biases (and, thus, issue a warning against relying on subjective assessments of leadership qualities in research as well as practice; Eagly & Karau, 2002; Lord & Maher, 1991; chapter 10; D. van Knippenberg, in press) and because they may set the stage for behavioral indicators of leadership effectiveness (i.e., followers are likely to be more open to the influence of leaders they perceive as possessing "the right stuff"; cf. B. van Knippenberg & van Knippenberg, 2005). A further integration of group identity and leadership categorization theories may have important value for the development of follower-centric approaches to leadership (cf. D. van Knippenberg, van Knippenberg, & Giessner, 2007) and, thus, for our understanding of an important aspect of the leadership process.

Group-based versus interpersonal leadership. The social identity analysis of leadership emphasizes the group-based nature of leadership processes more than most other approaches to leadership do. (The obvious exceptions are studies of shared leadership [chapter 11] and team leadership [Day, Gronn, & Salas, 2004].) In an interesting counterpoint to this, there is a long-standing research tradition in leadership that champions the interpersonal, dyadic, nature of leadership: leader–member exchange (LMX) theory (Dansereau, Graen, & Haga, 1975; Gerstner & Day, 1997; Graen & Uhl-Bien, 1995; chapter 9). LMX theory builds on the more general social exchange theory of human relations (Homans, 1958) to understand how leader–follower relationship quality develops over time and influences leadership effectiveness. In a nutshell, its basic tenet is that leader–follower relationships are based on the exchange of material (e.g., a bonus) and immaterial (e.g., respect) goods, and that the quality of the leader–follower relationship is captured by the quality of this social exchange. Exchange quality is understood here both in terms of the quality of the goods exchanged (i.e., better relationships involve more exchanges and of higher value) and in terms of the balance in the exchange: The value of goods received should match the value of goods given—There should be fairness in the exchange. The quality of the exchange relationship may differ from follower to follower, and a leader, thus, may have better relationships with some followers than with others. In LMX theory, it therefore is the interpersonal relationship between leader and follower that is key to leadership effectiveness, not the relationship between leader and followers in terms of their shared group membership.

At first blush, the LMX perspectives may seem in opposition to the social identity analysis. Again, however, the integration of these perspectives is relatively straightforward and lies in the moderating role of follower identity. Hogg et al. (2005) argued and showed that social identification moderates the extent to which followers approach the relationship with their leader in interpersonal terms or, rather, in terms of the shared group membership. Consistent with this proposition, their findings showed that a leadership style of approaching followers in terms of their membership in the work group as opposed to on an interpersonal basis (cf. LMX) was more effective, the more followers identified with the group. D. van Knippenberg, van Dick, and Tavares (2007) obtained comparable findings for organizational identification as moderator of the relationship between leader support (a core variable in social exchange analysis of organizational behavior; Rhoades & Eisenberger, 2002) and turnover intentions as an indicator of leadership effectiveness. Leader support (i.e., reflecting the leader's input in the social exchange relationship) was more effective with lower follower identification (i.e., when the relationship presumably was conceived of more in interpersonal terms). Here, too, it may be noted that studies like these are only a first step toward more fully exploring the potential for integration of these perspectives, but here, too, follower identity manifests itself as an important determinant of the relative impact of different leadership processes.

Social identity and charisma. The social identity analysis is unique in advancing the role of leader group prototypicality. In proposing an important role for leader group-oriented behavior, however, it identifies a clear area of overlap with research in charismatic/transformational leadership, which has similarly advanced the notion that leader self-sacrifice in pursuit of collective goals is an aspect of charismatic/transformational leadership (Choi & Mai-Dalton, 1998; Conger & Kanungo, 1987; Shamir et al., 1993). Charismatic and transformational leadership, although sometimes discussed as related but different, can be taken to refer largely to the same concept, which emphasizes the communication of a vision for the collective and personal risks and sacrifices in pursuing these visions (Bass, 1985; Bass & Riggio, 2006; Conger & Kanungo, 1987; Kirkpatrick & Locke, 1996; Shamir et al., 1993; chapter 8).

Clearly, then, the social identity analysis and analyses of charismatic/transformational leadership are in agreement that group-oriented behavior contributes to leadership effectiveness. From the perspective of the social identity analysis of leadership, however, this also implies that the group-oriented part of charismatic leadership is less important to effective leadership, the more group prototypical the leader is. Indeed, this is exactly the interpretation that B. van Knippenberg and van Knippenberg (2005) gave to the prototypicality × self-sacrifice interactions they observed. Further supporting this link, B. van Knippenberg and van Knippenberg showed that this interaction also holds for perceptions of leader charisma. In a related vein, Platow et al. (2006) showed that group prototypical leaders were seen as charismatic regardless of their rhetoric style, whereas nonprototypical leaders were seen as more charismatic when they appealed to the collective interest rather than the follower's self-interest. These studies suggest not only that group prototypicality contributes to leader charisma, but also that insights from the social identity analysis (e.g., regarding the moderating role of follower identification) may be integrated with insights from research in charismatic/transformational leadership to advance our understanding of leadership effectiveness.

Even so, the greater overlap between these perspectives probably is in the processes identified as mediating between leadership and outcomes. Both theories of charismatic and transformational leadership and the social identity analysis of leadership point to the importance of follower identity in translating leadership into follower action (Shamir et al., 1993; D. van Knippenberg & Hogg, 2003a)—i.e., the mediating, rather than the moderating, role of follower identity. This is the issue we turn to next.

Leadership as Shaping Identity

Follower identity is not only something that motivates responses to leadership; it is also something that may be affected by leadership. The important thing to realize here is that identity is not set in stone. Not only may identity change gradually over time (Sani, 2008; cf. the discussion of continuity of identity above), but also situational factors may have relatively instantaneous influences on identity. Part of our identity, sometimes referred to as the working self-concept (Lord & Brown, 2004; Markus & Nurius, 1986), is quite fluid and may vary as a function of what situational cues invite to the fore. Self-categorization theory's treatment of social identity salience (Turner et al., 1987; cf. note 1) is a case in point, where situational cues (e.g., a threat to the group) may render group identity salient (i.e., cognitively activated), whereas group identity may withdraw to the background again (e.g., to make place for more personal aspects of identity) once the situational cues that triggered its activation are no longer present. Aside from this relatively "on-and-off" influence captured by notions of the working self-concept and identity salience, self-conception may also undergo less short-lived changes under the influence of contextual factors. As one's team becomes more successful, for instance, one may increasingly grow to identify with it (cf. Tajfel & Turner, 1986). Given the important role of identity in motivation and behavior, an important aspect of leadership effectiveness may therefore revolve around leaders' ability to temporarily or more permanently change follower self-conception (Lord &

Brown, 2004; Shamir et al., 1993; D. van Knippenberg et al., 2004). Research has probably highlighted this nowhere more than in leadership's influence on collective identification.

One of the core challenges facing leadership is to unite a diverse group of individuals in the pursuit of shared team, organizational, or societal goals, objectives, and missions. Different people have different interests, and it is often not self-evident to individuals that they would prioritize the collective interest over their individual pursuits. Achieving such a transformation of motives (i.e., from self-interests to collective interests; De Cremer & Van Vugt, 1999), thus, is key in mobilizing followers' cooperative efforts to realize collective objectives (Burns, 1978). Along the lines discussed previously, collective identification may drive such a prioritization of the collective interest (Ashforth & Mael, 1989; De Cremer & Van Vugt, 1999; D. van Knippenberg, 2000a). As recognized by social identity analyses of leadership and analyses of charismatic/transformational leadership alike, leadership, thus, can mobilize and motivate followers for collective endeavors by building follower identification (Lord et al., 1999; Shamir et al., 1993; D. van Knippenberg & Hogg, 2003a).

In line with this analysis, a number of studies show that the effectiveness of aspects of leadership can be explained by their influence on follower identification (i.e., follower identification mediates the relationship between leadership and indicators of leadership effectiveness). Studies, for instance, linked charismatic/transformational leadership to follower empowerment via the mediating role of identification (Conger, Kanungo, & Menon, 2000; Kark, Shamir, & Chen, 2003; see also Shamir, Zakay, Breinin, & Popper, 1998). De Cremer and van Knippenberg (2002) established a mediating role for collective identification in a study of the interactive effects of leader self-sacrifice and leader procedural fairness, showing that self-sacrifice and procedural fairness attenuated each other's positive effect on follower cooperation because both resulted in higher follower identification (i.e., with one in place, the other had less value). De Cremer and van Knippenberg (2004) studied the interactive influence of leader self-sacrifice and self-confidence (self-confidence is also seen as an aspect of charismatic leadership) and showed that these aspects of charisma enhanced each other's influence on leadership effectiveness and that these effects were mediated by collective identification.

In combination with the evidence for the moderating role of follower identification in the leadership processes, this, thus, suggests a dynamic model (D. van Knippenberg & Hogg, 2003a) in which leadership that builds identification (e.g., group-oriented leadership) can set the stage for its future effectiveness (i.e., group-oriented leadership is more effective with higher follower identification). This is not to say that identification is the only process through which charismatic leadership (and leader procedural fairness) is effective (indeed, see below and, e.g., De Cremer & van Knippenberg, 2005; Dirks & Ferrin, 2002, on the role of trust), but it does testify to the important role that follower collective identification may play in the leadership process—in particular, in motivating cooperation and collective efforts.

These analyses also point to an issue that is far less explored in leadership research: the *content* of the collective identity. As D. van Knippenberg (2000a) argued, identification motivates the pursuit of the collective interest, but it is the perception of what *is* the collective interest that determines if and how identification translates into action (e.g., identification leads to performance only if performance is seen as important to the group). Reicher and Hopkins's (2001, 2003) analysis implies that such perceptions can be closely linked to perceptions of the collective identity itself and that leaders can, in this respect, be effective by acting as *entrepreneurs of identity*, actively shaping followers' understanding of what the collective identity is and, by implication, how it is best served (cf. Voss, Cable, & Voss, 2006). This is a process we know far less about, but based on our knowledge about the importance of leadership's influence on follower identification, it seems it should be higher on the research agenda than it currently is.

In relation to this issue, an important element of Reicher and Hopkins's (2001, 2003) analysis is that leadership may not only shape followers' understanding of the collective identity, but it may also affect follower perceptions of leader group prototypicality. Their analysis suggests, for instance, that political leaders like Thatcher, Sukharno, and Ghandi not only derived influence from their group prototypicality, but in fact, they actively construed a public self-image that conveyed their prototypicality. It is not so much that they just "happened to be" group prototypical, but rather that they actively contributed to the perception that they were. By and large, however, this work is qualitative and anecdotal, and important contributions are still to be made in complementing this work with quantitative, hypothesis-testing research. Although firmer conclusions should await the outcomes of such research, an important implication is that being an *entrepreneur of identity* not only can make one highly effective as a leader, but it may also be a competency that can, to a certain extent, be developed.

Being an entrepreneur of identity may be an aspect of leadership that is of particular importance in the context of group diversity where it may sometimes be challenging to see what unites and defines the group or what grounds there would be to see the leader as group prototypical. Under such conditions in particular, it may be an important leadership skill to be able to define group identity in such a way that it is able both to instill a sense of collective identity among group members and to engender the perception that the leader embodies this identity. As perhaps a somewhat extreme example of what this might look like, consider this brief excerpt from an influential speech given by U.S. President John F. Kennedy to an audience in West Berlin at the height of the cold war, just after the East Germans had added a second barrier behind the original Berlin Wall:

> Two thousand years ago, the proudest boast was *civis Romanus sum*. Today, in the world of freedom, the proudest boast is *Ich bin ein Berliner*. All free men, wherever they may live, are citizens of Berlin, and, therefore, as a free man, I take pride in the words *Ich bin ein Berliner*.

Mr. Kennedy was not born in Berlin and, indeed, was not even German. Out of context, the claim to be a citizen of Berlin—*Ich bin ein Berliner*—would seem to be merely a quaint touch, but what this quote shows is that what Mr. Kennedy was really doing was defining a group—*all free men, wherever they may live*—in which he and his audience share a membership. Especially against the backdrop of the notion, which was then more salient than ever, that America is the leader of the free world, by proudly claiming to be *ein Berliner*, Mr. Kennedy may have conveyed an image that fed straight into his audience's perception of him as a leader in the context of this shared group membership—as *their* leader.

To recap the discussion so far then, a social identity analysis of leadership suggests key roles for follower social identity, both in informing responses to leadership (prioritizing leader group prototypicality, group-oriented behavior, and procedural and interactional fairness at high levels of identification, and the matching of implicit leader prototypes and interpersonal leadership at lower levels of identification) and as a process translating leadership in contributions to the collective. There is more to identity than collective identification, however, and other aspects of identity and self-conception may also play an important role in leadership (D. van Knippenberg et al., 2004). Leadership research has highlighted self-evaluations, in particular in this respect, and to a more modest extent, future identities. These issues are discussed in the next two sections.

Self-Evaluations and Leadership

People are evaluators. They cannot help passing judgment on virtually anything they encounter, including other people and, indeed, themselves. Self-evaluations play an important role in motivation and therefore also in leadership. Self-evaluations are typically discussed either as self-esteem, which often tends to emphasize the evaluation of the social self (how well one is regarded by others; Brockner, 1988), or as the more capability-oriented concept of self-efficacy, one's assessments of one's capabilities to accomplish certain goals (Bandura, 1997). However, there is reason to believe that self-esteem and self-efficacy both are instantiations of the higher order concept of self-evaluations (Judge, Locke, & Durham, 1997). Of particular interest to leadership researchers, and especially in a social identity analysis of leadership, self-evaluations not only capture one's assessment of the individual self (i.e., self-esteem or self-efficacy) but may also capture one's (shared) assessment of the group, the collective self (collective self-esteem; Crocker & Luhtanen, 1990; collective efficacy; Bandura, 1997). Self-evaluations are important to motivation, because higher self-evaluations inspire higher achievement goals.

The clear implication for leadership, then, is that leadership may derive part of its effectiveness from building follower, individual, and collective self-esteem and self-efficacy, because higher levels of (collective) self-evaluation may inspire more ambitious achievement goals (Shamir et al., 1993). In support of this proposition, there is empirical evidence that charismatic/transformational leadership may affect follower self-evaluations (e.g., Dvir, Eden, Avolio, & Shamir, 2002; Kark et al., 2003; Kirkpatrick & Locke, 1996) and, thus, motivate higher levels of performance (Shea & Howell, 1999). Other research also has established other influences on follower self-evaluations, such as leader procedural fairness (De Cremer, van Knippenberg, van Knippenberg, Mullenders, & Stinglhamber, 2005), empowering leadership (Mathieu, Ahearne, & Taylor, 2007), and leader self-efficacy (Hoyt, Murphy, Halverson, & Watson, 2003; see also below).

An important thing to note, however, is that the evidence that leadership may build follower self-evaluations is more abundant and consistent than the evidence that higher follower performance follows from leadership's influence on self-evaluations (for a more extensive review, see D. van Knippenberg et al., 2004). A complication to take into account here is highlighted by the work of Vancouver and colleagues on self-efficacy (e.g., Vancouver, More, & Yoder, 2008). These authors argued and showed that whereas self-efficacy may indeed inspire more ambitious performance goals (which are good for performance), it may simultaneously inspire lower investment of effort (which is bad for performance). That is, high confidence in one's capabilities may actually motivate one to invest *less* effort—on the assumption that one will be able to achieve one's goals anyway. In relationship to leadership and performance, follower self-evaluations, thus, may be somewhat of a double-edged sword. It would, therefore, be particularly worthwhile for research to determine the conditions under which leadership's influence on follower self-evaluations can be expected to have desired behavioral effects.

Self-evaluations may also moderate responses to leadership. Research in organizational justice shows that low self-esteem may render individuals more sensitive to authorities' procedural fairness (Vermunt, van Knippenberg, van Knippenberg, & Blaauw, 2001; but see Brockner et al., 1998), suggesting the same might hold for leader procedural fairness and follower self-esteem. De Cremer (2003) showed exactly this. Other research more tentatively suggests that follower self-evaluations moderate responses to leadership (e.g., Murphy & Ensher, 1999), but this evidence is far from unequivocal (D. van Knippenberg et al., 2004). The current state of the science thus suggests that it may be worthwhile to consider follower self-evaluations both as a mediator and as a moderator of leadership effectiveness, but at the same time, it suggests that more definite conclusions should await more conclusive evidence.

Follower Identity Over Time

In a previous section, I have already addressed the notion of identity change and continuity of identity. This, in fact, points to a broader issue, which is that there is a temporal dimension to identity. People have a sense of the relationship between their past, present, and future identity, and they value a sense of continuity of identity (Sani, 2008; Shamir et al., 1993). The leadership implications of this were discussed in a previous section, and I merely recall them here to identify them as part of this broader issue of the temporal aspects of identity.

In addition to a sense of continuity of identity, there is another major component to the temporal aspect of identity: Individuals may also have more or less well-defined notions about who they *could* be in the future—about *possible selves* (Markus & Nurius, 1986; cf. Higgins, 1987). Such selves can take the form of ideal selves (images of who one ideally would be) as well as ought selves (images of who one should be). An ideal self for a young lawyer at a law firm at the start of her career may, for instance, be that of a successful senior partner. The importance of such possible selves lies in the fact that they may motivate and guide goal pursuit. Individuals tend to be more persistent and better at self-regulating their efforts in goal pursuit for goals that are tied to possible selves (Banaji & Prentice, 1994). The better articulated and developed a possible self, the more it may become a "self-guide" and regulate the individual's actions—that is, the more it may become a source of motivation.

Based on these notions regarding the motivating and self-regulating potential of possible selves, Lord et al. (1999) and D. van Knippenberg et al. (2004) have proposed in conceptual analyses that leadership may be more effective if it can invite follower formation of possible selves that are aligned with collective goals and missions. Building on these conceptual analyses, Stam, van Knippenberg, and Wisse (2010) showed that leader visionary speeches that more explicitly invite followers to form an ideal self based on the vision are more effective in motivating vision-congruent performance (mediated by possible selves), especially for followers with a promotion focus (Higgins, 1987) who are more sensitive to such ideal images. Possible selves, and, more generally, the temporal aspects of the self, are largely uncharted territory in leadership research, however, and here lies a clear challenge for future research efforts.

Possible selves and, more generally, the development of a particular identity over time not only are relevant to understanding the psychology of followers in the leadership process, but also may be of particular relevance to our understanding of the psychology of leaders. As will be discussed in the next section, self-conception as a leader may be an important driver of leader behavior, and among others, this raises the question of how identity as a leader develops over time.

Leader Identity

At the core of the identity approach to leadership is the notion that identity shapes perceptions, attitudes, and behavior and that identity, therefore, may be a powerful motivating force. Clearly, a focus on follower identity is instrumental in understanding leadership effectiveness, but an identity perspective may also be applied to understand what motivates leadership itself—leader identity can also be the focus of inquiry. Although the bottom line for leadership research is leadership effectiveness (i.e., in terms of effects on followers), there is also a long tradition in studying the determinants of leadership, specifically those aspects of leadership that are assumed to be highly predictive of leadership effectiveness, such as transformational leadership. The traditional perspective on these determinants has been a personality perspective (e.g., Judge & Bono, 2000; D. van Knippenberg, in press), but an identity perspective may be at least as suited to tackle this issue.

In recognition of this, research has recently started to consider the role of leader self and identity in shaping leadership. Some of this work is closely aligned with the social identity analysis of leadership (e.g., D. van Knippenberg et al., 2000) and has emphasized leader identity as a determinant of leader self-serving versus group-serving behavior. Giessner and van Knippenberg (2007, 2009) for instance focused on the extent to which the leader conceives of the self as group prototypical. They argued that self-perceived group prototypicality intrinsically motivates group-serving behavior. In support of their analysis, they showed that group prototypical leaders were group serving, irrespective of whether they were held accountable for their actions or not, whereas nonprototypical leaders were more group-serving when they were accountable than when they were not (i.e., accountability provides an extrinsic reason to refrain from self-serving behavior). In contrast, the group-orientedness of group prototypical leaders' behavior was more contingent on group norms (i.e., which would be more internalized by leaders conceiving of the self as group prototypical) than on the behavior of nonprototypical leaders. Focusing on the related issue of leader identification with the collective, van Dick, Hirst, Grojean, and Wieseke (2007) demonstrate how leader organizational identification may lay the basis for follower organizational identification.

Identity in terms of the group membership shared with followers is not the only important aspect of leader identity to consider. For leaders, an important part of their identity may also be role-related and revolve around the extent to which they conceive of themselves as a leader (cf. the contrast between the social identity analysis and leadership categorization theories)—leader self-definition as a leader or leader role identification (cf. Stets & Burke, 2000). It is not self-evident that people in formal leader roles would see themselves as leaders and would have a strong sense of self that emphasizes that leader role. Leaders differ in the extent to which being a leader is an important part of their identity (Rus, van Knippenberg, & Wisse, 2010; cf. Chan & Drasgow, 2001). This is no minor point, because just as group identification invites taking group prototypes as a referent, leader role identification may invite taking one's ideal type of a leader as a referent—leader role identification may influence leader actions.

In a qualitative case study, Kramer (2003) argued that self-conception in terms of the leader role may have a powerful motivating influence on leaders' behavior. Focusing his analysis on U.S. President Lyndon Johnson's decisions concerning America's involvement in Vietnam, Kramer suggests that Mr. Johnson made a number of decisions that were informed more by his conception of what it meant to be a great American president and his self-image as fitting that category than by sound judgment of what would be advisable courses of action (even when Mr. Johnson could be deemed very capable of arriving at these sound judgments). In a quantitative counterpoint to this, Rus et al. (2010) studied self-definition as a leader as a determinant of leader-self versus group-serving behavior. They argued and found that stronger self-definition as a leader invites leaders to rely more on normative information about what good leaders should do or what most leaders would do in making decisions that have consequences along the self-serving versus group-serving continuum.

Studies like these not only suggest that the effects of leader role identification are deserving of more research attention, they also beg the question of what leads to the development of a leader identity (see also chapter 4; Day & Harrison, 2007; Day, Harrison, & Halpin, 2009). Such development, in fact, need not be restricted to people in a formal leader role—individuals in non-leadership positions, too, may conceive of themselves to a greater or lesser extent in terms of their leadership qualities (van Quaquebeke, van Knippenberg, & Brodbeck, 2007). In that sense, the development of a leader identity can start well before one holds a formal leadership position and may express itself in leadership behavior even when one does not hold a formal leadership position (i.e., emergent leadership; see also chapter 11 on shared leadership). Lord and Hall (2005) accord the development of possible selves as a leader an important role in leadership development (cf. Ibarra, 1999). That is, it may not be so much seeing oneself as a leader in the present as it is having a future image of the self as a leader that motivates and guides leadership development. A possible self as a leader may invite one to develop the necessary leadership skills and to experiment with leadership behaviors. DeRue, Ashford, and Cotton (2009) argue that in collaborative contexts, this may invite mutually reinforcing processes, in which others' responses to one's leadership attempts may affirm one's emergent leader identity, which in turn may invite other acts of leadership that bolster others' acknowledgement of one's leadership (cf. Ridgeway, 2003).

Part of the challenge of this line of research is that there is good theory and emergent evidence to suggest that the development of leader identity is important, but that such identity development would typically be expected to take place over the course of many years (Day et al., 2009). Accordingly, empirical work to substantiate and stimulate theoretical developments, more or less by necessity, would have to be, at least in part, longitudinal in nature and cover larger time spans than is typically seen in leadership research. Such complications should not discourage us from undertaking this research, however, and there is clear promise in developing the analysis of leadership identity empirically.

Where the study of self-definition as a leader revolves around individuals' understanding of what it means to be a leader, a related but different focus is on individuals' assessment of their own capabilities as a leader: leadership self-efficacy (e.g., Anderson, Krajewski, Griffin, & Jackson, 2008; Paglis & Green, 2002; Singer, 1991). Following the basic self-efficacy logic outlined previously (Bandura, 1997), leaders with higher leadership self-efficacy are expected to engage more proactively with the leadership role and, thus, to be more effective. There is some evidence to suggest that this may indeed be the case (Chemers, Watson, & May, 2000; Hoyt et al., 2003; Ng, Ang, & Chan, 2008; Paglis & Green, 2002). The same caveat identified earlier would seem to apply here, however: Although leadership self-efficacy may indeed fuel leadership ambitions, it does not necessarily mean that leaders with higher leadership self-efficacy will exert greater leadership efforts in pursuit of their goals (cf. Vancouver et al., 2008).

Leadership research has a long history of studying leader personality as determinant of leader behavior and leadership effectiveness (chapter 6), and attention to the role of leader identity in this respect is still at an embryonic stage. Even so, given the somewhat modest success of the personality perspective on leadership (Judge, Bono, Ilies, & Gerhardt, 2002; D. van Knippenberg, in press), it seems worthwhile to explore the possibility that a leader identity perspective may complement the personality perspective and substantially add to our understanding of the determinants of leadership. More research efforts in this area seem clearly warranted.

The Road Ahead

In leadership, identity matters. Research in the social identity analysis, in particular, has yielded a substantial body of highly consistent results to support that conclusion. This evidence also seems strong enough to warrant further investigation of the less explored issues suggested by this analysis, such as the determinants of leaders' ability and motivation to be an entrepreneur of identity and to actively make the identity dynamics identified in the social identity analysis work for them. In other areas, such as the role of the temporal aspects of the self in leadership effectiveness or of leader identity, analyses are still quite nascent. Given the strong evidence for the viability of other aspects of the identity analysis, it would seem reasonable to suspect promise in these areas too, however, and to invest substantial research efforts in these emerging areas.

The identity perspective on leadership is also very much a perspective that engages with other perspectives in leadership (e.g., leadership categorization theories, LMX theory), rather than develops in isolation (a not uncommon problem in leadership research). In that sense, further development of the identity perspective may also be instrumental in providing integration in the leadership field and in building more broad-ranging accounts of leadership (D. van Knippenberg & Hogg, 2003a). From this perspective, too, the available evidence in the identity analysis of leadership would seem to issue a call to arms for further research in the area.

Note

1. Whereas identification captures the extent to which an individual conceives of the self in terms of the group membership, social identity salience refers to the extent that the identification is cognitively activated—is influential in the here and now rather than "dormant" (i.e., the fact that someone identifies with a group does not mean that this identification is always equally central to the person's thoughts and actions). For instance, the competition between one's group and another group may render one's group identification more salient than it would have been without the competition. Identification can be seen as the more chronic or enduring influence, whereas identity salience can be seen as the more contextual activation of that influence (Haslam, 2004). To a large extent, however, identification and salience may be expected to be functionally equivalent and, indeed to a certain extent, positively related. I will focus on the more enduring influence of identification, which is also more widely studied in the leadership literature, and take this to apply also to social identity salience.

Discussion Questions

1. If you look at recent elections, e.g., U.S. presidential elections, can you see the evidence that candidates try to use social identity dynamics to mobilize support? In what way? What effect does it appear to have? Do you see evidence that the winning candidate is getting more mileage out of these dynamics than the competition?

2. If you think of your work experience, what motivates you? To what extent is this related to how you see yourself, your sense of who you are? If you think of very good and very bad experiences you had with ("receiving") leadership, to what extent do these speak to your sense of identity? What do the answers to these questions tell you about the identity role of leadership in your own personal work experience?

3. Can you describe your own identity as a leader?—Do you have any? If you would imagine yourself as a leader, what would you ideally be like? What would it take to achieve this? What do the answers to these questions tell you about the development of (your) role identity as a leader?

Supplementary Reading

Wright, R. (2010, June 1). Is Steve Jobs big brother? *New York Times Online Opinionator.* http://opinionator.blogs.nytimes.com/2010/06/01/is-steve-jobs-big-brother/?scp=1&sq=%22steve%20jobs%22%20and%20%20%22big%20brother%22&st=cse

References

Abrams, D., & Hogg, M. A. (1990). Social identification, self-categorization and social influence. *European Review of Social Psychology, 1,* 195–228.

Anderson, D. W., Krajewski, H. T., Griffin, R. D., & Jackson, D. N. (2008). A leadership self-efficacy taxonomy and its relation to effective leadership. *The Leadership Quarterly, 19,* 595–608.

Ashforth, B. E., & Mael, F. (1989). Social identity theory and the organization. *Academy of Management Review, 14,* 20–39.

Banaji, M. R., & Prentice, D. A. (1994). The self in social contexts. *Annual Review of Psychology, 45,* 297–332.

Bandura, A. (1997). *Self-efficacy: The exercise of self-control.* New York: Freeman.

Bass, B. M. (1985). *Leadership and performance beyond expectations.* New York: Free Press.

Bass, B. M., & Riggio, R. E. (2006). *Transformational leadership.* Mahwah, NJ: Lawrence Erlbaum.

Brewer, M. B., & Brown, R. J. (1998). Intergroup relations. In D. T. Gilbert, S. T. Fiske, & G. Lindzey (Eds.), *Handbook of social psychology* (4th ed., pp. 554–594). Boston: McGraw-Hill.

Brockner, J. (1988). *Self-esteem at work.* Lexington, MA: Lexington Books.

Brockner, J., Heuer, L., Siegel, P. A., Wiesenfeld, B., Martin, C., Grover, S., et al. (1998). The moderating effect of self-esteem in reaction to voice: Converging evidence from five studies. *Journal of Personality and Social Psychology, 75,* 394–407.

Burns, J. M. (1978). *Leadership.* New York: Harper & Row.

Chan, K.-Y., & Drasgow, F. (2001). Toward a theory of individual differences and leadership: Understanding the motivation to lead. *Journal of Applied Psychology, 86,* 481–498.

Chemers, M. M., Watson, C. B., & May, S. (2000). Dispositional affect and leadership effectiveness: A comparison of self-esteem, optimism, and efficacy. *Personality and Social Psychology Bulletin, 26,* 267–277.

Choi, Y., & Mai-Dalton, R. R. (1998). On the leadership function of self-sacrifice. *The Leadership Quarterly, 9,* 475–501.

Cicero, L., Pierro, A., & van Knippenberg, D. (2007). Leader group prototypicality and job satisfaction: The moderating role of job stress and team identification. *Group Dynamics, 11,* 165–175.

Cicero, L., Pierro, A., & van Knippenberg, D. (in press). Leader group prototypicality and leadership effectiveness: The moderating role of role ambiguity. *British Journal of Management.*

Colquitt, J. A., Conlon, D. E., Wesson, M. J., Porter, C. O. L. H., & Ng, K. Y. (2001). Justice at the millennium: A meta-analytic review of 25 years of organizational justice research. *Journal of Applied Psychology, 86*, 425–445.

Conger, J. A., & Kanungo, R. N. (1987). Toward a behavioral theory of charismatic leadership in organizational settings. *Academy of Management Review, 12*, 637–647.

Conger, J. A., Kanungo, R. N., & Menon, S. T. (2000). Charismatic leadership and follower effects. *Journal of Organizational Behavior, 21*, 747–767.

Conner, D. R. (1995). *Managing at the speed of change: How resilient managers succeed and prosper where others fail.* New York: Villard Books.

Crocker, J., & Luhtanen, R. (1990). Collective self-esteem and ingroup bias. *Journal of Personality and Social Psychology, 58*, 60–67.

Dansereau, F., Graen, G., & Haga, W. J. (1975). A vertical dyad linkage approach to leadership within formal organizations: A longitudinal investigation of the role making process. *Organizational Behavior and Human Performance, 13*, 46–78.

Day, D. V., Gronn, P., & Salas, E. (2004). Leadership capacity in teams. *The Leadership Quarterly, 15*, 857–880.

Day, D. V., & Harrison, M. M. (2007). A multilevel, identity-based approach to leadership development. *Human Resource Management Review, 17*, 360–373.

Day, D. V., Harrison, M. M., & Halpin, S. M. (2009). *An integrative approach to leader development.* New York, NY: Routledge.

De Cremer, D. (2003). Why inconsistent leadership is regarded as procedurally unfair: The importance of social self-esteem concerns. *European Journal of Social Psychology, 33*, 535–550.

De Cremer, D., van Knippenberg, B., van Knippenberg, D., Mullenders, D., Stinglhamber, F. (2005). Rewarding leadership and fair procedures as determinants of self-esteem. *Journal of Applied Psychology, 90*, 3–12.

De Cremer, D., & van Knippenberg, D. (2002). How do leaders promote cooperation? The effects of charisma and procedural fairness. *Journal of Applied Psychology, 87*, 858–866.

De Cremer, D., & van Knippenberg, D. (2004). Leader self-sacrifice and leadership effectiveness: The moderating role of leader self-confidence. *Organizational Behavior and Human Decision Processes, 95*, 140–155.

De Cremer, D., & van Knippenberg, D. (2005). Cooperation as a function of leader self-sacrifice, trust, and identification. *Leadership and Organization Development Journal, 26*, 355–369.

De Cremer, D., van Knippenberg, D., van Dijke, M., & Bos, A. E. R. (2006). Self-sacrificial leadership and follower self-esteem: When collective identification matters. *Group Dynamics, 10*, 233–245.

De Cremer, D., & Van Vugt, M. (1999). Social identification effects in social dilemmas: A transformation of motives. *European Journal of Social Psychology, 29*, 871–893.

De Cremer, D., & Van Vugt, M. (2002). Intergroup and intragroup aspects of leadership in social dilemmas: A relational model of cooperation. *Journal of Experimental Social Psychology, 38*, 126–136.

DeRue, D. S., Ashford, S. J., & Cotton, N. C. (2009). Assuming the mantle: Unpacking the process by which individuals internalize a leader identity. In L. M. Roberts &

J. E. Dutton (Eds.), Exploring positive identities in organizations (pp. 217–236). New York: Routledge.

Dirks, K. T., & Ferrin, D. L. (2002). Trust in leadership: Meta-analytic findings and implications for research and practice. *Journal of Applied Psychology, 87*, 611–628.

Dvir, T., Eden, D., Avolio, B. J., & Shamir, B. (2002). Impact of transformational leadership on follower development and performance: A field experiment. *Academy of Management Journal, 45*, 735–744.

Eagly, A. H., & Karau, S. J. (2002). Role congruity theory of prejudice toward female leaders. *Psychological Review, 109*, 573–598.

Eden, D., & Leviatan, V. (1975). Implicit leadership theory as a determinant of the factor structure underlying supervisory behavior. *Journal of Applied Psychology, 60*, 736–741.

Fielding, K. S., & Hogg, M. A. (1997). Social identity, self-categorization, and leadership: A field study of small interactive groups. *Group Dynamics: Theory, Research, and Practice, 1*, 39–51.

Gerstner, C. R., & Day, D. V. (1997). Meta-analytic review of leader–member exchange theory: Correlates and construct issues. *Journal of Applied Psychology, 82*, 827–844.

Giessner, S. R., & van Knippenberg, D. (2007, April). *Leading FOR the team: Situational determinants of team-oriented leader behavior.* Paper presented at the 2007 Annual Meeting of the Society of Industrial and Organizational Psychology, New York.

Giessner, S. R., & van Knippenberg, D. (2008). "License to fail": Goal definition, leader group prototypicality, and perceptions of leadership effectiveness after leader failure. *Organizational Behavior and Human Decision Processes, 105*, 14–35.

Giessner, S. R., & van Knippenberg (2009, June). *When does a leader show fair behavior? Influences of group prototypicality and the social context.* Paper presented at the Erasmus Leadership Conference, Rotterdam, the Netherlands.

Giessner, S. R., van Knippenberg, D., & Sleebos, E. (2009). License to fail? How leader group prototypicality moderates the effects of leader performance on perceptions of leadership effectiveness. *The Leadership Quarterly, 20*, 434–451.

Graen, G. B., & Uhl-Bien, M. (1995). Relationship-based approach to leadership: Development of leader–member exchange (LMX) theory of leadership over 25 years: Applying a multi-level multi-domain approach. *The Leadership Quarterly, 6*, 219–247.

Hains, S. C., Hogg, M. A., & Duck, J. M. (1997). Self-categorization and leadership: Effects of group prototypicality and leader stereotypicality. *Personality and Social Psychology Bulletin, 23*, 1087–1100.

Haslam, S. A. (2004). *Psychology in organisations: The social identity approach* (2nd ed.). London: Sage.

Haslam, S. A., & Platow, M. J. (2001). Your wish is our command: The role of shared social identity in translating a leader's vision into followers' action. In M. A. Hogg & D. J. Terry (Eds.), *Social identity processes in organizational contexts* (pp. 213–228). Philadelphia, PA: Psychology Press.

Higgins, E. T. (1987). Self-discrepancy: A theory relating self and affect. *Psychological Review, 94*, 319–340.

Hirst, G., van Dick, R., & van Knippenberg, D. (2009). A social identity perspective on leadership and employee creativity. *Journal of Organizational Behavior, 30,* 963–982.

Hogg, M. A. (2001). A social identity theory of leadership. *Personality and Social Psychology Review, 5,* 184–200.

Hogg, M. A. (2003). Social identity. In M. R. Leary & J. P. Tangney (Eds.), *Handbook of self and identity* (pp. 462–479). New York: Guilford.

Hogg, M. A. (2007). Uncertainty-identity theory. In M. P. Zanna (Ed.), *Advances in experimental social psychology* (Vol. 39, pp. 69–126). San Diego, CA: Academic Press.

Hogg, M. A., Fielding, K. S., Johnson, D., Masser, B., Russell, E., & Svensson, A. (2006). Demographic category membership and leadership in small groups: A social identity analysis. *The Leadership Quarterly, 17,* 335-350.

Hogg, M. A., Hains, S. C., & Mason, I. (1998). Identification and leadership in small groups: Salience, frame of reference, and leader stereotypicality effects on leader evaluations. *Journal of Personality and Social Psychology, 75,* 1248–1263.

Hogg, M. A., Martin, R., Epitropaki, O., Mankad, A., Svensson, A., & Weeden, K. (2005). Effective leadership in salient groups: Revisiting leader–member exchange theory from the perspective of the social identity theory of leadership. *Personality and Social Psychology Bulletin, 31,* 991-1004.

Hogg, M. A., & van Knippenberg, D. (2003). Social identity and leadership processes in groups. *Advances in Experimental Social Psychology, 35,* 1–52.

Homans, G. C. (1958). Social behavior as exchange. *American Journal of Sociology, 63,* 597–606.

Hoyt, C. L., Murphy, S. E., Halverson, S. K., & Watson, C. B. (2003). Group leadership: Efficacy and effectiveness. *Group Dynamics: Theory, Research, and Practice, 7,* 259–274.

Ibarra, H. (1999). Provisional selves: Experimenting with image and identity in professional adaptation. *Administrative Science Quarterly, 44,* 764–791.

Janson, A., Levy, L., Sitkin, S., & Lind, A. E. (2008). Fairness and other leadership heuristics: A four-nation study. *European Journal of Work and Organizational Psychology, 17,* 251–272.

Judge, T. A., & Bono, J. E. (2000). Five-factor model of personality and transformational leadership. *Journal of Applied Psychology, 85,* 751–765.

Judge, T. A., Bono, J. E., Ilies, R., & Gerhardt, M. (2002). Personality and leadership: A qualitative and quantitative review. *Journal of Applied Psychology, 87,* 765–780.

Judge, T. A., Locke, E. A., & Durham, C. C. (1997). The dispositional causes of job satisfaction: A core self-evaluations approach. *Research in Organizational Behavior, 19,* 151–188.

Kark, R., Shamir, B., & Chen, G. (2003). The two faces of transformational leadership: Empowerment and dependency. *Journal of Applied Psychology, 88,* 246–255.

Kirkpatrick, S. A., & Locke, E. A. (1996). Direct and indirect effects of three core charismatic leadership components on performance and attitudes. *Journal of Applied Psychology, 81,* 36–51.

Koper, G., van Knippenberg, D., Bouhuijs, F., Vermunt, R., & Wilke, H. (1993). Procedural fairness and self-esteem. *European Journal of Social Psychology, 23,* 313–325.

Kramer, R. M. (2003). The imperatives of identity: The role of identity in leader judgment and decision making. In D. van Knippenberg & M. A. Hogg (Eds.), *Leadership and power: Identity processes in groups and organizations* (pp. 184–196). London: Sage.

Leary, M. R., & Tangney, J. P. (2003). *Handbook of self and identity.* New York: Guilford.

Lind, E. A., Kray, L., & Thompson, L. (2001). Primacy effects in justice judgments: Testing predictions from fairness heuristic theory. *Organizational Behavior and Human Decision Processes, 85,* 189–210.

Lind, E. A., & Tyler, T. R. (1988). *The social psychology of procedural justice.* New York: Plenum.

Lord, R. G., Binning, J. F., Rush, M. C., & Thomas, J. C. (1978). The effect of performance cues and leader behavior on questionnaire ratings of leadership behavior. *Organizational Behavior and Human Performance, 21,* 27–39.

Lord, R. G., & Brown, D. J. (2004). *Leadership processes and follower identity.* Mahwah, NJ: Lawrence Erlbaum.

Lord, R. G., Brown, D. J., & Freiberg, S. J. (1999). Understanding the dynamics of leadership: The role of follower self-concepts in the leader/follower relationship. *Organizational Behavior and Human Decision Processes, 78,* 1–37.

Lord, R., & Hall, R. (2003). Identity, leadership categorization, and leadership schema. In D. van Knippenberg & M. A. Hogg (Eds.), *Leadership and power: Identity processes in groups and organizations* (pp. 48–64). London: Sage.

Lord, R. G., & Hall, R. J. (2005). Identity, deep structure and the development of leadership skill. *The Leadership Quarterly, 16,* 591–615.

Lord, R. G., & Maher, K. J. (1991). *Leadership and information processing: Linking perceptions and performance.* Boston: Unwin Hyman.

Markus, H., & Nurius, P. (1986). Possible selves. *American Psychologist, 41,* 954–969.

Mathieu, J., Ahearne, M., & Taylor, S. R. (2007). A longitudinal model of leader and salesperson influences on sales force technology use and performance. *Journal of Applied Psychology, 92,* 528–537.

Meindl, J. R. (1995). The romance of leadership as a follower-centric theory: A social constructionist approach. *The Leadership Quarterly, 6,* 329–341.

Meindl, J. R., Ehrlich, S. B., & Dukerich, J. M. (1985). The romance of leadership. *Administrative Science Quarterly, 30,* 78–102.

Murphy, S. E., & Ensher, E. A. (1999). The effects of leader and subordinate characteristics in the development of leader–member exchange quality. *Journal of Applied Social Psychology, 29,* 1371–1394.

Ng, K.-Y., Ang, S., & Chan, K.-Y. (2008). Personality and leader effectiveness: A moderated mediation model of leadership self-efficacy, job demands, and job autonomy. *Journal of Applied Psychology, 93,* 733–743.

Paglis, L. L., & Green, S. G. (2002). Leadership self-efficacy and managers' motivation for leading change. *Journal of Organizational Behavior, 23,* 215–235.

Pierro, A., Cicero, L., Bonaiuto, M., van Knippenberg, D., & Kruglanski, A. W. (2005). Leader group prototypicality and leadership effectiveness: The moderating role of need for cognitive closure. *The Leadership Quarterly, 16,* 503–516.

Pierro, A., Cicero, L., Bonaiuto, M., van Knippenberg, D., & Kruglanski, A. W. (2007). Leader group prototypicality and resistance to organizational change: The moderating role of need for closure and team identification. *Testing, Psychometrics, Methodology in Applied Psychology, 14,* 27–40.

Platow, M. J., Hoar, S., Reid, S., Harley, K., & Morrison, D. (1997). Endorsement of distributively fair and unfair leaders in interpersonal and intergroup situations. *European Journal of Social Psychology, 27,* 465–494.

Platow, M. J., & van Knippenberg, D. (2001). A social identity analysis of leadership endorsement: The effects of leader ingroup prototypicality and distributive intergroup fairness. *Personality and Social Psychology Bulletin, 27,* 1508–1519.

Platow, M. J., van Knippenberg, D., Haslam, S. A., van Knippenberg, B., & Spears, R. (2006). A special gift we bestow on you for being representative of us: Considering leader charisma from a self-categorization perspective. *British Journal of Social Psychology, 45,* 303–320.

Reicher, S., & Hopkins, N. (2001). *Self and nation.* London: Sage.

Reicher, S., & Hopkins, N. (2003). On the science and art of leadership. In D. van Knippenberg & M. A. Hogg (Eds.), *Leadership and power: Identity processes in groups and organizations* (pp. 197–209). London: Sage.

Rhoades, L., & Eisenberger, R. (2002). Perceived organizational support: A review of the literature. *Journal of Applied Psychology, 87,* 698–714.

Ridgeway, C. L. (2003). Status characteristics and leadership. In D. van Knippenberg & M. A. Hogg (Eds.), *Leadership and power: Identity processes in groups and organizations* (pp. 65–78). London: Sage.

Rosch, E. (1978). Principles of categorization. In E. Rosch & B. B. Lloyd (Eds.), *Cognition and categorization,* (pp. 27–48). Hillsdale, NJ: Lawrence Erlbaum.

Rousseau, D. M. (1998). Why workers still identify with organizations. *Journal of Organizational Behavior, 19,* 217–233.

Rus, D., van Knippenberg, D., & Wisse, B. (2010). Leader self-definition and leader self-serving behavior. *The Leadership Quarterly, 21,* 509–529.

Sani, F. (2008). *Self-continuity: Individual and collective perspectives.* New York: Psychology Press.

Sedikides, C., & Brewer, M. B. (2001). *Individual self, relational self, collective self.* Philadelphia, PA: Psychology Press.

Shamir, B. (1999). Leadership in boundaryless organizations: Disposable or indispensable? *European Journal of Work and Organizational Psychology, 8,* 49–71.

Shamir, B., House, R., & Arthur, M. B. (1993). The motivational effects of charismatic leadership: A self-concept based theory. *Organization Science, 4,* 577–594.

Shamir, B., Pillai, R., Bligh, M. C., & Uhl-Bien M. (2007), *Follower-centered perspectives on leadership: A tribute to the memory of James R. Meindl.* Greenwich, CT: Information Age.

Shamir, B., Zakay, E., Breinin, E., & Popper, M. (1998). Correlates of charismatic leader behavior in military units: Subordinates' attitudes, unit characteristics, and superiors' appraisals of leader performance. *Academy of Management Journal, 41,* 387–409.

Shea, C. M., & Howell, J. M. (1999). Charismatic leadership and task feedback: A laboratory study of their effects on self-efficacy and task performance. *The Leadership Quarterly, 10,* 375–396.

Singer, M. (1991). The relationship between employee sex, length of service and leadership aspirations: A study from valence, self-efficacy and attribution perspectives. *Applied Psychology: An International Review, 40,* 417–436.

Stam, D., van Knippenberg, D., & Wisse, B. (2010). Focusing on followers: The role of regulatory focus and possible selves in explaining the effectiveness of vision statements. *The Leadership Quarterly. 21,* 457–468.

Stets, J. E., & Burke, P. J. (2000). Identity theory and social identity theory. *Social Psychology Quarterly, 63,* 284–297.

Tajfel, H., & Turner, J. C. (1986). The social identity theory of intergroup behavior. In S. Worchel & W. Austin (Eds.), *Psychology of intergroup relations* (pp. 7–24). Chicago: Nelson-Hall.

Thibaut, J., & Walker, L. (1975). *Procedural justice: A psychological analysis.* Hillsdale, NJ: Lawrence Erlbaum.

Turner, J. C., Hogg, M. A., Oakes, P. J., Reicher, S. D., & Wetherell, M. S. (1987). *Rediscovering the social group: A self-categorization theory.* Oxford, UK: Blackwell.

Tyler, T. R. (1999). Why people cooperate with organizations: An identity-based perspective. *Research in Organizational Behavior, 21,* 201–246.

Tyler, T. R., & Blader, S. (2000). *Cooperation in groups: Procedural justice, social identity, and behavioral engagement.* Philadelphia, PA: Psychology Press.

Tyler, T. R., & De Cremer, D. (2005). Process-based leadership: Fair procedures and reactions to organizational change. *The Leadership Quarterly, 16,* 529–545.

Ullrich, J., Christ, O., & van Dick, R. (2009). Substitutes for procedural fairness: Prototypical leaders are endorsed whether they are fair or not. *Journal of Applied Psychology, 94,* 235–244.

Vancouver, J. B., More, K. M., & Yoder, R. J. (2008). Self-efficacy and resource allocation: Support for a discontinuous model. *Journal of Applied Psychology, 93,* 35–47.

van Dick, R., Hirst, G., Grojean, M. W., & Wieseke, J. (2007). Relationships between leader and follower organizational identification and implications for follower attitudes and behaviour. *Journal of Occupational and Organizational Psychology, 80,* 133–150.

van Dijke, M., & De Cremer, D. (2008). How leader prototypicality affects followers' status: The role of procedural fairness. *European Journal of Work and Organizational Psychology, 17,* 226–250.

van Knippenberg, B., & van Knippenberg, D. (2005). Leader self-sacrifice and leadership effectiveness: The moderating role of leader prototypicality. *Journal of Applied Psychology, 90,* 25–37.

van Knippenberg, D. (2000a). Work motivation and performance: A social identity perspective. *Applied Psychology: An International Review, 49,* 357–371.

van Knippenberg, D. (2000b). Group norms, prototypicality, and persuasion. In D. J. Terry & M. A. Hogg (Eds.), *Attitudes, behavior, and social context: The role of norms and group membership* (pp. 157–170). Mahwah, NJ: Lawrence Erlbaum.

van Knippenberg, D. (2003). Intergroup relations in organizations. In M. West, D. Tjosvold, & K. G. Smith (Eds.), *International handbook of organizational teamwork and cooperative working* (pp. 381–399). Chichester, UK: Wiley.

van Knippenberg, D. (in press). Leadership: A person-in-situation perspective. In K. Deaux & M. Snyder (Eds.), *Oxford handbook of personality and social psychology.* New York: Oxford University Press.

van Knippenberg, D., De Cremer, D., & van Knippenberg, B. (2007). Leadership and fairness: The state of the art. *European Journal of Work and Organizational Psychology, 16,* 113–140.

van Knippenberg, D., Haslam, S. A., & Platow, M. J. (2007). Unity through diversity: Value-in-diversity beliefs as moderator of the relationship between work group diversity and group identification. *Group Dynamics, 11,* 207–222.

van Knippenberg, D., & Hogg, M. A. (2003a). A social identity model of leadership effectiveness in organizations. *Research in Organizational Behavior, 25,* 243–295.

van Knippenberg, D., & Hogg, M. A. (2003b). *Leadership and power: Identity processes in groups and organizations.* London: Sage.

van Knippenberg, D., Lossie, N., & Wilke, H. (1994). In-group prototypicality and persuasion: Determinants of heuristic and systematic message processing. *British Journal of Social Psychology, 33,* 289–300.

van Knippenberg, D., & Schippers, M. C. (2007). Work group diversity. *Annual Review of Psychology, 58,* 515–541.

van Knippenberg, D., & Sleebos, E. (2006). Organizational identification versus organizational commitment: Self-definition, social exchange, and job attitudes. *Journal of Organizational Behavior, 27,* 571–584.

van Knippenberg, D., van Dick, R., & Tavares, S. (2007). Social identity and social exchange: Identification, support, and withdrawal from the job. *Journal of Applied Social Psychology, 37,* 457–477.

van Knippenberg, D., van Knippenberg, B., & Bobbio, A. (2008). Leaders as agents of continuity: Self continuity and resistance to collective change. In F. Sani (Ed.), *Self-continuity: Individual and collective perspectives* (pp. 175–186). New York: Psychology Press.

van Knippenberg, D., van Knippenberg, B., De Cremer, D., & Hogg, M. A. (2004). Leadership, self, and identity: A review and research agenda. *The Leadership Quarterly, 15,* 825–856.

van Knippenberg, D., van Knippenberg, B., & Giessner, S. R. (2007). Extending the follower-centered perspective: Leadership as an outcome of shared social identity. In B. Shamir, R. Pillai, M. C. Bligh, & M. Uhl-Bien (Eds.), *Follower-centered perspectives on leadership: A tribute to the memory of James R. Meindl* (pp. 51–70). Greenwich, CT: Information Age.

van Knippenberg, D., van Knippenberg, B., Monden, L., & de Lima, F. (2002). Organizational identification after a merger: A social identity perspective. *British Journal of Social Psychology, 41,* 233–252.

van Knippenberg, D., van Knippenberg, B., & van Dijk, E. (2000). Who takes the lead in risky decision making? Effects of group members' individual riskiness and prototypicality. *Organizational Behavior and Human Decision Processes, 83,* 213–234.

van Quaquebeke, N., van Knippenberg, D., & Brodbeck, F. C. (2007, August). *The influence of subordinates' self-perceptions on their evaluations of and responses to leaders.* Paper presented at the Academy of Management Annual Meeting 2007, Philadelphia, PA, USA.

Vermunt, R., van Knippenberg, D., van Knippenberg, B., & Blaauw, E. (2001). Self-esteem and outcome fairness: Differential importance of procedural and outcome considerations. *Journal of Applied Psychology, 86,* 621–628.

Voss, Z. G., Cable, D. M., & Voss, G. B. (2006). Organizational identity and firm performance: What happens when leaders disagree about "who we are?" *Organization Science, 17,* 741–755.

Yorges, S. L., Weiss, H. M., & Strickland, O. J. (1999). The effect of leader outcomes on influence, attributions, and perceptions of charisma. *Journal of Applied Psychology, 84,* 428–436.

Yukl, G. (2002). *Leadership in organizations* (5th ed.). New York: Prentice Hall.

15

Ethics and Effectiveness

The Nature of Good Leadership

Joanne B. Ciulla

University of Richmond
University of Fort Hare

The moral triumphs and failures of leaders carry a greater weight and volume than those of most other people (Ciulla, 2003b). In leadership, we see morality and immorality magnified, which is why the study of ethics is fundamental to the study of leadership. The study of ethics concentrates on the nature of right and wrong and good and evil. It examines the relationships of people with each other and with other living things. Ethics explores questions related to what we should do and what we should be like as individuals, as members of a group or society, and in the different roles that we play in life. The role of a leader entails a distinctive type of human relationship. Some hallmarks of this relationship are power and/or influence, vision, obligation, and responsibility. By understanding the ethics of this relationship, we gain a better understanding of leadership because some of the central issues in ethics are also the central issues of leadership. They include personal challenges such as self-knowledge, self-interest, and self-discipline, and moral obligations related to justice, duty, competence, and the greatest good.

The challenges of leadership are not new, which is why we find some of the most perceptive work on leadership and ethics in ancient texts. History is

AUTHOR'S NOTE: Please address correspondence concerning this chapter to Joanne B. Ciulla, Professor & Coston Family Chair in Leadership and Ethics, The Jepson School of Leadership Studies, University of Richmond, Richmond, Virginia, 23173, USA. Phone: 804–320–2525 or 804–287–6083; e-mail: jciulla@richmond.edu.

A special thanks to Tammy Tripp for her help in preparing this chapter.

filled with wisdom and case studies on the morality of leaders and leadership. Ancient scholars from the East and West offer insights that enable us to understand leadership and formulate contemporary research questions in new ways. History, philosophy, and the humanities in general provide perspective and reveal certain patterns of leadership behavior and themes about leadership and morality that have existed over time. Perhaps the most important benefit of the humanities approach to leadership studies is that it does not allow us to study leader effectiveness without looking at the ethics of what leaders do and how and why they do it. In short, the humanities approach never lets us forget that the very nature of leadership is inextricably tied to the human condition, which includes the values, needs, and aspirations of human beings who live and work together.

The study of ethics and the history of ideas help us understand two overarching and overlapping questions that drive most leadership research. They are: What is leadership? And what is good leadership? The first is about what leadership is, or a descriptive question. The second is about what leadership ought to be, or a normative question. These two questions are sometimes confused in the literature. Progress in leadership studies rests on the ability of scholars to integrate the answers to these questions. In this chapter, I discuss the implications of these two questions for our understanding of leadership. I begin the chapter by looking at how the ethics and effectiveness question plays out in contemporary work on leadership ethics, and I discuss some of the ethical issues distinctive to leadership. Then I show some of the insights gleaned from the ancient literature and how they complement and provide context for contemporary research. In the end, I suggest some directions for research on ethics in the context of leadership studies.

Ethikos and Morale

Before I get started, a short note on the words *ethics* and *moral* is in order. Some people like to make a distinction between these two concepts. The problem with it is that everyone seems to distinguish the concepts in a different way. Like most philosophers, I use the terms interchangeably. As a practical matter, courses on moral philosophy cover the same material as courses on ethics. There is a long history of using these terms as synonyms of each other, regardless of their roots in different languages. In *De Fato* (II.i) Cicero substituted the Latin word *morale* for Aristotle's use of the Greek word *ethikos*. We see the two terms defining each other in the *Oxford English Dictionary*. The word *moral* is defined as "of or pertaining to the distinction between right and wrong, or good and evil in relation to the actions, volitions, or character of human beings; ethical," and "concerned with virtue and vice or rules of conduct, ethical praise or blame, habits of life, custom and manners" (*Compact Oxford English Dictionary*, 1991, p. 1114). Similarly, it defines *ethics* as "of or pertaining to morality" and "the science of morals, the moral principles by which a person is guided" (*Compact Oxford English*

Dictionary, 1991, p. 534). Perhaps the most compelling evidence for why these terms are not significantly different is that people rarely define the difference between them in the same way. They often tend to define the two terms in ways that best suit their argument or research agenda.

Ethics as Critical Theory

In 1992, I conducted an extensive search of literature from psychology, sociology, anthropology, political science, religion, and philosophy to find work on ethics and leadership (Ciulla, 1995). The results were disappointing both in terms of the quantity and quality of articles in contemporary books and journals. This is not to say that prominent leadership scholars ignored the subject or failed to see the importance of ethics to leadership. Missing were rigorous philosophic analyses of ethical issues that are distinctive to leaders and leadership. Philosophers differ from social scientists in their approach to ethics. Studies of charismatic, transformational, visionary, and authentic leadership often talk about ethics. In these studies, ethics is part of the social scientist's description of types or qualities of leaders and/or leader behaviors. From a philosopher's point of view, these studies offer useful empirical descriptions, but they do not offer a full analysis of the ethics of leadership. The study of ethics in any field, such as business or law, also serves as a critical theory. Philosophers usually question most of the assumptions in the field (which might explain why people often try to serve them hemlock!). My point here is not that philosophy is better than the social sciences, but that it brings out different aspects of leadership by employing different methods of analysis. If we are to gain an understanding of ethics and leadership, we will need both kinds of research and analysis.

Explanation and Understanding

The other striking thing I observed about the leadership literature was that writer after writer complained that researchers did not seem to be making much progress in understanding leadership (Hunt, 1991). Fortunately, I will not be adding my voice to that chorus of lamentation. Many things have changed in leadership studies since the early 1990s. Several initiatives are afoot to pull research together. The "full-range leadership theory" consolidates research on transformational and charismatic leadership theories and research with empirical findings on leadership behaviors (Antonakis & House, 2002). Also, more scholars from the humanities have entered the field, and more leadership scholars are doing interdisciplinary work. This is a substantial development because the humanities give us a different kind of knowledge than do the sciences and social sciences. The humanities provide a larger context in which we can synthesize what we know about leadership (Ciulla, 2008a, 2008b).

This context also shows us patterns of leadership that we can use to analyze contemporary problems. The challenge for today's leadership scholars is how to bring the two together. As C. P. Snow noted in his famous 1959 Rede lecture, there are "two cultures" of scholars, the humanities and the natural sciences. He said the sciences provide us with descriptions and explanations, but we need the humanities for understanding (Snow, 1998). Similarly, in 1962, Bennis observed that the science part of social science is not about the data the scientists produce, "nor is it barren operationalism—what some people refer to as 'scientism' or the gadgetry used for laboratory work. Rather it is what may be called the 'scientific temper' or 'spirit'" (Bennis, 2002, pp. 4–5). The temper and spirit of science include freedom and democratic values. Bennis (2002) argued that the scientist and citizen cannot be sharply separated and that empirical research had to be done from "a moral point of view" (p. 7). Although the quantity of research that focuses solely on ethics and leadership is still very small, this perspective on leadership is already changing the way some traditional social scientists think about their work.

Ethics as Exhortation

Whereas some of the leadership studies literature offers descriptive accounts of ethics, other parts of the literature treat ethics as an exhortation rather than an in-depth exploration of the subject. Researchers often tell us that leaders should be honest, have integrity, and so forth. For example, John Gardner makes his plea for ethical leaders in his working paper "The Moral Aspect of Leadership" (1987), later published in his book *On Leadership* (Gardner, 1990). In the chapter titled "The Moral Dimension of Leadership," Gardner begins by categorizing the different kinds of bad leaders, or what he called "transgressors," that we find in history. He said some leaders are cruel to their subjects; some encourage their subjects to be cruel to others; some motivate their subjects by playing on the cruelty of their subjects; some render their followers childlike and dependent; and some destroy processes that societies have set up to preserve freedom, justice, and human dignity (Gardner, 1990, pp. 67–68). Gardner picks an important and provocative place to start a discussion on ethics and leadership. However, he never takes us much beyond the "leaders shouldn't be like this" phase of analysis.

When Gardner gets to the meat of the chapter, he offers a series of eloquent and inspiring exhortations on the importance of caring, responsive leaders and empowering leaders who serve the common good. He does not tell us anything we do not already know, but he says it beautifully: "We should hope that our leaders will keep alive values that are not so easy to embed in laws—our caring for others, about honor and integrity, about tolerance and mutual respect, and about human fulfillment within a framework of values" (Gardner, 1990, p. 77). Missing in Gardner's discussion is what this means in terms of moral commitments and relationships. Why do so many leaders fail in these areas? What does it take to stay on the moral track? And what role can and do followers play in the moral behavior of leaders?

The Normative Aspects of Definitions

Leadership scholars often concern themselves with the problem of defining leadership. Some believe that if they could only agree on a common definition of leadership, they would be better able to understand it. This really does not make sense because scholars in history, biology, and other subjects do not all agree on the definition of their subject and, even if they did, it would not help them to understand it better. Furthermore, scholars do not determine the meaning of a word for the general public. Would it make sense to have an academic definition that did not agree with the way ordinary people understood the word? Social scientists sometimes limit the definition of a term so that they can use it in a study. Generally, the way people in a culture use a word and think about it determines the meaning of a word (Wittgenstein, 1968). The denotation of the word *leadership* stays basically the same in English. Even though people apply the term differently, all English-speaking leadership scholars know what the word means. Slight variations in its meaning tell us about the values, practices, and paradigms of leadership in a certain place and at a certain time.

Rost (1991) is among those who think that there has been little progress in leadership studies. He believed that there will be no progress in leadership studies until scholars agree on a common definition of leadership. He collected 221 definitions of leadership, ranging from the 1920s to the 1990s. All of these definitions generally say the same thing—leadership is about a person or persons somehow moving other people to do something. Where the definitions differ is in how leaders motivate their followers, their relationship to followers, who has a say in the goals of the group or organization, and what abilities the leader needs to have to get things done. I chose definitions that were representative of definitions from other sources from the same era. Even today, one can find a strong family resemblance in the ways various leadership scholars define leadership.

Consider the following definitions (all from American sources), and think about the history of the time and the prominent leaders of that era. What were they like? What were their followers like? What events and values shaped the ideas behind these definitions?

1920s: [Leadership is] the ability to impress the will of the leader on those led and induce obedience, respect, loyalty, and cooperation.

1930s: Leadership is a process in which the activities of many are organized to move in a specific direction by one.

1940s: Leadership is the result of an ability to persuade or direct men, apart from the prestige or power that comes from office or external circumstance.

1950s: [Leadership is what leaders do in groups.] The leader's authority is spontaneously accorded him by his fellow group members.

1960s: [Leadership is] acts by a person which influence other persons in a shared direction.

1970s: Leadership is defined in terms of discretionary influence. Discretionary influence refers to those leader behaviors under control of the leader, which he may vary from individual to individual.

1980s: Regardless of the complexities involved in the study of leadership, its meaning is relatively simple. Leadership means to inspire others to undertake some form of purposeful action as determined by the leader.

1990s: Leadership is an influence relationship between leaders and followers who intend real changes that reflect their mutual purposes.

Notice that in the 1920s, leaders "impressed" their will on those led. In the 1940s, they "persuaded" followers; in the 1960s, they "influenced" them; whereas in the 1990s, leaders and followers influenced each other. All of these definitions are about the nature of the leader–follower relationship. The difference between the definitions rests on normative questions: How should leaders treat followers? And how should followers treat leaders? Who decides what goals to pursue? What is and what ought to be the nature of their relationship to each other? One thing the definition debate demonstrates is the extent to which the very concept of leadership is a social, historical, and normative construction.

The Hitler Problem

Some scholars would argue that bullies and tyrants are not leaders, which takes us to what I have called "the Hitler problem" (Ciulla, 1995). The Hitler problem is based on how you answer the question, Was Hitler a leader? According to the morally unattractive definitions, he was a leader, perhaps even a great leader, albeit an immoral one. Heifetz (1994) argued that, under the "great man" and trait theories of leadership, you can put Hitler, Lincoln, and Gandhi in the same category because the underlying idea of the theory is that leadership is influence over history. However, when your concept of leadership includes ethical considerations, Hitler was not a leader at all. He was a bully or tyrant—or simply the head of Germany.

We see how ingrained ethical ideas are in the concept of a leader when scholars differentiate between leaders and "real leaders" or "true leaders."

Burns (1978) and Bass (1997) suggest that many leaders—transactional ones—are competent in that they promote exchanges among subordinates in their pursuit of collective outcomes, but that only transformational leaders are leaders in a strong moral sense. Extending this distinction, Bass attempts to separate leaders who fit the description of a transformational leader but are not ethical, from ethical leaders by distinguishing between transformational and pseudotransformational leaders or authentic transformational leaders (Bass & Steidlmeier, 1999). Brown, Treviño, and Harrison (2005) make this distinction between common leadership and ethical leadership explicit in their concept of ethical leadership: "the demonstration of normatively appropriate conduct through personal actions and interpersonal relations, and the promotion of such conduct to followers through two-way communication, reinforcement, and decision-making" (p. 120). Using Bennis and Nanus's (1985) characterization of leadership—"Managers are people who do things right and leaders are people who do right things" (p. 21)—one could argue that Hitler was neither unethical nor a leader. (Maybe he was a manager?) Bennis and Nanus are among those scholars who sometimes slip into using the term leader to mean a morally good leader. However, what appears to be behind this in Bennis and Nanus's comment is the idea that leaders are or should be a head above everyone else morally.

This normative strand exists throughout the leadership literature, most noticeably in the popular literature. Writers will say leaders are participatory, supportive, and so forth, when what they really mean is that leaders should have these qualities. Yet it may not even be clear that we really want leaders with these qualities. As former presidential spokesman David Gergen (2002) pointed out, leadership scholars all preach and teach that participatory, empowering leadership is best. A president like George W. Bush, however, exercises a top-down style of leadership. Few leadership scholars would prescribe such leadership in their work. Nonetheless, President Bush scored some of the highest approval ratings for his leadership in recent history (Gergen, 2002). A number of studies help explain this based on the context of Bush's leadership in post-9/11 America. For example, Pillai found that charismatic leadership is not only about personal characteristics but is also something that emerges in leaders during a crisis (Pillai, 1996). When people feel a loss of control, they look for decisive leaders. In the case of Bush, they may have found his autocratic leadership style comforting. As the crisis subsided later in his presidency, Bush's ratings hit rock bottom. Another explanation for this disparity between what leadership scholars preach and what people want reflects conflicting cultural values. The American ethos of rugged individualism may also help explain Bush's ratings. On one hand, Americans admire leaders who take bold, decisive, and autocratic action, but on the other hand, they do not want to work for them (Ruscio, 2004).

Philosopher Eva Kort offers a solution to the Hitler problem that goes beyond semantics. She notes that group actions, not relationships, reveal the features that identify what she calls "leadership proper" or "real" leadership from cases of "purported" leadership. Real leadership is ethical and effective leadership. Purported leadership is basically someone in a leadership role, telling people what to do. Kort uses a simple example to illustrate the normative and technical aspects of leadership. A concertmaster holds a formal leadership position. If he conducts the orchestra with instructions that the musicians know are bad, they will follow him because of his position. In this case, Kort says the concertmaster is merely a purported leader, not a leader proper. She writes: "It is only when the concertmaster does lead–participate in the plural action in (generally) the right sort of way–that the concertmaster is the leader in the proper sense" (Kort, 2008, p. 422). Notice how Kort's definition includes unavoidable judgments. Leaders are people whom we choose to follow because they seem competent and, where relevant, ethical. For Kort, leaders are those whose ideas are voluntarily endorsed and acted on by others in various situations. This is a useful way to understand how ethics and effectiveness are woven together in the concept of leadership. For Kort, the answer to the Hitler problem depends on whether followers freely choose to follow him because they endorse his ethics and think he is competent. Notice that this speaks directly to his leadership, but still does not account for cases where followers are unethical or morally mistaken or when they misjudge the competence of their leaders.

Moral Luck

The ultimate question about leadership is not, What is the definition of leadership? We are not confused about what leaders do, but we would like to know the best way to do it. The point of studying leadership is to answer the question, What is good leadership? The use of the word good here has two senses: morally good leadership and technically good leadership (i.e., effective at getting the job at-hand done). The problem with this view is that when we look at history and the leaders around us, we find some leaders who meet both criteria and some who only meet one. History only confuses the matter further. Historians do not write about the leader who was very ethical but did not do anything of significance. They rarely write about a general who was a great human being but never won a battle. Most historians write about leaders who were winners or who change history for better or for worse.

The historian's assessment of leaders also depends on what philosophers call moral luck. Moral luck is another way of thinking about the free will/ determinism problem in ethics. People are responsible for the free choices they make. We are generally not responsible for things over which we have no control. The most difficult ethical decisions leaders make are those where they cannot fully determine the outcome. Philosopher Bernard Williams (1982) described moral luck as intrinsic to an action based on how well a person thinks through a decision and whether his or her inferences are sound and turn out to be right. He stated that moral luck is also extrinsic to a decision. Things like bad weather, accidents, terrorists, mal-functioning machines, and so forth can sabotage the best-laid plans. Moral luck is an important aspect of ethics and leadership because it helps us think about decision making, risk assessment, and moral accountability.

Consider President George W. Bush's decision to invade Iraq. The morality of this decision is based on what Bush intended to do and the actual outcome of the war. His decision was allegedly based on the following argument:

1. Just because the U.N. weapons inspectors have not found weapons of mass destruction, does not mean that there are no weapons of mass destruction.

2. If there are weapons of mass destruction, Saddam Hussein will use them on the United States.

3. As president, Bush has a moral obligation to protect the public.

4. Therefore, we must go to war with Iraq.

Premises 1 and 2 were later modified to:

1a. Saddam Hussein is an evil leader who has used biological weapons on his own people.

2a. If given the chance, he will harm his people and use weapons of mass destruction on the United States and its allies.

Leaders must justify war with powerful moral arguments—genocide, self-defense, and so forth. Just wars are usually a last resort after other measures have failed. Leaders who go to war when there are other viable options or for personal, ideological, or economic designs are ethically problematic, especially when they fail. In the case of the Iraq war, Bush and the British Prime Minister Tony Blair both believed that the war was justified; however, their belief was allegedly based on the conditional premises 1, 1a and 2, 2a. Bush and Blair also may have had an ideological reason, which they considered a moral reason, for the war—to bring democracy to Iraq and eventually the Middle East.

Moral luck is when the consequences of the action justify the means and or intentions of the action. So in this case, we can imagine history revealing the following:

1. If sometime in the future, we discover weapons of mass destruction in Iraq and plans by Saddam Hussein to use weapons of mass destruction on the United States and other countries, then Bush and Blair's war initiative will appear ethical.

2. If we never find weapons or any evidence of Saddam Hussein's intentions, then the morality of their actions will continue to be hotly contested.

3. If we find evidence that Hussein was bluffing and had no weapons or plans to use weapons on anyone, then the war in Iraq will look like a waste of human life.

4. If in the next decade, an unforeseeable set of events produce democracy in Iraq, then Iraqis may celebrate the U.S. invasion and erect a statue of George Bush in Bagdad—history tells us that such strange things can happen.

In this case, the moral luck of leaders rests on whether they make the right choice or assessment of risk in a case of uncertainty. How they assess the risk and their intentions also matter, especially if they lose the war.

Some leaders are ethical but unlucky, whereas others are not as ethical but very lucky. Most really difficult moral decisions made by leaders are risky because they have imperfect or incomplete information and lack control over all of the variables that will affect outcomes. Leaders who fail at something are worthy of forgiveness when they act with deliberate care and for the right moral reasons, even though followers do not always forgive them or lose confidence in their leadership. Americans did not blame President Jimmy Carter for the botched attempt to free the hostages in Iran, but it was one more thing that shook their faith in his leadership. He was unlucky because if the mission had been successful, it might have strengthened people's faith in him as a leader and improved his chances of retaining the presidency.

The irony of moral luck is that leaders who are reckless and do not base their actions on sound moral and practical arguments are usually condemned when they fail and celebrated as heroes when they succeed. That is why Immanuel Kant (1785/1993) argued that because we cannot always know the results of our actions, moral judgments should be based on the right moral principles and not be contingent on outcomes. The reckless, lucky leader does not demonstrate moral or technical competency, yet because of the outcome, he or she often gets credit for having both. Because history usually focuses on outcomes, it is not always clear how much luck, skill, and morality figured in the success or failure of a leader. This is why we need to devote more study to the ethics of leaders' decision-making processes in addition to their actions and behavior.

_____ The Relationship Between Ethics and Effectiveness

History defines successful leaders largely in terms of their ability to bring about change for better or worse. As a result, great leaders in history include everyone from Gandhi to Hitler. Machiavelli was disgusted by Cesare Borgia the man, but impressed by Borgia as the resolute, ferocious, and cunning prince (Prezzolini, 1928, p. 11). Whereas leaders usually bring about change or are successful at doing something, the ethical questions waiting in the wings are always these; Was the change itself good? How did the leader go about bringing change? And what were the leader's intentions? A full analysis of the ethics and effectiveness of any action requires one to ask: Was it the right thing to do? Was it done the right way? Was it done for the right reason?

In my own work, I have argued that a good leader is an ethical and an effective leader (Ciulla, 1995). Whereas, this may seem like stating the obvious, the problem we face is that we do not always find ethics and effectiveness in the same leader. Some leaders are highly ethical but not very effective. Others are very effective at serving the needs of their constituents or organizations but not very ethical. United States Senator Trent Lott, who was forced to step from his position as Senate majority leader because of his insensitive racial comments, is a compelling example of the latter. Some of his African American constituents said that they would vote for him again, regardless of his racist comments because Lott had used his power and influence in Washington to bring jobs and money to the state. In politics, the old saying "He may be a son-of-a-bitch, but he's our son-of-a-bitch," captures the trade-off between ethics and effectiveness. In other words, as long as Lott gets the job done, we do not care about his ethics.

This distinction between ethics and effectiveness is not always a crisp one. Sometimes being ethical is being effective and sometimes being effective is being ethical. In other words, ethics is effectiveness in certain instances. There are times when simply being regarded as ethical and trustworthy makes a leader effective and other times when being highly effective makes a leader ethical. Given the limited power and resources of the secretary-general of the United Nations, it would be very difficult for someone in this position to be effective in the job if he or she did not behave ethically. The same is true for organizations. In the famous Tylenol case, Johnson & Johnson actually increased sales of Tylenol by pulling Tylenol bottles off their shelves after someone poisoned some of them. The leaders at Johnson & Johnson were effective because they were ethical.

The criteria that we use to judge the effectiveness of a leader are also not morally neutral. For a while, Wall Street and the business press lionized Al Dunlap ("Chainsaw Al") as a great business leader. Their admiration was based on his ability to downsize a company and raise the price of its stock. Dunlap apparently knew little about the nuts and bolts of running a business. When he failed to deliver profits at Sunbeam, he tried to cover up his losses and was fired. In this case and in many business cases, the criteria for effectiveness are practically and morally limited. It does not take great skill to get rid of employees, and taking away a person's livelihood requires a moral and a practical argument. Also, one of the most striking aspects of professional ethics is that often what seems right in the short run is not right in the long run or what seems right for a group or organization is not right when placed in a broader context. For example, Mafia families may have very strong internal ethical systems, but they are highly unethical in any larger context of society.

There are also cases when the sheer competence of a leader has a moral impact. For instance, there were many examples of heroism in the aftermath of the September 2001 terrorist attack on the World Trade Center. The most inspiring and frequently cited were the altruistic acts of rescue workers. Yet consider the case of Alan S. Weil, whose law firm Sidley, Austin, Brown, & Wood occupied five floors of the World Trade Center. Immediately after watching the Trade Center towers fall to the ground and checking to see if his employees got out safely, Weil got on the phone and within 3 hours had rented four floors of another building for his employees. By the end of the day, he had arranged for an immediate delivery of 800 desks and 300 computers. The next day, the firm was open for business with desks for almost every employee (Schwartz, 2001). We do not know if Mr. Weil's motives were altruistic or avaricious, but his focus on doing his job allowed the firm to fulfill its obligations to all of its stakeholders, from clients to employees.

On the flip side of the ethics effectiveness continuum are situations where it is difficult to tell whether a leader is unethical, incompetent, or stupid. As Price (2000, 2005) has argued, the moral failures of leaders are not always intentional. Sometimes moral failures are cognitive and sometimes they are normative. Leaders may get their facts wrong and think that they are acting ethically when, in fact, they are not. For example, in 2000, South African president Thabo Mbeki issued a statement saying that it was not clear that HIV caused AIDS. He thought the pharmaceutical industry was just trying to scare people so that it could increase its profits (Garrett, 2000). Coming from the leader of a country where about one in five people tests positive for HIV, this was a shocking statement. His stance caused outrage among public health experts and other citizens. It was irresponsible and certainly undercut the efforts to stop the AIDS epidemic. Mbeki understood the scientific literature but chose to put political and philosophical reasons ahead of scientific knowledge. (He has since backed away from this position.) When leaders do things like this, we want to know if they are unethical, misinformed, incompetent, or just stupid. Mbeki's actions seemed unethical, but he may have thought he was taking an ethical stand. His narrow mind-set about this issue made him recklessly disregard his more pressing obligations to stop the AIDS epidemic (Moldoveanu & Langer, 2002).

In some situations, leaders act with moral intentions, but because they are incompetent, they create unethical outcomes. Take, for instance, the unfortunate case of the Swiss charity Christian Solidarity International. Its goal was to free an estimated 200,000 Dinka children who were enslaved in Sudan. The charity paid between $35 and $75 a head to free enslaved children. The unintended consequence of the charity's actions was that it actually encouraged enslavement by creating a market for it. The price of slaves and the demand for them went up. Also, some cunning Sudanese found that it paid to pretend that they were slaves so that they could make money by being liberated. This deception made it difficult for the charity to identify those who really needed help from those who were faking it. Here the charity's intent and the means it used to achieve its goals were not unethical in relation to alleviating suffering in the short run; however, in the long run, the charity inadvertently created more suffering. This case illustrates the relationship between ethics and effectiveness. In short, the charity.

1. Did the right thing—trying to free children from slavery

2. But they did it the wrong way—buying the children is unethical because they took part in the buying and selling of a human being and ineffective because it created a market for slaves and increased rather than diminished slavery

3. They did it for the right reason—slavery violates the dignity and human rights of children

Deontological and Teleological Theories

The ethics-and-effectiveness question parallels the perspectives of deontological and teleological theories in ethics. From the deontological point of view, intentions are the morally relevant aspects of an act. As long as the leader acts according to his or her duty or on moral principles, then the leader acts ethically, regardless of the consequences, as was the case in the first moral luck example. From the teleological perspective, what really matters is that the leader's actions result in bringing about something morally good or "the greatest good." Deontological theories locate the ethics of an action in the moral intent of the leader and his or her moral justification for the action, whereas teleological theories locate the ethics of the action in its results. We need both deontological and teleological theories to account for the ethics of leaders. Just as a good leader has to be ethical and effective, he or she also has to act according to duty and with some notion of the greatest good in mind.

In modernity, we often separate the inner person from the outer person and a person from his or her actions. Ancient Greek theories of ethics based on virtue do not have this problem. In virtue theories, you basically are what you do. The utilitarian John Stuart Mill (1987) saw this split between the ethics of the person and the ethics of his or her actions clearly. He said the intentions or reasons for an act tell us something about the morality of the person, but the ends of an act tell us about the morality of the action. This solution does not really solve the ethics-and-effectiveness problem. It simply reinforces the split between the personal morality of a leader and what he or she does as a leader.

Going back to an earlier example, Mr. Weil may have worked quickly to keep his law firm going because he was so greedy he did not want to lose a day of billings, but in doing so, he also produced the greatest good for various stakeholders. We may not like his personal reasons for acting, but in this particular case, the various stakeholders may not care because they also benefited.

If the various stakeholders knew that Weil had selfish intentions, they would, as Mill said, think less of him but not less of his actions. This is often the case with business. When a business runs a campaign to raise money for the homeless, it may be doing it to sell more of its goods and improve its public image. Yet it would seem a bit harsh to say that the business should not have the charity drive and deny needed funds for the homeless. One might argue that it is sometimes very unethical to demand perfect moral intentions. Nonetheless, personally unethical leaders who do good things for their constituents are still problematic. Even though they provide for the greatest good, their people can never really trust them.

Moral Standards

People often say that leaders should be held to "a higher moral standard," but does that make sense? If true, would it then be acceptable for everyone else to live by lower moral standards? The curious thing about morality is that if you set the moral standards for leaders too high, requiring something close to moral perfection, then few people will be qualified to be leaders or will want to be leaders. For example, how many of us could live up to the standard of having never lied, said an unkind word, or reneged on a promise? Ironically, when we set moral standards for leaders too high, we become even more dissatisfied with our leaders because few are able to live up to our expectations. We set moral standards for leaders too low, however, when we reduce them to nothing more than following the law or, worse, simply not being as unethical as their predecessors. A business leader may follow all laws and yet be highly immoral in the way he or she runs a business. Laws are supposed to be either morally neutral or moral minimums about what is right. They do not and cannot capture the scope and complexity of morality. For example, an elected official may be law abiding and, unlike his or her predecessor, live by "strong family values." The official may also have little concern for the disadvantaged. Not caring about the poor and the sick is not against the law, but is such a leader ethical? So where does this leave us? On one hand, it is admirable to aspire to high moral standards, but on the other hand, if the standards are unreachable, then people give up trying to reach them (Ciulla, 1994, pp. 167–183). If the standards are too high, we may become more disillusioned with our leaders for failing to reach them. We might also end up with a shortage of competent people who are willing to take on leadership positions because we expect too much from them ethically. Some highly qualified people stay out of politics because they do not want their private lives aired in public. If the standards are too low, we become cynical about our leaders because we have lost faith in their ability to rise above the moral minimum.

History is littered with leaders who did not think they were subject to the same moral standards of honesty, propriety, and so forth, as the rest of society.

One explanation for this is so obvious that it has become a cliché—power corrupts. Winter's (2002) and McClelland's (1975) works on power motives and on socialized and personalized charisma offer psychological accounts of this kind of leader behavior. Maccoby (2000) and a host of others have talked about narcissistic leaders who, on the bright side, are exceptional and, on the dark side, consider themselves exceptions to the rules.

Hollander's (1964) work on social exchange demonstrates how emerging leaders who are loyal to and competent at attaining group goals gain "idiosyncrasy credits" that allow them to deviate from the groups' norms to suit common goals. As Price (2000) has argued, given the fact that we often grant leaders permission to deviate or be an exception to the rules, it is not difficult to see why leaders sometimes make themselves exceptions to moral constraints. This is why I think we should not hold leaders to higher moral standards than ourselves. If anything, we have to make sure that we hold them to the same standards as the rest of society. What we should expect and hope is that our leaders will fail less than most people at meeting ethical standards, while pursuing and achieving the goals of their constituents. The really interesting question for leadership development, organizational, and political theory is, What can we do to keep leaders from the moral failures that stem from being in a leadership role? Too many models of leadership characterize the leader as a saint or "father-knows-best" archetype who posses all the right values.

Altruism

Some leadership scholars use altruism as the moral standard for ethical leadership. In their book *Ethical Dimensions of Leadership*, Kanungo and Mendonca wrote (1996), "Our thesis is that organizational leaders are truly effective only when they are motivated by a concern for others, when their actions are invariably guided primarily by the criteria of the benefit to others even if it results in some cost to oneself" (p. 35). When people talk about altruism, they usually contrast altruism with selfishness, or behavior that benefits oneself at a cost to others (Ozinga, 1999). Altruism is a very high personal standard and, as such, is problematic for a number of reasons. Both selfishness and altruism refer to extreme types of motivation and behavior. Locke brings out this extreme side of altruism in a dialogue with Avolio (Avolio & Locke, 2002). Locke argued that if altruism is about self-sacrifice, then leaders who want to be truly altruistic will pick a job that they do not like or value, expect no rewards or pleasure from their job or achievements, and give themselves over totally to serving the wants of others. He then asked, "Would anyone want to be a leader under such circumstances?" (Avolio & Locke, 2002, pp. 169–171). One might also ask, "Would we even want such a person as a leader?" Whereas I do not agree with Locke's argument that leaders should act according to their self-interest, he does articulate the practical problem of using altruism as a standard of moral behavior for leaders. Avolio's argument against Locke is based on equally extreme cases. He draws on his work at West Point, where a central moral principle in the military is the willingness to make the ultimate sacrifice for the good of the group. Avolio also used Mother Teresa as one of his examples. In these cases, self-sacrifice may be less about the ethics of leaders in general and more about the jobs of military leaders and missionaries. The Locke and Avolio debate pits the extreme aspects of altruism against its heroic side. Here, as in the extensive philosophic literature on self-interest and altruism, the debate spins round and round and does not get us very far. Ethics is about the relationship of individuals to others, so in a sense both sides are right and wrong.

Altruism is a motive for acting, but it is not in and of itself a normative principle (Nagel, 1970). Requiring leaders to act altruistically is not only a tall order, but it does not guarantee that the leader or his or her actions will be moral. For example, stealing from the rich to give to the poor, or *Robinhoodism,* is morally problematic (Ciulla, 2003a). A terrorist leader who becomes a suicide bomber might have purely altruistic intentions, but the means that he uses to carry out his mission—killing innocent people—is not considered ethical even if his cause is a just one. One might also argue, as one does against suicide, that it is unethical for a person to sacrifice his or her life for any reason because of the impact that it has on loved ones. Great leaders such as Martin Luther King, Jr., and Gandhi behaved altruistically, but what made their leadership ethical was the means that they used to achieve their ends and the morality of their causes. We have a particular respect for leaders who are martyred for a cause, but the morality of King and Gandhi goes beyond their motives. Achieving their objectives for social justice while empowering and disciplining followers to use nonviolent resistance is morally good leadership.

People also describe altruism as a way of assessing an act or behavior, regardless of the agent's intention. For example, Worchel, Cooper, and Goethals (1988) defined altruism as acts that "render help to another person" (p. 394). If altruism is nothing more than helping people, then it is a more manageable standard, but simply helping people is not necessarily ethical. It depends on how you help them and what you help them do. It is true that people often help each other without making great sacrifices. If altruism is nothing more than helping people, then we have radically redefined the concept by eliminating the self-sacrificing requirement. Mendonca (2001) offered a further modification of altruism in what he called "mutual altruism." Mutual altruism boils down to utilitarianism and enlightened self-interest. If we follow this line of thought, we should also add other moral principles, such as the golden rule, to this category of altruism.

It is interesting to note that Confucius explicitly called the golden rule altruism. When asked by Tzu-Kung what the guiding principle of life is, Confucius answered, "It is the word altruism (*shu*). Do not do unto others what you do not want them to do to you" (Confucius, trans. 1963, p. 44).

The golden rule crops up as a fundamental moral principle in most major cultures because it demonstrates how to transform self-interest into concern for the interests of others. In other words, it provides the bridge between altruism and self-interest (others and the self) and allows for enlightened self-interest. This highlights another reason why altruism is not a useful standard for the moral behavior of leaders. The minute we start to modify altruism, it not only loses its initial meaning but it starts to sound like a wide variety of other ethical terms, which makes it very confusing.

Why Being a Leader Is Not in a Just Person's Self-Interest

Plato believed that leadership required a person to sacrifice his or her immediate self-interests, but this did not amount to altruism. In Book II of the *Republic,* Plato (trans. 1992) wrote:

> In a city of good men, if it came into being, the citizens would fight in order not to rule. . . . There it would be clear that anyone who is really a true ruler doesn't by nature seek his own advantage but that of his subjects. And everyone, knowing this, would rather be benefited by others than take the trouble to benefit them. (p. 347d)

Rather than requiring altruistic motives, Plato was referring to the stress, hard work, and the often thankless task of being a morally good leader. He implied that if you are a just person, leadership will take a toll on you and your life. The only reason a just person will take on a leadership role is out of fear of punishment. He stated further, "Now the greatest punishment, if one isn't willing to rule, is to be ruled by someone worse than oneself. And I think it is fear of this that makes decent people rule when they do" (Plato, trans. 1992, p. 347c). Plato's comment sheds light on why we sometimes feel more comfortable with people who are reluctant to lead than with those who are eager to do so. Today, as in the past, we worry that people who are too eager to lead want the power and position for themselves or that they do not fully understand the enormous responsibilities of leadership. Plato also tells us that whereas leadership is not in the just person's immediate self-interest, it is in their long-term interest. He argued that it is in our best interest to be just, because just people are happier and lead better lives than do unjust people (Plato, trans. 1992, p. 353e).

Whereas we admire self-sacrifice, morality sometimes calls upon leaders to do things that are against their self-interest. This is less about altruism than it is about the nature of both morality and leadership. We want leaders to put the interests of followers first, but most leaders do not pay a price for doing that on a daily basis, nor do most circumstances require them to calculate their interests in relation to the interests of their followers. The practice of leadership is to guide and look after the goals, missions, and aspirations of groups, organizations, countries, or causes. When leaders do this, they are doing their job; when they do not do this, they are not doing their job. Ample research demonstrates that self-interested people who are unwilling to put the interests of others first are often not successful as leaders (Avolio & Locke, 2002, pp. 186–188).

Looking after the interests of others is as much about what leaders do in their role as leaders as it is about the moral quality of leadership. Implicit in the idea of leadership effectiveness is the notion that leaders do their job. When a mayor does not look after the interests of a city, she is not only ineffective, she is unethical for not keeping the promise that she made when sworn in as mayor. When she does look after the interests of the city, it is not because she is altruistic, but because she is doing her job. In this way, altruism is built into how we describe what leaders do. Whereas altruism is not the best concept for characterizing the ethics of leadership, scholars' interest in altruism reflects a desire to capture, either implicitly or explicitly, the ethics-and-effectiveness notion of good leadership.

Transforming Leadership

In the leadership literature, transforming or transformational leadership has become almost synonymous with ethical leadership. Transformational leadership is often contrasted with transactional leadership. There is a parallel between these two theories and the altruism/self-interest dichotomy. Burns's (1978) theory of transforming leadership is compelling because it rests on a set of moral assumptions about the relationship between leaders and followers. Burns's theory is clearly a prescriptive one about the nature of morally good leadership. Drawing from Abraham Maslow's work on needs, Milton Rokeach's research on values development, and research on moral development from Lawrence Kohlberg, Jean Piaget, Erik Erickson, and Alfred Adler, Burns argued that leaders have to operate at higher need and value levels than those of followers, which may entail transcending their self-interests. A leader's role is to exploit tension and conflict within people's value systems and play the role of raising people's consciousness (Burns, 1978).

On Burns's account, transforming leaders have very strong values. They do not water down their values and moral ideals by consensus, but rather they elevate people by using conflict to engage followers and help them reassess their own values and needs. This is an area where Burns's view of ethics is very different from advocates of participatory leadership such as Rost. Burns wrote, "Despite his [Rost's] intense and impressive concern about the role of values, ethics, and morality in transforming leadership, he underestimates the crucial importance of these variables." Burns goes on to say, "Rost leans toward, or at least is tempted by, consensus procedures and goals that I believe erode such leadership" (Burns, 1991, p. xii).

The moral questions that drive Burns's (1978) theory of transforming leadership come from his work as a biographer and historian. When biographers or historians study a leader, they struggle with the question of how to judge or keep from judging their subject. Throughout his book, Burns used examples of a number of incidents where questionable means, such as lying and deception, are used to achieve honorable ends or where the private life of a politician is morally questionable. If you analyze the numerous historical examples in Burns's book, you find that two pressing moral questions shape his leadership theory. The first is the morality of means and ends (and this also includes the moral use of power). The second is the tension between the public and private morality of a leader. His theory of transforming leadership is an attempt to characterize good leadership by accounting for both of these questions.

Burns's distinction between transforming and transactional leadership and modal and end values offers a way to think about the question of what is a good leader in terms of the leader–follower relationship and the means and ends of his or her actions. Transactional leadership rests on the values found in the means or process of leadership. He calls these modal values. These include responsibility, fairness, honesty, and promise keeping. Transactional leadership helps leaders and followers reach their own goals by supplying lower-level wants and needs so that they can move up to higher needs. Transforming leadership is concerned with end values, such as liberty, justice, and equality. Transforming leaders raise their followers up through various stages of morality and need, and they turn their followers into leaders.

As a historian, Burns was very concerned with the ends of actions and the changes that leaders initiate. Consider, for example, Burns's (1978) two answers to the Hitler question. In the first part of the book, he stated quite simply that "Hitler, once he gained power and crushed all opposition, was no longer a leader—he was a tyrant" (pp. 2–3). A tyrant is similar to Kort's (2008) idea of a purported leader. Later in the book, Burns offered three criteria for judging how Hitler would fare before "the bar of history." He stated that Hitler would probably argue that he was a transforming leader who spoke for the true values of the German people and elevated them to a higher destiny. First, he would be tested by modal values of honor and integrity or the extent to which he advanced or thwarted the standards of good conduct in mankind. Second, he would be judged by the end values of equality and justice. Last, he would be judged on the impact that he had on the people that he touched (Burns, 1978). According to Burns, Hitler would fail all three tests. Burns did not consider Hitler a true leader or a transforming leader because of the means that he used, the ends that he achieved, and the impact he had as a moral agent on his followers during the process of his leadership. By looking at leadership as a process that is judged by a set of values, Burns's (1978) theory of good leadership is difficult to pigeonhole into one ethical theory. The most attractive part of Burns's theory is the idea that a leader elevates his or her followers and makes them leaders. Near the end of his book, he reintroduced this idea with an anecdote about why President Johnson did not run in 1968, stating, "Perhaps he did not comprehend that the people he had led—as a result in part of the impact of his leadership—had created their own fresh leadership, which was now outrunning his" (Burns, 1978, p. 424). All of the people that Johnson helped, the sick, the Blacks, and the poor, now had their own leadership. Burns (1978) noted, "Leadership begat leadership and hardly recognized its offspring. . . . Followers had become leaders" (p. 424).

Burns's and other scholars' use of the word value to talk about ethics is problematic because it encompasses so many different kinds of things— economic values, organizational values, personal values, and moral values. Values do not tie people together the way moral concepts like duty and utility do, because most people subscribe to the view that "I have my values and you have yours." Having values does not mean that a person acts on them. To make values about something that people do rather than just have, Rokeach (1973) offered a very awkward discussion of the "ought" character of values. "A person phenomenologically experiences 'oughtness' to be objectively required by society in somewhat the same way that he perceives an incomplete circle as objectively requiring closure" (p. 9). Whereas Burns offers a provocative moral account of leadership, it would be stronger and clearer if he used the richer and more dynamic concepts found in moral philosophy.[1] This is not philosophic snobbery, but a plea for conceptual clarity and completeness. The implications of concepts such as virtue, duty, rights, and the greatest good have been worked out for hundreds of years and offer helpful tools for dissecting the moral dynamics of leadership and the relationship between leaders and followers.

Transformational Leadership

Burns's (1978) theory has inspired a number of studies on transformational leadership. For example, Bass's (1985) early work on transformational leadership focused on the impact of leaders on their followers. In sharp contrast to Burns, Bass's transformational leaders did not have to appeal to the higher-order needs and values of their followers. He was more concerned with the psychological relationship between transformational leaders and their followers. Bass originally believed that there could be both good and evil transformational leaders, so he was willing to call Hitler a transformational leader. Bass has made an admirable effort to offer a richer account of ethics in his more recent work. Bass and Steidlmeier (1999) argued that only morally good leaders are authentic transformational leaders; the rest, like Hitler, are pseudotransformational. Bass and Steidlmeier described pseudotransformational leaders as people who seek power and position at the expense of their followers' achievements. The source of their moral shortcomings lies in the fact that they are selfish and pursue their own interests at the expense of their followers. Whereas Bass and Steidlmeier still depend on altruism as a moral concept, they also look at authentic transformational leadership in terms of other ethical concepts such as virtue and commitment to the greatest good.

Bass (1985) believed that charismatic leadership is a necessary ingredient of transformational leadership. The research on charismatic leadership opens up a wide range of ethical questions because of the powerful emotional and moral impact that charismatic leaders have on followers (House, Spangler, & Woycke, 1991). Charismatic leadership can be the best and the worst kinds of leadership, depending on whether you look at a Gandhi or a Charles Manson (Lindholm, 1990). Bass and Steidlmeier's (1999) recent work runs parallel to research by Howell and Avolio (1992) on charismatic leadership. Howell and Avolio studied charismatic leaders and concluded that unethical charismatic leaders are manipulators who pursue their personal agendas. They argued that only leaders who act on socialized, rather than personalized, bases of power are transformational.

Critics of Transformational and Charismatic Leadership Theories

There is plenty of empirical research that demonstrates the effectiveness of transformational leaders. Scholars are almost rhapsodic in the ways in which they describe their findings, and with good reason. These findings show that ethics and effectiveness go hand in hand. Shamir, House, and Arthur (1993) stated:

> Charismatic leaders . . . increase followers' self-worth through emphasizing the relationships between efforts and important values. A general sense of self-worth increases general self-efficacy; a sense of moral correctness is a source of strength and confidence. Having complete faith in the moral correctness of one's convictions gives one the strength and confidence to behave accordingly. (p. 582)

The problem with this research is that it raises many, if not more, questions about the ethics. What are the important values? Are the values themselves ethical? What does moral correctness mean? Is what followers believe to be moral correctness really morally correct?

Critics question the ethics of the very idea of transformational leadership. Keeley (1998) argued that transformational leadership is well and good as long as you assume that everyone will eventually come around to the values and goals of the leader. Drawing on Madison's concern for factions in Federalist No. 10, Keeley (1998) wondered, "What is the likely status of people who would prefer their own goals and visions?" (p. 123). What if followers are confident that the leader's moral convictions are wrong? Keeley observed that the leadership and management literature has not been kind to nonconformists. He noted that Mao was one of Burns's transforming heroes and Mao certainly did not tolerate dissidents. Whereas Burns's theory tolerated conflict, conflict is only part of the process of reaching agreement on values. Is it ethical for a leader to require everyone to agree on all values?

Price (2000) discussed another problem with the moral view of transformational leadership articulated by Burns (1978) and Bass and Steidlmeier (1999). The leaders they described are subject to making all sorts of moral mistakes, even when they are authentic, altruistic, and committed to common values. The fact that a leader possesses these traits does not necessarily yield moral behavior or good moral decisions. Price further argued that leaders and followers should be judged by adherence to morality, not adherence to their organizations' or society's values. "Leaders must be willing to sacrifice their other-regarding values when generally applicable moral requirements make legitimate demands that they do so" (Price, 2003, p. 80). Sometimes being a charismatic and transformational leader in an organization, in the sense described by some theorists, does not mean that you are ethical when judged against moral concepts that apply in larger contexts.

Solomon (1998) took aim at the focus on charisma in leadership studies. He stated charisma is the shorthand for certain rare leaders. As a concept it is without ethical value and without much explanatory value. Charisma is not a distinctive quality of personality or character, and according to Solomon, it is not an essential part of leadership. For example, Solomon (1998) stated, "Charisma is not a single quality, nor is it a single emotion or set of emotions. It is a generalized way of pointing to and emptily explaining an emotional relationship that is too readily characterized as fascination" (p. 95). He then went on to argue that research on trust offers more insight into the leader–follower relationship than does research into charisma. Solomon specifically talked about the importance of exploring the emotional process of how people give their trust to others.

Knocking Leaders Off Their Pedestals

Keeley's (1998), Price's (2000), and Solomon's (1998) criticisms of transformational and charismatic leadership theories raise two larger questions. First, scholars might be missing something about leadership when they study only exceptional types of leaders. Second, by limiting their study in this way, they fail to take into account the fact that even exceptional leaders get things wrong. Morality is a struggle for everyone, and it contains particular hazards for leaders. As Kant (1795/1983) observed,

> From such warped wood as is man made, nothing straight can be fashioned. . . . Man is an animal that, if he lives among other members of his species, has need of a master, for he certainly abuses his freedom in relation to his equals. He requires a master who will break his self-will and force him to obey a universally valid will, whereby everyone can be free. . . . He finds the master among the human species, but even he is an animal who requires a master. (p. 34)

The master for Kant (1785/1983) is morality. No individual or leader has the key to morality, and hence, everyone is responsible for defining and enforcing morality. We need to understand the ethical challenges faced by imperfect humans who take on the responsibilities of leadership, so that we can develop morally better leaders, followers, institutions, and organizations. At issue is not simply what ethical and effective leaders do, but what leaders have to confront and, in some cases, overcome to be ethical and effective. Some of these questions are psychological in nature, and others are concerned with moral reasoning.

Like many leadership scholars, Plato constructed his theory of the ideal leader—the philosopher king who is wise and virtuous. Through firsthand experience, Plato realized the shortcomings of his philosopher king model of leadership. Plato learned about leadership through three disastrous trips to the city-state of Syracuse. Plato visited Syracuse the first time at the invitation of the tyrant Dionysius I, but he soon became disgusted by the decadent and luxurious lifestyle of Dionysius's court. Plato returned to Athens convinced that existing forms of government at home and abroad were corrupt and unstable. He then decided to set up the Academy, where he taught for 40 years and wrote the *Republic.* In the *Republic,* Plato argued that the perfect state could come about only by rationally exploiting the highest qualities in people (although this sounds a bit like a transformational leadership, it is not). Plato firmly believed that the philosopher king could be developed through education. Hence, we might regard Plato's Academy as a leadership school.

About 24 years after his first visit, Dionysius's brother-in-law, Dion, invited Plato back to Syracuse. By this time, Dionysius I was dead. Dion had read the *Republic* and wanted Plato to come and test his theory of leadership education on Dionysius's very promising son Dionysius II. This was an offer that Plato could not refuse, although he had serious reservations about accepting it. Nonetheless, off Plato went to Syracuse. The trip was a disaster. Plato's friend Dion was exiled because of court intrigues. Years later, Plato returned to Syracuse a third time, but the visit was no better than the first two. In Epistle VII, Plato (trans. 1971a) reported that these visits changed his view of leadership:

> The more I advanced in years, the harder it appeared to me to administer the government correctly. For one thing, nothing could be done without friends and loyal companions, and such men were not easy to find ready at hand. . . . Neither could such men be created afresh with any facility. . . . The result was that I, who had at first been full of eagerness for a public career, as I gazed upon the whirlpool of public life and saw the incessant movement of shifting currents, at last felt dizzy. (p. 1575)

Plato seemed to have lost faith in his conviction that leaders could be perfected. He realized that leaders shared the same human weaknesses of their followers, but he also saw how important trust was in leadership. In the *Republic,* Plato had entertained a pastoral image of the leader as a shepherd to his flock. But in a later work, *Statesman,* he observed that leaders are not at all like shepherds. Shepherds are obviously quite different from their flocks, whereas human leaders are not much different from their followers (Plato, trans. 1971b). He noted that people are not sheep—some are cooperative and some are very stubborn. Plato's revised view of leadership was that leaders were really like weavers. Their main task was to weave together different kinds of people—the meek and the self-controlled, the brave and the impetuous—into the fabric of society (Plato, trans. 1971b).

Plato's ideas on leadership progressed from a profound belief that it is possible for some people to be wise and benevolent philosopher kings to a more modest belief that the real challenge of leadership is working successfully with people who do not always like each other, do not always like the leader, and do not necessarily want to live together. These are some of the key challenges faced by leaders today all over the world. Leadership is more like being a shepherd to a flock of cats or like pushing a wheelbarrow full of frogs (O'Toole, 1995).

Whereas Plato's image of the philosopher king in the *Republic* is idealistic, the *Statesman* and the early books of the *Republic* lay out some of the fundamental ethical issues of leadership; namely, moral imperfection and power. Near the end of the *Statesman,* Plato contended that we cannot always depend on leaders to be good and that is why we need rule of law (Plato, trans. 1971b). Good laws, rules, and regulations protect us from unethical leaders and serve to help leaders be ethical (similar to James Madison's concern for checks on leaders).

Plato, like many of the ancients, realized that the greatest ethical challenge for humans in leadership roles stems from the temptations of power. In Book II of the *Republic,* he provided a thought-provoking experiment about power and accountability. Glaucon, the protagonist in the dialogue, argued that the only reason people are just is because they lack the power to be unjust. He then told the story of the "Ring of Gyges" (Plato, trans. 1992). A young shepherd from Lydia found a ring and discovered that when he turned the ring on his finger, it made him invisible. The shepherd then used the ring to seduce the king's wife, attack the king, and take over the kingdom. Plato asks us to consider what we would do if we had power without accountability. One of our main concerns about leaders is that they will abuse their power because they are accountable to fewer people. In this respect, the "Ring of Gyges" is literally and figuratively a story about transparency. The power that leaders have to do things also entails the power to hide what they do.

Power carries with it a temptation to do evil and an obligation to do good. Philosophers often refer to a point made by Kant (1785/1993, p. 32) as "ought implies can," meaning you have a moral obligation to act when you are able to act effectively (similar to the free will/determinism question mentioned earlier—more power, more free will). It means that the more power, resources, and ability you have to do good, the more you have a moral obligation to do so. The notion of helpfulness, discussed earlier in conjunction with altruism, is derived from this notion of power and obligation. It is about the moral obligation to help when you can help.

The Bathsheba Syndrome

The moral foible that people fear most in their leaders is personal immorality accompanied by abuse of power. Usually, it is the most successful leaders who suffer the worst ethical failures. Ludwig and Longenecker (1993) called the moral failure of successful leaders the "Bathsheba syndrome," based on the biblical story of King David and Bathsheba. Ancient texts such as the Bible provide us with wonderful case studies on the moral pitfalls of leaders. King David is portrayed as a successful leader in the Bible. We first meet him as a young shepherd in the story of David and Goliath. This story offers an interesting leadership lesson. In it, God selects the small shepherd David over his brother, a strong soldier, because David "has a good heart." Then as God's hand-picked leader, David goes on to become a great leader, until we come to the story of David and Bathsheba (2 Samuel 11–12).

The story begins with David taking an evening stroll around his palace. From his vantage point on the palace roof, he sees the beautiful Bathsheba bathing. He asks his servants to bring Bathsheba to him. The king beds Bathsheba and she gets pregnant. Bathsheba's husband, Uriah, is one of David's best generals. King David tries to cover up his immoral behavior by calling Uriah home. When Uriah arrives, David attempts to get him drunk so that he will sleep with Bathsheba. Uriah refuses to cooperate, because he said it would be unfair to enjoy such pleasures while his men are on the front. (This is a wonderful sidebar about the moral obligations of leaders to followers.) David then escalates his attempt to cover things up by ordering Uriah to the front of a battle where he gets killed. In the end, the prophet Nathan blows the whistle on David and God punishes David.

The Bathsheba story has repeated itself again and again in history. Scandals ranging from Watergate to the President Clinton and Monica Lewinsky affair to Enron all follow the general pattern of this story (Winter, 2002, gives an interesting psychological account of the Clinton case). First, we see what happens when successful leaders lose sight of what their jobs are. David should have been focusing on running the war, not watching Bathsheba bathe. He was literally and figuratively looking in the wrong place. This is why we worry about men leaders who are womanizers getting distracted from their jobs. Second, because power leads to privileged access, leaders have more opportunities to indulge themselves and, hence, need more willpower to resist indulging themselves. David could have Bathsheba brought to him by his servants with no questions asked. Third, successful leaders sometimes develop an inflated belief in their ability to control outcomes. David became involved in escalating cover-ups.

The most striking thing about leaders who get themselves in these situations is that the cover-ups are usually worse than the crime. In David's case, adultery was not as bad as murder. Also, it is during the cover-up that leaders abuse their power as leaders the most. In Clinton's case, a majority of Americans found his lying to the public far more immoral than his adultery. Last, leaders learn that their power falls short of the ring of Gyges. It will not keep their actions invisible forever. Whistle-blowers such as Nathan in King David's case or Sharon Watkins in the Enron case call their bluff and demand that their leaders be held to the same moral standards as everyone else. When this happens, in Bible stories and everywhere else, all hell breaks loose. The impact of a leader's moral lapses causes great harm to their constituents.

Read as a leadership case study, the story of David and Bathsheba is about pride and the moral fragility of people when they hold leadership positions. It is also a cautionary tale about success and the lengths to which people will go to keep from losing it. What is most interesting about the Bathsheba syndrome is that it is difficult to predict which leaders will fall prey to it, because people get it after they have become successful. One can never tell how even the most virtuous person will respond to situations in various contexts and circumstances (Doris, 2005). If we are to gain a better understanding of ethics and leadership, we need to examine how leaders resist falling for the ethical temptations that come with power.

Self-Discipline and Virtue

The moral challenges of power and the nature of the leader's job explain why self-knowledge and self-control are, and have been for centuries, the most important factors in leadership development. Ancient writers, such as Lao tzu, Confucius, Buddha, Plato, and Aristotle, all emphasized good habits, self-knowledge, and self-control in their writing. Eastern philosophers, such as Lao tzu, Confucius, and Buddha, not only talked about virtues but also about the challenges of self-discipline and controlling the ego. Lao tzu warned against egotism when he stated, "He who stands on tiptoe is not steady" (Lao Tzu, trans. 1963, p. 152). He also tells us, "The best rulers are those whose existence is merely known by people" (Lao tzu, trans. 1963, p. 148). Confucius (trans. 1963) focused on the importance of duty and self-control. He stated, "If a man (the ruler) can for one day master himself and return to propriety, all under heaven will return to humanity. To practice humanity depends on oneself" (p. 38). He tied a leader's self-mastery and effectiveness together when he wrote, "If a ruler sets himself right, he will be followed without his command. If he does not set himself right, even his commands will not be obeyed" (Confucius, trans. 1963, p. 38).

In the "First Sermon," the Buddha described how people's uncontrolled thirst for things contributes to their own suffering and the suffering of others. Not unlike psychologists today, he realized that getting one's desires under control is the best way to end personal and social misery. This is a particular challenge for leaders because they often have the means to indulge their material and personal desires. Compassion is the most important virtue in Buddhist ethics because it keeps desires and vices in check. The Dalai Lama (1999) concisely summed up the moral dynamics of compassion in this way:

> When we bring up our children to have knowledge without compassion, their attitude towards others is likely to be a mixture of envy of those in positions above them, aggressive competitiveness towards their peers, and scorn for these less fortunate. This leads to a propensity toward greed, presumption, excess, and very quickly to loss of happiness. (p. 181)

Virtues are a fundamental part of the landscape of moral philosophy and provide a useful way of thinking about leadership development. What is important about virtues are their dynamics (e.g., how they interact with other virtues and vices) and their contribution to self-knowledge and self-control. The properties of a virtue are very different from the properties of other moral concepts such as values. Virtues are things that you have only if you practice them. Values are things that are important to people. I may value honesty but not always tell the truth. I cannot possess the virtue of honesty without telling the truth. As Aristotle mentioned, virtues are good habits that we learn from society and our leaders. Aristotle wrote quite a bit about leaders as moral role models, and much of what he said complements observations in research on transformational leadership. He noted, "Legislators make citizens good by forming habits in them" (Aristotle, trans. 1984). Whereas virtues come naturally to those who practice them, they are not mindless habits. People must practice them fully conscious of knowing that what they are doing is morally right.

Perhaps the most striking thing about the Greek notion of virtue (*areté*), which is also translated as excellence, is that it does not separate an individual's ethics from his or her occupational competence. Both Plato and Aristotle constantly used examples of doctors, musicians, coaches, rulers, and so forth to talk about the relationship between moral and technical or professional excellence. Aristotle (trans. 1984) wrote,

> Every excellence brings to good the thing to which it is the excellence and makes the work of that thing be done well. . . . Therefore, if this is true in every case, the excellence of man also will be the state which makes man good and which makes him do his work well. (p. 1747)

Excellence is tied to function. The function of a knife is to cut. An excellent knife cuts well. The function of humans, according to Aristotle, is to reason.

To be morally virtuous, you must reason well, because reason tells you how to practice and when to practice a virtue. If you reason well, you will know how to practice moral and professional virtues. In other words, reason is the key to practicing moral virtues and the virtues related to one's various occupations in life. Hence, the morally virtuous leader will also be a competent leader because he or she will do what is required in the job the right way. Virtue ethics does not differentiate between the morality of the leader and the morality of his or her leadership. An incompetent leader, like the head of the Swiss charity that tried to free the enslaved children, lacks moral virtue, regardless of his or her good intentions.

Conclusion

The more we explore how ethics and effectiveness are inextricably intertwined, the better we will understand leadership. The philosophic study of ethics provides a critical perspective from which we can examine the assumptions behind leadership and leadership theories. It offers another level of analysis that should be integrated into the growing body of empirical research in the field. The ethics of leadership has to be examined along a variety of dimensions:

1. The ethics of a leader as a person, which includes things like self-knowledge, discipline, intentions, and so forth

2. The ethics of the leader–follower relationship (i.e., how they treat each other)

3. The ethics of the process of leadership (i.e., command and control, participatory)

4. The ethics of what the leader does or does not do

These dimensions give us a picture of the ethics of what a leader does and how he or she does it. But even after an interdependent analysis of these dimensions, the picture is not complete. We then have to take one more step and look at all of these interdependent dimensions in larger contexts and time frames. For example, the ethics of organizational leadership would have to be examined in the context of the community, and so forth. One of the most striking distinctions between effective leadership and ethical *and* effective leadership is often the time frame of decisions. Ethics is about the impact of behavior and actions in the long and the short run. Leaders can be effective in the short run but unethical and ultimately ineffective in the long run. For example, we have all seen the problem of defining good business leadership based simply on the quarterly profits that a firm makes. Long-term ideas of effectiveness, such as sustainability, tend to be normative.

A richer understanding of the moral challenges that are distinctive to leaders and leadership is particularly important for leadership development. Whereas case studies of ethical leadership are inspiring and case studies of evil leaders are cautionary, we need a practical understanding of why it is morally difficult to be a good leader and a good follower. Leaders do not have to be power-hungry psychopaths to do unethical things, nor do they have to be altruistic saints to do ethical things. Most leaders are neither charismatic nor transformational leaders. They are ordinary men and women in business, government, nonprofits, and communities who sometimes make volitional, emotional, moral, and cognitive mistakes. More work needs to be done on ordinary leaders and followers and how they can help each other be ethical and make better moral decisions.

Aristotle (trans. 1984) said that happiness is the end to which we aim in life. The Greek word that Aristotle uses for happiness is *eudaimonea*. It means happiness, not in terms of pleasure or contentment, but as flourishing. A happy life is one in which we flourish as human beings, both in terms of our material and personal development and our moral development. The concept of *eudaimonea* gives us two umbrella questions that can be used to assess the overall ethics and effectiveness of leadership. Does a leader or a particular kind of leadership contribute to and/or allow people to flourish in terms of their lives as a whole? Does a leader or a particular kind of leadership interfere with the ability of other groups of people or other living things to flourish? Leaders do not always have to transform people for them to flourish. Their greater responsibility is to create the social and material conditions under which people can and do flourish (Ciulla, 2000). Change is part of leadership, but so is sustainability. Ethical leadership entails the ability of leaders to sustain fundamental notions of morality such as care and respect for persons, justice, and honesty, in changing organizational, social, and global contexts. Moreover, it requires people who have the competence, knowledge, and will to determine and do the right thing, the right way, and for the right reasons. The humanities offer one source of insight into the nature of right and wrong.

Lastly, leadership scholars have just begun to scratch the surface of other disciplines. History, philosophy, anthropology, literature, and religion all promise to expand our understanding of leaders and leadership. Ancient writers such as Plato, Aristotle, Lao tzu, and Confucius not only tell us about leadership, they also capture our imaginations. What makes a classic a classic is that its message carries themes and values that are meaningful to people from different cultures and different periods of history. They offer well-grounded ideas about who we are, what we should be like, and how we should live. These ideas will help us understand current empirical research on leadership and generate new ideas for research. To really understand leadership in terms of ethics and effectiveness, each one of us needs to put our ear to the ground of history and listen carefully to the saga of human hopes, desires, and aspirations, and the follies, disappointments, and triumphs of those who led and those who followed them. As Confucius once said, "A man who reviews the old as to find out the new is qualified to teach others."

Note

1. I have been arguing this point with Burns since 1991. We continue to be equally stubborn on our positions.

Discussion Questions

1. Who would you prefer to work for, an effective but ethically questionable leader or an ethical but ineffective leader? How do you weigh the costs and benefits of each type of leader?

2. Why does success have the potential to corrupt leaders? How is corruption from success different from corruption from power?

3. Think of examples where ethical considerations interfere with a leader's ability to be effective. Then think of ways in which a leader's ethics interfere with his or her ability to be effective. Should leaders always pick ethics over effectiveness?

4. How would you redefine effective leadership to take into account normative considerations?

Supplemental Readings

Ciulla, J. B. (1999). The importance of leadership in shaping business values. *Long Range Planning, 32,* 166–172.
Heifetz, R. A., & Laurie, D. L. (1997). The work of leadership. *The Harvard Business Review, 75,* 124–134.
Lipman-Blumen, J. (2006). *The allure of toxic leaders: Why we follow destructive bosses and corrupt politicians and how we can survive them.* New York: Oxford University Press.

Case Studies

Glynn, M., & Dowd, T. J. (2008). Charisma (un)bound: Emotive leadership in *Martha Stewart Living* magazine. *Journal of Applied Behavioral Science, 44,* 71–93.
Le Guin, U. (1975/2004). The ones who walk away from Omelas. In U. Le Guin, *The wind's twelve corners* (pp. 275–284). New York: Harper Perennial.

Available at http://harelbarzilai.org/words/omelas.txt. This story is about the problems of determining the right thing, right way, when you know the right reason.

Orwell, G. (1936). Shooting an elephant. Available at http://www.physics.ohio-state .edu/~wilkins/writing/Resources/essays/elephant.html. This is a short story about how followers influence the moral behavior of leaders. It is in collections, but also can be found in several sites online.

References

Antonakis, J., & House, R. J. (2002). An analysis of the full-range leadership theory: The way forward. In B. J. Avolio & F. J. Yammarino (Eds.), *Transformational and charismatic leadership: The road ahead* (pp. 3–33). Amsterdam: JAI.

Aristotle. (trans. 1984). *Nichomachean ethics* (W. D. Ross, Trans.). In J. Barnes (Ed.), *The complete works of Aristotle: The revised Oxford translation* (Vol. 2, pp. 1729–1867). Princeton, NJ: Princeton University Press.

Avolio, B. J., & Locke, E. E. (2002). Contrasting different philosophies of leader motivation: Altruism verses egoistic. *The Leadership Quarterly, 13,* 169–191.

Bass, B. M. (1985). *Leadership and performance beyond expectations.* New York: Free Press.

Bass, B. M. (1997). Does the transactional–transformational leadership paradigm transcend organizational and national boundaries? *American Psychologist, 52,* 130–139.

Bass, B. M., & Steidlmeier, P. (1999). Ethics, character, and authentic transformational leader behavior. *The Leadership Quarterly, 10,* 181–217.

Bennis, W. (2002). Towards a "truly" scientific management: The concept of organizational health. *Reflections, 4,* 4–13.

Bennis, W., & Nanus, B. (1985). *Leaders: Strategies for taking charge.* New York: HarperCollins.

Brown, M. E., Treviño, L. K., & Harrison, D. A. (2005). Ethical leadership: A social learning perspective for construct development and testing. *Organizational Behavior and Human Decision Processes, 97,* 117–134.

Burns, J. M. (1978). *Leadership.* New York: Harper & Row.

Burns, J. M. (1991). Foreword. In J. C. Rost, *Leadership for the twenty-first century* (pp. xi–xii). New York: Praeger.

Ciulla, J. B. (1994). Casuistry and the case for business ethics. In T. Donaldson & R. E. Freeman, (Eds.), *Business as a humanity* (pp. 167–183). Oxford, UK: Oxford University Press.

Ciulla, J. B. (1995). Leadership ethics: Mapping the territory. *Business Ethics Quarterly, 5,* 5–24.

Ciulla, J. B. (2000). *The working life: The promise and betrayal of modern work.* New York: Crown Books.

Ciulla, J. B. (2003a). The ethical challenges of nonprofit leaders. In R. E. Riggio & S. S. Orr (Eds.), *Improving leadership in nonprofit organizations* (pp. 63–75). San Francisco: Jossey-Bass.

Ciulla, J. B. (2003b). *The ethics of leadership.* Belmont, CA: Wadsworth.

Ciulla, J. B. (Ed). (2008a). *Leadership and the humanities.* Vol. 3 of J. B. Ciulla (Ed.), *Leadership at the crossroads.* Westport, CT: Praeger.

Ciulla, J. B. (Ed). (2008b). Leadership: Views from the humanities [Special issue]. *The Leadership Quarterly, 19*(4).

Compact Oxford English dictionary. (1991). Oxford, UK: Clarendon.

Confucius. (trans. 1963). Selections from the *Analects*. In W. Chan (Ed. & Trans.), *A source book in Chinese philosophy* (pp. 18–48). Princeton, NJ: Princeton University Press.

Dalai Lama XIV. (1999). *Ancient wisdom, modern world: Ethics for a new millennium* (T. Jinpa, Trans.). New York: Riverhead Books.

Doris, J. (2005). *Lack of character: Personality and moral behavior.* Cambridge, UK: Cambridge University Press.

Gardner, J. (1987). *The moral aspect of leadership.* Washington, DC: Leadership Studies Program, Independent Sector.

Gardner, J. (1990). *On leadership.* New York: Free Press.

Garrett, L. (2000, March 29). Added foe in AIDS war: Skeptics. *Newsday,* p. A6.

Gergen, D. (2002, November). *Keynote address.* Delivered at the meeting of the International Leadership Association, Seattle, WA.

Heifetz, R. A. (1994). *Leadership without easy answers.* Cambridge, MA: Harvard University Press.

Hollander, E. P. (1964). *Leaders, groups, and influence.* New York: Oxford University Press.

House, R. J., Spangler, W. D., & Woycke, J. (1991). Personality and charisma in the U.S. presidency: A psychological theory of effectiveness. *Administrative Science Quarterly, 36,* 334–396.

Howell, J. M., & Avolio, B. (1992). The ethics of charismatic leadership. *Academy of Management Executive, 6,* 43–54.

Hunt, J. G. (Ed.). (1991). *Leadership: A new synthesis.* Newbury Park, CA: Sage.

Kant, I. (1983). The idea for a universal history with a cosmopolitan intent. In T. Humphrey (Ed. & Trans.), *Perpetual peace and other essays on politics, history, and morals* (pp. 29–40). Indianapolis, IN: Hackett. (Original work published 1795)

Kant, I. (1993). *Foundations of the metaphysics of morals* (J. W. Ellington, Trans.). Indianapolis, IN: Hackett. (Original work published 1785)

Kanungo, R., & Mendonca, M. (1996). *Ethical dimensions of leadership.* Thousand Oaks, CA: Sage.

Keeley, M. (1998). The trouble with transformational leadership. In J. B. Ciulla (Ed.), *Ethics, the heart of leadership* (pp. 111–144). Westport, CT: Praeger.

Kort, E. D. (2008). What, after all, is leadership? "Leadership" and plural action. *The Leadership Quarterly, 19,* 409–425.

Lao tzu. (trans. 1963). The *Lao Tzu (Tao-te ching)*. In W. Chan (Ed. & Trans.), *A source book in Chinese philosophy* (pp. 139–176). Princeton, NJ: Princeton University Press.

Lindholm, C. (1990). *Charisma.* Cambridge, MA: Blackwell.

Ludwig, D., & Longenecker, C. (1993). The Bathsheba syndrome: The ethical failure of successful leaders. *The Journal of Business Ethics, 12,* 265–273.

Maccoby, M. (2000). Narcissistic leaders. *The Harvard Business Review, 78,* 69–75.

McClelland, D. C. (1975). *Power: The inner experience.* New York: Halsted.

Mendonca, M. (2001). Preparing for ethical leadership in organizations. *Canadian Journal of Administrative Sciences, 18,* 266–276.

Mill, J. S. (1987). What utilitarianism is. In A. Ryan, (Ed.), *Utilitarianism and other essays* (pp. 272–338). New York: Penguin Books.

Moldoveanu, M., & Langer, E. (2002). When "stupid" is smarter than we are: Mindlessness and the attribution of stupidity. In R. Sternberg (Ed.), *Why smart people can be so stupid* (pp. 212–231). New Haven, CT: Yale University Press.

Nagel, T. (1970). *The possibility of altruism.* Oxford, UK: Clarendon.

O'Toole, J. (1995). *Leading change: Overcoming the ideology of comfort and the tyranny of custom.* San Francisco: Jossey-Bass.

Ozinga, J. R. (1999). *Altruism.* Westport, CT: Praeger.

Pillai, R. (1996). Crisis and the emergence of charismatic leadership in groups: An experimental investigation. *Journal of Applied Social Psychology, 26,* 543–562.

Plato. (1971a). *Epistle VII* (L. A. Post, Trans.). In E. Hamilton & H. Cairns (Eds.), *The collected dialogues of Plato, including the letters* (pp. 1574–1603). Princeton, NJ: Princeton University Press.

Plato. (1971b). *Statesman* (J. B. Skemp, Trans.). In E. Hamilton & H. Cairns (Eds.), *The collected dialogues of Plato, including the letters* (pp. 1018–1085). Princeton, NJ: Princeton University Press.

Plato. (1992). *Republic* (G. M. A. Grube, Trans.). Indianapolis, IN: Hackett.

Prezzolini, G. (1928). *Nicolo Machiavelli, the Florentine* (R. Roeder, Trans.). New York: Brentano's.

Price, T. L. (2000). Explaining ethical failures of leadership. *The Leadership and Organizational Development Journal, 21,* 177–184.

Price, T. L. (2003). The ethics of authentic transformational leadership. *The Leadership Quarterly, 14,* 67–81.

Price, T. L. (2005). *Understanding ethical failures in leadership.* New York: Cambridge University Press.

Rokeach, M. (1973). *The nature of human values.* New York: Free Press.

Rost, J. (1991). *Leadership for the twenty-first century.* New York: Praeger.

Ruscio, K. P. (2004). *The leadership dilemma in modern democracy.* Northampton, MA: Edward Elgar.

Schwartz, J. (2001, September 16). Up from the ashes, one firm rebuilds. *New York Times,* sec. 3, p. 1.

Shamir, B., House, R. J., & Arthur, M. B. (1993). The motivational effects of charismatic leadership: A self-concept based theory. *Organizational Science, 4,* 577–594.

Snow, C. P. (1998). *The two cultures.* Cambridge, UK: Cambridge University Press.

Solomon, R. C. (1998). Ethical leadership, emotions, and trust: Beyond charisma. In J. B. Ciulla (Ed.), *Ethics, the heart of leadership* (pp. 83–102). Westport, CT: Praeger.

Williams, B. A. O. (1982). *Moral luck.* Cambridge, UK: Cambridge University Press.

Winter, D. G. (2002). The motivational dimensions of leadership: Power, achievement, and affiliation. In R. E. Riggio, S. E. Murphy, & F. J. Pirozzolo (Eds.), *Multiple intelligences and leadership* (pp. 118–138). Mahwah, NJ: Lawrence Erlbaum.

Wittgenstein, L. (1968). *Philosophical investigations* (G. E. M. Anscombe, Trans.). New York: Macmillan.

Worchel, S., Cooper, J., & Goethals, G. (1988). *Understanding social psychology.* Chicago: Dorsey.

PART V

Conclusion

16

The Crucibles of Authentic Leadership

Warren Bennis[1]

University of Southern California

I t was the practice of Ralph Waldo Emerson to ask old friends he had not seen in a while: "What's become clear to you since we last met?" As this revamped volume makes clear, those engaged in the study of leadership have learned an enormous amount in the century or so since the enterprise began to evolve from the study of "great" men. It would have been unthinkable a couple of decades ago that evolutionary theorists and biologists would have contributed to such a volume. Yet, as I make it clear later, truly understanding this mystical phenomenon called leadership will occur only if scientists from various disciplines work in collaboration.

The 20th century was marked by the emergence of some of the most powerful and disturbing leaders in human history. Millions died as a direct result of failed or evil leadership—in the death camps of the Third Reich but also in the Soviet Union and in famine-ravaged China. The misery inflicted by malicious leaders continues into the 21st century. Millions today face a similar fate in dictatorships like North Korea. The open tab in the form of a "butcher's bill" is a reminder of why we study leadership in the first place. Our very lives depend on it. That has never been truer than it is today, because one consequence of the extraordinary leadership of Franklin Delano Roosevelt was the creation of genuine weapons of mass destruction. I bring these matters up, not because any of you need a capsule history lesson, but because it is important to remember that the quality of all our lives is dependent on the quality of our leadership. The context in which we study leadership is very different from the

AUTHOR'S NOTE: Please address correspondence concerning this chapter to Warren Bennis, USC Marshall School of Business, Los Angeles, CA 90089–0808, USA. Phone: 213–740–0766; e-mail: warren.bennis@gmail.com.

context in which we study, say, astronomy. By definition, leaders wield power, and so we study them with the same self-interested intensity with which we study diabetes and other life-threatening diseases. Only when we understand leaders will we be able to control them. Today, studying leadership is still an important scientific imperative; scandal after scandal, economic crisis after crisis, ecological disaster after disaster, and the anticipated flowering of democracy in Arab countries can be partly traced back to failed leadership. It is through effective leadership that our human race and planet will prosper.

I would argue that context always counts when it comes to leadership, and in the next few pages, I want to examine certain enduring issues and questions related to leadership in today's milieu. I want to look at how recent events and trends are reshaping contemporary ideas about leadership.

In the United States at least, leadership studies changed in some basic way on September 11, 2001. As the nation watched, in horror, the television footage of people fleeing the World Trade Center and, in even greater horror, the collapse of the Twin Towers, I realized as so many others did that this was one of the transformational events of our time. One immediate consequence of the terrorist assaults on New York and the Pentagon was to make leadership a matter for public discussion in the United States in a way it has not been since World War II. Leadership became central to the public conversation—displacing the endless background noise about celebrity and pushing aside even worried talk about the sorry state of the economy. People in other parts of the world have been dealing with the ugly realities of international terrorism for decades, and to them, the stunned horror of Americans must have seemed more than a little naive. But the United States has long had the luxury of studying leadership with the leisurely detachment that only those in peaceful, prosperous nations can afford.

The assault on a nonmilitary target in the paradigmatic American city was more stunning, in many ways, than Pearl Harbor. Not since the Civil War had ideologically motivated violence occurred on such a scale in a city in the United States. Americans are still sorting out the consequences of the attacks of 9/11 and will continue to do so for decades. But with the collapse of the Twin Towers came a new awareness that leadership is more than a matter of who looks best on television. Since 9/11, government officials have been scrutinized for evidence of leadership ability with an intensity usually seen only in wartime. And indeed, in describing how then New York City Mayor Rudolph Giuliani and others responded to al Qaeda's assault, the media referred repeatedly to the larger-than-life leaders of World War II. The iconic leader du jour was unquestionably Winston Churchill. It was noted, for instance, that Karen Hughes, then special assistant to President George W. Bush, kept a plaque on her desk that bore Churchill's stirring line: "I was not the lion but it fell to me to give the lion's roar." The invocation of Churchill was a secular prayer for help, but it was also evidence of a shift in the very idea of leadership—a return to a more heroic, more inspirational definition than had been the fashion for decades. In the rubble of Ground Zero, people did not want a leader who could organize cross-functional teams; they longed for a leader for the ages, a sage and savior to lead them out of hell.

For those who have spent their lives studying leadership, 9/11 was a compelling reminder that war and other violent crises are inevitably crucibles from which leaders emerge. It was fascinating to watch how Rudy Giuliani was transformed in the days following the attacks from a lame-duck mayor with a reputation for mean spiritedness into "Churchill in a baseball cap," as one phrasemaker dubbed him. Almost daily, CNN and the *New York Times* released first-draft case studies of leadership in action. Giuliani's performance was so full of lessons about leadership that he published a best-selling book on the subject. Indeed, his behavior in the wake of the attacks underscored many truisms about leadership, including how it can emerge in unlikely candidates and how it frequently endures only as long as the crisis itself.

Giuliani, who served New York City tirelessly during those days, standing in for slain fathers of the bride and comforting both grieving relatives and the city as a whole, richly deserved to be named *Time* magazine's Person of the Year. But it remains to be seen whether he will again find himself in a position that allows his proven leadership ability to shine. History has a way of throwing leaders up and then covering them over, Ozymandias-style. After Churchill gave the lion's roar, he spent several decades as a Sunday painter. Giuliani, too, has quietly disappeared into a successful law practice after having made an unsuccessful bid for the 2008 Republican Party nomination in the presidential primaries. George W. Bush, too, and the Republicans collectively, paid a dear bill when the context shifted. Bush's post-9/11 stratospheric approval ratings fell just like the stock market did in the recent recession. The shift in context and the economic crisis of 2008 handed the presidency to Barack Obama.

Whatever else 9/11 meant, it was a vivid reminder that one of the sweeter uses of adversity continues to be its ability to bring leadership to the fore. What Abigail Adams wrote to son John Quincy Adams in the tumult of 1780 is still true today: "These are the times in which a genius would wish to live. It is not in the still calm of life, or in the repose of a pacific station, that great challenges are formed . . . . Great necessities call out great virtues." In 2001 and 2002, when Robert Thomas and I were doing the research for *Geeks & Geezers* (Bennis & Thomas, 2002), we interviewed almost 50 leaders—some 75 and older, the rest 35 and younger. In every case, we found that their leadership had emerged after some defining experience, or crucible, as we called it. These were often ordeals, and among the older leaders, they often occurred in wartime. The crucibles of our leaders included such personal tragedies as television journalist Mike Wallace's discovery of the body of his son after an accident in Greece and global business pioneer Sidney Rittenberg's harrowing 16 years in Chinese prisons, much of them in solitary confinement, often in the dark. Most people realize how crucibles can be transforming events. Political leaders have instrumentalized their "crucible" experiences and vie to take advantage of the media to communicate them in vivid ways.

They know that voters are more likely to trust those who have known suffering, yet voters are becoming wary of such efforts that smack of inauthenticity.

In a foreword to our book, David Gergen, head of the Center for Public Leadership at Harvard's John F. Kennedy School of Government, describes the crucible in which Harry Truman discovered that he was a leader. We tend to think of Truman as the one-time haberdasher whose leadership emerged only after the death of Roosevelt. But as Gergen recounts, Truman was tested during the Great War on the battlefields of France. The head of an artillery battery, he was in the Vosges Mountains when his position was shelled by the Germans. His men panicked, and Truman's horse panicked as well, falling on him and almost killing him. But as historian David McCullough wrote in his prize-winning biography of Truman, the future president crawled out from under his horse and overcame his own fear, screaming profanities at his men until most of them returned to their posts. Truman's men never forgot that his courage under fire had saved their lives, and Truman discovered that he had a taste for leadership as well as a gift for it.

Again and again, we found that something magical happens in the crucible—an alchemy whereby fear and suffering are transformed into something glorious and redemptive. This process reveals, if it does not create, leadership, the ability to inspire and move others to action. We found intelligence, optimism, and other traits traditionally associated with leadership present in all our subjects, but those traits are no guarantee that the alchemy of leadership will take place. Countless gifted people are broken by suffering. But our leaders discovered themselves in their crucibles, for reasons we still do not fully understand. However searing the experience, our leaders were able to make sense of it or organize meaning around it—meaning that subsequently attracted followers. Instead of being defeated by his or her ordeal, each of our leaders saw it as a heroic journey. Whatever their age, these men and women created their own legends. Without being untruthful, they constructed new, improved versions of themselves. In many cases—as in Truman's—the ordeal and the leader's interpretation of it led others to follow the newly revealed leader.

In the model of leadership development that grew out of that research, successful individuals all evidenced four essential competencies—adaptive capacity, the ability to engage others through shared meaning, a distinctive voice, and integrity. Often these abilities were evident to some degree before their ordeals, but they were intensified by the crucible experience. Of all these abilities, the most important was adaptive capacity. All our leaders had an extraordinary gift for coping with whatever life threw at them. I believe that adaptive capacity is essentially creativity—the ability to take disparate things and turn them into something new and useful. Indeed, it is no accident that there is a convergence between leadership studies and studies of creativity—a convergence that dates back to the first studies of Darwin, Einstein, and other geniuses, or thought leaders. When we speak of exemplary leadership, we are often talking about exemplary, creative problem solving—the discovery of new solutions to unprecedented problems.

But let's return to the lessons of 9/11. During the 1950s, no one who heard Marshall McLuhan speak so confidently of the global village or the extent to which the medium is the message had any idea how truly prescient he was. But the terrorist attacks of 2001 underscored that ours is indeed one world, albeit a profoundly splintered one, and that television and more recent technologies are its primary mediators. Here were multinational terrorists dispatched by an individual holed up in an apartment, or a cave, in Afghanistan or elsewhere in the Middle East. Digital technology was used to advance a medieval ideology, with orders and money transferred in a nanosecond halfway across the planet. Globalization has created a host of new dangers that require a new kind of leadership—one that is, above all, collaborative. It was the inability of security agencies in the United States to work effectively together that allowed the 9/11 terrorists to enter and remain in the country and to learn how to fly a jet into a skyscraper at American flight schools.

And global terrorism is only one contemporary threat that requires a multinational, collaborative response. Disease, poverty, and the oppression of minorities, women, and political dissidents are urgent international concerns. As the outbreak in 2003 of severe acute respiratory syndrome (SARS) or the much-hyped but relatively anodyne 2009 swine flu illustrated, the ability of almost anyone to jump on a plane and fly to some distant city has created the real possibility that future flights will spread deadly plagues with unprecedented ease and rapidity.

In the months that led up to the toppling of the regime of Iraq's Saddam Hussein in 2003, much was made in the media, and rightfully so, of President George W. Bush's failure to build a global coalition. His "either you're with us or against us" attitude and his decision to enter Iraq with support from only a handful of nations (Great Britain, Australia, and Poland, among them) was widely seen as a leadership failure, despite the defeat of Hussein in record time. The critique of the president reflected more than political differences on whether American military action was appropriate only if legitimized by the United Nations. The criticism reflected an understanding that coalition building is one of the essential competencies of all leaders—in some ways, the defining one. And again, leadership came to the fore long after the war was over: Securing the peace in Iraq has proven very difficult, and some of the disastrous consequences have been blamed on precipitous policies, bad planning, and lack of shared leadership. Iraqis were rid of their dictator only to be replaced by al Qaeda.

Among the committed coalition builders President Bush might have emulated was his father. Before the first Gulf War, President George Herbert Walker Bush doggedly wooed world leaders. When the president was not smiling over banquet tables himself, he dispatched his secretary of state, James Baker, on eight consensus-building trips abroad, trips that took Baker to 18 European capitals. The result was that the United States went to war as part of a genuine "coalition of the willing." We cannot know what father said to son in private conversation before the Iraqi conflict. But we do know what the older Bush counseled in a speech at Tufts University in February 2003. "You've got to reach out to the other person," he said, describing what leaders in an interconnected world must do. "You've got to convince them that long-term friendship should trump short-term adversity." The senior Bush was articulating what democratic leaders have always known. In a society in which power must be given freely, not coerced, leaders make alliances by persuading others that their interests and fates are intertwined. As I write this in 2010, it is clear that the United States needs allies more than ever, as disorder continues in post-Hussein Iraq and a growing number of Iraqis perceive the forces of the United States and her handful of allies as occupiers rather than liberators.

Coalition building is also an essential element of corporate leadership. Until American business was roiled by recent corporate scandals, we had long been guilty of treating chief executive officers (CEOs) and other business leaders as demigods whose success was a unilateral achievement resulting from their special genius. This tradition dates back at least as far as our deification of such business titans as Thomas Edison and Henry Ford, and it resurged during the late 1970s when Lee Iacocca was hailed as the savior of the American auto industry. In retrospect, the lionization of anyone connected with the battered U.S. auto industry seems like a cruel joke. But we forget, now that so many corporate heads have rolled, how recently CEOs were treated both as celebrities and as thought leaders whose public comments were scrutinized for hidden wisdom like tea leaves.

In many ways, the rise of the celebrity CEO was a regression to the era when great institutions were thought to be the lengthened shadows of great men. The late-20th-century version of that durable myth differed only in conceding that a few great institutions—such as the Martha Stewart empire—were lengthened shadows of great women. But as Patricia Ward Biederman and I wrote in *Organizing Genius* (Bennis & Biederman, 1997), one has almost always been too small a number for greatness. Whatever their sphere, authentic leaders know, even if they do not bruit it around, that their power is a consequence of their ability to recruit the talent of others to the collective enterprise. The Lone Ranger has never been as dead as he is today. In all but the simplest undertaking, great things are done by alliances, not by larger-than-life individuals, however powerful they may seem.

I doubt that the world was ever so simple that a single heroic leader, however capable, could solve its problems unilaterally. Today's world requires unprecedented coalition building. The European Union may be the paradigmatic response to this changed reality. For those of us who experienced World War II first-hand, it is heartening to see such a high level of economic and political cooperation among nations that were so recently at one another's throats. And more and more coalitions, created and maintained by collaborative leaders, will be required in the years ahead. That this volume now includes a section on shared leadership gives me hope that business schools and political science departments will pay more attention to leadership as a collaborative endeavor.

The pace of change is not slowing. It is accelerating as never before. Ever-changing problems require faster, smarter, more inventive solutions, solutions that can be achieved only collaboratively. In recent years, even the way leaders make decisions has changed. The day is all but over when a leader has the leisure to digest all the facts and then to act. As psychologist Karl Weick has pointed out, today's leaders are more often required to act first, assess the results of their actions, and then act again. Thanks to digital technology, facts can be collected and numbers crunched with unprecedented ease. In this new climate, information is always flooding in, and there is no final analysis, only constant evaluation and reevaluation. Action becomes one more way to gather information, which becomes the basis for further action. As Weick so eloquently put it, in such a world, leaders cannot depend on maps. They need compasses. And as never before, they need allies.

The ability to form and maintain alliances is not just a political tool. The successful older leaders that Robert Thomas and I interviewed made it a point to seek out and befriend talented younger people. Forming these social alliances was a strategy the older leaders used to stay in touch with a rapidly changing world. These social alliances helped keep the older leaders vital in a way their less successful, more isolated peers were not. The younger leaders also benefited from relationships with more seasoned, older friends. And this strategy of forming alliances is not limited to humans. Stanford neurobiologist Robert Sapolsky, who lived, for a time, as part of a group of Serengeti baboons, found that the older males most likely to survive were those who were able to form strong bonds with younger males. Teamed with youthful allies, the senior males were able to compensate for the losses brought about by age. Mentoring is a variation on this primal theme, a way for the young and the old to pool their wisdom and energy to their mutual benefit.

Because leaders have power, the question of whether they use it for good or ill continues to be desperately important. We could argue forever over whether Hitler was an authentic leader or whether leadership, by definition, implies a kind of virtue. Certainly, Hitler had many of the competencies of leadership—a vision, the ability to recruit others to it, insight into what his followers needed, if only in the most demonic parts of themselves. He had the unquenchable self-confidence that is associated with leadership, the ambition, the obsessive sense of purpose, the need to communicate it, and the oratorical gifts to do so. He even had a kind of twisted integrity, in that he was always what his followers knew him to be. My fear is that our concern over this question is a dead end. Like the problem, the solution may be a matter of semantics. Perhaps we should reserve the word *leader* for those whose leadership is morally neutral (if that is possible) or tilted toward the good. We might simply stop calling Hitler an evil leader and refer to him as a despot or simply as a Führer, the straightforward German word for leader until Hitler poisoned it.

To say that the problem of how to label bad leaders distracts us from more pressing concerns is not to say that morality and leadership are trivial matters. They are of the utmost important, now and forever. As Harvard Business

School scholar Lynn Sharp Paine says of morality and business, ethics may not always pay, but it always counts. Far more urgent than the issue of what to call bad leaders is the question of how to create a culture in which despots or even plain-vanilla corporate tyrants of the Al Dunlap ("Chainsaw Al") sort cannot flourish. In truth, I think we do that by creating the same kind of climate in which talented people blossom and the very best work can be done. Fertile, liberating environments almost always have two components: able leaders who listen and capable followers who speak out. There is a memorable story about Nikita Khrushchev on this point. After the death of Stalin, the Soviet premier was at a public meeting at which he denounced Stalin's reign of terror. After Khrushchev spoke, someone in the audience confronted him. "You were a confidant of Stalin's," a voice called out from the crowd. "What were you doing when Stalin was slaughtering his own people?" "Who said that?" Khrushchev demanded to know. There was no answer. "Who said that?" he asked again, pounding the podium. And then Khrushchev explained: "*That's* what I was doing!"

By his silence, Khrushchev proved himself a bad follower (albeit a live one). This is one of those areas in which the lessons of leadership cry out for application in the workplace. The corporate scandals of the past few years (not to mention the recent economic crisis triggered by liquidity problems in U.S. banks) have caused unprecedented havoc in the American economy, tumult that has rocked the linked economies of the world. And in nearly every case, those scandals resulted not simply from crooked accounting and other crimes but from the failure of corporate leadership to create a culture of candor. Enron is a perfect example. Long before the energy giant crashed and burned, key employees knew that the books were being manipulated in ways that were deceptive, if not illegal. Enron executive Sherron S. Watkins did the right thing and warned her bosses that "Enron could implode in a wave of accounting scandals." Naive but admirably concerned about the good of the organization, Watkins expected to be heard, if not rewarded. Instead, company chief financial officer (CFO) Andrew Fastow buried the evidence and immediately set out to get rid of Watkins. The problem at Enron, she said later, was that few were willing to speak truth to power. Employees, including management, knew better than to point out the increasingly obvious ethical lapses in the company's business practices. Critical talk was taboo at Enron. "You simply didn't want to discuss it in front of the water cooler," Watkins said.

It is one thing to remain silent when your life or that of your family is in danger. It is quite another to remain silent when other people's lives are at risk and the worst thing that can happen to you is losing your job. And yet many organizations implicitly demand silence and denial on the part of their employees, even at the cost of human lives. When the space shuttle *Challenger* exploded shortly after takeoff in 1986, killing all seven on board, the blame was ultimately put on the space shuttle's O-rings, which failed in the unseasonable cold the morning of the launch. Tragically, the potential flaw in the O-rings had been repeatedly noted by Roger Boisjoly, an engineer with NASA supplier Morton Thiokol. Only the day before, Boisjoly had made one more desperate attempt to warn his superiors that the crew was in danger. But the company suppressed the information. As for Boisjoly, the whistleblower got the reward that annoying truth tellers so often receive. He lost his job, and indeed never worked again as an engineer; he did, however, receive the Scientific Freedom and Responsibility Award from the American Association for the Advancement of Science. He now makes his living giving talks on organizational ethics.

To an outsider, it is almost impossible to imagine that any organization would prefer silence to honest criticism that saves lives. But such deadly organizational quietism happens all the time. And one tragedy is often not enough to bring about change. In a report prepared after the shuttle *Columbia*'s deadly failure in 2003, investigators put part of the blame on "a flawed institutional culture that plays down problems," according to the *New York Times*. Just as Boisjoly had been ignored when he raised his concerns in 1986, a new generation of space-program managers had chosen to ignore signs of potential problems, including e-mails from employees warning of flaws in the system. The fiery failure of the *Columbia* killed seven astronauts, whose deaths are attributable, at least in part, to managers who closed their minds to vital but unwanted news. NASA created a system that rewarded silence before safety, and that is what it got.

Corporate enthusiasm for collective ignorance has launched a thousand "Dilbert" cartoons. Movie mogul Samuel Goldwyn, famous for his malapropisms as well as his autocratic rule, is said to have snarled at his underlings after a string of box-office flops, "I want you to tell me what's the matter with MGM even if it means losing your jobs." Too often, that is exactly what happens. More recently, Compaq CEO Eckhard Pfeiffer lost dominance of the computer market to Gateway and Dell, not because he lacked talent but because he surrounded himself with an A-list of yes men and closed his office door to anyone who had the courage to tell him what he did not want to hear.

In the 2003 scandal at the *New York Times* that led to the resignations of Executive Editor Howell Raines and Managing Editor Gerald Boyd, insiders repeatedly told other media that the real problem was not the pathological behavior of rogue reporter Jayson Blair but a newsroom culture that rewarded a handful of favorites of questionable merit and marginalized everyone else. It was also a place where control was concentrated in the hands of a few, and dissent was unwelcome. Neither Raines nor Boyd listened when another editor warned that Blair must stop reporting for the *New York Times* immediately. Much has been made of Raines's role in the scandal, but the *Wall Street Journal* reported a disturbing example of Boyd's arrogant resistance to the truth as well. When the paper's national editor suggested a story to Boyd on the *Columbia* disaster, Boyd nixed it, saying it had already run that morning in *USA Today*. Investigations Editor Douglas Frantz subsequently brought Boyd a copy of *USA Today* to prove that the story had not appeared. Boyd, of course, should have acknowledged his mistake and ordered up the story. Instead, he told Frantz he should not embarrass his managing editor and handed Frantz a quarter to call his friend Dean Baquet, a former *Times* editor who had gone to the *Los Angeles Times*. In essence, Boyd told Frantz to hit the road. And like a number of other unhappy veterans of the *New York Times,* Frantz quit to go to Los Angeles.

Linda Greenhouse, who covers the Supreme Court for the *New York Times,* told *Journal* reporters Matthew Rose and Laurie Cohen: "There is an endemic cultural issue at the *Times* that is not a Howell creation, although it plays into his vulnerabilities as a manager, which is a top-down hierarchical structure. And it's a culture where speaking truth to power has never been particularly welcomed."

You would hope that leaders in any organization would have the ego strength to accept well-intentioned criticism from talented underlings. You would hope that leaders would be wise enough to know that what you do not want to hear is often the most valuable information you can get. This makes me wonder why organizations do not go out of their way to use findings from differential psychology. Although far from perfect, new, sophisticated psychometric tests can identify leaders who will be smart and relatively open-minded, honest, and assertive enough to lead in an effective way. You would also think that czar-like executive compensation packages would more than make up for any embarrassment corporate leaders feel when subordinates choose candor over ego massage. But such is rarely the case. Executive arrogance poisons the atmosphere in far too many organizations. It is especially deadly in idea-driven organizations (as more and more are) in which subordinates are often as talented as their leaders, or more so. In hard economic times, autocratic leaders may be able to retain talent. But as soon as the economy rebounds, talented people who do not respect the people they work for head for the door. At the height of the now battered New Economy, employers knew that talent was their treasure, and they treated their employees with respect. In hard times, employers often become arrogant again, forgetting that good times will return and that the talent will again take flight.

The band-aid that The New York Times Company Chairman Arthur Sulzberger Jr. put on the paper's leadership problem was to name former Executive Editor Joseph Lelyveld, whom Raines had succeeded, as his interim replacement. Well-liked by reporters and editors, Lelyveld seemed to understand, as Raines did not, that the *New York Times* was about the work, not about the executive editor. Lelyveld had decentralized control, giving editors and reporters more autonomy and more discretion to work on longer, thoughtful stories appropriate to journalists at the top of their game (in contrast, Raines liked to dispatch masses of reporters to cover a breaking news story, a process he called "flooding the zone"). And, unlike Raines, who assigned reporters to execute his story ideas for the front page, Lelyveld joked that he had trouble getting his story ideas into the paper—an off-hand reminder to his staff that he did not confuse himself with god. Interestingly, Lelyveld was repeatedly described by those who worked with him as "aloof."

He was not a charismatic leader, nor a warm, fuzzy one, just an able one whom people respected. Lelyveld understood that smart, capable people should be treated with respect—not just because it is the right thing to do but because it is good business. Lelyveld was also a reminder that leadership abilities are ultimately more important than leadership styles.

Future of Leadership Research

In reading the earlier chapters in this book, I was struck by how rich and varied the study of leadership has become over the past 20 years. My sense is that the field is now on the brink of the kind of major breakthroughs that revolutionized social psychology in the 1950s and 1960s. Inspired by the earlier chapters, I will focus on three topics, among others, that seem to demand further study.

Leadership and Globalization

The Global Leadership and Organizational Behavior Effectiveness (GLOBE) Project, in which social scientists from approximately 60 countries look at leadership from a cross-cultural perspective, is an important start. In a world made smaller by technology, it is more urgent than ever that we understand each other's symbols, values, and mind-sets. Only then can we hope to reach consensus on common goals, including how to ensure global peace and prosperity. In the past few years, Westerners have become acutely aware of how little they know about Islamic cultures, including how to speak their languages. One subject that cries out for more scrutiny is tribalism, a powerful force throughout the world that undermines globalization at every turn. The private sector has long been aware of the importance of understanding its audiences and markets. Advertising agencies regularly recruit new PhDs in cultural anthropology to study the customs and values of consumers. We need to turn even more experts loose on comparing cultures on such fundamental problems as what we mean when we use certain terms. This is essential, not just to understand those who oppose us but to ensure the forging of effective alliances.

As recounted in an issue of *Smithsonian*, British and American military had so much trouble communicating during World War II that the Allies asked anthropologist Margaret Mead to try to find out what the problem was. Writer Patrick Cooke explains: "Mead discovered that the two cultures possessed fundamentally different world views. One simple way to demonstrate this was to ask an English person and an American a single question: What's your favorite color?" The American would answer immediately with the color of his or her choice. The English person would answer with a question: "Favorite color for what? A flower? A necktie?" Cooke explains: "Mead concluded that Americans, raised in a melting pot, learned to seek a simple common denominator. To the British, this came across as unsophisticated. Conversely, the class-conscious British insisted on complex categories, each with its own set of values. Americans interpreted this tendency to subdivide as furtive." How right Churchill was that the English and the Americans were great nations separated by a common language!

From our vantage point, Mead's conclusions seem a little simple-minded. But you cannot help admiring the unidentified leader who recognized the Allies' communication problem as cultural and, instead of assigning blame, chose an expert to study the problem dispassionately. Effective leadership will increasingly depend on being able to decipher what people really mean when they do and say things that baffle us.

Leadership and the Media

Leadership is and always has been a performance art. Rhetoric first developed as a tool of leadership, and leadership continues to involve both artifice and the perception of authenticity. There is a tendency to think of image consciousness on the part of leaders as a modern phenomenon. But as historian Leo Braudy tells us, Alexander the Great facilitated the spread of his power by putting his image on the coins of his empire. We take as a given that television gave JFK an edge over Nixon during their debates because of the latter's five o'clock shadow and sour scowl. But do we yet know the real extent to which our public figures are created or undone by the media, and the nature of these processes? To understand leadership today, it is essential to see how the competitive pressures of the media affect the reputations and the behavior of public officials. And you cannot get a handle on modern leaders without at least trying to gauge where spin begins and reality ends. When President George W. Bush made his famous tailgate landing on the carrier *Abraham Lincoln*, associating himself with both the Great Emancipator and the pop-culture warriors of the movie *Top Gun*, did he do something qualitatively different than Alexander the Great, who associated his exploits with those of the deities of his time? What impact does the public's knowledge that reality is being manipulated have on its trust in its leaders? And how does the Internet affect modern leadership, given its ability to create buzz about an individual or vilify him or her with a keystroke? The mastery of Internet-based media by Obama's team apparently helped play a role in his victory over McCain. These are things we need to know in an age when television cameras can create seeming character and instant polling allows leaders to change their positions in midspeech.

Multidisciplinary Approaches to Leadership

It may be possible in the near future to develop a true science of leadership (it will always be an art, as well). Obviously, this scientific understanding has been a dream since the first postmortem examination of a leader's brain. But the technology now exists to make real strides. It sometimes seem as if every department in every university wants PET (positron emission tomography) and fMRI (functional magnetic resonance imaging) technology of its own, however many millions the machines cost. But there may be real gains to having leaders, nonleaders, and followers submit to brain scans in hopes of discovering more about the physiology of leadership. What happens in a follower's brain as the person hears a rousing speech? Do the brains of autocratic leaders show different patterns of activity than those of collaborative ones? What about their respective followers? There is also new work to be done on how hormones affect leadership and, too, how dominance and subordination affect hormones, mood, health, and other outcomes. Does bad management literally make people sick? One immediate benefit of a rigorous science of leadership would be better management, now too often based on tradition and clumsy improvisation. Integrating basic biological sciences in the study of management and leadership, as *The Economist* suggested in an article published in September 2010, may provide the next major paradigm shift in the organizational sciences.

Conclusion

Having studied leadership for the past six decades, I still find it remarkable how often leaders in talent-driven organizations (e.g., *New York Times*) forget what scholarship tells us about how to manage genius. They encourage competition among colleagues, instead of the more productive competition with outside organizations. They forget that most talented people chafe at bureaucracy and hierarchy. They forget that intrinsic rewards are the best motivators. They refuse to believe that work should feel like fun, or better than fun.

In the gifted groups that Biederman and I studied, the most successful leaders were those who saw themselves not as top dogs but as facilitators. Although many had healthy egos, they were far more concerned with the project than with shows of deference on the part of their subordinates. Indeed, they did not regard the others as subordinates; they saw them as colleagues or as fellow crusaders on a holy mission (whether that mission was creating the first personal computer or the first animated feature film). These leaders saw their primary responsibility as unleashing the talent of others so the collective vision could be realized. These leaders prided themselves on their ability to discover and cultivate talent and to recognize the best ideas that came across their desks. They concerned themselves with such issues as keeping the project moving forward, making sure everyone had the tools and information they needed, and protecting the group from outside interference. A spirited collegiality is the usual mood of these great groups. As head of the Manhattan Project, J. Robert Oppenheimer successfully fought the government's initial insistence on secrecy within the group. Oppenheimer understood that the free exchange of ideas was essential to the project's success because ideas ignite each other and create more ideas. At Los Alamos, candor within the group was so valued that no one was shocked when cheeky young Richard Feynman disagreed with legendary Nobelist Niels Bohr. If Los Alamos was not a genuine republic of ideas, Oppenheimer did all he could to make it feel like one. Inside the fence, he rewarded frankness and transparency as well as utter dedication to the urgent task at hand. The result was that the atomic bomb was built more quickly than anyone believed possible. The first mushroom cloud still hung in the air when some of the scientists realized that they had unleashed a terrible force on the world. But most spoke admiringly of Oppenheimer's leadership for the rest of their lives.

Even though Oppenheimer's scientists were part of the Allied war effort, he treated them as if they were free agents. Oppenheimer realized that the most heroic effort is given freely; it cannot be coerced. He did not order. He inspired.

Perhaps the best exchange on the limits of power is from Shakespeare's *Henry IV,* Pt. I. Glendower boasts to Hotspur: "I can call spirits from the vasty deep." And Hotspur responds: "Why, so can I, or so can any [person]; But will they come when you do call them?" (p. 52).Whatever the arena, genuine leaders find ways to make others want to come when they are called.

Note

1. Editors' note: Warren Bennis has just published a very engaging book about leadership and his life. It is titled *Still Surprised: A Memoir of a Life in Leadership*.

Supplementary Readings

Bennis, W. G., & Biederman, P. W. (1997). *Organizing genius: The secrets of creative collaboration*. Reading, MA: Addison-Wesley.

Bennis, W. G., & Biederman, P. W. (2010). *Still surprised: A memoir of a life in leadership*. San Francisco: Jossey-Bass.

Bennis, W. G., & Thomas, R. J. (2002). *Geeks & geezers: How era, values, and defining moments shape leaders*. Boston: Harvard Business School Press.

Author Index _____

Cable, D. M., 163, 184, 194, 347, 349, 458, 492
Cacioppo, J. T., 47, 195, 299, 342
Cage, J. H., 225
Calder, B. J., 10, 33, 43, 306, 337, 338
Caldu, X., 12
Camacho, A., 12
Camerer, C., 146, 150
Cameron, A. C., 279
Camobreco, J. F., 113, 115
Campbell, B. C., 12
Campbell, D. T., 458
Campbell, J. D., 194
Campbell, R. J., 41, 112, 113, 166
Campbell, W. K., 195
Campion, M. A., 119, 182
Cannon, J. P., 403
Cantor, N., 278
Cantor, N. W., 342
Capaldi, D. M., 80
Capra, F., 317
Carey, J. A., 455
Carli, L. L., 13, 168, 239, 439, 446, 449, 454, 455, 456, 457
Carlyle, T., 180, 364
Carpenter, J. P., 156, 162
Carr, L., 119
Carroll, J., 463
Carson, J., 368, 370, 373
Carson, J. B., 30, 32, 51, 67
Carson, K. P., 10
Carsten, M. K., 201, 306
Carte, T. A., 373
Carter, D. A., 446
Cartwright, E., 157
Case, B., 227
Cashman, J., 293, 294, 296
Cassirer, N., 440
Castaño, N., 394, 395
Castelnovo, O., 299, 300
Castro, S., 316
Cavaretta, F. L., 12, 38, 43
Caver, K. A., 13
Cha, S. E., 204
Chagnon, N. A., 148, 155, 167
Chaleff, I., 333, 364
Chan, A., 109
Chan, D., 32, 50
Chan, K. Y., 46, 72, 113, 115, 122, 496, 498
Chandler, T., 314
Charness, N., 55, 121, 125
Charteris-Black, J., 276
Chartrand, T. L., 341
Chatterjee, A., 195, 198
Chaturvedi, S., 80

Chaudhry, A., 49, 88, 300
Chemers, M. M., 218, 219, 221, 222, 231, 234, 235, 236, 239, 243, 245, 498
Chen, F., 71
Chen, G., 40, 242, 337, 402, 409, 491, 494
Chen, J. J., 456
Chen, N., 298
Chen, Z. X., 402, 409
Cheng, C. M., 341
Cherulnik, P. D., 47, 276, 349
Chesner, S. P., 161
Cheung, G. W., 73
Chhokar, J. S., 400, 419
Chi, D. T. K., 397
Chi, M. T. H., 121
Chia, R. C., 229, 230
Chiao, J. Y., 12
Chidambaram, L., 373
Chin, J. L., 13, 455
Chiu, W., 300, 314
Cho, S. B., 40
Choi, J., 82, 83
Choi, Y., 351, 481, 489
Chopin, S., 316
Christ, O., 351, 480
Christal, R. E., 181
Chun, J. U., 33
Churchland, P. S., 45
Cialdini, R. B., 453, 455
Cianciolo, A. T., 257, 263, 279, 332, 363
Cicero, L., 480, 483, 484
Cilliers, P., 54
Ciulla, J. B., 508, 510, 513, 518, 521, 523, 536
Clair, J. A., 339
Cober, R. T., 47
Coetsier, P., 399
Cogliser, C. C., 6, 8, 9, 10, 11, 257, 316
Cohen, F., 163, 165, 339
Cohen, G. L., 457
Cohen, J., 73, 79
Cohen, P., 73, 79
Cohen, S. G., 367
Colbert, A. E., 8, 72, 156, 191, 223, 335, 450
Collinson, D., 318, 320
Colquitt, J. A., 193, 485
Confucius, 523, 533
Conger, J. A., 30, 51, 52, 124, 125, 126, 180, 195, 198, 202, 257, 269, 270, 271, 272, 276, 305, 314, 363, 364, 365, 367, 372, 374, 375, 377, 378, 481, 482, 483, 489, 491
Conklin-Brittain, N., 449
Conlon, D. E., 485

Diekman, A. B., 451, 452, 462
Dienesch, R. M., 294, 296, 297, 303
Dierdorff, E. C., 231, 244
Digman, J. M., 181, 182
Dijkmans, M., 341
Dilchert, S., 181
Dimitruk, P., 72, 74
Dingler-Duhon, M., 196
Dinh, J. E., 33, 34, 56, 347
Dinko, R. L., 372
Dion, K. L., 372
Dionne, P. J., 67, 115
Dionne, S. D., 33, 67, 113, 232
Dipboye, R. L., 182
Dirks, K. T., 39, 204, 369, 491
DiStefano, C., 90, 92
Dixon, R. A., 80
Dodge, G. E., 236, 319, 339
Dodge, J., 305
Dolan, R. J., 153
Doney, P. M., 403
Donley, K. A., 47, 276
Donovan, J. A., 231
Donovan, J. J., 190, 198
Dorfman, P. W., 13, 72, 152, 155, 163, 164,
    165, 203, 204, 229, 234, 344, 369,
    394, 395, 399, 400, 401, 402, 403,
    408, 414, 415, 416, 417, 418, 419,
    420, 421, 426, 464
Doris, J., 533
Dougherty, T. W., 193, 458
Douglas, C., 301
Douglas, S. C., 297
Dovidio, J. F., 455
Downton, J. V., 260, 261
Dragoni, L., 39, 47, 50, 52
Drasgow, F., 46, 113, 115, 122, 496
Drath, W. H., 110, 114, 121, 125, 130, 304,
    305, 306, 308, 310, 318
Drazin, R., 34
Dreher, G. F., 458, 459
Dreher, J. C., 12
Drenth, P. J. D., 394, 396, 413
Driskell, J. E., 446, 455
Drory, A., 196
Drucker, P. F., 132, 366
Dubin, R., 29
Dubinsky, A., 335
Duck, J. M., 343, 350, 480, 482, 487
Duke, A., 302
Dukerich, J. M., 10, 205, 306,
    338, 395, 487, 488
Dumdum, U. R., 265
Dunbar, R. I. M., 146, 147, 159

Dupré, K. E., 449
Durham, C. C., 493
Duthie, N., 368, 371
Dutton, J. E., 334
Duxbury, L., 458
Dvir, T., 274, 494
Dweck, C. S., 118, 132
Dzieweczynski, J. L., 181

Eagly, A. H., 13, 168, 202, 231, 237, 239,
    437, 439, 442, 443, 444, 445, 446, 447,
    448, 449, 451, 452, 453, 454, 455, 456,
    462, 463, 487, 488
Earle, T., 148, 160
Earley, P. C., 414
Eby, L. T., 458
Eden, D., 10, 40, 228, 266,
    274, 337, 347, 487, 494
Edwards, J. E., 227
Edwards, J. R., 67, 71, 72, 73, 242
Eggins, R., 161
Ehrhart, M., 422
Ehrlich, S. B., 10, 30, 34, 205, 338,
    395, 487, 488
Eidelman, S., 340
Eisenberg, N. H., 193
Eisenberger, R., 489
Ekman, P., 340
El Hadidy, W., 310
Elliott, E. S., 118, 451
Ellis, A. D., 441
Elloy, D. F., 369
Ellsworth, P. C., 79
Ellyson, S. L., 455
Elmhirst, K., 370
Emmons, R. A., 195
Emrich, C. G., 11, 228, 276, 336, 414
England, P., 441
Engle, E. M., 306, 348
Ensari, N., 344, 349, 350
Ensher, E. A., 494
Ensley, M. D., 67, 373, 374, 381
Epitropaki, O., 13, 51, 155, 163, 228, 229,
    279, 342, 344, 345, 348, 489
Epley, N., 342
Eplion, D. M., 300
Epstein, D., 80
Erdheim, J., 194
Erdogan, B., 292, 294, 299
Erez, A., 193
Erez, M., 344, 400, 402
Erhardt, M. L., 446
Ericsson, K. A., 55, 121, 125, 127
Eriksson, P., 364

Salas, E., 364, 446, 455, 488
Salmond, K., 458, 459
Salzman, P. C., 448
Sanchez-Hucles, J. V., 455
Sanchez-Runde, C., 394
Sanfey, A., 153
Sani, F., 484, 490, 495
Saporta, I., 441
Sashkin, M., 272
Saucier, G., 199, 200
Sauer, E., 370
Say, J. B., 365
Saz-Carranza, A., 310, 318
Scandura, T. A., 50, 294, 296, 297, 303,
    307, 314, 316, 332, 396, 414
Scerbo, M. M., 349
Schafer, W. D., 450, 462
Schall, E., 305
Schaller, M., 12, 143, 144, 149, 164
Schaubroeck, J., 204
Schein, E., 53, 54, 400, 410, 422, 423, 424
Schein, V. E., 453
Schell, J., 340
Schermelleh-Engel, K., 72, 74
Schiemann, W., 299
Schippers, M. C., 481
Schippmann, J. S., 119
Schleicher, T. L., 456
Schmidt, A. M., 45, 48, 52
Schmidt, F. L., 8, 127, 201
Schmidt, S. M., 332
Schmieder, R. A., 406
Schmitt, D. P., 149, 450
Schmitt, N., 182
Schneider, B., 53, 190, 422
Schneider, F., 150
Schneider, R. J., 240
Schneider, S. C., 404, 409, 410
Schoenborn, S., 126, 276
Schriesheim, C. A., 4, 42, 78, 203, 221, 222,
    226, 227, 231, 232, 268, 303, 314, 316
Schriesheim, J. F., 226
Schubert, T. W., 347, 349
Schunk, D., 150
Schutz, A., 305
Schwab, A. E., 244
Schwartz, S. H., 198, 397, 398, 401,
    406, 407, 410, 411
Schwartz-Shea, P., 319
Schyns, B., 242
Scott, K. A., 341, 350
Scribner, M., 205
Scullen, S. E., 340
Sczesny, S., 349

Sedikides, C., 478
Seers, A., 316
Seibert, S. E., 379
Sejnowski, T. J., 45
Self, S. G., 83
Sellers, J. G., 12, 146, 151, 153
Seltzer, J., 264, 267
Senders, P. S., 161
Sessa, V. I., 166
Seuss, Dr., 331
Seymour, B., 153
Shah, J., 46
Shamir, B., 12, 13, 30, 40, 54, 269, 270, 271,
    274, 276, 278, 315, 334, 336, 337, 339,
    340, 368, 369, 371, 382, 477, 481, 487,
    489, 490, 491, 493, 494, 495, 528
Shane, S., 405, 407
Shartle, C. L., 235
Shaver, P. R., 299, 300
Shaw, M. E., 236
Shea, C. M., 494
Shelton, D., 201
Sherif, M., 161
Sherman, J. W., 347
Sherony, K. M., 292, 314
Shi, K., 399
Shils, E., 260, 401, 409
Shinar, E. H., 453
Shipper, F., 373, 376
Shoda, Y., 33, 43, 44, 45
Shondrick, S. J., 33, 34, 56, 347
Shore, L. M., 50, 294, 295
Shrader, C. B., 446
Shrout, P. E., 86
Sias, P., 290, 291, 292, 304, 308, 312
Siegel, P. A., 494
Sigerson, K., 457
Silverthorne, C., 396
Silzer, R. F., 119
Simkins, B. J., 446
Simmons, W. K., 349, 367
Simon, M., 194, 228
Simonton, D. K., 146, 163, 196
Simpson, J., 144, 150
Simpson, W. G., 446
Sims, H. P., Jr., 364, 366, 367, 368,
    372, 374, 379, 381, 382
Simsek, Z., 236
Sin, H.-P., 117, 131, 315
Sinclair, L., 455
Singer, J. D., 79, 80, 83, 153
Singer, M., 498
Sinha, J. B. P., 412, 415
Sinha, R. B., 412

Subject Index_____

About the Editors_____

David V. Day is the Woodside Professor of Leadership and Management at the University of Western Australia Business School. Professor Day has published more than 75 journal articles, books, and book chapters, many pertaining to the core topics of his primary research interests in leadership and leadership development. He is the lead author on the recently published book titled *An Integrative Approach to Leader Development: Connecting Adult Development, Identity, and Expertise* (Routledge, 2009) and is presently editing *The Oxford Handbook of Leadership and Organizations*, with an expected publication date of 2012. Day serves as an Associate Editor of the *Journal of Applied Psychology* and is on the editorial boards of *Human Performance, Journal of Management, The Leadership Quarterly, Organizational Behavior and Human Decision Processes, Organizational Psychology Review*, and *Personnel Psychology*. He is a Fellow of the American Psychological Association and the Society for Industrial and Organizational Psychology.

John Antonakis is Professor of Organizational Behaviour in the Faculty of Business and Economics of the University of Lausanne, Switzerland. Professor Antonakis's research is currently focused on predictors and outcomes of leadership, leadership development, strategic leadership, social cognition, as well as on causality. He has published more than 35 book chapters and articles included in journals such as *Science, The Leadership Quarterly, Journal of Operations Management, Human Relations, Personality and Individual Differences*, among others. He has coedited two books: *The Nature of Leadership* and *Being There Even When You Are Not: Leading Through Strategy, Structures, and Systems*. Antonakis is Associate Editor of *The Leadership Quarterly* and is on the editorial boards of the *Academy of Management Review, Human Relations, Leadership, Organizational Psychology Review, Organizational Research Methods*, and *Journal of Management Studies*.

About the Contributors _____

Susan Adams, PhD, recently graduated from the Illinois Institute of Technology in Chicago in Industrial and Organizational Psychology. There she worked with the Leadership Academy, where she coauthored a review of undergraduate leadership development programs for the Kravis-de-Roulet Leadership Conference, *The Future of Leadership Development*. She currently teaches for the psychology department of Northeastern Illinois University in Chicago. She has completed several conference presentations and publications in the areas of leadership emergence, communication processes, group decision making, and leadership development. Most recently, at the 2010 Academy of Management Annual Meeting in Montrèal, she presented her dissertation, *Communication Frequency and Content on Leader Emergence: Does Communication Medium Matter?*

Roya Ayman, PhD, is a professor and the division head, Industrial and Organizational Psychology division, College of Psychology, Illinois Institute of Technology. She has received awards and honorary positions such as faculty fellow of the Leadership Academy at Illinois Institute of Technology, fellow at Leadership Trust Foundation, Herefordshire, UK, and the Dean's leadership award. Among her scholarships, Professor Ayman was the coeditor of a book titled *Leadership Theory and Research: Perspectives and Directions*. Her recent article on *Leadership: Why Gender and Culture Matter* was published in *American Psychologist*. She is the Associate Editor of Journal of Management & Organization and serves on the editorial board of *The Leadership Quarterly, Journal of Management & Organization,* and *International Journal of Cross Cultural Management,* as well as serving as an ad hoc reviewer for many academic journals and conferences. As a practitioner, she has served on executive and advisory boards of nonprofit organizations and has designed and conducted training on diversity, cross-cultural interaction, and leadership development for many private and public sector multinational, international, and national organizations. She also served for two terms on the education and training-working group of the Governor's Commission on the Status of Women in Illinois. She has conducted workshops and leadership training in many countries such as Mexico, China's Wuhan and Inner Mongolia provinces, Switzerland, Luxemburg, Thailand, and Spain. She has consulted with the public and private sector for decades on leadership development and effectiveness.

Adam P. Barsky is a senior lecturer in the Department of Management and Marketing at the University of Melbourne. He earned his PhD in Industrial/ Organizational Psychology from Tulane University in 2004. His research is focused on affect and emotion in judgment and decision making, ethical behavior in organizations, and research methodology. His work has appeared in journals such as *Journal of Applied Psychology, Psychological Bulletin, Journal of Organizational Behavior, Journal of Management,* and *Journal of Business Ethics.*

Warren Bennis is University Professor and Distinguished Professor of Business Administration at the Marshall School and Founding Chairman of The Leadership Institute at the University of Southern California. He is one of the world's leading experts on leadership. A lecturer, consultant, and writer, Professor Bennis has been an advisor to four U.S. presidents, including John F. Kennedy and Ronald Reagan. He is the author of numerous books, including the classic *On Becoming a Leader* and *Leaders,* both translated into 21 languages. He co-chairs the advisory board of the Center for Public Leadership at Harvard University's Kennedy School of Government. Professor Bennis is a former Distinguished Research Fellow at Harvard Business School, former president of the University of Cincinnati, as well as the former Provost and Executive Vice President of SUNY-Buffalo.

Douglas J. Brown is an associate professor of psychology at the University of Waterloo. Professor Brown has published more than 40 journal articles, books, and book chapters. His current program of research is focused on investigating the intersection between the self, abusive supervision, and workplace deviance. Professor Brown is the coauthor of the book *Leadership Processes and Follower Self-Identity.* His journal articles have appeared in such outlets as *Personnel Psychology,* the *Journal of Applied Psychology, Organizational Behavior and Human Decision Processes, Journal of Management, Journal of Organizational Behavior, Human Performance,* and *The Leadership Quarterly.* Dr. Brown is currently on the editorial board of the *Journal of Applied Psychology* and is an Associate Editor at *Organizational Behavior and Human Decision Processes.*

Linda L. Carli holds a PhD in social psychology from the University of Massachusetts at Amherst. She was faculty member at the College of the Holy Cross and Mount Holyoke College before joining Wellesley, where she teaches courses in organizational, social, and applied psychology. An authority on social influence, gender discrimination, and the challenges faced by professional women, she is the author (with Alice Eagly) of *Through the Labyrinth: The Truth About How Women Become Leaders* (Harvard Business School Press, 2007). The book received the 2008 Distinguished

Publication Award from the Association of Women in Psychology; an article based on the book received a McKinsey Award as the second most significant article published in the *Harvard Business Review* in 2007. In 2001, she coedited (with Eagly) a volume of the *Journal of Social Issues* that focused on women leaders. She has developed and conducted diversity training workshops and negotiation and conflict resolution workshops for women leaders and has lectured widely on gender and diversity for business, academic, and other organizations.

Joanne B. Ciulla is Professor and Coston Family Chair in Leadership and Ethics at the Jepson School of Leadership Studies, University of Richmond where she is one of the founding faculty of the school. Ciulla also has visiting professorships at Nyenrode Business Universiteit and the University of Fort Hare in South Africa. She has a BA, MA, and PhD in philosophy and publishes extensively in the areas of leadership ethics and business ethics. Ciulla's books include *Ethics, the Heart of Leadership*; *The Working Life: The Promise and Betrayal of Modern Work*; and *The Ethics of Leadership*. She coauthored a business ethics text titled *Honest Work: A Business Ethics Reader* and coedited a collection of essays on *The Quest for Ethical Leaders: Essays in Leadership Ethics*. She edited the three-volume set, *Leadership at the Crossroads*. She sits on the editorial boards of *The Business Ethics Quarterly*, *Leadership,* and *The Leadership Quarterly* and edits the New Horizons in Leadership series for Edward Elgar Publishing. Professor Ciulla gives lectures and seminars all over the world and has worked with organizations such as the Aspen Institute, the World Economic Forum, and the Brookings Institution.

Deanne N. Den Hartog is currently full Professor of Organizational Behavior in the Faculty of Economics and Business of the University of Amsterdam, the Netherlands. She heads the HRM/OB section of the Amsterdam Business School there. Deanne studies transformational, ethical and cross-cultural leadership processes. Other research interests include team effectiveness, trust, and employees' proactive and innovative work behavior. She has published her work in leading journals, including *Journal of Applied Psychology, Journal of Organizational Behavior, Human Relations,* and *The Leadership Quarterly,* and serves on several different editorial boards, among others that of *The Leadership Quarterly* and the *Journal of Occupational and Organizational Psychology*. Deanne is an elected member of the Royal Holland Society of Sciences and Humanities, serves on the Board of Directors of the International Association of Applied Psychology, and recently received a Fellowship award from the Leadership Trust Foundation, UK.

Marcus W. Dickson is Professor of Organizational Psychology and Associate Department Chair in the Department of Psychology at Wayne State University in Detroit, Michigan, USA. Marcus's research has focused on issues of cross-cultural leadership (including serving as Co-Principal Investigator for Project GLOBE for several years) and on organizational climate and culture. He is currently researching organizational recovery following leadership betrayal. His work has appeared in *The Leadership Quarterly, Journal of Applied Psychology,* and other leading peer-reviewed outlets in the field, as well as in books such as *The Handbook of Organizational Culture and Climate.* He has served or is serving on the editorial boards of several journals, including *The Leadership Quarterly, Journal of Organizational Behavior,* and *Academy of Management: Learning and Education.*

Jessica E. Dinh is currently a graduate student at the University of Akron in Industrial Organizational Psychology. Her research interests include leadership, organizational justice, cognitive processing and social cognition, as well as emotions in the workplace. She coauthored a theoretical piece that was published in *The Leadership Quarterly* in December of 2010.

Alice H. Eagly is Professor of Psychology, James Padilla Chair of Arts and Sciences, Professor of Management & Organizations, and Faculty Fellow in the Institute for Policy Research, all at Northwestern University. She received her PhD from the University of Michigan and has held faculty positions at Michigan State University, University of Massachusetts in Amherst, and Purdue University. Her research interests include the study of leadership, gender, attitudes, prejudice, and stereotyping. She is the author of several books and numerous journal articles and chapters in edited books. Her most recent book is *Through the Labyrinth: The Truth About How Women Become Leaders,* co-authored with Linda Carli. She has won several awards, most recently the Gold Medal for Life Achievement in the Science of Psychology from the American Psychological Foundation and the Distinguished Scientific Contribution Award from the American Psychological Association. Eagly is on the editorial boards *of Journal of Personality and Social Psychology, Research Synthesis Methods, Psychology of Women Quarterly, Social Psychology Quarterly, Psychological Bulletin, Gender and Management, Personality and Social Psychology Review, Current Psychology, European Review of Social Psychology,* and *Social Psychology.*

Timothy A. Judge is the Franklin D. Schurz Professor of Management, Mendoza College of Business, University of Notre Dame. Timothy Judge received his PhD from the University of Illinois at Urbana-Champaign in 1990. Before entering the doctoral program at Illinois, he was a manager with Kohl's department stores in Wisconsin and Illinois. Previously, Judge has been a member of the faculties of Cornell University, the University of Iowa, and most recently, the University of Florida. He is a fellow of the Academy of Management, the American Psychological Association, and the American Psychological Society. He serves on the editorial review boards of eight journals, including *Academy of Management Journal, Journal of Applied Psychology,* and *Personnel Psychology.* Judge's research interests are in the areas of personality and individual differences, leadership, moods and emotions, and job attitudes.

David M. Long is currently a doctoral student in organizational behavior at the University of Florida's Warrington College of Business. He earned his MBA from the University of Florida. His research interests are in leadership, justice, and positive psychology. Before beginning his doctoral program, Long spent four years at The Home Depot working in several leadership roles. He also spent eight years in the US Navy as a Naval Aviator.

Robert G. Lord is a Distinguished Professor of Psychology at the University of Akron. He received his PhD from Carnegie-Mellon University in 1975. He has published more than 125 journal articles and book chapters in leading industrial/organizational, psychology, and management sources. His research focuses on motivation and self-regulation, leadership perceptions and leadership skill development, information processing, ethical leadership behavior, leader behavior measurement, complexity leadership theory, and alternative perspectives on knowledge. He received the 2009 Leadership Quarterly distinguished scholar award for career contribution to the study of leadership. He is an editorial board member of *Organizational Behavior and Human Decision Processes*, *The Leadership Quarterly*, and the *Journal of Applied Social Psychology*. He has coauthored the books *Leadership and Information Processing: Linking Perceptions and Performance* with Karen Maher, and *Leadership Processes and Follower Self-Identity* with Douglas Brown. He coedited *Emotions in the Workplace: Understanding the Structure and Role of Emotions in Organizational Behavior* with Richard Klimoski and Ruth Kanfer. Dr. Lord is a Fellow of the American Psychological Association and the Association for Psychological Sciences.

John Maslyn is an associate professor of management in the College of Business Administration at Belmont University in Nashville, Tennessee. Professor Maslyn's current research interests are in leader–member exchange and perceptions of politics. He has published in a number of journals and book series including the *Journal of Applied Psychology, Journal of Management, The Leadership Quarterly, Journal of Applied Social Psychology, European Journal of Work and Organizational Psychology, Journal of Organizational Behavior,* and *LMX Leadership: The Series,* and *Research in Multi-Level Issues,* and serves as a reviewer for a number of journals in management. He is a member of the Academy of Management and the Southern Management Association.

Sonia M. Ospina is an associate professor of public management and policy and Faculty Director of the Research Center for Leadership in Action at New York University's Wagner Graduate School of Public Service. Her current interests include leadership and democratic governance. She recently finished a multiyear, national research project on social change leadership in the United States. Working with 90 social change organizations, it aimed to produce theoretical insights and knowledge about how leadership happens in these contexts. The research was reported in 29 peer-reviewed articles and/or book chapters—including several in the *Leadership Quarterly* and the *Journal of Public Administration Research and Theory*—and will culminate in a book. Ospina is also coeditor with Mary Uhl-Bien of *Relational Leadership Theory: Advancing a Dialogue Among Perspectives,* forthcoming (2011). Ospina also explores issues of accountability in public management in Latin America, and she has produced two books on the topic.

Craig L. Pearce, PhD, is the Clifton Chair in Leadership and the Director of the Institute for Innovative Leadership at the University of Nebraska. He has pioneered the development of shared leadership theory and practice. His work has appeared in many top journals, is widely cited, has spawned many doctoral dissertations across the globe, and has received widespread acclaim in the practitioner community–including a feature article in the *Wall Street Journal.* He has received many awards for his work, including the Ascendant Scholar Award, the Asia Pacific HR Leadership Award, and an award from the Center for Creative Leadership for his work on shared leadership. His book *Shared Leadership: Reframing the Hows and Whys of Leadership* is published by Sage. His most recent book, *The Drucker Difference*, is published by McGraw-Hill and has been translated into 10 languages. His forthcoming book, *Share the Lead*, will be published by Stanford University Press. Professor Pearce is an active keynote speaker and consultant to organizations. His clients have included such organizations as American Express, British Bakeries, the Central Intelligence Agency of the United States, Fujitsu, the Metropolitan Water District of Southern California, Nielsen, Panda Express, Rayovac, Rover Group Serono, and the U.S. Army, among many others.

Mary Uhl-Bien is the Howard Hawks Chair in Business Ethics and Leadership at the University of Nebraska. Professor Uhl-Bien's current research interests are relational leadership, complexity leadership, and followership. Her work has been published in the top journals in the field, and her research on complexity leadership and implicit followership theories has been recognized with Best Paper awards from the Center for Creative Leadership and the Southern Management Association. She serves on the editorial boards of *Academy of Management Journal, Academy of Management Review, The Leadership Quarterly, Leadership,* and *The International Journal of Complexity in Leadership and Management,* and is Senior Editor of the Leadership Horizons series (Information Age Publishers). She is coeditor of *The Sage Handbook of Leadership* (Sage, 2011), and her co-edited book with Sonia Ospina on *Relational Leadership Theory: Advancing a Dialogue Among Perspectives* is forthcoming (2011). She is a founding member of the Network of Leadership Scholars and the LDRNET listserv in the Academy of Management.

Daan van Knippenberg is Professor of Organizational Behavior at the Rotterdam School of Management, Erasmus University Rotterdam, the Netherlands. He has published more than 140 scholarly articles, books, and book chapters, including in such outlets as *Academy of Management Journal, Annual Review of Psychology, Journal of Applied Psychology, Organization Science,* and *Organizational Behavior and Human Decision Processes,* many of which revolve around his key research interests in leadership, work group diversity, group decision making, creativity and innovation, and social identity processes in organizations. Daan is an associate editor of *Journal of Organizational Behavior* and founding editor of *Organizational Psychology Review*. He is also cofounder and director of the Erasmus Center for Leadership Studies, cofounder and co-organizer of the *New Directions in Leadership Research* conference organized by Duke University, Erasmus University, INSEAD, and The Wharton School, and a Fellow of the Society for Industrial and Organizational Psychology.

Mark Van Vugt is Professor of Social and Organizational Psychology, VU University Amsterdam, and holds honorary positions at the Universities of Oxford and Kent. His research concentrates on the study of group and organizational processes from an evolutionary and social psychological perspective. He is interested in themes such as the evolution and psychology of leadership, status, power, altruism, cooperation, and intergroup relations. He is also interested in applying insights from social and evolutionary psychology to understand and help to solve real-world problems related to business and management, environmental conservation, and other prosocial behaviors such as volunteering and charity work. Professor Van Vugt is a member of the team that won the prestigious £1.2 million British Academy grant "From Lucy to Language: The Archaeology of the Social Brain." He is the lead author of a popular science book on leadership titled *Naturally Selected*, a coauthor of the text *Applying Social Psychology*, and a consulting editor of various journals in social psychology. He is a member of the European Association for Experimental Social Psychology, the Society of Experimental Social Psychology, and the Society for Personality. He blogs on *Psychology Today* on understanding the human animal in the workplace.

Christina L. Wassenaar is a PhD in Management student at the Peter F. Drucker and Masatoshi Ito Graduate School of Management. Her area of research is primarily focused on shared leadership and how this philosophical theory can be developed in groups and organizations. She is also actively consulting with various academic institutions on strategic and financial planning, accreditation, and marketing/branding initiatives. For five years, she served as the Academic Director and Director of Executive Programs at the Drucker School, where she directed or was actively engaged in program and curriculum development, alumni and external affairs, career management, accreditation, faculty recruitment, student affairs, and other internal and externally related activities. While at the school, she was also deeply involved in student mentoring, the EMBA Council, the Drucker Centennial Planning committee, as well as other university-related and outside professional organizations.

Zhen Zhang is an assistant professor of management in the W. P. Carey School of Business at Arizona State University. He earned his PhD in Human Resources and Industrial Relations at the University of Minnesota. His research focuses on leadership process and development, the biological basis of organizational behavior, the intersection between organizational behavior and entrepreneurship, and research methods. His work has appeared or is forthcoming in several journals including *Journal of Applied Psychology*, *Personnel Psychology*, *Organizational Behavior and Human Decision Processes*, *The Leadership Quarterly*, *Journal of Business Venturing*, *Psychological Methods*, and *Organizational Research Methods*.

Michael J. Zyphur enjoys studying quantitative methods. His work utilizes a generalized latent variable modeling framework that includes structural equation models, multilevel models, multilevel structural equation models, and latent class cluster analysis/factor mixture models as special cases. For these purposes, his PhD in Industrial and Organization psychology granted in 2006 by Tulane University has come in handy, helping him publish papers in journals such as *Academy of Management Review*, *Psychological Methods*, *Structural Equation Modeling*, *Organizational Research Methods*, *Journal of Applied Psychology*, and *Organizational Behavior and Human Decision Processes*. He is currently employed by the University of Melbourne. He likes dogs, but does not currently own one.

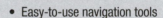